SHAKESPEARE'S
ROMAN PLAYS

AND THEIR BACKGROUND

BY

Mungo

M. W. MacCALLUM

M.A., Hon. LL.D., Glasgow

SOMETIME PROFESSOR OF MODERN LITERATURE
IN THE UNIVERSITY OF SYDNEY

WITH A FOREWORD BY

T. J. B. SPENCER

PROFESSOR OF ENGLISH LANGUAGE AND LITERATURE
AND DIRECTOR OF THE SHAKESPEARE INSTITUTE
UNIVERSITY OF BIRMINGHAM

MACMILLAN

LONDON · MELBOURNE

1967

Foreword © Macmillan & Co. Ltd 1967

First published 1910
Reprinted 1925, 1935
Reissued with a new foreword 1967

Published by
MACMILLAN & CO LTD
Little Essex Street London wc2
and also at Bombay Calcutta and Madras
Macmillan South Africa (Publishers) Pty Ltd Johannesburg
The Macmillan Company of Australia Pty Ltd Melbourne
The Macmillan Company of Canada Ltd Toronto

PRINTED IN GREAT BRITAIN BY
LOWE AND BRYDONE (PRINTERS) LTD., LONDON

TO

D. M. M·C.

" De Leev is Allens op de Welt,
Un de is blot bi di."

CONTENTS

CONTENTS

FOREWORD

Sir Mungo William MacCallum (1854–1942) was
a Scot, born in Glasgow, and a graduate of the
University of Glasgow. In 1887 he went to
Australia on appointment as Professor of Modern
Literature at the University of Sydney. He held
the chair for thirty-four years, and after his retirement became Vice-Chancellor and later Chancellor,
serving that university for a total of fifty years.
He received many honours, including the honorary
degrees of LL.D. of Glasgow University (1906) and
D.Litt. of Oxford University (1925); and he was
created K.C.M.G. in 1926.

His literary publications were varied, but
nothing was as important as his *Shakespeare's
Roman Plays and their Background*, which was
published in 1910 and reprinted in 1925 and 1935,
and is now reissued. Works of Shakespeare
criticism rarely survive their generation, unless
they are written by great masters of English
literature such as Johnson, Coleridge, or Hazlitt.
But MacCallum's *Shakespeare's Roman Plays* is
one of those few which have outlasted changes of
fashion in criticism. It remains an indispensable
book, even though the later interpreters of the
Roman plays have entered regions MacCallum
never knew.

Although written in a reasonably attractive
style, it is scarcely an inspiring work, for by
modern standards it is somewhat over-laboured

and over-explicit. No one would be aroused to a passionate love of Shakespeare by reading it. But MacCallum was sensible, intelligent, and modest. His purpose was straightforward, and he fulfilled it efficiently. He intended to give a full critical interpretation of three plays, *Julius Caesar, Antony and Cleopatra*, and *Coriolanus*, with something of the same thoroughness that A. C. Bradley had shown in his study of four plays in *Shakespearean Tragedy*, published a few years before (1904). His method was substantially the same as Bradley's. But the close relation between the three Roman plays and North's translation of Plutarch led MacCallum to a more extended source-study. His mind had, moreover, an historical rather than a metaphysical bias; and so he was more inclined to discuss pre-Shakespearian plays on Roman history (in Latin, French, and English) than to explore Hegelian theories of the dramatic experience. He gives nearly a quarter of his book (pp. 1–167) to an Introduction, before he gets down to the dissection of the three plays.

MacCallum's approach to the plays is basically that of studying the author's methods and achievements in characterization. He analyses and discriminates them with a critical subtlety which we now think more suited to the novel than to the drama. His elaborate interpretations of individual characters are not lacking in psychological insight. Their defect is that they rarely take account of the fact that we are dealing with stage-plays, where " characterization " means that the author provides a script for the actor to fill out by means of his impersonation. The visual impact of scenes and the means by which emotional situations are built up on the stage – these things MacCallum ignores. We have become a little uneasy at his kind of " realization " of characters in minute

detail, and are now more sensitive to other
qualities in Shakespeare – symbolic and imaginative meanings which transcend mere character-
building. Nevertheless, these character-studies
have a surprising staying-power, while other
fashionable modes of writing about the plays pass
away. The " interpretations " we are to give to
the dramatic figures of Caesar or Brutus or
Coriolanus remain subjects of critical debate.
They are, moreover, problems for the producer
and actor, and not merely for the literary critic;
perhaps, rather paradoxically, that is one cause
of the strength of the kind of Shakespeare criticism
we associate with Bradley and (to a lesser degree)
MacCallum.

Like Bradley, too, MacCallum depended upon
many predecessors; and by judicious absorption of
all that was of value in previous criticism he was
able to give his book a kind of definitiveness and
comprehensiveness. No one really needs any more,
after MacCallum, to turn to the works of Paul
Stapfer, whose two-volume *Shakespeare et
l'Antiquite* was translated into English in 1880 and
(rather oddly) was never mentioned by MacCallum;
or of F. A. T. Kreyssig, so warmly praised by
MacCallum (pp. xv–xvi) as he had been by Edward
Dowden and F. S. Boas, but little known in
England because untranslated. Unfortunately
MacCallum's allusions to the opinions of previous
critics are sometimes cryptic and unprovided with
references. The modern reader will get little help
from his casual dropping of names like " Klein "
(p. 310), " Mr. Watkiss Lloyd " (p. 519), " Captain
Mahan " (p. 265), " Professor Ingram " (p. 304),
or even " Lotze " (p. 89). Sometimes MacCallum
helpfully names the book of " Mr. Baker " (p. 267)
and of " M. Besnage " (p. 60) when he quotes from
these authors; but he does not tell his reader

where he can find the entertaining passage from Heine on p. 441. There is now no useful purpose to be served in documenting fully the obsolete criticism which MacCallum quotes.

Perhaps the most serious omission from MacCallum's discussion is *Titus Andronicus*. On p. 177 he briefly gives his reasons for ignoring the play. But these can no longer be felt to be satisfactory, for the subject of *The Most Lamentable Roman Tragedy of Titus Andronicus* was, in some respects, more typical " Roman history " for Shakespeare's contemporaries than *Coriolanus*. The contrast between *Titus Andronicus* and the three later plays shows Shakespeare's marvellous originality in his Plutarchan vision of Rome. Recent criticism has tended to reveal the importance of *Titus Andronicus* in Shakespeare's artistic development. (See Howard Baker, *Induction to Tragedy* (Baton Rouge, 1939; reissued, New York, 1965), E. M. W. Tillyard, *Shakespeare's History Plays* (1944), M. C. Bradbrook, *Shakespeare and Elizabethan Poetry* (1951), T. W. Baldwin, *On the Literary Genetics of Shakspere's Plays, 1592-1594* (Urbana, 1959).)

A useful summary of criticism of the Roman plays in the twentieth century is given by J. C. Maxwell in the tenth volume of *Shakespeare Survey* (1957). Some of this criticism is conveniently selected in *Discussions of Shakespeare's Roman Plays*, edited by Maurice Charney in the series " Discussions of Literature " (Boston, 1964). A brief general survey is by T. J. B. Spencer, *William Shakespeare: The Roman Plays* in the series " Writers and their Work " (1963), with a detailed bibliography. The following represents the principal work of a scholarly and critical kind on the Roman plays since MacCallum's book.

Among general studies, detailed attention has been given to the politics of the plays and to

Shakespeare's characterization of politicians in action. H. B. Charlton's pamphlet *Shakespeare: Politics and Politicians* (English Association, 1929), J. E. Philipps's *The State in Shakespeare's Greek and Roman Plays* (New York, 1940), John Palmer's *Political Characters of Shakespeare* (1945), which includes studies of Brutus and Coriolanus, are some of the most useful advances on MacCallum. In "Shakespeare and the Elizabethan Romans" (*Shakespeare Survey*, X (1957)) T. J. B. Spencer tries to interpret some aspects of the plays (including *Titus Andronicus*) strictly in terms of the notions of the Roman world which were usual among Shakespeare's contemporaries. An essay by J. Leeds Barroll on "Shakespeare and Roman History" (*Modern Language Review*, LIII (1958)) is a special study of medieval and Renaissance theories of world history, which have relevance to interpretations of the position of Julius Caesar and Octavius Caesar in the Divine scheme of things.

The new ways of experiencing the plays in more imaginative and symbolic terms are best represented by G. Wilson Knight's *The Imperial Theme*, first published in 1931 and revised in 1951. This has been highly influential. Maurice Charney's *Shakespeare's Roman Plays: The Function of Imagery in the Drama* (1961) is a more recent book which tries to combine theatrical and imaginative interpretations without losing sight of historical considerations. L. C. Knights in *Some Shakespearean Themes* (1959) and *Further Explorations* (1965), and D. A. Traversi in *The Roman Plays* (1963) have written with their characteristic method of moral probing.

Plutarch's *Lives* has become more accessible than MacCallum indicates. The four relevant lives had already been re-edited by R. H. Carr (Oxford, 1906) with valuable introduction and notes, super-

seding W. W. Skeat's edition of 1875; but
MacCallum seems not to have had access to it.
C. F. Tucker Brooke's edition of selected lives
(2 vols., 1909) is equally convenient, though offer-
ing less material for study. Complete editions of
North's translation were published in 1928 (8 vols.,
Shakespeare Head Press) and in 1929 (5 vols.,
Nonesuch Press); and a selection was edited by
Paul Turner (2 vols., 1963). The most recent
edition is *Shakespeare's Plutarch* by T. J. B. Spencer
(Penguin Books, 1964), with introduction, glossary,
and, at the foot of the page, the parallel passages
from Shakespeare's plays. The fifth volume of
Geoffrey Bullough's *Narrative and Dramatic Sources
of Shakespeare* (1964) is devoted to the Roman
plays and reprints extensive selections from
Plutarch and other sources. The question of
Shakespeare's use of Appian (see MacCallum,
Appendixes C and D) has been reconsidered in detail
by Ernest Schanzer in his *Shakespeare's Appian.
A Selection from the Tudor Translation of Appian's
Civil Wars* (Liverpool, 1956). The first volume of
Kenneth Muir's *Shakespeare's Sources* (1957) in-
cludes a discussion of the Roman plays.

Recent editions of the three Roman plays go
carefully over the same ground as MacCallum, but
they cannot be said to provide much more than
he does about Shakespeare's artistry in his use
of North's Plutarch. The New Variorum volumes
(*Julius Caesar*, 1913; *Antony and Cleopatra*, 1907;
Coriolanus, 1928) are already a little old-fashioned,
though their accumulations of critical comment
are useful and convenient. More important are
the volumes of the New Cambridge Shakespeare
(1949, 1950, and 1960, respectively) edited by
J. Dover Wilson, with many new insights on
points of detail; and the (new) Arden Shakespeare
now includes *Julius Caesar*, edited by T. S. Dorsch,

1955, and *Antony and Cleopatra*, edited by M. R. Ridley, 1954.

Julius Caesar

Harley Granville-Barker included a study of *Julius Caesar* from the producer's point of view in the first series of his *Prefaces to Shakespeare* (1927). The difficulties of interpreting Caesar and Brutus remain much as they were in MacCallum's book; and the debate continues. Among the many new attempts to clarify the issues the following essays may be mentioned: W. Warde Fowler, " The Tragic Element in Shakespeare's *Julius Caesar* " (1911), reprinted in his *Roman Essays and Interpretations* (1920); Sir Mark Hunter, " Politics and Character in Shakespeare's *Julius Caesar* ", in *Essays by Divers Hands*, x (1931); Ernest Schanzer, " The Problem of *Julius Caesar* ", in *Shakespeare Quarterly*, vi (1955); Adrien Bonjour, *The Structure of " Julius Caesar "* (Liverpool, 1958); and L. C. Knights, " Personality and Politics in *Julius Caesar* ", in his *Further Explorations*, 1965.

Antony and Cleopatra

A. C. Bradley's essay on this play, printed in his *Oxford Lectures on Poetry* (1909), appeared too late, MacCallum says (p. 313), for him to make use of it. Harley Granville-Barker's study appeared in the second series of his *Prefaces to Shakespeare* (1930). E. E. Stoll's vigorous rejection of sentimental or over-subtle interpretations of Cleopatra was printed in his *Poets and Playwrights* (Minneapolis, 1930); and Franklin Dickey in *Not Wisely But Too Well* (San Marino, 1957) gave an excellent analysis of the Elizabethan attitudes to love, in relation to this and other love-tragedies of Shakespeare.

Coriolanus

A. C. Bradley's British Academy lecture (1912) on *Coriolanus* was reprinted in *A Miscellany* (1929). Developing what MacCallum had said (p. 568) about Virgilia, J. Middleton Murry wrote agreeably on " A neglected heroine of Shakespeare " in *Countries of the Mind* (1922). D. A. Traversi's essay on *Coriolanus*, which appeared in *Scrutiny*, VI (1937–8), is his best piece of criticism.

In *Shakespeare's Satire* (1943) Oscar J. Campbell tries to show that the play belonged to a different category from tragedy; that is, " tragical satire ".

Harley Granville-Barker came late to *Coriolanus*, which was discussed at length in the last of his *Prefaces to Shakespeare* (Fifth Series, 1948). The contemporary background – which was a subject generally neglected by MacCallum – has been explored in various ways: by E. C. Pettet in " *Coriolanus* and the Midlands Insurrection of 1607 " in *Shakespeare Survey*, III (1950); by Kenneth Muir in " The Background of *Coriolanus* " in *Shakespeare Quarterly*, X (1959); and by W. G. Zeeveld in " *Coriolanus* and Jacobean Politics " in the *Modern Language Review*, LVII (1962). P. A. Jorgensen in *Shakespeare's Military World* (1956) describes in detail other aspects of the way Shakespeare and his contemporaries imagined warlike events and the soldier's profession.

The Shakespeare Institute   T. J. B. SPENCER
University of Birmingham
January 1967

PREFACE

SHAKESPEARE'S Roman plays may be regarded as forming a group by themselves, less because they make use of practically the same authority and deal with similar subjects, than because they follow the same method of treatment, and that method is to a great extent peculiar to themselves. They have points of contact with the English histories, they have points of contact with the free tragedies, but they are not quite on a line with either class. It seems, therefore, possible and desirable to discuss them separately.

In doing so I have tried to keep myself abreast of the literature on the subject ; which is no easy task when one lives at so great a distance from European libraries, and can go home only on hurried and infrequent visits. I hope, however, that there is no serious gap in the list of authorities I have consulted.

The particular obligations of which I am conscious I have indicated in detail. I should like, however, to acknowledge how much I owe throughout to the late F. A. T. Kreyssig, to my mind one of the sanest and most suggestive expositors that Shakespeare has ever had. I am the more pleased to avow my indebtedness, that at present in Germany Kreyssig is hardly receiving the learned, and in England has never received the popular, recognition that is his due. It is strange that while Ulrici's metaphysical lucubrations and Gervinus's somewhat ponderous commentaries found their translators and their public, Kreyssig's purely humane and literary appreciations were passed over. I once began to translate them myself, but "habent sua fata libelli," the time had gone by. It is almost exactly half a century ago since his lectures were first published; and now there is so much that he would wish to omit, alter, or amplify, that it would be unfair to present them after this lapse of years for the first time to the English public. All the same he has not lost his value, and precisely in dealing with the English and the Roman histories he seems to me to be at his best.

One is naturally led from a consideration of the plays to a consideration of their background; their antecedents in the drama, and their sources, direct and indirect.

The previous treatment of Roman subjects in Latin, French, and English, is of some interest, apart from the possible connection of this or that tragedy with Shakespeare's masterpieces, as showing by contrast the originality as well as the splendour of his achievement. For this chapter of my Introduction I therefore offer no apology.

On the other hand the sketches of the three "ancestors" of Shakespeare's Roman histories, and especially of Plutarch, need perhaps to be defended against the charge of irrelevancy.

In examining the plays, one must examine their relations with their sources, and in examining their relations with their sources, one cannot stop short at North, who in the main contributes merely the final form, but must go back to the author who furnished the subject matter. Perhaps, too, some of the younger students of Shakespeare may be glad to have a succinct account of the man but for whom the Roman plays would never have been written. Besides, Plutarch, so far as I know, has not before been treated exactly from the point of view that is here adopted. My aim has been to portray him mainly in those aspects that made him such a power in the period of the Renaissance, and gave him so great a fascination for men like Henry IV., Montaigne, and, of course, above all, Shakespeare. For the same reason I have made my quotations exclusively from Philemon Holland's translation of the *Morals* (1st edition, 1603) and North's translation of the *Lives* (Mr. Wyndham's reprint), as the Elizabethan versions show how he was taken by that generation.

The essay on Amyot needs less apology. In view of the fact that he was the immediate original of North, he has received in England far less recognition than he deserves. Indeed he has met with injustice. English writers have sometimes challenged his claim to have translated from the Greek. To me it has had the zest of a pious duty to repeat and enforce the arguments of French scholars which show the extreme improbability of this theory. Unfortunately I have been unable to consult the Latin version of 1470, except in a few transcripts from the copy in the British Museum : but while admitting that a detailed comparison of that with the Greek and the French would be necessary for the formal completion of the proof, I think it has been made practically certain that Amyot dealt with all his authors at first hand. At any rate he is a man, who, by rendering Plutarch into the vernacular and in many instances furnishing the first draught of Shakespeare's phrases, merits attention from the countrymen of Shakespeare.

Of North, even after Mr. Wyndham's delightful and admirable study, something remains to be said in supplement. And he too has hardly had his rights. The *Morall Philosophie* and the *Lives* have been reprinted, but the *Diall of Princes* is still to be seen only in the great libraries of Europe.

B

A hurried perusal of it two years ago convinced me that, apart from its historical significance, it was worthy of a place among the *Tudor Translations* and would help to clear up many obscurities in Elizabethan literature.

I at first hoped to discuss in a supplementary section the treatment of the Roman Play in England by Shakespeare's younger contemporaries and Caroline successors, and show that while in some specimens Shakespeare's reconciling method is still followed though less successfully, while in some antiquarian accuracy is the chief aim, and some are only to be regarded as historical romances, it ultimately tended towards the phase which it assumed in France under the influence of the next great practitioner, Corneille, who assimilated the ancient to the modern ideal of Roman life as Shakespeare never did and, perhaps fortunately, never tried to do. But certain questions, especially in regard to the sources, are complicated, and, when contemporary translations, not as yet reprinted, may have been used, are particularly troublesome to one living so far from Europe. This part of my project, therefore, if not abandoned, has to be deferred ; for it would mean a long delay, and I am admonished that what there is to do must be done quickly.

I have complained of the lack of books in Australia, but before concluding I should like to acknowledge my obligations to the book-loving colonists of an earlier generation, to whose irrepressible zeal for learning their successors owe access to many volumes that one would hardly expect to see under the Southern Cross. Thus a 1599 edition of Plutarch in the University Library, embodying the apparatus of Xylander and Cruserius, has helped me much in the question of Amyot's relations to the Greek. Thus, too, I was able to utilise, among other works not easily met with, the first complete trans-

lation of Seneca's Tragedies (1581), in the collection
of the late Mr. David Scott Mitchell, a "clarum et
venerabile nomen" in New South Wales. May I,
as a tribute of gratitude, inform my English readers
that this gentleman, after spending his life in collect-
ing books and manuscripts of literary and historical
interest, which he was ever ready to place at the
disposal of those competent to use them, bequeathed
at his death his splendid library to the State, together
with an ample endowment for its maintenance and
extension?

For much valuable help in the way of information
and advice, my thanks are due to my sometime
students and present colleagues, first and chiefly,
Professor E. R. Holme, then Mr. C. J. Brennan,
Mr. J. Le Gay Brereton, Mr. G. G. Nicholson,
Dr. F. A. Todd; also to Messrs. Bladen and Wright
of the Sydney Public Library for looking out books
and references that I required; to Mr. M. L. Mac-
Callum for making transcripts for me from books in
the Bodleian Library; to Professor Jones of Glasgow
University for various critical suggestions; above all
to Professor Butler of Sydney University, who has
pointed out to me many facts which I might have
overlooked and protected me from many errors into
which I should have fallen, and to Professor Ker of
University College, London, who has most kindly
undertaken the irksome task of reading through my
proofs.

M. W. MacCALLUM

UNIVERSITY OF SYDNEY,
27th April, 1909.

INTRODUCTION

CHAPTER I

ROMAN PLAYS IN THE SIXTEENTH CENTURY

PLAYS that dealt with the History of Rome were frequent on the Elizabethan stage, and all portions of it were laid under contribution. Subjects were taken from legends of the dawn like the story of Lucretia, and from rumours of the dusk like the story of Lucina; from Roman pictures of barbarian allies like Massinissa in the South, or barbarian antagonists like Caractacus in the North; as well as from the intimate records of home affairs and the careers of the great magnates of the Republic or Empire. But these plays belong more distinctively to the Stuart than to the Tudor section of the period loosely named after Elizabeth, and few have survived that were composed before the beginning of the seventeenth century. For long the Historical Drama treated by preference the traditions and annals of the island realm, and only by degrees did "the matter of Britain" yield its pride of place to "the matter of Rome the Grand." Moreover, the earlier Roman Histories are of very inferior importance, and none of them reaches even a moderate standard of merit till the production of Shakespeare's *Julius Caesar* in 1600 or 1601. In this department Shakespeare had not the light to guide him that

he found for his English Histories in Marlowe's
Edward II., or even in such plays as *The Famous
Victories of Henry V.* The extant pieces that
precede his first experiment, seem only to be grop-
ing their way, and it is fair to suppose that the
others which have been lost did no better. Their
interest, in so far as they have any interest at all,
lies in the light they throw on the gradual progress
of dramatic art in this domain. And they illustrate
it pretty fully, and show it passing through some of
the main general phases that may be traced in the
evolution of the Elizabethan Tragedy as a whole.
At the outset we have one specimen of the Roman
play in which the legitimate drama is just beginning
to disengage itself from the old Morality, and
another in which the unique Senecan exemplar is
transformed rather than translated to suit the primitive art of the time. Then we have several more
artistic specimens deriving directly or indirectly
from the French imitators of Seneca, which were
the most dignified and intelligent the sixteenth
century had to show. And lastly we have a specimen of what the Roman play became when elaborated by the scholar-playwrights for the requirements
of the popular London stage.

A survey of these will show how far the ground
was prepared for Shakespeare by the traditions of
this branch of the drama when he turned to cultivate
it himself.

I

APPIUS AND VIRGINIA.   THE TRANSLATION OF
OCTAVIA

The crudest if not the earliest of the series is
entitled *A new Tragicall Comedie of Apius and
Virginia*, by R.B., initials which have been supposed

with some probability to stand for Richard Bower, who was master of the Chapel Royal at Windsor in 1559. It was first printed in 1575, but must have been written some years before. A phrase it contains, "perhaps a number will die of the sweat," has been thought to refer to the prevalence of the plague in 1563, and it may be identified with a play on the same subject that was acted at that time by the boys of Westminster. At any rate several expressions show beyond doubt that it was meant for representation, but only on the old-fashioned scaffold which was soon to be out-of-date. Its character and scope belong too, in part, to a bygone age. The prologue proclaims its ethical intention with the utmost emphasis :

> You lordings all that present be, this Tragidie to heare
> Note well what zeale and loue heerein doth well appeare,
> And, Ladies, you that linked are in wedlocke bandes for euer
> Do imitate the life you see, whose fame will perish neuer :
> But Uirgins you, oh Ladies fair, for honour of your name
> Doo lead the life apparent heere to win immortall fame.[1]

It is written in commendation of chastity and rebuke of vice :

> Let not the blinded God of Loue, as poets tearm him so,
> Nor Venus with her venery, nor Lechors, cause of wo,
> Your Uirgins name to spot or file : deare dames, obserue the life
> That faire Verginia did obserue, who rather wish(ed) the knife
> Of fathers hand hir life to ende, then spot her chastety.
> As she did waile, waile you her want, you maids, of courtesie.
> If any by example heere would shun that great anoy,[2]
> Our Authour would rejoyce in hart, and we would leap for joy.

No Moral Play could be more explicit in its lesson, and the Moral Play has also suggested a large number of the personages. Conscience, Justice, Rumour, Comfort, Reward, Doctrine, Memory, are

---

[1] Quotations taken, with a few obvious emendations, from Mr. Farmer's reproduction in the Tudor Facsimile Texts.

[2] The hurt of impurity, not of death.

introduced, and some of them not only in scenes by themselves, but in association with the concrete characters.   Occasionally their functions are merely figurative, and can be separated from the action that is supposed to be proceeding : and then of course they hardly count for more than the attributes that help to explain a statue.   Thus, when Appius resolves to pursue his ruthless purpose, he exclaims :

> But out, I am wounded : how am I deuided !
> Two states of my life from me are now glided :

and the quaint stage direction in the margin gives the comment : " Here let him make as thogh he went out, and let Consience and Justice come out of[1] him, and let Consience hold in his hande a Lamp burning, and let Justice haue a sworde and hold it before Apius brest."   Thus, too, another stage direction runs : " Here let Consience speake within :

' Judge Apius, prince, oh stay, refuse : be ruled by thy friende :
What bloudy death with open shame did Torquin gaine in ende?'"

And he answers : " Whence doth this pinching sounde desende ? "   Here clearly it is merely the voice of his own feelings objectified : and in both instances the interference of the Abstractions is almost wholly decorative ; they add nothing to the reflections of Appius, but only serve to emphasise them.   This however is not always the case.   They often comport themselves in every respect like the real men and women.   Comfort stays Virginius from suicide till he shall see the punishment of the wicked. Justice and Reward (that is, Requital) summoned by the unjust judge to doom the father, pronounce sentence on himself.   In the end Virginius enters in company with Fame, Doctrina, and Memory.

---

[1] Altered unnecessarily to *out after* by Mr. Carew Hazlitt in his edition of Dodsley's *Old English Plays*. Appius' words imply that the two principles pass from his life, and the spectators are asked to imagine that they actually see the process.

Other of the characters, again, if more than general
ideas, are less than definite individuals. There is a
sub-plot not at all interwoven with the main plot,
in which the class types, Mansipulus, Mansipula,
and their crony, Subservus, play their parts. With
their help some attempt is made at presenting the
humours of vulgar life. They quarrel with each other,
but are presently reconciled in order to divert themselves together, and put off the business of their
master and mistress, hoping to escape the punishment for their negligence by trickery and good luck.
But we do not even know who their master and
mistress are, and they come into no contact with
either the historical or the allegorical figures.

The only personage who finds his way into both
compartments of the "Tragicall Comedie" is Haphazard the Vice, who gives the story such unity as
it possesses. His name happily describes the double
aspect of his nature. On the one hand he stands
for chance itself; on the other for dependence on
chance, the recklessness that relies on accident, and
trusts that all will end well though guilt has been
incurred. In this way he is both the chief seducer
and the chief agent, alike of the petty rogues and
of the grand criminal. To the former he sings :

Then wend ye on and folow me, Mansipulus,[1] Mansipula,
Let croping cares be cast away ; come folow me, come folow
me :
Subseruus is a joly loute
Brace[2] Haphazard, bould blinde bayarde ![3]
A figge for his uncourtesie that seekes to shun good company !

To Appius' request for advice he replies :

Well, then, this is my counsell, thus standeth the case,
Perhaps such a fetche as may please your grace :

[1] Text, *Mansipula*.
[2] Altered by Hazlitt to "brave." It probably means "embrace."
[3] A horse that does not see where it is going.

> There is no more wayes but *hap* or *hap not*,
> Either hap or els hapless, to knit up the knot :
> And if you will hazard to venter what falles,
> Perhaps that Haphazard will end all your thralles.

His distinctive note is this, that he tempts men by suggesting that they may offend and escape the consequences. In the end he falls into the pit that he has digged for others, and when his hap is to be hanged, like a true Vice he accepts the *contretemps* with jest and jape.

Yet despite the stock-in-trade that it takes over from Morality or Interlude, *Appius and Virginia* has specialties of its own that were better calculated to secure it custom in the period of the Renaissance. The author bestows most care on the main story, and makes a genuine attempt to bring out the human interest of the subject and the persons. In the opening scene he tries, in his well-meaning way, to give the impression of a home in which affection is the pervading principle, but in which affection itself is not allowed to run riot, but is restrained by prudence and obligation. Father, mother, and daughter sing a ditty in illustration of this sober love or its reverse, and always return to the refrain :

> The trustiest treasure in earth, as we see,
> Is man, wife, and children in one to agree ;
> Then friendly, and kindly, let measure be mixed
> With reason in season, where friendship is fixed.

There is some inarticulate feeling for effect in the contrast between the wholesomeness of this orderly family life and the incontinence of the tyrant who presently seeks to violate it. And the dramatic bent of the author—for it is no more than a bent—appears too in the portraiture of the parties concerned. The mingled perplexity and dread of Virginius, when in his consciousness of right he is summoned to the court, are justly conceived; and there is magnanimity in his answer to Appius' announcement that he must give judgment "as justice doth require":

> My lord, and reason good it is: your seruaunt doth request
> No parciall hand to aide his cause, no parciall minde or brest.
> If ought I haue offended you, your Courte or eke your Crowne,
> From lofty top of Turret hie persupetat me downe:
> If treason none by me be done, or any fault committed,
> Let my accusers beare the blame, and let me be remitted.

Similarly, the subsequent conflict in his heart between fondness for his daughter and respect for her and himself is clearly expressed. And her high-spirited demand for death is tempered and humanised by her instinctive recoil when he "proffers a blow":

> The gods forgeue thee, father deare! farewell: thy blow do
>   bend—
> Yet stay a whyle, O father deare, for fleash to death is fraile.
> Let first my wimple bind my eyes, and then thy blow assaile,
> Nowe, father, worke thy will on me, that life I may injoy.

But the most ambitious and perhaps the most successful delineation is that of Appius. At the outset he is represented as overwhelmed by his sudden yearning. Apelles, he thinks, was a "prattling fool" to boast of his statue; Pygmalion was fond "with raving fits" to run mad for the beauty of his work, for he could make none like Virginia. Will not the Gods treat him as they treated Salmacis, when Hermophroditus, bathing in the Carian fountain near the Lycian Marches, denied her suit?

>   Oh Gods aboue, bend downe to heare my crie
> As once ye[1] did to Salmasis, in Pond hard Lyzia by:
> Oh that Virginia were in case as somtime Salmasis,
> And in Hermofroditus stede my selfe might seeke my blisse!
> Ah Gods! would I unfold her armes complecting of my necke?
> Or would I hurt her nimble hand, or yeelde her such a checke?
> Would I gainsay hir tender skinne to baath where I do washe?
> Or els refuse her soft sweete lippes to touch my naked fleshe?
> Nay! Oh the Gods do know my minde, I rather would requier
> To sue, to serue, to crouch, to kneele, to craue for my desier.

[1] In original, *he*.

But out, ye Gods, ye bend your browes, and frowne to see me fare ;
Ye do not force ¹ my fickle fate, ye do not way my care.
Unrighteous and unequall Gods, unjust and eke unsure,
Woe worth the time ye made me liue, to see this haplesse houre.

This, we may suppose, is intended for a mad outbreak of voluptuous passion, "the nympholepsy
of some fond despair"; and, as such, it is not very
much worse than some that have won the applause
of more critical ages. It may suggest the style of
the Interlude in the *Midsummer-Night's Dream*, or
more forcibly, the "*King Cambyses'* vein" that was
then in vogue (for Preston's play of that name, published about a couple of years later than the probable
date when this was performed, is in every way the
nearest analogue to *Appius and Virginia* that the
history of our stage has to offer). But in comparison with the normal flow of the Moralities, the lines
have undoubtedly a certain urgency and glow. And
there are other touches that betray the incipient
playwright. Appius is not exhibited as a mere
monster ; through all his life his walk has been
blameless, and he is well aware of his "grounded
years," his reputation as judge, and the value of
good report. He is not at ease in the course he
now adopts ; there is a division in his nature, and he
does not yield to his temptation without forebodings
and remorse.

Consience he pricketh me contempnèd,
And Justice saith, Judgement wold haue me condemned :
Consience saith, crueltye sure will detest me ; ²
And Justice saith, death in thend will molest me :
And both in one sodden, me thinkes they do crie
That fier eternall my soule shall destroy.

But he always comes back to the supreme fact of his
longing for Virginia :

By hir I liue, by hir I die, for hir I joy or woe,
For hir my soule doth sinke or swimme, for her, I swere, I goe.

¹ Heed.   ² Make me detestable.

And there are the potentialities of a really powerful effect in the transition from his jubilant outburst when he thinks his waiting is at an end :

O lucky light! lo, present heere hir father doth appeare,

to his misgivings when he sees the old man is unaccompanied :

O, how I joy! Yet bragge thou not. Dame Beuty bides behinde.

And immediately thereafter the severed head is displayed to his view.

Nor was R. B., whether or not he was Richard Bower, Master of the Chapel children, quite without equipment for the treatment of a classical theme, though in this respect as in others his procedure is uncertain and fumbling in the highest degree. The typical personages of the under-plot have no relish of Latinity save in the termination of the labels that serve them as names, and they swear by God's Mother, and talk glibly of church and pews and prayer books, and a "pair of new cards." Even in the better accredited Romans of Livy's story there are anachronisms and incongruities. Appius, though ordinarily a judge, speaks of himself as prince, king or kaiser ; and references are made to his crown and realm. Nevertheless the author is not without the velleities of Humanism. He ushers in his prologue with some atrocious Latin Elegiacs, which the opening lines of the English are obliging enough to paraphrase :

Qui cupis aethereas et summas scandere sedes,
Vim simul ac fraudem discute, care, tibi.
Fraus hic nulla juvat, non fortia facta juvabunt :
Sola Dei tua te trahet tersa fides.
Cui placet in terris, intactae paludis [1] instar,
Vivere Virginiam nitere, Virgo, sequi :

[1] Professor Butler, to whom I am indebted for other emendations of the passage, which is very corrupt in the printed text, suggests *Palladis*, which gives a meaning, *the Virgin goddess*, and saves the metre. But I am not sure that R. B. had any bigoted objection to false quantities.

Quos tulit et luctus, discas et gaudia magna,
    Vitae dum parcae scindere fila parant.
Huc ades, O Virgo pariter moritura, sepulchro ;
    Sic ait, et facies pallida morte mutat."

Who doth desire the trump of fame to sound unto the skies,
Or els who seekes the holy place where mighty Joue he lies,
He must not by deceitfull mind, nor yet by puissant strength,
But by the faith and sacred lyfe he must it win at length ;
And what[1] she be that virgins lyfe on earth wold gladly leade,
The fluds that Virginia did fall[2] I wish her reade,
Her doller and hir doleful losse and yet her joyes at death :
"Come, Virgins pure, to graue with me," quoth she with latest
    breath.

In the same way there is throughout a lavish display
of cheap boyish erudition. Thus Virginius, reckoning up his services to Appius, soliloquises :

In Mars his games, in marshall feates, thou wast his only aide,
The huge Carrebd his[3] hazards thou for him hast[4] ofte assaied.
Was Sillas force by thee oft shunde or yet Lady Circe's[5] lande,
Pasiphae's[6] childe, that Minnotaur, did cause thee euer stande?

We are here indeed on the threshold of a very
different kind of art, of which, in its application to
Roman history, a sample had been submitted to the
English public two years previously in the *Octavia*
ascribed to Seneca.

The Latin Tragedy, merely because it was Latin,
and for that reason within the reach of a far
greater number of readers, was much better known
than the Greek at the period of the Renaissance.
But apart from its advantage in accessibility, it
attracted men of that age not only by its many
brilliant qualities but by its very defects, its tendency
to heightened yet abstract portraiture, its declamation,
its sententiousness, its violence, its unrestfulness. It
had both for good and bad a more modern bearing

---

[1] *I.e.* "whoever."
[2] Fall, causative ; "the tears she copiously shed."
[3] Charybdis.   [4] Original, *was*.
[5] So Hazlitt ; in the original *Adrice*.   [6] In the original, *Lacefaer*.

than the masterpieces of Hellenic antiquity, and in
some ways it corresponded more closely with the
culture of the sixteenth century than with our own.
It was therefore bound to have a very decisive
influence in shaping the traditions of the later stage ;
and the collection of ten plays ascribed to Seneca,
the poor remainder of a numerous tribe that may be
traced back to the third century before Christ,
furnished the pattern which critics prescribed for
imitation to all who would achieve the tragic crown.
And if this was true of the series as a whole, it was
also true of the play, which, whatever may be said
of the other nine, is certainly not by Seneca himself,
the poorest of them all, with most of the faults and
few of the virtues of the rest, *Octavia*, the sole
surviving example of the *Fabula Praetexta*, or the
Tragedy that dealt with native Roman themes.
The *Octavia*, however, was not less popular and
influential than its companions, and has even a claim
to especial attention inasmuch as it may be considered the remote ancestress of the Modern Historic
Play in general and of the Modern Roman Play
in particular. It inspired Mussato about 1300 to
write in Latin his *Eccerinis*, which deals with an
almost contemporary national subject, the fate of
Ezzelino : it inspired the young Muretus about 1544
to write his *Julius Caesar*, which in turn showed his
countrymen the way to treat such themes in French.
Before eight years were over they had begun to do
so, and many were the Roman plays composed by
the School of Ronsard. Certainly Seneca's method
would suit the historical dramatist who was not quite
at home in his history, for of local colour and visual
detail it made small account, and indeed was hardly
compatible with them. And it would commend
itself no less to men of letters who, without much
dramatic sympathy or aptitude, with no knowledge
of stage requirements, and little prospect of getting

their pieces performed, felt called upon *honoris causâ* to write dramas, which one of the most distinguished and successful among them was candid enough to entitle not plays but treatises. It is worth while to have a clear idea of the *Octavia* from which in right line this illustrious and forgotten progeny proceeded.

The date of the action is supposed to be 62 A.D. when Nero, who had for some time wished to wed his mistress, Poppaea Sabina, and had murdered his mother, partly on account of her opposition, divorced his virtuous wife, his step-sister Octavia, and exiled her to Pandataria, where shortly afterwards he had her put to death. The fact that Seneca is one of the persons in the piece, and that there are anticipatory references to Nero's death, which followed Seneca's compulsory suicide only after an interval of three years, sufficiently disposes of the theory that the philosopher himself was the author.

The text accepted in the sixteenth century suffered much, not only from the corruption of individual expressions, but from the displacement of entire passages. Greatly to its advantage it has been rearranged by later editors, but in the following account, their conjectures, generally happy and sometimes convincing, have been disregarded, as they were unknown to Thomas Nuce, who rendered it into English in 1561. In his hands, therefore, it is more loosely connected than it originally was, or than once more it has become for us ; and something of regularity it forfeits as well, for the dislocated framework led him to regard it as a drama in only four acts. Despite these flaws in his work he is a cleverer craftsman than many of his colleagues in Senecan translation, whose versions of the ten tragedies, most of them already published separately, were collected in a neat little volume in 1851.[1]

---

[1] It is from this that I quote. I have not been able to see either the first edition or the reprint for the Spenser Society.

An original "argument" summarises the story with sufficient clearness.

> Octauia, daughter to prince Claudius grace,
> To Nero espousd, whom Claudius did adopt,
> (Although Syllanus first in husbandes place
> Shee had receiu'd, whom she for Nero chopt[1]),
> Her parentes both, her Make that should have bene,
> Her husbandes present Tiranny much more,
> Her owne estate, her case that she was in,
> Her brother's death, (pore wretch), lamenteth sore.
> Him Seneca doth persuade, his latter loue,
> Dame Poppie, Crispyne's wife that sometime was,
> And eake Octauias maide, for to remoue.
> For Senecks counsel he doth lightly passe[2]
> But Poppie ioynes to him in marriage rites.
> The people wood[3] unto his pallace runne,
> His golden fourmed shapes[4]; which them sore spytes,
> They pull to ground : this uprore, now begunne,
> To quench, he some to griesly death doth send.
> But her close cased up in dreadful barge,
> With her unto Compania coast to wend
> A band of armed men, he gave in charge.

This programme the play proceeds to fill in.

In the first act Octavia, unbosoming herself to her nurse, relieves her heart of its woe and horror. She recounts the misfortunes of her house, the atrocities of her lord, his infidelities to her, her detestation of him. The nurse is full of sympathy, but admonishes her to patience, consoling her with assurances of the people's love, and reminding her of the truancies that the Empress of Heaven had also to excuse in her own husband and brother :

> Now, madam, sith on earth your powre is pight
> And haue on earth Queene Junos princely place,
> And sister are and wyfe to Neroes grace,
> Your wondrous restles dolours great appease.[5]

---

[1] Exchanged.

[2] Has small consideration.

[3] Mad.

[4] Statues.

[5] Tu quoque terris altera Juno
     Soror Augusti
     coniunxque graves vince dolores. (Line 224, ed. Peiper & Richter).
   This is now assigned to the chorus.

The chorus closes the act with a variation on the same themes, passing from praises of Octavia's purity and regrets for the ancient Roman intolerance of wrong, to the contrasted picture of Nero's unchallenged malignity.

The second act commences with a monologue by Seneca on the growing corruption of the age, which is interrupted by the approach of his master in talk with the Prefect. His words, as he enters, are :

> Dispatch with speede that we commaunded haue :
> Go, send forthwith some one or other slaue,
> That Plautius cropped scalpe, and Sillas eke,
> May bring before our face : goe some man seeke.[1]

Seneca remonstrates, but his remonstrances are of no avail ; and in a long discussion in which he advocates a policy of righteousness and goodwill and the sacredness of Octavia's claims, he is equally unsuccessful. The act, to which there is no chorus, concludes with Nero's determination to flout the wishes of the people and persist in the promotion of Poppaea :

> Why do we not appoynt the morrow next
> When as our mariage pompe may be context ?[2]

The third act is ushered in with one of those boding apparitions of which the Senecan Tragedy is so fond. The shade of Agrippina rises, the bridal torch of Nero and Poppaea in her hand :

> Through paunch of riuened earth, from Plutoes raigne
> With ghostly steps I am returnd agayne,
> In writhled wristes, that bloud do most desyre,
> Forguyding[3] wedlocke vyle with Stygian fire.[4]

---

[1] Perage imperata : mitte qui Plauti mihi
Sillaeque caesi referat abscissum caput.   (Line 449.)

[2] Quin destinamus proximum thalamis diem ?   (Line 604.)

[3] Guiding to ruin.

[4] Tellure rupta Tartaro gressum extuli
stygiam cruenta praeferens dextra facem
thalamis scelestis.   (Line 605.)

She bewails her crimes on her son's behalf and his parricidal ingratitude, but vengeance will fall on him at last.

> Although that Tyrant proude and scornful wight
> His court with marble stone do strongly dyght,
> And princelike garnish it with glistering golde :
> Though troupes of soldiours, shielded sure, upholde
> Their chieftaynes princely porch : and though yet still
> The world drawne drye with taskes even to his will
> Great heapes of riches yeeld, themselues to saue ;
> Although his bloudy helpe the Parthians craue,
> And Kingdomes bring, and goods al that they haue ;
> The tyme and day shall come, when as he shall,
> Forlorne, and quite undone, and wanting all,
> Unto his cursed deedes his life, and more,
> Unto his foes his bared throate restore.[1]

As she disappears, Octavia enters in conversation with the chorus, whom she dissuades from the expression of sympathy for her distress lest they should incur the wrath of the tyrant. On this suggestion they denounce the supineness of the degenerate Romans in the vindication of right, and exhort each other to an outbreak.

In the fourth act, Poppaea, terrified by an ominous dream of Nero stabbing her first husband, and of Agrippina, a firebrand in her grasp, leading her down through the earth, rushes across the stage, but is stayed by her nurse, who soothes and encourages her, and bids her return to her bridal chamber. Yet it seems as though her worst fears were at once to be realised. The chorus, acknowledging the charms of the new Empress, is interrupted by the hurried arrival of a messenger. He announces that

---

[1] Licet extruat marmoribus atque auro tegat
superbus aulam, limen armatae ducis
servent cohortes, mittat immensas opes
exhaustus orbis, supplices dextram petant
Parthi cruentam, regna divitias ferant :
veniet dies tempusque quo reddat suis
animam nocentem sceleribus jugulum hostibus
desertus ac destructus et cunctis egens.   (Line 636.)

the people are in uproar, overthrowing the statues
of Poppaea, and demanding the restitution of Octavia.
But to what purpose? The chorus sings that it is
vain to oppose the resistless arms of love. It is at
least vain to oppose the arms of Nero's soldiers.
Confident in their strength he enters, breathing forth
threatenings and slaughter, and expectant of a time
when he will exact a full penalty from the citizens:

> Then shall their houses fall by force of fire;
> What burning both, and buildings fayre decay,[1]
> What beggarly want, and wayling hunger may,
> Those villaines shall be sure to have ech day.[2]

Dreaming of the future conflagration, he is dissatisfied with the prefect, who tells him that the insurrection has been easily quelled with the death of one or
two, and meanwhile turns all his wrath against the
innocent cause of the riot. The play does not, however, end with the murder of Octavia. She informs
the chorus that she is to be dispatched in Agrippina's death-ship to her place of exile,

> But now no helpe of death I feele,
> Alas I see my Brothers boate:
> This is the same, whose vaulted keele
> His Mother once did set a flote.
> And now his piteous Sister I,
> Excluded cleane from spousall place
> Shall be so caried by and by;[3]
> No force hath virtue in this case.[4]

And the final song of the chorus, with a touch of
dramatic irony, wishes her a prosperous voyage, and

---

[1] Destruction of fair buildings.
[2] Mox tecta flammis concidant urbis meis,
ignes ruinae noxium populum premant
turpisque egestas saeva cum luctu fames.   (Line 847.)
[3] At once.
[4] Sed iam spes est nulla salutis:
fratris cerno miseranda ratem.
hac en cuius vecta carina
quondam genetrix
nunc et thalamis expulsa soror
miseranda vehar.   (Line 926.)

congratulates her on her removal from the cruel city
of Rome :

> O pippling puffe of western wynde,
> Which sacrifice didst once withstand,
> Of Iphigen to death assignde :
> And close in Cloude congealed clad
> Did cary hir from smoking aares [1]
> Which angry, cruell Virgin had ;
> This Prince also opprest with cares
> Saue from this paynefull punishment
> To Dian's temple safely borne :
> The barbarous Moores, to rudenesse bent,
> Then [2] Princes Courtes in Rome forlorne
> Haue farre more Cyuile curtesie :
> For there doth straungers death appease
> The angry Gods in heauens on hie,
> But Romayne bloude our Rome must please. [3]

There could be no greater contrast than between
Appius and Virginia, with its exits and entrances,
its changefulness and bustle, its mixture of the pom-
pous and the farcical ; and the monotonous declamation, the dismissal of all action, the meagreness of
the material in the *Octavia*. And yet they are more
akin than they at first sight appear. Disregard the
buffoonery which the mongrel "tragicall comedie"
inherited from the native stock, and you perceive
traits that suggest another filiation. The similarity
with the Latin Play in its English version is, of
course, misleading, except in so far as it shows how
the Senecan drama must present itself to an early

[1] Altars. [2] Than.

[3] Lenes aurae zephyrique leves
tectam quondam nube aetheria
qui vixistis raptam saevae
virginis aris Iphigeniam,
hanc quoque tristi procul a poena
portate precor templa ad Triviae.
Urbe est nostra mitior Aulis
et Maurorum * barbara tellus ;
hospitis illic caede litatur
numen superum.
civis gaudet Roma cruore.   (Line 1002.)

* Better reading, Taurorum.

Elizabethan in the light of his own crude art. The devices of the rhetorician were travestied by those who knew no difference between rhetoric and rant, and whose very rant, whether they tried to invent or to translate, was clumsy and strained. Hence the "tenne tragedies" of Seneca and the nearly contemporary Mixed Plays have a strong family resemblance in style. In all of them save the *Octavia* the resemblance extends from diction to verse, for in dialogue and harangue they employ the trailing fourteen-syllable measure of the popular play, while in the *Octavia* this is discarded for the more artistic heroic couplet. In this and other respects, T. N., as Nuce signs himself, is undoubtedly more at his ease in the literary element than others of the group ; nevertheless he is often content to fly the ordinary pitch of R. B. This is most obvious when their performances are read and compared as a whole, but it is evident enough in single passages. The Nurse, for example, says of Nero to Octavia :

> Eft steppèd into servile Pallace stroke,
> To filthy vices lore one easly broke,
> Of Divelish wicked wit this Princocks proude,
> By stepdames wyle prince Claudius Sonne auoude ;
> Whome deadly damme did bloudy match ylight,
> And thee, against thy will, for feare did plight.[1]

These words might almost suit the mouths of Appius and his victims.

But leaving aside the affinities due to the common use of English by writers on much the same plane of art, the London medley is not immeasurably different from or inferior to the Roman *Praetexta*, even when confronted with the latter in its native

---

[1] The original author has a right to complain :

> Intravit hostis hei mihi captam domum
> dolisque novercae principis factus gener
> idemque natus iuvenis infandi ingeni
> scelerum capacis dira cui genetrix facem
> accendit et te iunxit invitam metu.   (Line 155.)

dress. In both the characterisation is in the same rudimentary and obvious style, and shows the same predilection for easily classified types. There is even less genuine theatrical tact in the Latin than in the English drama. The chief persons are under careful supervision and are kept rigidly apart. Nero never meets Octavia or Poppaea, Poppaea and Octavia never meet each other. No doubt there are some successful touches : the first entrance of Nero is not ineffective ; the equivocal hopefulness of the last chorus is a thing one remembers : the insertion of Agrippina's prophecy and Poppaea's dream does something to keep in view the future requital and so to alleviate the thickening gloom. Except for these, however, and a few other felicities natural to a writer with long dramatic traditions behind him, the *Octavia* strikes us as a series of disquisitions and discussions, well-arranged, well-managed, often effective, sometimes brilliant, that have been suggested by a single impressive historical situation.

2

THE FRENCH SENECANS

These salient features are transmitted to the Senecan dramas of France, except that the characterisation is even vaguer, the declamation ampler, and the whole treatment less truly dramatic and more obviously rhetorical ; of which there is an indication in the greater relative prominence of monologue as compared with dialogue, and in the excessive predilection for general reflections,[1] many of them

---

[1] " Jodelle's und Garnier's Dramen sind reicher an Sentenzen als die Seneca's, Jodelle hat mehr als doppelt so viel." *Gedankenkreis . . . in Jodelle's und Garnier's Tragödien*, by Paul Kahnt, who gives the results of his calculations in an interesting table.

derived from Seneca and Horace, but many of them too of modern origin.

At the head of the list stands the *Julius Caesar* of Muretus, a play which, even if of far less intrinsic worth than can be claimed for it, would always be interesting for the associations with which it is surrounded.

Montaigne, after mentioning among his other tutors "Marc Antoine Muret," que le France et l'Italie recognoist pour le meilleur orateur du temps," goes on to tell us: "J'ay soustenu les premiers personnages ez tragedies latines de Buchanan, de Guerente et de Muret, qui se representerent en nostre college de Guienne avecques dignité: en cela, Andreas Goveanus, nostre principal, comme en toutes aultres parties de sa charge, feut sans comparaison le plus grand principal de France; et m'en tenoit on maistre ouvrier."

The *Julius Caesar* written in 1544 belongs to the year before Montaigne left Bordeaux at the age of thirteen, so he may have taken one of the chief parts in it, Caesar, or M. Brutus, or Calpurnia. This would always give us a kind of personal concern in Muret's short boyish composition of barely 600 lines, which he wrote at the age of eighteen and afterwards published only among his *Juvenilia*. But it has an importance of its own. Of course it is at the best an academic experiment, though from Montaigne's statement that these plays were presented "avecques dignité," and from the interest the principal took in the matter, we may suppose that the performance would be exemplary in its kind. Of course, too, even as an academic experiment it does not, to modern taste, seem on the level of the more elaborate tragedies which George Buchanan, "ce grand poëte ecossois," as Montaigne reverently styles his old preceptor, had produced at the comparatively mature age of from thirty-three to thirty-six, ere leaving Bordeaux two years before. It is inferior to the *Baptistes* and far inferior to the *Jephthes* in precision of portraiture and pathos of appeal. But in the sixteenth century, partly, no doubt, because the subject was of such secular importance and the treatment so congenial to learned theory, but also, no doubt, because the eloquence was sometimes so genuinely eloquent, and the Latin, despite a few licenses in metre and grammar, so racy of the classic soil, it obtained extraordinary fame and exercised extraordinary influence. For these reasons, as well as the additional one that it is now less widely known than it ought to be, a brief account of it may not be out of place.

The first act is entirely occupied with a soliloquy by Caesar, in which he represents himself as having attained the summit of earthly glory.

> Let others at their pleasure count their triumphs, and name themselves from vanquished provinces. It is more to be called Caesar : whoso seeks fresh titles elsewhere, takes something away thereby. Would you have me reckon the regions conquered under my command ? Enumerate all there are.[1]

Even Rome has yielded to him, even his great son-in-law admitted his power,

> and whom he would not have as an equal, he has borne as a superior.[2]

What more is to be done ?

> My quest must be heaven, earth is become base to me. . . . Now long enough have I lived whether for myself or

---

[1] Numerent triumphos, cum volent, alii suos,
Seque * subactis nominent provinciis.
Plus est vocari Caesarem ; quisquis novos
Aliunde titulos quaerit, is jam detrahit :
Numerare ductu vis meo victas plagas ?
Percurrito omnes.

[2] quemque noluerat parem,
Tulit priorem.

* Insert *ex*.

for my country. . . . The destruction of foes, the gift of laws to the people, the ordering of the year, the restoration of splendour to worship, the settlement of the world,—than these, greater things can be conceived by none, nor pettier be performed by me. . . . When life has played the part assigned to it, death never comes in haste and sometimes too late.[1]

The chorus sings of the immutability of fortune.

In the second act Brutus, in a long monologue, upbraids himself with his delay.

Does the virtue of thy house move thee nought, and nought the name of Brutus? Nought, the hard lot of thy groaning country, crushed by the tyrant and calling for thine aid? Nought the petitions in which the people lament that Brutus comes not to champion the state? If these things fail to touch thee, thy wife now gives thee rede enough that thou be a man ; who has pledged her faith to thee in blood, thus avouching herself the offspring of thine uncle.[2]

He raises and meets the objections which his understanding offers :

Say you he is not king but dictator? If the thing be the same, what boots a different name? Say you he shuns that name, and rejects the crowns they proffer him : this is pretence and mockery, for why then did he remove the tribunes? True, he gave me dignities and once my life ; with me my country outweighs them all. Whoso shows gratitude to a

[1] Coelum petendum est : terra jam vilet mihi. . . .
Jam vel mihi, vel patriae vixi satis. . . .
Hostes perempti, civibus leges datae,
Digestus annus, redditus sacris nitor,
Compostus orbis, cogitari nec queunt
Majora cuiquam, nec minora a me geri. . . .
Cum vita partes muneris functa est sui,
Mors propera nunquam, sera nonnunquam venit.

[2] Nihilne te virtus tuorum commovet,
Nomenque Bruti? nihil * gementis patriae,
Pressae a tyranno, opemque poscentis tuam
Conditio dura? nil libelli supplices,
Queis Brutum abesse civitatis vindicem
Cives queruntur? Haec parum si te movent,
Tua jam, vir ut sis, te satis conjux monet,
Fidem cruore quae tibi obstrinxit suam.
Testata sic se avunculi prolem tui.

* Certainly read *nil.*

tyrant against his country's interest, is ingrate while he seeks
to be stupidly grateful.[1]

And his conclusion is

> The sun reawakening to life saw the people under the yoke,
> and slaves : at his setting may he see them free.[2]

To him enters Cassius exultant that the day has
arrived, impatient for the decisive moment, scarce
able to restrain his eagerness. Only one scruple
remains to him ; should Antony be slain along with
his master ? Brutus answers :

> Often already have I said that my purpose is this, to
> destroy tyranny but save the citizens.
> *Cass.* Then let it be destroyed from its deepest roots, lest if
> only cut down, it sprout again at some time hereafter.
> *Brut.* The whole root lurks under a single trunk.
> *Cass.* Think'st thou so ? I shall say no more. Thy will be
> done : we all follow thy guidance.[3]

The chorus sings the glories of those who, like
Harmodius with his "amiculus," destroy the tyrants,
and the risks these tyrants run.

In the third act Calpurnia, flying in panic to her
chamber, is met by her nurse, to whom she discloses
the cause of her distress. She has dreamed that
Caesar lies dead in her arms covered with blood,

[1] At vero non rex iste, sed dictator est.
Dum res sit una, quid aliud nomen juvat?
At nomen illud refugit, et oblatas sibi
Rejicit coronas. Fingere hoc et ludere est.
Nam cur Tribunos igitur amovit loco?
At mihi et honores et semel vitam dedit.
Plus patria illis omnibus apud me potest.
Qui se tyranno in patriam gratum exhibet,
Dum vult inepte gratus esse, ingratus est.

[2] Phoebus renascens subditos cives jugo,
Servosque vidit : liberos videat cadens.

[3] Jam saepe dixi, id esse consilium mihi,
Salvis perimere civibus tyrannida.
Cass. Perimatur ergo ab infimis radicibus,
Ne quando posthac caesa rursum pullulet.
Bru. Latet sub uno tota radix corpore.
Cass. Itan' videtur? amplius nil proloquar.
Tibi pareatur ; te sequimur omnes ducem.

and stabbed with many wounds. The nurse points out the vanity of dreams and the unlikelihood of any attempt against one so great and beneficent, whose clemency has changed even foes to friends. Calpurnia, only half comforted, rejoins that she will at least beseech him to remain at home that day, and the chorus prays that misfortune may be averted.

In the fourth act Calpurnia tries her powers of persuasion. To her passionate appeal, her husband answers:

> What? Dost thou ask me to trust thy dreams?
> *Cal.* No; but to concede something to my fear.
> *Caes.* But that fear of thine rests on dreams alone.
> *Cal.* Assume it to be vain; grant something to thy wife.[1]

She goes on to enumerate the warning portents, and at length Caesar assents to her prayers since she cannot repress her terrors. But here Decimus Brutus strikes in:

> High-hearted Caesar, what word has slipped from thee?[2]

He bids him remember his glory:

> O most shameful plight if the world is ruled by Caesar and Caesar by a woman. . . . What, Caesar, dost thou suppose the Fathers will think if thou bidst them, summoned at thy command, to depart now and to return when better dreams present themselves to Calpurnia. Go rather resolutely and assume a name the Parthians must dread: or if this please thee not, at least go forth, and thyself dismiss the Fathers; let them not think they are slighted and had in derision.[3]

---

[1] Quid? Somniis me credere tuis postulas?
Cal. Non: sed timori ut non nihil tribuas meo.
Caes. At iste solis nititur somniis timor.
Cal. Finge esse vanum: tribuito aliquid conjugi.

[2] Magnanime Caesar, quod tibi verbum excidit?

[3] O statum deterrimum,
Si Caesar orbem, Caesarem mulier regit! . . .
Quid, Caesar, animi patribus credis fore,
Si te jubente convocatos jusseris
Abire nunc, redire, cum Calpurniae
Meliora sese objecerint insomnia?
Vade potius constanter, et nomen cape
Parthis timendum; aut, hoc minus si te juvat,
Prodito saltem, atque ipse patres mittito:
Ne negligi se, aut ludibrio haberi putent.

Caesar is bent one way by pity for his wife, another by fear of these taunts; but, at last, leaving Calpurnia to her misgivings, he exclaims :

> But yet, since even to fall, so it be but once, is better than to be laden with lasting fear; not if three hundred prophet-voices call me back, not if with his own voice the present Deity himself warn me of the peril and urge my staying here, shall I refrain.[1]

The chorus cites the predictions of Cassandra to show that it would sometimes be wise to follow the counsel of women.

In the fifth act Brutus and Cassius appear in triumph.

Brut. Breathe, citizens; Caesar is slain! . . . In the Senate which he erewhile overbore, he lies overborne.

Cass. Behold, Rome, the sword yet warm with blood, behold the hand that hath championed thine honour. That loathsome one who in impious frenzy and blind rage had troubled thee and thine, sore wounded by this same hand, by this same sword which thou beholdest, and gashed in every limb, hath spewed forth his life in a flood of gore.[2]

As they leave, Calpurnia enters bewailing the truth of her dream, and inviting to share in her laments the chorus, which denounces vengeance on the criminals. Then the voice of Caesar is heard in rebuke of their tears and in comfort of their distress. Only

---

[1] Sed tamen quando semel
Vel cadere praestat, quam metu longo premi ;
Non si tracentis vocibus vatum avocer,
Non si ipse voce propria praesens Deus
Moneat pericli, atque hic manendum suadeat,
Me continebo.

[2] *Brut.* Spirate cives ! Caesar interfectus est. . . .
In curia, quam oppresserat, oppressus jacet.

Cass. En, Roma, gladium adhuc tepentem sanguine ;
En dignitatis vindicem dextram tuae.
Impurus ille, qui furore nefario,
Rabieque caeca, te et tuos vexaverat,
Hac, hac manu, atque hoc, hocce gladio, quem vides,
Consauciatus, et omnibus membris lacer
Undam cruoris, et animum evomuit simul.

his shadow fell, but he himself is joined to the immortals.

> Weep no more: it is the wretched that tears befit. Those who assailed me with frantic mind—a god am I, and true is my prophecy—shall not escape vengeance for their deed. My sister's grandson, heir of my virtue as of my sceptre, will require the penalty as seems good to him.[1]

Calpurnia recognises the voice, and the chorus celebrates the bliss of the "somewhat" that is released from the prison house of the body.

It is interesting to note that Muretus already employs a number of the *motifs* that reappear in Shakespeare. Thus he gives prominence to the self-conscious magnanimity of Caesar: to the temporary hesitation of Brutus, with his appeal to his name and the letters that are placed in his way; to his admiration for the courage and constancy of Portia; to his final whole-heartedness and disregard of Caesar's love for him; to his prohibition of Mark Antony's death; to Cassius' vindictive zeal and eager solicitation of his friend; to Calpurnia's dream, and the contest between her and Decimus Brutus and in Caesar's own mind; to Caesar's fatal decision in view of his honour, and his rejection of the fear of death; to the exultation of Brutus and Cassius as they enter with their blood-stained swords after the deed is done. And more noticeable than any of these details, are the divided admiration and divided sympathy the author bestows both on Brutus and Caesar—which are obvious even in the wavering utterances of the chorus. We are far removed from the times when Dante saw Lucifer devouring Brutus and Cassius in two of his mouths with Judas between

---

[1] Desinite flere : lacrymae miseros decent.
Qui me furenti, (vera praemoneo Indiges)
Sunt animo adorti, non inultum illud ferent.
Heres meae virtutis, ut sceptri mei,
Nepos sororis, arbitratu pro suo
Poenos reposcet.

them ; or when Chaucer, making a composite monster of the pair, tells how "false Brutus-Cassius,"

"That ever hadde of his hye state envye,"

"stikede" Julius with "boydekins." But we are
equally far from the times when Marie - Joseph
Chénier was to write his tragedy of *Brutus et
Cassius, Les Derniers Romains.* At the renaissance
the characteristic feeling was enthusiasm for Caesar
and his assassin alike, though it was Shakespeare
alone who knew how to reconcile the two points of
view.[1]

Of the admiration which Muret's little drama
excited there is documentary proof. Prefixed to it
are a number of congratulatory verses, and among
the eulogists are not only scholars, like Buchanan,[2]
but literary men, members of the Pléiade—Dorat,
Baïf, and especially Jodelle, who has his compli-
mentary conceits on the appropriateness of the
author's name, Mark Antony, to the feat he has
accomplished.

But this last testimony leads us to the less explicit
but not less obvious indications of the influence
exercised by Muret's tragedy which appear in the
subsequent story of literary production. This influence was both indirect and direct. The example
of this modern Latin play could not but count for

[1] I am quite unable to agree with Herr Collischonn's view that
Muret's play is more republican in sentiment than that of Grévin. In
both there is some discrepancy and contradiction, but with Muret,
Caesar is a more prominent figure than Brutus, taking part in three
scenes, if we include his intervention after death, while Brutus appears
only in two, and to my mind Caesar makes fully as sympathetic an
impression. On the other hand, the alleged monarchic bias of Grévin's
work cannot be considered very pronounced, when, as M. Faguet
mentions in his *Tragédie française au XVIe Siècle*, "it was reprinted
in the time of Ravaillac with a preface violently hostile to the principle
of monarchy." But see Herr Collischonn's excellent introduction to his
Grévin's Tragödie " Caesar," Ausgaben und Abhandlungen, etc., LII.

[2] See Ruhnken's edition of Muretus. For the text I have generally
but not always used Collischonn's reprint.

something when Jodelle took the further step of treating another Roman theme in the vernacular. In the vernacular, too, Grévin was inspired to rehandle the same theme as Muretus, obtaining from his predecessor most of his material and his apparatus. These experiments again were not without effect on the later dramas of Garnier, two of which were to leave a mark on English literature.

The first regular tragedy as well as the first Roman history in the French language was the *Cléopatre Captive* of Jodelle, acted with great success in 1552 before Henry II. by Jodelle's friends, who at the subsequent banquet presented to him, in semi-pagan wise, a goat decked with flowers and ivy. The prologue [1] to the King describes the contents.

> " C'est une tragedie
> Qui d'une voix plainti᎓e et hardie
> Te represente un Romain, Marc Antoine,
> Et Cleopatre, Egyptienne royne,
> Laquelle après qu'Antoine, son amy,
> Estant desjà vaincu par l'ennemy,
> Se fust tué, ja se sentant captive,
> Et qu'on vouloit la porter toute vive
> En un triomphe avecques ses deux femmes,
> S'occit. Icy les desirs et les flammes
> De deux amants : d'Octavian aussi
> L'orgueil, l'audace et le journel soucy
> De son trophée emprains tu sonderas."

But this programme conveys an impression of greater variety and abundance than is justified by the piece. In point of fact it begins only after the death of Antony, who does not intervene save as a ghost in the opening scene, to bewail his offences and announce that in a dream he has bid Cleopatra join him before the day is out.[2] Nor do we hear

---

[1] *Ancien Théatre François*, Tome IV. ed Viollet Le Duc.

[2] As he puts it, rather comically to modern ears :
> 'Avant que ce soleil qui vient ores de naistre,
> Ayant tracé son jour, *chez sa tante se plonge.*

anything of "desirs et flammes" on his part; rather
he resents her seductions, and has summoned her to
share his torments :

> Or se faisant compagne en ma peine et tristesse
> Qui s'est faite long-temps compagne en ma liesse.

The sequel does little more than describe how
his command is carried out.   Cleopatra enters into
conversation with Eras and Charmium, and despite
their remonstrances resolves to obey.   The chorus
sings of the fickleness of fortune : (Act i.).   Octavianus, after a passing regret for Antony, arranges
with Proculeius and Agrippa to make sure of her
presence at his triumph.   The chorus sings of the
perils of pride : (Act ii.).   Octavianus visits the
Queen, dismisses her excuses, but grants mercy to
her and her children, and pardons her deceit when
her retention of her jewellery is exposed by Seleucus.
But Seleucus is inconsolable for his offence as well
as his castigation, and exclaims :

> Lors que la royne, et triste et courageuse,
> Devant Cesar aux chevaux m'a tiré,
> Et de son poing mon visage empiré,
> S'elle m'eust fait mort en terre gesir,
> Elle eust preveu à mon present desir,
> Veu que la mort n'eust point esté tant dure
> Que l'eternelle et mordante pointure
> Qui jà desjà jusques au fond me blesse
> D'avoir blessé ma royne et ma maistresse.

The chorus oddly enough discovers in her maltreat-
ment of the tale-bearer a proof of her indomitable
spirit, and an indication that she will never let
herself be led to Rome : (Act iii.).   Cleopatra now
explains that her submission was only feigned to
secure the lives of her children, and that she herself
has no thought of following the conqueror's car.
Eras and Charmium approve, and all three depart
to Antony's tomb to offer there a last sacrifice,
which the chorus describes in full detail : (Act

c

iv.).   Proculeius in consternation announces the
sequel :

> " J'ay veu (ô rare et miserable chose !)
> Ma Cleopatre en son royal habit
> Et sa couronne, au long d'un riche lict
> Peint et doré, blesme et morte couchée,
> Sans qu'elle fust d'aucun glaive touchée,
> Avecq Eras, sa femme, à ses pieds morte,
> Et Charmium vive, qu'en telle sorte
> J'ay lors blasmée :   'A a ! Charmium, est-ce
> Noblement faict ?'   'Ouy, ouy, c'est de noblesse
> De tant de rois Egyptiens venuë
> Un tesmoignage.'   Et lors, peu soustenuë
> En chancelant et s'accrochant en vain,
> Tombe a l'envers, restans un tronc humain."

The chorus celebrates the pitifulness and glory of
her end, and the supremacy of Caesar : (Act v.).

Thus, despite the promises of the prologue, the
play resolves itself to a single *motif*, the determination of Cleopatra to follow Antony in defiance
of Octavianus' efforts to prevent her.   Nevertheless,
simple as it is, it fails in real unity.   The ghost of
Antony, speaking, one must suppose, the final verdict,
pronounces condemnation on her as well as himself ;
yet in the rest of the play, even in the undignified
episode with Seleucus, Jodelle bespeaks for her
not only our sympathy but our admiration.   It is
just another aspect of this that Antony treats her
death as the beginning of her punishment, but to
her and her attendants and the women of Alexandria
it is a desirable release.   The recurrent theme of
the chorus, varied to suit the complexion of the
different acts, is always the same :

> Joye, qui dueil enfante
> Se meurdrist ; puis la mort,
> Par la joye plaisante,
> Fait au deuil mesme tort.

Half a dozen years later, in 1558, the *Confrères
de la Passion* were acting a play which Muretus had

more immediately prompted, and which did him greater credit. This was the *Cesar* of Jacques Grévin, a young Huguenot gentlemen who, at the age of twenty, recast in French the even more juvenile effort of the famous scholar, expanding it to twice the size, introducing new personages, giving the old ones more to do, and while borrowing largely in language and construction, shaping it to his own ends and making it much more dramatic. Indeed, his tragedy strikes one as fitter for the popular stage than almost any other of its class, and this seems to have been felt at the time, for besides running through two editions in 1561 and 1562, it was reproduced by the *Confrères* with great success in the former year. Of course its theatrical merit is only relative, and it does not escape the faults of the Senecan school. Grévin styles his *dramatis personae* rather ominously and very correctly "entre-parleurs"; for they talk rather than act. They talk, moreover, in long, set harangues even when they are conversing, and Grévin so likes to hear them that he sometimes lets the story wait. Nor do they possess much individuality or concrete life. But the young author has passion ; he has fire ; and he knows the dramatic secret of contrasting different moods and points of view.

He follows his exemplar most closely, and often literally, in the first three acts, though even in them he often goes his own way. Thus, after Caesar's opening soliloquy, which is by no means so Olympian as in Muret, he introduces Mark Antony, who encourages his master with reminders of his greatness and assurances of his devotion. In the second act, after Marcus Brutus' monologue, not only Cassius but Decimus has something to say, and there is a quicker interchange of statement and rejoinder than is usual in such a play. In the third act, the third and fourth of Muretus are combined, and after the conversation of Calpurnia with the Nurse, there follow her attempts to dissuade her husband from visiting the senate-house, the hesitation of Caesar, the counter-arguments of Decimus; and in conclusion, when Decimus has prevailed, the Nurse resumes her endeavours at consolation. The fourth act is entirely new, and gives an account of the assassination by the mouth of a Messenger, who is also a new person, to the distracted Calpurnia and her sympathetic Nurse. In the fifth Grévin begins by returning to his authority in the jubilant speeches of Brutus and Cassius, but one by Decimus is added; and rejecting the expedient of the ghostly intervention, he substitutes, much more effectively, that of Mark Antony, who addresses the chorus of soldiers, rouses them to vengeance, and having made sure of them, departs to stir up the people.

Altogether a creditable performance, and a distinct improvement on the more famous play that supplied the ground-work. One must not be misled by the almost literal discipleship of Grévin in particular passages, to suppose that even in language he is a mere imitator. The discipleship is of course undeniable. Take Brutus' outburst:

> Rome effroy de ce monde, exemple des provinces,
> Laisse la tyrannie entre les mains des Princes
> Du Barbare estranger, qui honneur luy fera,
> Non pas Rome, pendant que Brute vivera.

And compare:

> Reges adorent barbarae gentes suos,
> Non Roma mundi terror, et mundi stupor.
> Vivente Bruto, Roma reges nesciet.

So, too, after the murder Brutus denounces his victim:

> Ce Tyran, ce Cesar, ennemi du Senat. . . .
> Ce bourreau d'innocens, ruine de nos loix,
> La terreur des Romains, et le poison des droicts.

The lines whence this extract is taken merely enlarge Muretus' conciser statement :

> Ille, ille, Caesar, patriae terror suae,
> Hostis senatus, innocentium carnifex,
> Legum ruina, publici jures lues.

But generally Grévin is more abundant and more fervid even when he reproduces most obviously, and among the best of his purple patches are some that are quite his own. He indeed thought differently. He modestly confesses :

> Je ne veux pourtant nier que s'il se trouve quelque traict digne estre loué, qu'il ne soit de Muret, lequel a esté mon precepteur quelque temps es lettres humaines, et auquel je donne le meilleur comme l'ayant appris de luy.

All the same there is nothing in Muretus like the passage in which Brutus promises himself an immortality of fame :

> Et quand on parlera de Cesar et de Romme,
> Qu'on se souvienne aussi qu'il a esté un homme,
> Un Brute, le vangeur de toute cruauté,
> Qui aura d'un seul coup gaigné la liberté.
> Quand on dira, Cesar fut maistre de l'empire,
> Qu'on die quant-et-quant, Brute le sceut occire.
> Quand on dira, Cesar fut premier Empereur,
> Qu'on die quant-et-quant, Brute en fut le vangeur.
> Ainsi puisse a jamais sa gloire estre suyvie
> De celle qui sera sa mortelle ennemie.

Grévin's tragedy had great vogue, was preferred even to those of Jodelle, and was praised by Ronsard, though Ronsard afterwards retracted his praises when Grévin broke with him on religious grounds. His protestantism, however, would be a recommendation rather than otherwise in England, and one would like to know whether some of the lost English pieces on the same subject owed anything to the French drama. The suggestion has even been made that Shakespeare was acquainted with it. There are some vague resemblances in particular thoughts and phrases,[1] the closest of which occurs in Caesar's pronouncement on death :

> Il vault bien mieux mourir
> Asseuré de tout poinct, qu'incessament perir
> Faulsement par la peur.

This suggests :

> Cowards die many times before their deaths :
> The valiant never taste of death but once. (II. ii. 32.)

Herr Collischonn also draws attention to a coincidence in situation that is not derived from Plutarch. When the conspirators are discussing the chances of Caesar's attending the senate meeting, Cassius says :

> Encore qu'il demeure
> Plus long temps à venir, si fault il bien qu'il meure :

and Decimus answers :

> Je m'en vay au devant, sans plus me tormenter,
> Et trouveray moyen de le faire haster.

It is at least curious to find the same sort of addition, in the same circumstances and with the same speakers in Shakespeare.

> *Cassius.* But it is doubtful yet,
> Whether Caesar will come forth to-day, or no. . . .
> *Dec. Brut.* Never fear that : if he be so resolved,
> I can o'ersway him. . . .
> For I can give his humour the true bent
> And I will bring him to the Capitol.
> (II. i. 194, 202, 210.)

Such *minutiae*, however, are far from conclusive, especially since, as in the two instances quoted, which are the most significant, Plutarch, though he did not authorise, may at any rate have suggested them. The first looks like an expansion of Caesar's remark when his friends were discussing which death was the best : " Death unlooked for." The second

---

[1] Enumerated by Collischonn in his excellent edition, see above. He has, however, overlooked the one I give.

follows as a natural dramatic anticipation of the part
that Decimus actually played in inducing Caesar to
keep tryst. They may very well have occurred
independently to both poets ; or, if there be a connection, may have been transmitted from the older
to the younger through the medium of some forgotten English piece. There is more presumptive
evidence that Grévin influenced the *Julius Caesar*
of Sir William Alexander, Earl of Stirling ; but
Stirling's paraphrase of his authorities is so diffuse
that they are not always easy to trace. His apparent debts to Grévin may really be due to the later
and much more famous French Senecan Garnier,
two of whose works have an undoubted though not
very conspicuous place in the history of the English
Drama generally, and especially of the Roman Play
in England.

Cornélie, the earlier and less successful of the pair,
written in Garnier's twenty-eighth year, was performed at the Hôtel de Bourgogne in 1573, and was
published in 1574. The young author was not
altogether unpractised in his art, for already in 1568
he had written a drama on the subject of Portia,
but he has not yet advanced beyond his predecessors, and like them, or perhaps more obviously
than they, is at the stage of regarding the tragedy
"only as an elegy mixed with rhetorical exposi-
tions." The episode that he selected lent itself to
such treatment.

Cornelia, the daughter of Metellus Scipio, had
after the loss of her first husband, the younger
Cassius, become the wife of Pompey the Great, of
whose murder she was an eye-witness. Meanwhile
her father still made head against Caesar in Africa,
and the play deals with her regrets and suspense at
Rome till she learns the issue of this final struggle.
In the first act Cicero soliloquises on the woes of
the country, which he traces to her lust of conquest ;

and the chorus takes up the burden at the close. In the second Cornelia bewails her own miseries, which she attributes to her infidelity in marrying again : Cicero tries to comfort her and she refuses his comfort, both in very long harangues ; and the chorus describes the mutability of mortal things. In the third act she narrates an ominous dream in which the shade of Pompey has visited her. Scarcely has she left the stage when Cicero enters to announce the triumph of Caesar and the death of Scipio. Cornelia re-enters to receive the urn with Pompey's ashes, the sight of which stirs her to new laments for herself and imprecations against Caesar. The chorus dwells on the capriciousness of fortune. In the fourth act the resentment against Caesar is emphasised by Cassius in discourse with Decimus Brutus, and the chorus sings of Harmodios and Aristogeiton ; but after that Caesar and Antony come in and discuss the means to be taken for Caesar's safety, Antony advocating severity and caution, Caesar leniency and confidence. This act is closed by a chorus of Caesar's friends, who celebrate his services and virtues. The fifth act is chiefly occupied with the messenger's account of Scipio's last battle and death, at the end of which Cornelia at some length declares that when she has paid due funeral rites to husband and father, she will surrender her own life.

From this analysis it will be seen that *Cornélie* as a play is about as defective as it could be. The subject is essentially undramatic, for the heroine— and there is no hero—has nothing to do but spend her time in lamentations and forebodings, in eulogies and vituperations. Yet the subject is more suitable than the treatment. There is no trace of conflict, internal or external ; for the persons maintain their own point of view throughout, and the issue is a matter of course from the first. There is no entanglement or plot ; but all the speakers, as they enter in turn, are affected with a craving to deliver their minds either in solitude or to some congenial listener : and their prolations lead to nothing. Even the unity of interest, which the classicists so prized, and over-prized, is lacking here, despite the bareness of the theme. Cicero has hardly less to say than Cornelia, and in two acts she does not so much as appear, while in one of them attention is diverted from her sorrows to the dangers of Caesar. The heroine no doubt retains a certain kind of primacy, but save for that, M. Faguet's description would be literally correct : " The piece in the author's conception might be entitled *Thoughts of various persons concerning Rome at the Date of Thapsus.*"[1] The *Cornélie* is by no means devoid of merit, but that merit is almost entirely rhetorical, literary, and poetical. The language is never undignified, the metres are carefully manipulated ; the descriptions and reflections, many of them taken from Lucan, though sometimes stilted, are often elevated and picturesque. But the most dramatic passages are the conversations in the fourth act, where the *interlocuteurs*, as Garnier calls the characters with even more reason than Grévin calls those of his play *entreparleurs*, are respectively Decimus Brutus and Cassius, Caesar and Mark Antony : and this is typical for two reasons. In the first place, these scenes have least to do with the titular subject, and are, as it were, mere excrescences on the main theme. In the second place, they are borrowed, so far as their general idea is concerned, from Grévin, as Grévin in turn had borrowed them from Muretus ; and even details have been transmitted to the cadet in the trinity from each and both of his predecessors. Thus in the *Cornélie* Decimus not very suitably replaces or absorbs Marcus Brutus, but the whole

---

[1] *Tragédie Française au XVIe Siècle.*

tone and movement of the interview with Cassius
are the same in all the three plays, and particular
expressions reappear in Garnier that are peculiar to
one or other of his elder colleagues or that the later
has adapted from the earlier. For example, Garnier's Cassius describes Caesar as

> un homme effeminé
> Qui le Roy Nicomede a jeune butiné.[1]

There is no express reference to this scandal in
Muretus, but it furnishes Grévin's Decimus with a
vigorous couplet which obviously has inspired the
above quotation :

> N'endurons plus sur nous regner un Ganimede
> Et la moitié du lict de son Roy Nicomede.

Here, on the other hand, is an instance of Garnier
getting a phrase from Muretus that Grévin passed
over. Decimus says in excuse of his former patron :

> Encor' n'est il pas Roy portant le diadême :

to which Cassius replies :

> Non, il est Dictateur : et n'est-ce pas de mesme ?

In the Latin both objection and answer are put in
the lips of Marcus Brutus, but that does not affect
the resemblance.

> At vero non rex iste, sed dictator est.
> Dum res sit una, quid aliud nomen juvat ?

In other cases the parallelism is threefold. Thus
Garnier's Cassius exclaims :

> Les chevaux courageux ne maschent point le mors
> Sujets au Chevalier qu'avecque grands efforts ;
> Et les toreaux cornus ne se rendent domtables
> Qu'à force, pour paistrir les plaines labourables.
> Nous hommes, nous Romains, ayant le cœur plus mol,
> Sous un joug volontaire irons ployer le col.

---

[1] *Garnier's Tragédies*, ed. Foerster.

Grévin's Marcus Brutus said :

> Le taureau, le cheval ne prestent le col bas
> A l'appetit d'un joug, si ce n'est pas contraincte :
> Fauldra il donc que Rome abbaisse sous la craincte
> De ce nouveau tyran le chef de sa grandeur ?

In Muretus the same personage puts it more shortly :

> Generosiores frena detrectant equi :
> Nec nisi coacti perferunt tauri jugum :
> Roma patietur, quod recusant belluae.

In the scene between Caesar and Antony the resemblances are less marked in detail, partly owing to the somewhat different role assigned to the second speaker, but they are there ; and the general tendency, from the self-conscious monologue of Caesar with which it opens, to the dialogue in which he gives expression to his doubts, is practically the same in both plays.

And these episodes are of some importance in view of their subsequent as well as their previous history. Though neither entirely original nor entirely relevant, they seem, perhaps because of their comparative fitness for the stage, to have made a great impression at the time. It has been suggested that they were not without their influence on Shakespeare when he came to write his *Julius Caesar* : a point the discussion of which may be reserved. It is certain that they supplied Alexander, though he may also have used Grévin and even Muretus, with the chief models and materials for certain scenes in his tragedy on the same subject. Thus, he too presents Caesar and Antony in consultation, and the former prefaces this interchange of views with a high-flown declaration of his greatness. Thus, too, the substance of their talk is to a great extent adapted from Garnier and diluted in the process. Compare the similar versions

of the apology that Caesar makes for his action.   In
Alexander he exclaims :

> The highest in the heaven who knows all hearts,
> Do know my thoughts as pure as are their starres,
> And that (constrain'd) I came from forraine parts
> To seeme uncivill in the civill warres.
> I mov'd that warre which all the world bemoanes,
> Whil'st urged by force to free my selfe from feares ;
> Still when my hand gave wounds, my heart gave groanes ;
> No Romans bloud was shed, but I shed teares.[1]

It is very like what Garnier's Caesar says :

> J'atteste Jupiter qui sonne sur la terre,
> Que contraint malgré moy j'ay mené ceste guerre :
> Et que victoire aucune où j'apperçoy gesir
> Le corps d'un citoyen, ne me donne plaisir :
> Mais de mes ennemis l'envie opiniatre,
> Et le malheur Romain m'a contraint de combattre.

So, too, when Antony asserts that some are contriving Caesar's death, the speakers engage in a
dialectical skirmish :

> *Caesar.*   The best are bound to me by gifts in store.
> *Antony.*   But to their countrey they are bound farre more.
> *Caesar.*   Then loathe they me as th' enemy of the state ?
> *Antony.*   Who freedom love, you (as usurper) hate.
> *Caesar.*   I by great battells have enlarg'd their bounds.
> *Antony.*   By that they think your pow'r too much abounds.

The filiation with Garnier is surely unmistakable,
though it cannot be shown in every line or phrase.

> *Antoine.*   Aux ennemis domtez il n'y a point de foy.
> *Cesar.*   En ceux qui vie et biens de ma bonté reçoivent ?
> *Antoine.*   Voire mais beaucoup plus à la Patrie ils doivent.
> *Cesar.*   Pensent-ils que je sois ennemy du païs ?
> *Antoine.*   Mais cruel ravisseur de ses droits envahis.
> *Cesar.*   J'ay à Rome soumis tant de riches provinces.
> *Antoine.*   Rome ne peut souffrir commandement de Princes.

The scene with the conspirators Stirling treats very
differently and much more freely.   It had had, as

---

[1] Works of Sir William Alexander, Glasgow, 1872. *Julius Caesar*,
II. i.

we have seen, a peculiar history. In Muretus it was confined to Marcus Brutus and Cassius, in Grévin Decimus Brutus is added, in Garnier Decimus is retained and Marcus drops out. Alexander discriminates. He keeps one discussion for Marcus and Cassius, in so far restoring it to the original and more fitting form it had obtained from Muretus, though he transfers to Marcus some of the sentiments that Garnier had assigned to Decimus. But the half-apologetic rôle that Decimus plays in Garnier had impressed him, and he did not choose to forego the spice of variety which this contributed. So he invents a new scene for him in which Cicero takes the place of Cassius and solicits his support. But though the one episode is thus cut in two, and each of the halves enlarged far beyond the dimensions of the original whole, it is unquestionable that they owe their main suggestion and much of their matter to the *Cornélie*.

Since then Garnier, when his powers were still immature, could so effectively adapt these incidental passages, it is not surprising that he should by and by be able to stand alone, and produce plays in which the central interest was more dramatic.

Of these we are concerned only with *Marc Antoine*, which was acted with success at the Hôtel de Bourgogne in 1578, and was printed in the same year. In it Garnier has not altogether freed himself from his former faults. There are otiose personages who are introduced merely to supply general reflections : Diomedes, the secretary, on the pathos of Cleopatra's fall ; Philostratus, the philosopher, on the overthrow of the Egyptian monarchy. There is no inter-action of character on character, all the protagonists being so carefully excluded from each other that Octavianus does not meet Antony, Antony does not meet Cleopatra, Cleopatra does not meet Octavianus. The speeches are still over

long, and the "sentences" over abundant. Nevertheless there is a real story, there are real characters;
and the story and characters admit, or rather
demand, an effective alternation of passion.

The time comprises the interval between Antony's
final reverse and the suicide of Cleopatra: it is
short, but a good deal longer than what Jodelle
allowed himself in the companion play. Further,
the situation is much more complex and less confined, so that Garnier, while borrowing many *motifs*
from Jodelle, or from their common authority,
Plutarch, is able to avoid the monotony of *Cléopatre
Captive*. Nor does the coherence suffer. It is true
that the account of Antony's death, announced by
Dercetas, occurs as with Shakespeare in the fourth
act; but the play is rightly named after him and not
after the Queen. He is the principal and by far
the most interesting figure, and it is his tragic fate
to which all that precedes leads up, and which
determines all that follows.

The first act, as so often in these Senecan plays,
is entirely occupied with a soliloquy, which Antony
declaims; but even this has a certain share of
dramatic life, though rather after the fashion of a
dramatic lyric than of a dramatic scene. He rages
against what he supposes to be the crowning perfidy
of his mistress, he recalls all that his infatuation has
cost him; the worst of his woes is that they are
caused by her; but he must love her still. The
second act has at the opening and the close respectively the unnecessary monologues of Philostratus
and Diomedes, but they serve as setting for the
animated and significant conversation between Cleopatra and her women. From it we learn that of the
final treason at least she is innocent, but she is full
of remorse for the mischief that her love and her
caprices have done, and determines, despite the
claims of her children, to expiate it in death.

Then, entering the monument she despatches
Diomedes with her excuses to Antony. To him
we return in the third act, which is central in interest
as in position, and we hear him disburden his soul
to his friend Lucilius. His fluctuations of feeling,
shame at his undoing, passion for the fair undoer,
jealousy lest his conqueror should supplant him in
love as in empire, are delineated with sympathetic
power :

> Ait Cesar la victoire, ait mes biens, ait l'honneur
> D'estre sans compagnon de la terre seigneur,
> Ait mes enfans, ma vie au mal opiniâtre,
> Ce m'est tout un, pourveu qu'il n'ait ma Cleopatre :
> Je ne puis l'oublier, tant j'affole, combien
> Que de n'y penser point servoit non plus grand bien.

He remembers his past glory and past prowess, and
it stings him that he should now be overcome by an
inferior foe :

> un homme effeminé de corps et de courage
> Qui du mestier de Mars n'apprist oncque l'usage.

But he has only himself to blame, for he has debased
his life :

> N'ayant soing de vertu, ny d'aucune louange ;
> Ains comme un porc ventru touille dedans la fange,
> A cœur saoul me voitray en maints salles plaisirs,
> Mettant dessous le pied tous honnestes desirs.

Now it only remains for him to die. In the fourth
act Octavianus dwells on the arduousness of his
triumphs and the enormity of Antony's offences, in
order to justify a ruthless policy ; and a discussion
follows between him and Agrippa, like the one
between Julius and Antony in the *Cornélie*, except
that here the emperor and his adviser have their
parts reversed. When his resolution seems fixed
Dercetas enters in dismay with tidings that Antony
has sought to take his own life, and that mortally
wounded he has been drawn up into the monument

to breathe his last in Cleopatra's arms. For a
moment his conqueror's heart is touched. But only
for a moment. He speedily gives ear to the warning of Agrippa, that to secure her treasures and
preserve her life, Cleopatra must be seized. In the
fifth act she has all her preparations made to follow
her lord. In vain Euphron tries to stay her by
gathering her children round and predicting their
probable fate :

Eufron. Desja me semble voir
Cette petite enfance en servitude cheoir,
Et portez en trionfe, . . .
Et au doigt les monstrer la tourbe citoyenne.
Cleopatre. Hé ! plutost mille morts.

But she persists in her resolve and dismisses them.
Her only regret is that she has delayed so long,

Et ja fugitive Ombre avec toy je serois,
Errant sous les cyprès des rives escartees.

She has waited only to pay the due rites, but now
she is free to breathe her last on her lover's corpse :

Que de mille baisers, et mille et mille encore
Pour office dernier ma bouche vous honore.
Et qu'en un tel devoir mon corps affoiblissant
Defaille dessur vous, mon ame vomissant.

3

ENGLISH FOLLOWERS OF THE FRENCH SCHOOL.
"THE WOUNDS OF CIVIL WAR"

The *Marc Antoine* is the best tragedy on a Roman
theme, and one of the best imitations of Seneca that
France in the sixteenth century has to show. It
deserved to find admirers on the other side of the
Channel, and it did. Among the courtly and cultured circles in whose eyes the Latin drama was the
ideal and criterion to which all poets should aspire

and by which their achievements should be tested, it was bound to call forth no little enthusiasm. In England ere this similar attempts had been made and welcomed, but none had been quite so moving and interesting, above all none had conformed so strictly to the formal requirements of the humanist code. In *Gorboduc,* the first of these experiments, Sidney, lawgiver of the elect, was pleased to admit the "honest civility" and "skilful poetry," but his praises were not without qualification :

> As it is full of stately speeches and well sounding Phrases, clyming to the height of Seneca his stile, and as full of notable moralitie, which it doth most delightfully teach, and so obtayne the very end of Poesie : yet in troth it is very defectious in the circumstaunces: which greeveth mee, because it might not remaine as an exact model of all Tragedies. For it is faulty both in place, and time, the two necessary companions of all corporall actions. For where the stage should alwaies represent but one place, and the uttermost time presupposed in it, should be, both by Aristotles precept, and common reason, but one day : there is both many dayes, and many places, inartificially imagined.[1]

Nor in such respects were things much better in the *Misfortunes of Arthur*, by Thomas Hughes, which was composed in 1587, the year after Sidney's death. But meanwhile France had been blessed with a play at least the equal of these native products in poetry and pathos, and much more observant of the unities that scholars were proclaiming. If the scene was not absolutely unchanged, at least the changes were confined within the area of a single town. If the time was not precisely marked, and in Plutarch's narrative slightly exceeded the orthodox limits, still Garnier had so managed it that the occurrences set forth might easily be conceived to take place in a single day. It seems just the modern play that would have fulfilled the desire of Sidney's heart ; and since it was composed in a foreign tongue, what

---

[1] *Apologie for Poetrie*, Arber's reprint.

could be more fitting than that Sidney's sister, the famous Countess of Pembroke, who shared so largely in Sidney's literary tastes and literary gifts, should undertake to give it an English form ? It may have been on her part a pious offering to his *manes*, and in 1590, four years after her brother's death, her version was complete.[1] She was well fitted for her task, and she has discharged it well. Sometimes she may take her liberties, but generally she is wonderfully faithful, and yet neither in diction nor versification is she stiffer than many contemporary writers of original English verse. Here, for instance, is Diomed's eulogy of Cleopatra's charm :

> Nought liues so faire. Nature by such a worke
> Hir selfe, should seeme, in workmanship hath past.
> She is all heau'nlie : neuer any man
> But seing hir, was rauish'd with hir sight.
> The Allablaster couering of hir face,
> The corall colour hir two lipps engraines,
> Hir beamie eies, two sunnes of this our world,
> Of hir faire haire the fine and flaming golde,
> Hir braue streight stature and her winning partes
> Are nothing else but fiers, fetters, dartes.
> Yet this is nothing to th' enchaunting skilles,
> Of her coelestiall Sp'rite, hir training speache,
> Hir grace, hir Maiestie, and forcing voice,
> Whether she it with fingers speache consorte,
> Or hearing sceptred kings ambassadors
> Answer to eache in his owne language make.

This excellently preserves many details as well as the pervading tone of the original :

> Rien ne vit de si beau, Nature semble avoir
> Par un ouvrage tel surpassé son pouvoir :

[1] There is an edition of this by Miss Alice Luce, *Literarhistorische Forschungen*, 1897, but I am told it is out of print, and at any rate I have been unable to procure it. The extracts I give are transcripts from the British Museum copy, which is indexed thus : *Discourse of Life and Death written in French by P. Mornay. Antonius a tragedie, written also in French by R. Garnier. Both done in English by the Countesse of Pembroke, 1592.* This edition has generally been overlooked by historians of the drama, from Professor Ward to Professor Schelling (probably because it is associated with Mornay's tract), and,

Elle est toute celeste, et ne se voit personne
La voulant contempler, qu'elle ne passionne.
L'albastre qui blanchist sur son visage saint,
Et le vermeil coral qui ses deux lévres peint,
La clairté de ses yeux, deux soleils de ce monde,
Le fin or rayonnant dessur sa tresse blonde,
Sa belle taille droitte, et ses frians attraits,
Ne sont que feux ardents, que cordes, et que traits.
    Mais encor ce n'est rien aupres des artifices
De son esprit divin, ses mignardes blandices,
Sa maiestie, sa grace, et sa forçante voix,
Soit qu'ell' la vueille joindre au parler de ses doigts,
Ou que des Rois sceptrez recevant les harangues,
Elle vueille respondre à chacun en leurs langues.

The most notable privilege of which the translation makes use is to soften or refine certain expressions that may have seemed too vigorous to the high-bred English lady. This, for example, is her rendering of the lines already quoted in which Antony denounces his voluptuous life :

Careless of uertue, careless of all praise,
Nay, as the fatted swine in filthy mire,
With glutted heart I wallow'd in delights,
All thoughts of honor troden under foote.

Similarly, in Cleopatra's closing speech, the original expression, "mon ame vomissant," yields to a gentler and not less poetical equivalent :

A thousand kisses, thousand thousand more
Let you my mouth for honor's farewell give :
That, in this office, weake my limmes may growe
Fainting on you, and fourth *my soule may flowe*.

As the deviations are confined to details, it is not necessary to repeat the account of the tragedy as a whole. These extracts will show that Garnier's *Marc Antoine* was presented to the English public in a worthy dress ; and the adequacy of the workmanship, the appeal to cultivated taste, the prestige

as a rule, the translation of Garnier is said to have been first published in 1595. That and the subsequent editions bear a different title from the neglected first ; the *Tragedie of Antonie*, instead of *Antonius*.

of the great Countess as "Sidney's sister, Pembroke's mother," her personal reputation among literary men, procured it immediate welcome and lasting acceptance. Fifteen years after its first publication it had passed through five editions, and must have been a familiar book to Elizabethan readers who cared for such wares. Moreover, it directly evoked an original English play that followed in part the same pattern and treated in part the same theme.

In 1594 appeared the *Cleopatra* of Samuel Daniel, dedicated to Lady Pembroke with very handsome acknowledgments of the stimulus he had received from her example and with much modest deprecation of the supplement he offered. His muse, he asserts, would not have digressed from the humble task of praising Delia,

> had not thy well graced Antony
> (Who all alone, having remained long)
> Requir'd his Cleopatra's company.

These words suggest that it was not written at once after the Countess's translation : on the other hand there can have been no very long delay, as it was entered for publication in October, 1593. The first complete and authorised edition of *Delia* along with the *Complaint of Rosamond*, which Daniel does not mention, had been given to the world in 1592 ; and we may assume from his own words that the *Cleopatra* was the next venture of the young author just entering his thirties, and ambitious of a graver kind of fame than he had won by these amatorious exercises. He had no reason to be dissatisfied with the result, and perhaps from the outset his self-disparagement was not very genuine. His play was reprinted seven times before his death, and these editions show one complete revision and one thorough recast of the text. Poets are not wont to spend such pains on works that they do not value. The truth is that Daniel's *Cleopatra* may take its place beside his subsequent *Philotas* among the best original Senecan tragedies that Elizabethan England produced. Its claims, of course, are almost exclusively literary and hardly at all theatrical, though some of the changes in the final version of 1607 seem meant to give a little mobility to the slow-paced scenes. But from first to last it depends on the elegiac and rhetorical qualities that characterise the whole school, and in its undivided attention to them recalls rather Jodelle's *Cléopatre Captive* than Garnier's *Marc Antoine*. The resemblance to the earlier drama is perhaps not accidental. The situation is precisely the same, for the story begins after the death of Antony, and concludes with the account of Cleopatra's suicide. Thus, despite Daniel's statement, his play is not in any true sense a sequel to the one which the Countess had rendered, nor is it the case, as his words insinuate, that in the *Antonius* Cleopatra still delayed to join her beloved : on the contrary we take leave of her as she is about to expire upon his corpse. So though his patroness's translation may very well have suggested to him his heroine, it could not possibly prescribe to him his argument. And surely after Garnier had shown the more excellent way of treating the subject so as to include both the lovers, this truncated section of the history would not spontaneously occur to any dramatist as the material most proper for his needs. It seems more than likely that Daniel was acquainted with Jodelle's play, and that the precedent it furnished, determined him in his not very happy selection of the final episode to the exclusion of all that went before. A careful comparison of the two *Cleopatras* supports this view. No doubt in general treatment they differ widely, and most of the coincidences in

detail are due to both authors having exploited
Plutarch's narrative.   But this is not true of all.
There are some traits that are not to be accounted
for by their common pedigree, but by direct transmission from the one to the other.   Thus, to
mention the most striking, in Jodelle Seleucus is
made to express penitence for exposing the Queen's
misstatement about her treasure.   There is no
authority for this : yet in Daniel the new *motif*
reappears.   Of course it is not merely repeated
without modification.   In Jodelle it is to the chorus
that the culprit unbosoms himself ; in Daniel it is
to Rodon, the false governor who has betrayed
Caesarion, and who similarly and no less fictitiously
is represented as full of remorse for his more heinous
treason.   But imitators frequently try in this fashion
to vary or heighten the effect by duplicating the
rôles they borrow ; and Daniel has done so in a
second instance, when he happened to get his suggestion from Garnier.   In the *Marc Antoine*, as we
saw, there is the sententious but quite superfluous
figure of the philosopher Philostratus ; Daniel
retains him without giving him more to do, but
places by his side the figure of the equally sententious and superfluous philosopher Arius.   In Rodon
we have just such another example of gemination.
It is safe to say that the contrite Seleucus comes
straight from the pages of Jodelle ; and his presence, if there were any doubt, serves to establish
Daniel's connection with the first French Senecan
in the vernacular.

But the Countess's protégé differs from her not
only in reverting to an elder model : he distinctly
improves on her practice by substituting for her
blank verse his own quatrains.   The author of the
Defence of Ryme showed a right instinct in this.
Blank verse is doubtless the better dramatic measure,
but these pseudo-Senecan pieces were lyric rather

than dramatic, and it was not the most suitable for them. The justice of Daniel's method is proved by its success. He not only carried the experiment successfully through for himself, which might have been a *tour de force* on the part of the "well-languaged" poet, but he imposed his metre on successors who were less skilled in managing it, like Sir William Alexander.

Such, then, is the *Cleopatra* of Daniel, a play that, compared even with the contemporary classical dramas of France, belongs to a bygone phase of the art; a play that is no play at all, but a series of harangues interspersed with odds and ends of dialogue and the due choric songs; but that nevertheless, because it fulfils its own ideal so thoroughly, is admirable in its kind, and still has charms for the lover of poetry.

The first act is occupied with a soliloquy of Cleopatra,[1] in which she laments her past pleasure and glory, and proclaims her purpose of death.

> Thinke, Caesar, I that liu'd and raign'd a Queene,
> Do scorne to buy my life at such a rate,
> That I should underneath my selfe be seene,
> Basely induring to suruiue my state :
> That Rome should see my scepter-bearing hands
> Behind me bound, and glory in my teares ;
> That I should passe whereas Octauia stands,
> To view my misery, that purchas'd hers.[2]

She has hitherto lived only to temporise with Caesar for the sake of her children, but to her late-born

---

[1] That is, in the original version. Subsequently Daniel threw a later narrative passage describing Cleopatra's parting from Caesarion and Rodon into scenic form, introduced it here, and followed it up with a discussion between Caesar and his advisers. This seems to be one of his attempts to impart more dramatic animation to his play, and it does so. But as dramatic animation is not what we are looking for, the improvement is doubtful.

[2] Dr. Grosart's Edition.

love for Antony her death is due.   She remembers
his doting affection, and exclaims :

> And yet thou cam'st but in my beauties waine,
> When new appearing wrinckles of declining
> Wrought with the hand of yeares, seem'd to detaine
> My graces light, as now but dimly shining . . .
> Then, and but thus, thou didst loue most sincerely,
> O Antony, that best deseru'd it better,
> This autumn of my beauty bought so dearely,
> For which in more then death, I stand thy debter.

In the second act Proculeius gives an account of
Cleopatra's capture, and describes her apparent
submission, to Caesar, who suspects that it is pretence.   In the first scene of the third act Philostratus
and Arius philosophise on their own misfortunes,
the misfortunes of the land, and the probable fate
of Cleopatra's children.   The next scene presents
the famous interview between Caesar and Cleopatra,
with the disclosures of Seleucus, to which are added
Dolabella's avowal of his admiration, and Caesar's
decision to carry his prisoner to Rome.   In the
fourth act Seleucus, who has betrayed the confidence
of his mistress, bewails his disloyalty, to Rodon, who
has delivered up Caesarion to death; but they
depart to avoid Cleopatra, whom Dolabella has
informed of the victor's intentions, and who enters,
exclaiming :

> What, hath my face yet powre to win a louer?
> Can this torn remnant serue to grace me so,
> That it can Caesar's secret plots discouer,
> What he intends with me and mine to do?
> Why then, poore beauty, thou hast done thy last
> And best good seruice thou could'st doe unto me :
> For now the time of death reueal'd thou hast,
> Which in my life didst serue but to undoe me.

In the first scene of the fifth act Titius tells how
Cleopatra has sent a message to Caesar, and in the
second scene we learn the significance of this from
the Nuntius, who himself has taken her the asps.

Well, in I went, where brighter then the Sunne,
Glittering in all her pompeous rich aray,
Great Cleopatra sate, as if sh' had wonne
Caesar, and all the world beside, this day :
Euen as she was, when on thy cristall streames,
Cleare Cydnos, she did shew what earth could shew :
When Asia all amaz'd in wonder, deemes
Venus from heauen was come on earth below.
Euen as she went at firste to meete her loue,
So goes she now againe to finde him.
But that first, did her greatnes onely proue,
This last her loue, that could not liue behind him.

Her words to the asp are not without a quaint
pathetic tenderness, as she contrasts the "ugly
grimness" and "hideous torments" of other deaths
with this that it procures :

Therefore come thou, of wonders wonder chiefe,
That open canst with such an easie key
The doore of life : come gentle cunning thiefe
That from our selues so steal'st our selues away.

And her dallying with the accepted and inevitable
end is good :

Looke how a mother at her sonnes departing,
For some farre voyage bent to get him fame,
Doth entertaine him with an ydle parting
And still doth speake, and still speakes but the same :
Now bids farewell, and now recalles him backe,
Tels what was told, and bids againe farewell,
And yet againe recalles ; for still doth lacke
Something that Loue would faine and cannot tell :
Pleased he should goe, yet cannot let him goe.
So she, although she knew there was no way
But this, yet this she could not handle so
But she must shew that life desir'd delay.

But this is little more than by-play and make-believe.
She does the deed, and when Caesar's messengers
arrive, it is past prevention.

For there they found stretcht on a bed of gold,
Dead Cleopatra ; and that proudly dead,
In all the rich attire procure she could ;
And dying Charmion trimming of her head,

And Eras at her feete, dead in like case.
" Charmion, is this well done ? " sayd one of them.
" Yea, well," sayd she, "and her that from the race
Of so great Kings descends, doth best become."
And with that word, yields to her faithfull breath
To passe th' assurance of her loue with death.

One more example of the influence of the French
Senecans remains to be mentioned, and though, as
a translation, it is less important than Daniel's free
reproduction, the name of the translator gives it a
special interest. The stately rhetoric of the *Cornélie*
caught the fancy of Thomas Kyd, who from the
outset had found something sympathetic in Garnier's
style, and, perhaps in revolt from the sensationalism
of his original work, he wrote an English version
which was published in 1594. When this was so,
it need the less surprise us that the Senecan form
should still for years to come be cultivated by writers
who had seen the glories of the Elizabethan stage,
above all for what would seem the peculiarly appropriate themes of classic history : that Alexander
should employ it for his *Julius Caesar* and the rest
of his *Monarchic Tragedies* even after Shakespeare's
Julius Caesar had appeared, and that Ben Jonson
himself should, as it were, cast a wistful, backward
glance at it in his *Catiline*, which he supplies, not
only with a chorus, but with a very Senecan exposition by Sylla's ghost. If this style appealed to the
author of *The Spanish Tragedy*, it might well appeal
to the more fastidious connoisseurs in whom the
spirit of the Renaissance was strong. It was to
them Kyd looked for patronage in his new departure,
and he dedicates his *Cornelia* to the Countess of
Suffolk, aunt of the more memorable lady who had
translated the *Marc Antoine*.

In execution it hardly equals the companion piece :
the language is less flexible and graphic, and the
whole effect more wearisome ; which, however, may

be due in part to the inferior merit of the play Kyd
had to render, as well as to the haste with which
the rendering was made. But he aims at preserving
the spirit of the French, and does preserve it in no
small degree. The various metres of the chorus are
managed with occasional dexterity; the rhyme that
is mingled with the blank verse of the declamation
relieves the tedium of its somewhat monotonous
tramp, and adds point and effectiveness. A fair
specimen of his average procedure may be found in
his version of the metaphorical passage in Cassius'
speech, that, as has been pointed out, can be traced
back to Grévin and Muretus.

> The stiff-neckt horses champe not on the bit
> Nor meekely beare the rider but by force:
> The sturdie Oxen toyle not at the Plough
> Nor yeeld unto the yoke, but by constraint.
> Shall we then that are men and Romains borne,
> Submit us to unurged slauerie?
> Shall Rome, that hath so many ouerthrowne
> Now make herselfe a subject to her owne? [1]

Kyd was certainly capable of emphasis, both in the
good and the bad sense, which stands him in good
stead when he has to reproduce the passages adapted
from Lucan. These he generally presents in something of their native pomp, and indeed throughout
he shows a praiseworthy effort to keep on the level
of his author. The result is a grave and decorous
performance, which, if necessarily lacking in distinctive colour, since the original had so little, is
almost equally free from modern incongruities. It
can hardly be reckoned as such that Scipio grasps
his "cutlass," or that in similar cases the equivalent
for a technical Latin term should have a homely
sound. Perhaps the most serious anachronism

---

[1] Kyd, ed. Boas. The *Cornelia* has also been edited by H. Gassner;
but this edition, despite some considerable effort, I have been unable
to procure.

occurs when Cicero, talking of "this great town" of Rome, exclaims :

> Neither could the flaxen-haird high Dutch,
> (A martiall people, madding after Armes),
> Nor yet the fierce and fiery humord French . . .
> Once dare t'assault it.

Garnier is not responsible : he writes quite correctly:

> Ny les blons Germains, peuple enragé de guerre,
> Ny le Gaulois ardent.

This, however, is a very innocent slip. It was different when another scholar of the group to which Kyd belonged treated a Roman theme in a more popular way.

But before turning to him it may be well to say a word concerning the influence which these Senecan pieces are sometimes supposed to have had on Shakespeare's Roman plays that dealt with kindred themes.

And in the first place it may be taken as extremely probable that he had read them. They were well known to the Elizabethan public, the least famous of them, Kyd's *Cornelia*, reaching a second edition within a year of its first issue. They were executed by persons who must have bulked large in Shakespeare's field of vision. Apart from her general social and literary reputation, the Countess of Pembroke was mother of the two young noblemen to whom the first folio of Shakespeare's plays was afterwards dedicated on the ground that they had "prosequutted both them and the author living with so much favour." Some of Daniel's works Shakespeare certainly knew, for there are convincing parallelisms between the *Complaint of Rosamond* on the one hand, and the *Rape of Lucrece* and *Romeo and Juliet* on the other ; nor can there be much question about the indebtedness of Shakespeare's *Sonnets* to Daniel's *Delia*. Again, with Kyd's acting dramas Shakespeare was undoubtedly acquainted. He quotes *The Spanish Tragedy* in the *Taming of the Shrew, Much Ado About Nothing, King Lear*; and the same play, as well as *Solyman and Perseda*, if that be Kyd's, in *King John*: nor is it to be forgotten that many see Kyd's hand and few would deny Kyd's influence in *Titus Andronicus*, and that some attribute to him the lost *Hamlet*. All these things considered, Shakespeare's ignorance of the English Senecans would be much more surprising than his knowledge of them. Further, though his own method was so dissimilar, he would be quite inclined to appreciate them, as may be inferred from the approval he puts in Hamlet's mouth of *Æneas' tale to Dido*, which reads like a heightened version of the narratives that occur so plentifully in their pages. So there is nothing antecedently absurd in the conjecture that they gave him hints when he turned to their authorities on his own behalf.

Nevertheless satisfactory proof is lacking. The analogies with Garnier's *Marc Antoine* not accounted for by the obligation of both dramatists to Plutarch are very vague, and oddly enough seem vaguer in the translation than in the original. Of this there is a good example in Antony's words when he recalls to his shame how his victor

> Dealt on lieutenantry, and no practice had
> In the brave squares of war. (*A. and C.* III. x. 39.)

There is similarity of *motif*, and even the suggestion of something more, in his outburst in Garnier :

> Un homme effeminé de corps et de courage
> Qui du mestier de Mars n'apprist oncque l'usage.

But only the *motif* is left in the Countess of Pembroke's rendering :

> A man, a woman both in might and minde,
> In Marses schole who neuer lesson learn'd.

The alleged parallels are thus most apparent when
Shakespeare is collated with the French, and of
these the chief that do not come from Plutarch
have already been quoted in the description of the
Marc Antoine. They are neither numerous nor
striking. Besides Antony's disparagement of his
rival's soldiership there are only three that in any
way call for remark. In Garnier, Cleopatra's picture of her shade wandering beneath the cypress
trees of the Underworld may suggest, in Shakespeare, her lover's anticipation of Elysium, "where
souls do couch on flowers" (*A. and C.* IV. xiv. 51);
but there is a great difference in the tone of the
context. Her dying utterance:

> Que de mille baisers, et mille et mille encore
> Pour office dernier ma bouche vous honore:

is in the wording not unlike the dying utterance of
Antony:

> Of many thousand kisses the poor last
> I lay upon thy lips;   (*A. and C.* IV. xv. 20.)

but there is more contrast than agreement in the
ideas. Above all, Cleopatra's horror at the thought
of her children being led in triumph through Rome
and pointed at by the herd of citizens is close
akin to the feeling that inspires similar passages in
Shakespeare (*A. and C.* IV. xv. 23, v. ii. 55, v. ii.
207); but even here the resemblance is a little
deceptive, since in Shakespeare she feels this horror
for herself.

The correspondences between Shakespeare and
Daniel are equally confined to detail, but they are
more definite and more significant. It is Daniel
who first represents Cleopatra as scorning to be
made a spectacle in Rome; and her resentment at
Caesar's supposing

> That I should underneath my selfe be seene,

might have expressed itself in Shakespeare's phrase,

> He words me, girls, he words me, that I should not
> Be noble to myself.   (*A. and C.* v. ii. 191.)

Noteworthy, too, in the same passage, is her reluctance to pass before the injured Octavia, for there is no mention of this point in Plutarch, but Shakespeare touches on it twice. Further, her very noticeable references to her waning charms, her wrinkles, her declining years have their analogies in Shakespeare and in Shakespeare alone ; for Plutarch expressly says that she was "at the age when a woman's beawtie is at the prime." The tenderness in tone of her address to the asp is common and peculiar to both English poets ; and her adornment in preparation for death suggests to each of them, but not to Plutarch, her magnificence when she met Antony on the Cydnus.[1]

These coincidences are interesting, but they are not conclusive. They are none of them such as could not occur independently to two writers who vividly realised the meaning of Plutarch's *data* ; for he, as it were, gives the premises though he does not draw the inference. Thus he says nothing of Cleopatra's disdain for the Roman populace, but he does make the knowledge that she must go to Rome determine her to die. He says nothing of her recoil from the thought of Octavia seeing her in her humiliation, but he does tell us of her jealousy of Octavia's superior claims. He never hints that Cleopatra was past her bloom, but his praise of her as at her prime belongs to 41 B.C., and the closing incident to 30 B.C., when she was in her thirty-ninth year. He does not attribute to her any kindly greeting of the asp, but he does report that she chose it as providing the easiest and gentlest

---

[1] The last point is mentioned by Mr. Furness (Variorum Edition), who cites others, of which one occurs in Plutarch and the rest seem to me untenable or unimportant.

means of death. And though in describing her suicide he makes no reference to the meeting on the Cydnus, he dwells on the glorious array on both occasions, and the fancy naturally flies from one to the other. Each of these particulars separately might well suggest itself to more than one sympathetic reader. The most that can be said is that in their mass they have a certain cogency. In any case, however, characteristic and far-reaching as some of them are, they bear only on details of the conception.

The possible connection of *Julius Caesar* with the *Cornélie* is of a somewhat different kind. It is restricted almost entirely to the conversations between Cassius and Decimus Brutus on the one hand, and between Cassius and Marcus Brutus on the other. It is thought to show itself partly in particular expressions, partly in the general situation. So far as the former are concerned, it is neither precise nor distinctive ; and it is rather remarkable that, as in the case of the *Marc Antoine*, more is to be said for it when Shakespeare's phraseology is compared with that of the original than when it is compared with that of the translation.[1] In regard to the latter M. Bernage, the chief advocate of the theory, writes :

> In the English play (*Julius Caesar*), as in our own, Brutus and Cassius have an interview before the arrival of the Dictator ; the subject of their conversation is the same ; it is Cassius too who "strikes so much show of fire" (*fait jaillir l'etincelle*) from the soul of Brutus. . . . These characters are painted by Garnier in colours quite similar (to Shakespeare's), and he is momentarily as vigorous and great. In like manner . . . Caesar crosses the stage after the interview of the two conspirators ; he is moreover accompanied by Antony.[2]

In the whole tone and direction of the dialogue, too, Shakespeare resembles Garnier and does not

[1] See Appendix A. [2] *Étude sur Garnier*, 1880.

resemble Plutarch. The *Life* records one short sentence as Brutus' part of the colloquy, while Cassius does nothing more than explain the importance of the anonymous letters and set forth the expectations that Rome has formed of his friend. There is no denunciation in Plutarch of Caesar either for his overgrown power or for his "feeble temper"; there is no lament for the degeneracy of the Romans; there is no reference to the expulsion of the kings or appeal to Brutus' ancestry; all of these matters on which both the dramatists insist. And at the end the two friends are agreed on their policy and depart to prosecute their plans, while in Garnier as in Shakespeare Brutus comes to no final decision.

It would be curious if this conjecture were correct, and if this famous scene had influenced Shakespeare as it was to influence Alexander. There would be few more interesting cases of literary filiation, for, as we have seen, there is no doubt that here Garnier bases and improves on Grévin, and that Grévin bases and improves on Muretus; so the genealogy would run Muretus, Grévin, Garnier, Kyd, Shakespeare.

Here the matter may rest. The grounds for believing that Shakespeare was influenced by Garnier's *Marc Antoine* are very slight; for believing that he was influenced by Daniel's *Cleopatra* are somewhat stronger; that he was influenced by Garnier's *Cornélie* are stronger still; but they are even at the best precarious. In all three instances the evidence brought forward rather suggests the obligation as possible than establishes it as certain. But it seems extremely likely that Shakespeare would be acquainted with dramas that were widely read and were written by persons none of whom can have been strange to him; and in that case their stateliness and propriety may have affected him in other ways than we can trace or than he himself knew.

D

Meanwhile the popular play had been going its own way, and among other subjects had selected a few from Roman history. We may be certain that slowly and surely it was absorbing some of the qualities that characterised the imitations of the classics ; and this process was accelerated when university men, with Marlowe at their head, took a leading share in purveying for the London play-house. The development is clearly marked in the general history of the drama. Of the Roman play in this transition phase, as treated by a scholar for the delectation of the vulgar, we have only one specimen, but it is a specimen that despite its scanty merit is important no less for the name of the author than for the mode of the treatment. That author was Thomas Lodge, so well known for his songs, novels, pamphlets, and translations. As dramatist he is less conspicuous, and we possess only two plays from his hand. In one of them, *A Looking Glass for London and England*, which gives a description of the corruption and repentance of Nineveh, and was acted in 1591, he co-operated with Robert Greene. Of the other,[1] *The Wounds of Civill War: Lively set forth in the true Tragedies of Marius and Scilla: As it hath beene publicquely plaide in London, by the Right Honourable the Lord High Admirall his Servants*, he was sole author, and it is with it that we are concerned. It was printed in 1594, but was probably composed some years earlier.[2] In

[1] I quote from Dodsley's *Old English Plays*, ed. Hazlitt.

[2] Professor Ward calls attention to the stage direction (Act III.) : "Enter Sylla in triumph in his chair triumphant of gold, drawn by four Moors ; before the chariot, his colours, his crest, his captains, his prisoners ; . . . bearing crowns of gold and manacled." This, he points out, seems a reminiscence of the similar situation in *Tamburlaine II.*, Act iv. sc. 3. : "Enter Tamberlaine drawn in his chariot by the Kings of Trebizon and Soria, with bits in their mouths, reins in his left hand, and in his right hand a whip with which he scourgeth them." From this Professor Ward infers that Lodge's play belongs approximately to the same date as Marlowe's, possibly to 1587. It

any case it comes after the decisive appearance of
Marlowe ; but Lodge was far from rivalling that
master or profiting fully by his example, and indeed
is inferior to such minor performers as Peele or
Greene. Moreover, in the present case he adds to
his general dramatic disabilities, the incapacity to
treat classical history aright. In this respect, indeed,
he improves on the Senecan school by borrowing
graphic minutiae from Plutarch, such as the prefigura-
tion of Marius' future glory in his infancy by the
seven eagles, the account of the Gaul's panic in
Minturnae, or the unwilling betrayal of Antonius
by the slave. But on the other hand he astonishes
us by his failure to make use of picturesque incidents
which he must have known ; like Sulla's flight for
shelter to his rival's house, the relief of Marius by
the woman whom he had sentenced, the response of
the exile from the ruins of Carthage. And even

may be so, but there are some reasons for placing it later. The mixture
of rhyme and prose instead of the exclusive use of blank verse would
suggest that the influence of *Tamburlaine* was not very immediate.
It has some points of contact with the *Looking Glass* which Lodge
wrote along with Greene. It has the same didactic bent, though the
purpose is political rather than moral, for the *Wounds of Civill War*
enforces on its very title page the lesson that Elizabethans had so
much at heart, the need of harmony in the State. Like the *Looking
Glass* it deals rather with an historic transaction than with individual
adventures, for it summarises the whole disastrous period of the conflict
between Marius and Sulla. And like the *Looking Glass* it visualises
this by scenes taken alike from dignified and low life, the latter even
more out of place than the episodes of the Nineveh citizens and peasants
in the joint work. In so far one is tempted to put the two together
about 1591. And there is one detail that perhaps favours this view—
the introduction of the Gaul with his bad English and worse French.
In Greene's *James IV.* (c. 1590) the assassin hired to murder Queen
Dorothea is also a Frenchman who speaks broken English, and in
that play such a personage is quite in keeping, violating the probabilities neither of time nor of place. It is, therefore, much more
probable that, if he proved popular, Lodge would reproduce the same
character inappropriately to catch the applause of the groundlings,
than that Lodge should light on the first invention when that invention
was quite unsuitable, and that Greene should afterwards borrow it and
give it a fit setting. In the latter case we can only account for the
absurdity by supposing that Lodge carried much further the anachronism in *Cornelia* of "the fierce and fiery-humour'd French."

when he utilises Plutarch's touches, Lodge is apt to weaken or travesty them in his adaptation. The incident of the eagles, though it furnishes two of the best passages in the play, illustrates the enfeeblement. Plutarch had said :

> When Marius was but very young and dwelling in the contry, he gathered up in the lappe of his gowne the ayrie of an Eagle, in the which were seven young Eagles ; whereat his father and mother much wondering, asked the Sooth-sayers, what that ment ? They answered, that their sonne one day should be one of the greatest men in the world, and that out of doubt he should obtain seven times in his life the chiefest office of dignity in his contry.

Plutarch is not quite sure about the trustworthiness of this story, for the characteristic reason that " the eagle never getteth but two younge ones," and his hesitation may have led Lodge to modify the vivid and improbable detail. Favorinus the Minturnian tells the story thus :

> Yonder Marius in his infancy
> Was born to greater fortunes than we deem :
> For, being scarce from out his cradle crept,
> And sporting prettily with his compeers,
> On sudden seven young eagles soar'd amain,
> And kindly perch'd upon his tender lap.
> His parents wondering at this strange event,
> Took counsel of the soothsayers in this :
> Who told them that these seven-fold eagles' flight
> Forefigurèd his seven times consulship.

And this version, with only another slight variation, is repeated rather happily in the invented narrative of the presage of Marius' death :

> Bright was the day, and on the spreading trees
> The frolic citizens of forest sung
> Their lays and merry notes on perching boughs ;
> When suddenly appeared in the east
> Seven mighty eagles with their talons fierce,
> Who, waving oft above our consul's head,
> At last with hideous cry did soar away :
> When suddenly old Marius aghast,
> With reverend smile, determin'd with a sigh
> The doubtful silence of the standers-by.

"Romans," he said, "old Marius must die:
These seven fair eagles, birds of mighty Jove,
That at my birthday on my cradle sat,
Now at my last day warn me to my death."

But the other two passages Lodge modernises beyond recognition and beyond decency.

Of the attempt on Marius' life at Minturnae, Plutarch narrates very impressively:

Now when they were agreed upon it, they could not finde a man in the citie that durst take upon him to kill him; but a man of armes of the Gaules, or one of the Cimbres (for we finde both the one or the other in wryting) that went thither with his sword drawen in his hande. Now that place of the chamber where Marius lay was very darke, and, as it is reported, the man of armes thought he sawe two burninge flames come out of Marius eyen, and heard a voyce out of that darke corner, saying unto him: "O, fellowe, thou, darest thou come to kill Caius Marius?" The barbarous Gaule, hearing these words, ranne out of the chamber presently, castinge his sworde in the middest of the flower,[1] and crying out these wordes onely: "I can not kill Caius Marius."

Here is Lodge's burlesque with the Gaul nominated Pedro, whose name is as unsuitable to his language as is his language to his supposed nationality.

Pedro. Marius tu es mort. Speak dy preres in dy sleepe, for me sal cut off your head from your epaules, before you wake. Qui es stia?[2] What kinde of a man be dis?

Favorinus. Why, what delays are these? Why gaze ye thus?

Pedro. Notre dame! Jésu! Estiene! O my siniors, der be a great diable in ce eyes, qui dart de flame, and with de voice d'un bear cries out, "Villain, dare you kill Marius?" Je tremble; aida me, siniors, autrement I shall be murdered.

Pausanins. What sudden madness daunts this stranger thus?

Pedro. O, me no can kill Marius; me no dare kill Marius! adieu, messieurs, me be dead, si je touche Marius. Marius est un diable. Jesu Maria, sava moy!

exit fugiens.

[1] Floor.
[2] Probably: "Qui est lá?" the misprint of *i* for *l* is common.

Things are scarcely better in the episode of Antonius' betrayal. Plutarch has told very simply how the poor man with whom the orator took refuge, wishing to treat him hospitably, sent a slave for wine, and how the slave, by requiring the best quality for the distinguished guest, provoked the questions of the drawer. In Lodge the unsuspecting serving man becomes a bibulous clown who blabs the secret in a drunken catch that he sings as he passes the soldiers :

> O most surpassing wine,
> The marrow of the vine !
> More welcome unto me
> Than whips to scholars be.
> Thou art, and ever was,
> A means to mend an ass ;
> Thou makest some to sleep,
> And many mo to weep,
> And some be glad and merry.
> With heigh down derry, derry.
> Thou makest some to stumble
> A many mo to fumble
> And me have pinky neyne.[1]
> More brave and jolly wine !
> What need I praise thee mo,
> For thou art good, with heigh-ho ! . . .

(*To the Soldiers*) :

> You would know where Lord Antony is ? I perceive you.
> Shall I say he is in yond farm-house ?   I deceive you.
> Shall I tell you this wine is for him ?   The gods forfend.
> And so I end.

Lodge is not more fortunate with his additions. Thus, after Sylla's final resignation, two burghers with the very Roman names of Curtall and Poppy are represented as tackling the quondam dictator.

> *Curtall.* And are you no more master-dixcator, nor generality of the soldiers ?
> *Sylla.* My powers do cease, my titles are resign'd.

<hr>

1 Pink eyes.

Curtall. Have you signed your titles? O base mind, that being in the Paul's steeple of honour, hast cast thyself into the sink of simplicity. Fie, beast!

> Were I a king, I would day by day
> Suck up white bread and milk,
> And go a-jetting in a jacket of silk;
> My meat should be the curds,
> My drink should be the whey,
> And I would have a mincing lass to love me every day.

Poppy. Nay, goodman Curtall, your discretions are very simple; let me cramp him with a reason. Sirrah, whether is better good ale or small-beer? Alas! see his simplicity that cannot answer me; why, I say ale.

Curtall. And so say I, neighbour.

Poppy. Thou hast reason; ergo, say I, 'tis better be a king than a clown. Faith, Master Sylla, I hope a man may now call ye knave by authority.

Even more impertinent, because they violate the truth of character and misrepresent an historical person, are some of the liberties Lodge takes with Marius. Such is the device with the echo, which he transfers from the love scenes of poetical Arcady, where it is quite appropriate, to the mountains of Numidia, where it would hardly be in place even if we disregarded the temperament and circumstances of the exile.

Marius. Thus Marius lives disdain'd of all the gods,
> *Echo.* Gods!

Marius. With deep despair late overtaken wholly.
> *Echo.* O, lie!

Marius. And will the heavens be never well appeased?
> *Echo.* Appeased.

Marius. What mean have they left me to cure my smart?
> *Echo.* Art.

Marius. Nought better fits old Marius' mind then war.
> *Echo.* Then, war!

Marius. Then full of hope, say, Echo, shall I go?
> *Echo.* Go!

Marius. Is any better fortune then at hand?
> *Echo.* At hand.

Marius. Then farewell, Echo, gentle nymph, farewell.
> *Echo.* Fare well.

Marius (soliloquises). O pleasing folly to a pensive man!

Yet Lodge was a competent scholar who was by and by to translate *The Famous and Memourable Workes of Josephus, a Man of Much Honour and Learning among the Jewes*, and the *Works both Moral and Natural of Lucius Annaeus Seneca.* And already in this play he makes Sylla's genius, invisible to all, summon him in Latin Elegiacs audible only to him. If then the popular scenes in Shakespeare's Roman plays do not make a very Roman impression, it should be remembered that he is punctilious in comparison with the University gentleman who preceded him. Nor did the fashion of popularising antique themes with vulgar frippery from the present die out when Shakespeare showed a more excellent way. There is something of very much the same kind in Heywood's *Rape of Lucrece* which was published in 1608.

But these superficial laches are not the most objectionable things in the play. There is nothing organic in it. Of course its neglect of the unities of time and place is natural and right, but it is careless of unity in structure or even in portraiture. The canvas is crowded with subordinate figures who perplex the action without producing a vivid impression of their own characters. A few are made distinct by insistence on particular traits, like Octavius with his unbending civic virtue, or Antonius with his 'honey-dropping' and rather ineffectual eloquence, or Lepidus with his braggard temporising. The only one of them who has real individuality is the younger Marius, insolent, fierce, and cruel, but full of energy and filial affection, and too proud to survive his fortunes. He perhaps is the most consistent and sympathetic person in the piece ; which of itself is a criticism, for he occupies a much less important place than the two principals, expressly announced as the heroes in the title-page. It is difficult even to guess the intention of the

author in this delineation of them, and in any case
the result is not pleasing.   Marius, despite a certain
amount of tough fortitude—which for the rest is
not so indomitable as in Plutarch—and a rude
magnanimity displayed in the imaginary scene with
Sylla's daughter and wife, is far from attractive;
and it comes as a surprise that after all his violence
and vindictiveness he should meet his death "with
a reverend smile" in placid resignation.   But with
Sylla matters are worse.   He would be altogether
repulsive but for his courage, and Lodge seems to
explain him and his career only by appealing to his
own adopted epithet of Felix or Fortunate.   His
last words are:

> Fortune, now I bless thee
> That both in life and death would'st not oppress me.

And when, "to conclude his happiness," his sump-
tuous funeral is arranged, Pompey expresses the
same idea in the lines that close the play:

> Come, bear we hence this trophy of renown
> Whose life, whose death was far from Fortune's frown.

The problem of his strange story is not so much
stated as implied, and far less is there any attempt
at a solution.   After all his blood-guiltiness, he too,
like Marius, passes away in peace, but with him
the peacefulness rises to the serenity of a saint or
sage.   To his friend he exclaims:

> My Flaccus, worldly joys and pleasures fade;
> Inconstant time, like to the fleeting tide
> With endless course man's hopes doth overbear:
> Now nought remains that Sylla fain would have
> But lasting fame when body lies in grave.

To his wife, who soon after asks:

> How fares my lord?   How doth my gentle Sylla?

he replies still more devoutly:

> Free from the world, allied unto the heavens;
> Not curious of incertain chances now.

There is thus no meaning in the story. The rival
leaders are equally responsible for the Wounds of
Civil War, but end as happily as though they
had been benefactors of society. And this is by no
means presented as an example of tragic irony, in
which case something might be said for it, but as
the natural, fitting, and satisfactory conclusion. Yet
Plutarch tells of Marius' sleeplessness, drunkenness,
and perturbation, and of Sylla's debaucheries and
disease. These were hints, one might have thought,
that would have suited the temper of an Elizabethan
dramatist ; but Lodge passes them over.

It is the same with the public story. If Rome is
left in quiet it is only because Sylla's ruthlessness
has been ' fortunate ' ; it is not represented as the
rational outcome of what went before, nor is there
any suggestion of what was to follow after.

The merit of the play, such as it is, lies in its
succession of stirring scenes — but not the most
stirring that might have been selected—from the
career of two famous personalities in the history of
a famous State. It is almost incredible that in
barely more than half a dozen years after its publication London playgoers were listening to *Julius
Caesar* with its suggestive episodes, its noble characterisation, and full realisation of what the story
meant.

Yet Lodge's play is probably as good as any of
those based on Roman History till Shakespeare
turned his attention to such subjects. The titles of
a number of others have come down to us. Some
of these are of early date and may have approximated
to the type of *Apius and Virginia*. Others would
attempt the style of Seneca, either after the crude
fashion of *Gorboduc* or subsequently under the
better guidance of the French practitioners ; and
among these later Senecans were distinguished men
like Lord Brooke, who destroyed a tragedy on

Antony and Cleopatra in 1601, and Brandon, whose *Vertuous Octavia*, written in 1598, still survives.[1] In others again there may have been an anticipation or imitation of the more popular manner of Lodge. But the fact that they were never published, or have been lost, or, in one or two cases where isolated copies are extant, have not been thought worth reprinting, affords a presumption that their claims are inferior, and that in them no very characteristic note is struck. It is pretty safe to suppose that they did not contain much instruction for Shakespeare, and that none of them would bridge the gap between Lodge's medley and Shakespeare's masterpiece.

The progress made since the middle of the century was, of course, considerable. A pioneer performance, like *Apius and Virginia*, had the merit of pushing beyond the landmarks of the old Morality, and of bringing Roman story within the ken of English playgoers, but it did nothing more. It treated this precisely as it might have treated any other subject, and looked merely to the lesson, though, no doubt, it sought to make the lesson palatable with such dramatic condiments as the art of the day supplied. The Senecans, inspired by the *Octavia*, make a disinterested effort to detach and set forth the conception of old Roman greatness, as it was given that age to understand it, and these productions show no impropriety and much literary skill, but the outlines and colours are too vague to admit of reality or life. Lodge is realistic enough in his way, but it is by sacrificing what is significant and characteristic, and submerging the majesty of ancient Rome in the banalities and trivialities of his own time. No dramatist had been able at once to rise to the

---

[1] It is in the Dyce Collection in South Kensington and is inaccessible to me. It is described as claiming sympathy for Antony's neglected wife.

grandeur of the theme and keep a foothold on solid earth, to reconcile the claims of the ideal and the real, the past and the present. That was left for Shakespeare to do.

CHAPTER II

SHAKESPEARE'S TREATMENT OF HISTORY

THE turn of the centuries roughly bisects the dramatic career of Shakespeare. In the first half he had written many comedies and a few tragedies ; in the second he was to write many tragedies with a few plays which, on account of the happy ending and other traits, may be assigned to the opposite class. But beyond these recognised and legitimate subdivisions of the Romantic Drama, he had also before 1600 busied himself with that characteristic product of the Elizabethan Age, the Historical Play dealing with the national annals. In this kind, indeed, he had been hardly less abundant than in comedy, the proportions being nine of the one to eleven of the other. Then suddenly he leaves it aside, and returns to it only at the close in *Henry VIII.*, which moreover is but partially his handi-work.

Thus, while the tragic note is not inaudible in the earlier period of his activity nor the comic note in the later, the third, that sounded so loud in the sixteenth century, utterly or all but utterly dies away in the seventeenth.

Why this should be so it is impossible to say. It may be that the patriotic self-consciousness stirred by the defeat of the Armada and the triumph of England waned with the growing sense of internal grievances and the loss of external prestige, and that the national story no longer inspired such curiosity and delight. It may be that Shakespeare had exhausted the episodes which had a special attraction for contemporaries and himself. It may be that he found in the records of other lands themes that gave his genius freer scope and more fully satisfied the requirements of his art. Or all these considerations may have co-operated.

For the last of them there is at any rate this much to say, that, though the play on native history virtually disappears, the Historical Play as such survives and wins new triumphs. The Roman group resembles the English group in many ways, and, where they differ, it has excellences of its own.

What are the main points in which respectively they diverge or coincide?

(1) There is no doubt that it was patriotic enthusiasm that called into existence the Chronicle Histories so numerous in Elizabeth's reign, of which the best in Shakespeare's series are only the consummate flower. The pride in the present and confidence in the future of England found vent, too, in occupation with England's past, and since the general appetite could not be satisfied by the histories of every sort and size that issued from the press, the vigorous young drama seized the opportunity of extending its operations, and stepped in to supply the demand. Probably with a more definite theory of its aims, methods, and sphere there might have been less readiness to undertake the new department. But in the popular conception the play was little else than a narrative presented in scenes. The only requirement was that it should interest the spectators, and few troubled themselves about classic rule and precedent, or even about connected structure and arrangement. And when by and by the Elizabethan

Tragedy and Comedy became more organic and vertebrate, the Historic Play had secured recognition, and was able to persist in what was dramatically a more rudimentary phase and develop without regard to more exacting standards. Shakespeare's later Histories, precisely the superlative specimens of the whole species, illustrate this with conspicuous force. The subject of *Henry IV.*, if presented in summary, must seem comparatively commonplace ; the ' argument' of both parts, if analysed, is loose and straggling ; the second part to a great extent repeats at a lower pitch the *motifs* of the first ; yet it is hardly if at all less excellent than its predecessor, and together they represent Shakespeare's grand achievement in this kind. In *Henry V.*, which has merits that make it at least one of the most popular pieces that Shakespeare ever wrote, the distinctively narrative wins the day against the distinctively dramatic. Not only are some of the essential links supplied only in the story of the chorus, but there is no dramatic collision of ideas, no conflict in the soul of the hero, except in the scenes preliminary to Agincourt, not even much of the excitement of suspense. It is a plain straightforward history, admirably conveyed in scene and speech, all the episodes significant and picturesque, all the persons vividly characterised, bound to stir and inspire by its sane and healthy patriotism ; but in the notes that are considered to make up the *differentia* of a drama, whether ancient or modern, it is undoubtedly defective.

In proportion then as Shakespeare realised the requirements of the Chronicle History, and succeeded in producing his masterpieces in this domain, he deviated from the course that he pursued in his other plays. And this necessarily followed from the end he had in view. He wished to give, and his audience wished to get, passages from the history of their country set forth on the stage as pregnantly and attractively as possible ; but the history was the first and chief thing, and in it the whole species had its *raison d'être*. History delivered the material and prescribed the treatment, and even the selection of the episodes treated was determined less perhaps by their natural fitness for dramatic form, than by the influence of certain contemporary historic interests. For the points which the average Elizabethan had most at heart were—(1) The unity of the country under the strong and orderly government of securely succeeding sovereigns, who should preserve it from the long remembered evils of Civil War ; (2) Its rejection of Papal domination, with which there might be, but more frequently among the play-going classes, there was not associated the desire for a more radical reconstruction of the Church ; (3) The power, safety and prestige of England, which Englishmen believed to be the inevitable consequence of her unity and independence. So whatever in by-gone times bore on these matters and could be made to illustrate them, whether by parallel or contrast, was sure of a sympathetic hearing. And in this as in other points Shakespeare seems to have felt with his fellow-men and shared their presuppositions. At least all the ten plays on English history in which he is known to have had a hand deal with rivalry for the throne, the struggle with Rome, the success or failure in France accordingly as the prescribed postulates are fulfilled or violated. It may have been his engrossment in these concerns that sometimes led him to choose subjects which the mere artist would have rejected as of small dramatic promise.

When he turned to the records of antiquity, the conditions were very different. Doubtless to a man of the Renaissance classical history in its appeal came only second, if even second, to the history of his own land ; doubtless also to the man who was not a technical scholar, the history of Rome had far more familiar charm than the history of Greece. When, therefore, Shakespeare went outside his own England in search for historical themes, he was still addressing the general heart, and showed himself in closer accord with popular taste than, *e.g.* Chapman, whose French plays are perhaps next to his own among the best Elizabethan examples of the historical drama.   But we may be sure that Ambois and Biron and Chabot were much less interesting persons to the ordinary Londoner than Caesar and Antony and Coriolanus.   Not merely in treatment, but in selection of the material—which cannot fail to influence the treatment—Shakespeare was in touch with common feeling and popular taste.

All the same a great deal more was now required than in the case of the English series.   In that the story of a reign or the section of a reign, the chronicle of a flimsy conspiracy or a foreign campaign might furnish the framework for a production that would delight the audience.   It was otherwise when dramatist and spectators alike knew the history only in its mass, and were impressed only by the outstanding features.   Just as with individuals so with nations, many things become significant and important in those of our familiar circle that would seem trivial in mere strangers and acquaintances.   If the Roman plays were to be popular as the English ones had been, Shakespeare was bound to select episodes of more salient interest and more catholic appeal than such as had hitherto sometimes served his turn.   In the best of the English plays we constantly wonder that Shakespeare could get such results from stories that we should have thought in advance to be quite unfit for the stage.   But the fall of Caesar and the fate of those who sought to strangle the infant empire, the shock of opposing forces in Augustus and Antony and the loss of the world for Cleopatra's

love, the triumph and destruction of the glorious
renegade from whose wrath the young republic
escaped as by fire—that there are tragic possibilities
in themes like these is patent to a casual glance.   It
is significant that, while of the subjects handled in
the English histories only the episode of Joan of
Arc and the story of Richard III. have attracted the
attention of foreign dramatists, all the Roman plays
have European congeners.   One of the reasons may
be, that though the events described in the national
series are dramatic enough for national purposes,
they do not like the others satisfy the severer inter-
national test.

And to a difference in the character of the material
corresponds a difference in the character of the treatment.   The best of the English plays, as we have
seen, are precisely those that it would be hardest
to describe in terms of the ordinary drama.   The
juvenile *Richard III.* is the only one that could
nowadays without objection be included in a list
of Shakespeare's tragedies.   But with the Roman
plays it is quite the reverse.   In the main lines
of construction they are of tragic build ; there is
invariably a tragic problem in the hero's career ; and
it reaches a tragic solution in his self-caused ruin.
So they are always ranked with the Tragedies, and
though here and there they may show a variation
from Shakespeare's usual tragic technique, it would
occur-to no one to alter the arrangement.

(2) Yet ,these little variations may remind u's that
after all they were not produced under quite the same
presuppositions as plays like *Hamlet* and *Othello*, or
even *King Lear* and *Macbeth*.   In a sense they
remain *Histories*, as truly histories as any of their
English analogues.   The political vicissitudes and
public catastrophies do not indeed contribute the
chief elements of interest.   Here as everywhere
Shakespeare is above all occupied with the career

of individuals, with the interaction of persons and persons, and of persons and circumstances.   Nevertheless in these plays the characters are always exhibited in relation to the great mutations in the State.   Not merely the background but the environment and atmosphere are supplied by the large life of affairs.   It is not so in *Lear*, where the legend offered no tangible history on which the imagination could take hold ; it is only partially so in *Macbeth*, where Shakespeare knew practically nothing of the actual local conditions ; nor, had it been otherwise, was there anything in these traditions of prerogative importance for later times.   But in the Roman plays the main facts were accredited and known, and of infinite significance for the history of the world. They could not be overlooked, they had to be taken into account.

For the same reason they must no more be tampered with than the accepted facts of English History.   The two historical series are again alike in this, that they treat their sources with much more reverence than either the Comedies or the other Tragedies show for theirs.   Even in *Lear* the dramatist has no scruple about altering the traditional close ; even in *Macbeth* he has no scruple about blending the stories of two reigns.   But in dealing with the professedly authentic records whether of England or Rome, Shakespeare felt that he had to do with the actual, with what definitely had been ; and he did not conceive himself free to give invention the rein, as when with a light heart he reshaped the caprices of a novel or the perversions of a legend.   As historical dramatist he was subordinated to his subject much in the same way as the portrait painter.   He could choose his point of view, and manage the lights and shades, and determine the pose.   He could emphasize details, or slur them over, or even leave them out.

He could interpret and reveal, so far as in him lay, the meaning and spirit of history. But he had his marching orders and could no more depart from them to take a more attractive way of his own, than the portrait painter can correct the defects of his sitter to make him an Apollo. It cannot always have been easy to keep true to this self-denying ordinance. Despite the suitability of the subject in general suggestion and even in many particular incidents there must have been a recalcitrance to treatment here and there ; and traces of this may be detected, if the Roman plays are compared with the tragedies in which the genius of Shakespeare had quite unimpeded sway. To some of the chief of these traces Mr. Bradley has called attention. Thus there is in the middle of *Antony and Cleopatra*, owing to the undramatic nature of the historic material, an excessive number of brief scenes "in which the *dramatis personae* are frequently changed, as though a novelist were to tell his story in a succession of short chapters, in which he flitted from one group of his characters to another." In *Coriolanus*, "if Shakespeare had made the hero persist and we had seen him amid the flaming ruins of Rome, awaking suddenly to the enormity of his deed and taking vengeance on himself . . . that would merely have been an ending more strictly tragic [1] than the close of Shakespeare's play." In *Julius Caesar* the "famous and wonderful" quarrelscene between Brutus and Cassius is "an episode the removal of which would not affect the actual sequence of events (unless we may hold that but for the emotion caused by the quarrel and reconcilia-

---

[1] *I.e.* more tragic in the technical sense. Of course Mr. Bradley is quite aware that as it stands *Coriolanus* is "a much nobler play." It is right to add that he expresses no opinion whether the actual close of Shakespeare's play "was due simply to his unwillingness to contradict his historical authority on a point of such magnitude." At any rate, I am convinced that in his eyes that was a sufficient ground.

tion Cassius would not have allowed Brutus to overcome his objection to the fatal policy of offering battle at Philippi)." Mr. Bradley discusses this in another connection, and here, as we shall see, Shakespeare only partially adheres to his authority. In the same play, however, we have the episode of the poet Cinna's murder which, however useful in illustrating the temper of the mob and suggestive in other respects, is nevertheless a somewhat crude intrusion of history, for it leads to nothing and in no way helps on the action. But Shakespeare will put up with an occasional awkwardness in the mechanism rather than fail to give what he considers a faithful picture. As in the best English Histories he omits, he compresses, he even regroups; but he never consciously alters the sense, and to bring out the sense he utilises material that puts a little strain on his art.

Yet of course this does not mean that in the Roman any more than in the English plays he attempts an accurate reconstruction of the past. It may even be doubted whether such an attempt would have been intelligible to him or to any save one or two of his contemporaries. To the average Elizabethan (and in this respect Shakespeare was an average Elizabethan, with infinitely clearer vision certainly, but with the same outlook and horizon) the past differed from the present chiefly by its distance and dimness; and distinctive contrasts in manners and customs were but scantily recognised. A generation later French audiences could view the perruques and patches of Corneille's Romans without any sense of incongruity, and the assimilation of the ancient to the modern was in some respects much more thorough-going in Shakespeare's England. In all his classical pieces the impression of historic actuality and the genuine antique *cachet* is only produced when there

is a kind of inner kinship between the circumstances
to be represented and the English life that he knew.
There was a good deal of such correspondence
between Elizabethan life and Roman life, so the
Roman Tragedies have a breath of historic verisimilitude and even a faint suggestion of local
colour. There was much less between Elizabethan
life and Greek life, so *Timon* and *Troilus and
Cressida*, though true as human documents, have
almost nothing Hellenic about them. But even in
the Roman plays, so soon as there is anything that
involves a distinctive difference between Rome and
London Shakespeare is sure to miss it. Anachronisms in detail are of course abundantly unimportant, though a formidable list of them could be
computed. In *Julius Caesar* there are clocks that
strike, and the crowd throw up their sweaty night-
caps. The arrangements of the Elizabethan stage
furnish Cleopatra and Comminius with similes.
Menenius is familiar with funeral knells and bat-
teries and Galen's prescriptions.

These are *minutiae* on which students like Bacon
or Ben Jonson might set store, but in regard to
which Shakespeare was quite untroubled and careless. Perhaps they deserve notice only because
they add one little item to the mass of proof that
the plays were written by a man of merely ordinary
information, not by a trained scholar. But for
themselves they may be disregarded. It is not such
trifles that interfere with fidelity to antiquity. But
in weightier matters, too, Shakespeare shows an
inevitable limitation in reproducing a civilisation
that was in some aspects very different from his
own, and for which he had no parallel in his own
experience. He shows a precisely analogous limitation when he deals with themes from English
History that were partly alien to the spirit of the
time. Of this *King John* furnishes the grand

example. We all know why that troublesome
reign is memorable now, not merely to the constitutional historian, but to the man in the street and
the child on the school bench. Yet Shakespeare
makes no mention of Runnymede or the Great
Charter ; and we may assume that he, like most
Elizabethans, if interested in such matters at all,
would have been unsympathetic to a movement
that extorted liberties by civil strife. To him the
significant points are the disputed succession, the
struggle with the Pope, the initial invasion of
France by England when the Kingdom is of one
accord, and the subsequent invasion of England by
France, when it is divided against itself. So *King
John*, though very true to human nature and even
to certain aspects of the period, pays no heed
to the aspect which other generations have considered the most important of all, and one which
on any estimate is not to be overlooked. But if
Shakespeare thus misses a conspicuous feature in a
set of occurrences that took place among his own
people less than four hundred years before, we need
not wonder if he failed to detect the peculiar
features of ancient Rome as it existed at a further
distance of twelve or sixteen centuries. His approximation to the actual or alleged conditions varies
indeed in the different plays. It is closest in
Antony and Cleopatra. In that there is hardly a
personage or circumstance for which he had not
some sort of a clue. He knew about soldiers
of fortune like Enobarbus and pirate-adventurers
like Menas ; a ruler like Henry VII. had in him a
touch of Octavius, there were not a few notabilities
in Europe who carried a suggestion of Mark Antony,
the orgies of Cleopatra's court in Egypt were analogous to those of many an Italian or French court at
the Renaissance. It is all native ground to Shakespeare and he would feel himself at home. On the

other hand, he is least capable of seeing eye to eye the primitive republican life which on Plutarch's evidence he has to depict in *Coriolanus*. The shrewd, resolute, law-abiding Commons, whom some of the traditions that Plutarch worked up seem meant to exalt; the plebs that might secede to the Holy Mount, but would not rise in armed revolt; that secured the tribunate as its constitutional lever with which it was by and by to shift the political centre of gravity, this was like nothing that he knew or that anybody else knew about till half a century had elapsed. He could only represent it in terms of a contemporary city mob; and the consequence is that though he has given a splendid picture that satisfies the imagination and even realises some of Plutarch's hints, it is not true to the whole situation as envisaged by Plutarch.[1] *Julius Caesar* occupies a kind of intermediate position, and for that reason illustrates his method most completely. He could understand a good deal of the political crisis in Rome on which that story turns, from the existing conditions or recent memories of his own country. In both a period of civil turmoil had ended in the establishment of a strong government. In both there were nobles who from principle or interest were opposed to the change, so he could enter into the feelings of the conspirators. In both the centralisation of authority was the urgent need, so he could appreciate the indispensableness of the Empire, the 'spirit of Caesar.' But of zeal for the republican theory as such he knows nothing, and therefore his Brutus is only in part the Brutus of Plutarch.

Thus Shakespeare in his picture of Rome and Romans, does not give the notes that mark off Roman from every other civilisation, but rather

[1] Of course Shakespeare could not be expected to anticipate the later theories and researches that go to prove that the political power of plebs and tribunate has been considerably antedated.

those that it possessed in common with the rest, and especially with his own.   He even puts into it, without any consciousness of the discrepancy, qualities that are characteristic of Elizabethan rather than of Roman life.   And the whole result, the quickening of the antique material with modern feeling in so far as that is also antique, and occasionally when it is not quite antique, is due to the thorough realisation of the subject in Shakespeare's own mind from his own point of view, with all the powers not only of his reason, but of his imagination, emotion, passion, and experience.   Hence his delineations are in point of fact more truly antique than those of many much more scholarly poets, who can reproduce the minute peculiarities, but not, what is more central and essential, the living energy and principle of it all. This was felt by contemporaries. We have the express testimony of the erudite Leonard Digges, who after graduating as Bachelor in Oxford, continued his studies for many years in several foreign universities, and consequently was promoted on his return to the honorary degree of Master, a man who, with his academic training and academic status, would not be apt to undervalue literal accuracy.   But he writes :

> So have I seen when Caesar would appear,
> And on the stage at half-sword parley were
> Brutus and Cassius : oh ! how the audience
> Were ravish'd, with what wonder went they thence ;
> When some new day they would not brook a line
> Of tedious though well-labour'd *Catiline*,—
> Sejanus too was irksome.

Ben Jonson in *Sejanus* and *Catiline* tried to restore antiquity in its exclusive and exceptional traits. Shakespeare approached it on its more catholic and human side, interpreted it by those qualities in modern life that face towards the classical ideal, and even went the length of using at unawares some that were more typical of his new world.   And Jonson's

Roman plays were felt to be well-laboured and irksome, while his filled the spectators with ravishment and wonder.

In both series then, English and Roman alike, Shakespeare on the one hand loyally accepted his authorities and never deviated from them on their main route, but on the other he treated them unquestioningly from his own point of view, and probably never even suspected that their own might be different. This is the double characteristic of his attitude to his documents, and it combines pious regard for the assumed facts of History with complete indifference to critical research. He is as far as possible from submitting to the dead hand of the past, but he is also as far as possible from allowing himself a free hand in its manipulation. His method, in short, implies and includes two principles, which, if separated, may easily become antagonistic, and which, in point of fact, have led later schools of the historic drama in quite opposite directions. A short examination of these contrasted tendencies may perhaps help to throw a clearer light on Shakespeare's own position.

The one that lays stress on the artist's right to take counsel with his own ideas has been explained by Lessing in a famous passage of the *Hamburg Dramaturgy*, which is all the more interesting for the present purpose, that throughout it tacitly or expressly appeals to the practice of Shakespeare. Lessing starts with Aristotle's doctrine that poetry is more pregnant than history, and asks why, when this is so, the poet does not keep within the kingdom of his imagination, why more especially the dramatist descends to the lower artistic level of the historian to trespass on the domain of prosaic fact. And he answers that it is merely a matter of convenience. There is advantage to be gained from illustrious position and impressive associations ; and moreover the playwright finds it helpful that the audience should already have some idea of the story to be told, that they should, as it were, meet him half way, and bring to the understanding of his piece some general knowledge of the persons. He gains his purpose if he employs famous names which appear in a nimbus of associations, and saves time in describing their characters and circumstances ; and thus they attune our minds for what is to come and serve as so many labels by means of which, when we see a new play, we may inform ourselves what it is all about. The initial familiarity and the prestige it implies are fulcra for moving the interest of the beholders. The historical dramatist, therefore, must be careful not to alter the current conceptions of character ; but, with that proviso, he has almost unlimited powers, and may omit or recast or invent incidents, or forge an entirely new story, just as he pleases, so long, that is, as he leaves the character intact and does not interfere with our idea of the hero. In that case the historic label would be more of a hindrance than a help to our enjoyment.

Lessing's view of the Historic Drama (and there is no doubt that he thought he was describing the method of Shakespeare) is therefore that it is a free work of fiction woven around characters that are fairly well known. He was certainly wrong about Shakespeare, and his theory strikes us nowadays as strangely inadequate, but it had very important results. It directly influenced the dramatic art of Germany, and it would be hard to overestimate the share it had in determining Schiller's methods of composition. It was in the air at the time of the Romantic Movement in France, and is really the principle on which Hugo constructs his more impor-tant plays in this kind. Schiller's treatment of history is very free ; he invents scenes that have no shadow of foundation in fact, and yet are of crucial importance in his idealised narrative ; he invents subordinate persons who are hardly less conspicuous than the authentic principals, and who vitally affect the plot and action.   All his plays contain these licenses. Such episodes as the interview between Mary and Elizabeth, of Jeanne Darc's indulgence of her pity illustrate the first, such figures as Mortimer or Max and Thekla illustrate the second ; but what would *Mary Stuart* or the *Maid of Orleans* or *Wallenstein* be without them ?   And with Victor Hugo this emancipation from authority is pushed to even greater lengths.   Plays like *Le Roi s'amuse* or *Marion de Lorme* might recall the vagaries of early Elizabethan experiments like Greene's *James IV.*, were it not that they are works of incomparably higher genius.   Hugo has accepted the traditional view of a French king and a French court, but all the rest is sheer romance on which just here and there we detect the trail of an old *mémoire.*

Now, some of the extreme examples suggest a twofold objection to Lessing's account as a quite satisfactory explanation of the species.

In the first place, when the poet carries his privi- lege of independence so far, why should he not go a step further and invent his entire drama, names and all ?   As it is, we either know something of the real history or we do not.   If we do not, what is the advantage of appealing to it ?   If we do, will not such lordly disregard of facts stir up the same recal- citrance as disregard of traditional character, and shall we not be rather perplexed than aided by the conflict between our reminiscences and the state- ments of the play ?

And, in the second place, is the portrayer of human nature to take his historical persons as once for all given and fixed, so that he must leave the accepted estimate of them intact without attempting to modify it ?   Surely that would be to deprive the dramatist of his greater privilege and the drama of its greatest opportunity. For then we should only see a well-known character illustrated or described anew, displaying its various traits in this or that set of novel surroundings. But there would be little room for the sort of work that the historic drama is specially fitted to do, viz. the exposition of ambiguous or problematic natures, which will give us a different conception of them from the one we have hitherto had.

Hence there arose in Germany a view directly opposed to that of Lessing, and Lotze does not hesitate to recommend the most painstaking investigation and observance of the real facts. The poet, he thinks, will find scope enough in giving a new interpretation of the career and individuality of the hero, after he has used all the means in his power to bring home to his imagination the actual circumstances from which they emerged. Probably little was known in England of this theory of Lotze's, though utterances to the same effect occur in Carlyle, especially in his remarks on Shakespeare's English Histories ; yet it seems to give a correct account of the way in which most English historical dramas were constructed in the nineteenth century. Sir Henry Taylor, while calling *Philip van Artevelde* " a dramatic romance," is careful to state that " historic truth is preserved in it, as far as the material events are concerned." Mr. Swinburne, in his trilogy on Mary Stuart, versifies whole pages of contemporary writers (*e.g.* in the interview of Mary and Knox taken almost verbatim from Knox's *History of the Reformation*), and in his prose essay seems specially to value himself on his exact delineation of her career, and his solution of the problem of her strange nature. But the prerogative instance is furnished by Tennyson. In his dedication of *Harold*, he writes to Lord Lytton : " After old world records

like the Bayeux Tapestry and the Roman de Rou,
Edward Freeman's *History of the Norman Conquest*
and your father's historical romance treating of the
same theme have been mainly helpful to me in
writing this drama." He puts his antiquarian researches first, his use of the best modern critical
authorities second, and only in the third place an
historical romance, to which for the rest Freeman
has said that he owes something himself. Nor
would it be difficult to show that in *Queen Mary*
and *Becket* he has followed the same lines. And
on such lines it is clear that the historical dramatist's only aim must be to present in accurate though
artistic form a selection of the incidents and circumstances of the hero's life and times, and place them
in such mutual relation that they throw new light on
the nature and destiny of the man.

But from this point of view the functions of the
poet and the historian will tend to coalesce, and it is
just this that at first sight rouses suspicion. After
all can we so reproduce the past as to give it real
immediate truth? It is hardly possible by antiquarian knowledge quickened by ever so much
poetic power to galvanise into life a state of things
that once for all is dead and gone. And meanwhile
the mere effort to do so is apt to make the drama a
little frigid, as Tennyson's dramas are. We are
seldom carried away on a spontaneous stream of
passion; for after all the methods of the historian
and the poet are radically different, and the painful
mosaic work of the one is almost directly opposed
to the complete vision, the creation in one jet, which
may be rightly expected of the other.

But it is noteworthy that though the two schools
which we have just discussed, make appeal to
Shakespeare, his own procedure does not precisely
agree with that of one or other. He is too much of
the heaven-born poet for the latter; he has too

genuine a delight in facts for the former.   He has
points of contact with both, but in a way he is more
naïf and simple-minded than either.   He at the
same time accepts the current conception of character with Lessing, and respects the allegations of
history with Carlyle.   But though he begins with
the ordinary impression produced by his hero, he
does not stop there.   Such an impression is bound
to be incoherent and vague.   Shakespeare probes
and defines it ; he tests it in relation to the assumed
facts on which it is based ; he discovers the latent
difficulties, faces them, and solves them, and, starting with a conventional type, leaves us with an
individual man.   In doing this he treats the facts as
a means, not as an end, but he does not sophisticate
them.   We hardly ever find fictitious persons and
scenes in Schiller's style, and when we do the
exception proves the rule, for they have not the
same function as in Schiller's theatre.   Falstaff
plays his part aside, as it were, from the official
history, he belongs to the private life of Prince Hal,
and is impotent to affect the march of public events.
People like Lucius in *Julius Caesar*, or Nicanor in
Coriolanus, or Silius in *Antony and Cleopatra* do
not interfere in the political story ; they are present
to make or to hear comments, or at most to assist
the inward interpretation.   No unhistorical person
has historical work to do, and no unhistorical episode
affects the historical action.[1]   Yet he quite escapes
from the chill and closeness of the book-room.   He
engages in no critical investigations to sift out the
genuine facts.   He does not study old tapestry or
early texts.   Unhampered by the learned apparatus
of the scholar, undistracted by the need of pausing
to verify or correct, he speeds along on the flood-

---

[1] Even the intervention of the Bastard in *King John* was guaranteed
by the old play and was doubtless considered authentic by Shakespeare.

tide of his own inspiration, which takes the same course with the interests of the nation. For it is the reward of the intimate sympathy which exists between him and his countrymen, that he goes to work, his personal genius fortified and enlarged by the popular enthusiasms, patriotic or cosmopolitan. And nothing can withstand the speed and volume of the current. There is a great contrast between the broad free sweep of his Histories, English or Roman, that lift us from our feet and carry us away, and the little artificial channels of the antiquarian dramas, on the margin of which we stand at ease to criticise the purity of the distilled water. Yet none the less he is in a sense more obedient to his authorities than any writer of the antiquarian school. Just because, while desiring to give the truth as he knows it, he is careless to examine the accuracy or estimate the value of the documents he consults ; and just because, while determined to give a faithful narrative, he spares himself all labour of comparison and research and takes a statement of Holinshed or Plutarch as guaranteeing itself, he is far more in the hands of the guide he follows than a later dramatist would be. He takes the text of his author, and often he has not more than one : he accepts it implicitly and will not willingly distort it : he reads it in the light of his own insight and the spirit of the age, and tries to recreate the agents and the story from the more or less adequate hints that he finds.

Now, proceeding in this way it is clear that while in every case Shakespeare's indebtedness to his historical sources must be great, it will vary greatly in quality and degree according to the material delivered to him. The situations may be more or less dramatic, the narrative more or less firmly conceived. And among his sources Plutarch occupies quite an exceptional place. From no one else has he 'conveyed' so much, and no one else has he altered so little. And the reason is, that save Chaucer and Homer, on whom he drew for *Troilus and Cressida*, but from whom he could assimilate little that suited his own different ideas, no other writer contained so much that was of final and permanent excellence. To put it shortly, in Plutarch's *Lives* Shakespeare for the first and almost the only time was rehandling the masterpieces of a genius who stood at the summit of his art. It was not so in the English Histories. One does not like to say a word in disparagement of the Elizabethan chronicles, especially Holinshed's, on which the maturer plays are based. They are good reading and deserve to be read independently of the dramatist's use of them. But they are not works of phenomenal ability, and they betray the infancy of historical writing, not only in scientific method, which in the present connection would hardly matter, but in narrative art as well. Cowley in *his* Chronicle, *i.e.* the imaginary record of his love affairs, breaks off with a simile and jest at their expense. If, he says, I were to give the details,

> I more voluminous should grow—
> (Chiefly if I like them should tell
> All change of weathers that befell)
> Than Holinshed and Stowe.

Their intention is good, and they often realise it so as to interest and impress, but the introduction of such-like trifles as Cowley mentions, without much relevance or significance, may give us the measure of their technical skill. Again, though in the second and third part of *Henry VI.* Shakespeare was dealing with the work of Marlowe, we have to remember, first, that his originals were composite pieces not by Marlowe alone, and, further, that even Marlowe could not altogether escape the disabilities of a pioneer.

E

In Plutarch, however, Shakespeare levied toll on
no petty vassal like the compilers of the Chronicles,
or innovating conqueror like the author of *Tamburlaine*, but on the king by right divine of a
long-established realm.   And the result is that he
appropriates more, and that more of greater value,
than from any other tributary.

CHAPTER III

ANCESTRY OF SHAKESPEARE'S ROMAN PLAYS

I.

PLUTARCH [1]

PLUTARCH, born at Chaeronea in Boeotia, about 45 or 50 A.D., flourished in the last quarter of the first and the earliest quarter of the second century. He came of good stock, which he is not reluctant to talk about. Indeed, his habit of introducing or quoting his father, his grandfather, and even his great grandfather, gives us glimpses of a home in which the prescribed pieties of family life were warmly cherished ; and some of the references imply an atmosphere of simplicity, urbanity, and culture.

The lad was sent to Athens to complete his education under Ammonius, an eminent philosopher of that generation, though in Carlyle's phrase, 'now dim to us,' who also took part in what little administrative work was still intrusted to provincials, and more than once held the distinguished position of strategos. Thus, as in childhood Plutarch was trained in the best domestic traditions of elder Greece, so now he had before his eyes an example of such active citizenship as survived in the changed condition of things.

[1] See Plutarch's works *passim*, especially North's version of the *Lives* reprinted in the *Tudor Translations*, and the *Morals* translated by Philemon Holland (1603). See also Archbishop Trench's *Lectures on Plutarch*.

The same spirit of reverence for the past presided over his routine of study. His works afterwards show a wide familiarity with the earlier literature and philosophy of his country, and the foundations of this must have been laid in his student days. It was still in accordance with accepted precedents and his own reminiscent tastes, that when he set out on his travels, he should first, as so many of his predecessors were reported to have done, betake himself to the storied land of Egypt. We know that this must have been after 66 A.D., for in that year, when Nero made his progress through Greece, Plutarch tells us that he was still the pupil of Ammonius. We know, further, that he must have visited Alexandria, for he mentions that in his grandfather's opinion his father gave too large a banquet to celebrate their homecoming from that city. But he does not inform us how much of Egypt he saw, or how long was his stay, or in what way he employed himself. It is only a probable conjecture at most that his treatise on *Isis and Osiris* may be one of the fruits of this expedition.

Of another and later journey that took him to Italy, there is more to be said. Plutarch at an early age, whether before or after the Egyptian tour, had already been employed in public affairs. He tells us :

> I remember my selfe, that when I was but of yoong yeres I was sent with another in embassage to the Proconsul : and in that my companion staid about I wot not what behind, I went alone and did that which we had in commission to do together. After my returne when I was to give an account unto the State, and to report the effect of my charge and message back again, my father arose, and taking me apart, willed me in no wise to speak in the singular number and say, *I departed or went*, but, *We departed*; item not *I said* (or *quoth I*) but *We said*; and in the whole narration of the rest to joine alwaies my companion as if he had been associated and at one hand with me in that which I did alone.[1]

[1] *Instructions for them, etc.*

Such courtesy conciliates good will, and he was subsequently sent 'on public business' to Rome. This must have been before 90 A.D., when Rusticus, whom Plutarch mentions that he met, was condemned to death, and when the philosophers were expelled from the city ; and was probably some time after 74 A.D., the date of their previous expulsion, when, moreover, Plutarch was too young to be charged with matters so weighty as to need settlement in the capital. But it is not certain whether this was his only visit to Italy, and whether he made it in the reign of Vespasian or of Domitian. His story of a performing dog that took part in an exhibition in presence of Vespasian, has been thought to have the verisimilitude of a witnessed scene, and has been used to support the former supposition : his description of the sumptuousness of Domitian's buildings makes a similar impression, and has been used to support the latter. All this must remain doubtful, but some things are certain : that his business was so engrossing, and those who came to him for instruction were so numerous, that he had little time for the study of the Latin language ; that he delivered lectures, some of which were the first drafts of essays subsequently included in the *Moralia* ; that he had as his acquaintances or auditors several of the most distinguished men in Rome, among them Mestrius Florus, a table companion of Vespasian, Sosius Senecio, the correspondent of Pliny, and that Arulenus Rusticus afterwards put to death by Domitian, who on one occasion would not interrupt a lecture of Plutarch's to read a letter from the Emperor ; that he traversed Italy as far north as Ravenna, where he saw the bust of Marius, and even as Bedriacum, where he inspected the battlefields of 69 A.D.

But though Plutarch loved travel and sight-seeing, and though he was fully alive to the advantages of a great city, with its instructive society and its collections of books, his heart was in his native place, and he returned to settle there. " I my selfe," he says, " dwelle in a poore little towne, and yet doe remayne there willingly, least it should become lesse."[1] And in point of fact he seems henceforth only to have left it for short excursions to various parts of Greece. One of these exhibits him in a characteristic and amiable light. Apparently soon after his marriage a dispute had broken out between the parents of the newly wedded pair, and Plutarch in his conciliatory way took his wife, as we should say, 'on a pilgrimage,' to the shrine at Thespiae on Mount Helicon to offer a sacrifice to Love.[2] This is in keeping with all the express utterances and all the unconscious revelations he makes of his feeling for the sacredness of the family tie. He was one of those whose soul rings true to the claims of kith and kin. He thanks Fortune as a chief favour for the comradeship of his brother Timon, and delights to show off the idiosyncrasies of his brother Lamprias. We do not know when his marriage took place, but if Plutarch acted on his avowed principles, it must have been when he was still a young man, and it was a very happy one. As we should expect ; for of all the affections it is wedded love that he dwells on most fully, and few have spoken more nobly and sincerely of it than he. Again and again he gives the point of view, which is often said to have been attained by the Modern World only by the combined assistance of Germanic character and Christian religion. Thus he says of a virtuous attachment :

But looke what person soever love setleth upon in mariage, so as he be inspired once therewith, at the very first, like as it is in Platoes Common-wealth, he will not have these words in his mouth, *Mine* and *Thine*; for simply all goods are not common among all friends, but only those who being severed

[1] *Life of Demosthenes.*   [2] *Love.*

apart in body, conjoine and colliquate as it were perforce
their soules together, neither willing nor believing that they
should be twaine but one : and afterward by true pudicitie
and reverence one unto the other, whereof wedlock hath
most need. . . In true love there is so much continency,
modesty, loyalty and faithfulnesse, that though otherwhile it
touche a wanton and lascivious minde, yet it diverteth it from
other lovers, and by cutting off all malapert boldnesse, by
taking downe and debasing insolent pride and untaught
stubornesse, it placeth in lieu thereof modest bashfulnesse,
silence, and taciturnity ; it adorneth it with decent gesture
and seemly countenance, making it for ever after obedient
to one lover onely. . . For like as at Rome, when there
was a Lord Dictatour once chosen, all other officers of state
and magistrates valed bonnet, were presently deposed, and
laied downe their ensignes of authority ; even so those over
whom love hath gotten the mastery and rule, incontinently are
quit freed and delivered from all other lords and rulers, no
otherwise than such as are devoted to the service of some
religious place.[1]

His wife bore him at least five children, of whom
three died in childhood, the eldest son, "the lovely
Chaeron," and then their little daughter, born after
her four brothers, and called by her mother's name,
Timoxena. The letter of comfort which Plutarch,
who was absent at Tanagra, sent home after the
death took place, is good to read. There is perhaps
here and there a touch that suggests the professional
moralist and rhetorician : as when he recounts a
fable of Aesop's to enforce his advice ; or bids his
wife not to dwell on her griefs rather than her
blessings, like "those Criticks who collect and gather
together all the lame and defective verses of Homer,
which are but few in number ; and in the meane time
passe over an infinite sort of others which were by
him most excellently made" ; or warns her to look
to her health because, if "the bodie be evill entreated
and not regarded with good diet and choice keeping,
it becometh dry, rough and hard, in such sort as
from it there breathe no sweet and comfortable

[1] *Love.*

exhalations unto the soule, but all smoakie and bitter vapors of dolour griefe and sadnesse annoy her." These were the toll Plutarch paid to his age and to his training. But the tender feeling for his wife's grief, and the confidence in her dignified endurance of it are very beautiful and human. And his descriptions of the child's sweet nature, which he does not leave general, but after his wont lights up with special reminiscences, and which, he insists, they must not lose from mind or turn to bitterness but cherish as an abiding joy, strike the note that is still perhaps most comforting to mourners. After telling over her other winsome and gracious ways, he recalls :

She was of a wonderfull kinde and gentle nature ; loving she was againe to those that loved her, and marvellous desirous to gratifie and pleasure others : in which regards she both delighted me and also yielded no small testimonie of rare debonairetie that nature had endued her withall ; for she would make pretie means [1] to her nourse, and seeme (as it were) to intreat her to give the brest or pap, not only to other infants but also to little babies [2] and puppets and such like gauds as little ones take joy in and wherewith they use to play ; as if upon a singular courtesie and humanitie shee could finde in her heart to communicate and distribute from her owne table even the best things that shee had, among them that did her any pleasure. But I see no reason (sweet wife) why these lovely qualities and such like, wherein we took contentment and joy in her life time, should disquiet and trouble us now after her death, when we either think or make relation of them : and I feare againe, lest by our dolour and griefe, we abandon and put cleane away all the remembrance thereof ; like as Clymene desired to do when she said

"I hate the bow so light of cornel tree :
All exercise abroad, farewell for me,"

as avoiding alwaies and trembling at the commemoration of her sonne which should do no other good but renew her griefe and dolour ; for naturally we seeke to flee all that troubleth and offendeth us. We oughte therefore so to demeane ourselves, that, as whiles she lived, we had nothing

[1] = Coax.   [2] Dolls.

in the world more sweet to embrace, more pleasant to see or delectable to heare than our daughter; so the cogitation of her may still abide and live with us all our life time, having by many degrees our joy multiplied more than our heavinesse augmented.[1]

And then there is the confident expectation of immortality to mitigate the present pang of severance. But Plutarch and his wife had other consolations as well. Two sons, Aristobulus and a younger Plutarch, lived to be men, and to them he dedicated a treatise on the *Timaeus*. We know that one of them at least married and had a son in his father's lifetime. Beyond his domestic circle Plutarch had a large number of friends in Chaeronea and elsewhere, including such distinguished names as Favorinus the philosopher and Serapion the poet; and being, in Dr. Johnson's phrase, an eminently "clubbable man," he was often host and guest at banquets, fragments of the talk at which he has preserved in his *Symposiacs*. Almost the only rigorous line in his portrait is contributed by Aulus Gellius, his later contemporary, and the friend of their common friend Favorinus. Gellius [2] represents the philosopher Taurus as telling about "Plutarchus noster"—a phrase that shows the attachment men felt for him—a story of which Dryden gives the following free and amplified but very racy translation :

Plutarch had a certain slave, a saucy stubborn kind of fellow; in a word one of these pragmatical servants who never make a fault but they give a reason for it. His justifications one time would not serve his turn, but his master commanded that he should be stripped and that the law should be laid on his back. He no sooner felt the smart but he muttered that he was unjustly punished, and that he had done nothing to deserve the scourge. At last he began to bawl out louder; and leaving off his groaning, his sighs, and his lamentations, to argue the matter with more show of reason : and, as under such a master he must needs have gained a smattering of learning, he cried out that Plutarch

---

[1] *Epistle to Wife.*   [2] *Noctes Atticae*, I. xxvi.

was not the philosopher he pretended himself to be ; that he had heard him waging war against all the passions, and maintaining that anger was unbecoming a wise man; nay, that he had written a particular treatise in commendation of clemency ; that therefore he contradicted his precepts by his practices, since, abandoning himself over to his choler, he exercised such inhuman cruelty on the body of his fellow-creature. " How is this, Mr. Varlet ? " (answered Plutarch). " By what signs and tokens can you prove that I am in · passion ? Is it by my countenance, my voice, the colour of my face, by my words or by my gestures that you have discovered this my fury? I am not of opinion that my eyes sparkle, that I foam at the mouth, that I gnash my teeth, or that my voice is more vehement, or that my colour is either more pale or more red than at other times ; that I either shake or stamp with madness ; that I say or do anything unbecoming a philosopher. These, if you know them not, are the symptoms of a man in rage. In the meantime," (turning to the officer who scourged him) "while he and I dispute this matter, mind your business on his back."

This story, as we have seen, comes from one who was in a position to get authentic information about Plutarch, and it may very well be true ; but it should be corrected, or at least supplemented, by his own utterances in regard to his servants. " Sometimes," he says, " I use to get angry with my slaves, but at last I saw that it was better to spoil them by indulgence, than to injure myself by rage in the effort to amend them." And more emphatically :

As for me I coulde never finde in my hart to sell my drawght Oxe that hadde plowed my lande a longe time, because he coulde plowe no longer for age ; and much lesse my slave to sell him for a litle money, out of the contrie where he had dwelt a long time, to plucke him from his olde trade of life wherewith he was best acquainted, and then specially, when he shalbe as unprofitable for the buyer as also for the seller.[1]

Plutarch was thus fully alive to the social and domestic amenities of life, and to his responsibilities as householder, but he did not for them overlook other claims. He became priest of Apollo in Delphi, and for many years fulfilled the priestly

[1] *Cato Major.*

functions, taking part in the sacrifices, processions and dances even as an old man ; for philosopher as he was, his very philosophy supplied him with various contrivances for conformity . with the ancient cult, and he probably had no more difficulty about it than a modern Hegelian has with the Thirty-nine Articles. His deeper religious needs would be satisfied by the Mysteries, in which he and his wife were initiated.

He was equally assiduous in public duties, which he did not despise for the pettiness to which under the Roman domination they had shrunk. In his view even the remnants of self-government are to be jealously guarded and loyally employed, though they may concern merely parochial and municipal affairs, and for them vigilant training and discipline are required.

> Surely impossible it is that they should ever have their part of any great roial and magnificall joy, such as indeed causeth magnanimitie and hautinesse of courage, bringeth glorious honour abroad or tranquillitie of spirit at home, who have made choice of a close and private life within doors, never showing themselves in the world nor medling with publicke affaires of common weale ; a life, I say, sequestered from all offices of humanitie, far removed from any instinct of honour or desire to gratifie others, thereby to deserve thankes or winne favour : for the soul, I may tell you, is no base and small thing ; it is not vile and illiberal, extending her desires onely to that which is good to be eaten, as doe these poulpes [1] or pour cuttle fishes which stretch their cleies as far as to their meat and no farther : for such appetites as these are most quickly cut off with satietie and filled in a moment. But when the motives and desires of the minde tending to vertue and honestie, to honour and contentment of conscience are once growen to their vigour and perfection, they have not for their limit, the length and tearme onely of one man's life ; but surely the desire of honour and the affection to profit the societie of men, comprehending all aeternitie, striveth still to goe forward in such actions and beneficiall deedes as yield infinite pleasures that cannot be expressed. [2]

[1] Polypes.   [2] *That a man cannot live pleasantly, etc.*

He was true to his principles. He not only officiated as Archon of Chaeronea, but, "gracing the lowliest act in doing it," was willing to discharge the functions of a more subordinate post, which some thought beneath his dignity.

> Mine answer is to such as reprove me, when they find me in proper person present, at the measuring and counting of bricks and tiles, or to see the stones, sand and lime laid downe, which is brought into the citie: "It is not for myselfe that I builde, but for the citie and common-wealth."[1]

He was thus faithful over a few things; tradition made him ruler over many things. It is related that Trajan granted him consular rank and directed the governor of Achaia to avail himself of his advice. This was embellished by the report that he had been Trajan's preceptor; and in the Middle Ages a letter very magisterial in tone was fabricated from him to his imperial pupil. It was even said that in his old age Hadrian had made him governor of Greece.

There is a poetic justification for such legends. The government of Trajan and Hadrian was felt to be such that the precepts of philosophy might very fittingly have inspired it, and that the philosopher might very well have been the administrator of their policy. And indeed it is perhaps no fable that Plutarch had something to do with the better *régime* that was commencing; for his nephew Sextus of Chaeronea, who may have inherited something of his uncle's spirit, was an honoured teacher of Marcus Aurelius, and influenced his pupil by his example no less than by his teaching. The social renovation which was then in progress should be remembered in estimating Plutarch's career. Gibbon says: "If a man were called to fix the period in the History of the World, during which the condition of the human race was most happy and prosperous, he would, without hesitation, name that which elapsed

[1] *Instructions for them, etc.*

from the death of Domitian to the accession of Commodus." Probably this statement would need to be, if not greatly qualified, at least greatly amplified, before it commanded universal assent, but, as it stands, there is a truth in it which anyone can perceive. There was peace throughout a great portion of the world; there was good government within the Empire; there was a rejuvenescence of antique culture, literature, and conduct. Indeed, the upward tendency begins with the reigns of Vespasian and Titus, and even the thwarting influence of Domitian's principate would be felt in Rome rather than in the provinces. It was in this time of "reaction against corruption" that Plutarch flourished, and his later life especially fell well within that Indian summer of classical civilisation that Gibbon celebrates. The tradition that he survived till the accession of Antonine may be incorrect, but he certainly enjoyed eight years of Trajan's government, and, by Eusebius' statement, was still alive in the third year of Hadrian's reign. It is to his latter days that his *Lives* as a whole are assigned, partly on account of the casual reference to contemporary events that some of them contain.

Plutarch's character, circumstances, and career in a world which was reaching its close, well fitted him for the work that he did. This Greek citizen of the Roman Empire had cultivated his mind by study and travel, and had assimilated the wisdom of wide experience and pregnant memories which Antiquity had amassed in earlier times and to which this interval of revival was heir. Benevolent and dutiful, temperate and devout, with a deep sense of his public obligations and the ethos of his race, he sympathised with the best principles that had moulded the life of olden days, and that were emerging to direct the life of the present. And he combined his amplitude of traditional lore and enthusiasm for traditional virtue in a way that made him more than an antiquary or a moralist. The explorer and practitioner of antique ideas, in a sense he was their artist as well.

His treatment and style already suggest the manifold influences that went to form his mind. One of his charms lies in his quotations, which he culls, or rather which spring up of their own accord, from his reading of the most various authors of the most different times. He is at home in Greek literature, and likes to clinch his argument with a saying from the poets, for he seems to find that their words put his thought better than he could himself. But this affects his original expression. Dryden writes :

> Being conversant in so great a variety of authors, and collecting from all of them what he thought most excellent, out of the confusion or rather mixture of their styles he formed his own, which partaking of each was yet none of them, but a compound of them all :—like the Corinthian metal which had in it gold and brass and silver, and yet was a species in itself.

There may be a suggestion of the curious mosaic-worker in his procedure, something of artifice, or at least of conscious art ; and indeed his treatises are not free from a rhetorical and sometimes declamatory strain.[1] That in so far is what Courier means when

---

[1] Even in the narrative passages one is conscious that the descriptions have been worked up. Take, e.g. the following passage from the *Life of Marius* :—

Ἐπεὶ δὲ πολλοὺς τῶν Ἀμβρώνων οἱ Ῥωμαῖοι διαφθείραντες ἀνεχώρησαν ὀπίσω καὶ σκότος ἐπέσχεν, οὐχ ὥσπερ εὐτυχήματι τοσούτῳ τὸν στρατὸν ἐδέξαντο παιᾶνες ἐπινίκιοι καὶ πότοι κατὰ σκηνὰς καὶ φιλοφροσύναι περὶ δεῖπνα, καί, τὸ πάντων ἥδιστον ἀνδράσιν εὐτυχῶς μεμαχημένοις, ὕπνος ἤπιος, ἀλλ᾽ ἐκείνην μάλιστα τὴν νύκτα φοβερὰν καὶ ταραχώδη διήγαγον. Ἦν μὲν γὰρ αὐτοῖς ἀχαράκωτον τὸ στρατόπεδον καὶ ἀτείχιστον, ἀπελείποντο δὲ τῶν βαρβάρων ἔτι πολλαὶ μυριάδες ἀήττητοι καὶ συμμεμιγμένων τούτοις, ὅσοι διαπεφεύγεσαν, τῶν Ἀμβρώνων ὀδυρμὸς ἦν διὰ νυκτός, οὐ κλαυθμοῖς οὐδὲ στεναγμοῖς ἀνθρώπων ἐοικώς, ἀλλὰ θηρομιγής τις ὠρυγὴ καὶ βρύχημα μεμιγμένον ἀπειλαῖς καὶ θρήνοις ἀναπεμπόμενον ἐκ πλήθους

he says that Plutarch writes in the style of a *sophistes* ; but it was inseparable from his composite

τοσούτου τά τε πέριξ ὄρη καὶ τὰ κοῖλα τοῦ ποταμοῦ περιεφώνει. Καὶ κατεῖχε φρικώδης ἦχος τὸ πεδίον.

(XX. Döhner's Edition.)

Or take this from the *Life of Sulla* :—

Τὴν δὲ κραυγὴν καὶ ἀλαλαγμὸν οὐκ ἔστεγεν ὁ ἀὴρ ἐθνῶν τοσούτων ἅμα καθισταμένων εἰς τάξιν. Ἦν δὲ ἅμα καὶ τὸ κομπῶδες καὶ σοβαρὸν αὐτῶν τῆς πολυτελείας οὐκ ἀργὸν οὐδὲ ἄχρηστον εἰς ἔκπληξιν, ἀλλ' αἵ τε μαρμαρυγαὶ τῶν ὅπλων ἠσκημένων χρυσῷ τε καὶ ἀργύρῳ διαπρεπῶς αἵ τε βαφαὶ τῶν Μηδικῶν καὶ Σκυθικῶν χιτώνων ἀναμεμιγμέναι χαλκῷ καὶ σιδήρῳ λάμποντι πυροειδῆ καὶ φοβερὰν ἐν τῷ σαλεύεσθαι καὶ διαφέρεσθαι προσέβαλλον ὄψιν, ὥστε τοὺς Ῥωμαίους ὑπὸ τὸν χάρακα συστέλλειν ἑαυτοὺς καὶ τὸν Σύλλαν μηδενὶ λόγῳ τὸ θάμβος αὐτῶν ἀφελεῖν δυνάμενον βιάζεσθαί τε ἀποδιδράσκοντας οὐ βουλόμενον ἡσυχίαν ἄγειν καὶ φέρειν βαρέως ἐφυβρίζοντας ὁρῶντα κομπασμῷ καὶ γέλωτι τοὺς βαρβάρους.

(XVI. Döhner's Edition.)

This is very different from the unstudied charm of Herodotus. Even in North's translation, though something of the cunning has been lost in the selection and manipulation of the words, it is easy to see that the pictures are elaborate both in their general effect and their details.

Now the Romaines, after they had overcome the most parte of the Ambrons, retyring backe by reason the night had overtaken them, did not (as they were wont after they had geven such an overthrow) sing songes of victory and triumphe, nor make good chere in their tentes one with an other, and least of all sleepe : (which is the best and sweetest refreshing for men that have fought happely), but contrarily they watched all that night with great feare and trouble, bicause their campe was not trenched and fortified, and bicause they knewe also that there remained almost innumerable thowsandes of barbarous people, that had not yet fought : besides also that the Ambrons that had fled and scaped from the overthrow, did howle out all night with lowd cries, which were nothing like men's lamentacions and sighes, but rather like wild beastes bellowing and roaringe. So that the bellowinge of such a great multitude of beastly people, mingled together with threates and waylinges, made the mountains thereabouts and the running river to rebounde againe of the sounde and ecco of their cries marvellously : by reason whereof, all the valley that lay between both, thundered to heare the horrible and fearfull trembling.

The ayer was even cut a sunder as it were with the violence of the noyse and cries of so many sundry nations, which altogether did put them selves in battell ray. The sumptuousness of their furniture moreover, was not altogether superfluous and unprofitable, but served greatly to feare the beholders. For the glistering of their harnesse,

culture and academic training, and it does not interfere with his sincerity and directness.

His philosophy makes a similar impression. He
is an eclectic or syncretist, and has learned from
many of the mighty teachers of bygone times.
Plato is his chief authority, but Plato's doctrines are
consciously modified in an Aristotelian sense, while
nevertheless those aspects of them are made prominent which were afterwards elaborated by Neo-
Platonism strictly so called. But Plutarch, though
he has the good word of Neo-Platonic thinkers, is
not himself to be reckoned of their company. He
is comparatively untouched by their mysticism,
borrowed freely from the Theosophy of the East,
and he stands in closer lineal relation to the antique
Greek spirit than some, like Philo, who precede him
in time. He was so indifferent to the Semitic
habit of mind that, despite his almost omnivorous
curiosity, he never thought it worth while to instruct
himself in the exact nature of Judaism or its difference from the Syrian cult, far less to spend on
Christianity so much as a passing glance. He
approaches Neo-Platonism most nearly in certain
religious imaginings which, as he himself recognised,
have affinity with beliefs which prevailed in Persia
and Egypt; but even so, he hardly ceases to be
national, for these were the two countries with
which in days of yore Greece had the most important historic connections. And moreover, his interest

so richly trimmed and set forth with gold and silver, the cullers of
their arming coates upon their curaces, after the facion of the Medes
and Scythians, mingled with the bright glistering steele and shining
copper, gave such a showe as they went and removed to and fro, that
made a light as clere as if all had bene on a very fire, a fearfull thing
to looke upon. In so much as the Romaines durst not so much as
once goe out of the trenches of their campe, nor Sylla with all his perswasion coulde take away this great conceived feare from them :
wherefore, (and bicause also he would not compell them to goe forth
in this feare) he was driven not to stirre, but close to abide, (though
it grieved him greatly) to see the barbarous people so proudly and
villanously laugh him and his men to scorne.

in such surmises is not, in the first place, a speculative one, but springs from the hope of his finding some explanation of and comfort for the trials and difficulties of actual life. For on the whole he differs from Plato chiefly in his subordination of theory to practice. This compels him to accept loans from the very schools that he most criticises, the Stoics, the Sceptics, the Epicureans themselves. It is his pre-occupation with conduct, rather than eclectic debility, that makes him averse to any one-sided scheme, and inclined to supplement it with manifold additions. But as in his style, so in his thought, he blends the heterogeneous elements to his own purpose, and fixes on them the stamp of his own mind. It is not without reason that his various treatises are included under the common title of *Moralia*. He may dilate on the worship of *Isis and Osiris*, or *The Face appearing within the Roundle of the Moone*; he may discuss *Whether creatures be more wise, they of the land or those of the water; What signifieth this word Ei engraven over the Dore of Appolloes Temple in the City of Delphi*, and various other recondite matters; but the prevailing impression is ethical, and he is at his best when he is discoursing expressly on some moral theme, on *Unseemly and Naughty Bashfulnesse*, or *Brotherly Love*, or *Tranquillitie and Contentment of Mind*, or the *Pluralitie of Friends*, or the question *Whether this common Mot be well said 'Live Hidden.'* There is the background of serious study and philosophic knowledge, but against it is detached the figure of the sagacious and practical teacher, who wishes to make his readers better men and better women, but never forgets his urbanity and culture in his admonitions, and drives them home with pointed anecdote and apt quotation. And the substance of his teaching, though so sane and experimental that it is sometimes described as obvious and trite, has a generous, ideal, and even chivalrous strain, when he touches on such subjects as love, or devotion, or the claims of virtue ; and his sympathy goes out spontaneously to noble words or deeds or minds.

It is an easy step from the famous *Moralia* to the still more famous *Parallel Lives*. "All history," says Dryden, in reference to the latter, "is only the precepts of moral philosophy reduced into examples." This, at least, is no bad description of Plutarch's point of view ; and his methods do not greatly differ in the series of essays and in the series of biographies. In the essays he did not let himself be unduly hampered by the etiquette of the Moral Treatise, but expatiated at will among Collections and Recollections, and embroidered his abstract argument with the stories that he delights to tell. As historian, on the other hand, he is not tied down to historical narration and exposition, but indulges his moralising bent to the full. He is on the lookout for edification, and is seldom at a loss for a peg to hang a lecture on. And these discourses of his, though the material is sometimes the sober drab of the decent *bourgeois*, are always fine in texture, and relieved by the quaintness of the cut and the ingenuity of the garnishing : nor are they the less interesting that they do not belong to the regulation historical outfit. Such improving digressions, indeed, are among Plutarch's charms. "I am always pleased," says Dryden, "when I see him and his imitator Montaigne when they strike a little out of the common road ; for we are sure to be the better for their wandering. The best quarry does not always lie on the open field, and who would not be content to follow a good huntsman over hedges and ditches, when he knows the game will reward his pains." [1]

[1] There are so many good things, despite all the inevitable mistakes, in Dryden's *Life of Plutarch*, that one half regrets that Professor Ker's

Proceeding in this way it is not to be expected that Plutarch should compose his *Lives* with much care for dexterous design. Just as in his philosophy he has no rigidly consequent system of doctrine, so in his biographies he has no orderly or well-digested plan. The excellences that arise from a definite and vigorous conception of the whole are not those at which he aims. He would proceed very much at haphazard, were it not for the chronological clue; which, for the rest, he is very willing to abandon if a tempting by-path presents itself, or if he thinks of something for which he must retrace his steps. Yet, no more than in his metaphysics is he without an instinctive method of his own. The house is finished, and with all its irregularities it is good to dwell in; the journey is ended, and there has been no monotony on the devious track. There is this advantage indeed in his procedure over that of more systematic biographers, that it offers hospitality to all the suggestions that crowd for admission. None is rejected because it is out of place and insignificant. Gossip and allotria of every kind that do not make out their claims at first sight, and that the more ambitious historian would exclude as trivial, find an entry if they can show a far-off connection with the subject. And, lo and behold, they often turn out to be the most instructive of all.

But Plutarch welcomes them without scrutinising them very austerely. He submits their credentials to no stringent test. He is no severe critic of their authenticity. He takes them where he finds them, just as he picks up philosophic ideas from all quarters, even from the detested Epicureans, without

---

plan did not allow him to include at least part of it in his admirable selection. Thus, in excuse for omitting the catalogue of Plutarch's lost works, which had been given in full in the Paris edition : " But it is a small comfort to the merchant to pursue his bill of freight when he is certain his ship is cast away ; moved by the like reason, I have omitted that ungrateful task."

condemning them on account of their suspicious
source : it is enough for him if they adapt themselves
to his use. Nor does he educe from them all that
they involve. He does not even confront them with
each other, to examine whether opposite hints about
his heroes may not lead to fuller and subtler conceptions of them. This is the point of the charge
brought against him by St. Évremond, that he
might have carried his analysis further and penetrated more deeply into human nature. St. Évremond
notes how different a man is from himself, the same
person being just and unjust, merciful and cruel ;
"which qualities," proceeds the critic, "seeming to
belie each other in him, [Plutarch] attributes these
inconsistencies to foreign causes. He could never
. . . reconcile contrarieties in the same subject."
He never tried to do so. He collects a number of
vivid traits, which, like a number of minute lines, set
forth the likeness to his own mind, but he is ordinarily
as far from interrogating and combining his impressions as he is from subjecting them to any punctilious
test. He exhibits characters in the particular aspects
and manifestations which history or hearsay has
presented, and is content with the general sense
of verisimilitude that these successive indications,
credited or accredited, have left behind. But he
stops there, and does not study his manifold data
to construct from them a consistent complex individuality in its oneness and difference. And if this is
true of him as biographer, it is still truer of him as
historian. He touches on all sorts of historical subjects—war, policy, administration, government ; and
he has abundance of acute and just remarks on them
all. But it is not in these that his chief interest lies,
and it is not over them that he holds his torch. This
does not mean that he fails to perceive the main drift
of things or to appreciate the importance of statecraft. Mr. Wyndham, defending him against those

who have "denied him any political insight," very
justly shows that, despite "the paucity of his political
pronouncements," he has a "political bent." His
choice of heroes, in the final arrangement to which
they lent themselves, proves that he has an eye for
the general course of Greek and Roman history, for
the impotence into which the city state is sunk by
rivalry with neighbours in the one case, for its transmutation into an Empire on the other: "The tragedy
of Athens, the drama of Rome," says Mr. Wyndham,
"these are the historic poles of the *Parallel Lives.*"
And Plutarch has a political ideal: the "need of
authority and the obligation of the few to maintain
it—by a 'natural grace' springing on the one hand
from courage combined with forbearance, and leading, on the other, to harmony between the rulers
and the ruled—is the text, which, given out in the
Lycurgus, is illustrated throughout the *Parallel
Lives.*" So much indeed we had a right to expect
from the thoughtful patriot and experienced magistrate of Chaeronea. The salient outlines of the story
of Greece and Rome could hardly remain hidden
from a clear-sighted man with Plutarch's knowledge
of the past: the relations of governor and governed
had not only engaged him practically, but had
suggested to him one of his most pithy essays, *Prae-
cepta gerendae Reipublicae*, a title which Philemon
Holland paraphrases in stricter accordance with the
contents, *Instructions for them that manage Affaires
of State*. But this does not carry us very far.
Shakespeare in his English Histories shows at least
as much political discernment and political instinct.
He brings out the general lesson of the wars of
Lancaster and York, and in *Henry V.* gives his conception of the ideal ruler. But no one would say
that this series shows a conspicuous genius for
political research or political history. The same
thing is true, and in a greater degree, of Plutarch.

He is public-spirited, but he is not a publicist.   He has not much concern or understanding for particular measures and movements and problems, however critical they may be.   It is impossible to challenge the justice of Archbishop Trench's verdict, either in its general scope or in its particular instances, when he says :

> One who already knows the times of Marius and Sulla will obtain a vast amount of instruction from his several *Lives* of these, will clothe with flesh and blood what would else, in some parts, have been the mere skeleton of a story; but I am bold to say no one would understand those times from him. The suppression of the Catilinarian Conspiracy was the most notable event in the life of Cicero; but one rises from Plutarch's *Life* with only the faintest impression of what that conspiracy, a sort of anticipation of the French Commune, and having objects social rather than political, meant.   Or take his *Lives* of the Gracchi.   Admirable in many respects as these are, greatly as we are debtors to him here for important facts, whereof otherwise we should have been totally ignorant, few, I think, would affirm that he at all plants them in a position for understanding that vast revolution effected, with the still vaster revolution attempted by them, and for ever connected with their names.

In Plutarch the historian, as well as the biographer, is subordinate to the ethical teacher who wishes to enforce lessons that may be useful to men in the management of their lives.   He gathers his material for its "fine moral effects," not for "purposes of research." [1]

Plutarch, then, had already composed many disquisitions to commend his humane and righteous

---

[1] De Quincey says : "Nor do I believe Wordsworth would much have lamented on his own account if all books had perished, except the entire body of English poetry and Plutarch's Lives.· . . . I do not mean to insinuate that Wordsworth was at all in the dark about the inaccuracy or want of authentic weight attaching to Plutarch as historian, but his business with Plutarch was not for *purposes of research* ; he was satisfied with his *fine moral effects*." So too one of Plutarch's latest editors, Mr. Holden, says in a similar sense: "Plutarch has no idea of historic criticism. . . .   He thought far less of finding out and relating what actually occurred than of edifying his readers and promoting virtue."

ideas, and it was partly in the same didactic spirit that he seems to have written his *Parallel Lives*. At the beginning of the *Life of Pericles* he says :

> Vertue is of this power, that she allureth a mans minde presently to use her, and maketh him very desirous in his harte to followe her : and doth not frame his manners that beholdeth her by any imitation but by the only understanding and knowledge of vertuous deedes, which sodainely bringeth unto him a resolute desire to doe the like. *And this is the reason why methought I should continew still to write on the lives of noble men.*

And similar statements occur again and again. They clearly show the aim that he consciously had in view. The new generation was to be admonished and renovated by the examples of the leading spirits who had flourished in former times. And since he was addressing the whole civilised world, he took his examples both from Roman and from Grecian History, and arranged his persons in pairs, each pair supplying the matter for one book. Thus he couples Theseus and Romulus, Alcibiades and Coriolanus, Alexander and Caesar, Dion and Brutus, Demetrius and Antony. Such parallelism is a little far-fetched, and though some of the detailed comparisons with which it is justified, are not from Plutarch's hand, and belong to a later time, it of itself betrays a certain fondness for symmetry and antithesis, a leaning towards artifice and rhetoric which, as we have seen, the author owed to his environment. He wishes in an eloquent way to inculcate his lessons, and is perhaps, for the same reason, somewhat prone to exaggerate the greatness of the past, and show it in an idealised light. But this is by no means the pose of the histrionic revivalist. It corresponds to an authentic sentiment in his own nature, which loved to linger amid the glooms and glories of tradition, and pay vows at the shrine of the Great Departed. " The cradle of war and statecraft," says Mr. Wyndham, "was become a memory dear to him, and ever evolved by his personal contact with the triumphs of Rome. From this contrast flowed his inspiration for the *Parallel Lives*—his desire as a man to draw the noble Grecians, long since dead, a little nearer to the noonday of the living; his delight as an artist in setting the noble Romans, whose names were in every mouth, a little further into the twilight of more ancient Romance."

But this transfiguration of the recent and resurrection of the remoter past, in which Mr. Wyndham rightly sees something "romantic," does not lay Plutarch open to the charge of vagueness or unreality. He was saved from such vices by his interest in human nature and suggestive *ana* and picturesque incidents on the one hand, and by his deference for political history and civil society on the other.

He loved marked individualities: no two of his heroes are alike, and each, though in a varying degree, has an unmistakable physiognomy of his own. There is no sameness in his gallery of biographies, and even the legends of demigods yield figures of firm outline that resist the touch. This is largely due to his joy in details, and the imperious demand his imagination makes for them. In his *Life of Alexander* he uses words which very truly describe his own method, words which Boswell[1] was afterwards to quote in justification of his own similar procedure.

> The noblest deedes doe not alwayes shew men's vertues and vices, but often times a light occasion, a word, or some sporte, makes men's natural dispositions and manners appear more plaine, then the famous battells wonne wherein are slaine tenne thousande men, or the great armies, or cities wonne by siege or assault. For like as painters or drawers of pictures, which make no accompt of other parts of the bodie, do take the resemblaunces of the face and favor of the countenance, in the which consisteth the judgement of their maners and disposition; even so they must give us

---

[1] *Johnson's Life*, ed. B. Hill, i. 31.

leave to seeke out the signes and tokens of the minde only,
and thereby shewe the life of either of them, referring you
unto others to wryte the warres, battells and other great
thinges they did.[1]

So he likes to give the familiar traits and emphasise
the suggestive nothings that best discover character.
But his purpose is almost always to discover character, and, so far as his principal persons are concerned,
to discover great character. Though so assiduous
in sharking up their mannerisms, foibles, and oddities,
their tricks of gait or speech or costume, he is not
like the Man with the Muck Rake, and is not piling
together the rubbish of tittle-tattle just because
he has a soul for nothing higher. Still less does he
take the valet's view of the hero, and hold that he
is no hero at all because he can be seen in undress
or in relations that show his common human nature.
Reverence for greatness is the point from which he
starts, reverence for greatness is the star that guides
his course, and his reverence is so entire, that on
the one hand he welcomes all that will help him to
restore the great one in his speech and habit as he
lived, and on the other, he assumes that the greatness must pervade the whole life, and that flashes
of glory will be refracted from the daily talk and
walk. Like Carlyle, though in a more *naïf* and
simple way, he is a hero-worshipper; like Carlyle
he believes that the hero will not lose but gain by
the record of his minutest traits, and that these will
only throw new light on his essential heroism. In
the object he proposed to himself he has succeeded
well. "Plutarch," says Rousseau, almost reproducing the biographer's own words, "has inimitable
dexterity in painting great men in little things, and
he is so happy in his selection, that often a phrase,
a simile, a gesture suffices him to set forth a hero.
That is the true art of portraiture. The physiognomy

[1] *Life of Alexander.*

does not display itself in the main lines, nor the characters in great actions; it is in trifles that the temperament discloses itself." An interesting testimony; for Rousseau, when he sets up as character-painter, belongs to a very different school.

It is not otherwise with his narratives of actions or his descriptions of scenes, if action or scene really interest him; and there is little of intrinsic value, comic or tragic, vivacious or stately, familiar or weird, that does not interest him. Under his quick successive strokes, some of them so light that at first they evade notice, some of them so simple that at first they seem commonplace, the situation becomes visible and luminous. He knows how to choose the accessories and what to do with them. When our attention is awakened, we ask ourselves how he has produced the effect by means apparently so insignificant; and we cannot answer. Here he may have selected a hint from his authorities, there he may derive another from the mental vision he himself has evoked, but in either case the result is equally wonderful. Whether from his tact in reporting or his energy in imagining, he contrives to make us view the occurrence as a fact, and a fact that is like itself and like nothing else.

But again Plutarch was saved from wanton and empty phantasms by his political bias. He was not a politician or a statesman or an historian of politics or institutions, but he was a citizen with a citizen's respect for the State. "For himself," to quote Mr. Wyndham once more, "he was painting individual character, and he sought it among men bearing a personal stamp. But he never sought it in a private person, or a comedian, nor even in a poet or a master of the Fine Arts." He confines himself to public men, as we should call them, and never fails to recollect that they played their part on the public stage. And this not only gave a robustness of touch and breadth of stroke to his delineations ; the connection with well - known and certified events preserved him from the worst licenses to which the romantic and rhetorical temper is liable. Courier, indeed, says of him that he was " capable of making Pompey win the battle of Pharsalia, if it would have rounded his sentence ever so little." But though he may be credulous of details and manipulate his copy, and with a light heart make one statement at one time and a different one at another, the sort of liberty Courier attributes to him is precisely the one he does not take. Facts are stubborn things, and the great outstanding facts he is careful to observe : they bring a good deal else in their train.

2

AMYOT[1]

A book like the *Parallel Lives* was bound to achieve a great popularity at the Renaissance. That it was full of instruction and served for warning and example commended it to a generation that was but too inclined to prize the didactic in literature. Its long list of worthies included not a few of the names that were being held up as the greatest in human history, and these celebrities were exhibited not aloft on their official pedestals, but, however impressive and imposing the *mise en scène* might be, as men among men in the private and personal passages of their lives. And yet they were not private persons but historical magnates, the founders or leaders of world-renowed states : and as such they were particularly congenial to an age in which many of the best minds—More and Buchanan, L'Hôpital

[1] See De Blignières' *Essai sur Amyot*, and Amyot's translations *passim*, with the prefatory epistles.

and La Boëtie, Brand and Hutten—were awakening
to the antique idea of civic and political manhood,
and finding few unalloyed examples of it in the
feudalised West. It was not enough that Plutarch
was made more accessible in the Latin form. He
deserved a vernacular dress, and after various
tentative experiments this was first satisfactorily,
in truth, admirably, supplied by Bishop Amyot in
France.

Jacques Amyot was born in October, 1513, in
Melun, the little town on the Seine, some thirty miles
to the south-east of Paris. His parents were very
poor, but at any rate from his earliest years he was
within the sweep of the dialect of the Île de France,
and had no *patois* to unlearn when he afterwards
appeared as a literary man. Perhaps to this is due
some of the purity and correctness which the most
fastidious were afterwards to celebrate in his style.
These influences would be confirmed when as a lad
he proceeded to Paris to pursue his studies. His
instructors in Greek were—first, Evagrius, in the
college of Cardinal Lemoine, and afterwards, Thusan
and Danès, who, at the instance of Budaeus, had
just been appointed *lecteurs royaux* in Ancient
Philosophy and Literature. Stories are told of the
privations that he endured in the pursuit of scholarship, how his mother sent him every week a loaf by
the watermen of the Seine, how he read his books
by the light of the fire, and the like; but similar
circumstances are related of others, and, to quote
Sainte Beuve, are in some sort "the legend of the
heroic age of erudition." It is better authenticated
that he supported himself by becoming the domestic
attendant of richer students till he graduated as
Master of Arts at the age of nineteen. Then his
position began to improve. He became tutor in
important households, to the nephews of the Royal
Reader, and to the children of the Royal Secretary.

Through such patrons his ability and knowledge were made known to the King's sister, Marguérite de Valois, the beneficent patroness of literature and learning. He had proceeded to Bourges, it is said, to study law, but by her influence was appointed to discharge the more congenial functions of Reader in the Greek and Latin Languages, and was soon promoted to the full professorship. The University of Bourges was at the time the youngest in France save that of Bordeaux, having been founded less than three-quarters of a century before in 1463, when the Renaissance was advancing from conquest to conquest in Italy, and when Medievalism was moribund even in France. The new institution would have few traditions to oppose to the new spirit, and there was scope for a missionary of the New Learning. For some ten or twelve years Amyot remained in his post, lecturing two hours daily, in the morning on Latin, in the afternoon on Greek. No doubt such instruction would be elementary in a way; but even so, it was a laborious life, for in those days the classical teacher had few of the facilities that his modern colleague enjoys. It was, however, a good preparation for Amyot's peculiar mission, and he even found time to make his first experiments in the sphere that was to be his own. By 1546 he had completed a translation of the *Aethiopica* of Heliodorus, the famous Greek romance that deals with the loves and adventures of Theagenes and Chariclea. Amyot afterwards, on the authority of a manuscript which he discovered in the Vatican, identified the author with a Bishop of Tricca who lived in the end of the fourth century, and of whom a late tradition asserted that when commanded by the provincial synod either to burn his youthful effusion or resign his bishopric, he chose the latter alternative. "Heliodorus," says Montaigne, when discussing parental love, "ayma mieulx perdre la dignité, le proufit, la devotion d'une prelature si venerable, que de perdre sa fille, fille qui dure encores bien gentille, mais à l'aventure pourtant un peu curieusement et mollement goderonnee pour fille ecclesiastique et sacerdotale, et de trop amoureuse façon."[1]   In the case of the young French professor it had happier and opposite consequences, for it procured him from the king the Abbey of Bellozane. This gift, one of the last that Francis bestowed for the encouragement of letters, was partly earned, too, by a version of some of Plutarch's *Lives*, which Amyot presented to his royal patron and had executed at his command.

With an income secured Amyot was now in a position to free himself from the drudgery of class work, and follow his natural bent.   In those days not all the printed editions of the classics were very satisfactory, and some works of the authors in whom he was most interested still existed only in manuscript or were known only by name.   He set out for Italy in the hope of discovering the missing *Lives* of Plutarch and of obtaining better texts than had hitherto been within his reach, and seems to have remained abroad for some years.   For a moment he becomes a conspicuous figure in an uncongenial scene.   In May, 1551, the Council of Trent had been reopened, but Charles delayed the transaction of business till the following September. The Italian prelates, impatient and indignant, were hoping for French help against the emperor, but instead of the French Bishops there came only a letter from the "French King addressed to 'the Convention' which he would not dignify with the name of a council.   The King said he had not been consulted about their meeting.   He regarded them as a private synod got up for their own purposes by the Pope and the Emperor and he would have

[1] II. viii., *De l'affection des pères aux enfants.*

nothing to do with them."[1]   It was Amyot who was commissioned with the delivery and communication of the ungracious message.   Probably the selection of the simple Abbé was intended less as an honour to him than as an insult to the assemblage. At any rate it was no very important part that he had to play, but it was one which made him very uncomfortable.   He writes : " Je filois le plus doux que je pouvois, me sentant si mal et assez pour me faire mettre en prison, si j'eusse un peu trop avant parle."   He was not even named in the letter, and had not so much as seen it before he was called to read it aloud, so that he complains he never saw a matter so badly managed, "si mal cousu," but he delivered the contents with emphasis and elocution. " Je croy qu'il n'y eust personne en toute la compagnie qui en perdist un seul mot, s'il n'estoit bien sourd, de sorte que si ma commission ne gisoit qu'a présenter les lettres du roy, et à faire lecture de la proposition, je pense y avoir amplement satisfait."

But his real interests lay elsewhere, and he brought back from Italy what would indemnify him for his troubles as envoy and please him more than the honour of such a charge.   In his researches he had made some veritable finds, among them a new manuscript of Heliodorus, and Books XI. to XVII. of Diodorus Siculus' *Bibliotheca Historica*, only the two last of which had hitherto been known at all. His treatment of this discovery is characteristic,[2] both of his classical enthusiasm and his limitations as a classical scholar.   He did not, as the specialist of that and perhaps of any age would have done, edit and publish the original text, but contented himself with giving to the world a French translation.   But the *Historic Library* has neither the

[1] Froude, *Council of Trent*, chap. xii.

[2] See M. de Job's remarks in Petit de Julleville's *Littérature Française.*

allurement of a Greek romance nor the edification of Plutarch's *Lives* ; and in this version, which for the rest is said to be poor, Amyot for once appealed to the popular interest in vain.

The Diodorus Siculus appeared in 1554, and in the same year Henry II. appointed Amyot preceptor to his two sons, the Dukes of Orleans and Anjou, who afterwards became respectively Charles IX. and Henry III. As his pupils were very young their tuition cannot have occupied a great deal of his time, and he was able to pursue his activity as translator. In 1559, besides a revised edition of *Theagenes and Chariclea*, there appeared anonymously a rendering, probably made at an earlier date, of the *Daphnis and Chloe*, a romance even more "curieusement et mollement goderonnee pour fille ecclesiastique et sacerdotale" than its companion. But it is with his own name and a dedication to the King that Amyot published almost at the same date his greatest work, the complete translation of Plutarch's *Parallel Lives*. If his Heliodorus gave him his first step on the ladder of church preferment, his Plutarch was a stronger claim to higher promotion. Henry II., indeed, died before the end of the year, but the accession of Amyot's elder pupil in 1560, after the short intercalary reign of Francis II., was propitious to his fortunes, for the new king, besides bestowing on him other substantial favours, almost immediately named him Grand Almoner of France.

Amyot was an indefatigable but deliberate worker. Fifteen years had elapsed between his first appearance as translator and the issue of his masterpiece. Thirteen more were to elapse before he had new material ready for the press. The interval in both cases was filled up with preparation, with learned labour, with the leisurely prosecution of his plan. A revised edition of the *Lives* appeared in 1565 and a third in 1567, and all the time he was pushing on a version of Plutarch's *Moralia*. Meanwhile in 1570 Charles gave him the bishopric of Auxerre ; and without being required to disown the two literary daughters of his vivacious prime, "somewhat curiously and voluptuously frounced and of too amorous fashion" though they might be, he had yet to devote himself rather more seriously to his profession than he hitherto seems to have done. He set about it in his usual steady circumspect way. He composed sermons, first, it is said, writing them in Latin and then turning them into French ; he attended faithfully to the administration of his diocese ; he applied himself to the study of theological doctrine, and is said to have learned the *Summa* of St. Thomas Aquinas by heart.[1] These occupations have left their trace on his next work, which was ready by 1572. Not only are Plutarch's moral treatises perfectly consonant in tone with Amyot's episcopal office, but the preface is touched with a breath of religious unction, of which his previous performances show no trace. Perhaps the flavour is a little too pronounced when in his grateful dedication to his royal master he declares : "The Lord has lodged in you singular goodness of nature." The substantive needs all the help that can be wrung from the adjective, when used of Charles IX. in the year of St. Bartholomew. But Amyot, though the exhibiter of "Plutarch's men," was essentially a private student, and was besides bound by ties of intimacy and obligation to his former pupil, who had certainly done well by him. Nor was the younger brother behindhand in his acknowledgments. Charles died before two years were out (for Amyot had a way of dedicating books to kings who deceased soon after), and was lamented by Amyot in a simple and heartfelt Latin elegy.

[1] Twelve volumes !

F

But his regrets were quite disinterested, for when
Henry III. succeeded in 1574, he showed himself
as kind a master, and in 1578 decreed that the
Grand Almoner should also be Commander of the
Order of the Holy Ghost without being required to
give proofs of nobility.

Invested with ample revenues and manifold dignities, Amyot for the next eleven years lived a busy
and simple life, varying the routine of his administrative duties with music, of which he was a lover
and a practitioner ; with translations, never published and now lost, from the Greek tragedians,
who had attracted him as professor, and from St.
Athanasius, who appealed to him as bishop ; above
all, with the revision of his Plutarch, for which he
never ceased to collect new readings.   Then came
disasters, largely owing to his reputation for partiality and complaisance.   When the Duke and the
Cardinal of Guise were assassinated in 1589, he was
accused by the Leaguers of having approved the
crime and of having granted absolution to the King.
This he denied ; but his Chapter and diocesans rose
against him, the populace sacked his residence, and
he had to fly from Auxerre.   Nor were his woes
merely personal.   On August 3rd the House of
Valois, to which he was so much beholden, became
extinct with the murder of Henry III. ; and however worthless the victim may have been, Amyot
cannot have been unaffected by old associations of
familiarity and gratitude.   Six days later he writes
that he is "the most afflicted, desolate and destitute
poor priest I suppose, in France."   His private
distress was not of long duration.   He made peace
with the Leaguers, denounced the "politicians" for
supporting Henry IV., returned to his see, resumed
his episcopal duties, though he was divested of his
Grand Almonership, and was able to leave the large
fortune of two hundred thousand crowns.   But he

did not survive to see the establishment of the new dynasty or the triumph of Catholicism, for he died almost eighty years old in February, 1593, and only in the following June was Henry IV. reconciled to the Church. Perhaps had he foreseen this consummation Amyot would have found some comfort in the thought that a third pupil, a truer and greater one than those who were no more, would reign in their stead, and repair the damage their vice and folly had caused. "Glory to God!" writes Henry of Navarre to his wife, "you could have sent me no more pleasant message than the news of the zest for reading which has taken you. Plutarch always attracts me with a fresh novelty. To love him is to love me, for he was for long the instructor of my early years. My good mother, to whom I owe everything, and who had so great a desire to watch over my right attitude and was wont to say that she did not wish to see in her son a distinguished dunce, put this book in my hands when I was all but an infant at the breast. It has been, as it were, my conscience, and has prescribed in my ear many fair virtues and excellent maxims for my behaviour and for the management of my affairs."[1]

Amyot has exerted a far-reaching influence on the literature of his own country and of Europe. Though as a translator he might seem to have no more than a secondary claim, French historians of letters have dwelt on his work at a length and with a care that are usually conceded only to the

[1] Vive Dieu! vous ne m'auriés sceu rien mander qui me fust plus agréable que la nouvelle du plaisir de lecture qui vous a prins. Plutarque me soubrit toujours d'une fresche nouveauté ; l'aymer c'est m'aymer, car il a esté longtemps l'instituteur de mon bas age : ma bonne mère à laquelle je doibs tout, et qui avoit une affection si grande de veiller à mes bons deportmens, et ne vouloit pas (ce disoit-elle) voir en son filz un illustre ignorant, me mist ce livre entre les mains, encores que je ne feusse à peine plus un enfant de mamelle. Il m'a esté comme ma conscience et il m'a dicté à l'oreille beaucoup de bonnes honnestetés et maximes excellentes pour ma conduite, et pour le gouvernement de mes affaires.

achievements of creative imagination or intellectual discovery. And the reason is that his aptitude for his task amounts to real genius, which he has improved by assiduous research, so that in his treatment, the ancillary craft, as it is usually considered, rises to the rank of a free liberal art. He has the insight to divine what stimulus and information the age requires; the knowledge to command the sources that will supply them; the skill to manipulate his native idiom for the new demands, and suit his expression, so far as may be, both to his subject and to his audience. Among the great masters of translation he occupies a foremost place.

Of spontaneous and initiative power he had but little. He cannot stand alone. For Henry II. he wrote a *Projet de l'Eloquence Royal*, but it was not printed till long after his death; and of this and his other original prose his biographer, Roulliard, avows that the style is strangely cumbersome and laggard (*estrangement pesant et traisnassier*). Even in his prefaces to Plutarch he is only good when he catches fire from his enthusiasm for his author. Just as his misgivings at the Council of Trent, his commendations of his royal patrons, his concessions to his enemies of the League, suggest a defect in independent force of character, so the writings in which he must rely on himself show a defect in independent force of intellect.

Nor is he a specialist in scholarship. Already in 1635, when he had been less than a century in his grave, Bachet de Méziriac, expert in all departments of learning, exposed his shortcomings in a Discourse on Translation, which was delivered before the Academy. His critic describes him as "a promising pupil in rhetoric with a mediocre knowledge of Greek, and some slight tincture of Polite Letters"; and asserts that there are more than two thousand passages in which he has perverted the sense of his

author.   Even in 1580-81, during Amyot's lifetime,
Montaigne was forced to admit in discussion with
certain learned men at Rome that he was less
accurate than his admirers had imagined.   He was
certainly as far as possible from being a *Zunft-
gelehrter.*   His peculiar attitude is exactly indicated
by his treatment of the missing books of Diodorus
which it was his good fortune to light upon.   He is
not specially interested in his discovery, and has no
thought of giving the original documents to the
world.   At the same time he has such a reverence
for antiquity that he must do something about them.
So with an eye to his chosen constituency, his own
countrymen, he executes his vernacular version.

For of his own countrymen he always thought first.
They are his audience, and he has their needs in his
mind.   And that is why he made Plutarch the study
of his life.   His romances are mere experiments for
his pastime and equipment :[1] his Diodorus is a task
prescribed by accident and vocation: but his Plutarch
is a labour of love and of patriotism.   It was knowledge of antiquity for which the age clamoured and
of which it stood in need ; and who else could give
such a summary and encyclopaedia of Classical Life
as the polyhistor of Chaeronea, who interested himself in everything, from details of household management to the government of states, from ancestral
superstitions to the speculations of philosophers,
from after-dinner conversation to the direction of
campaigns ; but brought them all into vital relation
with human nature and human conduct?   Plutarch
appealed to the popular instinct of the time and to
the popular instinct in Amyot's own breast.   It is
his large applicability "distill'd through all the needful uses of our lives" and "fit for any conference

---

[1] As he himself states in the *Proesme* of *Théagène et Chariclée.*   He
has occupied himself with this only, " aux heures extraordinaires, pour
adoucir le travail d'autres meilleures et plus fructueuses traductions," so
as to be made "plus vif à la consideration des choses d'importance."

one can use " that, for example, arouses the enthusiasm of Montaigne. After mentioning that when he writes he willingly dispenses with the companionship or recollection of books, he adds :

> But it is with more difficulty that I can get rid of Plutarch: he is so universal and so full that on all occasions and whatever out-of-the-way subject you have taken up, he thrusts himself into your business, and holds out to you a hand lavish and inexhaustible in treasures and ornaments. I am vexed at his being so much exposed to the plunder of those who resort to him. I can't have the slightest dealings with him myself, but I snatch a leg or a wing.[1]

And again :

> I am above all grateful to [Amyot] for having had the insight to pick out and choose a book so worthy and so seasonable, to make a present of it to his country. We dunces should have been lost, if this book had not raised us out of the mire. Thanks to it we now dare to speak and write. With it the ladies can lecture the school-masters. It is our breviary.[2]

" In all kinds Plutarch is my man," he says elsewhere. And indeed it is obvious, even though he had not told us, that Plutarch with Seneca supplies his favourite reading, to which he perpetually recurs. " I have not," he writes, " systematically acquainted myself with any solid books except Plutarch and Seneca, from whom I draw like the Danaides, filling and pouring out continually."[3] To the latter he

[1] Je me puis plus malaysement desfaire de Plutarque ; il est si universel et si plein, qu'à toutes occasions, et quelque subject extravagant que vous ayez prins, il s'ingere à vostre besongne, et vous tend une main liberale et inespuisable de richesses et d'embellissements. Il m'en faict despit, d'estre si fort exposé au pillage de ceulx qui le hantent : je ne le puis si peu raccointer, que je n'en tire cuisse ou aile (iii. 5).

[2] Mais, surtout, je lui sçais bon gré d'avoir sceu trier et choisir un livre si digne et si à propos, pour en faire présent à son pais. Nous aultres ignorants estions perdus, si ce livre ne nous eust relevé du bourbier : sa mercy nous osons à cette heure et parler et escrire ; les dames en regentent les maistres d'eschole ; c'est notre bresviaire (ii. 4).

[3] Je n'ay dressé commerce avecques aulcun livre solide sinon Plutarque et Senecque, où je puyse comme les Danaïdes remplissant et versant sans cesse (i. 25).

could go for himself ; for the Greek he had to depend on Amyot. For combined profit and pleasure, he says, "the books that serve me are Plutarch, *since he is French*, and Seneca."[1] But it is to the former that he seems to give the palm.

> Seneca is full of smart and witty sayings, Plutarch of things: the former kindles you more and excites you, the latter satisfies you more and requites you better; he guides us while the other drives us.[2]

It is indeed impossible to imagine Montaigne without Plutarch, to whom he has a striking resemblance both in his free-and-easy homilies and in his pregnant touches. It is these things on which he dwells.

> There are in Plutarch many dissertations at full length well worth knowing, for in my opinion he is the master-craftsman in that trade ; but there are a thousand that he has merely indicated ; he only points out the track we are to take if we like, and confines himself sometimes to touching the quick of a subject. We must drag (the expositions) thence and put them in the market place. . . . It is a dissertation in itself to see him select a trivial act in the life of a man, or a word that does not seem to have such import.[3]

But Montaigne did not stand alone in his admiration. He himself, as we have seen, bears witness

---

[1] Les livres qui m'y servent, c'est Plutarque depuis qu'il est françois, et Seneque (ii. iv.). Of course Montaigne knew some Greek and read it more or less. He has even his own opinion about Plutarch's style (see page 104), and M. Faguet conjectures : "It is quite conceivable that Montaigne compared the translation with the text, and that it is a piece of mere affectation when he says he knows nothing of the Greek." But doubtless he read the French much more habitually and easily.

[2] Seneque est plein de poinctes et saillies, Plutarque de choses ; celuy là vous eschauffe plus et vous esmeut, cettuy ci vous contente davantage et vous paye mieulx ; il nous guide, l'aultre nous poulse (ii. 10).

[3] Il y a dans Plutarque beaucoup de discours estendus très dignes d'estre sceus, car, à mon gré, c'est le maistre ouvrier de telle besongne ; mais il y en a mille qu'il n'a que touchez simplement ; et guigne seule- ment du doigt par où nous irons, s'il nous plaist ; et se contente quelquefois de ne donner qu'une attaincte dans le plus vif d'un propos. Il les fault arracher de la, et mettre en place marchande. . . . Cela mesme de luy voir trier une legere action en la vie d'un homme, ou un mot qui semble ne porter cela, c'est un discours (i. 25).

to the widespread popularity of Amyot's Plutarch and the general practice of rifling its treasures. Indeed, Plutarch was seen to be so congenial to the age, that frequent attempts had been made before Amyot to place him within the reach of a larger circle than the little band of Greek scholars. In 1470, *e.g.* a number of Italians had co-operated in a Latin version of the *Lives*, published at Rome by Campani, and this was followed by several partial translations in French.[1] But the latter were immediately superseded, and even the former had its authority shaken, by Amyot's achievement.

This was due partly to its greater intelligence and faithfulness, partly to its excellent style.

In regard to the first, it should be remembered that the criticism of Amyot's learning must be very carefully qualified. Scholarship is a progressive science, and it is always easy for the successor to point out errors in the precursor, as Méziriac did in Amyot. Of course, however, the popular expositor was not a Budaeus or Scaliger, and the savants whom Montaigne met in Rome were doubtless justified in their strictures. Still the zeal that he showed and the trouble that he took in searching for good texts, in conferring them with the printed books and in consulting learned men about his conjectural emendations,[2] would suggest that he had the root of the matter in him, and there is evidence

---

[1] There were also translations in Italian, Spanish, and German ; but none of them had anything like the literary importance of Amyot's, and they were made from the Latin, not from the Greek. Of Hieronymus Boner, for instance, who published his *Plutarch, Von dem Leben der allerdurchlauchtigsten Griechen und Romern* (1st edition, Augsburg, 1534), it is misleading to say that he "anticipated" Amyot. Merzdorf writes of Boner's versions of Greek authors generally (*Allgemeine Deutsche Biographie*) that he "turned them into German not from the original Greek but from Latin translations. Moreover, one must not expect from him any exact rendering, but rather a kind of paraphrase which he accommodates to the circumstances of the time."

[2] See his preface, towards the close.

that expert opinion in his own days was favourable to his claims.[1]

At the time when he was translating the *Lives* into French two scholars of high reputation were, independently of each other, translating them into Latin. Xylander's versions appeared in 1560, those of Cruserius were ready in the same year, but were not published till 1564. They still hold their place and enjoy consideration. Now, they both make their compliments to Amyot. Xylander, indeed, has only a second-hand acquaintance with his publication, but even that he has found valuable :

> After I had already finished the greater part of the work, the *Lives of Plutarch* written by Amyot in the French language made their appearance. And since I heard from those who are skilled in that tongue, a privilege which I do not possess, that he had devoted remarkable pains to the book and used many good MSS., assisted by the courtesy of friends, I corrected several passages about which I was in doubt, and in not a few my conjecture was established by the concurrence of that translator.[2]

Cruserius, again, in his prefatory *Epistle to the Reader*, warmly commends the merits of Xylander and Amyot, but refers with scarcely veiled disparagement to the older Latin rendering, which nevertheless enjoyed general acceptance as the number of editions proves, and was considered the standard authority.

[1] In later days, too, Mr. Holden, who has busied himself with Plutarch, says "Amyot's version is more scholarlike and correct than those of Langhorne or Dryden and others."

[2] Cum jam majorem operis partem absolvissem, prodierunt Vitae Plutarchi gallicâ linguâ ab Amyoto conscriptae. Quem cum praeclaram ei libro operam impendisse ex iis qui linguae ejus sunt periti (quod mihi non datum est) et usum multis ac bonis codicibus audirem ; amicorum adjutus . . . officio, nonnullos, de quibus dubitabam, locos correxi ; in haud paucis mea conjectura est illius interpretis suffragio comprobata (Ed. 1560). Xylander's friends must have given him yeoman's help, for he frequently discusses Amyot's readings, generally adopting them ; and for the whole life of Cato, he even goes so far as to avow : "Amyoti versionem secutus sum, Graecis non satis integris."

> If indeed (he writes) I must not here say that I by myself have both more faithfully and more elegantly interpreted *Plutarch's Lives*, the translation of which into Latin a great number of Italians formerly undertook without much success; this at least I may say positively and justly that I think I have done this.[1]

On the other hand "Amiotus" has been a help to him. When he had already polished and corrected his own version, he came across this very tasteful rendering in Brussels six months after it had appeared. "This man's scholarship and industry gave me some light on several passages."[2] It is well then to bear in mind, when Amyot's competency is questioned, that by their own statement he cleared up things for specialists like Xylander and Cruserius. And this is all the more striking, that Cruserius, whom his preface shows to be very generous in his acknowledgments, has no word of recognition for his Italian predecessors even though Filelfo was among their number.[3] But his Epistle proceeds : "To whom (*i.e.* to Amyot) I will give this testimony that now-a-days it is impossible that anyone should render Plutarch so elegantly in the Latin tongue, as he renders him in his own."[2] And this praise of Amyot's style leads us to the next point.

If Amyot claims the thanks of Western Europe

[1] Ego quidem si dicere hîc non valeam, vitas me Plutarchi, quas plurimi sumpserunt antehac Itali Latine reddendas parum feliciter, me explicavisse unum et verius et mundius ; hoc certe dicere queo liquide et recte, esse arbitratum me hoc effecisse (*Epistola ad Lectorem*, 1561, edition 1599).

[2] Interea cum jam polivissem atque emendassem vitas meas Plutarchi, ostendit mihi Bruxellae, ubi agebam illustrissimi principis mei legatus, secretarius regius editas elegantissime ab Amioto linguâ gallicâ vitas Plutarchi, quae exierant tamen in publicum sex menses antequam eas viderem. Hujus viri mihi eruditio et diligentia aliquid lucis nonnullis in locis attulit. Cui ego hoc testimonium dabo : non posse fieri, ut quisquam hoc tempore Plutarchum tam vertat ornate linguâ Latina quam vertit ille suâ (*Ib.*).

[3] Amyot's own attitude is very similar. He cites the Latin versions in proof of the hardness of the original, and challenges a comparison of them with his own.

for giving it with adequate faithfulness a typical miscellany of ancient life and thought, his services to his country in developing the native language are hardly less important. Before him Rabelais and Calvin were the only writers of first-rate ability in modern French. But Rabelais' prose was too exuberant, heterogeneous and eccentric to supply a model; and Calvin, besides being suspect on account of his theology, was of necessity as a theologian abstract and restricted in his range. The new candidate had something of the wealth and universal appeal of the one, something of the correctness and purity of the other.

Since Plutarch deals with almost all departments of life, Amyot had need of the amplest vocabulary, and a supply of the most diverse locutions. Indeed, sometimes the copious resources of his vernacular, with which he had doubtless begun to familiarise himself among the simple folk of Melun, leave him in the lurch, and he has to make loans from Latin or Greek. But he does this sparingly, and only when no other course is open to him. Generally his thorough mastery of the dialect of the Île de France, the standard language of the kingdom, helps him out.

Yet he is far from adopting the popular speech without consciously manipulating it. He expressly states that he selects the fittest, sweetest, and most euphonious words, and such as are in the mouths of those who are accustomed to speak well. The ingenuousness of his utterance, which is in great measure due to his position of pioneer in a new period, should not mislead us into thinking him a careless writer. His habit of first composing his sermons in Latin and then translating them into French tells its own story. He evidently realised the superiority in precision and orderly arrangement of the speech of Rome, and felt it a benefit to submit to such discipline the artless *bonhomie* of his mother tongue.   But since he is the born interpreter, whose very business it was to mediate between the exotic and the indigenous, and assimilate the former to the latter, he never forgets the claims of his fellow Frenchmen and his native French.   He does not force his idiom to imitate a foreign model, but only learns to develop its own possibilities of greater clearness, exactitude, and regularity.

It is for these excellencies among others, "pour la naifeté et pureté du language en quoi il surpasse touts aultres,"[1] that Montaigne gives him the palm, and this purity served him in good stead during the classical period of French literature, which was so unjust to most writers of the sixteenth century, and found fault with Montaigne himself for his "Gasconisms."   Racine thought that Amyot's "old style" had a grace which could not be equalled in our modern language.   Fénelon regretfully looks back to him for beauties that are fallen into disuse.   Nor was it only men of delicate and poetic genius who appreciated his merits.   Vaugelas, the somewhat illiberal grammarian and purist, is the most enthusiastic of the worshippers.

> What obligation (he exclaims) does our language not owe to him, there never having been anyone who knew its genius and character better than he, or who used words and phrases so genuinely French without admixture of the provincial expressions which daily corrupt the purity of the true French tongue.   All stores and treasures are in the works of this great man.   And even to-day we have hardly any noble and splendid modes of speech that he has not left us ; and though we have cut out a half of his words and phrases, we do not fail to find in the other half almost all the riches of which we boast.

It will be seen, however, that in such tributes from the seventeenth century (and the same thing is true of others left unquoted), it is implied that

[1] ii. 4.

Amyot is already somewhat antiquated and out of
fashion. He is honoured as ancestor in the right
line of classical French, but he is its ancestor and
not a living representative. Vaugelas admits that
half his vocabulary is obsolete, Fénelon regrets his
charms just because their date is past, Racine wonders that such grace should have been attained in
what is not the modern language.

And this may remind us of the very important
fact, that Amyot could not on account of his position
deliver a facsimile of the Greek. Plutarch lived at
the close of an epoch, he at the beginning. The
one employed a language full of reminiscences and
past its prime ; the other, a language that was just
reaching self-consciousness and that had the future
before it. Both in a way were artists, but Plutarch
shows his art in setting his stones already cut, while
Amyot provides moulds for the liquid metal. At
their worst Plutarch's style becomes mannered and
Amyot's infantile. By no sleight of hand would it
have been possible to give in the French of the sixteenth century an exact reproduction of the Greek
of the second. Grey-haired antiquity had to learn
the accents of stammering childhood.

Sometimes Amyot hardly makes an attempt at
literal fidelity. The style of his original he describes
as "plein, serré et philosophistorique." With him
it retains the fulness, but the condensation, or rather
what a modern scholar describes as "the crowding
of the sentence,"[1] often gives place to periphrasis,
and of the "philosophistorique" small trace remains.
Montaigne praises him because he has contrived "to
expound so thorny and crabbed[2] an author with such

[1] Mr. Holden.

[2] Espineux et ferré (ii. iv.). Perhaps *ferré* should be rendered *difficult*
rather than *crabbed*. But even *thorny and difficult* are hardly words
that one would apply to Plutarch. Montaigne's meaning may perhaps
be illustrated by the criticism of Paley : "Plutarch's Greek is not like
Lucian's, fluent and easy, nor even clear. He uses many words not in

fidelity." What is most crabbed and thorny in
Plutarch he passes over or replaces with a loose
equivalent; single words he expands to phrases;
difficulties he explains with a gloss or illustration
that he does not hesitate to insert in the text; and
he is anxious to bring out the sense by adding more
emphatic and often familiar touches.

The result of it all undoubtedly is to lend Plutarch
a more popular and less academic bearing than he
really has. Some of Amyot's most attractive effects
either do not exist or are inconspicuous in his original.
The tendency to artifice and rhetoric in the pupil of
Ammonius disappears, and he is apt to get the credit
for an innocence and freshness that are more characteristic of his translator. M. Faguet justly points
out that Amyot in his version makes Plutarch " a
simple writer, while he was elegant, fastidious, and
even affected in his style." . . . He " emerges from
Amyot's hands as *le bon Plutarque* of the French
people, whereas he was certainly not that." Thus
it is beyond dispute that the impression produced is
in some respects misleading.

But there is another side to this. Plutarch in his
tastes and ideals did belong to an older, less sophisticated age, though he was born out of due time
and had to adapt his speech to his hyper-civilised
environment. Ampère has called attention to the
picture, suggested by the facts at our disposal, of
Plutarch living in his little Boeotian town, obtaining his initiation into the mysteries, punctually
fulfilling the functions of priest, making antiquities
and traditions his hobby. " There was this man
under the rhetorician," he adds, " and we must not
forget it. For if the rhetorician wrote, it was the

the ordinary Greek vocabulary; and he too often constructs long sentences, the thread of which separately as well as the connection cannot
be traced without close attention. Hence he is unattractive as a
writer.

other Plutarch who often dictated." Of course in a
way the antithesis is an unreal one. Plutarch was
after all, as every one must be, the child of his own
generation, and his aspirations were not confined to
himself. The *Sophistes* is, on the one hand, what
the man who makes antiquity and traditions his
hobby, is on the other. Still it remains certain that
his love was set on things which pertained to an
earlier and less elaborate phase of society, to " the
good old days" when they found spontaneous acceptance and expression. On him the ends of the world
are come, and he seeks by all the resources of his
art and learning to revive what he regards as its
glorious prime. His heart is with the men " of heart,
head, hand," but when he seeks to reveal them, he
must do so in the chequered light of a vari-coloured
culture.

Hence there was a kind of discrepancy between
his spirit and his utterance ; and Amyot, removing
the discrepancy, brings them into a natural harmony.
There is truth in the paradox that the form which
the good bishop supplies is the one that was meant
for the matter. "Amyot," says Demogeot, summing
up his discussion of this aspect of the question, "has
in some sort created Plutarch, and made him truer
and more complete than nature made him."

But though Plutarch's ideas seem from one point
of view to enter into their predestined habitation,
this does not alter the fact that they lose something
of their distinctive character in accommodating themselves to their new surroundings. It is easy to
exaggerate their affinity with the vernacular words,
as it is easy to exaggerate the correspondence
between author and translator. Thus Ampère, half
in jest, pleases himself with drawing on behalf of
the two men a parallel such as is appended to each
particular brace of *Lives*. Both of them lovers of
virtue, he points out, for example, that both had a

veneration for the past, of which the one strove to
preserve the memories even then beginning to
fade, and the other to rediscover and gather up the
shattered fragments.   Both experienced sad and
troublous times without having their tranquillity
disturbed, the one by the crimes of Domitian or the
other by the furies of St. Bartholomew's.   Both
belonged to the hierarchy, the one as priest of
Apollo, the other as Bishop of Auxerre.

But it is not hard to turn such parallels into so
many contrasts.   The past with which Plutarch was
busy was in a manner the familiar past of his native
country or at least of his own civilisation ; but Amyot
loved the past of that remote and alien world in
which for ages men had neglected their heritage
and taken small concern.   The sequestered life of
the provincial under the Roman Empire, a privacy
whence he emerges to whatever civil offices were
within his reach, is very different from the dislike
and refusal of public activity that characterises the
Frenchman in his own land at a time when learning
was recognised as passport to high position in the
State.   The priest of a heathen cult which he could
accept only when explained away by a rationalistic
idealism, and which was by no means incompatible
with his family instincts, was very different from the
celibate churchman who ended by submitting to the
terms imposed by the intolerance of the Holy
League.   The analogies are there, and imply perhaps a strain of intellectual kinship, but the contrasts
are not less obvious, and refute the idea of a perfect
unison.

Now, it is much the same if we turn from the
writers to their writings.   All translation is a compromise between the foreign material and the native
intelligence, but in Amyot the latter factor counts
most.   Classical life is very completely assimilated
to the contemporary life that he knew, but such

contemporary life was in some ways quite unlike
that which he was reproducing. There is an illusory
sameness in the effects produced as there is an illusion
of coincidence in the characters and careers of the
men who produce them, and this may have its cause
in real contact at certain points. But the gaps that
separate them are also real, though at the time they
were seldom detected. " Both by the details and
the general tone of his version," says M. Lanson,
"[Amyot] modernises the Graeco-Roman world, and
by this involuntary travesty he tends to check the
awakening of the sense for the differences, that is,
the historic sense. As he invites Shakespeare to
recognise the English *Mob* in the *Plebs Romana*,
so he authorises Corneille and Racine and even
Mademoiselle Scudéry to portray under ancient
names the human nature they saw in France."

And this tendency was carried further in Amyot's
English translator.

3

NORTH

Of Sir Thomas North, the most recent and direct
of the authorities who transmitted to Shakespeare
his classical material, much less is known than of
either of his predecessors. Plutarch, partly because
as original author he has the opportunity of express-
ing his own personality, partly because he uses this
opportunity to the full in frank advocacy of his views
and gossip about himself, may be pictured with fair
vividness and in some detail. Such information fails
in regard to Amyot, since he was above all the
mouthpiece for other men ; but his high dignities
placed him in the gaze of contemporaries, and his
reputation as pioneer in classical translation and
nursing-father of modern French ensured a certain

interest in his career. But North, like him a translator, had not equal prominence either from his position or from his achievement. Such honours and appointments as he obtained were not of the kind to attract regard. He was a mere unit in the Elizabethan crowd of literary importers, and belonged to the lower class who never steered their course "to the classic coast." He had no such share as Amyot in shaping the traditions of the language, but was one writer in an age that produced many others, some of them greater masters than he. Yet to us, as the immediate interpreter of Plutarch to Shakespeare, he is the most important of the three, the most famous and the most alive. Sainte-Beuve, talking of Amyot, quotes a phrase from Leopardi in reference to the Italians who have associated themselves forever with the Classics they unveiled: "Oh, how fair a fate! to be exempt from death except in company with an Immortal!" This fair fate is North's in double portion. He is linked with a great Immortal by descent, and with a greater by ancestry.

Thomas North, second son of the first Baron North of Kirtling, was born about 1535, to live his life, as it would seem, in straitened circumstances and unassuming work. Yet we might have anticipated for him a prosperous and eminent career. He had high connections and powerful patrons; his father made provision for him, his brother helped him once and again, a royal favourite interested himself on his behalf. His ability and industry are evident from his works; his honesty and courage are vouched for by those in a position to know; the efficiency of his public services received recognition from his fellow-citizens and his sovereign. But with all these advantages and qualifications he was even in middle age hampered by lack of means, and he never had much share in the pelf and pomp of life. Perhaps his occupation with larger concerns than personal aggrandisement may have interfered with his material success. At any rate, in his narrower sphere he showed himself a man of public interest and public spirit, and the authors with whom he busies himself are all such as commend ideal rather than tangible possessions as the real objects of desire. And we know besides that he was an unaggressive man, inclined to claim less than his due ; for in one of his books he professes to get the material only from a French translation, when it is proved that he must have had recourse to the Spanish original as well.

This was his maiden effort, *The Diall of Princes*, published in 1557, when North was barely of age and had just been entered a student of Lincoln's Inn ; and with this year the vague and scanty data for his history really begin. He dedicates his book to Queen Mary, who had shown favour to his father, pardoning him for his support of Lady Jane Grey, raising him to the peerage, and distinguishing him in other ways. But on the death of Mary, Lord North retained the goodwill of Elizabeth, who twice kept her court at his mansion, and appointed him Lord Lieutenant of Cambridgeshire and the Isle of Ely. The family had thus considerable local influence, and it was not diminished when, on the old man's death in 1564, Roger, the first son, succeeded to the title. Before long the new Lord North was made successively an alderman of Cambridge, Lord Lieutenant of the County, and High Steward ; while Thomas, who had benefited under his father's will, was presented to the freedom of the town. All through, the career of the junior appears as a sort of humble pendant to that of the senior, and he picks up his dole of the largesses that Fortune showers on the head of the house. What he had been doing in the intervening years we do not know, but he cannot have abandoned his literary pursuits, for in 1568, when he received this civic courtesy, he issued a new edition' of the *Diall*, corrected and enlarged; and he followed it up in 1570 with a version of Doni's *Morale Filosofia*.

Meanwhile the elder brother was advancing on his brilliant course. He had been sent to Vienna to invest the Emperor Maximilian with the Order of the Garter; he had been commissioned to present the Queen on his return with the portrait of her suitor, the Archduke Charles; he had held various offices at home, and in 1574 he was appointed Ambassador Extraordinary to congratulate Henry III. of France on his accession, and to procure if possible toleration for the Huguenots and a renewal of the Treaty of Blois. On this important legation he was accompanied by Thomas, who would thus have an opportunity of seeing or hearing something of Amyot, the great Bishop and Grand Almoner who was soon to be recipient of new honours from his royal pupil and patron, and who had recently been drawing new attention on himself by his third edition of the *Lives* and his first edition of the *Morals*.[1] It may well be that this visit suggested to Thomas North his own masterpiece, which he seems to have set about soon after he came home in the end of November. At least it was to appear in January, 1579, before another lustre was out; and a translation even from French of the entire *Lives*, not only unabridged but augmented (for biographies of Hannibal and Scipio are added from the versions of Charles de l'Escluse),[2] is a task of years rather than of months.

---

[1] I do not know what authority Mr. Wyndham has for his statement that Amyot's version of the *Morals* "fell comparatively dead." It is, of course, much less read nowadays, but at the time it ran through three editions in less than four years (1572, 1574, 1575), and for the next half century there are frequent reprints.

[2] These, translated from the Latin collection of 1470, to which they had been contributed by Acciaiuoli, were included in Amyot's third edition.

The embassage, despite many difficulties to be overcome, had been a success, and Lord North returned to receive the thanks and favours he deserved. He stood high in the Queen's regard, and in 1578 she honoured him with a visit for a night. He was lavish in his welcome, building, we are told, new kitchens for the occasion; filling them with provisions of all kinds, the oysters alone amounting to one cart load and two horse loads; rifling the cellars of their stores, seventy-four hogsheads of beer being reinforced with corresponding supplies of ale, claret, white wine, sack, and hippocras; presenting her at her departure with a jewel worth £120 in the money of the time. In such magnificent doings he was by no means unmindful of his brother, to whom shortly before he had made over the lease of a house and household stuff. Yet precisely at this date, when Thomas North was completing or had completed his first edition of the *Lives*, his circumstances seem to have been specially embarrassed. Soon after the book appeared Leicester writes on his behalf to Burleigh, stating that he "is a very honest gentleman and hath many good parts in him which are drowned only by poverty." There is perhaps a certain incongruity between these words and the accounts of the profusion at Kirtling in the preceding year.

Meanwhile Lord North, to his reputation as diplomatist and courtier sought to add that of a soldier. In the Low Countries he greatly distinguished himself by his capacity and courage; but he was called home to look after the defences of the eastern coast in view of the expected Spanish invasion, and this was not the only time that the Government resorted to him for military advice.

No such important charge was entrusted to Thomas, but he too was ready to do his duty by his country in her hour of need, and in 1588 had command of three hundred men of Ely. In the interval between this and the distressful time of 1579 his position must have improved; for in 1591, in reward it may be for his patriotic activity, the Queen conferred on him the honour of knighthood, which in those days implied as necessary qualification the possession of land to the minimum value of £40 a year. This was followed by other acknowledgments and dignities of moderate worth. In 1592 and again in 1597 he sat on the Commission of Peace for Cambridgeshire. In 1598 he received a grant of £20 from the town of Cambridge, and in 1601 a pension of £40 a year from the Queen. These amounts are not munificent, even if we take them at the outside figure suggested as the equivalent in modern money.[1] They give the impression that North was not very well off, that in his circumstances some assistance was desirable, and a little assistance would go a long way. At the same time they show that his conduct deserved and obtained appreciation. Indeed, the pension from the Queen is granted expressly "in consideration of the good and faithful service done unto us."

He also benefited by a substantial bequest from Lord North, who had died in 1600, but he was now an old man of at least sixty-six, and probably he did not live long to enjoy his new resources. Of the brother Lloyd records: "There was none better to represent our State than my Lord North, who had been two years in Walsingham's house, four in Leicester's service, had seen six courts, twenty battles, nine treaties, and four solemn jousts, whereof he was no mean part." In regard to the younger son, even the year of whose death we do not know, the parallel summary would run : " He served a few months in an ambassador's suite ; he commanded a local force, he was a knight, and sat on the Com-

---

[1] That is, if we multiply them by eight.

mission of Peace ; he made three translations, one of which rendered possible Shakespeare's Roman Plays." [1]

This is his "good and faithful service" unto us, not that he fulfilled duties in which he might have been rivalled by any country justice or militia captain. And, "a good and faithful servant," he had qualified himself for his grand performance by a long apprenticeship in the craft. Like Amyot, he devotes himself to translation from first to last, but unlike Amyot he knows from the outset the kind of book that it is given him to interpret. He is not drawn by the fervour of youth to "vain and amatorious romance," nor by conventional considerations to the bric-a-brac of antiquarianism. From the time that he has attained the years of discretion and comes within our knowledge, he applies his heart to study and supply works of solid instruction.

> Souninge in moral vertu was his speche,
> And gladly wolde he lerne, and gladly teche.

It is characteristic, too, both of his equipment and his style, that though he may have known a little Greek and certainly knew some Latin, as is shown by a few trifling instances in which he gives Aymot's expressions a more learned turn, he never used an ancient writer as his main authority, but confined himself to the adaptations and translations that were current in modern vernaculars.

Thus his earliest work is the rendering, mainly from the French, of the notable and curious forgery of the Spanish Bishop, Antonio de Guevara, alleged by its author to have been derived from an ancient manuscript which he had discovered in Florence. It was originally entitled *El Libro Aureo de Marco*

[1] Most of the facts of the foregoing sketch are taken from the articles on the Norths in the *Dictionary of National Biography*, which, however, must not be considered responsible for the inferences.

Aurelio, Emperador y eloquentissimo Orator, but afterwards, when issued in an expanded form, was rechristened, *Marco Aurelio con el Relox de Principes.* It has however little to do with the real Marcus Aurelius, and the famous *Meditations* furnish only a small ingredient to the work. It is in some ways an imitation of Xenophon's *Cyropaedia*, that is, it is a didactic romance which aims at giving in narrative form true principles of education, morals, and politics. But the narrative is very slight, and most of the book is made up of discussions, discourses, and epistles, the substance of which is in many cases taken with a difference from Plutarch's *Moralia.* These give the author scope to endite "in high style"; and in his balanced and erudite way of writing, which with all its tastelessness and excess has a far-off resemblance to Plutarch's more rhetorical effects, as well as in his craze for allusions and similes, he anticipates the mannerisms of the later Euphuists. But despite the moralisings and affectations (or rather, perhaps, on account of them, for the first fell in with the ethical needs of the time, and the second with its attempts to organise its prose), the book was a great favourite for over a hundred years, and Casaubon says that except the Bible, hardly any other has been so frequently translated or printed. Lord Berners had already made his countrymen acquainted with it in shorter form, but North renders the *Diall of Princes* in full, and even adds another treatise of Guevara's, *The Favored Courtier*, as fourth book to his second edition.

It is both the contents and the form that attract him. In the title page he describes it as "right necessarie and pleasaunt to all gentylmen and others which are louers of vertue"; and in his preface he says that it is "so full of high doctrine, so adourned with auncient histories, so authorised with grave sentences, and so beautified with apte similitudes, that I knowe not whose eies in reding it can be weried, nor whose eares in hearing it not satisfied."

That North's contemporaries agreed with him in liking such fare is shown by the publication of the new edition eleven years after the first, and even more strikingly by the publication of John Lily's imitation eleven years after the second. For Dr. Landmann has proved beyond dispute that the paedagogic romance of *Euphues*, in purpose, in plan, in its letters and disquisitions, its episodes and persons, is largely based on the *Diall*. He has not been quite so successful in tracing the distinctive tricks of the Euphuistic style through North to Guevara. It has to be remembered that North's main authority was not the Spanish *Relox de Principes*, but the French *Orloge des princes*; and at the double remove a good many of the peculiarities of Guevarism were bound to become obliterated : as in point of fact has occurred. It would be a mistake to call North a Euphuistic writer, though in the *Diall*, and even in the *Lives*, there are Euphuistic passages. Still, Guevara did no doubt affect him, for Guevara's was the only elaborate and architectural prose with which he was on intimate terms. He had not the advantage of Amyot's daily commerce with the Classics, and constant practice in the equating of Latin and French. In the circumstances a dash of diluted Guevarism was not a bad thing for him, and at any rate was the only substitute at his disposal. To the end he sometimes uses it when he has to write in a more complex or heightened style.

But if the Spanish Bishop were not in all respects a salutary model, North was soon to correct this influence by working under the guidance of a very different man, the graceless Italian miscellanist,

Antonio Francesco Doni. That copious and auda-
cious conversationalist could write as he talked, on
all sorts of themes, including even those in which
there was no offence, and seldom failed to be entertaining. He is never more so than in his *Morale
Filosofia*, a delightful book to which and to himself
North did honour by his delightful rendering. The
descriptive title runs : " The Morall Philosophie of
Doni : drawne out of the auncient writers. A worke
first compiled in the Indian tongue, and afterwards
reduced into diuers other languages : and now lastly
Englished out of Italian by Thomas North." This
formidable announcement is a little misleading, for
the book proves to be a collection of the so-called
Fables of Bidpai, and though the lessons are not
lacking, the main value as well as the main charm
lies in the vigour and picturesqueness of the little
stories.[1]

Thus in both his prentice works North betrays the
same general bias. They are both concerned with
the practical and applied philosophy of life, and both
convey it through the medium of fiction : in so far
they are alike. But they are unlike, in so far as the
relative interest of the two factors is reversed, and
the accent is shifted from the one to the other. In
the *Diall* the narrative is almost in abeyance, and
the pages are filled with long-drawn arguments and
admonitions. In the *Fables* the sententious purpose
is rather implied than obtruded, and in no way
interferes with the piquant adventures; which are
recounted in a very easy and lively style.

North was thus a practised writer and translator,
with a good knowledge of the modern tongues, when
he accompanied his brother to France in 1574. In
his two previous attempts he had shown his bent
towards improving story and the manly wisdom of
the elder world; and in the second, had advanced in

[1] A charming reprint was edited by Mr. Joseph Jacobs in 1888.

appreciation of the concrete example and the racy presentment. If he now came across Amyot's Plutarch, we can see how well qualified he was for the task of giving it an English shape, and how congenial the task would be. Of the *Moral Treatises* he already knew something, if only in the adulterated concoctions of Guevara, but the *Lives* would be quite new to him, and would exactly tally with his tastes in their blend of ethical reflection and impressive narrative. There is a hint of this double attraction in the opening phrase of the title page: "The Lives of the Noble Grecians and Romans compared by that grave learned *Philosopher* and *Historiographer*, Plutarch of Chaeronea." The philosophy and the history are alike signalised as forming the equipment of the author, and certainly the admixture was such as would appeal to the public as well as to the translator.

The first edition of 1579, imprinted by Thomas Vautrouillier and John Wight, was followed by a second in 1595, imprinted by Richard Field for Bonham Norton. Field, who was a native of Stratford-on-Avon, and had been apprenticed to Vautrouillier before setting up for himself, had dealings with Shakespeare, and issued his *Venus and Adonis* and *Rape of Lucrece*. But whether or no his fellow townsman put him in the way of it, it is certain that Shakespeare was not long in discovering the new treasure. It seems to leave traces in so early a work as the *Midsummer-Night's Dream*, which probably borrowed from the life of *Theseus*, as well as in the *Merchant of Venice*, with its reference to " Cato's daughter, Brutus' Portia "; though it did not inspire a complete play till *Julius Caesar*. In 1603 appeared the third edition of North's Plutarch, enlarged with new Lives which had been incorporated in Amyot's collection in 1583: and this some think to have been the particular authority for

Antony and Cleopatra and *Coriolanus*.[1]   And again a fourth edition, with a separate supplement bearing the date of 1610, was published in 1612 ; and of this the famous copy in the Greenock Library has been claimed as the dramatist's own book.   If by any chance this should be the case, then Shakespeare must have got it for his private delectation, for by this time he had finished his plays on ancient history and almost ceased to write for the stage.   But apart from that improbable and crowning honour, there is no doubt about the value of North's version to Shakespeare as dramatist, and the four editions in Shakespeare's lifetime sufficiently attest its popularity with the general reader.

[1] The whole question about the editions which Shakespeare read is a complicated one.   Two things are pretty certain : (1) He must have used the first edition for *Midsummer-Night's Dream*, which was in all likelihood composed before 1595, when the second appeared.   (2) He must have used the first or second for *Julius Caesar*, which was composed before 1603, when the third appeared.   It is more difficult to speak positively in regard to *Antony and Cleopatra* and *Coriolanus*. It has been argued that the former cannot have been derived from the first two editions, because in them Menas' remark to Sextus Pompeius runs :

"Shall I cut the gables of the ankers, and make thee Lord not only of Sicile and Sardinia, but of the whole Empire of Rome besides ? "

In the third edition this is altered to *cables*, and this is the form that occurs in Shakespeare :

"Let me cut the cable ;
And, when we are put off, fall to their throats :
All there is thine."   (*A. and C.* II. vii. 77.)

But this change is a very slight one that Shakespeare might easily make for himself on the same motives that induced the editor of the *Lives* to make it.   And though attempts have been made to prove that the fourth edition was used for *Coriolanus*, there are great difficulties in accepting so late a date for that play, and one phrase rather points to one of the first two editions (see Introduction to *Coriolanus*).   If this is really so, it affects the case of *Antony and Cleopatra* too, for it would be odd to find Shakespeare using the first or second edition for the latter play, and the third for the earlier one.   Still, such things do occur, and I think there is a tendency in those who discuss this point to confine Shakespeare over rigidly to one edition.   In the twentieth century it is possible to find men reading or re-reading a book in the first copy that comes to hand without first looking up the date on the title page.   Was this practice unknown in Shakespeare's day?

This popularity is well deserved. Its permanent excellences were sure of wide appreciation, and the less essential qualities that fitted Plutarch to meet the needs of the hour in France, were not less opportune in England. North's prefatory " Address to the Reader " describes not only his own attitude but that of his countrymen in general.

> There is no prophane studye better than Plutarke. All other learning is private, fitter for Universities then cities, fuller of contemplacion than experience, more commendable in the students them selves, than profitable unto others. Whereas stories, (*i.e.* histories) are fit for every place, reache to all persons, serve for all tymes, teache the living, revive the dead, so farre excelling all other bookes as it is better to see learning in noble mens lives than to reade it in Philosophers writings. Nowe, for the Author, I will not denye but love may deceive me, for I must needes love him with whome I have taken so much payne, but I bileve I might be bold to affirme that he hath written the profitablest story of all Authors. For all other were fayne to take their matter, as the fortune of the contries where they wrote fell out ; But this man, being excellent in wit, in learning, and experience, hath chosen the speciall actes, of the best persons, of the famosest nations of the world. . . . And so I wishe you all the profit of the booke.

This passage really sums up one half the secret of Plutarch's fascination for the Renaissance world. The aim is profit, and profit not merely of a private kind. The profit is better secured by history than by precept, just as the living example is more effectual than the philosophic treatise. And there is more profit in Plutarch than in any other historian, not only on account of his personal qualifications, his wit, learning, and experience, but on account of his subject-matter, because he had the opportunity and insight to choose the prerogative instances in the annals of mankind. Only it should be noted that the profit is conceived in the most liberal and ideal sense. It is the profit that comes from contact with great souls in great surroundings, not the profit of the trite and unmistakable moral. This Amyot had already clearly perceived and set forth in a fine passage of which North gives a fine translation. The dignity of the historian's office is very high :

> Forasmuch as his chiefe drift ought to be to serve the common weale, and that he is but as a register to set downe the judgements and definitive sentences of God's Court, whereof some are geven according to the ordinarie course and capacitie of our weake naturall reason, and other some goe according to God's infinite power and incomprehensible wisedom, above and against all discourse of man's understanding.

In other words history is not profitable as always illustrating a simple retributive justice. It may do that, but it may also do otherwise. Some of its awards are mysterious or even inscrutable. The profit it yields is disinterested and spiritual, and does not lie in the encouragement of optimistic virtue. And this indicates how it may be turned to account. The stuff it contains is the true stuff for Tragedy.

The remaining half of Plutarch's secret depends on the treatment, which loses nothing in the hands of those who now must manage it; of whom the one, in Montaigne's phrase, showed "the constancy of so long a labour," and the other, in his own phrase, "took so much pain," to adapt it aright. But just as the charm of style, though undiminished, is changed when it passes from Plutarch to Amyot, so too this takes place to some degree when it passes from Amyot to North. North was translating from a modern language, without the fear of the ancients before his eyes. Amyot had translated from Greek, and was familiar with classical models. Not merely does this affect the comparative fidelity of their versions, as it was bound to do, for North, with two intervals between, and without the instincts of an accurate scholar, could not keep so close as even Amyot had done to the first original. Indeed he sometimes, though not often, violates the meaning of the French, occasionally misinterpreting a word, as when he translates Coriolanus' final words to his mother : " Je m'en revois (i.e. *revais, retourne*) vaincu par toy seule," by "I *see* myself vanquished by you alone"; more frequently misconstruing an idiom, as when he goes wrong with the negative in passages like the following: "Ces paroles feirent incontinent penser à Eurybides et craindre que les Atheniens ne s'en voulussent aller et les abandonner"; which he renders : "These wordes made Eurybides presently thinke and feare that the Athenians would *not* goe, and that they would forsake them."[1]

But the same circumstance affects North's mode of utterance as well. It is far from attaining to Amyot's habitual clearness, coherence, and correctness. His words are often clumsily placed, his constructions are sometimes broken and more frequently charged with repetitions, he does not always find his way out of a complicated sentence with his grammar unscathed or his meaning unobscured. One of the few Frenchmen who take exception to Amyot's prose says that "it trails like the ivy creeping at random, instead of flying like the arrow to its mark." This is unfair in regard to Amyot; it would be fairer, though still unfair, in regard to North. Compare the French and English versions of the passage that deals with Mark Antony's "piscatory eclogue." Nothing could be more lucid or elegant than the French.

Il se meit quelquefois à pescher à la ligne, et voyant qu'il ne pouvoit rien prendre, si en estoit fort despit et marry à cause que Cléopatra estoit présente. Si commanda secrettement à quelques pescheurs, quand il auroit jeté sa ligne, qu'ilz se plongeassent soudain en l'eau, et qu'ilz allassent accrocher à son hameçon quelques poissons de ceulx qu'ilz auroyent eu peschés auparavent; et puis retira aussi deux or

[1] Themistocles.

trois fois sa ligne avec prise. Cleopatra s'en aperceut incontinent, toutes fois elle feit semblant de n'en rien sçavoir, et
de s'esmerveiller comme il peschoit si bien; mais apart, elle
compta le tout à ses familiers, et leur dit que le lendemain ilz
se trouvassent sur l'eau pour voir l'esbatement. Ilz y vin-
drent sur le port en grand nombre, et se meirent dedans des
bateaux de pescheurs, et Antonius aussi lascha sa ligne, et
lors Cleopatra commanda à lun de ses serviteurs qu'il se has-
tast de plonger devant ceulx d'Antonius, et qu'il allast attacher
a l'hameçon de sa ligne quelque vieux poisson sallé comme
ceulx que lon apporte du païs de Pont. Cela fait, Antonius
qui cuida qu'il y eust un poisson pris, tira incontinent sa ligne,
et adonc comme lon peult penser, tous les assistans se prirent
bien fort à rire, et Cleopatra, en riant, lui dit: "Laisse-nous,
seigneur, à nous autres Ægyptiens, habitans [1] de Pharus et
de Canobus, laisse-nous la ligne; ce n'est pas ton mestier.
Ta chasse est de prendre et conquerer villes et citez, païs et
royaumes."

The flow of the English is not so easy and
transparent.

On a time he went to angle for fish, and when he could
take none, he was as angrie as could be, bicause Cleopatra
stoode by. Wherefore he secretly commaunded the fisher
men, that when he cast in his line, they should straight dive
under the water, and put a fishe on his hooke which they had
taken before: and so snatched up his angling rodde and
brought up a fish twise or thrise. Cleopatra found it straight,
yet she seemed not to see it, but wondred at his excellent
fishing: but when she was alone by her self among her owne
people, she told them howe it was, and bad them the next
morning to be on the water to see the fishing. A number of
people came to the haven, and got into the fisher boates to
see this fishing. Antonius then threw in his line, and Cleopatra straight commaunded one of her men to dive under
water before Antonius men and to put some old salte fish
upon his baite, like unto those that are brought out of the
contrie of Pont. When he had hong the fish on his hooke,
Antonius, thinking he had taken a fishe in deede, snatched
up his line presently. Then they all fell a-laughing. Cleopatra laughing also, said unto him: "Leave us, (my lord),
Ægyptians (which dwell in the contry of Pharus and Canobus) your angling rodde: this is not thy profession; thou must
hunt after conquering realmes and contries."

[1] Greek Βασιλεῦσιν. Does the *habitans* come from the 1470 Latin
version? A later emendation is ἁλιεῦσιν.

This specimen is in so far a favourable one for North, that in simple narrative he is little exposed to his besetting faults, but even here the superior deftness of the Frenchman is obvious. We leave out of account little mistranslations, like *on a time* for *quelquefois*,[1] or *the fishermen* for *quelques pescheurs*,[1] or *alone by herself* for *apart*. We even pass over the lack of connectedness when *they* (*i.e.* the persons informed) *in great number*[1] becomes the quite indefinite *a number of people*, and the omission of the friendly nudge, so to speak, *as you can imagine, comme lon peult penser*. But to miss the point of the phrase *pour voir l'esbatement, to see the sport*, and translate it *see the fishing*, and then clumsily insert the same phrase immediately afterwards where it is not wanted and does not occur; to change the order of the *fishe* and the *hooke* and entangle the connection where it was quite clear, to change *s'esmerveiller* to *wondred*, the infinitive to the indicative past, and thus cloud the sense; to substitute the ambiguous and prolix *When he had hong the fish on his hooke*, for the concise and sufficient *cela fait*—to do all this and much more of the same kind elsewhere was possible only because North was far inferior to Amyot in literary tact. In the English version we have often to interpret the words by the sense and not the sense by the words; and this is a demand which is seldom made by the French.

But there are compensations. All modern languages have in their analytic methods and common stock of ideas a certain family resemblance, in which those of antiquity do not share; and in particular

[1] Yet in these three cases, where North is certainly behind Amyot as a narrator, he is more faithful to the Greek. This is the sort of thing that makes one ask whether he was not really in closer contact with the original than he professes to have been. One remembers his similar modesty in regard to the *Diall*, which, nominally from the French, really made use of the Spanish as well.

G

French is far closer akin to English than Greek to French. Since North had specialised in the continental literature of his day and was now dispensing the bounty of France, his allegiance to the national idiom was virtually undisturbed, even when he made least change in his original. He may be more licentious than Amyot in his treatment of grammar, and less perspicuous in the ordering of his clauses, but he is equal to him or superior in word music, after the English mode; and he is even richer in full-blooded words and in phrases racy of the soil. Not that he ever rejects the guidance of his master, but it leads him to the high places and the secret places of his own language. So while he is quick to detect the rhythm of the French and makes it his pattern, he sometimes goes beyond it; though he can catch and reproduce the cadences of the music-loving Amyot, it is sometimes on a sweeter or a graver key. Take, for instance, that scene, the favourite with Chateaubriand, where Philip, the freedman of Pompey, stands watching by the headless body of his murdered master till the Egyptians are sated with gazing on it, till they have "seen it their bellies full" in North's words. Amyot proceeds :

Puis l'ayant lavé de l'eau de la mer, et enveloppé d'une sienne pauvre chemise, pour ce qu'il n'avoit autre chose, il chercha au long de la greve ou il trouva quelque demourant d'un vieil bateau de pescheur, dont les pieces estoyent bien vieilles, mais suffisantes pour brusler un pauvre corps nud, et encore non tout entier. Ainsi comme il les amassoit et assembloit, il survint un Romain homme d'aage, qui en ses jeunes ans avoit esté à la guerre soubs Pompeius : si luy demanda : "Qui est tu, mon amy, qui fais cest apprest pour les funerailles du grand Pompeius?" Philippus luy respondit qu'il estoit un sien affranchy. "Ha," dit le Romain, "tu n'auras pas tout seul cest honneur, et te prie vueille moy recevoir pour compagnon en une si saincte et si devote rencontre, à fin que je n'aye point occasion de me plaindre en tout et partout de m'estre habitué en païs estranger,

ayant en recompense de plusieurs maulx que j'y ay endurez,
rencontré au moins ceste bonne adventure de pouvoir toucher
avec mes mains, et aider a ensepvelir le plus grand Capitaine
des Romains. "

This is very beautiful, but to English ears, at
least, there is something in North's version, copy
though it be, that is at once more stately and more
moving.

> Then having washed his body with salt water, and
> wrapped it up in an old shirt of his, because he had no
> other shift to lay it in,[1] he sought upon the sands and found
> at the length a peece of an old fishers bote, enough to serve
> to burne his naked bodie with, but not all fully out.[2] As he
> was busie gathering the broken peeces of this bote together,
> thither came unto him an old Romane, who in his youth had
> served under Pompey, and sayd unto him : "O friend, what
> art thou that preparest the funeralls of Pompey the Great."
> Philip answered that he was a bondman of his infranchised.
> "Well," said he, "thou shalt not have all this honor alone, I
> pray thee yet let me accompany thee in so devout a deede,
> that I may not altogether repent me to have dwelt so long in
> a straunge contrie where I have abidden such miserie and
> trouble ; but that to recompence me withall, I may have this
> good happe, with mine owne hands to touche Pompey's
> bodie, and to helpe to bury the only and most famous
> Captaine of the Romanes."[3]

On the other hand, while anything but a purist in
the diction he employs, North's foreign loans lose
their foreign look, and become merely the fitting
ornament for his native home-spun.   It is chiefly on
the extraordinary wealth of his vocabulary, his
inexhaustible supply of expressions, vulgar and
dignified, picturesque and penetrating, colloquial

[1] Amyot probably and North certainly has mistaken the sense.
After washing and shrouding the body "ἄλλο δε οὐδὲν ἔχων ἀλλὰ
περισκοπῶν"; but having nothing else to carry out the funeral rites
with, such as pine wood, spices, etc., but looking about on the beach,
he found, etc.

[2] A misunderstanding on North's part where Amyot translates the
Greek quite adequately.   The rendering should be "a poor naked
body and moreover an incomplete one," *i.e.* with the head wanting.

[3] *Pompeius.*

and literary, but all of them, as he uses them, of indisputable Anglicity—it is chiefly on this that his excellence as stylist is based, an excellence that makes his version of Plutarch by far the most attractive that we possess. It is above all through these resources and the use he makes of them that his book distinguishes itself from the French; for North treats Amyot very much as Amyot treats Plutarch; heightening and amplifying; inserting here an emphatic epithet and there a homely proverb; now substituting a vivid for a colourless term, now pursuing the idea into pleasant side tracks. Thus Amyot describes the distress of the animals that were left behind when the Athenians set out for Salamis, with his average faithfulness.

> Et si y avoit ne sçay quoi de pitoyable qui attendrissoit les cueurs, quand on voyoit les bestes domestiques et privées, qui couroient ça et là avec hurlemens et signifiance de regret après leurs maistres et ceulx qui les avoient nourries, ainsi comme ilz s'embarquoient: entre lesquelles bestes on compte du chien de Xantippus, pere de Pericles, que ne pouvant supporter le regret d'estre laissé de son maistre, il se jeta dedans la mer après luy, et nageant au long de la galère où il estoit, passa jusques en l'isle de Salamine, là où si tost qu'il fust arrivé, l'aleine luy faillit, et mourut soudainement.

But this account stirs North's sympathy, and he puts in little touches that show his interest and compassion.

> There was besides, a certain pittie that made mens harts to yerne, when they saw the *poore doggs, beasts and cattell* ronne up and doune, *bleating, mowing, and howling out aloude* after their masters in token of sorowe, whan they did imbarke. Amongst them there goeth a *straunge* tale of Xanthippus dogge, who was Pericles father; which, for sorowe his master had left him behind him, dyd caste him self after into the sea, and swimming still by the galley's side wherein his master was, he held on to the Ile of Salamina, where so sone as *this poor curre* landed, his breath fayled him, and dyed instantly.[1]

[1] *Themistocles.*

Similarly, when he recounts the story how the Gauls entered Rome, North cannot restrain his reverence for Papirius or his delight in his blow, or his indignation at its requital. Amyot had told of the Gaul :

> qui prit la hardiesse de s'approcher de Marcus Papyrius, et luy passa tout doulcement [1] la main par dessus sa barbe qui estoit longue. Papyrius luy donna de son baston si grand coup sur la teste, qu'il la luy blecea ; dequoy le barbare estant irrité, desguaina son espée, et l'occit.

North is not content with such reserve.

> One of them went boldely unto M. Papyrius and layed his hand fayer and softely upon his long beard. But Papyrius gave him such a *rappe on his pate* with his staffe, that the *bloude ran about his eares.* This *barbarous beaste* was in *such a rage with the blowe* that he drue out his sworde and slewe him.[2]

Or sometimes the picture suggested is so pleasant to North that he partly recomposes it and adds some gracious touch to enhance its charm. Thus he found this vignette of the peaceful period that followed Numa :

> Les peuples hantoient et trafiquoient les uns avec les autres sans crainte ni danger, et s'entrevisitoient en toute cordiale hospitalité, comme si la sapience de Numa eut été une vive source de toutes bonnes et honnestes choses, de laquelle plusieurs fleuves se fussent derivés pour arroser toute l'Italie.

This is how North recasts and embellishes the last sentence :

> The people did trafficke and frequent together, without feare or daunger, and visited one another, making great cheere : *as if out of the springing fountain of Numa's wisdom many pretie brookes and streames of good and honest life had ronne over all Italie and had watered it.*[3]

But illustrations might be multiplied through pages. Enough have been given to show North's debts to

---

[1] Represents πράως. Amyot leaves out ἥψατο τοῦ γενείου, *caught the chin*: *si grand*, and *estant irrité*, are added.

[2] *Furius Camillus.* [3] *Numa Pompilius.*

the French and their limits. With a few unimportant errors, his rendering is in general wonderfully faithful and close, so that he copies even the sequence of thought and modulation of rhythm. He sometimes falls short of his authority in simplicity, neatness, and precision of structure. On the other hand he sometimes excels it in animation and force, in volume and inwardness. But, and this is the last word on his style, even when he follows Amyot's French most scrupulously, he always contrives to write in his own and his native idiom. And hence it came that he once for all naturalised Plutarch among us. His was the epoch-making deed. His successors, who were never his supersessors, merely entered into his labours and adapted Plutarch to the requirements of the Restoration, or of the eighteenth or of the nineteenth century. But they were adapting an author whom North had made a national classic.

> Plutarch was a Greek, to be sure, and a Greek no doubt he is still. But as when we think of a Devereux . . . we call him an Englishman and not a Norman, so who among the reading public troubles himself to reflect that Plutarch wrote Attic prose of such and such a quality? Scholars know all about it to be sure, as they know that the turkeys of our farm-yards come originally from Mexico. Plutarch however is not a scholar's author, but is popular everywhere as if he were a native.[1]

But one aspect of this is that North carries further the process which Amyot had begun of accommodating antiquity to current conceptions. The atmosphere of North's diction is so genuinely national that objects discerned through it take on its hue. Under his strenuous welcome the noble Grecian and Roman immigrants from France are forced to make themselves at home, but in learning the ways of the English market-place they forget something of the

[1] *Quarterly Review*, 1861.

Agora and the Forum.   Perhaps this was inevitable, since they were come to stay.

And the consequence of North's method is that he meets Shakespeare half way.   His copy may blur some of the lines in the original picture, but they are lines that Shakespeare would not have perceived.   He may present Antiquity in disguise, but it was in this disguise alone that Shakespeare was able to recognise it.   He has in short supplied Shakespeare with the only Plutarch that Shakespeare could understand.   The highest compliment we can pay his style is, that it had a special relish for Shakespeare, who retained many of North's expressions with little or no alteration.   The highest compliment we can pay the contents is, that, only a little more modernised, they furnished Shakespeare with his whole conception of antique history.

The influence of North's Plutarch on Shakespeare is thus of a twofold kind.   There is the influence of the diction, there is the influence of the subject-matter; and in the first instance it is more specifically the influence of North, while in the second it is more specifically the influence of Plutarch.

It would be as absurd as unfair to deny Shakespeare's indebtedness to North not only in individual turns and phrases, but in continuous discourse. Often the borrower does little more than change the prose to poetry.   But at the lowest he always does that; and there is perhaps in some quarters a tendency to minimise the marvel of the feat, and so, if not to exaggerate the obligation, at least to set it in a false light.   He has nowhere followed North so closely through so many lines as in Volumnia's great speech to her son before Rome ; and, next to that, in Coriolanus' great speech to Aufidius in Antium.   In these passages the ideas, the arrangement of the ideas, the presentation of the ideas are practically the same in the translator and in the dramatist : yet, with a few almost imperceptible touches, a few changes in the order of construction, a few substitutions in the wording, the language of North, without losing any directness or force, gains a majestic volume and vibration that are only possible in the cadences of the most perfect verse. These are the cases in which Shakespeare shows most verbal dependence on his author, but his originality asserts itself even in them. North's admirable appeal is not Shakespeare's, Shakespeare's more admirable appeal is not North's.[1]

Similarly there has been a tendency to over-estimate the loans of the Roman Plays from Plutarch. From this danger even Archbishop Trench has not altogether escaped in an eloquent and well-known passage which in many ways comes very near to the truth. After dwelling on the freedom with which Shakespeare generally treats his sources, for instance the novels of Bandello or Cinthio, deriving from them at most a hint or two, cutting and carving, rejecting or expanding their statements at will, he concludes :

> But his relations with Plutarch are very different—different enough to justify or almost to justify the words of Jean Paul when in his *Titan* he calls Plutarch "der biographische Shakespeare der Weltgeschichte." What a testimony we have here to the true artistic sense and skill which, with all his occasional childish simplicity[2] the old biographer possesses, in the fact that the mightiest and completest artist of all times, should be content to resign himself into his hands and simply to follow where the other leads.

To this it might be answered in the first place that Shakespeare shows the same sort of fidelity in kind, though not in degree, to the comparatively inartistic chronicles of his mother country. That is,

---

[1] The relations of the various versions—Greek, Latin, French, and English—are illustrated by means of this speech in Appendix B.

[2] Childish simplicity does not strike one as a correct description of Plutarch's method.

it is in part, as we have seen, his tribute not to the historical author but to the historical subject. Granting, however, the superior claims of Plutarch, it is yet an overstatement to say that Shakespeare is content to resign himself into his hands, and simply to follow where the other leads. Delius, after an elaborate comparison of biography and drama, sums up his results in the protest that " Shakespeare has much less to thank Plutarch for than one is generally inclined to suppose."

Indeed, however much Plutarch would appeal to Shakespeare in virtue both of his subjects and his methods, it is easy to see that even as a "grave learned philosopher and historiographer" he is on the hither side of perfection. He interrupts the story with moral disquisitions, and is a little apt to preach, and often, through such intrusions and irrelevancies, or the adherence of the commonplace, his most impressive touches fail of their utmost possible effect : at least he does not always seem aware of the full value of his details, of their depth and suggestiveness when they are set aright. Yet he is more excellent in details than in the whole : he has little arrangement or artistic construction ; he is not free from contradictions and discrepancies; he gives the bricks and mortar but not the building, and occasionally some of the bricks are flawed or the mortar is forgotten. And his stories have this inorganic character, because he is seldom concerned to pierce to the meaning that would give them unity and coherence. He moralises, and only too sententiously, whenever an opportunity offers ; but of the principles that underlie the conflicts and catastrophes which in his free-and-easy way he describes, he has at best but fragmentary glimpses.

And in all this the difference between the genial moralist and the inspired tragedian is a vast one— so vast that when once we perceive it, it is hard to

retain a fitting sense of the points of contact.   In
Shakespeare, Plutarch's weaknesses disappear, or
rather are replaced by excellences of precisely the
opposite kind.   He rejects all that is otiose or dis-
cordant in speech or situation, and adds from other
passages in his author or from his own imagination,
the circumstances that are needed to bring out its
full poetic significance.   He always looks to the
whole, removes discrepancies, establishes the inner
connection ; and at his touch the loose parts take
their places as members of one living organism.
And in a sense, "he knows what it is all about."
In a sense he is more of a philosophic historian than
his teacher.   At any rate, while Plutarch takes his
responsibilities lightly in regard both to facts and
conclusions, Shakespeare, in so far as that was
possible for an Elizabethan, has a sort of intuition
of the principles that Plutarch's narrative involves ;
and while adding some pigment from his own
thought and feeling to give them colour and visible
shape, accepts them as his pre-suppositions which
interpret the story and which it interprets.

Thus the influences of North's Plutarch, whether
of North's style or of Plutarch's matter, though no
doubt very great, are in the last resort more in the
way of suggestion than of control.   But they do not
invariably act with equal potency or in the same proportion.   Thus *Antony and Cleopatra* adheres most
closely to the narrative of the biographer, which is
altered mainly by the omission of details unsuitable
for the purpose of the dramatist; but the words,
phrases, constructions, are for the most part conspicuously Shakespeare's own.   Here there is a
maximum of Plutarch and a minimum of North.   In
Coriolanus, on the other hand, apart from the
unconscious modifications that we have noticed,
Shakespeare allows himself more liberty than elsewhere in chopping and changing the substance; but

lengthy passages and some of the most impressive ones are incorporated in the drama without further alteration than is implied in the transfiguration of prose to verse. Here there is the maximum of North with the minimum of Plutarch. *Julius Caesar*, as in the matter of the inevitable and unintentional misunderstandings, so again here, occupies a middle place. Many phrases, and not a few decisive suggestions for the most important speeches, have passed from the *Lives* into the play: one sentence at least it is hard to interpret without reference to the context; but here as a rule, even when he borrows most, Shakespeare treats his loans very independently. So, too, though he seldom wittingly departs from Plutarch, he elaborates the new material throughout, amplifying and abridging, selecting and rejecting, taking to pieces and recombining, not from one Life but from three. Here we have the mean influence both of Plutarch and of North.

In so far therefore *Julius Caesar* gives the norm of Shakespeare's procedure; and with it, for this as well as on chronological grounds, we begin.

JULIUS CAESAR

CHAPTER I

POSITION OF THE PLAY BETWEEN THE HISTORIES AND THE TRAGEDIES. ATTRACTION OF THE SUBJECT FOR SHAKESPEARE AND HIS GENERATION. INDEBTEDNESS TO PLUTARCH

ALTHOUGH *Julius Caesar* was first published in the Folio of 1623, seven years after Shakespeare's death, there is not much doubt about its approximate date of composition, which is now placed by almost all scholars near the beginning of the seventeenth century. Some of the evidence for this is partly external in character.

(1) In a miscellany of poems on the death of Elizabeth, printed in 1603, and entitled *Sorrowes Joy*, the lines occur :

> They say a *comet* woonteth to appeare
> When *Princes* baleful destinie is neare:
> So *Julius* starre was seene with fiery crest,
> Before his fall to *blaze* among the rest.

It looks as though the suggestion for the idea and many of the words had come from Calpurnia's remonstrance,

> When beggars die there are no *comets seen:*
> The heavens themselves *blaze* forth the death of *princes.* [1]
>
> (II. ii. 30.)

[1] Pointed out by Mr. Stokes, *Chronological Order, etc.* Might not some of the expressions come, however, from Virgil's list of the portents

Another apparent loan belongs to the same year. In 1603 Drayton rewrote his poem of *Mortimeriados* under the title of *The Barons' Wars*, altering and adding many passages. One of the insertions runs :

> Such one he was, of him we boldely say,
>> In whose riche soule all soueraigne powres did sute,
> In *whome in peace th(e) elements all lay*
>> *So mixt* as none could soueraignty impute ;
> As all did gouerne, yet all did obey.
>> His liuely temper was so absolute,
> That 't seemde when heauen his modell first began,
> In him it *shewd perfection in a man.*

Compare Antony's verdict on Brutus :

> His life was gentle, and *the elements*
> *So mix'd* in him, that Nature might stand up
> And say to all the world, "This *was a man.*" (v. v. 73.)

Some critics have endeavoured to minimise this coincidence on the ground that it was a common idea that man was compounded of the four elements. But that would not account for such close identity of phrase. There must be some connection; and that Drayton, not Shakespeare, was the copyist, is rendered probable by the circumstance that Drayton, in 1619, *i.e.* after Shakespeare's death, makes a still closer approach to Shakespeare's language.

> He was a man, then, boldly dare to say,
>> In whose rich soul the virtues well did suit;
> In whom, *so mix'd the elements all lay*,
>> That none to one could sovereignty impute ;
> As all did govern, yet all did obey :
>> He of a temper was so absolute
> As that it seem'd, when *Nature* him began,
> She meant to show *all that might be in man.*[1]

(2) Apart, however, from these apparent adaptations in 1603, there is reason to conjecture that the play had been performed by May in the previous year. At that date, as we know from Henslowe's *Diary*,

that accompanied Caesar's death? Compare especially "nec diri toties *arsere cometae*" (*G.* i. 488).

[1] Collier's Shakespeare.

Drayton, Webster and others were engaged on a
tragedy on the same subject called *Caesar's Fall*.
Now it is a well ascertained fact that when a drama
was a success at one theatre, something on a similar
theme commonly followed at another. The entry
therefore, that in the early summer of 1602 Henslowe had several playwrights working at this
material, apparently in a hurry, since so many are
sharing in the task, is in so far presumptive evidence
that Shakespeare's *Julius Caesar* had been produced
in the same year or shortly before.

(3) But these things are chiefly important as con-
firming the probability of another allusion, which
would throw the date a little further back still.   In
Weever's *Mirror of Martyrs* there is the quatrain:

> The many headed multitude were drawne
> By Brutus speech, that Caesar was ambitious,
> When eloquent Mark Antony had showne
> His vertues, who but Brutus then was vicious.[1]

Now this has a much more specific reference to
the famous scene in the Play than to anything in
Plutarch, who, for instance, even in the *Life of
Brutus*, which gives the fullest account of Brutus'
dealings with the citizens, does not mention the
substance of his argument and still less any insistence on Caesar's ambition, but only says that he
"made an oration unto them to winne the favor
of the people, and to justifie what they had done";
and this passage, which contains the fullest notice of
Brutus' speeches, like the corresponding one in the
Life of Caesar, attributes only moderate success to
his appeal in the market place, while it goes on to
describe the popular disapproval as exploding
before the intervention of Antony.[2]   Thus it seems

[1] Mr. Halliwell-Phillips' discovery.

[2] "Brutus and his confederates came into the market place to
speake unto the people, who gave them such audience, that it seemed
they neither greatly reproved, nor allowed the fact : for by their great

fairly certain that a knowledge of Shakespeare's play is presupposed by the *Mirror of Martyrs*, which was printed in 1601.

On the other hand, it cannot have been much earlier. The absence of such a typical "tragedy" from Meres' list in 1598 is nearly proof positive that it was not then in existence.

After that the *data* are less definite. *A Warning for Fair Women*, printed in 1599, contains the lines :

> I have given him fifteen wounds,
> Which will be fifteen *mouths* that do accuse me :
> In every mouth there is a bloody *tongue*
> Which will *speak*, although he holds his peace.

It is difficult not to bring these into connection with Antony's words :

> Over thy wounds now do I prophesy—
> Which like dumb *mouths* do ope their ruby lips
> To beg the voice and utterance of my *tongue*.   (III. i. 259.)

And again :

> I tell you that which you yourselves do know,
> Show you sweet Caesar's wounds, poor, poor dumb *mouths*,
> And bid them *speak* for me : but were I Brutus
> And Brutus Antony, there were an Antony
> Would ruffle up your spirits and put a *tongue*
> In every *wound*.   (III. ii. 228.)

But in this Shakespeare may have been the debtor not the creditor : and other coincidences like the " Et tu, Brute," in *Acolastus his Afterwit* [1] (1600) may be due to the use of common or current authorities.

silence they showed that they were sorry for Caesar's death and also that they did reverence Brutus." *Julius Caesar*.

"When the people saw him in the pulpit, although they were a multitude of rakehells of alle sortes, and had a good will to make some sturre, yet being ashamed to doe it for the reverence they bare unto Brutus, they kept silence to heare what he would say. When Brutus began to speak they gave him quiet audience ; howbeit immediately after, they shewed that they were not all contented with the murther. For when another called Cinna would have spoken and began to accuse Caesar ; they fell into a great uprore among them, and marvelously reviled him." *M. Brutus*.

[1] By S. Nicholson.

One little detail has been used as an argument that the play was later than 1600. Cassius says :

There was a Brutus once that would have brook'd
The eternal devil to keep his state in Rome
As easily as a king. (I. ii. 159.)

Here obviously the word we should have expected is *infernal* not *eternal*. It has been conjectured[1] that the milder expression was substituted in deference to the increasing disapproval of profane language on the stage ; and since three plays published in 1600 use *infernal*, the inference is that *Julius Caesar* is subsequent to them. One fails to see, however, why Shakespeare should admit the substantive and be squeamish about the adjective : in point of fact, much uglier words than either find free entry into his later plays. And one has likewise to remember that the *Julius Caesar* we possess was published only in 1623, and that such a change might very well have been made in any of the intervening years, even though it were written before 1600. The most then that can be established by this set of inferences, is that it was produced after Meres' *Palladis Tamia* in 1598 and before Weever's *Mirror of Martyrs* in 1601.

The narrowness of the range is fairly satisfactory, and it may be further reduced. It has been surmised that perhaps Essex' treason turned Shakespeare's thoughts to the story of another conspiracy by another high-minded man, and that Caesar's reproach, "Et tu, Brute," derived not from the Parallel Lives but from floating literary tradition, would suggest to an audience of those days the feeling of Elizabeth in regard to one whom Shakespeare had but recently celebrated as "the general of our gracious Empress." At any rate the time seems suitable. Among Shakespeare's serious plays *Julius Caesar* most resembles in style *Henry V.*,

[1] By Mr. Wright, *Clarendon Press Edition.*

written between March and September 1599, as the
above allusion to Essex' expedition shows,[1] and
Hamlet, entered at Stationers' Hall in 1602, as
"latelie acted." But the connection is a good deal
closer with the latter than with the former, and
extends to the parallelism and contrast between the
chief persons, both of them philosophic students
called upon to make a decision for which their temperament and powers do not fit them, and therefore
the one of them deciding wrong and the other
hardly deciding at all. Both pieces contain references to the story of Caesar, but those in *Hamlet*
accord better with the tone of the tragedy. Thus
the chorus says of Henry's triumph :

> The mayor and all his brethren in best sort,
> Like to the senators of the antique Rome,
> With the plebeians swarming at their heels,
> Go forth to fetch their conquering Caesar in.
>
> (v. prologue 25.)

Would this passage have been penned if Shakespeare had already described how the acclamations of
the plebs were interrupted by the tribunes, and how
among the senators there were some eager to make
away with the Victor?

But the two chief references in *Hamlet* merely
abridge what is told more at large in the Play.
Polonius says : "I did enact Julius Caesar : I was
killed i' the Capitol. Brutus killed me" (III. ii. 108),
which is only a bald summary of the central situation.
Hamlet says :

> In the most high and palmy state of Rome,
> A little ere the mightiest Julius fell,
> The graves stood tenantless, and the sheeted dead
> Did squeak and gibber in the Roman streets :
> As stars with trains of fire and dews of blood,
> Disasters in the sun ; and the moist star
> Upon whose influence Neptune's empire stands
> Was sick almost to doomsday with eclipse.   (I. i. 113.)

---

[1] *Henry V.* v. prologue 30.

This reads like a condensed anthology from the descriptions of Casca, Cassius and Calpurnia, eked out with a few hints from another passage in Plutarch that had not hitherto been utilised.[1]

Even the quatrain :

> Imperious Caesar, dead and turn'd to clay,
> Might stop a hole to keep the wind away :
> O, that that earth which kept the world in awe,
> Should patch a wall to expel the winter's flaw !   (v. i. 236.)

is in some sort the ironical development of Antony's thought :

> O mighty Caesar ! dost thou lie so low ?
> Are all thy conquests, glories, triumphs, spoils,
> Shrunk to this little measure ?   (III. i. 148.)

> But yesterday the word of Caesar might
> Have stood against the world : now lies he there,
> And none so poor to do him reverence.   (III. ii. 123.)

Owing to Weever's reference we cannot put *Julius Caesar* after *Hamlet*, but it seems to have closer relations with *Hamlet* than with *Henry V*. It is not rash to place it between the two, in 1600 or 1601. This does not however mean that we necessarily have it quite in its original form. On the contrary, there are indications that it may have been revised some time after the date of composition.

Thus Ben Jonson in his *Discoveries* writes of Shakespeare : " His wit was in his own power : would the rule of it had been so too ! Many times

---

[1] Calpùrnia speaks of the appearance of comets at the death of princes, but merely in a general way, not as a presage then to be observed : and there is no mention in the play of disasters in the sun or eclipses of the moon. Near the end of the *Life of Caesar*, Plutarch records the first two portents, and his language suggests the idea of a solar, which, for variety's sake, might easily be changed to a lunar eclipse. "The great comet which seven nightes together was seene very bright after Caesar's death, the eight night after was never seene more. Also the *brightnes of the sunne was darkened*, the which all that yeare through was very pale, and shined not out, whereby it gave but small heate."

he fell into those things could not escape laughter, as when he said in the person of Caesar, one speaking to him, 'Caesar, thou dost me wrong,' he replied, 'Caesar did never wrong but with just cause,' and such like; which were ridiculous." Most people would see in this a very ordinary example of the figure called Paradox, and some would explain *wrong* in such a way that even the paradox disappears : but the alleged *bêtise* tickled Ben's fancy, for he recurs to it to make a point in the Introduction to the *Staple of News*. One of the persons says : " I can do that too, if I have cause "; to which the reply is made : "Cry you mercy; you never did wrong but with just cause."

Now in the present play there is no such expression. The nearest analogue occurs in the conclusion of the speech, in which Caesar refuses the petition for Publius Cimber's recall,

> Know, Caesar doth not wrong, nor without cause
> Will he be satisfied. (III. i. 47.)

It has been suggested [1] that Jonson simply misquoted the passage. But it is not likely that Ben would consciously or unconsciously pervert the authentic text by introducing an absurdity, still less by introducing an absurdity that few people find absurd. In his criticisms on Shakespeare he does not manufacture the things to which he objects, but regards them from an unsympathetic point of view. It seems probable, therefore, that he has preserved an original reading, that was altered out of deference for strictures like his : and this in so far supports the theory that the play was corrected after its first appearance.

So, too, with the versification. The consideration of certain technicalities, such as the weak ending, would place *Julius Caesar* comparatively early, but

[1] By Mr. Verity, *Julius Caesar*, 198.

there are others that yield a more ambiguous result.
It may have been revived and revised about 1607
when the subject was again popular.

And perhaps it has survived only in an acting
edition. It is unusually short : and, that Shakespeare's plays were probably abridged for the stage.
we know from comparison of the Quarto with the
Folio *Hamlets*. The same argument has been used
in regard to *Macbeth*.

Still granting the plausibility up to a certain
point of this conjecture, its importance must not be
exaggerated. It does not affect the fact that *Julius
Caesar* belongs essentially to the very beginning of
the century, and that it is an organic whole as it
stands. If abridged, it is still full, compact and
unattenuated. If revised, its style, metre and treatment are still all characteristic of Shakespeare's early
prime. The easy flow of the verse, the luminous
and pregnant diction, the skilful presentation of the
story in a few suggestive incidents, all point to a time
when Shakespeare had attained complete mastery of
his methods and material, and before he was driven
by his daemon to tasks insuperable by another and
almost insuperable by him,

> Reaching that heaven might so replenish him
> Above and through his art.

It is perhaps another aspect of the perfect and
harmonious beauty, which fulfils the whole play and
every part of it, that while there is none of the
speeches "that is in the bad sense declamatory,
none that does not gain by its context nor can be
spared from it without some loss to the dramatic
situation," there are many "which are eminently
adapted for declamation";[1] that is, for delivery by
themselves. In the later plays, on the other hand,

---

[1] The late Mr. H. Sidgwick, "Julius Caesar and Coriolanus," in
Essays and Addresses.

it is far more difficult to extract any particular jewel from its setting.

It is pretty certain then that *Julius Caesar* is the first not only of the Roman Plays, but of the great series of Tragedies. The flame-tipped welter of *Titus Andronicus*, the poignant radiance of *Romeo and Juliet* belong to Shakespeare's pupilage and youth. Their place is apart from each other and the rest in the vestibule and forecourt of his art. The nearest approach to real Tragedy he had otherwise made was in the English History of *Richard III*. And now when that period of his career begins in which he is chiefly occupied with the treatment of tragic themes, it is again to historical material that he has recourse, and he chooses from it the episode which was probably of supreme interest to the Europe of his day. Since Muretus first showed the way, the fate of Caesar had again and again been dramatised in Latin and in the vernacular, in French and in English. It was a subject that to a genius of the second rank might have seemed hackneyed, but a genius of the highest rank knows that the common is not hackneyed but catholic, and contains richer possibilities than the recondite. Shakespeare had already been drawn to it himself. The frequent references in his earlier dramas show how he too was fascinated by the glamour of Caesar. In the plays adapted by him, he inserts or retains tributes to Caesar's greatness, to the irony or injustice of his fate. Bedford in his enthusiasm for the spirit of Henry V., as ordained to prosper the realm and thwart adverse planets, can prefer him to only one rival,

> A far more glorious star thy soul will make
> Than Julius Caesar. (*H. VI.* A. i. i. 155.)

Suffolk, in his self-conceit and self-pity, seeks for examples of other celebrities who have perished by ignoble hands, and compared with his victim, even Brutus seems on the level of the meanest and most unscrupulous.

> A Roman sworder and banditto slave
> Murder'd sweet Tully : Brutus' bastard hand
> Stabb'd Julius Caesar : savage islanders
> Pompey the Great : and Suffolk dies by pirates.
> (*H. VI*. B. iv. i. 134.)

Margaret, when her boy is slaughtered at Tewkesbury, thinks of Caesar's murder as the one deed which can be placed beside it, and which it even transcends in horror.

> They that stabb'd Caesar shed no blood at all,
> Did not offend, nor were not worthy blame,
> If this foul deed were by to equal it.
> (*H. VI*. C. v. v. 53.)

It is the same if we turn to Shakespeare's indisputably spontaneous utterances. He sees Caesar's double merit with pen and sword. Says the little Prince Edward :

> That Julius Caesar was a famous man :
> With what his valour did enrich his wit,
> His wit set down to make his valour live.
> Death makes no conquest of this conquerer :
> For now he lives in fame, though not in life.
> (*R. III*. iii. i. 84.)

Rosalind laughs at the self-consciousness of his prowess as she laughs at the extravagance of love in Troilus and Leander, but evidently Shakespeare, just as he was impressed by their stories in Chaucer and Marlowe, was impressed in Plutarch with what she calls the "thrasonical brag of ' I came, saw, and overcame.'" Don Armado is made to quote it in his role of invincible gallant (*L.L.L.* iv. i. 68) ; and Falstaff parodies it by applying to himself the boast of "the hooked-nosed fellow of Rome" when Sir John Coleville surrenders (*H. IV*. B. iv. iii. 45). For to Shakespeare there are no victories like

Caesar's.   The false announcement of Hotspur's
success appeals to them for precedent :

> O, such a day
> So fought, so follow'd and so fairly won,
> Came not till now to dignify the times
> Since Caesar's fortunes.   (*H. IV.* B. i. i. 20.)

We have already noticed the references to his
triumphs, his fate, the ironical contrast between the
was and the *is* in *Henry V.* and *Hamlet*, the History
and the Tragedy that respectively precede and
succeed the play of which he is titular hero.   But
Shakespeare keeps recurring to the theme almost to
the end.   When in *Measure for Measure* the dis-
reputable Pompey is conveyed to prison, it suggests a
ridiculous parallel with that final triumph of Caesar's
when the tribunes saw far other

> tributaries follow him to Rome
> To grace in captive bonds his chariot wheels.

" How now, noble Pompey," says Lucio as the go-
between passes by behind Elbow and the officers,
" what, at the wheels of Caesar? art thou led in
triumph ? " (III. ii. 46).   In *Antony and Cleopatra*,
of course the incumbent presence of " broad-fronted
Caesar" is always felt.   But in Cymbeline, too, it
haunts us.   Now his difficulties in the island, since
there were difficulties even for him, are used as by
Posthumus, to exalt the prowess of the Britons,

> When Julius Caesar
> Smiled at their lack of skill, but found their courage
> Worthy his frowning at :   (II. iv. 21.)

or by the Queen :

> A kind of conquest
> Caesar made here ; but made not here his brag
> Of "came" and "saw" and "overcame."   (III. i. 22.)

But the dominant note is rather of admiration for

> Julius Caesar, whose remembrance yet
> Lives in men's eyes, and will to ears and tongues
> Be theme and hearing ever.   (III. i. 2.)

Or if the fault that Brutus enforced is brought to view, the very fault becomes a grandiose and super-human thing :

> Caesar's ambition,
> Which swell'd so much, that it did almost stretch
> The sides o' the world.   (III. i. 49.)

The subject then was one of wide-spread interest and had an abiding fascination for Shakespeare himself.   After leaving national history in *Henry V.* he seems to have turned to the history of Rome for the first Tragedy of his prime in a spirit much like that in which he had gone to the English Chronicles. And he goes to it much in the same way.   It has been said that in most of the earlier series " Holinshed is hardly ever out of the poet's hands." [1] Substituting Plutarch for Holinshed the expression is true in this case too.   An occasional phrase like the *Et tu, Brute*, he obtained elsewhere, most probably from familiar literary usage, but con-ceivably from the lost Latin play of Dr. Eedes or Geddes.   Stray hints he may have derived from other authorities ; for instance, though this is not certain, a suggestion or two from Appian's *Civil Wars* for Mark Antony's Oration. [2]   It is even possible that he may have been directed to the conception and treatment of a few longer passages by his general reading : thus, as we have seen, it has been maintained not without plausibility that the first conversation between Brutus and Cassius can be traced to the corresponding scene in the *Cornélie*. [3]   But in Plutarch he found practically all the stuff and substance for his play, except what was contributed by his own genius ; and any other ingredients are nearly imperceptible and altogether

[1] Mr. Churton Collins, *Studies in Shakespeare.*   See also Mr. Boswell Stone, *Shakespere's Holinshed.*

[2] See Appendix C.

[3] See Introduction, pages 60-61, and Appendix A.

negligible. Plutarch, however, has given much.
All the persons except Lucius come from him, and
Shakespeare owes to him a number of their characteristics down to the minutest traits.   Cassius' leanness
and Antony's sleekness, Brutus' fondness for his
books and cultivation of an artificial style, Caesar's
liability to the falling sickness and vein of arrogance
in his later years, are all touches that are taken over
from the Biographer.   So too with the events and
circumstances, and in the main, the sequence in
which they are presented.   Plutarch tells of the
disapproval with which the triumph over Pompey's
sons was regarded ; of the prophecy of danger on
the Ides of March ; of the offer of the crown on the
Lupercal ; of the punishment of the Tribunes ; of
Cassius' conference with Brutus ; of the anonymous
solicitations that are sent to the latter ; of the
respect in which he was held ; of his relations with
his wife, and her demand to share his confidence ;
of the enthusiasm of the conspirators, their contempt
for an oath, their rejection of Cicero as confederate,
their exemption of Antony at Brutus' request ; of
Ligarius' disregard of his illness ; of the prodigies
and portents that preceded Caesar's death ; of
Calpurnia's dream, her efforts to stay her husband
at home and the counter arguments of Decius
Brutus ; of Artemidorus' intervention, the second
meeting with the sooth-sayer ; of Portia's paroxysm
of anxiety ; of all the details of the assassination
scene ; of the speeches to the people by Brutus and
Antony ; of the effects of Caesar's funeral ; of the
murder of the poet Cinna ; of the proscription of
the Triumvirate ; of the disagreement of Brutus
and Cassius on other matters and with reference to
Pella, and the interruption of the intruder ; of the
apparition of the spirit, and the death of Portia ; of
Brutus' discussion with Cassius on suicide ; of his
imprudence at Philippi ; of the double issue and

repetition of the battle ; of the death of Cassius and Brutus on their own swords ; of the surrender of Lucilius ; of Antony's eulogy of Brutus. There is, thus hardly a link in the action that was not forged on Plutarch's anvil.

And even the words of North have in many cases been almost literally transcribed. Says Lucilius when brought before Antony :

> I dare assure thee, that no enemie hath taken, nor shall take Marcus Brutus alive; and I beseech God keepe him from that fortune. For wheresoever he be found, alive or dead ; he will be found like him selfe.   (*Brutus.*)

Compare :

> I dare assure thee that no enemy
> Shall ever take alive the noble Brutus :
> The gods defend him from so great a shame !
> When you do find him, or alive or dead,
> He will be found like Brutus, like himself.   (v. iv. 21.)

Or take the passage—considering its length, the exactest reproduction of all—in which Portia claims full share in her husband's secrets. The sentiment is what we are accustomed to regard as modern ; but Plutarch, who himself viewed marriage as a relation in which there was no Mine nor Thine,[1] has painted the situation with heart-felt sympathy. After describing the wound she gives herself to make trial of her firmness, he proceeds :

> Then perceiving her husband was marvelously out of quiet, and that he coulde take no rest : even in her greatest payne of all, she spake in this sorte unto him : "I being, O Brutus (sayed she), the daughter of Cato, was maried unto thee, not to be thy bedde fellowe and companion at bedde and at borde onelie, like a harlot ; but to be partaker also with thee, of thy good and evill fortune. Nowe for thy selfe, I can finde no cause of faulte in thee as touchinge our matche : but for my parte, howe may I showe my duetie towardes thee, and howe muche I woulde doe for thy sake, if

---

[1] See page 98.

I cannot constantlie beare a secret mischaunce or griefe with thee, which requireth secrecy and fidelity? I confesse, that a woman's wit commonly is too weake to keepe a secret safely: but yet, Brutus, good educacion, and the companie of vertuous men, have some power to reforme the defect of nature. And for my selfe, I have this benefit moreover: that I am the daughter of Cato, and wife of Brutus. This notwithstanding, I did not trust to any of these things before; untill that now I have found by experience, that no paine nor griefe whatsoever can overcome me.' With those wordes she shewed him her wounde on her thigh, and told him what she had done to prove her selfe. Brutus was amazed to heare what she sayd unto him, and lifting up his handes to heaven, he besought the goddes to give him grace he might bring his enterprise to so good passe, that he might be founde a husband, worthie of so noble a wife as Porcia."

(*Marcus Brutus.*)

It is hardly necessary to point out how closely Shakespeare follows up the trail.

> *Portia.* Within the bond of marriage, tell me, Brutus,
> Is it excepted I should know no secrets
> That appertain to you? Am I yourself
> But, as it were, in sort or limitation;
> To keep with you at meals, comfort your bed,
> And talk to you sometimes? Dwell I but in the suburbs
> of your good pleasure? If it be no more,
> Portia is Brutus' harlot, not his wife.
> *Brutus.* You are my true and honourable wife,
> As dear to me as are the ruddy drops
> That visit my sad heart.
> *Portia.* If this were true, then should I know this secret.
> I grant I am a woman; but withal,
> A woman that Lord Brutus took to wife;
> I grant I am a woman; but, withal,
> A woman well-reputed, Cato's daughter.
> Think you I am no stronger than my sex,
> Being so father'd and so husbanded?
> Tell me your counsels, I will not disclose 'em:
> I have made strong proof of my constancy,
> Giving myself a voluntary wound,
> Here, in the thigh: can I bear that with patience,
> And not my husband's secrets?
> *Brutus.*   O ye gods,
> Render me worthy of this noble wife.

(II. i. 280.)

Here we have "the marriage of true souls"; and though the prelude to this nuptial hymn, a prelude that heralds and enhances its sweetness, is veriest Shakespeare, when the main theme begins and the climax is reached, he is content to resign himself to the ancient melody, and re-echo, even while he varies, the notes.

North's actual slips or blunders are received into the play. Thus the account of the assassination runs: "Caesar was driven . . . against the base whereupon Pompey's image stood, which ranne all of a goare blood." The last clause, probably by accident, adds picturesqueness to Amyot's simple description, "qui en fust toute ensanglantee," and is immortalised in Antony's bravura:

> Even at the base of Pompey's statua
> Which all the while ran blood.   (III. ii. 192.)

More noticeable is the instance of Brutus' reply to Cassius' question, what he will do if he lose the battle at Philippi. Amyot's translation is straightforward enough.

> Brutus luy respondit: "Estant encore jeune et non assez experimenté es affaires de ce monde, je feis ne sçay comment un discours de philosophie, par lequel je reprenois et blasmois fort Caton d'estre desfait soymesme" etc.

That is:

> Brutus answered him: "When I was yet young and not much experienced in the affairs of this world, I composed, somehow or other, a philosophic discourse in which I greatly rebuked and censured Cato for having made away with himself!"

North did not notice where the quotation began; connected *feis* with *fier* in place of *faire*, probably taking it as present not as past; and interpreted *discours* as *principle*, which it never meant and never can mean, instead of *dissertation*. So he translates:

> Brutus answered him, *being yet but a young man, and not over-greatly experienced in the world*: I *trust* (I know not how)

a certaine rule of Philosophie, by the which I did greatly
blame and reprove Cato for killing of him selfe ; as being no
godly or lawful acte, touching the goddes ; nor concerning
men, valliant ; not to give place and yeld to divine providence,
and not constantly and paciently to take whatsoever it pleaseth
him to send us, but to drawe backe, and flie : but being nowe in
the middest of the daunger, I am of a contrary mind.   For if
it be not the will of God, that this battell fall out fortunate for
us : I will looke no more for hope, neither seeke to make any
new supply for warre againe, but will rid me of this miserable
world, and content me with my fortune.   For, I gave up my
life for my country in the Ides of Marche, for the which I
shall live in another more glorious worlde.   (*Marcus Brutus.*)

It is possible that North used *trust* in the first
sentence as a preterite equal to *trusted*, just as he
uses *lift* for *lifted*.   But Shakespeare at least took
it for a present: so he was struck by the contradiction which the passage seems to contain.   He got
over it, and produced a new effect and one very true
to human nature, by making Brutus' latter sentiment
the sudden response of his heart, in defiance of his
philosophy, to Cassius' anticipation of what they
must expect if defeated.

> *Brutus.*   Even by the rule of that philosophy
> By which I did blame Cato for the death
> Which he did give himself, I know not how,
> But I do find it cowardly and vile,
> For fear of what might fall, so to prevent
> The time of life: arming myself with patience
> To stay the providence of some higher powers
> That govern us below.
> *Cassius.*   Then if we lose this battle.
> You are contented to be led in triumph
> Thorough the streets of Rome ?
> *Brutus.*   No, Cassius, no: think not, thou noble Roman,
> That ever Brutus will go bound to Rome ;
> He bears too great a mind.   But this same day
> Must end that work the ides of March begun ;
> And whether we shall meet again I know not.
> Therefore our everlasting farewell take.   (v. i. 101.)

This last illustration may show us, however, that
Shakespeare, even when he seems to copy most

literally, always introduces something that comes from himself. Despite his wholesale appropriation of territory that does not in the first instance belong to him, the produce is emphatically his own. It is like the white man's occupation of America and Australasia, and can be justified only on similar grounds. The lands remain the same under their new as under their old masters, but they yield undreamed-of wealth to satisfy the needs of man. Never did any one borrow more, yet borrow less, than Shakespeare. He finds the clay ready to his hand, but he shapes it and breathes into it the breath of life, and it becomes a living soul.

CHAPTER II

SHAKESPEARE'S TRANSMUTATION OF HIS MATERIAL

THE examples given in the previous chapter may serve to show that from one point of view it is impossible to exaggerate Shakespeare's dependence on Plutarch. But this is not the only or the most important aspect of the case. He alters and adds quite as much as he gets. No slight modification of the story is implied by its mere reduction to dramatic shape, at least when the dramatiser is so consummate a playwright as Shakespeare. And it is very interesting to observe the instinctive skill with which he throws narrated episodes, like that of the death of Cassius, into the form of dialogues and scenes. But the dramatisation involves a great deal more than this. Shakespeare has to fix on what he regards as the critical points in the continuous story, to rearrange round them what else he considers of grand importance, and to bridge in some way the gaps between. These were prime essentials in all his English historical pieces. The pregnant moments have to be selected; and become so many ganglia, in which a number of filaments chronologically distinct are gathered up; yet they have to be exhibited not in isolation, but as connected with each other, and all belonging to one system. And in *Julius Caesar* this is the more noticeable, as it makes use of more sources than one. The main authority is the *Life of Brutus*, but the *Life of Caesar* also is employed very freely, and the *Life of Antony* to some extent. The scope and need for insight in this portion of the task are therefore proportionately great.

Thus the opening scene refers to Caesar's defeat of the sons of Pompey in Spain, for which he celebrated his triumph in October, 45 B.C. But Shakespeare dates it on the 15th February, 44 B.C., at the Lupercalian Festival.[1] Then, in the account of Caesar's chagrin at his reception, he mixes up, as Plutarch himself to some extent does, two quite distinct episodes, one of which does not belong to the Lupercalia at all.[2] Lastly, it was only later that the Tribunes were silenced and deprived of their offices for stripping the images, not of Caesar's "trophies," but of "diadems,"[3] or, more specifically, of the "laurel crown"[4] Antony had offered him.

The next group of events is clustered round the assassination, and they begin on the eve of the Ides, the 14th March. But at first we are not allowed to feel that a month has passed. By various artifices the flight of time is kept from obtruding itself. The position of the scene with the storm, which ushers in this part of the story, as the last of the first act instead of the first of the second, of itself associates it in our minds with what has gone before. Then

[1] Possibly he may have found a suggestion for this in Plutarch's expression that at the Lupercalia, Caesar was "apparelled in a triumphant manner" (*Julius Caesar*); or, more definitely "apparelled in his triumphing robe" (*Marcus Antonius*).

[2] In the *Julius Caesar* it is at an interview with the Senate in the market place that Caesar, in his vexation, bares his neck to the blow, and afterwards pleads his infirmity in excuse ; and nothing of the kind is recorded in connection with the offer of the crown at the Lupercalia. In the *Marcus Antonius* the undignified exhibition, as Plutarch regards it, is referred to the Lupercalia, and the previous incident is not mentioned.

[3] *Julius Caesar.*   [4] *Marcus Antonius.*

there are several little hints that we involuntarily
expand in the same sense.   Thus Cassius has just
said :

> I will this night,
> In several hands, in at his windows throw,
> As if they came from several citizens,
> Writings all tending to the great opinion
> That Rome holds of his name ; wherein obscurely
> Caesar's ambition shall be glanced at.   (I. ii. 319.)

And now we hear him say :

> Good Cinna, take this paper,
> And look you lay it in the praetor's chair,
> Where Brutus may but find it : and throw this
> In at his window ; set this up with wax
> Upon old Brutus' statue.   (I. iii. 142.)

We seem to see him carrying out the programme
that he has announced for the night of the Lupercalia.   Yet there are other hints,—the frequency with
which Brutus has received these instigations (II. i.
49), his protracted uncertainty since Cassius first
sounded him (II. i. 61), the fact that he himself has
had time to approach Ligarius,—which presently
make us realise that the opening scenes of the drama
are left a long way behind.

And in this section, too, Shakespeare has crowded
his incidents.   The decisive arrangements of the
conspirators, with their rejection of the oath, are dated
the night before the assassination ; Plutarch puts
them earlier.   Then, according to Plutarch, there was
a senate meeting the morning after Caesar's murder ;
and Antony, having escaped in slave's apparel,
proposed an amnesty for the perpetrators, offered his
son as hostage, and persuaded them to leave the
Capitol.   On the following day dignities were distributed among the ringleaders and a public funeral
was decreed to Caesar.   Only then did the reading
of the will, the speech of Antony, and the *émeute*
of the people follow, and the reading of the will

H

preceded the speech.   After a while Octavius comes
from Apollonia to see about his inheritance.

In the play, on the other hand, Antony's seeming
agreement with the assassins is patched up a few
minutes after the assassination.   Octavius, summoned by the dead Caesar, is already within seven
leagues of Rome.   Antony at once proceeds with
the corpse to the market place.   He has hardly
made his speech and then read the will, when, as
the citizens rush off in fury, he learns that Octavius
has arrived.

A lengthy interval elapses between the end of
Act III. and the beginning of Act IV., occupied, so
far as Rome and Italy were concerned, with the
rivalry and intrigues of Antony and Octavius, and
the discomfiture of the former (partly through
Cicero's exertions), till he wins the army of Lepidus
and Octavius finds it expedient to join forces with
him and establish the Triumvirate.   But of all this
not a word in Shakespeare.   He dismisses it as
irrelevant, and creates an illusion of speed and con-
tinuity, where there is none.   The servant who
announces the arrival of Octavius, tells Antony :

> He and Lepidus are at Caesar's house.   (III. xi. 269.)

"Bring me to Octavius," says Antony.   And the
fourth act opens "at a house in Rome," "Antony,
Octavius and Lepidus seated at a table," just finish-
ing the lists of the proscription.   The impression
produced is that their conference is direct sequel to
the popular outbreak and the conspirators' flight.
Yet it is November, 43 B.C., and nineteen or twenty
months have gone by since the Ides of March.
And the progress of time is indicated as well as
concealed.   Antony announces as a new and alarm-
ing piece of news

> And now, Octavius,
> Listen great things :—Brutus and Cassius
> Are levying powers.   (IV. i. 40.)

This too covers a gap in the history and hurries on the connection. The suggestion is that they are beginning operations at last, and that hitherto they have been inactive. Their various intermediate adventures and wanderings are passed over. We are carried forward to their grand effort, and are reintroduced to them only when they meet again at Sardis in the beginning of 42 B.C., just before the final movement to Philippi, where the battle was fought in October of the same year.

And this scene also is "compounded of many simples." The dispute which the poet[1] interrupts, the difference of opinion about Pella, the appearance of the Spirit, are all located at Sardis by Plutarch, but he separates them from each other ; the news of Portia's death is undated, the quarrel about money matters took place at Smyrna, and other traits are derived from various quarters. Here they are all made

> To join like likes, and kiss like native things.

Then at Philippi itself, not only are some of the speeches transferred from the eve to the day of the engagement ; but a whole series of operations, and two pitched battles, twenty days apart, after the first of which Cassius, and after the second of which Brutus, committed suicide, are pressed into a few hours.

It will thus be seen that though the action is spread over a period of three years, from the triumphal entry of Caesar in October, 45 B.C., till the victory of his avengers in October, 42 B.C., Shakespeare concentrates it into the story of five eventful days, which however do not correspond to the five separate acts, but by "overlapping" and other contrivances produce the effect of close sequence,

---

[1] In the *Lives* Faonius or Phaonius, properly Favonius, a follower of Cato. (*Marcus Brutus.*)

while in point of fact, historically, they are not consecutive at all.

In the first day there is the exposition, enforcing the predominance of Caesar and the revulsion against it (Act i. i. and ii.) ; assigned to the 15th February, 44 B.C.

In the second day there is the assassination with its immediate preliminaries and sequels (Act i. iii., Act ii., Act iii.) all compressed within the twenty-four hours allowed to a French tragedy, viz. within the interval between the night before the Ides of March and the next afternoon or evening.[1]

In the third day there is the account of the Proscription in November, 43 B.C. (Act iv. i.). In the fourth day the meeting of Brutus and Cassius, which took place early in 42 B.C., and the apparition of the boding spirit, are described (Act iv. ii. and iii.). Both these days are included in one act.

The fifth day is devoted to the final battle and its accessories, and must be placed in October, 42 B.C. (Act v.).

But the selection, assortment and filiation of the *data* are not more conspicuous in the construction of the plot than in the execution of the details. There will be frequent occasion to touch incidentally on these and similar processes in the discussion of other matters, but here it may be well to illustrate them separately, so far as that is possible when nearly every particular instance shows the influence of more than one of them.

Thus while Shakespeare's picture of the very perfect union of Brutus and Portia is taken almost in its entirety from Plutarch, who was himself so keenly alive to the beauty of such a wedlock, the charm of

[1] Cassius says at the end of the long opening scene of the series : " It is after midnight " (Act i. iii. 163). In the last scene of the group, Cinna, on his way to Caesar's funeral, is murdered by the rioters apparently just after they have left Antony.

the traits he adopts is heightened by the absence of
those he rejects.   Probably indeed he did not know,
for Plutarch does not mention it, that Brutus had
been married before, and had got rid of his first wife
by the simple and regular expedient of sending her
home to her father.   But he did know that Portia,
too, had a first husband, Bibulus, "by whom she
had also a young sonne."   The ideal beauty of their
relation is unbrushed by any hint of their previous
alliances.

So, too, he attributes the coolness between Brutus
and Cassius at the beginning of the story merely to
Brutus' inward conflicts, and to Cassius' miscon-
struction of his pre-occupation.   In point of fact,
it had a more definite and less creditable cause.
According to Plutarch, they had both been strenuous
rivals for the position of City Praetor, Brutus recommended by his "vertue and good name," Cassius
by his "many noble exploytes" against the Parthians.
Caesar, saying "Cassius cause is juster, but Brutus
must be first preferred," had given Brutus the chief
dignity and Cassius the second: therefore "they grew
straunge together for the sute they had for the prae-
torshippe."   But it would not answer Shakespeare's
purpose to show Brutus as moved by personal ambitions, or either of them as aspiring for honours that
Caesar could grant.

There are few better examples of the way in which
Shakespeare rearranges his material than the employment he makes of Plutarch's enumeration of the
portents that preceded the assassination.   It is given
as immediate preface to the catastrophe of the Ides.

Certainly, destenie may easier be foreseene then avoyded;
considering the straunge and wonderfull signes that were
sayd to be seene before Caesars death.   For touching the
fires in the element, and spirites running up and downe in the
night, and also these solitarie birdes to be seene at noone
dayes sitting in the great market place: are not all these
signes perhappes worth the noting in such a wonderfull

chaunce as happened?   But Strabo the Philosopher wryteth, that divers men were seene going up and downe in fire : and furthermore, that there was a slave of the souldiers, that did cast a marvelous burning flame out of his hande, insomuch as they that saw it, thought he had been burnt, but when the fire was out, it was found he had no hurt.   Caesar selfe also doing sacrifice unto the Goddes, found that one of the beastes which was sacrificed had no hart : and that was a straunge thing in nature, how a beast could live without a hart. Furthermore, there was a certain soothsayer that had geven Caesar warning long time affore, to take heede of the day of the Ides of Marche (which is the fifteenth of the moneth), for on that day he should be in great daunger.   That day being come, Caesar going into the Senate house, and speaking merily to the Soothsayer, tolde him, ‘ The Ides of Marche be come ’ :   ‘ So be they ’, softly aunswered the Soothsayer, ‘ but yet are they not past.’   And the very day before, Caesar supping with Marcus Lepidus, sealed certaine letters as he was wont to do at the bord : so talke falling out amongst them, reasoning what death was best : he preventing their opinions, cried out alowde, ‘ Death unlooked for.’   Then going to bedde the same night as his manner was, and lying with his wife Calpurnia, all the windowes and dores of his chamber flying open, the noyse awooke him, and made him affrayed when he saw such light : but more when he heard his wife Calpurnia, being fast a sleepe weepe and sigh, and put forth many fumbling and lamentable speaches.   For she dreamed that Caesar was slaine, and that she had him in her armes. [1]

It is interesting to note how Shakespeare takes this passage to pieces and assigns those of them for which he has a place to their fitting and effective position.   Plutarch’s reflections on destiny and Caesar’s opinions on death he leaves aside.   The first warning of the soothsayer he refers back to the Lupercalia, and the second he shifts forward to its natural place.   Calpurnia’s outcries in her sleep and her prophetic dream, the apparition of the ghosts mentioned by her among the other prodigies, the lack of the heart in the sacrificial beast, are reserved for the scene of her expostulation with Caesar, and are dramatically distributed between the various

[1] *Julius Caesar.*

speakers, Caesar, the servant, Calpurnia herself.
Shakespeare relies on the fiery heavens and the fire-
girt shapes, the flaming hand and the boding bird
for his grand effect, and puts them in a setting where
they gain unspeakably in supernatural awe. Of
course Shakespeare individualises Plutarch's hints
and adds new touches. But the main terror is due
to something else. We are made to view these portents in the reflex light of Casca's panic. He has
just witnessed them, or believes that he has done so,
and now breathless, staring, his naked sword in his
hand, the storm raging around, he gasps out his
amazement at Cicero's composure :

> Are not you moved, when all the sway of earth
> Shakes like a thing unfirm? O Cicero,
> I have seen tempests, when the scolding winds
> Have rived the knotty oaks, and I have seen
> The ambitious ocean swell and rage and foam,
> To be exalted with the threatening clouds :
> But never till to-night, never till now,
> Did I go through a tempest dropping fire.
> Either there is a civil strife in heaven,
> Or else the world, too saucy with the gods,
> Incenses them to send destruction.
>   *Cicero.* Why, saw you anything more wonderful?
>   *Casca.* A common slave—you know him well by sight—
> Held up his left hand, which did flame and burn
> Like twenty torches join'd, and yet his hand,
> Not sensible of fire, remain'd unscorch'd.
> Besides,—I ha' not since put up my sword—
> Against the Capitol I met a lion,
> Who glared upon me, and went surly by,
> Without annoying me : and there were drawn
> Upon a heap a hundred ghastly women,
> Transformed with their fear ; who swore they saw
> Men all in fire walk up and down the streets.
> And yesterday the bird of night did sit
> Even at noon-day upon the market place
> Hooting and shrieking. When these prodigies
> Do so conjointly meet, let not men say,
> 'These are their reasons : they are natural' :
> For, I believe, they are portentous things
> Unto the climate that they point upon.   (I. iii. 3.)

Here the superstitious thrill rises to a paroxysm of dread ; but the effect of dispersing the subsidiary presages through so many scenes is to steep the whole play in an atmosphere of weird presentiment, till Caesar passes up to the very doors of the Capitol.

But besides selecting and rearranging the separate details, Shakespeare establishes an inner connection between them even when in Plutarch they are quite isolated from each other. This is well exemplified by the manner in which the biography and the drama treat the circumstance that the conspirators were not sworn to secrecy. Plutarch says :

> The onlie name and great calling of Brutus did bring on the most of them to geve consent to this conspiracie. Who having never taken othes together, nor taken or geven any caution or assurance, nor binding them selves one to an other by any religious othes, they all kept the matter so secret to them selves, and could so cunninglie handle it, that notwithstanding the goddes did reveal it by manifeste signes and tokens from above, and by predictions of sacrifices, yet all this would not be believed. (*Marcus Brutus.*)

The drama puts it thus :

> *Brutus.* Give me your hands all over, one by one.
> *Cassius.* And let us swear our resolution.
> *Brutus.* No, not an oath : if not the face of men
> The suffrance of our souls, the time's abuse,
> If these be motives weak, break off betimes : (II. i. 112.)

and so on through the rest of his magnificent speech that breathes the pure spirit of virtue and conviction. The nobility of Brutus that is reverenced by all, the conspiracy of Romans that is safe-guarded by no vows, move Plutarch's admiration, but he does not associate them. Shakespeare traces the one to the other and views them as cause and effect.

Shakespeare thus greatly alters the character of Plutarch's narrative by his ceaseless activity in sifting it, ordering it afresh, and reading into it an

internal nexus that was often lacking in his authority.
But this last proceeding implies that he also makes
additions, and these are not only numerous and
manifold, but frequently quite explicit and very
far-reaching. It is important to note that Plutarch
has furnished nothing more than stray hints, and
often not even so much, for all the longer passages
that have impressed themselves on the popular
imagination. Cassius' description of the swimming
match and of Caesar's fever, Brutus' soliloquy, his
speech on the oath, his oration and that of Mark
Antony, even, when regarded closely, his dispute
with Cassius, are all virtually the inventions of
Shakespeare. The only exception is the conversation with Portia, and even in it, though the climax,
as we have seen, closely reproduces both Plutarch's
matter and North's expression, the fine introduction
is altogether Shakespearian.

But it is not the purple patches alone of which
this is true. The more carefully one examines the
finished fabric, the more clearly one sees that the
dramatist has not merely woven and fashioned and
embroidered it, but has provided most of the stuff.

Sometimes the new matter is a possible or
plausible inference from the premises he found in
his author.

Thus Plutarch represents the populace as on the
whole favourable to Caesar, but the tribunes as
antagonistic. He also records, concerning the celebration of Caesar's victory over Pompey's sons in
Spain :

> The triumph he made into Rome for the same did as
> much offend the Romanes, and more, then anything he had
> ever done before ; bicause he had not overcome Captaines
> that were straungers, nor barbarous kinges, but had destroyed
> the sonnes of the noblest man in Rome, whom fortune had
> overthrown. And bicause he had plucked up his race by
> the rootes men did not thinke it meete for him to triumphe
> so for the calamaties of his contrie. (*Julius Caesar.*)

This is all, but it is enough to give the foundation for the opening scene, which otherwise, both in dialogue and declamation, is an entirely free creation.

Sometimes again Shakespeare has realised the situation so vividly that he puts in some trait from the occurrences as in spirit he has witnessed them, something of the kind that may very well have happened, though there is no trace of it in the records. Thus he well knows what an unreasonable monster a street mob can be, how cruel in its gambols, how savage in its fun So in the account of the poet Cinna's end, though the gist of the incident, the mistake in identity, the disregard of the explanation, are all given in Plutarch, Shakespeare's rioters wrest their victim's innocent avowal of celibacy to a flout at marriage, and meet his unanswerable defence, "I am Cinna the poet," with the equally unanswerable retort, "Tear him for his bad verses." (III. iii. 23.)

Some of these new touches do more than lend reality to the scene. Though not incompatible with Plutarch's account, they give it a turn that he might disclaim and certainly does not warrant, but that belongs to Shakespeare's conception of the case. Thus after describing the "holy course" of the Lupercal, and the superstition connected with it, Plutarch mentions that Caesar sat in state to witness the sport, and that Antony was one of the runners. There is nothing more ; and Calpurnia is not even named. Shakespeare's introduction of her is therefore very curious. Whatever else it means, it shows that he imagined Caesar as desirous, certainly, of having an heir, and, inferentially, of founding a dynasty.[1]

Occasionally, however, the dramatist's insertions directly contradict the text of the *Lives*, if a more striking or more significant effect is to be attained,

[1] Genée, *Shakespeare's Leben und Werke.*

and if no essential fact is falsified. Thus Plutarch tells of Ligarius :

> [Brutus] went to see him being sicke in his bedde, and sayed unto him : " O Ligarius, in what a time art thou sicke ! " Ligarius risinge uppe in his bedde and taking him by the right hande, sayed unto him : "Brutus," sayed he, "if thou hast any great enterprise in hande worthie of thy selfe, I am whole." *(Marcus Brutus.)*

Shakespeare, keeping the phrases quoted almost literally, emphasises the effort that Ligarius makes, emphasises too the magnetic influence of Brutus, by representing the sick man as coming to his friend's house, as well as by amplifying his words :

> *Lucius.* Here is a sick man that would speak with you. . .
> *Brutus.* O, what a time have you chose out, brave Caius,
> To wear a kerchief ! Would you were not sick !
> *Ligarius.* I am not sick, if Brutus have in hand
> Any exploit worthy the name of honour . . .
> By all the gods that Romans bow before
> I here discard my sickness ! Soul of Rome !
> Brave son, derived from honourable loins !
> Thou, like an exorcist, hast conjured up
> My mortified spirit. Now bid me run,
> And I will strive with things impossible ;
> Yea, get the better of them. . . .
> . . . With a heart new-fired I follow you,
> To do I know not what : but it sufficeth
> That Brutus leads me on. (II. i. 310.)

So too Plutarch describes the collapse of Portia in her suspense as more complete than does the play, and makes Brutus hear of it just after the critical moment when the conspirators fear that Lena has discovered their plot :

> Nowe in the meane time, there came one of Brutus men post hast unto him, and tolde him his wife was a dying. . . . When Brutus heard these newes, it grieved him, as is to be presupposed : yet he left not of the care of his contrie and common wealth, neither went home to his house for any newes he heard.

In Shakespeare not only is this very effective dramatic touch omitted, but Portia sends Brutus an encouraging message. As her weakness increases upon her, she collects herself for a final effort and manages to give the command :

> Run, Lucius, and commend me to my lord :
> *Say, I am merry* : come to me again
> And bring me word what he doth say to thee.   (II. iv. 44.)

Shakespeare may perhaps have been unwilling to introduce anything into the assassination scene that might distract attention from the decisive business on hand, but the alteration is chiefly due to another cause.   These, the last words we hear Portia utter, were no doubt intended to bring out her forgetfulness of herself and her thought of Brutus even in the climax of her physical distress.

This, of course, does not affect our general estimate of Portia ; but Shakespeare has no scruple about creating an entirely new character for a minor personage, and, in the process, disregarding the hints that he found and asserting quite the reverse.   Thus Plutarch has not much to say about Casca, so Shakespeare feels free to sketch him after his own fancy as rude, blunt, uncultured, with so little education that, when Cicero speaks Greek, it is Greek to him.   This is a libel on his up-bringing.   Plutarch in one of the few details he spares to him, mentions that, when he stabbed Caesar, "they both cried out, Caesar in Latin, 'O vile traitor, Casca, what doest thou?' and Casca in Greek to his brother: 'Brother, helpe me.'"

But some of Shakespeare's interpolations are, probably unawares to himself, of a vital and radical kind, and affect the conception of the chief characters and the whole idea of the story.   Take, for example, Brutus' soliloquy, as he rids himself of his hesitations and scruples.   This, from beginning to end, is the handiwork of Shakespeare :

> It must be by his death : and, for my part
> I know no personal cause to spurn at him,

But for the general.   He would be crown'd :
How that might change his nature, that's the question.
It is the bright day that brings forth the adder,
And that craves wary walking.   Crown him ?—that :—
And then, I grant, we put a sting in him,
That at his will he may do danger with.
The abuse of greatness is, when it disjoins
Remorse from power : and, to speak truth of Caesar,
I have not known when his affections sway'd
More than his reason.   But 'tis a common proof
That lowliness is young ambition's ladder,
Whereto the climber upward turns his face :
But when he once attains the topmost round,
He then unto the ladder turns his back,
Looks in the clouds, scorning the base degrees
By which he did ascend.   So Caesar may ;
Then lest he may, prevent.   And, since the quarrel
Will bear no colour for the thing he is,
Fashion it thus ; that what he is, augmented,
Would run to these and these extremities :
And therefore think him as a serpent's egg,
Which, hatch'd, would as his kind, grow mischievous,
And kill him in the shell.   (II. i. 10.)

These words are so unlike, or, rather, so opposite
to all that we should have expected, that Coleridge
cannot repress his amazement.   He comments :

> This speech is singular :—at least, I do not at present see
> into Shakespeare's motive, his *rationale*, or in what point of
> view he meant Brutus' character to appear.   For surely . . .
> nothing can seem more discordant with our historical pre-
> conceptions of Brutus, or more lowering to the intellect of
> the Stoico-Platonic tyrannicide, than the tenets here attributed
> to him—to him, the stern Roman republican ; namely,—that
> he would have no objection to a king, or to Caesar, a
> monarch in Rome, would Caesar but be as good a monarch as
> he now seems disposed to be.   (*Lectures and Notes of* 1818.)

And this in a way is the crucial statement of Brutus'
case.   Here he has tried to get rid of the assumptions
that move himself and the rest, and seeks to find
something that will satisfy his reason.   It is thus a
more intimate revelation of his deliberate principles,
though not necessarily of his subconscious instincts
or his untested opinions, than other utterances in

which he lets feeling or circumstance have sway. Of these there are two that do not quite coincide with it. One of them is not very important, and in any case would not bring him nearer to the antique conception. In his plea for a pure administration of affairs, he asks Cassius :

> What, shall one of us,
> That struck the foremost man of all this world
> But for supporting robbers, shall we now
> Contaminate our fingers with base bribes ?   (IV. iii. 21.)

But this, one feels, is merely an *argumentum ad hominem*, brought forward very much in after-thought for a particular purpose. At the time, neither in Brutus' speeches to himself or others, nor in the discussions of the conspirators, is Caesar accused of countenancing peculation, or is this made a handle against him. And if it were, it would not be incompatible with acquiescence in a royal government.[1]

[1] On this passage Coleridge has the note : " This seemingly strange assertion of Brutus is unhappily verified in the present day. What is an immense army, in which the lust of plunder has quenched all the duties of the citizen, other than a horde of robbers, or differenced only as fiends from ordinarily reprobate men ? Caesar supported, and was supported by, such as these ;—and even so Buonaparte in our days." On this interpretation Brutus' charge would come to nothing more than this, that Caesar had employed large armies. I believe there is a more definite reference to one passage or possibly two in the *Marcus Antonius*.

" (a) Caesar's friends that governed under him, were cause why they hated Caesars government . . . by reason of the great insolencies and outragious parts that were committed : amongst whom Antonius, that was of greatest power, and that also committed greatest faultes, deserved most blame. But Caesar, notwithstanding, when he returned from the warres of Spayne, made no reckoning of the complaints that were put up against him : but contrarily, bicause he found him a hardy man, and a valliant Captaine, he employed him in his chiefest affayres.

" (b) Now it greved men much, to see that Caesar should be out of Italy following of his enemies, to end this great warre, with such great perill and daunger : and that others in the meane time abusing his name and authoritie, should commit such insolent and outragious parts unto their citizens. This me thinkes was the cause that made the conspiracie against Caesar increase more and more, and layed the reynes of the brydle upon the souldiers

The other is the exclamation with which he "pieces out" the anonymous letter that Cassius had left unfinished :

Shall Rome stand under one man's awe?   What, Rome?
(II. i. 52.)

This certainly has somewhat of the republican ring. It breathes the same spirit as Cassius' own avowal :

I had as lief not be, as live to be
In awe of such a thing as I myself;   (I. ii. 95.)

except that Cassius feels Caesar's predominance to be a personal affront, while Brutus characteristically extends his view to the whole community. But here Brutus is speaking under the excitement of Cassius' "instigation," and making himself Cassius' mouthpiece to fill in the blanks. Assuredly the declaration is not on that account the less personal to himself; nevertheless in it Brutus, no longer attempting to square his action with his theory, falls back on the blind impulses of blood that he shares with the other aristocrats of Rome. And in this, the most republican and the only republican sentiment that falls from his lips, which for the rest is so little republican that it might be echoed by the loyal subject of a limited monarchy, it is only the negative aspect of the matter and the public *amour propre* that are considered. Of the positive essence of republicanism, of enthusiasm for a state in which all the lawful authority is derived from the whole body of fully qualified citizens, there is, despite Brutus' talk of freemen and slaves and Caesar's ambition, no trace whatever in any of his utterances from first to last. It has been said that Plutarch's Brutus could live nowhere but in a self-governing common-

neckes, whereby they durst boldlier commit many extorsions, cruelties, and robberies."
Plutarch is speaking of Antony in particular, but surely this is the sort of thing that was in Shakespeare's mind.

wealth ; Shakespeare's Brutus would be quite at
home under a constitutional king and need not have
found life intolerable even in Tudor England. This
indeed is an exaggeration. True, in his soliloquy
he bases his whole case on the deterioration of
Caesar's nature that kingship might bring about ;
and if it were proved, as it easily could be from
instances like that of Numa, which Shakespeare and
therefore Shakespeare's Brutus knew, that no such
result need follow, his entire sorites would seem to
snap. But though the form of his reflection is
hypothetical and the hypothesis will not hold, the
substance is categorical enough. Brutus has such
inbred detestation of the royal power that practically
he assumes it must beyond question be mischievous
in its moral effects. This, however, is no reasoned
conviction, though it is the starting-point for what
he means to be a dispassionate argument, but a
dogma of traditional passion. And even were it
granted it would not make Brutus a true representative of classic republicanism. Shakespeare has
so little comprehension of the antique point of view
that to him a thoughtful and public-spirited citizen
can find a rational apology for violent measures only
by looking at Caesar's future and not at all by
looking at Caesar's past. This Elizabethan Brutus
sees nothing to blame in Caesar's previous career.
He has not known "when his affections (*i.e.*
passions) sway'd more than his reason," and implies
that he has not hitherto disjoined "remorse (*i.e.*
scrupulousness) from power." Yet as Coleridge
pertinently asks, was there nothing "in Caesar's
past conduct as a man" to call for Brutus' censure ?
"Had he not passed the Rubicon," and the like?
But such incidents receive no attention. Perhaps
Shakespeare thought no more of Caesar's crossing
the Rubicon to suppress Pompey and put an end to
the disorders of Rome, than of Richmond's crossing

the Channel to suppress Richard III., and put end to the Wars of the Roses. At any rate he makes no mention of these and similar grounds of offence, though all or most of them were set down in his authority.[1]

Shakespeare's position may be thus described. He read in Plutarch that Brutus, the virtuous Roman, killed Caesar, the master-spirit of his own and perhaps of any age, from a disinterested sense of duty. That was easy to understand, for Shakespeare would know, and if he did not know it from his own experience his well-conned translation of Montaigne would teach him, that the best of men are determined in their feeling of right by the preconceptions of race, class, education and the like. But he also read that Brutus was a philosophic student who would not accept or obey the current code without scrutinising it and fitting it into his theory. Of the political theory, however, which such an one would have, Shakespeare had no knowledge or appreciation. So whenever Brutus tries to harmonise his purpose with his idealist doctrine, he has to be furnished with new reasons instead of the old and obvious ones. And these are neither very clear nor very antique. They make one

[1] Coleridge's exact words, in continuation of the passage already discussed may be quoted. "How too could Brutus say that he found no personal cause, none in Caesar's past conduct as a man? Had he not passed the Rubicon? Had he not entered Rome as a conqueror? Had he not placed his Gauls in the Senate?—Shakespeare, it may be said, has not brought these things forward.—True ;—and this is just the cause of my perplexity. What character did Shakespeare mean his Brutus to be?"

The verbal answer to this is of course that *personal cause* refers not to Caesar but to Brutus, and means that Brutus has no private grievance ; but the substance of Coleridge's objection remains unaffected, for Brutus proceeds to take Caesar's character up to the present time under his protection.

It may be noted, however, that Plutarch says nothing about the Gauls. If Shakespeare had known of it, it would probably have seemed to him no worse than the presence of the Bretons, "those overweening rags of France," as Richard III. calls them, in the army of the patriotic and virtuous Richmond.

inclined to quote concerning him the words of Caesar spoken to Cicero in regard to the historical Brutus :

> I knowe not what this young man woulde, but what he woulde he willeth it vehemently. (*Marcus Brutus.*)

For what is it that he would ? The one argument with which he can excuse to his own heart the projected murder, is that the aspirant to royal power, though hitherto irreproachable, may or must become corrupted and misuse his high position. This is as different from the attitude of the ancient Roman as it well could be. It would never have occurred to the genuine republican of olden time that any justification was needed for despatching a man who sought to usurp the sovereign place ; and if it had, this is certainly the last justification that would have entered his head.

But the introspection, the self-examination, the craving for an inward moral sanction that will satisfy the conscience, and the choice of the particular sanction that does so, are as typical of the modern as they are alien to the classical mind. It is clear that an addition of this kind is not merely mechanical or superficial. It affects the elements already given, and produces, as it were, a new chemical combination. And this particular instance shows how Shakespeare transforms the whole story. He reanimates Brutus by infusing into his veins a strain of present feeling that in some ways transmutes his character ; and, transmuting the character in which the chief interest centres, he cannot leave the other *data* as they were. He can resuscitate the past in its persons, its conflicts, its palpitating vitality just because he endows it with his own life. It was an ancient belief that the shades of the departed were inarticulate or dumb till they had lapped a libation of warm blood ; then they would

speak forth their secrets. In like manner it is the
life-blood of Shakespeare's own passion and thought
that throbs in the pulses of these unsubstantial dead
and gives them human utterance once more. This,
however, has two aspects. It is the dead who
speak ; but they speak through the life that Shakespeare has lent them. The past is resuscitated; but
it is a resuscitation, not the literal existence it had
before. Nor in any other way can the phantoms of
history win bodily shape and perceptible motion for
the world of breathing men.

This may be illustrated by comparing Shakespeare's *Julius Caesar* with the *Julius Caesar* of
Sir William Alexander, afterwards Earl of Stirling,
which seems to have been written a few years later
than its more illustrious namesake. Alexander was
an able man and a considerable poet, from whom
Shakespeare himself did not disdain to borrow hints
for Prospero's famous reflections on the transitori-
ness of things. He used virtually the same sources
as Shakespeare, like him making Plutarch his chief
authority, and to supplement Plutarch, betaking
himself, as Shakespeare may also have done, to the
tradition set in France by Muretus, Grévin, and
Garnier. So they build on much the same sites
and with much the same timber. But their methods
are as different as can well be imagined. Alexander
is by far the more scrupulous in his reproduction of
the old-world record. He adopts the Senecan type
of tragedy, exaggerating its indifference to movement and fondness for lengthy harangues ; and this
enables him to preserve much of the narrative in its
original form without thorough reduction to the
category of action. This also in large measure
exempts him from the need of reorganising his
material : practically a single situation is given, and
whatever else of the story is required, has to be
conveyed in the words of the persons, who can

repeat things just as they have been reported. And
proceeding in this way Alexander can include as
much as he pleases of Plutarch's abundance, a privilege of which he avails himself to the utmost. Few
are the details that he must absolutely reject, for
they can always be put in somebody's mouth ; he is
slow to tamper with Plutarch's location of them ; and
he never connects them more closely than Plutarch
has authorised. He does not extract from his docu-
ment inferences that have not already been drawn,
nor falsify it with picturesque touches that have not
been already supplied, and he would not dream of
contradicting it in small things or great. Even
Brutus' republicanism is sacred to the author of this
" Monarchic Tragedy," though he was to be Secretary
of State to Charles I. and noted for his advocacy of
Divine Right. He has a convenient theory to justify
Brutus as much as is necessary from his point of
view. He makes him explain :

> If Caesar had been born or chused our prince
> Then those, who durst attempt to take his life,
> The world of treason justly might convince.
> Let still the states, which flourish for the time,
> By subjects be inviolable thought :
> And those (no doubt) commit a monstrous crime,
> Who lawfull soveraignty prophane in ought :
> And we must think (though now thus brought to bow)
> The senate, king ; a subject Caesar is :
> The soveraignty whom violating now
> The world must damne, as having done amisse.

Brutus' motives, which Shakespeare sophisticates,
can thus be left him. But does this bit of reasoning,
which reads like a passage from the *Leviathan*, and
explains why King James called Alexander " My
philosophical poet," really come nearer the historic
truth than the heart - searching of Shakespeare's
Brutus ? And does Alexander, taking Brutus' convictions at second hand and manufacturing an apology
for them, do much more to revive the real Brutus,

than Shakespeare, whose fervid imagination drives
him to realise Brutus' inmost heart, and who just
for that reason

> seeks into him
> For that which is not in him?

Here and generally Alexander gives the exacter,
if not the more faithful transcript, but the main
truth, the truth of life, escapes him ; and therefore,
too, despite all his painstaking fidelity, he is apt to
miss even the vital touches that Plutarch gives.
We have seen with what reverent accuracy Shakespeare reproduces the conversation between Brutus
and Portia. In a certain way Alexander is more
accurate still. Portia pleads :

> I was not (Brutus) match'd with thee to be
> A partner onely of thy boord and bed ;
> Each servile whore in those might equall me,
> Who but for pleasure or for wealth did wed.
> No, Portia spoused thee minding to remaine
> Thy fortunes partner, whether good or ill : . . .
> If thus thou seek thy sorrows to conceale
> Through a distrust, or a mistrust of me,
> Then to the world what way can I reveale,
> How great a matter I would do for thee?
> And though our sexe too talkative be deem'd,
> As those whose tongues import our greatest pow'rs,
> For secrets still bad treasurers esteem'd,
> Of others greedy, prodigall of ours :
> "Good education may reforme defects,"
> And this may leade me to a vertuous life,
> (Whil'st such rare patterns generous worth respects)
> I Cato's daughter am, and Brutus wife.
> Yet would I not repose my trust in ought,
> Still thinking that thy crosse was great to beare,
> Till I my courage to a tryall brought,
> Which suffering for thy cause can nothing feare :
> For first to try how that I could comport
> With sterne afflictions sprit-enfeebling blows,
> Ere I would seek to vex thee in this sort,
> (To whom my soule a dutious reverence owes) ;
> Loe, here a wound which makes me not to smart,
> No, I rejoyce that thus my strength is knowne ;
> Since thy distresse strikes deeper in my heart,
> Thy griefe (lifes joy !) makes me neglect mine owne.

And Brutus answers :

> Thou must (deare love !) that which thou sought'st, receive ;
> Thy heart so high a saile in stormes still beares,
> That thy great courage does deserve to have
> Our enterprise entrusted to thine eares.

Here, with the rhetorical amplification which was the chief and almost sole liberty that Alexander allowed himself, Plutarch's train of thought is more closely followed than by Shakespeare himself. King James's " philosophical poet " does not even suppress the tribute to education, but rather calls attention to the edifying "sentence" by the expedient less common west of the Channel than among his French masters, of placing it within inverted commas.　But, besides lowering the temperature of the whole, he characteristically omits the most important passage, at least in so far as Brutus is concerned, his prayer that " he might be founde a husband, worthie of so noble a wife as Porcia."

Suppose that a conscientious draughtsman and a painter of genius were moved to reproduce the impression that a group of antique statuary had made on them, using the level surface which alone is at their disposal.　The one might choose his station, and set down with all possible precision in his black and white as much as was given him to see.　The other taking into account the different conditions of the pictorial and the plastic art, might visualise what seemed to him the inmost meaning to his own mind in his own way, and represent it, the same yet not the same, in all the glory of colour.　The former would deliver a version more useful to the historian of sculpture were the original to be lost, but one in which we should miss many beauties of detail, and from which the indwelling spirit would have fled. The latter would not give much help to an antiquarian knowledge of the archetype, but he might transmit its inspiration, and rouse kindred feelings in an even greater degree just because they were mingled with others that came from his own heart.

The analogy is, of course, an imperfect one, for the problem of rendering the solid on the flat is not on all fours with the problem of converting Plutarch's *Lives* to modern plays. But it applies to this extent, that in both cases the task is to interpret a subject, that has received one kind of treatment, by a treatment that is quite dissimilar. And the difference between William Alexander and William Shakespeare is very much the difference between the conscientious draughtsman and the inspired artist.

CHAPTER III

THE TITULAR HERO OF THE PLAY

THE modification of Brutus' character typifies and involves the modification of the whole story, because the tragic interest is focussed in his career. This must be remembered, if we would avoid misconception. It has sometimes been said that the play suffers from lack of unity, that the titular hero is disposed of when it is half through, and that thereafter attention is diverted to the murderer. But this criticism is beside the point. Really, from beginning to end, Brutus is the prominent figure, and if the prominent figure should supply the name, then, as Voltaire pointed out, the drama ought properly to be called *Marcus Brutus*. If we look at it in this way, there is no lack of unity, though possibly there is a misnomer. Throughout the piece it is the personality of Brutus that attracts our chief sympathy and concern. If he is dismissed to a subordinate place, the result is as absurd as it would be were Hamlet thus treated in the companion tragedy; while, his position, once recognised, everything becomes coherent and clear.

But when this is the case, why should Shakespeare not say so? Why, above all, should he use a false designation to mix the trail?

It has been answered that he was wholly indifferent to labels and nomenclature, that he gives his plays somewhat irrelevant titles, such as *Twelfth Night*, or lets people christen them at their fancy, *What You Will*, or *As You Like It*. Just in the same way, as a shrewd theatrical manager with his eye on the audience, he may have turned to account the prevalent curiosity about Caesar, without inquiring too curiously whether placard and performance tallied in every respect.

And doubtless such considerations were not unknown to him. Shakespeare, as is shown by the topical allusions in which his works abound, by no means disdained the maxim that the playwright must appeal to the current interests of his public, even to those that are adventitious and superficial. At the same time, it is only his comedies, in which his whole method is less severe, that have insignificant or arbitrary titles. There is no instance of a tragedy being misnamed. On the contrary, the chief person or persons are always indicated, and in this way Shakespeare has protested in advance against the mistake of viewing *King Lear* as a whole with reference to Cordelia, or *Macbeth* as a whole with reference to Lady Macbeth.

But in the second place, *Julius Caesar*, both in its chronological position and in its essential character, comes as near to the Histories as to the Tragedies; and the Histories are all named after the sovereign in whose reign most of the events occurred. He may not have the chief role, which, for example, belongs in *King John* to the Bastard, and in *Henry IV.* to Prince Hal. He may even drop out in the course of the story, which, for example, in the latter play is continued for an entire act after the King's death : but he serves, as it were, for a landmark, to date and localise the action. It is not improbable that this was the light in which Shakespeare regarded Caesar. In those days people did not make fine distinctions. He was generally viewed as first in the regular succession of Emperors, and in so far could be considered to have held the same sort of position in Rome, as any of those who had sat on the throne of England.

But this is not all. Though it is manifest that Brutus is the principal character, the *protagonist*, the chief representative of the action, the central figure among the living agents, the interest of his career lies in its mistaken and futile opposition to Julius, to the idea of Caesarism, to what again and again, in the course of the play, is called "the spirit of Caesar." The expression is often repeated. Brutus declares the purpose of the conspirators :

> We all stand up against the spirit of Caesar ;
> And in the spirit of men there is no blood :
> O, that we then could come by Caesar's spirit,
> And not dismember Caesar. (II. i. 167.)

Antony, above the corpse, sees in prophetic anticipation,

> Caesar's spirit ranging for revenge. (III. i. 273.)

The ghost of Caesar proclaims what he is,

> Thy evil spirit, Brutus. (IV. iii. 282.)

And at the close Brutus apostrophises his dead victim :

> Thy spirit walks abroad, and turns our swords
> In our own proper entrails. (V. iii. 95.)

It is really Caesar's presence, his genius, his conception that dominates the story. Brutus is first among the struggling mortals who obey even while resisting their fate, but the fate itself is the imperialist inspiration which makes up the significance of Caesar, and the play therefore is fitly named after him.[1]

This is brought home to us in a variety of ways.

In the first place, Shakespeare makes it abundantly clear that the rule of the single master-mind is the only admissible solution for the problem of the time.

[1] See Professor Dowden, *Shakespeare's Mind and Art.*

Caesar, with his transcendent gifts, was chosen by Providence to preserve the Roman State from shipwreck, and steer it on its triumphant course ; and even if the helmsman perished, the course was set. Shakespeare was guided to this view by Plutarch. The celebrant of the life of ancient Greece was indeed very far from idealising the man who consolidated the supremacy of Rome. He records impartially and with appreciation, some of his noble traits, and without extenuation many that were not admirable. But he "honours his memory" very much "on this side idolatry," reserves his chief enthusiasm for Brutus, and never seems to take a full view of Caesar's unique greatness in the mass. None the less, he is now and again forced to admit that he was the man, and his were the methods that the emergency required. Thus talking of the bribery and violence that then prevailed in Rome he remarks :

> Men of deepe judgement and discression seeing such furie and madnes of the people, thought them selves happy if the common wealth were no worse troubled, then with the absolut state of a Monarchy and soveraine Lord to governe them. Furthermore, there were many that were not affraid to speake it openly, that there was no other help to remedy the troubles of the common wealth, but by the authority of one man only that should commaund them all.[1]

Again, commenting on the accident by which Brutus did not learn of the victory that might have averted his final defeat, he has the weighty reflection ;

> Howbeit the state of Rome (in my opinion) being now brought to that passe, that it could no more abide to be governed by many Lordes, but required one only absolute Governor: God, to prevent Brutus that it shoulde not come to his government, kept this victorie from his knowledge.[2]

And in one of those comparisons that Montaigne loved, he is more emphatic still :

> Howbeit Caesars power and government when it came to be established, did in deede much hurte at his first entrie

[1] *Julius Caesar.*   [2] *Marcus Brutus.*

and beginning unto those that did resist him: but afterwardes
unto them that being overcome had received his government.
it seemed he had rather the name and opinion[1] onely of a
tyranne, then otherwise that he was so in deed.   For there
never followed any tyrannicall nor cruell act, but contrarilie,
it seemed that he was a mercifull Phisition, whom God had
ordeyned of speciall grace to be Governor of the Empire of
Rome, and to set all thinges againe at quiet stay, the which
required the counsell and authoritie of an absolute Prince.
. . . But the fame of Julius Caesar did set up his friends
againe after his death, and was of such force, that it raised a
young stripling, Octavius Caesar, (that had no meanes nor
power of him selfe) to be one of the greatest men of Rome.[2]

On these isolated hints Shakespeare seizes.   He
amplifies them and works them out in his conception
of the situation.

The vast territory that is subject to Rome, of
which we have glimpses as it stretches north and
west to Gaul and Spain, of which we visit the
Macedonian and Asiatic provinces in the east and
south, has need of wise and steady government.
But is that to be got from the Romans?   The
plebeians are represented as fickle and violent, greedy
and irrational, the dupes of dead tradition parasites
in the living present.   They have shouted for Pompey, they strew flowers for Caesar : they can be
tickled with talk of their ancient liberties, they can be
cajoled by the tricks of shifty rhetoric : they cheer
when their favourite refuses the crown, they wish to
crown his "better parts" in his murderer : they
will not hear a word against Brutus, they rush off
to fire his house : they tear a man to pieces on
account of his name, and hold Caesar beyond parallel
on account of his bequest.

Nor are things better with the aristocrats.   Cassius,
the moving spirit of the opposition, is, at his noblest,
actuated by jealousy of greatness.   And he is not
always at his noblest.   He confesses that had he

[1] Reputation.   [2] *The comparison of Dion with Brutus.*

been in Caesar's good graces, he would have been on Caesar's side. This strain of servility is more apparent in the flatteries and officiousness of Decius and Casca. And what is its motive? Cassius seeks to win Antony by promising him an equal voice in disposing of the dignities : and he presently uses his position for extortion and the patronage of corruption. Envy, ambition, cupidity are the governing principles of the governing classes : and their enthusiasm for freedom means nothing more than an enthusiasm for prestige and influence, for the privilege of parcelling out the authority and dividing the spoils. What case have these against the Man of Destiny, whose genius has given compass, peace, and security to the Roman world? But their plea of liberty misleads the unpractical student, the worshipper of dreams, memories, and ideals, behind whose virtue they shelter their selfish aims, and whose countenance alone can make their conspiracy respectable. With his help they achieve a momentary triumph. But of course it leads not to a renovation of the republic, but to domestic confusion and to a multiplication of oppressors. So far as the populace is concerned, the removal of the master means submission to the unprincipled orator, who, with his fellow triumvirs, cheats it of its inheritance and sets about a wholesale proscription. So far as the Empire is concerned, the civil war is renewed, and the provincials are pillaged by the champions of freedom. Brutus sees too late that it is vain to strive against the "spirit of Caesar," which is bound to prevail, and which, though it may be impeded, cannot be defeated. He is ruined with the cause he espoused, and confesses fairly vanquished :

O Julius Caesar, thou art mighty yet.[1]   (v. iii. 94.)

[1] All this is so obvious that it can hardly be overlooked, yet overlooked it has been, though it has frequently been pointed out. In his not very sympathetic discussion of this play, Dr. Brandes makes the

Again, though it may seem paradoxical to say so, the all-compelling power of Caesar's ideal is indicated in the presentation of his own character. This at first sight is something of a riddle and a surprise. Shakespeare, as is shown by his many tributes elsewhere, had ample perception and appreciation of Caesar's greatness. Yet in the play called after him it almost seems as though he had a sharper eye for any of the weaknesses and foibles that Plutarch records of him, and even went about to exaggerate them and add to them.

Thus great stress is laid on his physical disabilities. When the crown is offered him, he swoons, as Casca narrates, for, as Brutus remarks, he is subject to the falling sickness. There is authority for these statements. But Cassius describes how his strength failed him in the Tiber and how he shook with fever in Spain, and both these touches are added by Shakespeare. Nor is it the malcon-

truly astounding statement : "As Shakespeare conceives the situation, the Republic which Caesar overthrew, might have continued to exist but for him, and it was a criminal act on his part to destroy it. . . . 'If we try to conceive to ourselves' wrote Mommsen in 1857, 'a London with the slave population of New Orleans, with the police of Constantinople, with the non-industrial character of modern Rome, and agitated by politics after the fashion of the Paris of 1848, we shall acquire an approximate idea of the republican glory, the departure of which Cicero and his associates in their sulky letters deplore.' Compare with this picture Shakespeare's conception of an ambitious Caesar striving to introduce monarchy into a well-ordered republican state" (Brandes, *William Shakespeare*). Of course Shakespeare had not read Mommsen or any of Mommsen's documents, save Plutarch ; and if he had, neither he nor any one else of his age, was capable of Mommsen's critical and constructive research. But considering the *data* that Plutarch delivered him he shows marvellous power in getting to the gist of the matter. I think we rise with a clearer idea, after reading him than after reading Plutarch, of the hopelessness and vanity of opposing the changes that Caesar represented, of the effeteness of the republican system ("Let him be Caesar!" cries the citizen in his strange recognition of Brutus' achievement), of the chaos that imperialism alone could reduce to rule. If Shakespeare's picture of Rome is that of "a well-ordered republican state," one wonders what the picture of a republic in decay would be. And where does Dr. Brandes find that Shakespeare viewed Caesar's enterprise as a criminal act?

tents alone who signalise such defects. Caesar
himself admits that he is deaf, though of his deafness
history knows nothing.

And not only does Shakespeare accentuate these
bodily infirmities ; he introduces them in such a way
and in such a connection that they convey an
ironical suggestion and almost make the Emperor
ridiculous. At the great moment when he is putting
by the coronet tendered him by Antony that he
may take with the more security and dignity the
crown which the Senate will vote him, precisely
then he falls down in a fit. This indeed is quasi-
historical, but the other and more striking instances
are forged in Shakespeare's smithy. It is just after
his overweening challenge to the swimming-match
that he must cry for aid : " Help me, Cassius, or I
sink " (I. ii. 3). In his fever, as Cassius maliciously
notes,

> That tongue of his that bade the Romans
> Mark him and write his speeches in their books,
> Alas, it cried ' Give me some drink, Titinius,'
> As a sick girl. (I. ii. 125.)

A pretty saying to chronicle. He says superbly to
Mark Antony, "Always I am Caesar"; and in the
very next line follows the anticlimax :

> Come on my right hand, for this ear is deaf. (I. ii. 213.)

But if his physical defects, which after all have
little to do with the real greatness of the man
save in the eyes of spiteful detractors, are thus
brought into satirical relief, much more is this the
case with his mental and moral failings, which of
course concern the heart of his character.

Already on his first appearance, we see this lord
of the world the credulous believer in magic rites.
At the Lupercal he enjoins Calpurnia to " stand
directly in Antonius' way" and Antony to touch her
in his " holy chase " (I. ii. 3 and 8), and he impresses

on Antony the observance of all the ritual : " Leave
no ceremony out " (I. ii. II).   It was not ever thus.
The time has been when he held these things at
their true value, and it is only recently, as watchful
eyes take note, that his attitude has changed.

> He is superstitious grown of late,
> Quite from the main opinion he held once
> Of fantasy, of dreams and ceremonies.   (II. i. 195.)

And this is no mere invention of the enemy.   He
does have recourse to sacrifice, he does inquire of the
priests " their opinions of success " (II. ii. 5) ; though
afterwards, on the news of the portent, he tries to
put his own interpretation on it :

> The gods do this in shame of cowardice :
> Caesar should be a beast without a heart,
> If he should stay at home to-day for fear.   (II. ii. 41.)

He is really impressed by his wife's cries in her
sleep, as appears from his words to himself, when he
has not to keep up appearances before others, but
enters, perturbed, in his nightgown, and seems urged
by his anxiety to consult the oracles.   He affects to
dismiss the signs and omens :

> These predictions
> Are to the world in general as to Caesar ;   (II. ii. 28.)

But it is clear that he attaches importance to them,
for, when Decius gives Calpurnia's dream an aus-
picious interpretation, he accepts it, and once again
changing his mind, presently resolves to set out :

> How foolish do your fears seem now, Calpurnia !
> I am ashamed I did yield to them.
> Give me my robe, for I will go.   (II. ii. 105.)

Thus we see a touch of self-deception as well as
of superstition in Caesar, and this self-deception
reappears in other more important matters.   He
affects an absolute fearlessness :

> Of all the wonders that I yet have heard,
> It seems to me most strange that men should fear.
>
> (II. ii. 33.)

His courage, of course, is beyond question ; but is there not a hint of the theatrical in this overstrained amazement, in this statement that fear is the most unaccountable thing in all his experience? One recalls the story of the young soldier who said that he knew not what it was to be afraid, and received his commander's answer : " Then you have never snuffed a candle with your fingers." That was the reproof of bravado by bravery in the mouth of a man so fearless that he could afford to acknowledge his acquaintance with fear. And surely Caesar could have afforded to do so too. We see and know that he is the bravest of the brave, but if anything could make us suspicious, it would be his constant harping on his flawless valour. So, too, he says of Cassius :

> I fear him not:
> Yet if my name were liable to fear,
> I do not know the man I should avoid
> So soon as that spare Cassius . . .
> I rather tell thee what is to be fear'd
> Than what I fear ; for always I am Caesar. (I. ii. 198, 211.)

Why should he labour the point? If he has not fears, he has at least misgivings in regard to Cassius, that come very much to the same thing. His anxiety is obvious, as he calls Antony to his side to catechise him on his opinions of the danger.

In the same way he prides himself on his inaccessibility to adulation and blandishments.

> These couchings and these lowly courtesies
> Might fire the blood of ordinary men,
> And turn pre-ordinance and first decree
> Into the law of children. Be not fond
> To think that Caesar bears such rebel blood,
> That will be thaw'd from the true quality
> With that which melteth fools ; I mean, sweet words,
> Low crooked court'sies and base spaniel fawning.
>
> (III. i. 36.)

We may believe that he does indeed stand secure against the grosser kinds of parasites and their more

I

obvious devices; but that does not mean that he
cannot be hoodwinked by meaner men who know
how to play on his self-love.   Decius says :

> I can o'ersway him : for he loves to hear
> That unicorns may be betray'd with trees,
> And bears with glasses, elephants with holes,
> Lions with toils, and men with flatterers ;
> But when I tell him he hates flatterers,
> He says he does, being then most flattered.
> Let me work.   (II. i. 203.)

And Decius makes his words good.

In like manner he fancies that he possesses an
insight that reads men's souls at a glance.   When
he hears the cry : " Beware the Ides of March," he
gives the command, "Set him before me ; let me
see his face."   A moment's inspection is enough :
"He is a dreamer: let us leave him: pass" (I. ii. 24).
Yet he fails to read the treachery of the conspirators,
though they are daily about him, consults with
Decius whom he "loves," and bids Trebonius be
near him.

And then he elects to pose as no less immovable
in resolution than infallible in judgment.   When we
have been witnesses of all his vacillation and shilly-
shally about attending the senate meeting—now he
would, now he would not, and again he would—it is
hard to suppress the jeer at the high-sounding words :

> I could be well moved, if I were as you :
> If I could pray to move, prayers would move me :
> But I am constant as the northern star,
> Of whose true-fix'd and resting quality
> There is no fellow in the firmament.
> The skies are painted with unnumber'd sparks,
> They are all fire, and every one doth shine,
> But there's but one in all doth hold his place :
> So in the world : 'tis furnish'd well with men,
> And men are flesh and blood, and apprehensive ;
> Yet in the number I do know but one
> That unassailable holds on his rank,
> Unshaked of motion : and that I am he,
> Let me a little show it, even in this.   (III. i. 58.)

Now, all these things are wholly or mainly the fabrications of Shakespeare. In Plutarch Caesar does not direct Calpurnia to put herself in Antony's way, nor is there any indication that he attached importance to the rite. It is in the wife and not in the husband that Plutarch notes an unexpected strain of credulity, remarking with reference to her dream : " Capurnia untill that time was never geven to any feare or supersticion." [1] Plutarch cites noble sayings of Caesar's in regard to fear, for instance that " it was better to dye once, than alwayes to be affrayed of death:" [2] but he never attributes to him any pretence of immunity from human frailty, and makes him explicitly avow the feeling in the very passage where in Shakespeare he disclaims it. " ' As for those fatte men, with smooth comed heades,' quoth he, ' I never reckon of them : but these pale visaged and carian leane people, I feare them most.' " The dismissal of the soothsayer after a contemptuous glance is unwarranted by Plutarch. There is no authority for his defencelessness among flatterers, or for his illusion that he is superior to their arts. Yielding in quite a natural way and without any hesitation to the solicitations of Calpurnia and the reports of the bad omens, Caesar in Plutarch resolves to stay at home, but afterwards is induced to change his mind by Decius' very plausible arguments. There is no hint of unsteadiness in his conduct, as there described ; nor in the final scene is there any of the ostentation but only the reality of firmness in his rejection of Metellus Cimber's petition.

Considering all this it is not difficult to understand the indignation of the critics who complain that Shakespeare has here given a libel rather than a portrait of Caesar, and has substituted impertinent cavil for sympathetic interpretation. And some of Shakespeare's apologists have accepted this state-

[1] *Julius Caesar.*   [2] *Ibid.*

ment of the case, but have sought to defend the supposed travesty on the ground that it is prescribed by the subject and the treatment. Thus Dr. Hudson suggests [1] that "the policy of the drama may have been to represent Caesar, not as he was indeed, but as he must have appeared to the conspirators ; to make us see him as they saw him ; in order that they might have fair and equal justice at our hands." With a slight variation this is also the opinion of Gervinus: [2] "The poet, if he intended to make the attempt of the conspirators his main theme, could not have ventured to create too great an interest in Caesar : it was necessary to keep him in the background, and to present that view of him which gave reason for the conspiracy." And alleging, what would be hard to prove, that in Plutarch, Caesar's character "altered much for the worse, shortly before his death," he continues, in reference to his arrogance : "It is intended with few words to show him at that point when his behaviour would excite those free spirits against him." But this explanation will hardly bear scrutiny. In the first place : if Shakespeare's object had been to provide a relative justification for the assassins, he could have done so much more naturally and effectively by adhering to the *data* of the *Life*. Among them he could have found graver causes of resentment against Caesar than any of those he invents, which at the worst are peccadillos and affectations rather than real delinquencies. And Plutarch does not slur them over: on the contrary the shadows in his picture are strongly marked, and he lays a long list of offences to Caesar's score ; culminating in what he calls the "shamefullest part" that he played, to wit, his support of Clodius. Here was matter enough for the dramatic *Advocatus Diaboli*. It would have

---

[1] *Shakespeare, His Life, Art and Characters.*
[2] *Shakespeare Commentaries.*

been as easy to weave some of these damaging stories into the reminiscences of Cassius, as to concoct harmless fictions about Caesar's having a temperature and being thirsty, or his failing to swim a river in flood. All these by-gone scandals, whether domestic or political, would have immensely strengthened the conspirators' case, especially with a precisian like Brutus. But Shakespeare is silent concerning them, and Brutus, as we have seen, gives Caesar in regard to his antecedents a clean bill of health. Of course almost all Caesar's previous history is taken for granted and left to the imagination, but the dubious passages are far more persistently kept out of sight than such as tend to his glory. And that is the bewildering thing, if Shakespeare's delineation was meant to explain the attitude of the faction. It is surely an odd way of winning our good will for a man's murderers to keep back notorious charges against him of cruelty, treason and unscrupulousness, to certify that he has never abused his powers or let his passion over-master his reason, and then to trump up stories that he gives himself airs and is deaf in one ear. It reminds one of Swift's description of Arbuthnot: "Our doctor has every quality and virtue that can make a man amiable or useful; but, alas, he hath a sort of slouch in his walk." Swift, however, was not explaining how people might come to think that Dr. Arbuthnot should be got rid of.

Again his tendency to parade by no means alters the fact, that he does possess in an extraordinary degree the intellectual and moral virtues that he would exaggerate in his own eyes and the eyes of others. Independence, resolution, courage, insight must have been his in amplest store or he would never have been able to

Get the start of the majestic world
And bear the palm alone;   (I. ii. 130.)

and there is evidence of them in the play. He is not moved by the deferential prayers of the senators : he does persist in the banishment of Publius Cimber ; he has in very truth read the heart and taken the measure of Cassius :

> Such men as he be never at heart's ease,
> Whiles they behold a greater than themselves ; (i. ii. 208.)

he neither shrinks nor complains when the fatal moment comes. The impression he makes on the unsophisticated mind, on average audiences and the elder school of critics, is undoubtedly an heroic one. It is only minute analysis that discovers his defects, and though the defects are certainly present and should be noted, they are far from sufficing to make the general effect absurd or contemptible. If they do so, we give them undue importance. It was not so that Shakespeare meant them to be taken. For he has invented for his Caesar not only these trivial blemishes, but several conspicuous exhibitions of nobility, which Plutarch nowhere suggests ; and this should give pause to such as find in Shakespeare's portrait merely a wilful or wanton caricature. Thus in regard to the interposition of Artemidorus, Shakespeare read in North :

> He marking howe Caesar received all the supplications that were offered him, and that he gave them straight to his men that were about him, pressed neerer to him and sayed : "Caesar, reade this memoriall to your selfe, and that quickely, for they be matters of great waight and touch you neerely." Caesar tooke it of him, *but coulde never reade it, though he many times attempted it,* for the multitude of people that did salute him : but holding it still in his hande, keeping it to him selfe, went on withall into the Senate house.[1]

Compare this with the scene in the play :

> *Artemidorus.*   Hail, Caesar ! read this schedule.
> *Decius.*   Trebonius doth desire you to o'er-read,
> At your best leisure, this his humble suit.

[1] *Julius Caesar.*

Artemidorus. O Caesar, read mine first, for mine's a suit
That touches Caesar nearer : read it, great Caesar.
    Caesar.   What touches us ourself shall be last served.
                                                        (III. i. 3.)

Can one say that Shakespeare has defrauded Caesar
of his magnanimity ?

Or again observe, in the imaginary conclusion to
the unrecorded remonstrances of Calpurnia, how
loftily he refuses to avail himself of the little white
untruths that after all pass current as quite excusable
in society. They are beneath his dignity. He
turns to Decius :

    Caesar.   You are come in very happy time,
To bear my greeting to the senators
And tell them that I will not come to-day ;
Cannot, is false, and that I dare not falser :
I will not come to-day : tell them so, Decius.
    Calpurnia. Say he is sick.
    Caesar.   Shall Caesar send a lie?
Have I in conquest stretch'd mine arm so far,
To be afeard to tell graybeards the truth ?
Decius, go tell them Caesar will not come . . .
The cause is in my will : I will not come.   (II. ii. 60.)

But this last instance is not merely an example of
Shakespeare's homage to Caesar's grandeur and his
eagerness to enhance it with accessories of his own
contrivance. It gives us a clue to the secret of his
additions both favourable and the reverse, and points
the way to his conception of the man. For observe
that this refusal of Caesar's to make use of a falsehood is an afterthought. A minute before he has,
also in words that Shakespeare puts in his mouth,
fully consented to the proposal that he should feign
illness. He pacifies Calpurnia :

    Mark Antony shall say I am not well ;
    And, for thy humour, I will stay at home.   (II. ii. 55.)

This compliance he makes to his wife, but in presence of Decius Brutus he recovers himself and
adopts the stricter standard. What does this imply ?

Does it not mean that in a certain sense he is playing a part and aping the Immortal to be seen of
men ?

Let us consider the situation. Caesar, a man with
the human frailties, mental and physical, which are
incident to men, is nevertheless endowed by the
Higher Powers with genius that has raised him far
above his fellows. By his genius he has conceived
and grasped and done much to realise the sublime
idea of the Roman Empire. By his genius he has
raised himself to the headship of that great Empire
which his own thought was creating. Private
ambitions may have urged and doubtful shifts may
have helped his career. He himself feels that
within his drapery of grand exploits there is something that will not bear scrutiny ; and hence his
mistrust of Cassius :

> He is a great observer and he looks
> Quite through the deeds of men.   (I. ii. 201.)

But these things are behind him and a luminous
veil is drawn over them, beyond which we discern
him only as "the foremost man of all this world,"
"the noblest man that ever lived in the tide of times,"
devoted to the cause of Rome, fighting and conquering for her ; filling her public treasuries, her general
coffers, with gold ; sympathising with her poor to
whom it will be found only after his death that he
has left his wealth. The only hints of unrighteous
dealing on his part are given in Artemidorus' statement to himself : "Thou hast wronged Caius
Ligarius," and in Brutus' statement about him that
he was slain "but for supporting robbers." But it
is never suggested that he himself was guilty of
robbery : and the wrong to Ligarius, who was
accused "for taking parte with Pompey," and
"thanked not Caesar so muche for his discharge,
as he was offended with him for that he was brought

in daunger by his tyrannicall power,"[1] hardly deserves the name, at least in the common acceptation. Besides Shakespeare has a large tolerance for the practical statesman when dowered with patriotism, insight, and resolution ; and will not lightly condemn him because he must use sorry tools, and takes some soil from the world, and is not unmoved by personal interests. Provided that his more selfish aims coincide with the good of the whole, and that he has veracity of intellect to understand, with steadiness of will to satisfy the needs of the time, Shakespeare will vindicate for him his share of prosperity, honour, and desert. And this seems to be, in glorified version, his view of Caesar. The only serious charge he brings against him in the play, the only charge to which he recurs elsewhere, is that he was ambitious. But ambition is not wholly of sin, and brings forth good as well as evil fruit. Indeed when a man's desire for the first place merges in the desire for the fullest opportunity, and that again in the desire for the task he feels he can do best, it is distinguishable from a virtue, if at all, only by the demand that he shall be the agent. So is it, to compare celebrities of local and of universal history, with the ambitious strain in the character of Henry IV.; it is not incompatible with sterling worth that commands solid success ; it spurs him to worthy deeds that redeem the offences it exacts; and these offences themselves in some sort "tend the profit of the state." No doubt with both men their ambition brings its own Nemesis, the ceaseless care of the one, the premature death of the other. But that need not prevent recognition of their high qualities, or their just claims, or their providential mandate. Such men are ministers of the Divine Purposes, as Plutarch said in regard to Caesar ; and in setting forth the essential meaning of his career, Shakespeare can scorn the

---

[1] Marcus Brutus.

base degrees by which he did ascend. Partly his
less creditable doings were necessary if he was to
mount at all ; partly they may have seemed venial
to the subject of the Tudor monarchy ; at worst,
when compared with the splendour of his achievement, they were spots in the sun.   In any case
they were not worth consideration.   With them
Shakespeare is not concerned, but with the plenary
inspiration of Caesar's life, the inspiration that made
him an instrument of Heaven and that was to bring
peace and order to the world.   So he passes over
the years of effort and preparation, showing their
glories but slightly and their trespasses not at all.
He confines himself to the time when the summit
is reached and the dream is fulfilled.   Then to his
mind begins the tragedy and the transfiguration.

He represents Caesar, like every truly great man,
as carried away by his own conception and made a
slave to it.   What a thing was this idea of Empire,
this " spirit of Caesar," of which he as one of earth's
mortal millions was but the vehicle and the organ !
He himself as a human person cannot withhold
homage from himself as the incarnate *Imperium*.
Observe how he speaks of himself habitually in the
third person.   Not " I do this," but " Caesar does
this," " Caesar does that," alike when talking to the
soothsayer, to his wife and to the senate.[1]   It is
almost as though he anticipated its later use as a
common noun equivalent to Emperor : for in all
these passages he describes, as it were, what the
Emperor's action and attitude should be.   And that
is the secret of the strange impression that he makes.

---

[1] Of course the substitution of the third for the second or first person
is very noticeable all through this play, and may have been due to an
idea on Shakespeare's part that such a mode of utterance suited the
classical and Roman majesty of the theme.   But this rather confirms
than refutes the argument of the text, for the usage is exceptionally
conspicuous in regard to Caesar, in whom the majesty of Rome is
summed up.

It is a case, an exaggerated case, of *noblesse oblige*. The Caesar, the first of those Caesars who were to receive their apotheosis and be hailed as *Divi Augusti*, must in literal truth answer Hobbes' description of the State, and be a mortal god.   He must be fearless, omniscient, infallible, without changeableness or shadow of turning : does he not represent the empire?   He has to live up to an impossible standard, and so he must affect to be what he is not.   He is the martyr of the idea that has made his fortune. He must not listen to his instincts or his misgivings; there is no room in the Caesar for timidity or mistake or fickleness.   But, alas ! he is only a man, and as a man he constantly gives the lie to the majesty which the spirit of Caesar enjoins.   We feel all the more strongly, since we are forced to the comparison, the contrast between the shortcomings of the individual and the splendour of the ideal role he undertakes. And not only that.   In this assumption of the Divine, involving as it does a touch of unreality and falsehood, he has lost his old surety of vision and efficiency in act.   He tries to rise above himself, and pays the penalty by falling below himself, and rushing on the ruin which a little vulgar shrewdness would have avoided.   But his mistake is due to his very greatness, and his greatness encompasses him to the last, when with no futile and undignified struggle, he wraps his face in his mantle and accepts the end. Antony does not exaggerate when he says :

> O, what a fall was there, my countrymen !
> Then I, and you, and all of us fell down ;   (III. ii. 194.)

for it was the Empire that fell.   But to rise again ! For the idea of Caesarism, rid of the defects and limitations of its originator, becomes only the more invincible, and the spirit of Caesar begins its free untrammelled course.

The greatness of his genius cannot be fully

realised unless the story is carried on to the final triumph at Philippi, instead of breaking off immediately after his bodily death. It is in part Shakespeare's perception of this and not merely his general superiority of power, that makes his Caesar so much more impressive than the Caesar of contemporary dramatists that seem to keep closer to their theme.

Not only then is *Julius Caesar* the right name for the play, in so far as his imperialist idea dominates the whole, but a very subtle interpretation of his character is given when, as this implies, he is viewed as the exponent of Imperialism. None the less Brutus is the leading personage, if we grant precedence in accordance with the interest aroused.

CHAPTER IV

THE EXCELLENCES AND ILLUSIONS OF BRUTUS

THUS Shakespeare has his Act of Oblivion for all
that might give an unfavourable impression of
Caesar's past, and presents him very much as the
incarnate principle of Empire, with the splendours
but also with the disabilities that must attend the
individual man who feels himself the vehicle for
such an inspiration.

He somewhat similarly screens from view whatever in the career of Brutus might prejudice his
claims to affection and respect : and carries much
further a process of idealization that Plutarch had
already begun. For to Plutarch Brutus is, so to
speak, the model republican, the paragon of private
and civic virtue. The promise to the soldiers before
the second battle at Philippi of two cities to sack,
calls forth the comment : "In all Brutus' life there
is but this only fault to be found" : and even this,
as the marginal note remarks, is "wisely excused";
on the plea, namely, that after Cassius' death the
difficulties were very great and the best had to be
made of a bad state of things. But no other mis-
conduct is laid to his charge : his extortionate
usury and his abrupt divorce are passed over in
silence. All his doings receive indulgent construction, and the narrative is often pointed with a formal
éloge. In the *Comparison*, where of course such

estimates are expected, attention is drawn to his
rectitude, "only referring his frendschippe and
enmitie unto the consideracion of justice and
equitie"; to "the marvelous noble minde of him,
that for fear never fainted nor let falle any part of
his corage"; to his influence over his associates
so that "by his choyce of them he made them
good men"; to the honour in which he was held
by his "verie enemies." But already the keynote
is struck in the opening page :

> This Marcus Brutus . . . whose life we presently wryte,
> having framed his manners of life by the rules of vertue and
> studie of philosophie, and having employed his wit, which
> was gentle and constant, in attempting of great things : me
> thinkes he was rightly made and framed unto vertue.

And the story often deviates from its course into
little backwaters of commendation, as when after
some censure of Cassius, we are told :

> Brutus in contrary manner, for his vertue and valliantnes,
> was well-beloved of the people and his owne, esteemed of
> noble men, and hated of no man, not so much as of his
> enemies: bicause he was a marvelous lowly and gentle
> person, noble minded, and would never be in any rage, nor
> caried away with pleasure and covetousness, but had ever an
> upright mind with him, and would never yeeld to any wronge
> or injustice, the which was the chiefest cause of his fame, of
> his rising, and of the good will that every man bare him : for
> they were all perswaded that his intent was good.

This conception Shakespeare adopts and purifies.
He leaves out the shadow of that one fault that
Plutarch wisely excused : he leaves out too the
unpleasant circumstance, which Plutarch apparently
thought needed no excuse, that Brutus was applicant for and recipient of offices at the disposal of
the all-powerful dictator. There must be nothing
to mar the graciousness and dignity of the picture.
Shakespeare wishes to portray a patriotic gentleman
of the best Roman or the best English type, such
"a gentleman or noble person" as it was the aim

of Spenser's *Faerie Queene* " to fashion in vertuous and gentle discipline," such a gentleman or noble person as Shakespeare's generation had seen in Spenser's friend, Sir Philip Sidney. So Plutarch's summaries are expanded and filled in partly with touches that his narrative supplies, partly with others that the summaries themselves suggest.

To the latter class belongs the winning courtesy with which Brutus at his first appearance excuses himself to Cassius for his preoccupation. His inward trouble might well have stirred him to irritability and abruptness ; but he only feels that it has made him remiss, and that an explanation is due from him :

> Vexed I am
> Of late with passions of some difference,
> Conceptions only proper to myself,
> Which give some soil perhaps to my behaviours :
> But let not therefore my good friends be grieved—
> Among which number, Cassius, be you one—
> Nor construe any further my neglect,
> Than that poor Brutus, with himself at war,
> Forgets the shows of love to other men. (I. ii. 39.)

So with his friends. Shakespeare invents the character of Lucius to show how attentive and considerate Brutus is as master. He apologises for having blamed his servant without cause.

> Bear with me, good boy, I am much forgetful. (IV. iii. 255.)

He notes compassionately that the lad is drowsy and overwatched (IV. iii. 241). At one time he dispenses with his services because he is sleeping sound (II. i. 229). At another he asks a song from him not as a right but as a favour (IV. iii. 256). And immediately thereafter the master waits, as it were, on the nodding slave, and removes his harp lest it should be broken.

But it is to his wife that he shows the full wealth of his affectionate nature. He would fain keep from

her the anxieties that are distracting his own mind :
but when she claims to share them as the privilege
and pledge of wifehood, with his quick sympathy he
sees it at once :

> You are my true and honourable wife,
> As dear to me as are the ruddy drops
> That visit my sad heart.   (II. i. 288.)

And yielding to her claim as a right, he recognises
that it is a claim that comes from an ideally noble
and loving soul, and prays to be made worthy of
her.   What insight Shakespeare shows even in his
omissions !   This is the prayer of Plutarch's Brutus
too, but he lifts up his hands and beseeches the
gods that he may " bring his enterprise to so goode
passe that he mighte be founde a husband worthie
of so noble a wife as Porcia."   Shakespeare's Brutus
does not view his worthiness as connected with any
material success.

And these words are also an evidence of his
humble-mindedness.   However aggressive and overbearing he may appear in certain relations, we never
fail to see his essential modesty.   If he interferes,
as often enough he does, to bow others to his will,
it is not because he is self-conceited, but because he
is convinced that a particular course is right ; and
where right is concerned, a man must come forward
to enforce it.   But for himself he has no idea of the
high estimation in which his character and parts are
held.   When Cassius insinuates that everyone thinks
him the man for the emergency, if he would only
realise it, his reply is a disclaimer : he has never
supposed, and shrinks from imagining, that he is fit
for such a role.   Yet such is his personality that, as
all of the faction feel, his help is absolutely necessary
if the conspiracy is to have a chance of approval.
Cinna exhorts Cassius to win him to the party,
Casca bears witness to his popular credit and to the

value of his sanction in recommending the enterprise, Ligarius is willing to follow any course if Brutus leads, the cynical Cassius admits his worth and their great need of him.

For his amiable and attractive virtues are saved from all taint of weakness by an heroic strain, both high-spirited and public-spirited, both stoical and chivalrous. Challenged by the solicitations of Cassius he for once breaks through his reticence, and discloses his inward temper. We may be sure that even then he speaks less than he feels.

> If it be aught toward the general good,
> Set honour in one eye, and death i' the other,
> And I will look on both indifferently:
> For let the gods so speed me, as I love
> The name of honour more than I fear death. (I. ii. 85.)

This elevated way of thinking has been fostered and confirmed by study, just as in the case of Sidney, and by study of much the same kind. Plutarch says:

> Now touching the Greecian Philosophers, there was no sect nor Philosopher of them, but he heard and liked it: but above all the rest, he loved Platoes sect best, and did not much give himself to the new or meane Academy as they call it, but altogether to the old Academy.

He has striven to direct his life by right reason, and has pondered its problems under the guidance of his chosen masters. His utterance, which Plutarch quotes, on suicide, shows how he has sought Plato's aid for a standard by which to judge others and himself.[1] His utterance, which Shakespeare invents, on the death of Portia, shows how he has schooled himself to fortitude, and suggests the influence of a different school.

> We must die, Messala:
> With meditating that she must die once,
> I have the patience to endure it now. (IV. iii. 190.)

[1] Compare the argument in the *Phaedo*, with its conclusion: "Then there may be reason in saying that a man should wait and not take his own life till God summons him." Jowett's *Plato*, Vol. I.

He is essentially a thinker, a reader, a student.
Plutarch had told how on the eve of Pharsalia, when
his companions were resting, or forecasting the
morrow, Brutus "fell to his booke and wrote all day
long till night, wryting a breviarie of Polybius."
And in his last campaign :

> His heade ever busily occupied to thinke of his affayres,
> . . . after he had slumbered a little after supper, he spent all
> the rest of the night in dispatching of his waightiest causes,
> and after he had taken order for them, if he had any leysure
> left him, he would read some booke till the third watch of the
> night, at what tyme the Captaines, pety Captaines and
> Colonells, did use to come unto him.

Shakespeare only visualises this description when
he makes him find the book, that in his troubles and
griefs he has been "seeking for so," in the pocket of
his gown, with the leaf turned down where he
stopped reading.

Does then Shakespeare take over Plutarch's
favourite, merely removing the single stain and
accenting all the attractions, to confront him as the
embodiment of republican virtue, with Caesar,
against whom too no evil is remembered, as the
embodiment of imperial majesty ? Will he show
the inevitable collision between two political principles each worthily represented in its respective
champion ?

This has been said, and there are not wanting
arguments to support it. It is clear that the contrast is not perplexed by side issues. Brutus has no
quarrel with Caesar as a man, and no justification is
given for the conspiracy in what Caesar has done.
On the contrary, his murderer stands sponsor for his
character, acknowledges his supreme greatness, and
loves him as a dear friend. But neither on the other
hand is anything introduced that might divert our
sympathies from Brutus by representing him as
bound by other than the voluntary ties of affection

and respect. And this is the more remarkable that in Plutarch there are two particulars full of personal pathos which Shakespeare cannot have failed to note, and which lend themselves to dramatic purposes, as other dramatists have proved. One of them, employed by Voltaire, would darken the assassination to parricide. In explanation of the indulgence with which Caesar treated Brutus, Plutarch says:

> When he was a young man, he had been acquainted with Servilia, who was extreamelie in love with him. And bicause Brutus was borne in that time when their love was hottest, he perswaded him selfe that he begat him.[1]

And then follows what can be alleged in proof. "What of anguish," says Mr. Wyndham, "does this not add to the sweep of the gesture wherewith the hero covered his face from the pedant's sword!"

This is a mere casual hint; but the other point finds repeated mention in the *Life*, and is dwelt upon though explained away in the *Comparison*. It is the circumstance that Brutus had fought on Pompey's side, and that thereafter Caesar had spared him, amnestied his friends, and loaded him with favours.

> The greatest reproache they could make against Brutus was : that Julius Caesar having saved his life, and pardoned all the prisoners also taken in battell, as many as he made request for, taking him for his frende, and honoring him above all his other frends, Brutus notwithstanding had imbrued his hands in his blood.[2]

Plutarch indeed instances this as the grand proof of Brutus' superiority to personal considerations ; but it looks bad, and certainly introduces a new element into the moral problem. At all events, though it involves in a specially acute form that conflict of duties

---

[1] Voltaire decorously invents a secret marriage !

[2] *The comparison of Dion with Brutus.*

which the drama loves, and was so used by Shakespeare's contemporaries, as early as Muretus and as
late as Alexander, Shakespeare dismisses it.

Attention is concentrated on the single fact that
Brutus felt it his duty to take the life of Caesar, and
no obligations of kinship or gratitude are allowed to
complicate the one simple case of conscience.

The victim and the sacrificer are thus set before
us, each with an unstained record, and in only those
personal relations that arise from warm and reverent
friendship.

Of their mutual attachment we are left in no doubt,
nor are we ever suffered to forget it. Cassius in talk
to himself, bears witness that Caesar "loves Brutus"
(i. ii. 317). Antony, in his speech to the people,
appeals to this as a notorious fact :

> Brutus, as you know, was Caesar's angel :
> Judge, O you Gods, how dearly Caesar loved him.
>
> (iii. ii. 185.)

But the strongest testimony is Caesar's own cry, the
cry of astonishment and consternation, whether from
the betrayed when the beloved is the traitor, or from
the condemned when the beloved is the judge:

> Et tu Brute !   Then fall, Caesar !   (iii. i. 77.)

Nor is less stress laid on Brutus' feeling. He avows
it in the Forum, as before he had assured Antony
that "he did love Caesar when he struck him" (iii.
i. 182). Cassius tells him :

> When thou didst hate him worst, thou lovedst him better
> Than ever thou lovedst Cassius.   (iv. iii. 106.)

But here again the most pathetic evidence is to be
found in the assassination scene itself. When Brutus
stoops in the guise of petitioner, we cannot suppose
it is merely with treacherous adroitness :

> I kiss thy hand, but not in flattery, Caesar.   (iii. i. 52.)

Knowing the man, do we not feel that this is the
last tender farewell ?

But though all this is true it cannot be maintained, in view of the soliloquy before the conspirators' meeting, that Shakespeare makes Brutus the mouthpiece of republicanism, as he makes Caesar the mouthpiece of imperialism. The opposition of principles is present, but it is of principles on a different plane.

Caesar, the spirit of Caesar, is indeed the spirit of Empire, the spirit of practical greatness in the domains of war, policy, organisation : of this he is the exponent, to this he is the martyr. Brutus' spirit is rather the spirit of loyalty to duty, which finds in him its exponent and martyr too.

He is lavishly endowed by nature with all the inward qualities that go to make the virtuous man, and these he has improved and disciplined by every means in his power. His standard is high, but he is so strenuous and sincere in living up to it, that he is recognised as no less pre-eminent in the sphere of ethics, than Caesar in the sphere of politics. Indeed their different ideals dominate and impel both men in an almost equal degree. And in each case this leads to a kind of pose. It appears even in their speech. The balanced precision of the one tells its own tale as clearly as the overstrained loftiness of the other, and is as closely matched with the part that he needs must play. Obviously Brutus does not like to confess that he has been in the wrong. No more in the σώφρων than in the Emperor is there room for any weakness. After his dispute with Cassius he assumes rather unjustifiably that he has on the whole been in the right, that he has been the provoked party, and that at worst he has shown momentary heat. But even this slight admission, coming from him, fills Cassius with surprise.

Brutus. When I spoke that, I was ill-temper'd too.
Cassius. Do you confess so much? Give me your hand.
(IV. iii. 116.)

The Ideal Wise Man must not yield to anger any
more than to other passions, and it costs Brutus
something to own that he has done so.   But he
minimises his confession by accepting Cassius'
apology for his rash humour and promising to overlook any future offences, as though none could be
laid to his own door.   We like him none the worse
for this, his cult of perfection is so genuine : but
sometimes the cult of perfection becomes the assumption and obtrusion of it.   Read the passage where
Messala tells him of Portia's death.

> *Messala.* Had you letters from your wife, my lord ?
> *Brutus.* No, Messala.
> *Messala.* Nor nothing in your letters writ of her ?
> *Brutus.* Nothing, Messala.
> *Messala.*   That, methinks, is strange.
> *Brutus.* Why ask you ? hear you aught of her in yours ?
> *Messala.* No, my lord.
> *Brutus.* Now, as you are a Roman, tell me true.
> *Messala.* Then like a Roman bear the truth I tell :
> For certain she is dead, and by strange manner.
> *Brutus.* Why, farewell, Portia.   (IV. iii. 181.)

Now Brutus had received earlier tidings.   He may
profess ignorance to save himself the pain of explanation, though surely it would have been simpler to say,
" I know all."   But the effect is undoubtedly to
bring his self-control into fuller relief in presence of
Messala and Titinius even than in the presence of
Cassius a few minutes before ; for then he was announcing what he already knew, here he would seem
in the eyes of his informants to be encountering the
first shock.   Too much must not be made of this,
for Cassius who is aware of the circumstances, is no
less impressed than the others, and Cassius would
have detected any hollow ring.   But at the least it
savours of a willingness to give a demonstration, so
to speak, in Clinical Ethics.

A man like this whose desires are set on
building up a virtuous character, but who is not free

from the self-consciousness and self-confidence of the specialist in virtue, is exposed to peculiar dangers. His interests and equipment are in the first place for the inward life, and his chief concern is the well-being of his soul. But precisely such an one knows that he cannot save his own soul alone. It is not open to him to disregard the claims of his fellows or the needs of the world, so he is driven to take in hand matters for which he has no inclination or aptitude. He may be quite aware of his unfitness for the work and shrink from investing himself with qualities which he knows he does not possess. All the same, if the call comes, the logic of his nature will force him to essay the ungrateful and impossible task ; and he will be apt to imagine a call when there is none. So it is with Brutus. It is true that many of the best respect do look up to him and designate him as their leader : it is none the less true that the unsigned instigations which he takes for the voice of Rome, are the fabrications of a single schemer. He would not be Brutus if he suspected or shirked the summons. This votary of duty cannot acknowledge a merely fugitive and cloistered virtue ; this platonic theorist can easily be hood-winked by the practised politician. So Brutus, who is so at home in his study with his book, who is so exemplary in all the private relations of friend, master and husband ; predestined, one would say, for the serene labours of philosophic thought and the gracious offices of domestic affection, sweeps from his quiet anchorage to face the storms of political strife, which such as he are not born to master but which they think they must not avoid.

It is a common case ; and many have by their very conscientiousness been hurried into a false position where they could not escape from committing blunders and incurring guilt. But generally the blunders are corrigible and the guilt is venial. It is

Brutus' misfortune, that his very greatness, his moral ascendancy with the prestige it bestows, gives him the foremost place, and shifts on his shoulders the main responsibility for all the folly and crime.

For it is inevitable that he should proceed as he does. Yet it is not easy for him. There is a conflict in this sensitive and finely tuned spirit, which, with all his acquired fortitude, bewrays itself in his bearing to Cassius before any foreign suggestion has entered his mind, which afterwards makes him unlike himself in his behaviour to his wife, which drives sleep from his eyes for nights together, which so jars the rare harmony of his nature, in Antony's view his chief perfection, that he seems to suffer from an insurrection within himself. And it is not hard to understand why this should be. Morality is the guiding principle of Brutus' character, but what if it should be at variance with itself? Now two sets of moral forces are at strife in his heart. There are the more personal sentiments of love and reverence for Caesar and of detestation for the crime he contemplates. Even after his decision he feels the full horror of conspiracy with its "monstrous visage"; how much more must he feel the horror of assassinating a friend! On the other side are the more traditional ethical obligations to state, class, and house. It is almost as fatal to this visionary to be called Brutus, as it is to the poet to be called Cinna. For a great historic name spares its bearer a narrow margin of liberty. It should be impossible for a Bourbon to be other than a legitimist; it would be impossible for a Romanoff to abandon the Orthodox Church; it is impossible for a Brutus to accept the merest show of royal power. The memory of his stock is about him. Now Cassius reminds him of his namesake who would brook the eternal devil in Rome as easily as a king; now the admonition is affixed with wax upon Old

Brutus' statue; now he himself recalls the share his ancestors had in expelling the Tarquin. If such an one acquiesced in the coronation of Caesar, he must be the basest renegade, or more detached from his antecedents than it is given a mortal man to be. And in Brutus there is no hint of such detachment. The temper that makes him so attentive and loyal to the pieties of life, is the very temper that vibrates to all that is best in the past, and clings to the spirit of use and wont. Let it again be repeated that Brutus reveals himself to Shakespeare very much in the form of a cultured and high-souled English nobleman, the heir of great traditions and their responsibilities, which he fulfils to the smallest jot and tittle; the heir also of inevitable preconceptions.

But in Brutus there is more than individual morality and inherited ethos: there is superimposed on these the conscious philosophic theory with which his actions must be squared. He has to determine his conduct not by instinct or usage, but by impersonal, unprejudiced reason. It is to this tribunal that in the last resort he must appeal; and in that strange soliloquy of his he puts aside all private preferences on the one hand, all local considerations on the other, and discusses his difficulty quite as an abstract problem of right and wrong. He sees that if the personal rule of Caesar is to be averted, half measures will not suffice. There are no safeguards or impediments that can prevent the supremacy of so great a man if he is allowed to live. This is his starting point: "It must be by his death." But then the question arises: is the death of such an one permissible? And in answering it Brutus seems at the first glance to show admirable intellectual candour. He acquits Caesar of all blame; the quarrel "will bear no colour for the thing he is." What could be more dispassionate and impartial, what more becoming the philosopher? There is no sophistication of the facts in the interest of his party. But immediately there follow the incriminating words :

> Fashion it thus; that what he is, augmented,
> Would run to these and these extremities. (II. i. 30.)

There is a sophistication of the inference. Surely this line of argument is invented to support a foregone conclusion. Already that hint to his conscience, "Fashion it thus," betrays the resolve to make out a case. And does the mere future contingency justify the present infliction of death? Brutus is appealing to his philosophy : by his philosophy he is judged : for just about this date he was condemning the suicide of Cato because he found it

> Cowardly and vile,
> *For fear of what might fall,* so to prevent
> The time of life. (v. i. 104.)

But the argument is the same in both cases, and if it does not excuse self-murder, still less does it excuse the murder of others.

The truth is that Brutus, though he personates the philosopher, is less of one than he thinks. It is not his philosophy but his character that gives him strength to bear the grief of Portia's death ; as Cassius says :

> I have as much of this in art as you,
> But yet my nature could not bear it so. (IV. iii. 194.)

At the end he casts his philosophy to the winds rather than go bound to Rome: he "bears too great a mind" (v. i. 113). And just as on these occasions he is independent or regardless of it, so here he tampers with it to get the verdict that is required. For even in his own eyes he has to play the part of the ideally wise and virtuous man ; and though the obligations of descent and position, the consideration in which he is held, the urgings of a malcontent,

and (as he believes not altogether without reason)
the expectations formed of him by his fellow citizens,
supply his real motives for the murder, he needs to
give it the form of ideal virtue and wisdom before
he can proceed to it.

Now, however, he persuades himself that he has
the sanction of reason and conscience, and he acts
on the persuasion. His hesitations are gone. He
can face without wincing the horror of conspiracy.
With an impassioned eloquence, which he nowhere
else displays, he can lift the others to the level of
his own views. No doubts or scruples becloud his
enthusiasm now.

> If not the face of men,
> The sufferance of our souls, the time's abuse—
> If these be motives weak, break off betimes,
> And every man hence to his idle bed;
> So let high-sighted tyranny range on
> Till each man drop by lottery. (II. i. 114.)

His certainty has advanced by leaps and bounds.
A few minutes ago there was no complaint against
Caesar as he was or had been, but it could be alleged
that he might or would change: now his tyranny,
lighting by caprice on men, is announced as a positive
fact of the future or even of the present. But by
this time Brutus is assured that the plot is just and
that the confederates are the pick of men, both plot
and confederates so noble that for them an ordinary
pledge would be an insult:

> Unto bad causes swear
> Such creatures as men doubt: but do not stain
> The even virtue of our enterprise,
> Nor the insuppressive metal of our spirits,
> To think that or our cause or our performance
> Did need an oath. (II. i. 132.)

He carries them away with him. They abandon
the oath; they accept all his suggestions; we feel
that their thoughts are ennobled by his intervention,

that, as Plutarch noted to be the effect of his fellowship, he has made them better men, at least for the
time.

Meanwhile it is a devout imagination, an unconscious sophistry that lends him his power ; and this
brings its own Nemesis at its heels.   In the future
Brutus will be disillusioned of the merit of the
exploit.   In the present, persuading his associates
of its unparalleled glory, he makes them take their
measures to suit.   He will not hear of the murder of
Antony, for that would be bloody and unnecessary.
And his clemency is based on disparagement of
Antony's abilities and contempt for his moral character.   Of this "limb of Caesar," as he calls him,
"who can do no more than Caesar's arm when
Caesar's head is off," he cries :

> Alas, good Cassius, do not think of him :
> If he love Caesar, all that he can do
> Is to himself, take thought and die for Caesar :
> And that were much he should ; for he is given
> To sports, to wildness and much company.   (II. i. 185.)

It is not so in Plutarch :

> Brutus would not agree to it.   First for that he sayd it was
> not honest : secondly, bicause he told them there was hope
> of chaunge in him.   For he did not mistrust, but that
> Antonius being a noble minded and coragious man (when
> he should knowe that Caesar was dead) would willingly helpe
> his contrie to recover her libertie, having them an example
> unto him to follow their corage and vertue.

In this hope of converting a *rusé* libertine like
Antony, there is no doubt a hint of idealism, but it
is not so marked as in the high-pitched magnanimity
of Shakespeare's Brutus, who denies a man's powers
of mischief because his life is loose.

Yet though Antony would always be a source of
danger, the conspirators might find compensation in
the reputation for leniency they would gain, and the
danger might be reduced were effective steps taken

to render him innocuous. But this is only the beginning of Brutus' mistakes. If indeed they had not
begun before. With his masterful influence he has
dissuaded his friends from applying to Cicero, on the
ground that Cicero will not share in any scheme of
which he is not the author. It may be so, but one
would think it was at least an experiment well worth
the trying. Apart from the authority of his years
and position, there would have been the spell of his
oratory; and of that they were soon to be sorely
in need, again through Brutus' crotchet that their
course evinced its own virtue, and that virtue was a
sufficient defence.

> "The first fault that he did," says Plutarch, "was, when
> he would not consent to his fellow conspirators, that Antony
> should be slayne: and therefore he was justly accused, that
> thereby he had saved a stronge and grievous enemy of their
> conspiracy. The second fault was when he agreed that
> Caesars funeralls should be as Antony would have them : the
> which in deede marred all."

This hint Shakespeare works out. He sees
clearly that this further blunder marred all, and
heightens the folly of it in various ways. For in
Plutarch the question is debated in the Senate,
after it has been determined that the assassins
shall be not only pardoned but honoured and after
provinces have been assigned to them, Crete to
Brutus, Africa to Cassius, and the like. Only
then, when their victory seems complete and
assured, do they discuss the obsequies.

> Antonius thinking good his testament should be red
> openly, and also that his body should be honorably buried,
> and not in hugger mugger, least the people might thereby
> take occasion to be worse offended if they did otherwise :
> Cassius stowtly spake against it. But Brutus went with the
> motion and agreed unto it.

That is the amount of his error : that when all
seemed to be going well with the faction, Antony,
who had shown himself in seeming and for the

time their most influential friend, commended the
proposal on opportunist grounds, and Cassius
opposed it, but Brutus supported it and voted
with the majority.   In the Play his responsibility
is undivided, and all the explanatory circumstances
have disappeared.   He is not one member of an
approving Senate, who, when the assassination
seems once for all a *chose jugée*, accepts a suggestion, made apparently in the interests of peace
and quiet, by the man to whom, more than to
anyone else, the settlement of the affair is due.
While the position is still critical, without any
evidence of Antony's good will, without any pressure of public opinion or any plea of political
expediency, he endows the helpless suppliant with
means to undo what has been done and destroy
those who have done it.   No wonder that Cassius
when he hears Brutus giving Antony permission to
speak in the market place, interrupts : " Brutus, a
word with you," and continues in the alarmed aside :

> You know not what you do : do not consent
> That Antony speak in his funeral :
> Know you how much the people may be moved
> By that which he will utter?   (III. i. 232.)

But Brutus waves his remonstrance aside.   He is
now so besotted by his own sophisms that he
will listen to no warning.   He thinks all risk will
be averted by his going into the pulpit first to
show the "reason" of Caesar's death.   He has
quite forgotten that the one reason that he could
allege to himself was merely a hazardous conclusion
from doubtful premises ; and this forsooth is to
satisfy the citizens of Rome.   But meanwhile since
their deed is so irreproachable and disinterested, the
conspirators must act in accordance, and show their
freedom from any personal motive by giving Caesar
all due rites :

> It shall advantage more than do us wrong.

The infatuation is almost incredible, and it springs not only from generosity to Antony and Caesar, but from the fatal assumption of the justice of his cause, and the Quixotic exaltation the assumption brings with it.

For were it ever so just, could this be brought home to the Roman populace? Brutus, who is never an expert in facts, has been misled by the inventions of Cassius, which he mistakes for the general voice of Rome. Here, too, Shakespeare departs from his authority to make the duping of his hero more conspicuous. For in Plutarch these communications are the quite spontaneous incitements of the public, not the contrivances of one dissatisfied aristocrat.

> But for Brutus, *his frendes and contrie men*, both by divers procurementes, and sundrie rumors of the citie, and by many bills also, did openlie call and procure him to doe that he did. For, under the image of his auncestor Junius Brutus, that drave the kinges out of Rome, they wrote: "O, that it had pleased the goddes that thou wert now alive, Brutus: and againe that thou wert with us nowe." His tribunall (or chaire) where he gave audience during the time he was praetor, was full of such billes: "Brutus, thou art a sleepe, and art not Brutus in deede."

All these in Plutarch are worth their face value, but in Shakespeare they are not: and it is one of the ironies of Brutus' career that he takes them as appeals from the people when they are only the juggleries of Cassius. So far from objecting to Imperialism, the citizens when most favourable to Brutus call out, "Let him be Caesar!" "Caesar's better parts shall be crowned in Brutus" (III. ii. 56). This is the acme of his success and the prologue to his disillusionment.

But even if the case of the conspirators could be commended to the populace, Brutus is not the man to do it. It is comic and pathetic to hear him reassuring Cassius with the promise to speak first as though he could neutralise in advance the arts of Antony. Compare his oration with that of his rival. First, in the matter of it, there is no appeal to the imagination or passions, but an unvarnished series of arguments addressed exclusively to the logical reason. Such a speech would make little impression on an assembly of those who are called educated men, and to convince an audience like the artisans of Rome (for such was Shakespeare's con- conception of the People), it is ridiculously inadequate. But the style is no less out of place. The diction is as different as possible from the free and fluent rhetoric of Antony. Shakespeare had read in Plutarch :

> They do note in some of his Epistells, that he counter- feated that briefe compendious maner of speach of the Lacedaemonians. As when the warre was begonne, he wrote unto the Pergamenians in this sorte : " I understand you have geven Dolabella money ; if you have done it willingly, you confesse you have offended me : if against your wills, shewe it then by geving me willinglie." An other time againe unto the Samians : " Your counsels be long, your doinges be slowe, consider the ende." And in an other Epistell he wrote unto[1] the Patareians : " The Xanthians despising my good wil, have made their contrie a grave of dispaire : and the Patareians that put them selves into my protection, have lost no jot of their libertie. And therefore whilest you have libertie, either choose the judgement of the Patareians, or the fortune of the Xanthians."

Thus prompted Shakespeare makes Brutus affect the balanced structure of Euphuism. Not only in his oration. Read his words to Cassius at their first interview :

> That you do love me, I am nothing jealous ;
> What you would work me to, I have some aim ;
> How I have thought of this and of these times,
> I shall recount hereafter ; for this present,
> I would not, so with love I might entreat you,
> Be any further moved. What you have said

---

[1] *i.e.* in reference to.

I will consider : what you have to say
I will with patience hear, and find a time
Both meet to hear and answer such high things. (I. ii. 161.)

Nothing could be more neat, accurate and artificial
than this Euphuistic arrangement of phrases. It at
once suggests the academic studious quality of
Brutus' expression whenever he gives thought to
it.   But it is a style unsuitable to, one might
almost say incompatible with, genuine passion.   So
it is noteworthy that when he lets himself go in
answer to Cassius and introduces the personal
accent, he abandons his mannerisms.   And could
the symmetrical clauses of his oration move the
popular heart?   It has a noble ring about it,
because it is sincere, with the reticence and sobriety
which the sincere man is careful to observe when
he is advocating his own case.   But that is not
the sort of thing that the Saviour of his Country
as Brutus thought himself to be, will find fit to
sway a mob.   Nevertheless his eloquence was
notorious.   Plutarch states that when his mind
" was moved to followe any matter, he used a
kind of forcible and vehement perswasion that
calmed not till he had obteyned his desire."   There
is a rush of emotion in his words when he is
denouncing the conventional pledge or wanton
bloodshed, but if any personal interest is involved,
the springs are dry.   In the Forum it is characteristic that he speaks with far more warmth—a
transition indicated not only by the change of
style, but, after Shakespeare's wont, by the substitution of verse for prose—when he no longer
pleads for himself but tries to get a hearing for
Mark Antony.

And this is the man with his formal dialectic and
professorial oratory, impassioned only on behalf of
his enemy, who thinks that by a temperate statement of the course which he has seduced his reason

K

to approve, he can prevent the perils of a speech by Caesar's friend. He does not even wait to hear it: but if he did, what could he effect against the sophistries and rhetorical tricks, the fervour and regret, the gesticulation and tears of Antony's headlong improvisation?

CHAPTER V

THE DISILLUSIONMENT OF BRUTUS. PORTIA

BRUTUS had been doubly duped, by his own subtlety and his own simplicity in league with his conscientiousness; for in this way he was led to idealise his deed as enjoined both by the inward moral code and the demands of his country, and such self-deception avenges itself as surely as any intentional crime. He is soon disabused in regard to the wishes of Rome and its view of the alleged wrongs it has suffered from Caesar. His imagination had dwelt on the time when his ancestors drove out the Tarquin; now he himself must ride "like a madman" through the gates. It is not only the first of his reverses but a step towards his enlightenment, for it helps to show that he has been mistaken in the people. Still, the momentary mood of the populace may not always recognise its best interests and real needs, and may not coincide with the true *volonté générale*. There is harder than this in store for Brutus. By the time we meet him again at Sardis a worse punishment has overtaken him, and his education in disappointment has advanced, though he does his utmost to treat the punishment as fate and not to learn the lessons it enforces.

This scene has won the applause of the most dissimilar minds and generations. We have seen how Leonard Digges singles it out as the grand attraction of the play, by which, above all others, it transcends the laboured excellences of *Catiline* or *Sejanus*. It excited the admiration and rivalry of the greatest genius of the Restoration period. Scott says of the dispute between Antony and Ventidius in *All for Love* : "Dryden when writing this scene had unquestionably in his recollection the quarrel between Brutus and Cassius, which was so justly a favourite in his time, and to which he had referred as inimitable in his prologue to *Aureng-Zebe*.

> But spite of all his pride, a secret shame
> Invades his breast at Shakespeare's sacred name :
> Awed, when he hears his godlike Romans rage,
> He in a just despair would quit the stage ;
> And to an age less polished, more unskilled,
> Does with disdain the foremost honours yield."

In the eighteenth century Dr. Johnson, though he finds *Julius Caesar* as a whole "somewhat cold and unaffecting," perhaps because Shakespeare's "adherence to the real story and to Roman manners" has "impeded the natural vigour of his genius," excepts particular passages and cites "the contention and reconciliation of Brutus and Cassius" as universally celebrated. And Coleridge goes beyond himself in his praise: "I know no part of Shakespeare that more impresses on me the belief of his being super-human, than this scene between Brutus and Cassius. In the Gnostic heresy it might have been credited with less absurdity than most of their dogmas, that the Supreme had employed him to create, previously to his function of representing characters." Yet it is not merely in the revelation of character that the scene is unique. More than any other single episode, more than all the rest together, it lays bare the significance of the story in its tragic pathos and its tragic irony. And the wonder of it is increased rather than lessened when we take note that it is a creation not out of nothing but out of chaos. For there is hardly a suggestion, hardly a detail, that Shakespeare did not find in Plutarch, but here in confused mixture, there in inert isolation, and nowhere with more than the possibilities of being organised. It is Shakespeare, who, to borrow from Milton's description of the beginning of his Universe, "founded and conglobed like things to like, and vital virtue infused and vital warmth."

The nucleus of this passage is found just after the account of Brutus' exploits in Lycia.

About that tyme, Brutus sent to pray Cassius to come to the citye of Sardis, and so he did. Brutus understanding of his comming, went out to meete him with all his frendes. There both their armies being armed, they called them both Emperors. Nowe, as it commonly hapneth in great affayres betwene two persons, both of them having many friends, and so many Captaines under them; there ranne tales and complaints betwixt them. Therefore, before they fell in hand with any other matter, they went into a little chamber together, and bad every man avoyde, and did shut the dores to them. Then they beganne to powre out their complaints one to the other, and grew hot and lowde, earnestly accusing one another, and at length fell both a weeping. Their friends that were without the chamber hearing them lowde within, and angry betwene them selves. they were both amased and affrayd also lest it would grow to further matter: but yet they were commaunded that no man should come to them. Notwithstanding, one Marcus Phaonius, that had bene a friend and follower of Cato while he lived, and tooke upon him to counterfeate a Philosopher, not with wisedom and discretion, but with a certaine bedlem and frantick motion: he would needes come into the chamber, though the men offered to keepe him out. But it was no boote to let Phaonius, when a mad moode or toy tooke him in the head: for he was a hot hasty man, and sodaine in all his doings, and cared for never a Senator of them all. Now, though he used this bold manner of speeche after the profession of the Cynick Philosophers (as who would say, doggs), yet this boldnes did no hurt many times, bicause they did but laugh at him to see him so mad. This Phaonius at that time, in despite of the doore keepers, came into the chamber, and with a certain scoffing and

mocking gesture which he counterfeated of purpose, he
rehearsed the verses which old Nestor sayd in Homer:

> My lords, I pray you harken both to mee,
> For I have seene moe yeares than suchye three.

Cassius fell a laughing at him: but Brutus thrust him out
of the chamber, and called him dogge, and counterfeate
Cynick. Howbeit his comming in brake their strife at that
time, and so they left eche other.

Here there seems little enough to tempt the dramatist; the two generals quarrel, Phaonius bursts in,
Cassius laughs at him, Brutus turns him out, but
the interruption temporarily patches up a truce
between them. And this petty incident is made
the most pregnant in Shakespeare's whole play;
and that by apparently such simple means. To
get the meaning out of it, or to read the meaning
into it, he does little more, so far as the mechanical
aspects of his treatment are concerned, than collect
a few other notices scattered up and down the pages
of his authority. He had found in an earlier
digression Cassius described as

> a hot cholerick and cruell man, that would often tymes be
> caried away from justice for gayne: it was certainly thought
> that he made warre, and put him selfe into sundry daungers,
> more to have absolute power and authoritie, than to defend
> the liberty of his contrie.

Again after describing Brutus' success with the
Patareians, Plutarch proceeds:

> Cassius, about the selfe same tyme, after he had compelled
> the Rhodians every man to deliver all the ready money they
> had in gold and silver in their houses, the which being
> brought together, amounted to the summe of eyght thousande
> talents: yet he condemned the citie besides, to paye the
> summe of five hundred talents more. When Brutus in
> contrary manner, after he had leavyed of all the contrye
> of Lycia but a hundred and fiftye talents onely: he departed
> thence into the contrye of Ionia, and did them no more
> hurt.

Previously with reference to the first meeting
of the fugitives after they collected their armies

and before they came to Sardis at all, Plutarch
narrates :

> Whilst Brutus and Cassius were together in the citie of
> Smyrna : Brutus prayed Cassius to let him have some part
> of his money whereof he had great store, bicause all that he
> could rappe and rend of his side, he had bestowed it in
> making so great a number of shippes, that by meanes of them
> they should keepe all the sea at their commaundement.
> Cassius' friendes hindered this request, and earnestly
> disswaded him from it : perswading him, that it was no
> reason that Brutus should have the money which Cassius
> had gotten together by sparing, and leavied with great evil
> will of the people their subjects, for him to bestowe liberally
> uppon his souldiers, and by this meanes to winne their good
> willes, by Cassius charge. This notwithstanding, Cassius
> gave him the third part of his totall summe.

Then at Sardis, but not on occasion of the dispute
interrupted by Phaonius, mention is made of the
affair with Pella :

> The next daye after, Brutus, upon complaynt of the
> Sardians did condemne and noted Lucius Pella for a
> defamed person, that had been a Praetor of the Romanes,
> and whome Brutus had given charge unto : for that he was
> accused and convicted of robberie, and pilferie in his office.
> This judgement much misliked Cassius; bicause he him selfe
> had secretly (not many dayes before) warned two of his
> friends, attainted and convicted of the like offences, and
> openly had cleered them : but yet he did not therefore leave
> to employ them in any manner of service as he did before.
> And therefore he greatly reproved Brutus, for that he would
> shew him selfe so straight and seveare in such a tyme, as was
> meeter to beare a little, then to take thinges at the worst.
> Brutus in contrary manner aunswered, that he should remember
> the Ides of Marche, at which tyme they slue Julius Caesar :
> who nether pilled nor polled the contrye, but onely was a
> favorer and suborner of all them that did robbe and spoyle,
> by his countenaunce and authoritie. And if there were any
> occasion whereby they might honestly sette aside justice and
> equitie : they should have had more reason to have suffered
> Caesar's friendes, to have robbed and done what wronge and
> injurie they had would, then to beare with their owne men.
> For then, sayde he, they could but have sayde they had
> bene cowards : "and now they may accuse us of injustice, beside
> the paynes we take, and the daungèr we put our selves into."

Lastly at the end of the *Life of Brutus*, Shakespeare would find a short notice of the death of Portia. No indication is given of the date at which this took place, except that Plutarch seems on the whole to discredit the idea that she survived her husband.

> And for Porcia, Brutus wife: Nicolaus the Philosopher, and Valerius Maximus doe wryte. that she determining to kill her selfe (her parents and frendes carefullie looking to her to kepe her from it) tooke hot burning coles, and cast them into her mouth, and kept her mouth so close, that she choked her selfe. There was a letter of Brutus found wrytten to his frendes, complayning of their negligence, that his wife being sicke, they would not helpe her, but suffered her to kill her selfe, choosing to dye rather than to languish in paine. Thus it appeareth, that Nicolaus knewe not well that time, sith the letter (at the least if it were Brutus letter) doth plainly declare the disease and love of this Lady, as also the maner of her death.

Now in Shakespeare's scene all these detached jottings find their predestined place, and together have an accumulated import of which Plutarch has only the remotest guess. They are so combined as to bring out at once the ideal aspect of Brutus' deed, and its folly and disastrousness in view of the facts. He maintains his manhood under the most terrible ordeal, which is well; he clings to his illusion in the face of the clearest proof, which is not so well. He is gathering evil fruit where he looked for good, but he refuses to admit that the tree was corrupt; and of the prestige that his clear conscience confers, he still makes baneful use. He is raised to the heroic by his persistence in regarding the murder as an act of pure and disinterested justice, but for that very reason he makes his blunders, and puts himself and others in the wrong.

Perhaps indeed his loss of temper is to be ascribed to another cause. He is in a tense, over-wrought state, when the slightest thing will provoke an outbreak. In Cassius' view his private and personal

sorrow, the only one Cassius could understand,
might quite well, apart from all the rest, have driven
him to greater violence :

> How 'scaped I killing when I cross'd you so ?   (IV. iii. 150.)

No wonder he uses stinging words to his friend,
taxes him most unfairly with the boast of being a
better soldier, and flings aside Cassius' temperate
correction of "elder," with the contemptuous, "If
you did, I care not." No wonder he drives out the
poet, while Cassius merely laughs at him. Yet even
here, though he is undoubtedly the angrier and
more unreasonable in the quarrel, his moral dignity
just before has saved him from an indiscretion into
which Cassius falls. When the other begins to
complain before the soldiers, Brutus checks him :

> Cassius, be content ;
> Speak your griefs softly ; I do know you well.
> Before the eyes of both our armies here,
> Which should perceive nothing but love from us,
> Let us not wrangle : Bid them move away ;
> Then in my tent, Cassius, enlarge your griefs,
> And I will give you audience.   (IV. ii. 41.)

In the onset of misfortune Brutus does not forget
his weightier responsibilities, though the strain of
resisting it may impair his suavity. The fine balance
of his nature that was overthrown by suspense,
may well be shaken by his afflictions. For they
are more numerous than Cassius knew and more
poignant than he could understand.

Portia's suicide with all its terrible accessories
Brutus brings into relation with himself. It is
absence from him, and, as his love tells him, distress
at the growing power of his enemies that caused
her madness. The ruin of that home life which
was his native element, the agony and death of the
wife he worshipped, are the direct consequences of
his own act.

And with this private there has come also the public news. The proscription has already swept away seventy senators; Cicero, despite his "silver hairs," his "judgment," and his "gravity" being one; and the number given, according to Messala, is an understatement. Brutus had talked of each man's dropping by lottery under Caesar's rule, but however much Caesar had degenerated, would he have decreed a more wholesale and indiscriminate slaughter than this? Was there anything in his career as described by Brutus himself, that foreshadowed a callousness like that of the Triumvirs in pricking down and damning their victims, among them the most illustrious members of Brutus' own class? And the perpetrators, far from injuring their cause by these atrocities, are in a position to take the field with a "mighty power." So the civil war with all its horrors and miseries will run its full course.

But even that is not the worst. Brutus has to realise that his associates were not the men he supposed them. Their hands are not clean, their hearts are not pure, even his brother Cassius connives at corruption and has "an itching palm" himself. Even when the *soi disant* deliverers wield the power, what are things better than they would have been under Caesar who was at least personally free from such reproach and whose greatness entitled him to his place in front? Surely there are few more pathetic passages even in Shakespeare than the confession of disillusionment wrung from Brutus by the force of events, a confession none the less significant that he admits disillusion only as to the results and still clings to his estimate of the deed itself.

> Remember March, the ides of March remember:
> Did not great Julius bleed for justice' sake?
> What villain touch'd his body, that did stab,

And not for justice ?   What, shall one of us,
That struck the foremost man of all this world
But for supporting robbers, shall we now
Contaminate our fingers with base bribes,
And sell the mighty space of our large honours
For so much trash as may be grasped thus ?
I had rather be a dog, and bay the moon,
Than such a Roman.   (IV. iii. 18.)

It has come to this.   In anticipating the effects of
Caesar's rule, he had said he "had rather be a
villager than to repute himself a son of Rome" in
the probable conditions.   But his attempt at remedy
has resulted in a situation even more intolerable.
He would rather be a dog than such Romans as the
confederates whom he sought to put in Caesar's
place are disclosing themselves to be.

It says much for his intrinsic force, that when all
these things rise up in judgment against him, he can
still maintain to himself and others the essential
nobility of the deed that has brought about all the
woe and wrong; and without any faint-hearted
penitence, continue to insist that their doings must
conform to his conception of what has been done :
that if that conception conflicts with the facts, it is
the facts that must give way.   Yet on that very
account he is quite impracticable and perverse, as
every enthusiast for abstract justice must be, who
lets himself be seduced into crime on the plea of
duty, and yet shapes his course as though he were
not a criminal.

Brutus has brought about an upturn of society
by assassinating the one man who could organize
that society.   His own motives were honourable,
though not so unimpeachable as he assumed, but
they could not change wrong into right and they
could not be taken for granted in others than himself.   Now in the confusions that ensue he finds, to
his horror, that revolutions are not made with rose
water, that even champions of virtue have to reckon

with base and dirty tools.   So he condemns Pella
for bribery.   Cassius judges the case better.   He
sees that Pella is an efficient and useful officer of
whose services he does not wish to be deprived.
He sees that in domestic broils the leaders must
not be too particular about their instruments, that,
according to the old proverb, you must go into
the water to catch fish.   But Brutus will not
go into the water.   He thinks that an assassin
should only have Galahads in his troops.   And
sometimes his offended virtue becomes even a little
absurd.   He is angry with Cassius for not giving
him money, but listen to his speech :

> I did send to you
> For certain sums of gold, which you denied me :
> For I can raise no money by vile means :
> By heaven, I had rather coin my heart,
> And drop my blood for drachmas, than to wring
> From the hard hands of peasants their vile trash
> By any indirection : I did send
> To you for gold to pay my legions,
> Which you denied me : was that done like Cassius ?
> Should I have answer'd Caius Cassius so ?
> When Marcus Brutus grows so covetous
> To lock such rascal counters from his friends,
> Be ready, gods, with all your thunderbolts ;
> Dash him to pieces !   (IV. iii. 69.)

What does all this come to ?   That the superfine
Brutus will not be guilty of extortion, but that
Cassius may : and then Brutus will demand to share
in the proceeds.   All this distress and oppression
are his doing, or at least the consequences of his
deed, and he would wash his hands of these inevitable accompaniments.   He would do this by using
Cassius as his *âme damnée* while yet interfering
in Cassius' necessary measures with his moral
rebukes.[1]

---

[1] It will be noticed that in this episode Shakespeare has altered
Plutarch's narrative in two respects.   In the first place Cassius did

This of course is between Cassius and himself, and if Cassius chooses to submit, it is his own concern. But Brutus plays the Infallible to such purpose, that, what with his loftiness of view, his earnestness, and his marvellous fortitude, he obtains an authority over Cassius' mind that has disastrous results. Though Cassius is both the better and the elder soldier, he must needs intermeddle with Cassius' plan of campaign. Here, as so often, Shakespeare has no warrant for his most significant touch. Plutarch had said that Cassius, against his will, was overruled by Brutus to hazard their fortunes in a single battle. But that was afterwards, at Philippi. There is no hint that Cassius was opposed to the movement from Sardis to Philippi, and it is on this invented circumstance that Shakespeare lays most stress. In the play Brutus, in the teeth of his fellow generals' disapproval, insists on their leaving their vantage ground on the hills, chiefly as it appears because he dislikes the impositions they are compelled to lay on the people round about:

> They have grudged us contribution;   (iv. iii. 206.)

and because he has a vague belief that this is the nick of time;

> There is a tide in the affairs of men,
> Which, taken at the flood, leads on to fortune;
> Omitted, all the voyage of their lives
> Is bound in shallows and in miseries.   (iv. ii. 218.)

give money to the amount of "the thirde part of his totall summe." This is not very important, as in the play he disclaims having ever refused it. But in the second place Brutus was neither so scrupulous nor so unsuccessful in raising supplies, but had used them in a quite practical way, that Captain Mahan would thoroughly approve, in developing his sea power: "all that he could rappe and rend . . . he had bestowed it in making so great a number of shippes that by meanes of them they should keepe all the sea at their commaundement."

These are the arguments which he opposes to
Cassius' skilled strategy.   He will not even listen
to Cassius' rejoinder :

> *Cassius.*   Hear me, good brother—
> *Brutus.* Under your pardon :   (IV. iii. 212.)

and he runs on.   The spiritual dictator carries his
point, as he always does, and as here especially
he is bound to do, when their recent trial of strength
has ratified his powers afresh.   Cassius is hypnotised into compliance, "Then, with your will, go
on."   But Brutus is wrong.   He is doing the very
thing that the Triumvirs would have him do and
dare not hope he will do.   Octavius, when he hears
of the movement, exclaims :

> Now, Antony, our hopes are answered :
> You said the enemy would not come down,
> But keep the hills and upper regions :
> It proves not so.   (v. i. 1.)

The adoption of Brutus' plan, which he secured in
part through the advantage he had gained in the
quarrel, leads directly to the final catastrophe.

Here then we have the gist of the whole story.
The tribulations of Brutus that ensue on his grand
mistake, the wreck of his dearest affections, the
butchery at Rome, the oppression of the provinces,
the appalling discovery that his party is animated
by selfish greed and not by righteous zeal, and that
Caesar bore away the palm in character as well as
ability ; the dauntless resolution with which despite
his vibrant sensibility he bears up against the rudest
blows ; the sustaining consciousness that he himself
acted for the best, and the pathetic imagination even
now that the rest must live up to his standard ; the
warrant this gives him to complete the outward ruin
of the cause that already is rotten within—all this is
brought home to us in a passage of little more than
two hundred lines.   It is not merely a masterpiece

in characterisation; it at once garners the harvest
of the past and sows the seeds of the future. Nor
is the execution inferior to the conception; the
passion of the verse, the fluctuation of the dialogue,
provide the fit medium for the pregnancy and wealth
of the matter.[1]

But the scene is not yet at an end. Even now
we are not for a moment allowed to forget Brutus,
the considerate gentleman and cultured student, in
Brutus, the political pedant and the incompetent
commander. We have a momentary glimpse of
him with Lucius, unassuming and gentle, claiming
the indulgence, consulting the comfort, tending the
needs of his slave. This moving little passage is,

---

[1] Two objections have been made to this scene, or, rather to the
whole act. The first, in Mr. Bradley's words that it has a "tendency
to drag" (*Shakespearian Tragedy*), is put more uncompromisingly by
Mr. Baker (*Development of Shakespeare as a Dramatist*); "[Shake-
speare] produced in *Julius Caesar* a fourth act probably not entirely
successful even in his own day"; and afterwards he refers to it as
"ineffective to-day." In view of Digges' testimony, it is difficult to see
how Mr. Baker can say that it was not entirely successful in Shakespeare's day. As to the impression it makes now, one must largely
depend on one's own feeling and experience. Certainly I myself have
never been conscious that it dragged or was ineffective, nor have I
noted that it failed to stir the audience. I have never been present at
a first-rate performance, but I have seen it creditably presented in
Germany, England and Australia; and on every occasion it seemed
to me that the quarrel scene was the most popularly successful in the
play. This statement is, I believe, strictly accurate, for having
Digges' lines in my mind I was on the watch to see whether the taste
of the Elizabethan coincided with the taste of a later generation.
The second criticism is that in the economy of the piece it leads to
nothing, "unless," as Mr. Bradley says, "we may hold that but for the
quarrel and reconciliation, Cassius would not have allowed Brutus to
overcome his objection to the fatal policy of offering battle at
Philippi." This is quite true, though the proviso is a most important
one. But it does very manifestly connect with what has gone before,
and gives the essence and net result of the story. We could sooner
dispense with the Fifth Act than the Fourth, for the Fifth may with
less injustice be described as an appendix than the Fourth as an
episode. Not only is it less unique in kind, but for the most part it
works out issues that can easily be foreseen and that to some extent
are clearly indicated here. Of course this is not to say that it could
be rejected without mutilating the play, for it works them out far more
impressively than we could do in our own imaginations, even with
Plutarch to help us.

as we have seen, entirely due to Shakespeare, and it seems to be introduced for the sake partly of the dramatic contrast with the prevailing trouble and gloom, partly of the indication it gives that Brutus is still unchanged at heart. In the stress of his suffering he may be irritable and overbearing with Cassius, but he has more than a woman's tenderness for the boy.

His habit of reading at night is mentioned by Plutarch, but when we consider the circumstances, has it not a deeper meaning here? His love for Portia we know, but after his brief references to her death, he seems to banish her from his mind, and never, not even in his dying words, does her name cross his lips again. Is this an inadvertence on Shakespeare's part, or an omission due to the kinship of *Julius Caesar* with the Chronicle History? Is it not rather that he conceives Brutus as one of those who are so bound up in their affections that they fear to face a thought of their bereavement lest they should utterly collapse? Is it fanciful to interpret that search for his book with the leaf turned down, in the light of Macaulay's confession on the death of his sister: " Literature has saved my life and my reason ; even now I dare not in the intervals of business remain alone a minute without a book"?

But this little interlude, which sets Brutus before us with all his winsome and pathetic charm, leads back to the leading *motif*, the destruction he has brought on himself by his own error, though he may face it like a man and keep the beauty of his soul unsoiled. Here, too, Plutarch points the way, but Shakespeare advances further in it. What he found was the following bit of hearsay:

> One night very late (when all the campe tooke quiet rest) as he was in his tent with a little light, thinking of waighty matters, he thought he heard one come in to him,

and casting his eye towards the doore of his tent, that he
saw a wonderfull straunge and monstruous shape of a body
comming towards him, and sayd never a word.   So Brutus
boldly asked what he was, a god, or a man, and what cause
brought him thither.   The spirit aunswered him, " I am thy
evill spirit, Brutus, and thou shalt see me by the citie of
Philippes."   Brutus beeing no otherwise affrayd, replyed again
unto it : " Well, then, I shall see thee agayne."   The spirit
presently vanished away : and Brutus called his men unto
him, who tolde him that they heard no noyse, nor sawe
any thinge at all.

Shakespeare's Brutus is not at the outset so
unconcerned as Plutarch's.   Instead of "being no
otherwise affrayd," his blood runs cold and his hair
"stares."   On the other hand, he is free from the
perturbation that seizes Plutarch's Brutus when he
reflects, and that drives him to tell his experience
to Cassius, who "did somewhat comfort and quiet
him."   The Brutus of the play breathes no word of
the visitation, though it is repeated at Philippi,
till a few minutes before his death, and then in
all composure as a proof that the end is near, not
as a horror from which he seeks deliverance.   He
needs not the support of another, and even in the
moment of physical panic he has moral courage
enough : he summons up his resolution, and when
he has "taken heart" the spectre vanishes.   This
means, too, that it has a closer connection with his
nerves, with his subjective fears and misgivings,
than the "monstruous shape" in Plutarch, and
similarly, though he alleges that Lucius and his
attendants have cried out in their sleep, they are
unaware of any feeling or cause of fright.   And the
significance of this is marked by the greatest change
of all.   Shakespeare gives a personality to Plutarch's
nameless phantom : it is individualised as the ghost
of Caesar, and thus Caesar's spirit has become
Brutus' evil genius, as Brutus had been Caesar's
angel.   The symbolism explains itself, but is saved
from the tameness of allegory by the superstitious

dread with which it is enwrapped. The regrets and
forebodings of Brutus appear before him in outward
form. All day the mischievousness of his intervention has been present to his mind : now his accusing
thoughts take shape in the vision of his murdered
friend, and his vague presentiments of retribution
at Philippi leap to consciousness in its prophetic
words. But all this does not abash his soul or shake
his purpose. He only hastens the morning march.

Thus he moves to his doom, and never was he
so great. He is stripped of all adventitious aids.
His private affections are wrecked, and the thought
of his wife has become a torture. Facts have given
the lie to his belief that his country has chosen him
as her champion. He can no longer cherish the
dream that his course has been of benefit to the
Roman world. He even seems at last to recognise
his own guilt, for not only does he admit the might
of Caesar's spirit in the suicide of Cassius, but when
his own turn comes, his dying words sound like a
proffer of expiation :

> Caesar, now be still ;
> I kill'd not thee with half so good a will. (v. v. 50.)

The philosophic harness in which he felt so secure,
he has already found useless in the hour of need,
and fit only to be cast aside. So he stands naked
to the blows of fate, bereft of his love, his illusions,
his self-confidence, his creed. He has to rely solely
on himself, on his own nature and his own character.
Moreover his nature, in so far as it means temperament, is too delicate and fine for the rough practical
demands on it. Suspense is intolerable to his
sensitive and eager soul. Ere the battle begins,
he can hardly endure the uncertainty :

> O that a man might know
> The end of this day's business ere it come !
> But it sufficeth that the day will end,
> And then the end is known. (v. i. 123.)

The patience in which he tries to school himself cannot protect him from a last blunder. He gives the word too soon and his impetuosity ruins all. No doubt he is not so unsuccessful as Titinius thinks, but he has committed the unpardonable fault of fighting for his own hand without considering his partner. Thus his imprudence gives the final blow to the cause that all through he has thwarted and ennobled.

But in inward and essential matters his character victoriously stands the test, and meets all the calls that are made upon it. Even when his life-failure stares him in the face, he does not allow it a wider scope than its due, or let it disturb his faith in the purity of his motives.

> I am Brutus, Marcus Brutus, I :
> Brutus, my country's friend.   (v. iv. 7.)

Even now he can see himself aright, and be sure of the truth of his patriotism. Even now he can prefer the glory of this "losing day" to the "vile conquest" of such men as the authors of the proscription. And he is not without more personal consolations. When none of his friends will consent to kill him, their very refusal, since it springs from love, fills his soul with triumph. It is characteristic that this satisfaction to his private affections ranks with him as supreme at the end of all.

> Countrymen,
> My heart doth joy that yet in all my life
> I found no man but he was true to me.   (v. v. 33.)

We need not bemoan his fate : he is happy in it : indeed there is nothing that he could live for in the world of the Triumvirs, and this is what he himself desires :

> My bones would rest,
> That have but labour'd to attain this hour. (v. v. 41.)

At the side of this rare and lofty nature, we see the kindred figure of his wife, similar in her noble

traits, similar in her experiences, the true mate of
his soul.   Their relations are sketched in the merest
outline, or, to be more correct, are implied rather
than sketched.   Only in some eighty lines of one
scene do we see them together and hear them
exchange words.   In only one other scene does
Portia appear. when we witness her tremors on the
morning of the assassination.   And in a third we
hear of her death in detached notices, which, with
the comments they call forth, barely amount to
twenty lines.   Yet the impression made is indelible
and overpowering, not only of the lady's own character, but of the perfect union in which she and
Brutus lived.   There is no obtrusion of their love :
it does not exhale in direct professions.   On her
part, the claim to share his troubles, the solicitude
for his success, the distraction because of his absence
and danger ; on his, the acceptance of her claim, two
brief outbursts of adoration—and his reticence at
her death.   For he is not the man to wear his heart
on his sleeve ; and the more his feelings are stirred
the less inclined is he to prate of them.   Just as
after slaying Caesar though " he loved him well," he
never alludes to the anguish he must have endured,
so after his " Farewell, Portia," he turns to the claims
of life ("Well, to our work alive ! "), and never even
in soliloquy refers to her again.   Even in the first
pang of bereavement, the one hint of grief it can
extort from him is the curt retort, " No man bears
sorrow better."   We might fail to recognise all that
it meant for him if we did not see his misery reflected
in the sympathy and consternation of other men ; in
the hesitating reluctance of Messala, to break, as he
thinks, the news ; in the dismay of Cassius and his
wonder at Brutus' self-control.   Cassius indeed cannot
but recur to it despite the prohibition, " Speak no
more of her."   When they have sat down to business
his thoughts hark back to the great loss : " Portia,

art thou gone?" "No more, I pray you," repeats
Brutus, who cannot brook the mention of her, and
he plunges into the business of the hour.

And this woman, of whom Brutus felt that he was
unworthy, and prayed to be made worthy, noble and
devoted as himself, is involved too in his misfortunes.
On her also a greater load is laid than she can bear.
He is drawn by his political, and she by her domestic
ideal into a position that overstrains the strength of
each. She demands, as in Plutarch, though perhaps
with rather less of the dignity of the Roman matron
and rather more of the yearning of the affectionate
wife, to share in her husband's secrets. She does
this from no curiosity, intrusiveness or jealousy, but
from her unbounded love and her exalted conception
of the marriage tie. And she is confident that she
can bear her part in her husband's cares.

She has a great spirit, but it is lodged in a fragile
and nervous frame. Does she make her words
good? She gains her point, but her success is
almost too much for her. She can endure pain but
not suspense : like Brutus she is martyr·to her sense
of what is right. We presently find her all but
ruining the conspiracy by her uncontrollable agita
tion. The scene where she waits in the street serves
the function in the main story of heightening our
excitement by means of hers, in expectation of what
will presently be enacted at the Capitol; but it is
even more important for the light it throws on her
character. She may well confess : " I have a man's
heart, but a woman's might." Her feverish anxiety
quite overmasters her throughout, and makes her
do and say things which do not disclose the plot
only because the bystanders are faithful or unobser-
vant. She sends the boy to the senate house without
telling him his errand. She meaningly bids him

take good note
What Caesar doth, what suitors press about him. (II. iv. 15.)

She interrupts herself with the fancy that the revolt has begun. She plies the soothsayer with suspicious questions that culminate in the most indiscreet one on his wish to help Caesar :

> Why, know'st thou any harm's intended towards him ?
>
> (II. iv. 31.)

Then she almost commits herself, and has to extemporise a subterfuge, before, unable to hold out any longer, she retires on the point of fainting, though even now her love gives her strength to send a cheering message to her lord.

For her as for Brutus the burden of a duty, which she assumes by her own choice, but which one of her nature must assume, is too heavy. And in the after consequences, for which she is not directly responsible, but which none the less flow from the deed that she has encouraged and approved, it is the same inability to bear suspense, along with her craving for her husband's presence and success, that drives her through madness to death.

CHAPTER VI

THE REMAINING CHARACTERS

FAR beneath this pair are the other conspirators who rise up against the supremacy of Caesar.

Among these lower natures, Cassius is undoubtedly the most imposing and most interesting.

The main lines of his character are given in Caesar's masterly delineation, which follows Plutarch in regard to his spareness, but in the other particulars freely elaborates the impression that Plutarch's whole narrative produces.

> Yond Cassius has a lean and hungry look :
> He thinks too much : such men are dangerous . . .
>   He reads much ;
> He is a great observer, and he looks
> Quite through the deeds of men ; he loves no plays,
> As thou dost, Antony ; he hears no music ;
> Seldom he smiles, and smiles in such a sort
> As if he mock'd himself and scorn'd his spirit
> That could be moved to smile at anything.
> Such men as he be never at heart's ease
> Whiles they behold a greater than themselves,
> And therefore are they very dangerous.

(I. ii. 194 and 201.)

Lean, gaunt, hungry, disinclined to sports and revelry, spending his time in reading, observation, and reflection—these are the first traits that we notice in him. He too, like Brutus, has learned the lessons of philosophy, and he finds in it the rule of life.   He chides his friend for seeming to fail in the practice of it :

> Of your philosophy you make no use,
> If you give place to accidental evils.   (iv. iii. 145.)

And even when he admits and admires Brutus' self-mastery, he attibutes it to nature, and claims as good a philosophic discipline for himself.   There is, however, a difference between them even in this point.   Brutus is a Platonist with a Stoic tinge ; Cassius is an Epicurean.   That strikes us at first as strange, that the theory which identified pleasure with virtue should be the creed of this splenetic solitary : but it is quite in character.   Epicureanism appealed to some of the noblest minds of Rome, not as a cult of enjoyment, but as a doctrine that freed them from the bonds of superstition and the degrading fear of death.   This was the spirit of Lucretius, the poet of the sect :

> Artis
> Religionum animum nodis exsolvere pergo :

and one grand *motif* of his poem is the thought that this death, the dread of which makes the meanness of life, is the end of all consciousness, a refuge rather than an evil : " What ails thee so, O mortal, to let thyself loose in too feeble grievings ? Why weep and wail at death ? . . .   Why not rather make an end of life and labour ? "   And these are the reasons that Cassius is an Epicurean.   At the end, when his philosophy breaks down, he says :

> You know that I held Epicurus strong
> And his opinion : now I change my mind,
> And partly credit things that do presage.   (v. i. 77.)

He has hitherto discredited them.   And we seem to hear Lucretius in his noble utterance :

> Nor stony tower, nor walls of beaten brass,
> Nor airless dungeon, nor strong links of iron,
> Can be retentive to the strength of spirit :

> But life, being weary of these worldly bars,
> Never lacks power to dismiss itself.   (I. iii. 93.)

Free from all superstitious scruples and all thought of superhuman interference in the affairs of men, he stands out bold and self-reliant, confiding in his own powers, his own will, his own management :

> Men at some time are masters of their fates :
> The fault, dear Brutus, is not in our stars
> But in ourselves, that we are underlings.   (I. ii. 139.)

And the same attitude of mind implies that he is rid of all illusions. He is not deceived by shows. He looks quite through the deeds of men. He is not taken in by Casca's affectation of rudeness. He is not misled by Antony's apparent frivolity. He is not even dazzled by the glamour of Brutus' virtue, but notes its weak side and does not hesitate to play on it. Still less does Caesar's prestige subdue his criticism. On the contrary, with malicious contempt he recalls his want of endurance in swimming and the complaints of his sick-bed, and he keenly notes his superstitious lapses. He seldom smiles and when he does it is in scorn. We only once hear of his laughing. It is at the interposition of the poet, which rouses Brutus to indignation ; but the presumptuous absurdity of it tickles Cassius' sardonic humour.

For there is no doubt that he takes pleasure in detecting the weaknesses of his fellows. He has obvious relish in the thought that if he were Brutus he would not be thus cajoled, and he finds food for satisfaction in Caesar's merely physical defects. Yet there is as little of self-complacency as of hero-worship in the man. He turns his remorseless scrutiny on his own nature and his own cause, and neither maintains that the one is noble or the other honourable, nor denies the personal alloy in his motives. This is the purport of that strange

soliloquy that at first sight seems to place Cassius
in the ranks of Shakespeare's villains along with his
Iagos and Richards, rather than of the mixed
characters, compact of good and evil, to whom
nevertheless we feel that he is akin.

> Well, Brutus, thou art noble : yet, I see,
> Thy honourable metal may be wrought
> From that it is disposed : therefore it is meet
> That noble minds keep ever with their likes :
> For who so firm that cannot be seduced ?
> Caesar doth bear me hard : but he loves Brutus :
> If I were Brutus now and he were Cassius,
> He should not humour me.   (I. ii. 312.)

It frequently happens that cynics view themselves
as well as others in their meaner aspects. Probably
Cassius is making the worst of his own case and is
indulging that vein of self-mockery and scorn that
Caesar observed in him.[1] But at any rate the
lurking sense of unworthiness in himself and his
purpose will be apt to increase in such a man
his natural impatience of alleged superiority in his
fellows. He is jealous of excellence, seeks to
minimise it and will not tolerate it. It is on this
characteristic that Shakespeare lays stress. Plutarch
reports the saying "that Brutus could evill away
with the tyrannie and that Cassius hated the tyranne,
making many complayntes for the injuries he had
done him"; and instances Caesar's appropriation of
some lions that Cassius had intended for the sports,
as well as the affair of the city praetorship. But in
the play these specific grievances are almost effaced
in the vague statement, "Caesar doth bear me
hard"; which implies little more than general ill-
will. It is now resentment of pre-eminence that
makes Cassius a malcontent. Caesar finds him
"very dangerous" just because of his grudge at

[1] This explanation is offered with great diffidence, but it is the only
one I can suggest for what is perhaps the most perplexing passage in
the play, not even excepting the soliloquy of Brutus.

greatness; and his own avowal that he "would as lief not be as live to be in awe" of a thing like himself, merely puts a fairer colour on the same unamiable trait. He may represent republican liberty and equality, at least in the aristocratic acceptation, but it is on their less admirable side. His disposition is to level down, by repudiating the leader, not to level up, by learning from him. In the final results this would mean the triumph of the second best, a dull and uniform mediocrity in art, thought and politics, unbroken by the predominance of the man of genius and king of men. And it may be feared that this ideal, translated into the terms of democracy, is too frequent in our modern communities. But true freedom is not incompatible with the most loyal acknowledgment of the master-mind; witness the utterance of Browning's Pisan republican:

> The mass remains—
> Keep but the model safe, new men will rise
> To take its mould.

Yet notwithstanding this taint of enviousness and spite, Cassius is far from being a despicable or even an unattractive character. He may play the Devil's Advocate in regard to individuals, but he is capable of a high enthusiasm for his cause, such as it is. We must share his calenture of excitement, as he strides about the streets in the tempest that fills Casca with superstitious dread and Cicero with discomfort at the nasty weather. His republicanism may be a narrow creed, but at least he is willing to be a martyr to it; when he hears that Caesar is to wear the crown, his resolution is prompt and Roman-like:

> I know where I will wear this dagger then:
> Cassius from bondage will deliver Cassius.   (I. iii. 89.)

And surely at the moment of achievement, whatever was mean and sordid in the man is consumed

in his prophetic rapture that fires the soul of Brutus
and prolongs itself in his response.

> *Cassius.*   How many ages hence
> Shall this our lofty scene be acted over
> In states unborn and accents yet unknown !
>   *Brutus.* How many times shall Caesar bleed in sport
> That now on Pompey's basis lies along
> No worthier than the dust ! [1]   (III. i. 111.)

And even to individuals if they stand the test
of his mordant criticism, he can pay homage and
admiration. The perception that Brutus may be
worked upon is the toll he pays to his self-love,
but, that settled, he can feel deep reverence and
affection for Brutus' more ideal virtue. Perhaps
the best instance of it is the scene of their dispute.
Brutus, as we have seen, is practically, if not
theoretically, in the wrong, and certainly he is much
the more violent and bitter ; but Cassius submits to
receive his forgiveness and to welcome his assurance
that he will bear with him in future. This implies
no little deference and magnanimity in one who so
ill brooks a secondary role. But he does give the
lead to Brutus, and in all things, even against his
better judgment, yields him the primacy.

And then it is impossible not to respect his

---

[1] What a strange effect these words are apt to produce on auditor
and reader ! " How true ! " we say, " The prophecy is fulfilled. This
is happening now." And then the reflection comes that just because
that is the case there is no prophecy and no truth in the scene ; the
whole is being enacted, in sport. We experience a kind of vertigo, in
which we cannot distinguish the real and the illusory and yet are
conscious of both in their highest potence. And this is a characteristic
of all poetry, though it is not always brought so clearly before the
mind. In Shakespeare something of the kind is frequent : compare
the reference to the " squeaking Cleopatra " in *Antony and Cleopatra*,
which is almost exactly parallel ; compare too his favourite device of
the play within the play, when we see the actors of a few minutes ago,
sitting like ourselves as auditors ; and thus, on the one hand their own
performance seems comparatively real, but on the other there is the
constant reminder that we are in their position, and the whole is
merely spectacular. Dr. Brandes has some excellent remarks in this
connection on Tieck's Dramas in his *Romantic School in Germany*.

thorough efficiency. In whatsoever concerns the management of affairs and of men, he knows the right thing to do, and, when left to himself, he does it. He sees how needful Brutus is to the cause and gains him—gains him, in part by a trickery, which Shakespeare without historical warrant ascribes to him; but the trickery succeeds because he has gauged Brutus' nature aright. He takes the correct measure of the danger from Antony, of his love for Caesar and his talents, which Brutus so contemptuously underrates. So, too, after the assassination, when Brutus says,

> I know that we shall have him well to friend;

he answers,

> I wish we may : but yet I have a mind
> That fears him much ; and my misgiving still
> Falls shrewdly to the purpose. (III. i. 144.)

Brutus seeks to win Antony with general considerations of right and justice, Cassius employs a more effective argument :

> Your voice shall be as strong as any man's
> In the disposing of new dignities. (III. i. 177.)

He altogether disapproves of the permission granted to Antony to pronounce the funeral oration. He grasps the situation when the civil war breaks out much better than Brutus :

> In such a time as this it is not meet
> That every nice offence should bear his comment.
> (IV. iii. 7.)

His plans of the campaign are better, and he has a much better notion of conducting the battle.

All such shrewd sagacity is entitled to our respect. Yet even in this department Cassius is outdone by the unpractical Brutus, so soon as higher moral qualities are required, and the wisdom of the fox yields to the wisdom of the man. We have seen

that however passionate and wrong-headed Brutus
may be in their contention, he has too much sense
of the becoming to wrangle in public, as Cassius
begins to do. Another more conspicuous example
is furnished by the way in which they bear anxiety.
Shakespeare found an illustration of this in Plutarch,
which he has merely dramatised.

> When Caesar came out of his litter : Popilius Laena, that
> had talked before with Brutus and Cassius, and had prayed
> the goddes they might bring this enterprise to passe, went
> into Caesar and kept him a long time with a talke. Caesar
> gave good eare unto him. Wherefore the conspirators (if
> so they should be called) not hearing what he sayd to Caesar,
> but conjecturing by that he had told them a little before,
> that his talke was none other but the verie discoverie of their
> conspiracie : they were affrayed everie man of them, and one
> looking in an others face, it was easie to see that they all
> were of a minde, that it was no tarying for them till they
> were apprehended, but rather that they should kill them
> selves with their owne handes. And when Cassius and
> certaine other clapped their handes on their swordes under
> their gownes to draw them : Brutus marking the counten-
> aunce and gesture of Laena, and considering that he did use
> him selfe rather like an humble and earnest suter, then like
> an accuser : he sayd nothing to his companions (bicause
> there were amongst them that were not of the conspiracie)
> but with a pleasaunt countenaunce encouraged Cassius.
> And immediatlie after, Laena went from Caesar, and kissed
> his hande ; which shewed plainlie that it was for some matter
> concerning him selfe, that he had held him so long in talke.

Shakespeare, by rejecting the reason for the dumb
show, is able to present this scene in dialogue, and
thus bring out the contrast more vividly. Cassius
believes the worst, loses his head, now hurries on
Casca, now prepares for suicide. But Brutus, the
disinterested man, is less swayed by personal hopes
and fears, keeps his composure, urges his friend to
be constant, and can calmly judge of the situation.
It is the same defect of endurance that brings about
Cassius' death. Really things are shaping well for
them, but he misconstrues the signs just as he has

misconstrued the words of Lena, and kills himself owing to a mistake ; as Messala points out :

> Mistrust of good success hath done this deed.   (v. iii. 66.)

This want of inward strength explains the ascendancy which Brutus with his more dutiful and therefore more steadfast nature exercises over him, though Cassius is in many ways the more capable man of the two.   They both have schooled themselves in the discipline of fortitude, Brutus in Stoic renunciation, Cassius in Epicurean independence ; but in the great crises where nature asserts herself, Brutus is strong and Cassius is weak.   And as often happens with men, in the supreme trial their professed creeds no longer satisfy them, and they consciously abandon them.   But while Cassius in his evil fortune falls back on the superstitions [1] which he had ridiculed Caesar for adopting on his good fortune, Brutus falls back on his feeling of moral dignity, and gives himself the death which theoretically he disapproves.

Yet, when all is said and done, what a fine figure Cassius is, and how much both of love and respect he can inspire.   Plutarch's story of his death already bears witness to this, but Shakespeare with a few deeper strokes marks his own esteem.

Cassius thinking in deede that Titinnius was taken of the enemies, he then spake these wordes : " Desiring too much to live, I have lived to see one of my best frendes taken, for my sake, before my face."   After that, he gote into a tent where no bodie was, and tooke Pyndarus with him, one of his freed bondmen, whom he reserved ever for suche a pinche, since the cursed battell of the Parthians, when Crassus was slaine, though he notwithstanding scaped from that overthrow ; but then casting his cloke over his head, and holding out his bare neck unto Pindarus, he gave him his head to be striken of.   So the head was found severed from the bodie : but

[1] The trait is taken from Plutarch who, after enumerating the sinister omens before Philippi, adds : " the which beganne somewhat to alter Cassius minde from Epicurus opinions."

after that time Pindarus was never seene more. Whereupon some tooke occasion to say that he had slaine his master without his commaundement. By and by they knew the horsemen that came towards them, and might see Titinnius crowned with a garland of triumphe, who came before with great speede unto Cassius. But when he perceived by the cries and teares of his frends which tormented them selves the misfortune that had chaunced to his Captaine Cassius by mistaking; he drew out his sword, cursing him selfe a thousand times that he had taried so long, and so slue him selfe presentlie in the fielde. Brutus in the meane time came forward still, and understoode also that Cassius had bene over throwen: but he knew nothing of his death, till he came verie neere to his campe. So when he was come thither, after he had lamented the death of Cassius, calling him the last of all the Romanes, being impossible that Rome should ever breede againe so noble and valliant man as he: he caused his bodie to be buried, and sent it to the citie of Thassos, fearing least his funerals within the campe should cause great disorder.

In the play Pindarus is not yet enfranchised, and though he gains his freedom by the fatal stroke, would rather remain a slave than return to his native wilds at such a price. Titinius places his garland on the dead man's brow, and in fond regret slays himself, not with his own but with Cassius' sword. Brutus, with hardly a verbal change, repeats the eulogy that Plutarch puts in his mouth,

> The last of all the Romans, fare thee well!
> It is impossible that ever Rome
> Should breed thy fellow.

But he does not stop here. Flushed with his initial success, he expects to triumph and to live, and the years to come seem darkened with grief for his "brother":

> Friends, I owe more tears
> To this dead man than you shall see me pay.
> I shall find time, Cassius, I shall find time. (v. iii. 99.)

The minor conspirators, with the adherents of the cause and the humbler dependents, are of course sketched very slightly, as proportion requires, but they have all something to individualise them in gait or pose. Even in the crowded final act, where, as in the chronicle histories which Shakespeare was leaving behind him, a number of persons are introduced with whom we are almost or entirely unacquainted, there is no monotony in the subordinate figures. They are distinguished from or contrasted with each other in their circumstances, sentiments or fate. Thus Pindarus and Strato are both described as servants, they are both attached to their masters, they are both reluctantly compelled to assist in their masters' death. Should we have thought it possible to differentiate them in the compass of the score or so of lines at the dramatist's disposal? But Cassius' slave, who, since his capture, has been kept like a dog to do whatever his owner might bid him, will not abide the issue and uses his new liberty to flee beyond the Roman world. Strato, to whom Brutus characteristically turns because he is " a fellow of a good respect " with " some snatch of honour " in his life, claims Brutus' hand like an equal before he will hold the sword, confronts the victors with praise of the dead, hints to Messala that Brutus' course is the one to follow, and has too much self-respect to accept employment with Octavius till Messala "prefers," that is, recommends him.

So too with the three captains, all on the losing side, all devoted to their leaders. Titinius, who seems to feel that his love for Cassius exceeds that of Brutus

> (Brutus, come apace,
> And see how I regarded Caius Cassius)

will not outlive him. Lucilius is quite ready to die for his general, but spared by the generosity of Antony, survives to exult that Brutus has fulfilled his prophecy and been "like himself." Messala, who brought word of Portia's death, must now

L

tell the same tale of Cassius with the same keen sympathy for Brutus' grief; and though Strato seems to censure him for consenting to live " in bondage," he shows no bondman's mind when he grounds his preferment of Strato to Octavius on the fact of Strato's having done "the latest service to my master."

More prominent, but still in the background, are the subaltern members of the faction in Rome. Ligarius, the best of them, with his fiery enthusiasm and personal fealty to Brutus, is an excellent counterpart to the ingratiating and plausible Decius, the least erected spirit of the group. Between them comes Casca, the only one who may claim a word or two of comment, partly because he is sketched in some detail, partly because he is practically an original creation. Plutarch has only two particulars about him, the one that he was the first to strike Caesar and struck him from behind ; the other that when Caesar cried out and gripped his hand, he shouted to his brother in Greek. Shakespeare, as we have seen, summarily rejects his acquaintance with Greek, but the stab in the back sets his fancy to work, and he constructs for him a character and life-history to match.

Casca is a man who shares with Cassius the jealousy of greatness—"the envious Casca," Antony described him—but is vastly inferior to Cassius in consistency and manhood. He seems to be one of those alert, precocious natures, clever at the uptake in their youth and full of a promise that is not always fulfilled : Brutus recalls that "he was quick mettle when we went to school" (I. ii. 300). Such sprightly youngsters, when they fail, often do so from a certain lack of moral fibre. And so with Casca. He appears before us at first as the most obsequious henchman of Caesar. When Caesar calls for Cal-purnia, Casca is at his elbow : " Peace, ho ! Caesar speaks." When Caesar, hearing the soothsayer's shout, cries, "Ha! who calls?" Casca is again ready : "Bid every noise be still : peace yet again!" Cassius would never have condescended to that. For Casca resents the supremacy of Caesar as much as the proudest aristocrat of them all : he is only waiting an opportunity to throw off the mask. But meanwhile in his angry bitterness with himself and others he affects a cross-grained bluntness of speech, "puts on a tardy form," as Cassius says, plays the satirist and misanthrope, as many others conscious of double dealing have done, and treats friend and foe with caustic brutality. But it is characteristic that he is panic-stricken with the terrors of the tempestuous night, which he ekes out with super-stitious fancies. It illustrates his want both of inward robustness and of enlightened culture. We remember that Cicero's remark in Greek was Greek to him, and that Greek was as much the language of rationalists then, as was French of the eighteenth century *Philosophes*. Nor is it less characteristic that even at the assassination he apparently does not dare to face his victim. Antony describes his procedure

> Damned Casca, like a cur, behind
> Struck Caesar on the neck. (v. i. 43.)

Yet even Casca is not without redeeming qualities. His humour, in the account he gives of the corona-tion fiasco, has an undeniable flavour : its very tartness, as Cassius says, is a "sauce to his good wit." And there is a touch of nobility in his avowal :

> You speak to Casca, and to such a man
> That is no fleering tell-tale. Hold, my hand :
> Be factious for redress of all these griefs,
> And I will set this foot of mine as far
> As who goes farthest. (I. iii. 116.)

But among those little vignettes, that of Cicero is decidedly the masterpiece. For this Shakespeare got no assistance from any of the three Lives on which he drew for the rest of the play. Indeed the one little hint they contained he did not see fit to adopt. In the *Marcus Brutus* Plutarch says of the conspirators :

> For this cause they durst not acquaint Cicero with their conspiracie, although he was a man whome they loved dearlie and trusted best : for they were affrayed that he being a coward by nature, and age also having increased his feare, he would quite turne and alter all their purpose.

In the play their reason for leaving him out is very different :

> He will never follow anything
> That other men begin. (II. i. 151.)

It seems to me, however, highly probable that Shakespeare had read the *Life of Cicero* and obtained his general impression from it, though he invents the particular traits. The irritable vanity and self-consciousness of the man, which Brutus' objection implies, are, for example, prominent features in Plutarch's portrait. So too is his aversion for Caesar and Caesarism, which makes him view the offer of the crown, abortive though it has been, as a personal offence : Brutus observes that he

> Looks with such ferret and such fiery eyes
> As we have seen him in the Capitol
> Being cross'd in conference with some senators.
> (I. ii. 186.)

But he is very cautious, and even when venting his vexation in one of those biting gibes to which, by Plutarch's statement, he was too prone, he takes care to veil it in the safe obscurity of a foreign language. " He spoke Greek . . . but those that understood him smiled at one another and shook their heads " (I. ii. 282). This has sometimes been misinterpreted. Shakespeare has been taxed with the absurdity of making Cicero deliver a Greek speech in a popular assemblage. Surely he does nothing of the kind. It is a sally that he intends for his friends, and he takes the fit means for keeping it to them ; much as St. John might talk French, if he wished to be intelligible only to those who had made the Grand Tour and so were in a manner of his own set. Plutarch lays stress on his familiarity with Greek, as also on his study of the Greek Philosophers. This may have left some trace in the description of his bearing in contrast to Casca's, when they meet in the storm. Cool and sceptical, he cannot guess the cause of Casca's alarm. Even when the horrors of earthquake, wind and lightning, are described in detail, he asks unmoved :

> Why, saw you anything more wonderful?   (I. iii. 14.)

And after the enumeration of the portents, he critically replies :

> Indeed, it is a strange-disposed time :
> But men may construe things after their fashion,
> Clean from the purpose of the things themselves.
>
> (I. iii. 32.)

And then after a passing reference[1] to current affairs, he bids Casca good night. To him the moral of the whole tempest is : " This disturbed sky is not to walk in." Opinions may differ as to this being the real Cicero ; none will deny that it is a living type.

Apart from the main group of personages, more or less antagonistic to Caesar, stands the brilliant figure of his friend and avenger, the eloquent Mark Antony. Shakespeare conceives him as a man of genius and feeling but not of principle, resourceful and daring, ambitious of honour and power, but unscrupulous in his methods and a voluptuary in

---

[1] Trivial to him, to us full of tragic meaning.

his life. Caesar tells him that he is "fond of plays" and "revels long o' nights." Cassius calls him a "masker and a reveller." Brutus says that he is given "to sports, to wildness and much company."

He makes his first appearance as the tool of Caesar. With Asiatic flattery, as though in the eastern formula, to hear were to obey, he tells his master :

> When Caesar says "do this," it is perform'd.   (i. ii. 10.)

He perceives his unspoken desires, his innermost wishes, and offers him the crown. It is no wonder that Brutus should regard him but as a "limb of Caesar," or that Trebonius, considering him a mere time-server, should prophesy that he will "live and laugh" hereafter at Caesar's death. But they are wrong. They do not recognise either the genuineness of the affection that underlies his ingratiating ways, or the real genius that underlies his frivolity. Here, as everywhere, Cassius' estimate is the correct one. He fears Antony's "ingrafted love" for Caesar, and predicts that they will find in him "a shrewd contriver." Of the love indeed there can be no question. It is proved not only by his public utterances, which might be factitious, nor by his deeds, which might serve his private purposes, but by his words, when he is alone with his patron's corpse.

> O, pardon me, thou bleeding piece of earth,
> That I am meek and gentle with these butchers !
> Thou art the ruins of the noblest man
> That ever lived in the tide of times.
> Woe to the hand that shed this costly blood !
>
> (iii. i. 254.)

It is worth noting the grounds that Antony in this solitary outburst alleges for his love of Caesar. He is moved not by gratitude for favours past or the expectation of favours to come, but solely by the supreme nobility of the dead. To the claims of nobility, in truth, Antony is always responsive and he is ready to acknowledge it in Brutus too. "This was the noblest Roman of them all"; so he begins his heartfelt tribute to his vanquished foe. This generous sympathetic strain in his nature is one of the things that make him dangerous. He is far from acting a part in his laments for Caesar. He feels the grief that he proclaims and the greatness he extols. His emotions are easily stirred, especially by worthy objects, and he has only to give them free rein to impress other people.

But along with this he has a subtle, scheming intellect; he is as much a man of policy as a man of sentiment. After the flight of Brutus and Cassius, we see him planning how he and his colleagues may cut down Caesar's bequests, of which in his speech he had made so much; how he may shift some of the odium of his proceedings on to Lepidus' back; how they may best arrange to meet the opposition. This mixture of feeling and diplomacy is especially shown in his words and deeds after the assassination. He does not shrink from any base compliance. His servant appears before the murderers, and at his bidding "kneels," "falls down," lies "prostrate" in token of submission, promising that his master will follow Brutus' fortunes. But even here it is on the understanding that Caesar's death shall be justified; and when he himself enters he gives his love and grief free scope.

> O mighty Caesar, dost thou lie so low?
> Are all thy conquests, glories, triumphs, spoils,
> Shrunk to this little measure? Fare thee well.
> I know not, gentlemen, what you intend,
> Who else must be let blood, who else is rank:
> If I myself, there is no hour so fit
> As Caesar's death's hour, nor no instrument
> Of half that worth as those your swords, made rich

With the most noble blood of all this world.
I do beseech ye, if you bear me hard,
Now, whilst your purpled hands do reek and smoke,
Fulfil your pleasure.   Live a thousand years,
I shall not find myself so apt to die ;
No place will please me so, no mean of death,
As here by Caesar, and by you cut off,
The choice and master spirits of this age.   (III. i. 148.)

What could be more loyal on the one hand, or more
discreet on the other ?   For, as he is well aware, if
he comes to terms with the assassins at all, he is
liable to an alternative accusation.   Either his love
for Caesar was genuine, and then his reconciliation
with the murderers implies craven fear ; or, if he
can freely take their part, his previous homage to
Caesar was mere pretence.   As he himself says :

My credit now stands on such slippery ground,
That one of two bad ways you must conceit me,
Either a coward or a flatterer.   (III. i. 191.)

And what more dexterous course could he adopt
than to assert his devotion to Caesar without
restraint, with undiminished emphasis : and at the
same time to profess his respect for the conspirators,
" the choice and master spirits of this age," and his
readiness to join them *if* they prove that Caesar
deserved to die.   This honourable and reasonable
attitude, which honour and reason would in reality
prescribe, must especially impress Brutus, to whom
Antony is careful chiefly to address himself.   He
enters a doubtful suppliant ; at the end of the scene
not only are his life and credit safe, but he has won
from Brutus' magnanimity the means to overthrow
him.

It is characteristic of Antony that he has no
scruple about using the vantage ground he has
thus acquired.   He immediately determines to
employ the liberty of speech accorded him against
the men who have granted it.   To Octavius'

servant, who enters ere he has well ended his soliloquy, he says :

> Thou shalt not back till I have borne this corse
> Into the market place : there shall I try,
> In my oration, how the people take
> The cruel issue of these bloody men.　　(III. i. 291.)

He does not hesitate, though this course will involve in ruin those who have generously spared him and given him the weapons against themselves. Not even for his country's sake will he pause, though, with his prescient imagination, he sees in all their lurid details the horrors of the

> Domestic fury and fierce civil strife　　(I. iii. 263.)

that must inevitably ensue.

And he effects his purpose, without any other help, by his wonderful address to the citizens. Perhaps nowhere else in History or Literature do we find the procedure of the demagogue of Genius set forth with such masterly insight. For Antony shows himself a demagogue of the most profligate description, but as undeniably the very genius of the art of moving men. Consider the enormous difficulties of his position. He is speaking under limitation and by permission before a hostile audience that will barely give him a hearing, and his task is to turn them quite round, and make them adore what they hated and hate what they adored. How does he set about it?

He begins with an acknowledgment and compliment to Brutus : " For Brutus' sake I am beholding to you." He disclaims the intention of even praising the dead. He cites the charge of ambition, but not to reply to it, merely to point out that any ambition has been expiated. But then he insinuates arguments on the other side : Caesar's faithfulness and justice in friendship, the additions not to his private but to the public wealth that his victories secured,

his pitifulness to the poor, his refusal of the crown.
Really these things are no arguments at all.   They
have either nothing to do with the case, or are
perfectly compatible with ambition, or may have
been its very means or may have been meant to
cloak it.   Such indeed we know that in part at
least they were.   But that does not signify so far
as Antony's purpose is concerned.   They were all
matters well known to the public, fit to call forth
proud and grateful and pleasing reminiscences of
Caesar's career.   The orator has managed to praise
Caesar while not professing to do so : if he does not
disprove what Brutus said, yet in speaking what he
does know, he manages to discredit Brutus' authority.
And now these regretful associations stirred, he can
at any rate ask their tears for their former favourite.
Have they lost their reason that they do not at least
mourn for him they once loved ?   And here with a
rhetorical trick, which, to his facile, emotional nature,
may have also been the suggestion of real feeling,
his utterance fails him ; he must pause, for his
" heart is in the coffin there with Caesar."

We may be sure that whatever had happened to
his heart his ear was intent to catch the murmurs of
the crowd.   They would satisfy him.   Though he
has not advanced one real argument, but has only
played as it were on their sensations, their mood
has changed.   Some think Caesar has had wrong,
some are convinced that he was not ambitious, all
are now thoroughly favourable to Antony.

He begins again.   And now he strikes the note
of contrast between Caesar's greatness yesterday
and his impotence to-day.   It is such a tragic fall
as in itself might move all hearts to terror and pity.
But what if the catastrophe were undeserved ?
Antony could prove that it was, but he will keep
faith with the conspirators and refrain.   Nevertheless he has the testament, though he will not read

it, which, read, would show them that Caesar was their best friend.

Compassion, curiosity, selfishness are now enlisted on his side. Cries of " The will! The will!" arise. He is quick to take advantage of these. Just as he would not praise Caesar, yet did so all the same ; so he refuses to read the will, for they would rise in mutiny—this is a little preliminary hint to them—if they heard that Caesar had made them his heirs.

Renewed insistence on the part of the mob, renewed coyness on the part of Antony ; till at last he steps down from the pulpit, taking care to have a wide circle round him that as many as possible may see. But he does not read the will immediately. Partly with his incomparable eye to effect, partly out of the fullness of his heart (for the substance of his words is the same as in his private soliloquy), he stands rapt above the body. Caesar's mantle recalls proud memories of the glory of Caesar and of Rome, the victory over the Barbarian.[1] And this mantle is pierced by the stabs of assassins, of Cassius, of Casca, of Brutus himself. He has now advanced so far that he can attack the man who was the idol of the

---

[1] Plutarch's account of Caesar's personal prowess in the battle with the Nervii, and of the honours decreed him by the Senate, shows why Shakespeare chose this exploit for special mention : " Had not Caesar selfe taken his shield on his arme, and flying in amongest the barbarous people, made a lane through them that fought before him ; and the tenth legion also seeing him in daunger, ronne unto him from the toppe of the hill, where they stoode in battell,* and broken the ranckes of their enemies ; there had not a Romane escaped a live that day. But taking example of Caesar's valliantnes, they fought desperatly beyond their power, and yet could not make the Nervians flie, but they fought it out to the death, till they were all in manner slaine in the field. . . . The Senate understanding it at Rome, ordained that they shoulde doe sacrifice unto the goddes, and keepe feasts and solemne processions fifteene dayes together without intermission, having never made the like ordinaunce at Rome, for any victorie that ever was obteined. Bicause they saw the daunger had bene marvelous great, so many nations rising as they did in armes together against him : and further the love of the people unto him made his victorie much more famous.

* battle order

mob but a few minutes before. And he makes his
attack well. The very superiority of Brutus to personal claims, the very patriotism which none could
appreciate better than Antony, and to which he does
large justice when Brutus is no more, this very
disinterestedness he turns against Brutus, and despite
all he owes him, accuses him of black ingratitude.
There is so much speciousness in the charge that it
would be hard to rebut before a tribunal of sages :
and when Antony makes his *coup*, withdrawing the
mantle and displaying the mutilated corpse,

> Kind souls, what, weep you when you but behold
> Our Caesar's vesture wounded? Look you here,
> Here is himself, marr'd, as you see, with traitors :
> (III. ii. 199.)

the cause of Brutus is doomed. Antony has a right
to exult, and he does so. There is the triumphant
pride of the artist in his art, when, on resuming, he
represents Brutus as the rhetorician and himself as
the unpractised speaker. He is no orator as Brutus
is, and—with sublime effrontery—that was probably
the reason he was permitted to address them. But

> Were I Brutus
> And Brutus Antony, there were an Antony
> Would ruffle up your spirits and put a tongue
> In every wound of Caesar, that should move
> The stones of Rome to rise and mutiny. (III. ii. 230.)

Note the last words: for though Antony feels entitled
to indulge in this farcing and enjoys it thoroughly,
he does not forget the serious business. He keeps
recurring more and more distinctly to the suggestion
of mutiny, and for mutiny the citizens are now more
than fully primed. All this, moreover, he has achieved
without ever playing his trump card. They have
quite forgotten about the will, and indeed it is not
required. But Antony thinks it well to have them
beside themselves, so he calls them back for this last
maddening draught.

And all the while, it will be observed, he has
never answered Brutus' charge on which he rested
his whole case, that Caesar was ambitious. Yet
such is the headlong flight of his eloquence, winged
by genius, by passion, by craft, that his audience
never perceive this. No wonder : it is apt to escape
even deliberate readers.

Such a man will go fast and far. We next see
him practically the ruler of Rome, swaying the
triumvirate, treating Octavius as an admiring pupil
whom he will tutor in the trade, ordering about or
ridiculing the insignificant and imitative Lepidus.[1]

But he has the *hybris* of genius, unaccompanied
by character and undermined by licence. It would
be an anomaly if such an one were to be permanently successful. Shakespeare was by and by,
though probably as yet he knew it not, to devote
a whole play to the story of his downfall ; here he
contents himself with indicating his impending
deposition and the agent who shall accomplish it.
There is something ominous about the reticence,
assurance, and calm self-assertion of the "stripling
or springall of twenty years" as Plutarch calls
Octavius. At the proscription Lepidus and even
Antony are represented as consenting to the death
of their kinsfolk : Octavius makes demands but no
concessions. When Lepidus is ordered off on his
errand, and Antony, secure in his superiority, explains
his methods, Octavius listens silent with just a hint
of dissent, but we feel that he is learning his lessons
and will apply them in due time at his teacher's
expense. Already he appropriates the leadership.
Before Philippi, Antony assigns to him the left wing
and he calmly answers :

> Upon the right hand I, keep thou the left.
> *Antony.* Why do you cross me in this exigent ?
> *Octavius.* I do not cross you : but I will do so. (v. i. 18.)

[1] In Plutarch Antony treats Lepidus with studied deference.

All these touches are contributed by Shakespeare, but the last is especially noticeable, because, though the words and the particular turn are his own, the incident itself is narrated not of Antony and Octavius but of their opponents.

> Then Brutus prayed Cassius he might have the leading of the right winge, the whiche men thought was farre meeter for Cassius : both bicause he was the elder man, and also for that he had the better experience. But yet Cassius gave it him.

Octavius too has a higher conception of the dignity of his position. In that strange scene, another of Shakespeare's additions, when the adversaries exchange *gabs*, like the heroes of the old Teutonic lays or the *Chansons de Gestes*, it is Antony who suggests the somewhat unseemly proceeding and it is Octavius who breaks it off. And at the close he, as it were, constitutes himself the heir of Brutus' reputation, and assumes as a matter of course that he has the right and duty to provide for Brutus' followers and take order for Brutus' funeral.

> All that served Brutus, I will entertain them . . .
> According to his virtue let us use him
> With all respect and rites of burial
> Within my tent his bones tonight shall lie.
> (v. v. 60 and 76.)

For the first of these statements there is no warrant in Plutarch, and the second contradicts the impression his narrative produces ; for in all the mention he makes of the final honours 'paid to Brutus, he gives the credit to Antony.

> Antonius, having found Brutus bodie, he caused it to be wrapped up in one of the richest cote armors he had. Afterwards also, Antonius understanding that this cote armor was stollen, he put the theefe to death that had stollen it, and sent the ashes of his bodie to Servilia his mother.
>
> *Marcus Brutus.*

And more explicitly in the *Marcus Antonius* :

> (Antony) cast his coate armor (which was wonderfull rich and sumptuous) upon Brutus bodie, and gave commaundement to one of his slaves infranchised to defray the charge of his buriall.

By means of these additions and displacements Shakespeare shows the young Octavius with his tenacity and self-control already superseding his older and more brilliant colleague. We see in them the beginning as well as the prophecy of the end.

CHAPTER I

POSITION OF THE PLAY AFTER THE GREAT TRAGEDIES. SHAKESPEARE'S INTEREST IN THE SUBJECT

IT may be taken as certain that Shakespeare did not at once set about continuing the story which he had brought to the end of one of its stages in *Julius Caesar* and of the future progress of which he had in that play given the partial programme. *Antony and Cleopatra* belongs to a different phase of his development.

Though not published, so far as we know, till it appeared in the Folio Edition of 1623, there is not much difficulty in finding its approximate date ; and that, despite its close connection with *Julius Caesar* in the general march of events and in the re-employment of some of the characters, was some half-dozen years after the composition of its predecessor. The main grounds for this opinion, now almost universally accepted, are the following:

1. We learn from the *Stationers' Register* that the publisher, Edward Blount, had entered a "booke called *Antony and Cleopatra*" on May 20th, 1608. Some critics have maintained that this could not be Shakespeare's in view of the fact that in November, 1623, license was granted

to the same Blount and the younger Jaggard, with whom he was now co-operating, to include in the collected edition the Shakespearian piece among sixteen plays of which the copies were "not formerly entered to other men." But the objection hardly applies, as the previous entry was in Blount's favour, and, though he is now associated with Jaggard, he may not have thought it necessary, because of a change of firm as it were, to describe himself as "another man." Even, however, if the authorship of the 1608 play be considered doubtful, its publication is significant. For, as has often been pointed out, it was customary when a piece was successful at one theatre to produce one on a similar subject at another. The mere existence, then, of an *Antony and Cleopatra* in the early months of 1608, is in so far an argument that about that time the great *Antony and Cleopatra* was attracting attention.

2. There is evidence that in the preceding years Shakespeare was occupied with and impressed by the *Life of Antony*.

(*a*) Plutarch tells how sorely Antony took to heart what he considered the disloyalty of his followers after Actium.

> He forsooke the citie and companie of his frendes, and built him a house in the sea, by the Ile of Pharos, upon certaine forced mountes which he caused to be cast into the sea, and dwelt there, as a man that banished him selfe from all mens companie; saying he would live Timons life, bicause he had the like wrong offered him, that was affore offered unto Timon: and that for the unthankefulnes of those he had done good unto, and whom he tooke to be his frendes he was angry with all men, and would trust no man.

In reference to this withdrawal of Antony's to the Timoneon, as he called his solitary house, Plutarch inserts the story of Timon of Athens, and there is reason to believe that Shakespeare made his contributions to the play of that name just before he wrote *Macbeth*, about the year 1606.[1]

(*b*) In *Macbeth* itself he has utilised the *Marcus Antonius* probably for one passage and certainly for another. In describing the scarcity of food among the Roman army in Parthia, Plutarch says :

> In the ende they were compelled to live of erbes and rootes, but they found few of them that men doe commonly eate of, and were enforced to tast of them that were never eaten before : among the which there was one that killed them, and *made them out of their witts*. For he that had once eaten of it, his memorye was gone from him, and he knewe no manner of thing.

Shakespeare is most likely thinking of this when after the disappearance of the witches, he makes Banquo exclaim in bewilderment :

> Were such things here as we do speak about ?
> Or have we eaten on the insane *root*
> That *takes the reason prisoner*.   (I. iii. 83.)

In any case *Macbeth* contains an unmistakable reminiscence of the soothsayer's warning to Antony.

> He . . . told Antonius plainly, that his fortune (which of it selfe was excellent good, and very great) was altogether bleamished, and obscured by Caesars fortune : and therefore he counselled him utterly to leave his company, and to get him as farre from him as he could. "For thy Demon," said he (that is to say, the good angell and spirit that kepeth thee), "is affraied of his, and being coragious and high when he is alone, becometh fearefull and timerous when he commeth neere unto the other."

Shakespeare was to make use of this in detail when he drew on the *Life* for an independent play.

> O Antony, stay not by his side :
> Thy demon, that's thy spirit which keeps thee, is
> Noble, courageous, high, unmatchable
> Where Caesar's is not ; but, near him, thy angel
> Becomes a fear, as being o'erpower'd : therefore
> Make space enough between you.   (II. iii. 18.)

---

[1] See Bradley, *Shakespearian Tragedy*.

But already in *Macbeth* it suggests a simile, when the King gives words to his mistrust of Banquo :

> There is none but he
> Whose being I do fear : and, under him,
> My Genius is rebuked ; as, it is said,
> Mark Antony's was by Caesar.[1]   (III. i. 54.)

More interesting and convincing is a coincidence that Malone pointed out in Chapman's *Bussy d'Ambois*, which was printed in 1607, but was probably written much earlier. Bussy says to Tamyra of the terrors of Sin :

> So our ignorance tames us, that we let
> His [2] shadows fright us : and like *empty clouds*
> In which our faulty apprehensions forge
> The forms of *dragons*, *lions*, elephants,
> When they *hold no proportion*, the sly charms
> Of the Witch Policy makes him like a monster.
>   (III. i. 22.)

Compare Antony's words :

> Sometime we see a *cloud that's dragonish :*
> A vapour sometimes like a bear or lion . . .
> . . . .   Here I am Antony :
> Yet *cannot hold this visible shape.*   (IV. xiv. 2 and 13.)

It is hard to believe that there is no connection between these passages, and if there is Shakespeare must have been the debtor ; but as *Bussy d'Ambois*

---

[1] I have said nothing of other possible references and loans because they seem to me irrelevant or doubtful. Thus Malone drew attention to the words of Morose in Ben Jonson's *Epicoene* : " Nay, I would sit out a play that were nothing but fights at sea, drum, trumpet and target." He thought that this remark might contain ironical allusion to the battle scenes in *Antony and Cleopatra,* for instance the stage direction at the head of Act III., Scene 10 : " Canidius marcheth with his land army one way over the stage : and Taurus, the lieutenant of Caesar the other way. After their going in is heard the noise of a sea-fight." But even were this more certain than it is, it would only prove that *Antony and Cleopatra* had made so much impression as to give points to the satirist some time after its performance : it would not help us to the date. For *Epicoene* belongs to 1610, and no one would place *Antony and Cleopatra* so late.

[2] *i.e.* Sin's.

was acted before 1600, this loan is without much value as a chronological indication.

3. Internal evidence likewise points to a date shortly after the composition of *Macbeth*.

(*a*) In versification especially valuable indications are furnished by the proportion of what Professor Ingram has called the light and the weak endings. By these terms he denotes the conclusion of the verse with a syllable that cannot easily or that cannot fully bear the stress which the normal scansion would lay upon it. In either case the effect is to break down the independence of the separate line as unit, and to vest the rhythm in the couplet or sequence, by forcing us on till we find an adequate resting-place. It thus has some analogy in formal prosody to enjambement, or the discrepancy between the metrical and the grammatical pause in prosody when viewed in connection with the sense. Now the employment of light and weak endings, on the one hand, and of enjambement on the other, is, generally speaking, much more frequent in the plays that are considered to be late than in those that are considered to be early. The tendency to enjambement indeed may be traced farther back and proceeds less regularly. But the laxity in regard to the endings comes with a rush and seems steadily to advance. It is first conspicuous in *Antony and Cleopatra* and reaches its maximum in *Henry VIII*. In this progress however there is one notable peculiarity. While it is unmistakable if the percentage be taken from the light and weak endings combined, or from the weak endings alone, it breaks down if the light endings be considered by themselves. Of them there is a decidedly higher proportion in *Antony and Cleopatra* than in *Coriolanus*, which nevertheless is almost universally held to be the later play. The reason probably is that the light endings mean a less revolutionary departure from the more rigid system and would therefore be the first to be attempted. When the ear had accustomed itself to them, it would be ready to accept the greater innovation. Thus the sudden outcrop of light and weak endings in *Antony and Cleopatra*, the preponderance of the light over the weak in that play, the increase in the total percentage of such endings and especially in the relative percentage of weak endings in the dramas that for various reasons are believed to be later, all confirm its position after *Macbeth* and before *Coriolanus*.

(*b*) The diction tells the same tale. Whether we admire it or no, we must admit that it is very concise, bold and difficult. Gervinus censures it as "forced, abrupt and obscure"; and it certainly makes demands on the reader. But Englishmen will rather agree with the well-known eulogy of Coleridge : "*Feliciter audax* is the motto for its style comparatively with that of Shakspere's other works, even as it is the general motto of all his works compared with those of other poets. Be it remembered, too, that this happy valiancy of style is but the representative and result of all the material excellences so expressed." But in any case, whether to be praised or blamed, it is a typical example of Shakespeare's final manner, the manner that characterises *Coriolanus* and the Romances, and that shows itself only occasionally or incompletely in his preceding works.

4. A consideration of the tone of the tragedy yields similar results. It has been pointed out [1] that there is a gradual lightening in the atmosphere of Shakespeare's plays after the composition of *Othello* and *Lear*. In them, and especially in the latter, we move in the deepest gloom. It is to them that critics point who read in Shakespeare

---

[1] Bradley, *Shakespearian Tragedy*.

a message of pessimism and despair. And though there are not wanting, for those who will see them, glimpses of comfort and hope even in their horror of thick darkness, it must be owned that the misery and murder of Desdemona, the torture and remorse of Othello, the persecution of Lear, the hanging of Cordelia, are more harrowing and appalling than the heart can well endure. But we are conscious of a difference in the others of the group. Though Macbeth retains our sympathy to the last, his story does not rouse our questionings as do the stories of these earlier victims. We are well content that he should expiate his crimes, and that a cleaner hand should inherit the sceptre : we recognise the justice of the retribution and hail the dawn of better times. In *Coriolanus* the feeling is not only of assent but of exultation. True, the tragedy ends with the hero's death, but that is no unmitigated evil. He has won back something of his lost nobility and risen to the greatest height his nature could attain, in renouncing his revenge : after that what was there that he could live for either in Corioli or Rome ?

Antony and Cleopatra has points of contact with both these plays, and shows like them that the night is on the wane. Of course in one way the view of life is still disconsolate enough. The lust of the flesh and the lust of the eye and the pride of life : ambitious egoism, uninspired craft and conventional propriety ; these are the forces that clash in this gorgeous mêlée of the West and the East. At the outset passion holds the lists, then self-interest takes the lead, but principle never has a chance. We think of Lucifera's palace in the *Faerie Queene*, with the seven deadly sins passing in arrogant gala before the marble front, and with the shifting foundations beneath, the dungeons and ruins at the rear. The superb shows of life are displayed in all their superbness and in all their vanity. In the end their worshippers are exposed as their dupes. Antony is a cloud and a dream, Cleopatra no better than "a maid that milks and does the meanest chares": yet she sees that it is "paltry to be Caesar," and hears Antony mock at Caesar's luck. Whatever the goal, it is a futile one, and the objects of human desire are shown on their seamy side. We seem to lose sight of ideals, and idealism would be out of place. Even the passing reference to Shakespeare's own art shows a dissipation of the glamour. In *Julius Caesar* Brutus and Cassius had looked forward to an immortality of glory on the stage and evidently regard the theatre as equal to the highest demands, but now to Cleopatra it is only an affair of vulgar makeshifts that parodies what it presents.

> I shall see
> Some squeaking Cleopatra boy my greatness
> I' the posture of a whore. (v. ii. 219.)

In so far the impression produced is a cheerless one, and Gervinus has gone so far as to say: "There is no great or noble character among the personages, no really elevated feature in the action of this drama whether in its politics or its love affairs." This is excessive : but it is true that, as in *Timon*, the suggestion for which came from the same source and the composition of which may be dated a short time before, no very spiritual note is struck and no very dutiful figure is to the fore. And the background is a lurid one. "A world-catastrophe!" says Dr. Brandes, "(Shakespeare) has no mind now to write of anything else. What is sounding in his ears, what is filling his thoughts, is the crash of a world falling in ruins. . . . The might of Rome, stern and austere, shivered at the touch of Eastern voluptuousness. Everything sank, everything fell,—character and will, dominions and principalities, men and women. Everything was worm-eaten, serpent-bitten, poisoned by sensuality—everything tottered and collapsed."

Yet though the sultry splendours of the scenes seem to blast rather than foster, though the air is laden with pestilence, and none of the protagonists has escaped the infection, the total effect is anything but depressing. As in *Macbeth* we accept without demur the penalty exacted for the offence. As in *Coriolanus* we welcome the magnanimity that the offenders recover or achieve at the close. If there is less of acquiescence in vindicated justice than in the first, if there is less of elation at the triumph of the nobler self than in the second, there is yet something of both. In this respect too it seems to stand between them and we cannot be far wrong if we place it shortly after the one and shortly before the other, near the end of 1607.

And that means too that it comes near the end of Shakespeare's tragic period, when his four chief tragedies were already composed and when he was well aware of all the requirements of the tragic art. In his quartet of masterpieces he was free to fulfil these requirements without let or hindrance, for he was elaborating material that claimed no particular reverence from him. But now he turns once more to authorised history and in doing so once more submits to the limitations that in his practice authorised history imposed. Why he did so it is of course impossible to say. It was a famous story, accessible to the English public in some form or other from the days of Chaucer's *Legend of Good Women*, and at an early age Shakespeare was attracted by it, or at least was conversant with Cleopatra's reputation as one of the world's paragons of beauty. In *Romeo and Juliet* Mercutio includes her in his list of those, Dido,

Hero, Thisbe and the rest, who in Romeo's eyes are nothing to his Rosaline ; compared with that lady he finds "Cleopatra a gipsy."[1]   And so indeed she was, for gipsy at first meant nothing else than Egyptian. and Skelton, in his *Garland of Laurel*, swearing by St. Mary of Egypt, exclaims :

> By Mary gipcy,
> Quod scripsi scripsi.

But in current belief the black-haired, tawny vagrants, who, from the commencement of the sixteenth century, despite cruel enactments cruelly enforced, began to swarm into England, were of Egyptian stock.   And precisely in this there lay a paradox and riddle, for according to conventional ideas they were anything but comely, and yet it was a matter of common fame that a great Roman had thrown away rule, honour and duty in reckless adoration of the queen of the race.   Perhaps Shakespeare had this typical instance in his mind when in *Midsummer Night's Dream* he talks of the madness of the lover who
> Sees Helen's beauty in a brow of Egypt.   (v. i. 11.)

For to the end the poet ignores the purity of Cleopatra's Greek descent, and seems by many touches to imagine her as of the same type as those undesirable immigrants against whom the penal laws were of so little avail.   Nevertheless he accepts the fact of her charm, and, in *As You Like It*, among the contributions which the "Heavenly Synod" levied on the supreme examples of womankind for the equipment of Rosalind, specifies "Cleopatra's majesty."[2]   It is not the quality on which he was afterwards to lay stress, it is not the quality that Plutarch accentuates, nor is it likely to have been suggested by the gipsies he had seen.   But there was another source on which he may have drawn.   Next to the story of

[1] II. iv. 44.   [2] III. ii. 154.

Julius Caesar, the story of Antony and Cleopatra was perhaps the prerogative Roman theme among the dramatists of the sixteenth century [1] and was associated with such illustrious personages as Jodelle and Garnier in France, and the Countess of Pembroke and Daniel in England. It is, as we have seen, highly probable that Shakespeare had read the versions of his compatriots at any rate, and their dignified harangues are just of the kind to produce the impression of loftiness and state.

Be that as it may, Cleopatra was a familiar name to Shakespeare when he began seriously to immerse himself in her history. We can understand how it would stir his heart as it filled in and corrected his previous vague surmises. What a revelation of her witchcraft would be that glowing picture of her progress when, careless and calculating, she condescended to obey the summons of the Roman

---

[1] Besides the plays discussed in the Introduction as having a possible place in the lineage of Shakespeare's, others were produced on the Continent, which in that respect are quite negligible but which serve to prove the widespread interest in the subject. Thus in 1560 Hans Sachs in Germany composed, in seven acts, one of his homespun, well-meant dramas that were intended to edify spectator or reader. Thus in 1583 Cinthio in Italy treated the same theme, and it has been conjectured, by Klein, that his *Cleopatra* was known to Shakespeare. Certainly Shakespeare makes use of Cinthio's novels, but the particulars signalised by Klein, that are common to the English and to the Italian tragedy, which latter I have not been able to procure, are, to use Klein's own term, merely "external," and are to be explained, in so far as they are valid at all, which Moeller (*Kleopatra in der Tragödien-literatur*) disputes, by reference to Plutarch. An additional one which Moeller suggests without attaching much weight to it, is even less plausible than he supposes. He points out that Octavius' emissary, who in Plutarch is called Thyrsus, in Cinthio becomes Tireo, as in Shakespeare he similarly becomes Thyreus ; but he notes that this is also the name that Shakespeare would get from North. As a matter of fact, however, in the 1623 folio of *Antony and Cleopatra* and in subsequent editions till the time of Theobald, this personage, for some reason or other as yet undiscovered, is styled Thidias ; so the alleged coincidence is not so much unimportant as fallacious. A third tragedy, Montreuil's *Cléopatre*, which like Cinthio s is inaccessible to me, was published in France in 1595 ; but to judge from Moeller's analysis and the list of *dramatis personae*, it has no contact with Shakespeare's.

conqueror and answer the charge that she had helped Brutus in his campaign.

> When she was sent unto by divers letters, both from Antonius him selfe and also from his frendes, she made so light of it, and mocked Antonius so much, that she disdained to set forward otherwise, but to take her barge in the river of Cydnus, the poope whereof was of gold, the sailes of purple, and the owers of silver, which kept stroke in rowing after the sounde of the musicke of flutes, howboyes, citherns, violls, and such other instruments as they played upon in the barge. And now for the person of her selfe: she was layed under a pavillion of cloth of gold of tissue, apparelled and attired like the goddesse Venus, commonly drawen in picture: and hard by her, on either hand of her, pretie faire boyes apparelled as painters doe set forth god Cupide, with little fannes in their hands, with which they fanned wind upon her. Her ladies and gentlewomen also, the fairest of them were apparelled like the nymphes Nereides (which are the mermaides of the waters) and like the Graces, some stearing the helme, others tending the tackle and ropes of the barge, out of which there came a wonderfull passing sweete savor of perfumes, that perfumed the wharfes side pestered[1] with innumerable multitudes of people. Some of them followed the barge all alongest the rivers side: others also ranne out of the citie to see her comming in. So that in thend, there ranne such multitudes of people one after an other to see her, that Antonius was left post alone in the market place, in his Imperiall seate to geve audience: and there went a rumor in the peoples mouthes that the goddesse Venus was come to play with the god Bacchus,[2] for the generall good of all Asia. When Cleopatra landed, Antonius sent to invite her to supper with him. But she sent him word againe, he should doe better rather to come and suppe with her. Antonius therefore to shew him selfe curteous unto her at her arrivall, was contented to obey her, and went to supper to her: where he found such passing sumptuous fare that no tongue can expresse it.

Only by a few touches has Shakespeare excelled his copy in the words of Enobarbus: but he has merely heightened and nowhere altered the effect.

The barge she sat in, like a *burnished throne,*
Burn'd on the water: the poop was beaten gold:

[1] obstructed. [2] Antony had already been worshipped as that deity.

Purple the sails and so perfumed that
The winds *were love-sick* with them : the oars were silver,
Which to the tune of flutes kept stroke and made
The water which they beat to follow faster,
As amorous of their strokes.   For her own person,
It beggar'd all description : she did lie
In her pavilion—cloth-of-gold of tissue—
O'er picturing that Venus where we see
The fancy outwork nature : on each side her
Stood pretty dimpled boys, like smiling Cupids
With divers-colour'd fans, whose wind did seem
To glow the delicate cheeks which they did cool,
And what they did undid. . . .
Her gentlewomen, like the Nereides
So many mermaids, *tended her i' the eyes*
And made their bends adornings : at the helm
A seeming mermaid steers : the *silken* tackle
Swell with the touches of those flower-soft hands
That *yarely* frame the office.   From the barge
A *strange invisible* perfume hits the sense
Of the adjacent wharfs : and Antony,
Enthroned i' the market-place, did sit alone,
Whistling the air : *which, but for vacancy,*
Had gone to gaze on Cleopatra too,
And made a gap in nature. . . .
Upon her landing, Antony sent to her,
Invited her to supper : she replied
It should be better he became her guest ;
Which she entreated : our courteous Antony,
Whom ne'er the word of " No " woman heard speak,
Being barber'd ten times o'er, goes to the feast
And for his ordinary pays his heart
For what his eyes eat only.
                                                    (II. ii. 196.)

And the impression of all this magnificence had not
faded from Shakespeare's mind when in after years
he wrote his *Cymbeline.*   Imogen's chamber

                                        is hang'd
With tapestry of silk and silver ; the story
Proud Cleopatra, when she met her Roman,
And Cydnus swell'd above the banks, or for
The press of boats or pride.[1]
                                                    (II. iv. 68.)

[1] It is rather strange that Shakespeare, whose "accessories" are
usually relevant, should choose such a subject for the decoration of
Imogen's room.   Mr. Bradley, in a note to his essay on *Antony and
Cleopatra* says : "Of the 'good' heroines, Imogen is the one who has

But it was not only the prodigality of charm that would enthral the poet. In the relation of the lovers, in the character of Cleopatra, in the nature of her ascendancy, there is something that reminds us of the story of passion enshrined in the *Sonnets*. No doubt it is uncertain whether these in detail are to be regarded as biographical, but biographical they are at the core, at least in the sense that they are authentic utterance of feelings actually experienced. No doubt, too, the balance of evidence points to their composition, at least in the parts that deal with his unknown leman, early in Shakespeare's career; but for that very reason the memories would be fitter to help him in interpreting the poetry of the historical record, for as Wordsworth says: "Poetry is emotion recollected in tranquillity." So once more Shakespeare may have been moved to "make old offences of affections new," that is, to infuse the passion of his own youth into this tale of "old unhappy far-off things." His bygone sorrows of the *Sonnets* come back to him when he is writing the drama, mirror themselves in some of the situations and sentiments, and echo in the wording of a few of the lines. It is of course easy to exaggerate the importance of these reminiscences. The Dark Lady has been described as the original of Cleopatra, but the original of Cleopatra is the Cleopatra of Plutarch, and in many ways she is unlike the temptress of the poet. She is dowered with a marvellous beauty which all from Enobarbus to Octavius acknowledge, while the other is "foul" in all eyes save those of her lover; her face "hath not the power to make love groan";

---

most of [Cleopatra's] spirit of fire and air." This is one of the things one sees to be true as soon as one reads it: can it be that their creator has brought them into association through some feeling, conscious or unconscious, of their kinship in this important respect?

I regret that Mr. Bradley's admirable study, which appeared when I was travelling in the Far East, escaped my notice till a few days ago, when it was too late to use it for my discussion.

and in her there is no hint of Cleopatra's royalty of soul. Nor is the devotion of Antony the devotion of the sonneteer; it is far more absolute and un-questioning, it is also far more comrade-like and sympathetic; at first he exults in it without shame, and never till the last distracted days does suspicion or contempt enter his heart. Still less is his passing spasm of jealousy at the close like the chronic jealousy of the poet. It is a vengeful frenzy that must find other outlets as well as the self-accusing remonstrances and impotent rebukes of the lyrical complaints. The resemblance between sonnets and play is confined to the single feature that they both tell the story of an unlawful passion for a dark woman—for this was Shakespeare's fixed idea in regard to Cleopatra—whose character and reputation were stained, whose influence was pernicious, and whose fatal spells depended largely on her arts and intellect. But this was enough to give Shake-speare, as it were, a personal insight into the case, and a personal interest in it, to furnish him with the key of the situation and place him at the centre.

And there was another point of contact between the author and the hero of the tragedy. It is stated in Plutarch's account of Antony : "Some say that he lived three and fiftie yeares : and others say six and fiftie." But the action begins a decade, or (for, as we shall see, there is a jumbling of dates in the opening scenes like that which we have noted in the corresponding ones of *Julius Caesar*) more than a decade before the final catastrophe. Thus Shakespeare would imagine Antony at the outset as between forty-two and forty-six, practically on the same *niveau* of life as himself, for in 1607-1608 he was in his forty-fourth year. They had reached the same stadium in their career, had the same general outlook on the future, had their great

triumphs behind them, and yet with powers hardly
impaired they both could say,

> Though grey
> Do something mingle with our younger brown, yet ha' we
> A brain that nourishes our nerves, and can
> Get goal for goal of youth.   (IV. viii. 19.)

There would be a general sympathy of attitude, and
it even extends to something in the poet himself
analogous to the headlong ardour of Antony.   In
the years that had elapsed since Shakespeare gave
the first instalment of his story in *Julius Caesar*, a
certain change had been proceeding in his art.   The
present drama belongs to a different epoch of his
authorship, an epoch not of less force but of less
restrained force, an epoch when he works perhaps
with less austerity of stroke and less intellectualism,
but—strange that it should be so in advancing years
—with more abandonment to the suggestions of
imagination and passion.   In all these respects the
fortunes of Antony and Cleopatra would offer him a
fit material.   In the second as compared with the
first Roman play, there is certainly no decline.   The
subject is different, the point of view is different, the
treatment is different, but subject, point of view and
treatment all harmonise with each other, and the
whole in its kind is as great as could be.

Perhaps some such considerations may explain
why Shakespeare, after he had been for seven years
expatiating on the heights of free tragic invention,
yet returned for a time to a theme which, with his
ideas of loyalty to recorded fact, dragged him back
in some measure to the embarrassments of the
chronicle history.   It was all so congenial, that he
was willing to face the disadvantages of an action
that straggled over years and continents, of a multi-
plicity of short scenes that in the third act rise to a
total of thirteen and in the fourth to a total of fifteen,
of a number of episodic personages who appear

without preparation and vanish almost without note. He had to lay his account with this if he dramatised these transactions at all, for to him they were serious matters that his fancy must not be allowed to distort. Indeed he accepts the conditions so unreservedly, and makes so little effort to evade them, that his mind seems to have taken the ply, and he resorts to the meagre, episodical scene, not only when Plutarch's narrative suggests it, but when he is making additions of his own and when no very obvious advantage is to be secured. This is the only explanation that readily presents itself for the fourth scene of the second act, which in ten lines describes Lepidus' leave-taking of Mecaenas and Agrippa.[1] There is for this no authority in the *Life*; and what object does it serve? It may indicate on the one hand the punctilious deference that Octavius' ministers deem fit to show as yet to the incompetent Triumvir, and on the other his lack of efficient energy in allowing his private purposes to make him two days late at the *rendezvous* which he himself has advocated as urgent. But these hints could quite well have been conveyed in some other way, and this invented scene seems theatrically and dramatically quite otiose. Nevertheless, and this is the point to observe, it so fits into the pattern of the chronicle play that it does not force itself on one's notice as superfluous.

It is partly for this reason that *Antony and Cleopatra* holds its distinctive place among Shakespeare's masterpieces. On the one hand there is no play that springs more spontaneously out of the heart of its author, and into which he has breathed

---

[1] Of course the division into scenes is not indicated in the Folio, but a new "place" is obviously required for this conversation. Of course, too, change of scene did not mean so much on the Elizabethan as on the modern stage, but it must always have counted for something. Every allowance made, the above criticism seems to me valid.

a larger portion of his inspiration ; and on the other there is none that is more purely historical, so that in this respect it is comparable among the Roman dramas to *Richard II.* in the English series.   This was the double characteristic that Coleridge emphasised in his *Notes on Shakespeare's Plays* : " There is not one in which he has followed history so minutely, and yet there are few in which he impresses the notion of angelic strength so much—perhaps none in which he impresses it more strongly.   This is greatly owing to the manner in which the fiery force is sustained throughout, and to the numerous momentary flashes of nature counteracting the historical abstraction."   The angelic strength, the fiery force, the flashes of nature are due to his complete sympathy with the facts, but that makes his close adherence to his authority all the more remarkable.

M

CHAPTER II

ANTONY AND CLEOPATRA, A HISTORY, TRAGEDY,
AND LOVE POEM; AS SHOWN BY ITS RELA-
TIONS WITH PLUTARCH

THE obligations to Plutarch, though very great, are
of a somewhat peculiar kind. Shakespeare does not
borrow so largely or so repeatedly from the diction
of North as in *Coriolanus* or even in *Julius Caesar.*
His literal indebtedness is for the most part confined
to the exploitation here and there of a few short
phrases or sentences, generally of a not very
distinctive character. Thus Octavia is described as
"having an excellent grace, wisedom and honestie,
joined unto so rare a beawtie"; which suggests her
"beauty, wisdom, modesty," in the play (II. ii. 246).
Thus, after the scourging of Thyreus, Antony sends
Caesar the message:

> "If this mislike thee," said he, "thou hast Hipparchus [1]
> one of my infranchised bondmen with thee : hang him if thou
> wilt, or whippe him at thy pleasure, that we may cry quittaunce."

This becomes:
> If he mislike
> My speech and what is done, tell him he has
> Hipparchus, my enfranchised bondman, whom
> He may at pleasure whip, or hang, or torture,
> As he shall like, to quit me.   (III. xiii. 147.)

[1] The irony of the proposal, which Plutarch indicates but does not
stress, is entirely lost in Shakespeare. We have already been told
that Hipparchus "was the first of all his (*i.e.* Antony's) infranchised
bondmen that revolted from him and yelded unto Caesar"; so Caesar
is invited to retaliate on one of his own adherents.

So, too, Plutarch says of Dolabella's disclosure to Cleopatra :

> He sent her word secretly as she had requested him, that Caesar determined to take his journey through Suria, and that within three dayes he would sende her away before with her children.

The words are closely copied in Dolabella's statement :

> Caesar through Syria
> Intends his journey, and within three days
> You with your children will he send before :
> Make your best use of this : I have perform'd
> Your pleasure and my promise. (v. ii. 200.)

It is only now and then that such small loans stand out as examples of the "happy valiancy of style" that characterises the drama as a whole. For instance, at the end when Cleopatra is dead and Charmian has applied the asp, the brief interchange of question and answer which Plutarch reports could not be bettered even by Shakespeare.

> One of the souldiers seeing her, angrily sayd unto her : "Is that well done, Charmion ?" "Verie well," sayd she againe, "and meete for a Princes discended from a race of so many noble Kings."

Shakespeare knows when he is well off and accepts the goods the gods provide.

> *1st Guard.* Charmian, is this well done?
> *Charmian.* It is well done and fitting for a princess
> Descended from so many royal kings. (v. ii. 238.)

Perhaps the noblest and one of the closest of these paraphrases is in the scene of Antony's death. With his last breath he persuades her

> that she should not lament nor sorowe for the miserable chaunge of his fortune at the end of his dayes : but rather that she should thinke him the more fortunate, for the former triumphes and honors he had received, considering that while he lived he was the noblest and greatest Prince of the world, and that now he was overcome, not cowardly but valiantly, a Romane by an other Romane.

Shakespeare's Antony says :

> The miserable change now at my end
> Lament nor sorrow at : but please your thoughts
> In feeding them with those my former fortunes
> Wherein I lived, the greatest prince o' the world,
> The noblest : and do now not basely die,
> Not cowardly put off my helmet to
> My countryman,—a Roman by a Roman
> Valiantly vanquish'd.   (IV. xv. 51.)

As a rule, however, even these short reproductions
are not transcripts.   Shakespeare's usual method is
illustrated in his recast of Antony's pathetic protest
to Caesar that

> he made him angrie with him, bicause he shewed him
> selfe prowde and disdainfull towards him, and now specially
> when he was easie to be angered, by reason of his present
> miserie.

Shakespeare gives a more bitter poignancy to the
confession.

> Look, thou say
> He makes me angry with him, for he seems
> Proud and disdainful, *harping on what I am,*
> *Not what he knew I was : he makes me angry;*
> And at this time most easy 'tis to do 't,
> *When my good stars, that were my former guides,*
> *Have empty left their orbs, and shot their fires*
> *Into the abysm of hell.*   (III. xiii. 140.)

Much the same estimate holds good of the longer
passages derived from North, which for the rest
are but few.   The most literal are as a rule
comparatively unimportant.   A typical specimen
is the list of complaints made by Antony against
Octavius, and Octavius' rejoinder :

> And the chiefest poyntes of his accusations he charged him
> with, were these: First, that having spoyled Sextus Pompeius
> in Sicile, he did not give him his parte of the Ile.   Secondly.
> that he did deteyne in his handes the shippes he lent him to
> make that warre.   Thirdly, that having put Lepidus their

companion and triumvirate out of his part of the Empire,
and having deprived him of all honors : he retayned for
him selfe the lands and revenues thereof, which had been
assigned to him for his part. . . . Octavius Caesar aunswered
him againe : that for Lepidus, he had in deede deposed him,
and taken his part of the Empire from him, bicause he did
overcruelly use his authoritie.   And secondly, for the conquests he had made by force of armes, he was contented
Antonius should have his part of them, so that he would
likewise let him have his part of Armenia.

Shakespeare copies even Caesar's convenient reticence as to the borrowed vessels.

> *Agrippa.*   Who does he accuse ?
> *Caesar.* Caesar : and that, having in Sicily
> Sextus Pompeius spoil'd, we have not rated him
> His part o' the isle : then does he say, he lent me
> Some shipping unrestored : lastly, he frets
> That Lepidus of the triumvirate
> Should be deposed ; and, being, that we detain
> All his revenue.
> *Agrippa.*   Sir, this should be answer'd.
> *Caesar.* 'Tis done already, and the messenger gone.
> I have told him Lepidus was grown too cruel :
> That he his high authority abused,
> And did deserve his change : for what I have conquer'd
> I grant him part : but then, in his Armenia,
> And other of his conquer'd kingdoms, I
> Demand the like.   (III. vi. 23.)

Less matter-of-fact, because more vibrant with its
fanfare of names, but still somewhat of the nature
of an official schedule, is the list of tributaries in
Antony's host.

(He) had with him to ayde him these kinges and subjects
following : Bocchus king of Lybia, Tarcondemus king of
high Cilicia, Archelaus king of Cappadocia, Philadelphus
king of Paphlagonia, Mithridates king of Comagena, and
Adallas king of Thracia.   All the which were there every
man in person.   The residue that were absent sent their
armies, as Polemon king of Pont, Manchus king of Arabia.
Herodes king of Iury; and furthermore, Amyntas king of
Lycaonia, and of the Galatians : and besides all these he had
all the ayde the king of Medes sent unto him.

The long bead-roll of shadowy potentates evidently delights Shakespeare's ear as it would have delighted the ear of Milton or Victor Hugo[1]:

> He hath assembled
> Bocchus, the king of Libya ; Archelaus
> Of Cappadocia ; Philadelphos king
> Of Paphlagonia ; the Thracian king, Adallas ;
> King Malchus of Arabia ; king of Pont ;
> Herod of Jewry ; Mithridates, king
> Of Comagene ; Polemon and Amyntas,
> The kings of Mede and Lycaonia,
> With a more larger list of sceptres.   (III. vi. 68.)

Still, of the longer passages that show throughout a real approximation to North's language, the two already quoted, the soothsayer's warning to Antony, and the description of Cleopatra on the Cydnus are the most impressive : and even they, and especially the latter, have been touched up and revised. Shakespeare's general procedure in the cases where he borrows at all is a good deal freer, and may be better illustrated from the passage in which Octavius recalls the bygone fortitude of Antony.

> These two Consuls (Hircius and Pansa) together with Caesar, who also had an armye, went against Antonius that beseeged the citie of Modena, and there overthrew him in battell : but both the Consuls were slaine there. Antonius flying upon this overthrowe, fell into great miserie all at once : but the chiefest want of all other, and that pinched him most, was famine.   Howbeit he was of such

---

[1] It is interesting to note that it had already caught the fancy of Jodelle, though being more faithful to the text in enumerating only the kings who were actually present and taking no liberties with the names and titles, he failed to get all the possible points out of it. Agrippa says to Octavian :

> Le Roy Bocchus, le Roy Cilicien
> Archelaus, Roy Capadocien,
> Et Philadelphe, et Adalle de Thrace,
> Et Mithridate, usoyent-ils de menace
> Moindre sus nous que de porter en joye
> Nostre despouille et leur guerriere proye,
> Pour a leurs Dieux joyeusement les pendre
> Et maint et maint sacrifice leur rendre ?   Acte II.

a strong nature, that by pacience he would overcome any adversitie, and the heavier fortune lay upon him, the more constant shewed he him selfe. . . . It was a wonderfull example to the souldiers, to see Antonius that was brought up in all finenes and superfluitie, so easily to drink puddle water, and to eate wild frutes and rootes: and moreover it is reported, that even as they passed the Alpes, they did eate the barcks of trees, and such beasts, as never man tasted of their flesh before.

This is good, but Shakespeare's version visualises as well as heightens Antony's straits and endurance, and brings them into contrast with his later effeminacy.

> When thou once
> Wast beaten from Modena, where thou slew'st
> Hirtius and Pansa, consuls, at thy heel
> Did famine follow: whom thou fought'st against,
> Though daintily brought up, with patience more
> Than savages could suffer: thou didst drink
> The stale of horses, and the gilded puddle
> Which beasts would cough at: thy palate then did deign
> The roughest berry on the rudest hedge:
> Yea, like the stag, when snow the pasture sheets,
> The barks of trees thou browsed'st; on the Alps
> It is reported thou didst eat strange flesh,
> Which some did die to look on: and all this—
> It wounds thine honour that I speak it now—
> Was borne so like a soldier, that thy cheek
> So much as lank'd not.   (I. iv. 56.)

But including such elaborations, the number of passages repeated or recast from North is not considerable. In the whole of the first act this description of the retreat from Modena is the only one of any consequence, and though the percentage increases as the play proceeds, and they are much more frequent in the second half, even in the fifth act, the proportion of easily traceable lines is fifty-seven to four hundred and forty-six, or barely more than an eighth.

Much more numerous and generally much more noteworthy than the strictly verbal suggestions are those that, conveyed altogether in Shakespeare's

phrase, give such immediate life to the play, whether
they supply episodes for acting or merely material
for the dialogue. Sometimes a whole paragraph is
distilled into a sentence, like that famous bit of
domestic chit-chat that must have impressed Plutarch
when a boy.

> I have heard my grandfather Lampryas report, that one
> Philotas a Physition, born in the citie of Amphissa, told him
> that he was at the present time in Alexandria, and studied
> physicke: and that having acquaintance with one of Antonius
> cookes, he tooke him with him to Antonius house, (being a
> young man desirous to see things) to shew him the wonderfull
> sumptuous charge and preparation of one only supper. When
> he was in the kitchin, and saw a world of diversities of meates,
> and amongst others eight wilde boares rosted whole: he
> began to wonder at it, and sayd, "Sure you have a great
> number of ghestes to supper." The cooke fell a laughing,
> and answered him: "No," (quoth he), "not many ghestes,
> nor above twelve in all: but yet all that is boyled or roasted
> must be served in whole, or else it would be marred straight.
> For Antonius peradventure will suppe presently, or it may
> be in a pretie while hence, or likely enough he will deferre
> it longer, for that he hath dronke well to day, or else hath
> had some other great matters in hand: and therefore we doe
> not dresse one supper only, but many suppers, bicause we
> are uncerteine of the houre he will suppe in."

In what strange ways has the gossip of the in-
quisitive medical student been transmitted through
Lampryas and his grandchild to furnish an arabesque
for Shakespeare's tapestry! And, when we know
its history, what a realistic touch does this anecdote
lend to Mecaenas' badinage, though Shakespeare
has raised the profuse to the sublime by transferring
the banquet from the evening to the morning, suppressing the fact of the relays, and insinuating that
this was nothing out of the common!

> *Mecaenas.* Eight wild boars roasted whole at a breakfast,
> and but twelve persons there: is this true?
> *Enobarbus.* This was but as a fly by an eagle: we had
> much more monstrous matter of feast, which worthily
> deserved noting.   (II. ii. 183.)

Or again we are told of Cleopatra's precautions after Actium.

> Now to make proofe of those poysons which made men dye with least paine, she tried it upon condemned men in prison. For when she saw the poysons that were sodaine and vehement, and brought speedy death with grievous torments : and in contrary manner, that suche as were more milde and gentle, had not that quicke speede and force to make one dye sodainly : she afterwardes went about to prove the stinging of snakes and adders, and made some to be applied unto men in her sight, some in one sorte, and some in an other. So when she had dayly made divers and sundrie proofes, she found none of all them she had proved so fit as the biting of an Aspicke, the which only causeth a heavines of the head, without swounding or complaining, and bringeth a great desire also to sleepe, with a little swet on the face, and so by little and little taketh away the sences and vitall powers, no living creature perceiving that the pacientes feele any paine. For they are so sorie when any bodie waketh them, and taketh them up ; as those that being taken out of a sound sleepe, are very heavy and desirous to sleepe.

This leaves a trace only in three lines of Caesar's reply when the guard detects the aspic's trail ; but these lines gain in significance if we remember the fuller statement.

> Most probable
> That so she died : for her physician tells me
> She hath pursued conclusions infinite
> Of easy ways to die.   (v. ii. 356.)

Apart from the great pivots and levers of the action Plutarch has supplied numbers of these minor fittings. Including with them the more literal loans, from which they cannot always be discriminated, we find in addition to the instances already cited the following unmistakable reminiscences : in Act i., Antony's proposal to roam the streets with Cleopatra ; in Act ii., the motive assigned for Fulvia's rising, Antony's ambiguous position as widower, Sextus Pompeius' courtesy to Antony's mother, Charmian's description of the fishing, the conditions

of peace offered to Pompey, Pompey's flout at the
seizure of his father's house, the bantering of Antony
in regard to Cleopatra, the banquet on the galley,
Menas' suggestion and Pompey's reply ; in Act III.,
Ventidius' halt in his career of victory and its reason,
Octavia's distraction between the claims of husband
and brother, the overthrow of Pompey and deposition of Lepidus, the account of the coronation of
Cleopatra and her children, Enobarbus' remonstrance
against Cleopatra's presence in the armament, the
allusion' to the war being managed by her eunuch
and her maids, the comparison of Octavius' and
Antony's navies, the name Antoniad given to Cleopatra's admiral, Antony's challenge to Octavius, the
soldier's appeal to fight on land, many particulars
about the battle of Actium, Antony's dismissal of his
friends with treasure, the embassage of Euphronius
and Octavius' reply, Thyreus' commission, Antony's
renewed challenge, the birthday celebration ; in
Act IV., Octavius' answer to the challenge, Antony's
disquieting speech at the banquet, the supposed
departure of his divine patron, the defection of
Enobarbus, the reference to the treason of Alexas
and others, Antony's successful sally, his return in
triumph and embrace of Cleopatra ere he doffs his
armour, her gift to the valiant soldier, the death of
Enobarbus, the posting of the footmen on the hills
before the final catastrophe, the presage of swallows
building on Antony's ship, the fraternization of the
fleets, Antony's rage at Cleopatra, her flight to the
tomb, the message of her death, Antony's revulsion
of feeling at the news, Eros' plighted obligation and
his suicide, the mortal wound Antony gives himself,
the second message from Cleopatra, his conveyance
to the monument, Cleopatra's refusal to undo the
locks and her expedient of drawing him up, several
particulars in the last interview, such as the commendation of Proculeius ; in Act V., Dercetas'

announcement to Octavius of Antony's death, Octavius' reception of the tidings and his reference to their correspondence, his plans for Cleopatra, the interview of Proculeius with Cleopatra at the Monument, his unobserved entrance, the exclamation of the waiting-woman, Cleopatra's attempted suicide, the visit of Octavius, his threats concerning Cleopatra's children, her concealment of her treasure, the disclosure of Seleucus, her indignation at him and apology to Octavius, Octavius' reception of it, Dolabella's sympathy with the captive queen, the arrival of the countryman with the figs, the dressing in state, the death of Cleopatra and Iras before the soldiers enter, Charmian's last service in adjusting the diadem, Octavius' appreciation of Cleopatra's courage and command for her burial beside Antony.

This enumeration shows how largely Shakespeare is indebted to Plutarch, and also how his obligations are greatest in the later portion of the play. They become conspicuous a little before the middle of the third act, and the proportion is maintained till the close ; for though there are not so many in the fifth act, it is considerably shorter than the fourth or than the last eight scenes of the third.

Shakespeare however obtains from Plutarch not merely a large number of his details, but the general programme of the story and the presuppositions of the portraiture, as will appear from a short summary of Plutarch's narrative, into which, for clearness' sake, I insert the principal dates.

After Philippi, Antony gave himself up to a life of ostentation and luxury, interrupted by flashes of his nobler mood, first in Greece and subsequently in Asia. Then came his meeting with Cleopatra on the Cydnus, and in his passion for her all that was worthiest in his nature was smothered. Despite pressing public duties he accompanied her on her return to Alexandria, where he wasted his time in

"childish sports and idle pastimes." In the midst
of his dalliance the tidings arrive with which the
play opens, in 41 B.C., of the contest of his brother
Lucius and his wife Fulvia, first with each other and
then with Octavius, of their defeat and expulsion
from Italy ; as well as of the inroad of the Parthians
under Labienus as far as Lydia and Ionia.

> Then began Antonius with much a doe to rouse him selfe
> as if he had been wakened out of a deepe sleepe, and as a
> man may say comming out of a great dronkennes.

He sets out for Parthia, but in obedience to the
urgent summons of Fulvia, changes his course for
Italy. On the way he falls in with fugitives of his
party who tell him that his wife was sole cause of
the war and had begun it only to withdraw him
from Cleopatra. Soon afterwards Fulvia, who was
"going to meete with Antonius" fell sick and died
at Sicyon in 40 B.C.—"by good fortune" comments
Plutarch, as now the colleagues could be more
easily reconciled. The friends of both were indis-
posed to "unrippe any olde matters" and a composition was come to whereby Antony obtained the
East, Octavius the West, and Lepidus Africa.
This agreement, since Antony was now a widower
and "denied not that he kept Cleopatra, but so did
he not confesse that he had her as his wife," was
confirmed by Antony's marriage, which every one
approved, with Octavius' dearly loved half-sister
Octavia, and it was hoped that "she should be a
good meane to keepe good love and amitie betwext
her brother and him."

Meanwhile Sextus Pompeius in Sicily had been
making himself troublesome with his pirate allies,
and as he had showed great courtesy to Antony's
mother, it seemed good to make peace with him
An interview accordingly took place at Misenum in
39 B.C. as a result of which he was granted Sicily

and Sardinia on the conditions mentioned in the play.

Antony was now able to resume his plans for punishing the Parthians and sent Ventidius against them while he still remained in Rome. But moved by the predominance of Octavius and the warning of the soothsayer, he resolved to take up his own jurisdiction, and with Octavia and their infant daughter set out for Greece, where he heard the news of Ventidius' success in 38 B.C.

In 37 B.C., offended at some reports, he returned to Italy with Octavia, who had now a second daughter and was again with child. By her intercession good relations were restored between the brothers-in-law, each lending the other the forces of which he most stood in need. Octavius employed the borrowed ships against Sextus Pompeius, Antony was to employ the borrowed soldiers against the Parthians.

Leaving his wife and children in Octavius' care, Antony proceeded directly to Asia.

> Then beganne this pestilent plague and mischiefe of Cleopatraes love (which had slept a longe tyme and seemed to have bene utterlie forgotten and that Antonius had geven place to better counsell) againe to kindle and to be in force, so soone as Antonius came neere unto Syria.

He sends for her and to the scandal of the Romans pays her extravagant honours, showers kingdoms upon her, and designates their twin children the Sun and the Moon.

He does not, however, in seeming, neglect his expedition to Parthia, but gathers a huge and well appointed host wherewith to invade it. Nevertheless

> this so great and puisant army which made the Indians quake for feare, dwelling about the contry of the Bactrians and all Asia also to tremble : served him to no purpose, and all for the love he bore to Cleopatra. For the earnest great desire he had to lye all winter with her, made him begin his

warre out of due time, and for hast to put all in hazard, being
so ravished and enchaunted with the sweete poyson of her
love, that he had no other thought but of her, and how he
might quickly returne againe: more then how he might
overcome his enemies.

Not only did Antony choose the wrong season, but
in his hurry he left all his heavy engines behind him
and thus threw away his chances in advance. The
campaign was a series of disasters and ended in an
inglorious retreat. The only credit that can be
given to him from beginning to end is for efficiency
in misfortune and sympathy with his soldiers. Yet
even these were impaired by his fatal passion.

The greate haste he made to returne unto Cleopatra,
caused him to put his men to great paines, forcing them to
lye in the field all winter long when it snew unreasonably,
that by the way he lost eight thowsand of his men.

Arrived at the Syrian coast he awaits her coming.

And bicause she taried longer then he would have had her,
he pined away for love and sorrow. So that he was at such a
straight, that he wist not what to doe, and therefore to weare
it out, he gave him selfe to quaffing and feasting. But he was
so drowned with the love of her, that he could not abide to
sit at the table till the feast were ended: but many times
while others banketted, he came to the sea side to see if she
were comming.

Meanwhile, in 36 B.C., during the Parthian expedition, Sextus Pompeius had been defeated, his death,
not mentioned by Plutarch, following in the ensuing
year, and Lepidus had been deposed by Octavius,
who gave no account of the spoils. On the other
hand, in 34 B.C., Antony, who had overrun and seized
Armenia, celebrated his triumph not in Rome but in
Alexandria.

Grievances were thus accumulating on both sides,
and Octavia once more seeking to mediate, took
ship to join her husband with the approval of
Octavius, who foresaw the upshot, and regarded it
as likely to put his brother-in-law in the wrong.

Antony bade her stop at Athens, promising to come to her, but afterwards, fearing lest Cleopatra should kill herself for grief, he broke tryst, and Octavia returned to Rome where she watched over his interests as best she might. Antony in the meantime accompanied Cleopatra to Egypt and gave the Romans new offence by paying her divine honours and parcelling out the East among her and her children.

Then came the interchange of uncompromising messages in 33 B.C., and Antony bade Octavia leave his house. The appeal to arms was inevitable, and as the taxation to which Octavius was compelled to resort in view of his rival's great preparation roused general discontent, it was Antony's cue to invade Italy. But he continued to squander his time in feasts and revels, and in such and other ways further alienated his friends in Rome.

In 32 B.C. Octavius declared war against Cleopatra, and had Antony deprived of his authority. The battle of Actium followed on the 2nd September, 31 B.C. But Antony, after his retirement to Egypt, in some measure recovered from his first despondency at the defeat, and even when he found himself forsaken by allies and troops, continued to live a life of desperate gaiety. After an ignominious attempt at negotiation and a flicker of futile success, the final desertion of his fleet, for which he blamed Cleopatra, put an end to his resistance, and he killed himself in 30 B.C., less, however, in despair at his overthrow than for grief at Cleopatra's alleged death.

> (He) said unto him selfe: "What doest thou looke for further, Antonius, sith spitefull fortune hath taken from thee the only joy thou haddest, for whom thou yet reservedst thy life."

After mentioning how Antony's son, Antyllus, and Cleopatra's son, Caesarion, were betrayed to death by their governors, Plutarch describes how Cleopatra for a while is deterred from suicide chiefly by fears

for her other children.   Hearing, however, Octavius'
definite plans for her, she obtains leave to offer a last
oblation at Antony's tomb, and thereafter takes her
own life.   The biography concludes with a notice of
Octavia's care for all Antony's children, not only
Fulvia's and her own, but those of whom Cleopatra
was mother.

It will be seen from this sketch that no incidents
of political importance are added, few are altered,
and very few omitted by Shakespeare.   Of course
the dramatic form necessitates a certain concentra-
tion, and this of itself, even were there no farther
motive, would account for the occasional synchronis-
ing of separate episodes.   Thus the news of Fulvia's
death and Sextus Pompeius' aggression is run together
with the news of the wars of Fulvia and Lucius and
the advance of the Parthians.   Thus between the
second marriage and the final breach it was convenient to condense matters, and, in doing this, to
omit Antony's flying visit to Italy, blend Octavia's
first and second attempts at mediation, and represent
her as taking leave of her husband at Athens.   In
the same way the months between the battle of
Actium and the death of Antony, and the days
between the death of Antony and that of Cleopatra
might easily be compressed without any hurt to the
sentiment of the story.   But even of this artistic
license Shakespeare avails himself far less systematically than in *Julius Caesar*.   There, as we saw, the
action is crowded into five days, though with considerable intervals between some of them.   There
is no such arrangement in *Antony and Cleopatra*.
Superficially this play is one of the most invertebrate
in structure that Shakespeare ever wrote.   It gives
one the impression of an anxious desire to avoid
tampering with the facts and their relations even
when history does not furnish ready - made the
material that bests fits the drama.

And in the main this impression is correct. Shakespeare supplies a panorama of some ten eventful years in which he can not only cite his chapter and verse for most of the official *data*, but reproduces, with amazing fidelity, the general contour of the historical landscape, in so far as it was visible from his point of view. And yet his allegiance to the letter has often been exaggerated and is to a great extent illusory. This does not mean merely that his picture fails to approve itself as the truth, the whole truth and nothing but the truth, when tested by the investigations of modern scholars. His position and circumstances were not theirs. He took Plutarch's *Marcus Antonius* as his chief and almost sole authority, resorting possibly for suggestions of situation and phrase to the Senecan tragedies on the same theme, probably for the descriptions of Egypt to Holland's translation of Pliny or Cory's translation of Leo, and almost certainly for many details about Sextus Pompeius [1] to the 1578 version of Appian ; but always treating the *Life* not only as his inexhaustible storehouse, but as sufficient guarantee for any statement that it contained. In short he could give the history of the time, not as it was but as Plutarch represented it, and as Plutarch's representation explained itself to an Elizabethan. It is hardly to his discredit if he underestimates Cleopatra's political astuteness, and has no guess of the political projects that recent criticism has ascribed to Antony, for of these things his author has little to say. It is hardly to his credit, if, on Appian's hint, he realises the importance of Sextus Pompeius' insular position and naval power, for he lived in the days of Hawkins and Drake.

But he is not slavishly literal even in his adherence to Plutarch. He adopts his essential and many of his subsidiary facts : he follows his lead in the broad

[1] See Appendix D.

course of events; he does not alter the main lines of the story. But it is surprising to find how persistently he rearranges and regroups the minor details, and how by this means he gives them a new significance. The portions of the play where he has made the narrative more compact are also, roughly speaking, those in which he has taken most liberties in dislocating the sequence, and the result is not merely greater conciseness but an original interpretation. Yet on the other hand we must not either misconstrue the meaning or overstate the importance of this procedure. In the first place it affects not so much the history of events as the portraiture of the persons. In the second place, even in the characterisation it generally adds vividness and depth to the presentation rather than alters the fundamental traits. Thus in Plutarch the soothsayer's warning to Antony follows, in Shakespeare it precedes, the composition with Pompey. From the chronicler's point of view this transposition is abundantly unimportant, but it does make a difference in our estimate of Antony: his consequent decision shows more levity and rashness in the play than in the biography. Yet in both his whole behaviour at this juncture is distinctly fickle and indiscreet; so the net result of the displacement is to sharpen the lines that Plutarch has already drawn. And this is true in a greater or less degree of most of the cases in which Shakespeare reshuffles Plutarch's notes. On the whole, despite dramatic parallax and changed perspective, *Antony and Cleopatra* is astonishingly faithful to the facts as they were supposed to be. Shakespeare could hardly have done more in getting to the heart of Plutarch's account, and in reconstructing it with all its vital and essential characteristics disentangled and combined afresh in their rational connection. And since after all Plutarch " meant right " this implies that Shakespeare is not only true to Plutarch, but virtually true to what is still considered the spirit of his subject.[1]

Indeed his most far-reaching modifications concern in the main the manner in which the persons appeal to our sympathies, and in which he wishes us to envisage their story ; and these perhaps in a preliminary view can better be indicated by what he has suppressed than by what he has added or recast. There is one conspicuous omission that shows how he deals with character ; there are several minor ones that in their sum show how he prescribes the outlook.

To begin with the former, it is impossible not to be struck by the complete deletion of the Parthian fiasco, which in Plutarch occupies nearly a fifth of the whole *Life*, or a fourth of the part with which Shakespeare deals in this play. It thus bulks large in Antony's career, and though in the main it may be unsuitable for dramatic purposes, it is nevertheless connected in its beginning, conduct and close, with the story of his love for Cleopatra. Yet we have only one far off and euphemistic reference to it in the words of Eros, when Antony bids him strike.

> The gods withhold me !
> Shall I do that which all the Parthian darts,
> Though enemy, lost aim, and could not ? (iv. xiv. 69.)

Why this reticence in regard to one of the most ambitious enterprises with which the name of Antony was associated ? The truth is that the whole management of the campaign detracts grievously

[1] This may be said even if we accept Professor Ferrero's arguments that Antony's infatuation for Cleopatra was invented or exaggerated by opponents, and that their relation was to a great extent invented or prescribed by their ambitions. Antony would still be the profligate man of genius, captivated by Asiatic ideals and careless of the interests of Rome. His policy at the close would still, by Professor Ferrero's own admission, be traceable to the ascendancy which Cleopatra had established over him. And the picture of contemporary conditions would still retain a large measure of truth.

from the glamour of "absolute soldiership" with which the dramatist surrounds his hero and through which he wishes us to view him. His silence in regard to it is thus a hint of one far-reaching and momentous change Shakespeare has made in the impression the story conveys, and that is in the character of Antony himself. In the biography he is by no means so grandiose a figure, so opulent and magnificent a nature, as he appears in the play. Gervinus sums up the salient features of Plutarch's Antony in the following sentence:

> A man who had grown up in the wild companionship of a Curio and a Clodius, who had gone through the high school of debauchery in Greece and Asia, who had shocked everybody in Rome during Caesar's dictatorship by his vulgar excesses, who had made himself popular among the soldiers by drinking with them and encouraging their low amours, a man upon whom the odium of the proscriptions under the rule of the triumvirate especially fell, who displayed a cannibal pleasure over Cicero's bloody head and hand, who afterwards renewed in the East the wanton life of his youth, and robbed in grand style to maintain the vilest gang of parasites and jugglers, such a man depicted finally as the prey of an elderly and artful courtesan, could not possibly have been made the object of dramatic interest. It is wonderful how Shakespeare on the one hand preserved the historic features of Antony's character, so as not to make him unrecognisable, and yet how he contrived on the other to render him an attractive personage.

The array of charges Gervinus compiles from Plutarch is not exaggerated. Indeed it could be enlarged and emphasised. Dishonesty in money matters, jealousy of his subordinates, an occasional lack of generalship that almost becomes inefficiency, might be added to the list. But Plutarch's picture contains other traits that he does not seek to reconcile with those that repel us, but drops in casually and by the way: and in Shakespeare these are brought to the front. Valour, endurance, generosity, versatility, resourcefulness, self-know-

ledge, frankness, simplicity after a fashion, width
of outlook, power of self-recovery, are all attributed
to Antony even by his first biographer, though
these qualities are overweighted by the mass of
his delinquencies. Shakespeare shows them in
relief; while the more offensive characteristics, like
his youthful licentiousness, are relegated to his
bygone past, or, like his jealousy and vindictiveness,
are merely suggested by subordinate strokes, such
as the break in Ventidius' triumphant campaign, or
the merciless scourging of Thyreus. It is sometimes said that Shakespeare's Brutus is historically
correct and that his Mark Antony is a new creation.
The opposite statement would be nearer the truth.
We feel that both the biographer and the dramatist
have given a portrait of Cleopatra's lover, and that
both portraits are like; but the one painter has
been content with a collection of vivid traits which
in their general effect are ignoble and repulsive:
the other in a sense has idealised his model, but
it is by reading the soul of greatness through the
sordid details, and explaining them by the conception of Antony, not perhaps at his best but at
his grandest. He is still, though fallen, the Antony
who at Caesar's death could alter the course of
history; a dissolute intriguer no doubt, but a man
of genius, a man of enthusiasms, one who is equal
or all but equal to the highest occasion the world
can present, and who, if he fails owing to the lack
of steadfast principle and virile will that results from
voluptuous indulgence and unscrupulous practisings,
yet remains fascinating and magnificent even in his
ruin. And by means of this transfiguration, Shakespeare is able to lend absorbing interest to his
delineation of this gifted, complex, and faulty soul,
and to rouse the deepest sympathy for his fate.
Despite his loyalty to the historical record he lifts
his argument above the level of the Chronicle

History, and makes it a true tragedy. In its deference for facts, *Antony and Cleopatra* is to be ranked with such pieces as *Richard II.* and *Henry VIII.*, but in its real essence it claims another position. "The highest praise, or rather the highest form of praise, of this play," says Coleridge, "is the doubt which the perusal always occasions in me, whether *Antony and Cleopatra* is not, in all exhibitions of a giant power in its strength and vigour of maturity, a formidable rival of *Macbeth, Lear, Hamlet,* and *Othello.*"

In another aspect the more obvious of the minor omissions are in their general tendency not less typical of the way in which Shakespeare deals with his subject. For what are those that strike us at first sight? To begin with, many instances of Octavia's devotion, constancy and principle are passed over, and she is placed very much in the shade. Then there is no reference to the children that sprang from her union with Antony, indeed their existence is by implication denied, and she seems to be introduced as another Iseult of the White Hands. Antony cries to Cleopatra,

> Have I my pillow left unpress'd in Rome,
> Forborne the getting of a lawful race,
> And by a gem of women, to be abused
> By one that looks on feeders?   (III. xiii. 106.)

Further, the tragic stories of Antony's son Antyllus and of Cleopatra's son Caesarion are left unused, Antyllus not being mentioned at all, Caesarion only by the way; though Daniel does not scruple to include both accessories within the narrower limits of a Senecan tragedy. More noticeable still, however, is the indifference with which the children of Antony and Cleopatra are dismissed. They are barely alluded to, though the Queen's anxiety for their preservation, which supplies acceptable matter not only to Daniel but to Jodelle and Garnier, is

avouched by Plutarch's statement and driven home
by North's vigorous phrase. Plutarch describes her
distress of body and mind after Antony's death and
her own capture.

> She fell into a fever withal: whereof she was very glad,
> hoping thereby to have good colour to absteine from meate,
> and that so she might have dyed easely without any trouble.
> . . . But Caesar mistrusted the matter, by many conjectures
> he had, and therefore did put her in feare, and threatned her
> to put her children to shameful death. With these threats
> Cleopatra for feare yelded straight, *as she would have yelded
> unto strokes ;* and afterwards suffred her selfe to be cured and
> dieted as they listed.

Shakespeare makes no use of this save in the
warning of Octavius :

<blockquote>
If you seek
To lay on me a cruelty, by taking
Antony's course, you shall bereave yourself
Of my good purposes, and put your children
To that destruction which I'll guard them from,
If thereon you rely.   (v. ii. 128.)
</blockquote>

But here the threat is significant of Octavius' character, not of Cleopatra's, who makes no reply to it,
and remains absolutely unaffected by it. Indeed
she shows more sense of motherhood in her dying
reference to the asp as " her baby at her breast,"
than in all the previous play.

It cannot be doubted that the effect of all these
omissions is to concentrate the attention on the
purely personal relations of the lovers. And the
prominence assigned to them also appears if we
compare the *Life* and the drama as a whole.

It will be noted that in direct quotation, in incident
and allusion, in general structure, Shakespeare owes
far more to his authority in the last half of the play
than in the first : for the closer observance of, and
the larger loans from, the biography begin with the
central scenes of the third act. But it is at this
stage of the narrative that Cleopatra, for a while in

the background, once more becomes the paramount person ; and few are the allusions to her from the period of Actium that Shakespeare suffers to escape him. Moreover such independent additions as there are in the latter portion of the play, have mostly to do with her ; and in six of the invented scenes in the earlier acts she has the chief or at least a leading role. Clearly, when she is in evidence, Shakespeare feels least need to supplement, and when she is absent he has to fill in the gap. And this is significant of his whole conception. Gervinus tries to express the contrast between the Antony of Plutarch and the Antony of Shakespeare by means of a comparison. "We are inclined," he writes, "to designate the ennobling transformation which the poet undertook by one word : he refined the crude features of Mark Antony into the character of an Alcibiades." In a way that is not ill said, so far as it goes ; but it omits perhaps the most essential point. The great thing about Shakespeare's Antony is his capacity for a grand passion. We cannot talk of Alcibiades as a typical lover in the literature of the world, but Antony has a good right to his place in the " Seintes Legende of Cupyde." When three quarters of a century after Shakespeare Dryden ventured to rehandle the theme in the noble play that almost justifies the audacity of his attempt, he called his version, *All for Love or the World well lost*. We have something of the same feeling in reading Shakespeare, and we do not have it in reading Plutarch. Plutarch has no eyes for the glory of Antony's madness. He gives the facts or traditions that Shakespeare reproduced, but he regards the whole affair as a pitiable dotage, or, at best, as a calamitous visitation—regards it in short much as the Anti-Shakesperians do now. After describing the dangerous tendencies in Antony's mixed nature. he introduces his account of the meeting at the

Cydnus, with the deliberate statement which the rest of his story merely works out in detail :

> Antonius being thus inclined, the last and extreamest mischiefe of all other (to wit, the love of Cleopatra) lighted on him, who did waken and stirre up many vices yet hidden in him, and were never seene to any ; and if any sparke of goodnesse or hope of rising were left him, Cleopatra quenched it straight and made it worse than before.

Similarly his final verdict in the *Comparison of Demetrius and Marcus Antonius* is unrelenting :

> Cleopatra oftentimes unarmed Antonius, and intised him to her, making him lose matters of importaunce, and verie needeful jorneys, to come and be dandled with her about the rivers of Canobus and Taphosiris. In the ende as Paris fledde from battell and went to hide him selfe in Helens armes ; even so did he in Cleopatraes armes, or to speak more properlie, Paris hidde him selfe in Helens closet, but Antonius to followe Cleopatra, fledde and lost the victorie. . . . He slue him selfe (to confesse a troth) cowardly and miserably.

Shakespeare by no means neglects this aspect of the case, as Dryden tends to do, and he could never have taken Dryden's title for his play. Nevertheless, while agreeing with Plutarch, he agrees with Dryden too. To him Antony's devotion to Cleopatra is the grand fact in his career, which bears witness to his greatness as well as to his littleness, and is at once his perdition and his apotheosis. And so in the third place this is a love tragedy, and has its relations with *Romeo and Juliet* and *Troilus and Cressida*, the only other attempts that Shakespeare made in this kind : as is indicated even in their designations. For these are the only plays that are named after two persons, and the reason is that in a true love story both the lovers have equal rights. The symbol for it is an ellipse with two foci not a circle with a single centre.[1]

---

[1] Even in *Othello* the conspicuous place is reserved for the Moor, and in him it is jealousy as much as love that is depicted.

It has sometimes been pointed out that what is generally considered the chief tragic theme and what was an almost indispensable ingredient in the classic drama of France, is very seldom the *Leit-motif* of a Greek or a Shakespearian masterpiece. In this triad however Shakespeare has made use of it, and it is interesting to note the differences of treatment in the various members of the group.   In *Romeo and Juliet* he idealises youthful love with its raptures, its wonders, its overthrow in collision with the harsh facts of life.   *Troilus and Cressida* shows the inward dissolution of such love when it is unworthily bestowed, and suffers from want of reverence and loftiness.   In *Antony and Cleopatra* love is not a revelation as in the first, nor an illusion as in the second, but an infatuation.   There is nothing youthful about it, whether as adoration or inexperience.   It is the love that seizes the elderly man of the world, the trained mistress of arts, and does this, as it would seem, to cajole and destroy them both.   It is in one aspect the love that Bacon describes in his essay with that title.

He that preferred Helena, quitted the gifts of Juno and Pallas.   For whosoever esteemeth too much of Amorous Affection quitteth both Riches and Wisedom.   This Passion hath his Flouds in the very times of Weaknesse, which are great Prosperitie and great Adversitie, though this latter hath beene lesse observed.   Both which times kindle Love, and make it more fervent, and therefore shew it to be the Childe of Folly.   They doe best, who, if they cannot but admit Love, yet make it keepe Quarter, And sever it wholly from their serious Affaires and Actions of life; For if it checke once with Businesse, it troubleth Men's Fortunes, and maketh Men that they can no wayes be true to their owne Ends. . . . In Life it doth much mischiefe, Sometimes like a Syren, Sometimes like a Fury.   You may observe that amongst all the great and worthy Persons (whereof the memory remaineth, either Ancient or Recent), there is not One that hath beene transported to the mad degree of Love; which shewes that great Spirits and great Businesse doe keepe out this weake Passion.   You must except, never the lesse, Marcus Antonius the halfe partner of the Empire of Rome.

Part Siren, part Fury, that in truth is precisely how Plutarch would personify the love of Antony: and yet it is just this love that makes him memorable. Seductive and destructive in its obvious manifestations, nevertheless for the great reason that it was so engrossing and sincere, it reveals and unfolds a nobility and depth in his character, of which we should otherwise never have believed him capable.

These three aspects of this strange play, as a chronicle history, as a personal tragedy and as a love poem, merge and pass into each other, but in a certain way they successively become prominent in the following discussion.

CHAPTER III

THE ASSOCIATES OF ANTONY

THE political setting of *Julius Caesar* had been the struggle between the Old Order and the New. The Old goes out with a final and temporary flare of success; the New asserts itself as the necessary solution for the problem of the time, but is deprived of its guiding genius who might best have elicited its possibilities for good and neutralised its possibilities for evil. In *Antony and Cleopatra* we see how its mastery is established and confirmed despite the faults and limitations of the smaller men who now represent it. But in the process very much has been lost. The old principle of freedom, which, even when moribund, serve to lend both the masses and the classes activity and self-consciousness, has quite disappeared. The populace has been dismissed from the scene, and, whenever casually mentioned, it is only with contempt. Octavius describes it :

> This common body,
> Like to a vagabond flag upon the stream,
> Goes to and back, lackeying the varying tide,
> To rot itself with motion.   (I. iv. 44.)

Antony has passed so far from the sphere of his oratorical triumph, that he thinks of his late supporters only as "the shouting plebeians," who cheapen their sight-seeing "for poor'st diminutives, for doits" (IV. xiii. 33). His foreign Queen has been taught his scorn of the Imperial people, and pictures them as "mechanic slaves, with greasy aprons, rules, and hammers," and with "their thick breaths, rank of gross diet" (v. ii. 208). Beyond these insults there is no reference to the plebs, except that, as we learn from Octavius, he and Antony have both notified it of their respective grievances against each other; but this is a mere formality that has not the slightest effect on the progress of events, and no citizen or group of citizens has part in the play.

Even the idea of the State is in abeyance. The sense of the majesty of Rome, which inspired both the conspirators and their opponents, seems extinct. No enterprise, whether right or wrong, is undertaken in the name of patriotism. On the very outposts of the Empire, where, in conflict with the national foe, the love of country is apt to burn more clearly than amidst the security and altercation of the capital, we see a general, in the moment of victory, swayed in part by affection for his patron, in part by care for his own interest, but not in the slightest degree by civic or even chivalrous considerations. When Ventidius is urged by Silius to pursue his advantage against the Parthians, he replies that he has done enough :

> Who does i' the wars more than his captain can
> Becomes his captain's captain : and ambition,
> The soldier's virtue, rather makes choice of loss,
> Than gain which darkens him.
> I could do more to do Antonius good,
> But 't would offend him ; and in his offence
> Should my performance perish.   (III. i. 21.)

And not only is Silius convinced ; he gives his full approval to Ventidius' policy :

> Thou hast, Ventidius, that
> Without the which a soldier, and his sword,
> Grants scarce distinction.   (III. i. 27.)

Are things better with Octavius' understrappers ?
They serve him well and astutely, but there is no
hint that their service is prompted by any large
public aim, and its very efficacy is due in great
measure to its unscrupulousness. Agrippa and
Mecaenas are ready for politic reasons to suggest
or support the marriage of the chaste and gentle
Octavia with a voluptuary like Mark Antony, whose
record they know perfectly well, and pay decorous
attentions to Lepidus while mocking him behind his
back : Thyreus and Proculeius make love to the
employment, when Octavius commissions them to
cajole and deceive Cleopatra ; Dolabella produces
the pleasantest impression, just because, owing to a
little natural manly feeling, he palters with his prescribed obligations to his master. But in none of
them all is there a trace of any liberal or generous
conception of duty ; they are human instruments,
more or less efficient, more or less trustworthy,
who make their career by serving the purposes of
Octavius' personal ambition.

Or turn to the court of Alexandria with its
effeminacy, wine-bibbing, and gluttony. Sextus
Pompeius talks of its "field of feasts," its "epicurean cooks," its "cloyless sauce" (II. i. 22, *et seq.*).
Antony palliates his neglect of the message from
Rome with the excuse that, having newly feasted
three kings, he did "want of what he was i' the
morning" (II. ii. 76). But even in the morning,
as Cleopatra recalls, he can be drunk to bed ere
the ninth hour, and then let himself be clad in
female garb (II. v. 21).

It is not indeed to Egypt that this intemperance
is confined. The contagion has spread to the West,
as we see from the picture of the orgy on board the
galley at Misenum ; a picture we may take in a
special way to convey Shakespeare's idea of the
conditions, since he had no authority for it, but

freely worked it up from Plutarch's innocent statement that Pompey gave the first of the series of
banquets on board his admiral galley, "and there
he welcomed them and made them great cheere."
But in the play all the boon companions, and not
merely the home-comers from the East, cup each
other till the world goes round ; save only the sober
Octavius, and even he admits that his tongue "splits
what it speaks." "This is not yet an Alexandrian
feast," says Pompey. "It ripens towards it," answers
Antony (II. vii. 102). It ripens towards it indeed ;
but more in the way of crude excess than of curious
corruption. In that the palace of the Ptolemies
with its eunuchs and fortune-tellers, its male and
female time-servers and hangers-on, is still inimitable
and unchallenged. It is interesting to note how
Shakespeare fills in the previous history of Iras and
Charmian, whom Plutarch barely mentions till he
tells of their heroic death. In the drama they are
introduced at first as the products of a life from
which all modesty is banished by reckless luxury
and smart frivolity. Their conversation in the
second scene serves to show the unabashed *proter-
vitas* that has infected souls capable of high loyalty
and devotion.[1] And their intimate is the absolutely

[1] If the ideas were in Shakespeare's mind that Professor Zielinski
of St. Petersburg attributes to him (*Marginalien Philologus*, 1905),
the gracelessness of Charmian passes all bounds. "(Die) muntre Zofe
wünscht sich vom Wahrsager allerhand schöne Sachen : 'lass mich
an einem Nachmittag drei Könige heiraten, und sie alle als Wittwe
überleben ; lass mich mit fünfzig Jahren ein Kind haben, dem Herodes
von Judaea huldigen soll : lass mich Octavius Caesar heiraten, etc.'
Das 'Püppchen' dachte sich Shakespeare jünger als ihre Herrin :
fünfzig würde sie also—um Christi Geburt. Ist es nun klar, was das
für ein Kind ist, dem Herodes von Judaea huldigen soll.' Ἐπὰν εὕρητε,
ἀπαγγείλατέ μοι, ὅπως κᾀγὼ ἐλθὼν προσκυνήσω αὐτῷ, sagt er selber, Matth.
ii. 18. Und wem sagt er es? Den Heiligen drei Königen. Sollten
es nicht dieselben sein, die auch in Charmian's Wunschzettel stehen ?
Der Einfall ist einer Mysterie würdig : Gattin der heiligen drei Könige,
Mutter Gottes, and römische Kaiserin dazu." Worthy of a mystery,
perhaps ! but more worthy of a scurrilous lampoon. It might perhaps
be pointed out, that, if fifty years old at the beginning of the Christian

contemptible Lord Alexas, with his lubricity, officiousness and flatteries, who, when evil days come, will persuade Herod of Jewry to forsake the cause of his patrons and will earn his due reward (IV. vi. 12). For there is no moral cement to hold together this ruinous world. After Actium the deserters are so numerous that Octavius can say:

> Within our files there are,
> Of those that served Mark Antony but late,
> Enough to fetch him in.   (IV. i. 12.)

There is not even decent delay in their apostasy. The battle is hardly over when six tributary kings show "the way of yielding" to Canidius, who at once renders his legions and his horse to Caesar (III. x. 33). Shakespeare heightens Plutarch's statement in regard to this, for in point of fact Canidius waited seven days on the chance that Antony might rejoin them, and then, according to Plutarch, merely fled without changing sides: but the object is to set forth the universal demoralisation and instability, and petty qualifications like that implied in the week's delay or abandonment of the post instead of desertion to the enemy are dismissed as of no account. In another addition, for which he has likewise no warrant, Shakespeare clothes the prevalent temper in words. When Pompey rejects the unscrupulous device to obtain the empire, Menas is made to exclaim:

> For this,
> I'll never follow thy pall'd fortunes more.   (II. vii. 87.)

Menas is a pirate, but he speaks the thought of the time; for it is only to fortune that the whole

---

era, Charmian could only be ten at the opening of the play: but this is a small point, and I think it very likely that Shakespeare intended to rouse some such associations in the mind of the reader as Professor Zielinski suggests. Mr. Furness is rather scandalised at the "frivolous irreverence," but it fits the part, and where is the harm? One remembers Byron's defence of the audacities in *Cain* and objection to making "Lucifer talk like the Bishop of London, *which would not be in the character of the former.*"

generation is faithful. Everywhere the cult of material good prevails, whether in the way of acquisition or enjoyment ; and that can give no sanction to payment of service apart from the results.

The corroding influence of the *Zeitgeist* even on natures naturally honest and sound is vividly illustrated in the story of Enobarbus : and the study of his character is peculiarly interesting and instructive, because he is the only one of the more prominent personages who is practically a new creation in the drama, the only one in whose delineation Shakespeare has gone quite beyond the limits supplied by Plutarch, even while making use of them. Lepidus and Pompey, with whom he proceeds in a somewhat similar fashion, are mere subordinates. Octavius and even Cleopatra are only interpreted with new vividness and insight. Antony himself is exhibited only with the threads of his nature transposed, as, for example, when a fabric is held up with its right side instead of its seamy side outwards. But for Enobarbus, who often occupies the front of the stage, the dramatist found only a few detached sentences that suggested a few isolated traits, and while preserving these intact, he introduces them merely as component elements in an entirely original and complex personality. It is therefore fair to suppose that the character of Enobarbus will be of peculiar importance in the economy of the piece.

Plutarch refers to him thrice. The first mention is not very noticeable. Antony, during his campaign in Parthia, had on one occasion to announce to his army a rather disgraceful composition with the enemy, according to which he received permission to retreat in peace.

> But though he had an excellent tongue at will, and very gallant to enterteine his souldiers and men of warre, and that he could passingly well do it, as well, or better then any

Captaine in his time, yet being ashamed for respects, he
would not speake unto them at his removing, but willed
Domitius Ænobarbus to do it.

Thus we see Enobarbus designated for a somewhat
invidious and trying task, and this implies Antony's
confidence in him, and his own efficiency.

Then we are told that when the rupture with
Caesar came,

Antonius, through the perswasions of Domitius, commaunded Cleopatra to returne againe into Ægypt, and there
to understand [1] the successe of this warre,

a command, which, however, she managed to over-
rule. Here again in Enobarbus' counsel we see
the hard-headed and honest officer, who wishes
things to be done in the right way, and risks ill
will to have them so done. It is on this passage
that Shakespeare bases the outburst of Cleopatra
and the downright and sensible remonstrance of
Enobarbus.

Cle. I will be even with thee, doubt it not.
Eno. But why, why, why?
Cle. Thou hast forespoke my being in these wars,
And say'st it is not fit.
Eno. Well, is it, is it? (III. vii. I.)

More remotely too this gave Shakespeare the hint
for Enobarbus' other censures on Antony's conduct
of the campaign.

Thirdly, in the account of the various misfortunes
that befell Antony before Actium, and the varying
moods in which he confronted them, Shakespeare
read :

Furthermore, he dealt very friendely and courteously with
Domitius, and against Cleopatraes mynde. For, he being
sicke of an agewe when he went and tooke a little boate to
goe to Caesars campe, Antonius was very sory for it, but yet
he sent after him all his caryage, trayne and men : and the
same Domitius, as though he gave him to understand that he
repented his open treason, he died immediately after.

[1] Observe or await.

This, of course, supplied Shakespeare with the episodes of Enobarbus' desertion and death, though he altered the date of the first, delaying it till the last flicker of Antony's fortune; and the manner of the second, making it the consequence, which the penitent deliberately desires, of a broken heart.

But this is all that Plutarch has to say about the soldier. He is capable; he is honest and bold in recommending the right course; when Antony wilfully follows the wrong one, he forsakes him; but, touched perhaps by his magnanimity, dies, it may be, in remorse.

Now see how Shakespeare fills in and adds to this general outline. Practical intelligence, outspoken honesty, real capacity for feeling, are still the fundamental traits, and we have evidence of them all from the outset. But, in the first place, they have received a peculiar turn from the habits of the camp. Antony, rebuking and excusing his bluntness, says:

Thou art a soldier only, speak no more. (II. ii. 109.)

Indeed he is a soldier, if not only, at any rate chiefly and essentially; and a soldier of the adventurer type, carrying with him an initial suggestion of the more modern gentlemen of fortune like Le Balafré or Dugald Dalgetty, who would fight for any cause, and offered their services for the highest reward to the leader most likely to secure it for them. He has also their ideas of a soldier's pleasures, and has no fancy for playing the ascetic. In Alexandria he has had a good time, in his own sphere and in his own way indulging in the feasts and carouses and gallantries of his master. He tells Mecaenas, thoroughly associating himself with the exploits of Antony:

We did sleep day out of countenance, and made the night light with drinking. (II. ii. 181.)

He speaks with authority of the immortal breakfast at which the eight wild boars were served, but makes little of it as by no means out of the way. Similarly he identifies himself with Antony in their love affairs when Antony announces his intention of setting out at once :

> Why, then, we kill all our women : we see how mortal an unkindness is to them : if they suffer our departure, death's the word.   (I. ii. 137.)

And after the banquet on the galley, when the exalted personages, "these great fellows," as Menas calls them, have retired more than a little disguised in liquor, he, fresh from the Egyptian Bacchanals, stays behind to finish up the night in Menas' cabin.

Yet he has a certain contempt for the very vices in which he himself shares, at least if their practitioners are overcome by them and cannot retain their self-command even in their indulgence. When Lepidus succumbs, this more seasoned vessel jeers at him :

> There's a strong fellow, Menas ! [*pointing to the attend-*
> *Men.* Why?   *ant who carries off Lepidus.*]
> *Eno.* A' bears the third part of the world, man : see'st not ?
>   (II. vii. 95.)

Nor does he suffer love to interfere with business :

> Under a compelling occasion, let women die : it were pity to cast them away for nothing : though, between them and a great cause, they should be esteemed nothing.   (I. ii. 141.)

His practical shrewdness enables him, though of a very different nature from Cassius, to look, like Cassius, quite through the deeds of men. He always lays his finger on the inmost nerve of a situation or complication. Thus when Mecaenas urges the need of amity on the Triumvirs, Enobarbus' disconcerting frankness goes straight to the point that the smooth propriety of the other evades :

> If you borrow one another's love for the instant, you may, when you hear no more words of Pompey, return it again : you shall have time to wrangle in when you have nothing else to do.   (II. ii. 103.)

Antony silences him, saying he wrongs this presence ; but Octavius sees he has hit the nail on the head though in a somewhat indecorous way :

> I do not much dislike the matter, but
> The manner of his speech.   (II. ii. 113.)

Just in the same way he takes the measure of the arts and wiles and affectations of Cleopatra and her ladies, and admits no cant into the consolations which he offers Antony on Fulvia's death :

> Why, sir, give the gods a thankful sacrifice . . . Your old smock brings forth a new petticoat ; and indeed the tears live in an onion that should water this sorrow.
>   (I. ii. 167.)

Yet he is by no means indifferent to real charm, to the spell of refinement, grace and beauty. Like many who profess cynicism, and even in a way are really cynical, he is all the more susceptible to what in any kind will stand his exacting tests, especially if it contrast with his own rough jostling life of the barracks and of the field. It is in his mouth that Shakespeare places that incomparable description of Cleopatra on the Cydnus, and there could be no more fitting celebrant of her witchery. Of course the poetry of the passage is supposed in part to be due to the theme, and is a tribute to Cleopatra's fascinations ; but Enobarbus has the soul to feel them and the imagination to portray them. Indeed she has no such enraptured eulogist as he. He may object to her presence in the camp and to her inter-ference in the counsels of war ; but that is only because, like Bacon, he believes that "they do best, who if they cannot but admit love, make it keep quarter, and sever it wholly from their serious affairs and actions of life"; it is not because he

underrates her enchantment or would advise Antony
to forego it. On the contrary, he seems to reproach
his general when, in a passing movement of remorse,
Antony regrets having ever seen her :

> O, sir, you then had left unseen a wonderful piece of
> work ; which not to have been blest withal would have dis-
> credited your travel. (I. ii. 159.)

And he not only sees that Antony, despite the most
sacred of ties, the most urgent of interests, will
inevitably return to her : the enthusiasm of his
words shows that their predestinate union has his
full sympathy and approval.

> *Mec.* Now Antony must leave her utterly.
> *Eno.* Never ; he will not ;
> Age cannot wither her, nor custom stale
> Her infinite variety : other women cloy
> The appetites they feed : but she makes hungry
> Where most she satisfies. (II. ii. 238.)

And this responsiveness to what is gracious, has
its complement in his responsiveness to what is
magnificent. He has an ardent admiration for his
" Emperor." He is exceeding jealous for his honour,
and has no idea of the mighty Antony stooping his
crest to any power on earth. When Lepidus begs
him to entreat his captain " to soft and gentle
speech " towards Octavius, he retorts with hot pride
and zeal, like a clansman's for his chief :

> I shall entreat him
> To answer like himself : if Caesar move him,
> Let Antony look over Caesar's head
> And speak as loud as Mars. By Jupiter,
> Were I the wearer of Antonius' beard,
> I would not shave't to-day. (II. ii. 3.)

He glories even in Antony's more doubtful qualities,
his lavishness, his luxury, his conviviality, his success
in love, for in all these his master shows a sort of
royal exuberance ; and they serve in the eyes of this
practical but splendour-loving veteran to set off his

more technical excellences, the "absolute soldiership," the "renowned knowledge" on which he also
dwells (III. vii. 43 and 46). But with all his
enthusiasm for Antony, he is from the first critical
of what he considers his weaknesses and mistakes,
just as with all his enthusiasm for Cleopatra he has
a keen eye for her affectations and interferences.
Knowing Antony's real bent, he sees the inex-
pedience of the Roman marriage, and foretells the
result :

> *Men.* Then is Caesar and he for ever knit together.
> *Eno.* If I were bound to divine of this unity, I would not
> prophesy so.
> *Men.* I think the policy of that purpose made more in the
> marriage than the love of the parties.
> *Eno.* I think so too. But you shall find, the band that
> seems to tie their friendship together will be the very strangler
> of their amity. (II. vi. 122.)

He is as contemptuous of Antony's easy emotionalism as of Octavius' politic family affection. At
the parting of brother and sister, Enobarbus and
Agrippa exchange the asides :

> *Eno.* Will Caesar weep?
> *Agr.* He has a cloud in's face.
> *Eno.* He were the worse for that, were he a horse ;
> So is he, being a man.
> *Agr.*   Why, Enobarbus,
> When Antony found Julius Caesar dead,
> He cried almost to roaring: and he wept
> When at Philippi he found Brutus slain.
> *Eno.* That year, indeed, he was troubled with a rheum ;
> What willingly he did confound he wail'd,
> Believe't, till I wept too. (III. ii. 51.)

It is therefore not hard to understand how, when
Antony wilfully sacrifices his advantages and rushes
on his ruin, his henchman's feelings should be outraged and his fidelity should receive a shock. After
the flight at Actium, Cleopatra asks him : "Is Antony
or we in fault for this?" And Enobarbus, though
he had opposed the presence and plans of the

Queen, is inexorable in laying the blame on the right shoulders :

> Antony only, that would make his will
> Lord of his reason.   (III. xiii. 3.)

He is raised above the common run of the legionaries by his devotion to his master ; but his devotion is half instinctive, half critical ; and, as a rational man, he can suppress in his nature the faithful dog. For the tragedy of Enobarbus' position lies in this : that in that evil time his reason can furnish him with no motive for his loyalty except self-interest and confidence in his leader's capacity ; or, failing these, the unsubstantial recompense of fame. He is not Antony's man from principle, in order to uphold a great cause,—no one in the play has chosen his side on such a ground ; and fidelity at all costs to a person is a forgotten phrase among the cosmopolitan materialists who are competing for the spoils of the Roman world. So what is he to do? His instincts pull him one way, his reason another, and in such an one instincts unjustified by reason lose half their strength. At first he fights valiantly on behalf of his inarticulate natural feeling. When Canidius deserts, he still refuses in the face of evidence to accept the example :

> I'll yet follow
> The wounded chance of Antony, though my reason
> Sits in the wind against me.   (III. x. 35.)

But Antony's behaviour in defeat, his alternations between the supine and the outrageous, shake him still more ; and only the allurement of future applause, not a very cogent one to such a man in such an age, wards off for a while the negative decision :

> Mine honesty and I begin to square.
> The loyalty well held to fools does make
> Our faith mere folly : yet he that can endure
> To follow with allegiance a fall'n lord
> Does conquer him that did his master conquer,
> And earns a place i' the story.   (III. xiii. 41.)

The paltering of Cleopatra however is a further object lesson :

> Sir, sir, thou art so leaky,
> That we must leave thee to thy sinking, for
> Thy dearest quit thee. (III. xiii. 63.)

Then the observation of Antony's frenzy of wrath and frenzy of courage finally convinces him that the man is doomed, and he forms his resolution :

> Now he'll outstare the lightning. To be furious
> Is to be frighted out of fear : and in that mood
> The dove will peck the estridge ; and I see still
> A diminution in our captain's brain
> Restores his heart : when valour preys on reason,
> It eats the sword it fights with. I will seek
> Some way to leave him. (III. xiii. 195.)

There is something inevitable in his recreancy, for the principle that Menas puts in words is the presupposition on which everybody acts ; and Antony himself can understand exactly what has taken place :

> O, my fortunes have
> Corrupted honest men ! (IV. v. 16.)

Enobarbus' heart is right, but in the long run it has no chance against the convincing arguments of the situation. And yet his heart has shown him the worthy way, and, in his despair and remorse, it recovers hold of the truth that his head had made him doubt. Observe however that even his revulsion of feeling is brought about by the appeal to his worldly wisdom ; it is not by their unassisted power that the discredited whispers of conscience make themselves heard and regain their authority. Enobarbus' penitence, though sudden, is all rationally explained, and is quite different from the miraculous conversions of some wrong-doers in fiction, who in an instant are awakened to grace for no conceivable cause and by no intelligible means. He is made to realise that he has taken wrong measures in his own interest, by Octavius' treatment of the other deserters.

> Alexas did revolt; and went to Jewry on
> Affairs of Antony; there did persuade
> Great Herod to incline himself to Caesar
> And leave his master Antony: for this pains
> Caesar hath hang'd him.   Canidius and the rest
> That fell away have entertainment, but
> No honourable trust.   I have done ill:
> Of which I do accuse myself so sorely,
> That I will joy no more.   (IV. vi. 11.)

Then the transmission to him of his treasure with increase, makes him feel that after all loyalty might have been a more profitable investment:

> O Antony,
> Thou mine of bounty, how would'st thou have paid
> My better service, when my turpitude
> Thou dost so crown with gold!   (IV. vi. 31.)

But he does not stop here.   It is only in this way that his judgment, trained by the time to test all things by material advantage, can be convinced. But when it is convinced, his deeper and nobler nature finds free vent in self-recrimination and self-reproach.   He goes on:

> This blows my heart:
> If swift thought break it not, a swifter mean
> Shall outstrike thought: but thought will do't, I feel.
> I fight against thee!   No: I will go seek
> Some ditch wherein to die; the foul'st best fits
> My latter part of life.   (IV. vi. 35.)

And this too is most natural.   Antony's generosity restores to him his old impression of Antony's magnificence which he had lost in these last sorry days. With that returns his old enthusiasm, and with that awakes the sense of his own transgression against such greatness.   He is ready now in expiation to sacrifice the one thing that in the end made him still shrink from treason.   He had tried to steady himself, as we have seen, with the thought that the glory of loyalty would be his, if he remained faithful to the last. Now he demands the brand of treachery for his name, though he fain would have Antony's pardon for himself:

> O Antony,
> Nobler than my revolt is infamous,
> Forgive me in thine own particular:
> But let the world rank me in register
> A master-leaver and a fugitive. (IV. ix. 18.)

Thus he dies heart-broken and in despair. Personal attachment to an individual, the one ethical motive that lingers in a world of self-seekers to give existence some dignity and worth, is the inspiration of his soul. But even this he cannot preserve unspoiled: on accepted assumptions he is forced to deny and desecrate it. He succumbs less through his own fault than through the fault of the age; and this is his grand failure. When he realises what it means, there is no need of suicide: he is killed by "swift thought," by the consciousness that his life with this on his record is loathsome and alien, a "very rebel to his will," that only "hangs on him" (IV. ix. 14).

Among the struggling and contentious throng of worldlings and egoists who to succeed must tread their nobler instincts underfoot, and even so do not always succeed, are there any honest and sterling characters at all? There are a few, in the background, barely sketched, half hid from sight. But we can perceive their presence, and even distinguish their gait and bearing, though the artist's purpose forbade their portrayal in detail.

First of these is Scarus, the simple and valiant fightingman, who resents the infatuation of Antony and the ruinous influence of Cleopatra as deeply as Enobarbus, but whose unsophisticated soldier-nature keeps him to his colours with a troth that the less naïf Enobarbus could admire but could not observe. It is from his mouth that the most opprobrious epithets are hurled on the absconding pair, the "ribaudred nag of Egypt, whom leprosy o'ertake," and "the doting mallard," "the noble ruin of her magic" who has kissed away kingdoms and provinces. But as soon as he hears they have fled toward Peloponnesus, he cries:

> 'Tis easy to't; and there will I attend
> What further comes. (III. x. 32.)

He attends to good purpose, and is the hero of the last skirmish; when Antony's prowess rouses him to applause, from which he is too honest to exclude reproach:

> O my brave emperor, this is fought indeed!
> Had we done so at first, we had droven them home
> With clouts about their heads. (IV. vii. 4.)

Then halting, bleeding, with a wound that from a T has been made an H, he still follows the chase. It is a little touch of irony, apt to be overlooked, that he, who has cursed Cleopatra's magic and raged because kingdoms were kissed away, should now as grand reward have his merits commended to "this great fairy," and as highest honour have leave to raise her hand—the hand that cost Thyreus so dear —to his own lips. Doubtless, despite his late outbreak, he appreciates these favours as much as the golden armour that Cleopatra adds. Says Antony,

> He has deserved it, were it carbuncled
> Like holy Phoebus car. (IV. viii. 28.)

He has: for he is of other temper than his nameless and featureless original in Plutarch, who is merely a subaltern who had fought well in the sally.

> Cleopatra to reward his manlines, gave him an armor and head peece of cleene gold: howbeit the man at armes when he had received this rich gift, stale away by night and went to Caesar.

Not so Scarus. He is still at his master's side on the disastrous morrow and takes from him the last orders that Antony as commander ever gave.

In this Roman legionary the spirit of military obligation still asserts its power; and the spirit of domestic obligation is as strong in the Roman matron Octavia. Shakespeare has been accused of travestying this noble and dutiful lady. He certainly does not do that, and the strange misstatement has arisen from treating seriously Cleopatra's distortion of the messenger's report, or from taking that report, when the messenger follows Cleopatra's lead, as Shakespeare's deliberate verdict. If the messenger says that she is low-voiced and not so tall as her rival, is that equivalent to the "dull of tongue, and dwarfish" into which it is translated? And finding it so translated, is it wonderful that the browbeaten informant should henceforth adopt the same style himself, and exaggerate her deliberate motion to creeping, her statuesque dignity to torpor, the roundness of her face to deformity—which Cleopatra at once interprets as foolishness—the lowness of her forehead to as much as you please, or, in his phrase, "as she would wish it." Agrippa, on the other hand speaks of her as one,

> whose beauty claims
> No worse a husband than the best of men :
> Whose virtue and whose general graces speak
> That which none else can utter. (II. ii. 130.)

Mecaenas, too, pays his tribute to her "beauty, wisdom, modesty" (II. ii. 246). And if the praises of the courtiers are suspect, they are not more so than the censures with which Cleopatra flatters herself or is flattered. But if we dismiss, or at least discount, both sets of overstatements, and with them Antony's own phrase, "a gem of women," uttered in the heat of jealous contrast, there are other conclusive evidences of the opinion in which she is held. Enobarbus speaks of her "holy, cold, and still conversation" (II. vi. 131). Antony thinks of her as patient, even when he threatens Cleopatra with her

vengeance by personal assault (IV. xii. 38). Cleopatra,
with her finer intuition, even when recalling Antony's
threat, conjectures more justly what that vengeance
would be :

> Your wife Octavia, with her modest eyes
> And still conclusion, shall acquire no honour
> Demuring upon me.   (IV. XV. 27.)

And elsewhere she asserts that she will not

> once be chastised with the sober eye
> Of dull Octavia.   (V. ii. 54.)

It is easy to construct her picture from these hints.
Calm, pure, devout, submissive ; quite without viva-
city or initiative, she presents the old-fashioned ideal
of womanhood, that finds a sphere subordinate
though august, by the domestic hearth. And this
is in the main Plutarch's conception of her too. But
there are differences. The sacrifices of the lady to
the exigencies of statecraft is emphasised by the
historian : " She was maryed unto him as it were
of necessitie, bicause her brother Caesars affayres so
required it," and that even in her year of mourning,
so that a dispensation had to be obtained ; since it
was " against the law that a widow should be maried
within tenne monethes after her husbandes death."
Nevertheless her association with Antony is far more
intimate in Plutarch than in Shakespeare ; she is
the mother of his children, feels bound to him, and
definitely takes his side. When relations first become
strained between the brothers-in-law, and not, as in
the drama, just before the final breach, she plays the
peace maker, but successfully and on Antony's behalf.
She seeks out her brother ; tells him she is now the
happiest woman in the world ; if war should break
out between them, " it is uncertaine to which of them
the goddes have assigned the victorie or overthrowe.
But for me, on which side soever victorie fall, my
state can be but most miserable still." In Shake-

speare this petition, eked out with reminiscences
of the appeal of Blanch in *King John*, and with
anticipations of the appeal of Volumnia in *Coriolanus*,
is addressed to Antony, and the even balance of her
sympathies is accented and reiterated in a way for
which Plutarch gives no warrant.

In the *Life* again, even when Antony has rejoined
Cleopatra, has showered provinces on her and his
illegitimate children, and, after the Parthian campaign, is living with her once more, Octavia insists
on seeking him out and brings him

> great store of apparell for souldiers, a great number of
> horse, summe of money, and gifts, to bestow on his friendes
> and Captaines he had about him : and besides all those, she
> had two thowsand souldiers chosen men, all well armed, like
> unto the Praetors bands.

She has to return from Athens without seeing
Antony, but, despite Caesar's command, she still
lives in her husband's house, still tries to heal the
division, looks after his children and promotes the
business of all whom he sends to Rome.

> Howbeit thereby, thinking no hurt, she did Antonius
> great hurt. For her honest love and regard to her husband,
> made every man hate him, when they sawe he did so un-
> kindly use so noble a Lady.

And finally, when Antony sent her word to leave
his house, she took with her all his children save
Fulvia's eldest son who was with his father, and
instead of showing resentment, only bewailed and
lamented " her cursed hap that had brought her to
this, that she was accompted one of the chiefest
causes of this civill warre."

Her even more magnanimous care for all Antony's
offspring without distinction, when Antony is no
more, belongs of course to a later date ; but all
the previous instances of her devotion to his interest
fall well within the limits of the play, and yet Shakespeare makes no use of them.

It does not suit him to suggest that Antony ever
deviated from his passion for Cleopatra or bestowed
his affection elsewhere : indeed, on the eve of his
marriage, he reveals his heart and intentions clearly
enough.   But Shakespeare also knows that without
affection to bring it out, there will be no answering
affection in a woman like Octavia.   She will be true
to all her obligations, so long as they are obligations,
but no love will be roused to make her do more than
is in her bond.   And of love there is in the play as
little trace on her part as on Antony's.   It is brother
and sister, not husband and wife, that exchange
the most endearing terms : " Sweet Octavia," " My
dearest sister," and " my noble brother," " most dear
Caesar "; while to Antony she is " Octavia," " gentle
Octavia," or at most " Dear Lady," and to her he is
" Good my lord."   At the parting in Rome Caesar
has a cloud in his face and her eyes drop tears like
April showers.   At the parting in Athens there is
only the formal permission to leave, on the one
hand, and the formal acknowledgment on the other.
Evidently, if, as she says, she has her.

heart parted betwixt two friends
That do afflict each other,   (III. vi. 77.)

or if Antony describes her equipoise of feeling as

the swan's down-feather,
That stands upon the swell at full of tide,
And neither way inclines,   (III. ii. 48.)

it is not because she regards them both with equal
tenderness.   Her brother has her love ; her husband,
so long as he deserves it, has her duty.   But when
he forfeits his claim, she has done with him, unlike
Plutarch's Octavia, who pursues him to the end, and
beyond the end, with a self-forgetfulness that her
mere covenant could never call forth.   Of all this
there is nothing in the play.   Her appeal to Antony
in defence of Caesar is far warmer than her appeal

to Caesar on behalf of Antony, and when she definitely hears that Antony has not only joined Cleopatra against her brother but has installed Cleopatra in her own place, she merely says, " Is it so ?" and falls silent.   No wonder.   She is following Antony's instructions to the letter :

> Let your best love draw to that point, which seeks
> Best to preserve it.   (III. iv. 21.)

And again ;

> When it appears to you where this begins,
> Turn your displeasure that way ; for our faults
> Can never be so equal that your love
> Can equally move with them.   (III. iv. 33.)

But this tacit assumption, fully borne out by her previous words, that the claims of husband and brother are equal in her eyes, and that the precedence is to be determined merely by a comparison of faults, shows how little of wifely affection Octavia felt, though doubtless she would be willing to fulfil her responsibilities to the smallest jot and tittle.

The hurried, loveless and transitory union, into which Antony has entered only to suit his convenience, for as Enobarbus says, " he married but his occasion here," and into which Octavia has entered only out of deference to her brother who "uses his power unto her," has thus merely a political and moral but no emotional significance. This Roman marriage lies further apart from the love story of Antony than the marriage in Brittany does from the love story of Tristram.   This diplomatic alliance interferes as little with Octavia's sisterly devotion to Octavius as the political alliances of Marguerite d'Angoulême interfered with her sisterly devotion to Francis I.   And much is gained by this for the play.   In the first place the hero no longer, as in the biography, offends us by fickleness in his grand idolatry and infidelity to a second attachment, on the one hand, or by ingratitude to a long-suffering and loving wife on the other. But just for that reason Octavia does not really enter into his life, and claims no full delineation. She is hardly visible, and does not disturb our sympathies with the lovers or force on us moral regards by demuring on them and chastising them with her sober eyes. Nevertheless visible at intervals she is, and then she seems to tell of another life than that of Alexandrian indulgence, a narrower life of obligations and pieties beside which the carnival of impulse is both glorified and condemned. And she does this not less effectually, but a great deal less obtrusively, that in her shadowy form as she flits from the mourning-chamber to the altar at the bidding of her brother, and from Athens to Rome to preserve the peace, we see rather the self-devoted sister than the devoted wife. For in the play she is sister first and essentially, and wife only in the second place because her sisterly feeling is so strong.

Still more slightly sketched than the domestic loyalty of Octavia or even than the military loyalty of Scarus, is the loyalty of Eros the servant ; but it is the most affecting of all, for it is to the death. Characteristically, he who obtains the highest spiritual honours that are awarded to any person in the play, is one of a class to which in the prime of ancient civilisation the possibilty of any moral life would in theory have been denied. Morality was for the free citizen of a free state : the slave was not really capable of it. And indeed it is clear that often for the slave, who might be only one of the goods and chattels of his owner, the sole chance of escape from a condition of spiritual as well as physical servitude would lie in personal enthusiasm for the master, in willing self-absorption in him. But in a world like that of *Antony and Cleopatra* such personal enthusiasm, as we have seen, is almost the highest thing that remains. So it is the quondam slave, Eros the freedman, bred in the cult of it, who bears away the palm. Antony commands him to slay him :

> When I did make thee free, sworest thou not then
> To do this when I bade thee ?   Do it at once ;
> Or thy precedent services are all
> But accidents unpurposed.   Draw, and come.
>
> (IV. xiv. 81.)

But Eros by breaking his oath and slaying himself, does his master a better service. He cheers him in his dark hour by this proof of measureless attachment :

> Thus do I escape the sorrow
> Of Antony's death. (IV. xiv. 94.)

CHAPTER IV

THE POLITICAL LEADERS

So much for the freedman whom Antony hails as his master, thrice nobler than himself. But what about his betters, the "great fellows" as Menas calls them, his rivals and associates in Empire?

Let us run through the series of them; and despite his pride of place we cannot begin lower than with the third Triumvir.

Lepidus, the "slight unmeritable man, meet to be sent on errands," as he is described in *Julius Caesar*, maintains the same character here, and is hardly to be talked of "but as a property." In the first scene where he appears, when he and Octavius are discussing Antony's absence, he is a mere cypher. Even in this hour of need, Octavius unconsciously and as a matter of course treats Antony's negligence as a wrong not to them both but only to himself. The messenger never addresses Lepidus and assumes that the question is between Caesar and Pompey alone. At the close this titular partner "beseeches" to be informed of what takes place, and Octavius acknowledges that it is his "bond," but clearly it is not his choice.

No doubt on the surface he pleases by his moderate and conciliatory attitude. When Octavius is indicting his absent colleague, Lepidus is frank in his excuse:

> I must not think there are
> Evils enow to darken all his goodness :
> His faults in him seem as the spots of heaven,
> More fiery by night's blackness.   (I. iv. 10.)

Knowing the zeal and influence of Enobarbus, he recommends his mediation as a becoming and worthy deed, and tries to mitigate his vehemence :

> Your speech is passion :
> But, pray you, stir no embers up.   (II. ii. 12.)

And when the Triumvirs meet, the counsels of forbearance, which Shakespeare assigns to him and which in Plutarch are not associated with his name, are just in the right tone :

> Noble friends,
> That which combined us was most great, and let not
> A leaner action rend us.   What's amiss
> May it be gently heard : when we debate
> Our trivial difference loud, we do commit
> Murder in healing wounds : then, noble partners,
> The rather, for I earnestly beseech,
> Touch you the sourest points with sweetest terms,
> Nor curstness grow to the matter.   (II. ii. 17.)

But all this springs from no real kindliness or public spirit.   Pompey understands the position :

> Lepidus flatters both,
> Of both is flatter'd : but he neither loves,
> Nor either cares for him.   (II. i. 14.)

It is mere indolence and flaccidity of temper that makes him ready to play the peace-maker, and his efforts are proof of incompetence rather than of nobility.   He is so anxious to agree with everybody and ingratiate himself with both parties, that he excites the ridicule not only of the downright Enobarbus, but of the reticent and diplomatic Agrippa :

Eno.   O, how he loves Caesar !
Agr. Nay, but how dearly he adores Mark Antony !
Eno. Caesar?   Why, he's the Jupiter of men.
Agr. What's Antony?   The god of Jupiter.

Eno. Spake you of Caesar? How! the nonpareil!
Agr. O Antony! O thou Arabian bird!
Eno. Would you praise Caesar, say "Caesar": go no further.
Agr. Indeed, he plied them both with excellent praises.

(III. ii. 7.)

He will be all things to all men that he himself may
be saved; and his love of peace runs parallel with
his readiness for good cheer. He likes to enjoy
himself and soon drinks himself drunk. The very
servants see through his infirmity:

> *Sec. Serv.* As they pinch one another by the disposition,
> he cries out "no more"; reconciles them to his entreaty
> and himself to the drink.[1] (II. vii. 6.)

And they proceed to draw the moral of the whole
situation. Lepidus' ineptitude is due to the same
circumstance that brings Costard's criticism on Sir
Nathaniel when the curate breaks down in the
pageant. "A foolish mild man; an honest man,
look you, and soon dashed. He is a marvellous
good neighbour, faith, . . . but, for Alexander,—
alas, you see how 'tis,—a little o'erparted." Lepidus
too is a marvellous good neighbour, but for a Triumvir,
—alas, you see how 'tis,—a little o'erparted. He is
attempting a part or role that is too big for him.
He is in a position and company where his nominal
influence goes for nothing and his want of perception
puts him to the blush.

---

[1] I take this much discussed passage to refer to the friction that
inevitably arises in such a gathering. The guests are of such different
disposition or temperament, that especially after their late misunderstandings they are bound to chafe each other. We have an example
of it. Pompey plays the cordial and tactful host to perfection, but
even he involuntarily harks back to his grievance:

> O, Antony,
> You have my father's house,—But, what? we are friends.

I think the meaning of the second servant's remark is that when such
little *contretemps* occur, as they could not but do in so ill-assorted a
company, Lepidus in his role of peace-maker interferes to check them,
and drowns the difference in a carouse. But the result is that he
befuddles himself.

Sec. Serv. Why, this it is to have a name in great men's fellowship: I had as lief have a reed that will do me no service as a partizan I could not heave.

First Serv. To be called into a huge sphere, and not to be seen to move in't, are the holes where eyes should be, which pitifully disaster the cheeks. (II. vii. 12.)

In his efforts at *bonhomie*, he becomes so bemused that even Antony, generally so affable and courteous, does not trouble to be decently civil, and flouts him to his wine-sodden face, with impertinent school-boy jests about the crocodile that is shaped like itself, and is as broad as it has breadth, and weeps tears that are wet. Caesar, ever on the guard, asks in cautious admonition: "Will this description satisfy him?" But Antony is scornfully aware that he may dismiss punctilios:

With the health that Pompey gives him; else he is a very epicure. (II. vii. 56.)

His deposition, which must come in the natural course of things, is mentioned only casually and contemptuously:

Caesar, having made use of him in the wars 'gainst Pompey, presently denied him rivality: would not let him partake in the glory of the action: and not resting here, accuses him of letters he had formerly wrote to Pompey: upon his own appeal, seizes him: so the poor third is up, till death enlarge his confine. (III. v. 7.)

Accused of letters written to Pompey! So he had been at his old work, buttering his bread on both sides. His suppression is one of the grievances Antony has against Caesar, who has appropriated his colleague's revenue; and it is interesting to note the defence that Caesar, who never chooses his grounds at random, gives for his apparent arbitrariness:

I have told him, Lepidus was grown too cruel;
That he his high authority abused,
And did deserve his change. (III. vi. 32.)

So this friend of all the world may be accused of
inhumanity and misrule.   The charge is plausible.
Shakespeare could not here forget that at the proscription, Lepidus is represented as acquiescing in
the death of his own brother-in-law to secure the
death of Antony's nephew.   Still his alleged cruelty
may only have been a specious pretext on Octavius'
part to screen his own designs, and even to transfer
his own offences to another man's shoulders.   Pompey
says, in estimating the chances of his venture,

> Caesar gets money where
> He loses hearts.   (II. i. 13.)

Appian refers to these exactions, but in Plutarch
there is as yet no mention of Octavius making himself unpopular by exorbitant imposts, and only at a
later time is he said to have done so in preparing
for his war with Antony.   The subsequent passage,
which Shakespeare does not use, or hardly uses, in
its proper place, may have suggested the present
statement :

> The great and grievous exactions of money did sorely
> oppresse the people. . . .   Hereuppon there arose a wonder-
> full exclamation and great uprore all Italy over : so that
> among the greatest faults that ever Antonius committed,
> they blamed him most for that he delayed to give Caesar
> battell. . . .   When such a great summe of money was de-
> maunded of them, they grudged at it, and grewe to mutinie
> upon it.

Does Shakespeare, by antedating Caesar's oppressive
measures, mean to insinuate his own gloss on the
charge of cruelty against Lepidus that he found in
Plutarch ?   At any rate in that case Octavius would
be merely following the course that Antony had
already laid down :

> Though we lay these honours on this man,
> To ease ourselves of divers slanderous loads,
> He shall but bear them as the ass bears gold,
> To groan and sweat under the business,
> Either led or driven, as we point the way :

And having brought our treasure where we will,
Then take we down his load, and turn him off,
Like to the empty ass, to shake his ears,
And graze in commons.   (*J. C.* IV. i. 19.)

Octavius certainly carries out Antony's programme
in the result, and it would add to the irony of the
situation if he had also done so in the process, and,
while exploiting Lepidus' resources, had incidentally
eased himself of a slanderous load.   No wonder that
Antony is annoyed.   But if he frets at his colleague's
undoing, we may be sure that apart from personal
chagrin, it is only because Octavius' influence has
been increased and his own share of the spoils with-
held.   Of personal regret there is nothing in his
reported reception of the news.   Lepidus the man,
Antony dismisses with an angry gesture and
exclamation : he

                                            spurns
The rush that lies before him ; cries, " Fool, Lepidus ! "
                                        (III. v. 17.)

Sextus Pompeius who at one time had a fair
chance of entering into a position equal or superior
to that of Lepidus, comes higher in the scale than
he.   He has a certain feeling for righteousness :

If the great gods be just, they shall assist
The deeds of justest men.   (II. i. 1.)

He has a certain nobility of sentiment that enables
him to rise to the occasion.   When to his surprise he
learns that he will have to reckon with the one man
he dreads, he cries :
                            But let us rear
The higher our opinion, that our stirring
Can from the lap of Egypt's widow pluck
The ne'er-lust-wearied Antony.   (II. i. 35.)

So, when told that he looks older, his reply is
magnanimous :
                            Well, I know not
What counts harsh Fortune casts upon my face ;
But in my bosom shall she never come,
To make my heart her vassal.   (II. vi. 55.)

Antony confesses that he owes him thanks for generous treatment:

> He hath laid strange courtesies and great
> Of late upon me.   (II. ii. 157.)

We presently get to hear what these were, and must admit that he acted like a gentleman:

> Though I lose
> The praise of it by telling, you must know,
> When Caesar and your brother were at blows,
> Your mother came to Sicily, and did find
> Her welcome friendly.   (II. vi. 43.)

He has moreover a certain filial piety for the memory of his father, and a certain afterglow of free republican sentiment:

> What was't
> That moved pale Cassius to conspire; and what
> Made the all-honour'd, honest Roman, Brutus,
> With the arm'd rest, courtiers of beauteous freedom,
> To drench the Capitol: but that they would
> Have one man but one man? And that is it
> Hath made me rig my navy: at whose burthen
> The anger'd ocean foams; with which I meant
> To scourge the ingratitude that despiteful Rome
> Cast on my noble father.   (II. vi. 14.)

But even if all this were quite genuine, it would not suffice to form a really distinguished character. In the first place Sextus never penetrates to the core of things but lingers over the shows. Thus he has no grip of his present strength or of the insignificance to which he relegates himself by his composition. For Shakespeare differs from Plutarch, and follows Appian, in making his rising a very serious matter.[1] It is this that in the play, and in complete contradiction of the *Life*, is the chief motive for Antony's return to Italy: and he gives his reasons. He says that Pompey "commands the empire of the sea" (I. ii. 191),—a great exaggeration of Plutarch's statement that he " so scored[2] all the sea thereabouts

---

[1] See Appendix D.   [2] Scoured.

(*i.e.*, near Sicily) that none durst peepe out with a sayle." He continues, that "the slippery people" begin to throw all the dignities of Pompey the Great upon his son (I. ii. 193), though there is no hint of this popular support in the history. And he concludes that Pompey's

> . . . quality, going on,
> The sides o' the world may danger.   (I. ii. 198.)

In Plutarch it is not prudence but courtesy that moves the Triumvirs to negociate with him. His hospitality to Antony's mother is expressly mentioned as the cause of their leniency ; "*therefore* they thought good to make peace with him." Similarly Shakespeare may have warrant from Appian, but he certainly has not warrant from Plutarch, to represent Octavius as listening in dismay to reports of malcontents "that only have fear'd Caesar" (I. iv. 38) crowding to Pompey's banners from love of him ; or as harassed by Antony's absence, when this occasion "drums him from his sport" (I. iv. 29) ; or as driven by fear of Pompey to "cement their divisions and bind up the petty difference" (II. i. 48). In all these ways Shakespeare treats the trifling disturbance of Plutarch's account as a civil war waged by not unequal forces. And even after the tension has been somewhat relieved by Antony's arrival, Octavius bears witness in regard to Pompey's strength by land that it is

> Great and increasing : but by sea
> He is an absolute master.   (II. ii. 165.)

Obviously then Shakespeare conceives Pompey as having much to hope for, and much to lose. But Pompey does not realise his own power. By the treaty he throws away his advantages. In the division of the world he only gets Sicily and Sardinia, which were his already ; and in return he must rid all the sea of pirates, and send wheat to Rome. By

the first provision he deprives himself of recruits like
Menas and Menecrates ; by the second, he caters for
his scarce atoned enemies.   Surely there is justification for Menas' aside ; "Thy father, Pompey,
would ne'er have made this treaty" (II. vi. 84), and
his like remark to Enobarbus : "Pompey doth this
day laugh away his fortune" (II. vi. 109).   He
practically gives over the contest which he has a fair
prospect of winning, and allows himself to be cajoled
of the means by which he might at least gain security
and power.   But the most that he obtains is a paper
guarantee for a fraction of the spoils ; though he
ought to have known that such guarantees are rotten
bands with rivals like Octavius, who will only wait
the opportunity, that must now inevitably come, to
set them aside.

But besides, this magnanimity, which he is so fond
of parading, is not only insufficient, even were it
quite sterling coin ; in his case it rings counterfeit.
We cannot forget that his noble sentiments about
justice are uttered to Menas and Menecrates, "great
thieves by sea."   Is Pompeius Magnus to be
avenged, is freedom to be restored by the help of
buccaneers who find it expedient to "deny" what
they have done by water ?   Surely all this is not
very dexterous make-believe, intended to impose on
others or himself.   Even his rejection of Menas'
scheme for doing away with the Triumvirs, though
it shows his regard for appearances, does not imply
any honourable feeling of the highest kind.   For
listen to his words :

> Ah, this thou should'st have done,
> And not have spoke on't ! In me, 'tis villany ;
> In thee 't had been good service.   Thou must know,
> 'Tis not my profit that does lead mine honour ;
> Mine honour, it.   Repent that e'er thy tongue
> Hath so betray'd thine act : being done unknown,
> I should have found it afterwards well done ;
> But must condemn it now.   (II. vii. 79.)

Here he shows no moral scruple, but only anxiety about his reputation. He would have no objection to reap the reward of crime, and would even after a decorous interval approve it; but he will not commit or authorise it, because he wishes to pose in his own eyes and the eyes of others as the man of justice, principle and chivalry. He is one of the people who "would not play false and yet would wrongly win," and who often excite more contempt than the resolute malefactor. And the reason is that their abstention from guilt arises not from tenderness of conscience but from perplexity of intellect. They confound shadow and substance; for by as much as genuine virtue is superior to material success, by so much is material success superior to the illusion of virtue. In the case of Pompey, the treachery of Octavius is almost excused by the ostentation, obtuseness, and half-heartedness of the victim. It is fitting that after being despoiled of Italy he should owe his death to a mistake. This at least is the story, not found in Plutarch, which Shakespeare in all probability adopts at the suggestion of Appian. It is not given as certain even by Appian, who leaves it open to question whether he was killed by Antony's command or not. But perhaps Shakespeare considers that his futile career should end futilely through the overzeal of an agent who misunderstands his master's wishes; so he makes Eros tell how Antony

> Threats the throat of that his officer
> That murder'd Pompey. (III. v. 19.)

It suits the dramatist too to free his hero from complicity in such a deed, and exhibit him as receiving the news with generous indignation and regret. Yet such regret is very skin-deep. Even Antony's chief complaint in regard to Pompey's

overthrow is that he gets none of the unearned
increment; or, as Octavius says,

> that, having in Sicily
> Sextus Pompeius spoil'd, we had not rated him
> His part o' the isle.   (III. vi. 24.)

Higher still in our respect, if not in our affection,
but even in our respect not very high, is Octavius
at the head of his statesmen, politicians, men of the
world, his Mecaenases, Agrippas and the rest, with
their *savoir faire* and *savoir vivre*. They never let
themselves go in thought or in deed; all their words
and behaviour are disciplined, reserved, premeditated.
Antony's description of their principal is no doubt
true, and it breathes the contempt of the born
soldier, who has drunk delight of battle with his
peers, for the mere deviser of calculations and
combinations :

> He at Philippi kept
> His sword e'en like a dancer ; while I struck
> The lean and wrinkled Cassius ; and 'twas I
> That the mad Brutus ended : he alone
> Dealt on lieutenantry, and no practice had
> In the brave squares of war.   (III. xi. 35.)

Nor is there any prestige of genius or glamour of
charm to conciliate admiration for such men. Theirs
are the practical, rather uninteresting natures, that
generally rise to the top in this workaday world.
They know what they wish to get; they know what
they must do to get it; and the light from heaven
never shines on their eyes either to glorify their path
or to lead them astray.

The most obvious trait, as Kreyssig remarks, in
the somewhat bourgeois personality of Octavius is
his sobriety, in every sense of the word : a self-
contained sobriety, which, though supposed to be
a middle-class virtue, is in him pushed so far as
to become almost aristocratic. For it fosters and
cherishes his self-esteem ; and his self-esteem rises

to an enormous and inflexible pride, which finds expression alike in his dignity and in his punctiliousness. In both respects it is outraged by the levity of Antony, which he resents as compromising himself. His colleague must

> No way excuse his soils, when we do bear
> So great weight in his lightness. (i. iv. 24.)

A man like this, fast centred in himself, cannot but despise the impulse-driven populace; he could never have courted it to sway it to his purposes, as Antony did of old ; to him it is a rotting water-weed. This temper, lofty and imposing in some respects, is apt to attach undue importance to form and etiquette, as when the "manner" of Enobarbus' interruption, not its really objectionable because all too incontrovertible matter, arouses his disapproval : but it is a difficult temper to take liberties with. None of his counsellors dreams of venturing with him on the familiarity which Enobarbus, Canidius, and even the common soldier, employ as a matter of course with Antony. And this is partly due to his lack of sympathy, to his deficient social feeling. Such an one plumes himself on being different from and superior to his fellows. He is like the Prince of Arragon in the *Merchant of Venice* :

> I will not choose what many men desire,
> Because I will not jump with common spirits
> And rank me with the barbarous multitudes.
> (*M. of V.* ii. ix. 3.)

It is because Antony's vices are those of the common spirits and the barbarous multitudes that Octavius despises him :

> You shall find there
> A man who is the abstract of all faults
> That all men follow. (i. iv. 8.)

His own failings do not lie in the direction of vulgar indulgence. He is a foe to all excess. When the feasters pledge him, he objects to the compulsory carouse :

> I could well forbear 't.
> It's monstrous labour, when I wash my brain,
> And it grows fouler. . . ..
>   I had rather fast from all four days
> Than drink so much in one.   (II. vii. 105.)

And he can address a dignified remonstrance and rebuke to his less temperate associates :

> What would you more ?   Pompey, good night.   Good brother,
> Let me request you off : our graver business
> Frowns at this levity.   Gentle lords, let's part :
> You see we have burnt our cheeks. . . .
>   The wild disguise hath almost
> Antick'd us all.   (II. vii. 126.)

A man of this kind will be externally faultless in all the domestic requirements, a good husband and a good brother, in so far as rigid fidelity to the nuptial tie and scrupulous care for his sister's provision are concerned.   He is honestly shocked at Antony's violation of his marriage bond.   We feel that if Cleopatra did really entertain the idea of subduing him by her charms, it was nothing but an undevout imagination.   One might as well think to set on fire " a dish of skim milk," as Hotspur calls men of this sort.

But the better side of this is his genuine family feeling.   His love for his sister may be limited and alloyed, but it is unfeigned.   It has sometimes been pointed out that his indignation at Octavia's scanty convoy when she returns from Athens to Rome, is stirred quite as much on his own behalf as on hers :

> Why have you stolen upon us thus ?   You come not
> Like Caesar's sister. . . .   You are come
> A market-maid to Rome ; and have prevented
> The ostentation of our love, which, left unshown,
> Is often left unlov'd.   (III. vi. 42.)

It is quite true that he thinks of what is due to himself, but he does not altogether forget her claims ;

and even when he regrets the defective "ostentation" of love—a term that is apt to rouse suspicion, no doubt, but less so in Elizabethan than in modern ears—he bases his regret on the just and valid ground that without expression love itself is apt to die. That behind his own "ostentation" of fondness (which of course he is careful not to neglect, for it is a becoming and creditable thing), there is some reality of feeling, is proved by the parting scene. His affectionate farewell and even his gathering tears might be pretence; but he promises to send her regular letters:

> Sweet Octavia,
> You shall hear from me still. (III. ii. 58.)

It really means something when a man like Octavius, busy with the affairs of the whole world, spares time for frequent domestic correspondence.

And yet this admirable brother has not hesitated to arrange for his sister a "mariage de convenance" with Antony, a man whom he disapproves and dislikes. From the worldly point of view it is certainly the most brilliant match she could make; and this perhaps to one of Octavius' arid nature, with its total lack of sympathy, imagination and generous ideals, may have seemed the main consideration. All the same we cannot help feeling that he was thinking mainly of himself, and, though with some regrets, has sacrificed her to the exigencies of statecraft. Menas and Enobarbus, shrewd and unsentimental observers, agree that policy has made more in the marriage than love. So much indeed is obvious, even if its purpose is what on the face of it it professes to be, the reconcilement of the men it makes brothers-in-law. But, as we shall see, Octavius may have a more tortuous device in it than this.

Treating it meanwhile, however, as an expedient for knitting the alliance with his rival, what inference does it suggest? If for the sake of his own interests, Octavius shows himself far from scrupulous in regard to the sister whom he loves and whose material well-being is his care, what may we expect of him in the case of those who are indifferent or dangerous or hostile?

He has no hesitation about ousting his colleague Lepidus, or ruining the reconciled rebel Pompeius, despite his compacts with both. Then it is Antony's turn; and Antony is a far more formidable antagonist, with all his superiority in material resources, fertility of genius, proven soldiership and strategic skill. It is not because Octavius is the greater man that he succeeds. It is, in the first place, because he concentrates all his narrow nature to a single issue, while Antony with his greater width of outlook disperses his interest on many things at once. How typical of each are the asides with which respectively they enter their momentous conference. Antony is already contemplating other contingencies:

> If we compose well here, to Parthia :
> Hark, Ventidius. (ii. ii. 15.)

Octavius will not be diverted from the immediate business :

> I do not know,
> Mecaenas ; ask Agrippa. (ii. ii. 16.)

So, too, when the composition has taken place, Antony squanders his strength in the invasion of Parthia, the conquest of Armenia and other annexations, not to mention his grand distraction in Egypt. But Octavius pursues his one purpose with the dogged tenacity of a sleuth hound, removes Pompey who might be troublesome, seizes the resources of Lepidus, and is able to oppose the solid mass of the West to Antony's loose congeries of Asiatic allies and underlings, whose disunited crowd seems to typify his own unreconciled ambitions.

But even so it is not so much that Octavius wins, as that Antony loses. In another sense than he means, the words of the latter are true :

> Not Caesar's valour hath o'erthrown Antony,
> But Antony's hath triumph'd on itself.   (IV. xv. 14.)

It is his extraordinary series of blunders, perversities, and follies that play into his antagonist's hands and give him the trick, though that antagonist holds worse cards and is less expert in many points of the game.

But in so far as Octavius can claim credit for playing it, it is due to cunning and chicane rather than to any wisdom or ability of the higher kind. At the outset he prepares a snare for Antony, into which Antony falls, and by the fall is permanently crippled. It seems more than probable that the marriage with Octavia was suggested, not to confirm the alliance, but to provoke a breach at a more convenient season. The biographer expressly assigns the same sort of ulterior motive to a later act of apparent kindliness, when Octavia was again used as the unconscious pawn. When she, just before the final breach, insists on setting out to join her husband, Plutarch explains :

> Her brother Octavius was willing unto it, not for his (*i.e.* Antony's) respect at all (as most authors doe report) as for that he might have an honest culler to make warre with Antonius if he did misuse her, and not esteeme of her as she ought to be.

This was quite enough to suggest to Shakespeare a similar interpretation of the marriage project from the first. He does not indeed expressly state but he virtually implies it, as appears if we realise the characters and circumstances of those concerned. At the time the match is being arranged, Enobarbus quite clearly foresees and openly predicts the upshot to Mecaenas and Agrippa. Will they, and especially Agrippa, who is nominal author of the plan and announces it as "a studied not a present thought," have overlooked so probable an issue? Will it never have occurred to the circumspect and calculating Octavius, who evidently leads up to Agrippa's intervention and proposal? Or if through some incredible inadvertence it has hitherto escaped them all, will not the vigilant pair of henchmen hasten to inform their master of the unexpected turn that things seem likely to take? Not at all. Despite the convinced and convincing confidence of Enobarbus' prophecy, they waive it aside. Mecaenas merely replies with diplomatic decorum :

> If beauty, wisdom, modesty, can settle
> The heart of Antony, Octavia is
> A blessed lottery to him.   (II. ii. 247.)

No doubt. But though Touchstone says, "Your If is your only peacemaker," it can also be a very good peace-breaker on occasion. In Enobarbus' opinion (and in his own way Octavius is just as shrewd), Octavia with her "holy, cold and still conversation" is no dish for Antony. But though this is now expressly pointed out to Octavius' confidants, the marriage goes on as though nothing could be urged against it. The reason is that nothing can, from the point of view of the contrivers. If it turns out well, so far good ; if it turns out ill, so much the better. Only when it is an accomplished fact, does Caesar give a glimpse of what it involves in the sinister exhortation :

> Let not the piece of virtue which is set
> Betwixt us, as the cement of our love,
> To keep it builded, be the ram to batter
> The fortress of it.   (III. ii. 28.)

Thus when Antony returns to Cleopatra, as he was bound to do, Octavius manages to represent himself as the aggrieved party, as champion of the sanctity of the hearth, the vindicator of old Roman pieties ;

and in this way gains a good deal of credit at the outset of the quarrel.

And for the fortunate conduct of it, he is indebted, apart from Antony's demoralisation, to his adroitness in playing on the weakness of others, rather than to any nobler strength in himself.   Thus he irritates Antony's reckless chivalry, both vain and grandiose, by defying him to give battle by sea at Actium.   Antony is not bound even by any punctilio of honour to consent, for Octavius has twice declined a similar challenge.

> *Ant.*   Canidius, we
> Will fight with him by sea.
> > *Cle.*   By sea !   What else ?
> > *Can.* Why will my lord do so ?
> > *Ant.*   For that he dares us to't.
> > *Eno.* So hath my lord dared him to single fight.
> > *Can.* Ay, and to wage this battle at Pharsalia,
> Where Caesar fought with Pompey ; but these offers,
> Which serve not for his vantage, he shakes off ;
> And so should you.   (III. vii. 28.)

But Octavius knows his man, and this appeal to his audacity, enforced by the command of Cleopatra, determines Antony like a true knight-errant to the fatal course.

This passage is of great significance in Shakespeare's delineation of Octavius, because, though suggested by Plutarch, it completely alters the complexion and some of the facts of Plutarch's story. That records the two-fold challenge of Antony, but represents it as answering, not preceding the message of Octavius.   Moreover that message contains no reference to a naval combat and has nothing in common with the shape it assumes in the play.

> Octavius Caesar sent unto Antonius, to will him to delay no more time, but to come on with his army into Italy : and that for his owne part he would give him safe harber, to lande without any trouble, and that he would withdraw his armie from the sea, as farre as one horse could runne, until he had put his army ashore, and had lodged his men.

That is, in the original Octavius takes the lead in dare-devilry, and seems voluntarily to suggest such terms as even Byrhtnoth at the Battle of Maldon conceded only by request. Shakespeare could not fit this in with his conception of the cold-blooded politician, and substitutes for it a proposal that will put the enemy at a disadvantage; while at the same time he accentuates Octavius' unblushing knavery, by making him apply this provocation after he has twice rejected offers that do not suit himself.

Again, having won his first victory through Cleopatra's flight, Caesar cynically reckons for new success on her corruptibility:

> From Antony win Cleopatra: promise,
> And in our name, what she requires; add more,
> From thine invention, offers: women are not
> In their best fortunes strong; but want will perjure
> The ne'er-touch'd vestal: try thy cunning, Thyreus.
> (III. xii. 24.)

This scheme indeed miscarries owing to Antony's intervention, but meanwhile it has become unnecessary owing to the torrent of deserters. So Octavius is sure of his case, and can dismiss with ridicule the idea of a single fight. In Plutarch he does so too, but with the implied brag that he would certainly be victor: "Caesar answered him that he had many other wayes to dye then so;" when the *he* stands for Antony: but owing to North's fortunate ambiguity Shakespeare takes it as referring to the speaker:

> Let the old ruffian know
> I have many other ways to die; mean time
> Laugh at his challenge.
> (IV. i. 4.)

A more subtle contumely; for it implies that Caesar with scornful impartiality acknowledges Antony's superiority as a *sabreur*, but can afford to dismiss that as of no moment. His response has already been annotated in advance by Enobarbus, when Antony was inditing his cartel :

> Yes, like enough, high-battled Caesar will
> Unstate his happiness, and be staged to the show,
> Against a sworder ! . . . That he should dream,
> Knowing all measures, the full Caesar will
> Answer his emptiness !   Caesar, thou hast subdued
> His judgement too.   (III. xiii. 29.)

Octavius has by this time the ball at his feet, and can even cast the contemptuous alms of his pity on " poor Antony," as he calls him (IV. i. 16).   Nor are his expectations deceived, for he reckons out everything :

> Go, charge Agrippa.
> Plant those that have revolted in the van,
> That Antony may seem to spend his fury
> Upon himself.   (IV. vi. 8.)

And though he suffers a momentary check, he presently achieves the final triumph through the treason and baseness of Antony's Egyptian followers, on which he rightly felt he might rely.

And when he has won the match he makes use of his advantage with more appearance than reality of nobleness.   He wishes to have not only the substantial rewards of victory, but the shows and trappings of it as well.   He seeks to preserve Cleopatra alive,

> for her life in Rome
> Would be eternal in our triumph.   (V. i. 65.)

This is the secret of his clemency and generosity, that he would have her " grace in captive bonds his chariot wheels."   And if he has another reason for sparing her, it is not for the sake of clemency and generosity in themselves, but for the parade of these qualities : as indeed Proculeius unconsciously lets out in the naïf advice he gives her :

> Do not abuse my master's bounty by
> The undoing of yourself : let the world see
> His nobleness well acted, which your death
> Will never let come forth.   (V. ii. 44.)

And ably does Octavius play his role : he "extenuates rather than enforces," gilds his covert threats with promises, and dismisses the episode of the unscheduled treasure with Olympian serenity. His only fault is that he rather overacts the part. His excess of magnanimity, when by nature he is far from magnanimous, tells Cleopatra all she needs to know, and leaves little for the definite disclosures of Dolabella :

> He words me, girls, he words me, that I should not
> Be noble to myself.   (v. ii. 191.)

But, though not magnanimous, he is intelligent : and his intelligence enables and enjoins him to recognise greatness when it is no longer opposed to his own interest, and when the recognition redounds to his own credit, by implying that the conqueror is greater still.   His panegyrics on Antony, and afterwards on Cleopatra, are very nearly the right things to say and are very nearly said in the right way.   When he hears of his rival's suicide, his first exclamation does not ill befit the occasion :

> The breaking of so great a thing should make
> A greater crack : . . . the death of Antony
> Is not a single doom ; in the name lay
> A moiety of the world.   (v. i. 14.)

But this disinterested emotion does not last long. The awe at fallen greatness soon leads to comparisons with the living greatness that has proved its match.   The obsequious bystanders find this quite natural and point it out without a hint of sarcasm :

> *Agr.*   Caesar is touch'd.
> *Mec.* When such a spacious mirror's set before him,
> He needs must see himself.

So Octavius proceeds to a recital of Antony's merits in which he bespeaks a double portion of the praise he seems to dispense :

O Antony!
I have follow'd thee to this ; but we do lance
Diseases in our bodies : I must perforce
Have shown to thee such a declining day,
Or look on thine : we could not stall together
In the whole world : but yet let me lament,
With tears as sovereign as the blood of hearts,
That thou, my brother, my competitor,
In top of all design, my mate in empire,
Friend and companion in the front of war,
The arm of mine own body, and the heart
Where mine his thoughts did kindle,—that our stars,
Unreconciliable, should divide
Our equalness to this.   (v. i. 35.)

And here, as business calls, he breaks off and post-
pones the rest to "some meeter season." Similarly
when he finds Cleopatra dead he has the insight
to do her justice :

Bravest at the last,
She levell'd at our purposes, and, being royal,
Took her own way.   (v. ii. 238.)

Then follows the official valediction :

She shall be buried by her Antony :
No grave upon the earth shall clip in it
A pair so famous.   High events as these
Strike those that make them ; and their story is
No less in pity than *his glory which
Brought them to be lamented.*   (v. ii. 361.)

So the last word is a testimonial to himself.

These are eulogies of the understanding, not of
the heart. They are very different in tone from
the tributes of Antony to his patron Julius or his
opponent Brutus. The tears and emotion, genuine
though facile, of the latter are vouched for even by
the sarcasms of Agrippa and Enobarbus. Octavius'
utterance, when he pronounces his farewell, is broken,
we may be sure, by no sob and choked by no passion.
His *éloge* has been compared to a funeral sermon,
and will not interfere with the victor's appetite for
the fruits of victory. But though his feeling is

not stirred to the depths, he is fairly just and fairly acute. He is no contemptible character, this man who carries off the palm from one of infinitely richer endowment. The contrast between the two rivals, and the justification of the success of the less gifted, is summed up in a couple of sentences they exchange at the banquet off Misenum. When Octavius shrinks from the carouse, Antony bids him : " Be a child o' the time" (II. vii. 106). '' Possess it, I'll make answer," is Octavius' reply and reproof.

CHAPTER V

MARK ANTONY

" BE a child o' the time," says Antony, and he carries out his maxim to the letter. Only that time could bring forth such a devotee of the joys of life and lavish on him such wealth of enjoyment. But the time was one that devoured its own children. Those who chose to be merely its products, must accept its ordinances, and it was cruel as well as indulgent. It was the manlier as well as the safer course for the child to possess the time, to repudiate its stock, and, if might be, to usurp the heritage.

We must bear the counter admonition of Octavius in mind when we approach the personage to whom it was addressed. All who have a wide range of interests, and with these warmth of imagination and spontaneity of impulse, must feel that their judgment is apt to be bribed by the attractions of Mark Antony. He is so many-sided, so many-ways endowed, so full of vitality and vigour, potentially so affluent and bright, that we look to find his life a clear and abundant stream, and disbelieve our senses when we see a turbid pool that loses itself in the sands. If we listen to the promptings of our blood, we hail him as demi-god, but the verdict of our reason is that he is only a futility. And both estimates base on Shakespeare who inspires and reconciles them both.

Of course we are apt to carry with us to the present play the impression we have received from the sketch of Antony in *Julius Caesar*. And not without grounds. He is still a masquer and a reveller, he is still a shrewd contriver. But we gradually become aware of a difference. First, the precedence that these characteristics takes is reversed. In *Julius Caesar* it is the contriving side of his nature that is prominent, and the other is only indicated by the remarks of acquaintances : in *Antony and Cleopatra*, it is his love of pleasure that is emphasised, while of his contrivance we have only casual glimpses. And the contrast is not merely an alteration in the point of view, it corresponds to an alteration in himself ; in the earlier drama he subordinates his luxury to his schemes, and in the latter he subordinates his schemes to his luxury. But this is not all. In the second place, his two main interests have changed in the degree of what may be called their organisation. In *Julius Caesar* he concentrates all his machinations on the one object of overthrowing the tyrannicides and establishing his power ; his pleasures, however notorious, are random and disconnected dissipations without the coherence of a single aim. In *Antony and Cleopatra*, however manifold they may be, they are all subdued to the service of his master passion, they are all focussed in his love for Cleopatra ; while his strategy is broken up to mere shifts and expedients that answer the demand of the hour. Passion has become not only the regulative but the constitutive force in his character.

When the action begins, he is indemnifying himself with a round of indulgence for the strenuous life between the fall of Julius and the victories at Philippi, some of the toils and privations of which, passed over in the earlier play, Octavius now recalls in amazement at the contrast. It is not so strange.

One remembers Professor von Karsteg's indictment
of the English that they spare no pains because
they live for pleasure. "You are all in one mass,
struggling in the stream to get out and lie and
wallow and belch on the banks. You work so
hard that you have all but one aim, and that is
fatness and ease!"[1] Something similar strikes us
in Antony. It is natural that action should be
followed by reaction and that abstinence should
lead to surfeit. It is doubly natural, when effort
and discipline are not prized for themselves or
associated with the public good, but have only
been accepted as the means to a selfish aim. By
them he has acquired more than mortal power : why
should he not use it in his own behoof, oblivious
of every call save the prompting of desire? A
vulgar attitude, we may say ; but it is lifted above
vulgarity by the vastness of the orbit through which
his desire revolves. It is grandiose, and almost
divine ; in so far at least as it is a circle whose
centre is everywhere and whose circumference is
nowhere. He has a gust for everything and for
everything in the highest degree, for each several
pleasure and its exact antithesis. In what does
he not feel zest ? Luxury, banqueting, drunkenness, appeal to him, so that Pompey prays they
"may keep his brain fuming" (II. i. 24). Or he
acts the god, and with Cleopatra as Isis, dispenses
sovereignty from the "tribunal silver'd," as they
sit on their "chairs of gold" (III. vi. 3). Or he
finds a relish in vulgar pleasures, and with the
queen on his arm, mingles incognito in the crowd,
wandering through the streets "to note the qualities
of people" (I. i. 52). Or he goes a-fishing, in which
art he is a novice and presently becomes a dupe,
when he pulls up the salt-fish "with fervency"
(II. v. 18). And a willing dupe, the conscious

[1] *The Adventures of Harry Richmond.*

humorous dupe of love to his tricksy enchantress,
he is pleased to be in many other ways :

> That time,—O times !—
> I laugh'd him out of patience ; and that night
> I laugh'd him into patience ; and next morn,
> Ere the ninth hour, I drunk him to his bed :
> Then put my tires and mantles on him, whilst
> I wore his sword Philippian.   (II. v. 18.)

In short his breathless pursuit of all sorts of
experiences more than justifies the scandalised
summary of Octavius :

> He fishes, drinks, and wastes
> The lamps of night in revel ; is not more manlike
> Than Cleopatra ; nor the queen of Ptolemy
> More womanly than he.   (I. iv. 4.)

And he goes on to describe how Antony has been
so indiscriminate as

> to tumble on the bed of Ptolemy ;
> To give a kingdom for a mirth ; to sit
> And keep the turn of tippling with a slave ;
> To reel the streets at noon, and stand the buffet
> With knaves that smell of sweat.   (I. iv. 17.)

Yet, however he may seem to sink in his pleasures,
he is never submerged ; such is his joyousness and
strength that they seem to bear him up and carry
him along rather than drag him down. As Cleopatra perceives :

> His delights
> Were dolphin-like ; they show'd his back above
> The element they lived in.   (v. ii. 88.)

It is this demand to share in all the *Erdgeist* has
to offer, that raises Antony above the level of the
average sensualist.   His dissipations impose by
their catholicity and heartiness.   His blithe eagerness never flags and nothing mundane leaves him
unmoved :

> There's not a minute of our lives should stretch
> Without some pleasure now.   (I. i. 46.)

This is his ideal, an infinity of pastimes under the presidency of his love ; and any ideal, no matter what, always dignifies those whom it inspires. But it also demands its sacrifice ; and in the present case Antony with a sort of inverse sublimity offers up to it all that the ambitious, the honourable or the virtuous man counts good.

For a life like his is hardly compatible even in theory with the arduous functions of the commander, the governor, the administrator ; and in practice it inevitably leads to their neglect. In the opening scene we see him leave unheard the momentous tidings from Rome, and turn aside to embrace his royal paramour. His followers are filled with angry disgust :

> Nay, but this dotage of our general's
> O'erflows the measure : those his goodly eyes
> That o'er the files and musters of the war
> Have glow'd like plated Mars, now bend, now turn,
> The office and devotion of their view
> Upon a tawny front. (I. i. I.)

The general voice cries out against him at home, where his faults are taunted

> With such full licence as both truth and malice
> Have power to utter. (I. ii. 112.)

His newly arrived friends find the worst libels verified, as Demetrius admits :

> I am full sorry
> That he approves the common liar, who
> Thus speaks of him at Rome. (I. i. 59.)

Octavius is not unduly severe in his condemnation :

> To confound such time,
> That drums him from his sport, and speaks as loud
> As his own state and ours,—'tis to be chid
> As we rate boys, who, being mature in knowledge,
> Pawn their experience to their present pleasure,
> And so rebel to judgement. (I. iv. 28.)

Nor is he without qualms himself. Sudden revulsions of feeling disturb his riots when "a Roman thought hath struck him" (I. ii. 87). He feels that stopping short in his labours and relaxing his energy, he gives his baser tendencies the sway, and cries:

> O, then we bring forth weeds,
> When our quick minds lie still.   (I. ii. 113.)

This, however, makes things worse rather than better. It does not rouse him to any constant course, it only perplexes his purpose. He does not wish to give up anything: the life at Rome and the life at Alexandria both tug at his heart-strings; and he cannot see that the Eastern and the Western career are not to be reconciled. It is still nominally open to him to make a choice, but at any rate the choice must be made. It must often have occurred to him to throw aside his civil ties, and to set up as independent Emperor with his Egyptian Queen. And apart from old associations there were only two reasons why he should not: lingering respect for his marriage with Fulvia, whom in a way he still loved, and dread of the avenging might of Rome directed by all the craft of Octavius. These impediments are suddenly removed; and their removal belongs to Shakespeare's conception. It may be traced in part to his own invention, in part perhaps to the suggestion of Appian, but in any case it is of far-reaching significance.

In the biography the situation is fundamentally different, though superficially alike. There Antony is threatened at once in the West and the East. Octavius has driven his wife and brother out of Italy; Labienus, the old foe of Caesarism, has led the Parthians into the provinces. It is to meet these dangers that Antony leaves Egypt, and to the Parthian as the more pressing he addresses himself first. Only at Fulvia's entreaty does he alter his plan and sail for home with two hundred ships; but her opportune death facilitates a composition with Octavius. Then the alliance between them having been confirmed, and the petty trouble with Sextus Pompeius having been easily settled, Antony is able with ampler resources to turn against the troublesome Parthians.

These are the facts as Caesar narrates them; and according to them Antony had no option but to break off his love affair and set out to face one or both of the perils that menaced him; the peril from Octavius who has defeated him in his representatives, the peril from Labienus who has overrun the Near East. These items are not wanting in Shakespeare, and as the news of them arrives, his Antony exclaims as Plutarch's might have done:

> These strong Egyptian fetters I must break,
> Or lose myself in dotage.   (I. ii. 120.)

But even as he speaks a second messenger arrives who supplements the tidings of the first with new circumstances that are really of much later date and quite different significance in Plutarch, and that entirely alter the complexion of affairs. He hears by word of mouth that Fulvia is dead, and, apparently by letter, that Sextus Pompeius stands up against Caesar and commands the empire of the sea. In Plutarch he is called to Rome by the fact not of Fulvia's being dead but of her being alive; and her death only prepares the way for a reconciliation when he is already nearing home. Still less is his return connected with the enterprise of Pompey which is mentioned only after the reconciliation is accomplished, and, as we have seen, is treated quite as a detail. But Shakespeare, inserting these matters here and viewing them as he does, dismisses altogether or in part the motive which Plutarch

implies for Antony's behaviour. Indeed they should
rather be reasons for his continuing and proceeding
further in his present course.   One main objection
to his connection with Cleopatra is removed, and
the way is smoothed to marriage with his beloved.
All danger from Rome is for the time at an end ;
and the opportunity is offered for establishing himself in Egypt while Pompey and Octavius waste
each other's strength, or for making common cause
with Pompey, who, as we know, is well inclined to
him and takes occasion to pay him court.

But in Shakespeare's Antony, the very removal
of external hindrances gives new force to those
within his own heart. Regrets and compunctions
are stirred. The memory of his wife rises up with
new authority, the entreaties of his friends and the
call of Rome sound with louder appeal in his ears :

> Not alone
> The death of Fulvia, with more urgent touches,
> Do strongly speak to us : but the letters too
> Of many our contriving friends in Rome
> Petition us at home.   (I. ii. 186.)

With a man of his emotional nature, precisely the
opportunity so procured to carry out one set of his
wishes, gives the other set the mastery.   Of his
wife's death he exclaims :

> There's a great spirit gone !   Thus did I desire it :
> What our contempt doth often hurl from us,
> We wish it ours again ; the present pleasure,
> By revolution lowering, does become
> The opposite of itself : she's good, being gone ;
> The hand could pluck her back that shoved her on.
> I must from this enchanting queen break off. (I. ii. 126.)

It is no doubt the nobler and more befitting course
that he proposes to himself, but it is so only on the
condition that he follows it out with his whole heart.
If he takes it up to let it go ; if one half or more

than one half of his soul lingers with the flesh-pots of Egypt, then nothing could be more foolish and calamitous. He merely throws away the grand chance of realising his more alluring ambition, and advances no step to the sterner and loftier heights. For he will patch up the Roman Triumvirate and rehabilitate the power of Octavius to his own hurt, unless he resolves henceforth to act as a Roman Triumvir and as the dominant partner with Octavius; and he will never again have so good an occasion for legitimising and thus excusing his relation with Cleopatra. This latter step was so obviously the natural one that Octavius almost assumes he must have taken it. On making his proposal for the match with Octavia, Agrippa says: "Great Antony is now a widower," but Octavius interrupts:

> Say not so, Agrippa:
> If Cleopatra heard you, your reproof
> Were well deserved of rashness. (II. ii. 122.)

But though he thus shrinks from the irrevocable choice, we see clearly enough at his departure from Egypt that the impulse towards Rome must soon be spent, and that therefore his refusal to commit himself, and his whole enterprise, show rather weakness and indecision than resolution and strength. To soothe Cleopatra he tells her:

> Be prepared to know
> The purposes I bear; which are, or cease,
> As you shall give the advice. By the fire
> That quickens Nilus' slime, I go from thence
> Thy soldier, servant, making peace or war
> As thou affect'st. (I. iii. 66.)

He is speaking too true when he says:

> Our separation so abides, and flies,
> That thou, residing here, go'st yet with me,
> And I, hence fleeting, here remain with thee. (I. iii. 102.)

And his last message runs :

> Say, the firm Roman to great Egypt sends
> This treasure of an oyster ; at whose foot,
> To mend the petty present, I will piece
> Her opulent throne with kingdoms : all the east,
> Say thou, shall call her mistress.   (I. v. 44.)

And with these pledges like so many mill-stones round his neck, he sets off to swim in the dangerous cross-currents of Roman politics. It is true that pledges do not weigh over heavily with him, but in this case their weight is increased by his inner inclinations.

So the reconciliation with Octavius is hollow from the first, and being hollow it is a blunder. Antony of course is able to blind himself to its hollowness and to conduct the negociations with great adroitness. His dignified and frank apology is just what he ought to say, supposing that the particular end were to be sought at all, and it has an air of candour that could not well be consciously assumed :

> As nearly as I may,
> I'll play the penitent to you : but mine honesty
> Shall not make poor my greatness, nor my power
> Work without it.   Truth is, that Fulvia,
> To have me out of Egypt, made wars here ;
> For which myself, the ignorant motive, do
> So far ask pardon as befits mine honour
> To stoop in such a case.   (II. ii. 91.)

But this is only another instance of the born orator's faculty for throwing himself into a situation, and feeling for the time what it is expedient to express. It is a fatal gift, which betrays him oftener than it helps. If it prompts his moving utterances over the bodies of Caesar and Brutus, and in so far directly or indirectly assists his cause, it nevertheless even then to some cynical observers like Enobarbus suggests a spice of hypocrisy. Hypocrisy it is not, but it comes almost to the same

thing; for the easily aroused emotion soon subsides
after it has done its work and yields to some quite
contrary impulsion. But meanwhile the worst of it
is, that it carries away the eloquent speaker, and
hurries him in directions and to distances that are
not for his good. With Antony's real and permanent
bias, even a temporary reconcilement with Octavius
is a mistake; but what shall we say of his marriage
with Octavia? Yet he jumps at it at once; and
with that convincing air of sincerity that can only
be explained by his really liking it for the moment,
exclaims :

> May I never
> To this good purpose, that so fairly shows,
> Dream of impediment! Let me have thy hand :
> Further this act of grace : and from this hour
> The heart of brothers govern in our loves
> And sway our great designs. (II. ii. 146.)

And again he realises just what is proper to feel
and say to his betrothed, and says it so that we are
sure he feels it so long as he is speaking :

> My Octavia,
> Read not my blemishes in the world's report:
> I have not kept my square : but that to come
> Shall all be done by the rule. (II. iii. 4.)

Yet she has barely left him, when, at the warning
of the soothsayer, and the thought of Octavius'
success in games of chance and sport, he resolves
to outrage the still uncompleted marriage and return
to his Egyptian bondage :

> I will to Egypt:
> For though I make this marriage for my peace,
> I' the East my pleasure lies. (II. iii. 38.)

But when this is his fixed determination, why make
the marriage at all? Does he fail to see that it will
bring not peace but a sword? Yet he is so hood-
winked by immediate opportunism that he bears his
share in making Pompey harmless to the mighty
brother-in-law he is just about to offend. And

knowing his own heart as he does, he can nevertheless assume an air of resentment at the veiled menace
in Octavius' parting admonition : "Make me not
offended in your mistrust " (III. ii. 33).

He has truly with all diligence digged a pit for
himself. Already he is the wreck of the shrewd contriver whose machinations Cassius so justly feared.
And this collapse of faculty, this access of presumption and hebetude belong to Shakespeare's conception of the case. In Plutarch the renewed agreement of the Triumvirs is expedient and even
necessary ; the marriage scheme is adopted in good
faith and for a period serves its purpose ; the granting of terms to Pompey is an unimportant act of grace.

Nevertheless some powers of contrivance Shakespeare's Antony still retains. He despatches the
capable Ventidius on the Parthian campaign, and he
has the credit and *éclat*, when

> with his banners and his well-paid ranks,
> The ne'er-yet-beaten horse of Parthia
> (Are) jaded out o' the field.   (III. i. 32.)

He himself over-runs and conquers Armenia, and
other Asiatic kingdoms, and with his new prestige
and resources is able to secure the support of a
formidable band of subject kings. When Octavia
has returned to Rome and he to Egypt, and war
breaks out, he is still, thanks to these allies and to
his own veteran legionaries whom he has so often
led to victory and spoil, the master of a power that
should more than suffice to make the fortune his.

But in his infatuation he throws all his advantages
away. He pronounces on himself the verdict which
his whole story confirms :

> When we in our viciousness grow hard—
> O misery on't !—the wise gods seel our eyes ;
> In our own filth drop our clear judgements ; make us
> Adore our errors ; laugh at's, while we strut
> To our confusion.   (III. xiii. 111.)

Of the preliminary blunder, which Plutarch signalises as "among the greatest faults that ever Antonius committed," viz., his failure to give Octavius battle, when universal discontent was excited at home by Octavius' exactions, there is no mention, or only a very slight and doubtful one in the play. When Eros has told the news of Pompey's overthrow and Lepidus' deposition, Enobarbus at once foresees the sequel :

> Then, world, thou hast a pair of chaps, no more :
> And throw between them all the food thou hast,
> They'll grind the one the other. (III. v. 14.)

And presently he continues :

> Our great navy's rigg'd.
> *Eros.* For Italy and Caesar. More, Domitius,
> My lord desires you presently ; my news
> I might have told hereafter.
> *Eno.* 'Twill be nought :
> But let it be. Bring me to Antony. (III. v. 20.)

Here we seem to have a faint reminiscence of Plutarch's statement. Eros takes for granted as the obvious course, that the great navy ready to start will make an immediate descent on the enemy's stronghold. Enobarbus, who understands Antony, knows that nothing will come of it, and that their destination is Egypt. In point of fact we learn in the next scene that Antony has arrived in Alexandria and there kept his state with Cleopatra.

But if Shakespeare glides over this episode, he dwells with all the greater detail on the array of imbecilities with which Antony follows it up. First, despite the advice of Enobarbus, he lets Cleopatra be present in the war. Then to please her caprice, and gratify his own fantastic chivalry, he sets aside the well-based objections of Enobarbus, of Canidius, of the common soldiers ; and accepts Octavius' challenge to fight at sea, though his ships are heavy, his mariners inexpert, and he himself and his veterans are more used to the dry land. Even so the inspiration of his soldiership and generalship is giving him a slight superiority, when the panic of Cleopatra withdraws her contingent of sixty ships :

> Yon ribaudred nag of Egypt,—
> Whom leprosy o'ertake !—i' the midst o' the fight,
> When vantage like a pair of twins appear'd,
> Both as the same, or rather ours the elder,
> The breese upon her, like a cow in June,
> Hoists sail and flies.   (III. x. 10.)

Not all is lost even then.   But Antony follows the fugitive, when, if he were true to himself, the day might still be retrieved.   This is the view that Shakespeare assigns to Canidius ; and while all the previous items he derived from Plutarch, only distributing them among his persons, and adding to their picturesqueness and force, this is an addition of his own to heighten the ignominy of Antony's desertion :

> Had our general
> Been what he knew himself, it had gone well.   (III. x. 25.)

And the explanation of his " most unnoble swerving," if in one way an excuse, in another is an extra shame to his manhood, and too well justifies Enobarbus' dread of Cleopatra's influence :

> Your presence needs must puzzle Antony ;
> Take from his heart, take from his brain, from's time,
> What should not then be spared.   (III. vii. 11.)

The authority for the idea that Antony was in a manner hypnotised by her love, Shakespeare found, like so much else, in the *Life*, but he enhances the effect immeasurably, first by putting the avowal in Antony's own lips, and again by the more poignant and pitiful turn he gives it.   Plutarch says :

> There Antonius shewed plainely, that he had not onely lost the corage and hart of an Emperor, but also of a valliant man, and that he was not his owne man : (proving that true which an old man spake in myrth that the soule of a lover lived in

another body, and not in his owne) he was so caried away
with the vaine love of this woman, as if he had bene glued
into her, and that she could not have removed without
moving of him also.

Antony cries in the play:

> O, whither hast thou led me, Egypt? . . .
> Thou knew'st too well
> My heart was to thy rudder tied by the strings,
> And thou shouldst tow me after: o'er my spirit
> Thy full supremacy thou knew'st, and that
> Thy beck might from the bidding of the gods
> Command me . . .
> You did know
> How much you were my conqueror: and that
> My sword, made weak by my affection, would
> Obey it on all cause. (III. x. 51.)

But in Shakespeare's view the final decision was
not reached even at the battle of Actium. Despite
that disaster and the subsequent desertions, Antony
is still able to offer no inconsiderable resistance in
Egypt. In direct contradiction of Plutarch's statement, he says, after the reply to Euphronius and the
scourging of Thyreus:

> Our force by land
> Hath nobly held; our sever'd navy too
> Have knit again, and fleet, threatening most sea-like.
> (III. xiii. 169.)

Whether this be fact or illusion, it shows that in his
own eyes at least some hope remains: but in the
hour of defeat he was quite unmanned and seemed
to give up all thought of prolonging the struggle.
When for the first time after his reverse we meet
him in Alexandria, he prays his followers to "take
the hint which his despair proclaims" (III. xi. 18),
and to leave him, with his treasure for their reward.
This circumstance Shakespeare obtained from Plutarch, but in Plutarch it is not quite the same. There
the dismissal takes place at Taenarus in the Peloponnesus, the first stopping-place at which Antony

touches in his flight, and apparently is dictated by
the difficulty of all the fugitives effecting their escape.
At any rate he was very far even then from despair-
ing of his cause, for in the previous sentence we
read that he "sent unto Canidius, to returne with
his army into Asia, by Macedon"; and some time
later we find him, still ignorant of the facts, continuing to act on the belief "that his armie by
lande, which he left at Actium, was yet whole." [1]
Here on the other hand he has succeeded in reaching
his lair, and it is as foolish as it is generous to throw
away adherents and resources that might be of help
to him at the last. But he is too despondent to
think even of standing at bay. He tells his friends:

> I have myself resolved upon a course
> Which has no need of you. (III. xi. 9.)

That course was to beseech Octavius by his
schoolmaster,

> To let him breathe between the heavens and earth,
> A private man in Athens. (III. xii. 14.)

Here he touches the bottom mud of degradation
and almost sinks to the level of Lepidus who did
obtain permission to live under surveillance at
Circeii "till death enlarged his confine." And here
too Shakespeare follows Plutarch, but here too with
a difference. For in the biography this incident
comes after some time has elapsed, and new dis-
appointments and new indulgences have made
deeper inroads in Antony's spirit. In one aspect
no doubt he is less pitiable in thus being brought
to mortification by degrees. In Shakespeare he
adopts this course before ever he has seen the
Queen, and in so far shows greater weakness of
character. Like Richard II. he bows his head at

---

[1] He learns the truth however before he sends Euphronius as
delegate.

once, and without an effort takes "the sweet way to despair." Yet just for that reason he is from another point of view less ignoble. It is the sudden sense of disgrace, the amazement, the consternation at his own poltroonery that turns his knees to water. But the very immediacy and poignancy of his self-disgust is a guarantee of surviving nobility that needs only an occasion to call it forth. The occasion comes in the refusal of his own petition and the conditional compliance with Cleopatra's. Antony's answer to this slighting treatment is his second challenge. This too Shakespeare obtained from Plutarch, but of this too he altered the significance and the date. In Plutarch it is sent after Antony's victorious sally, apparently in elation at that trifling success, and is recorded without other remark than Octavius' rejoinder. In Shakespeare it is the retort of Antony's self-consciousness to the depreciation of his rival, and it is the first rebound of his relaxed valour. When the victor counts him as nought he is stung to comparisons, and feels that apart from success and external advantages he is still of greater worth :

> Tell him he wears the rose
> Of youth upon him ; from which the world should note
> Something particular : his coin, ships, legions,
> May be a coward's ; whose ministers would prevail
> Under the service of a child as soon
> As i' the command of Caesar : I dare him, therefore,
> To lay his gay comparisons apart,
> And answer me declined, sword against sword,
> Ourselves alone. (III. xiii. 20.)

Of course it is absurd and mad ; and the madness and absurdity are brought out, in the play, not in the *Life*, by the comments of Enobarbus, Octavius and Mecaenas. Indeed at this juncture Antony's valour, or rather his desperation, does not cease to prey on his reason. His insult to Caesar in the scourging of his messenger is less an excess of audacity than the gnash of the teeth in the last agony : as Enobarbus remarks :

> 'Tis better playing with a lion's whelp
> Than with an old one dying.   (III. xiii. 94.)

Octavius may treat these transports of a great spirit in the throes as mere bluster and brutality, and find in them a warrant for his ruthless phrase, "the old ruffian." There is a touch of the ruffian in Antony's wild outbursts. Even the mettlesome vein in which he commands another gaudy night on Cleopatra's birthday is open to Enobarbus' disparagement : that a diminution of his captain's brain restores his heart. Truly the last shreds of prudence are whirled away in his storm of recklessness and anguish and love. At the defiant anniversary feast his soul is so wrung with gratitude to his true servants and grief at the near farewell, that he must give his feelings words though they will discourage rather than hearten the company. Cleopatra does not understand it, for her own nature has not the depth of Antony's, and deep can only call to deep. "What means this?" she asks.

> *Eno.*   'Tis one of those odd tricks which sorrow shoots
> Out of the mind.   (IV. ii. 14.)

Again, in amazement at his tearful pathos, she exclaims : "What does he mean?" And with an effort at cynicism, Enobarbus, who has scoffed at Antony's emotion over the bodies of Caesar and Brutus, replies : "To make his followers weep"; for Enobarbus tries to think that it is merely the orator's eloquence that runs away with him in his melting mood. Nevertheless his own sympathies are touched for the moment : " I, an ass, am onion-eyed." In truth none can mistake the genuine feeling of Antony's words, though at the hint he can

at once change their tone and give them an heroic
and even a sanguine turn.[1]

> Know, my hearts,
> I hope well of to-morrow; and will lead you
> Where rather I'll expect victorious life
> Than death and honour.
>   (IV. ii. 41.)

But whatever deductions be made, Antony's last
days in Alexandria bring back a St. Martin's summer
of genial power and genial nobility that are doubly
captivating when set off against the foil of Caesar's
coldness. The grand proportions of his nature, that
are obscured in the vintage time of success and
indulgence, show forth again when the branches are
bare. No doubt he again and again does the wrong
things, or at least the things that lead to no useful
result. His patron god deserts him as in Plutarch,
but that god in Shakespeare is not Bacchus but
Hercules, and he departs earlier than in the story
and not on the last night before the end; for the
withdrawal of the divine friend is now less the
presage of death than the symbol of inefficacy.
Antony's insight and judgment may be failing; his
flashes of power may be like his flashes of jealousy,
and indicate the dissolution of his being. Still when
all is said and done, he seems to become bolder,
grander, more magnanimous, as the fuel is cut off
from his inward fire and it burns and wastes in its
own heat. His reflux of heroism cannot save him
against the material superiority and concentrated
ambition of Octavius, for it is not the consequent
energy that commands success and that implies a
consequent purpose in life: but all the more impressive and affecting is this gallant fronting of fate.

---

[1] Which latter for the rest may be found in North but not in
Plutarch. "To salve that he had spoken he added this more unto it,
that he would not leade them to battell, where he thought not rather
safely to returne with victorie, then valliantly to dye with honor."
Cf. μὴ προάξειν ἐπὶ τὴν μάχην, ἐξ ἧς αὐτῷ θάνατον εὐκλεᾶ μᾶλλον ἢ σωτηρίαν
ζητεῖν καὶ νίκην.

As Cleopatra arms him for his last little victory, he cries with his old self-consciousness :

> O love,
> That thou couldst see my wars to-day, and knew'st
> The royal occupation ! thou shouldst see
> A workman in 't. (IV. iv. 15.)

He welcomes the time for battle:

> This morning, like the spirit of a youth,
> That means to be of note, begins betimes. (IV. iv. 26.)

Cleopatra recognises his greatness and his doom :

> He goes forth gallantly.   That he and Caesar might
> Determine this great war in single fight !
> Then, Antony,—but now—well, on. (IV. iv. 36.)

That day he does well indeed, He pursues the recreant Enobarbus with his generosity and the vanquished Romans with his valour. He returns victorious and jubilant to claim his last welcoming embrace.

> O thou day o' the world,
> Chain mine arm'd neck ; leap thou, attire and all,
> Through proof of harness to my heart, and there
> Ride on the pants triumphing. (IV. viii. 13.)

Then the morrow brings the end. His fleet deserts, and for the moment he suspects Cleopatra as the cause, and overwhelms her with curses and threats. The suspicion is natural, and his nature is on edge at the fiasco, which this time is no fault of his.

> The soul and body rive not more in parting
> Than greatness going off.[1] (IV. xiii. 5.)

---

[1] A familiar thought with Shakespeare.   Compare Anne's reference to Katherine in *Henry VIII.* :

> O, God's will ! much better
> She ne'er had known pomp : though't be temporal,
> Yet, if that quarrel, fortune, do divorce
> It from the bearer, 'tis a sufferance panging
> As soul and body's severing. (II. iii. 12.)

This scene is almost certainly Shakespeare's.

But his mood changes. Even before he hears Cleopatra's disclaimer and the news of her alleged death, he has become calm, and only feels the futility of it all ; he is to himself "indistinct, as water is in water" (IV. xiv. 10). Then comes the message that his beloved is no more, and his resolution is fixed :

> Unarm me, Eros ; the long day's task is done,
> And we must sleep. (IV. xiv. 36.)

His thoughts are with his Queen in the Elysian fields where he will ask her pardon,[1] and he only stays for Eros' help. But when Eros chooses his own rather than his master's death, Antony in his large-hearted way gives him the praise, and finds in his act a lesson.

> Thrice-nobler than myself !
> Thou teachest me, O valiant Eros, what
> I should, and thou couldst not. (IV. xiv. 95.)

The wound he deals himself is not at once fatal. He lives long enough to comfort his followers in the heroic words :

> Nay, good my fellows, do not please sharp fate
> To grace it with your sorrows : bid that welcome
> Which comes to punish us, and we punish it
> Seeming to bear it lightly. Take me up :
> I have led you oft : carry me now, good friends,
> And have my thanks for all.[2]

---

[1] Dido and her Æneas shall want troops,
And all the haunt be ours. (IV. xiv. 52.)

We have not got much further in explaining Shakespeare's allusion than when Warburton made the Warburtonian emendation of Sichaeus for Æneas. Shakespeare had probably quite forgotten Virgil's

> Illa solo fixos oculos aversa tenebat :
> . . . . atque inimica refugit
> In nemus umbriferum. (Æ. vi. 469.)

Perhaps he remembered only that Æneas, ancestor and representative of the Romans, between his two authorised marriages with ladies of the "superior" races, intercalated the love-adventure, which alone seized the popular imagination and which of all the deities Venus alone approved, with an African queen.

[2] No word of this in Plutarch.

He has heard the truth about Cleopatra, and only importunes death that he may snatch that one last interview sacred to his love of her, his care for her, and to that serene, lofty dignity which now he has attained. The world seems a blank when this full life is out ; and looking at the race that is left, we feel inclined to echo Cleopatra's words above the corpse :

O, wither'd is the garland of the war,
The soldier's pole is fall'n : young boys and girls
Are level now with men ; the odds is gone,
And there is nothing left remarkable
Beneath the visiting moon. (IV. xv. 64.)

CHAPTER VI

CLEOPATRA

To Cleopatra, the lodestar, the temptress, the pre-destined mate of Antony, we now turn : and perhaps even Shakespeare has no more marvellous creation than she, or one in which the nature that inspires and the genius that reveals, are so fused in the ideal truth. Campbell says : " He paints her as if the gipsy herself had cast her spell over him, and given her own witchcraft to his pencil." The witchcraft everybody feels. It is almost impossible to look at her steadily, or keep one's head to estimate her aright. She is the incarnate poetry of life without duty, glorified by beauty and grace ; of impulse without principle, ennobled by culture and intellect. But however it may be with the reader, Shakespeare does not lose his head. He is not the adept mesmerised, the sorcerer ensorcelled. Such avatars as the Egyptian Queen have often been described by other poets, but generally from the point of view either of the servile devotee or of the unsympathetic censor. Here the artist is a man, experienced and critical, yet with the fires of his imagination still ready to leap and glow. He stands in right relation to the laws of life ; and his delineation is all the more impressive and all the more aesthetic, the more remorselessly he sacrifices the

P

one-sided claims of the conception in which he delights to the laws of tragic necessity.

Cleopatra is introduced to us as a beauty of a somewhat dusky African type in the full maturity, or perhaps a little past the maturity, of her bloom. The first trait is for certain historically wrong.[1] The line of the Ptolemies was of the purest Grecian breed, with a purity of which they were proud, and which they sought to preserve by close intermarriage within their house.   But Shakespeare has so impressed his own idea of Cleopatra on the world that later painters and poets have followed suit ever since.   Tennyson, in the *Dream of Fair Women* tells how she summons him :

> I, turning. saw throned on a flowery rise
> One sitting on a crimson scarf unroll'd,
> A Queen with swarthy cheeks and bold black eyes,
> Brow-bound with burning gold.

Hawthorne in his *Transformation*, describing Story's statue of Cleopatra, which here he attributes to Kenyon, goes further :

> The face was a marvellous success.   The sculptor had not shunned to give the full Nubian lips and the other characteristics of the Egyptian physiognomy.   His courage and integrity had been abundantly rewarded : for Cleopatra's beauty shone out richer, warmer, more triumphantly beyond comparison, than if, shrinking timidly from the truth, he had chosen the tame Grecian type.

Hawthorne goes astray through taking Shakespeare's picture, or rather another picture which Shakespeare's suggested to his own fancy, as a literal portrait ; but his very mistake shows how incongruous a fair Cleopatra would now seem to us.

Not often or obtrusively, but of set purpose and beyond the possibility of neglect, does Shakespeare

---

[1] Wrong ; even if on numismatic evidence her features be considered to fall short of and deviate from the Greek ideal.   Professor Ferrero describes her face as " bouffie."

refer to her racial peculiarities. Philo talks of her
"tawny front" (i. i. 6), and both he and Antony call
her a gipsy with reference not merely to the wily
and vagabond character with which these landlopers
in Shakespeare's day were stigmatised, but surely
to the darkness of her complexion as well. But the
most explicit and the most significant statement is
her own :

> Think on me,
> That am with Phoebus' amorous pinches black. (i. v. 27.)

This is one of her ironical exaggerations ; but does
it not suggest something torrid and tropical, something of the fervours of the East and South, that
burn in the volcanic fires of Othello and the im-
pulsive splendours of Morocco ? Does it not recall
the glowing plea of the latter,

> Mislike me not for my complexion,
> The shadow'd livery of the burnish'd sun,
> To whom I am a neighbour and near bred.
> (*M. of V.*, ii. i. 1.)

The sun has indeed shone on her and into her.
She has known the love and adoration of the
greatest.

> Broad-fronted Caesar,
> When thou wast here above the ground. I was
> A morsel for a monarch : and great Pompey
> Would stand and make his eyes grow in my brow ;
> There would he anchor his aspect and die
> With looking on his life. (i. v. 29.)

Shakespeare magnifies the glories of her conquests,
for it was not Pompey the Great but his son who
had been her lover of old. But these experiences
were only the preparation for the grand passion of
her life. She has outgrown them ; and if the first
freshness is gone, the intoxication of fragrance, the
flavour and lusciousness are enhanced. However
much she believed herself engrossed by these early

fancies, now that she is under the spell of her
Antony, her "man of men," she looks back on
them as of her

salad days
When (she) was green in judgement, cold in blood. (I. v. 73.)

Talking of her preparations to meet Antony, Plutarch says :

> Gessing by the former accesse and credit she had with
> Julius Caesar and Cneus Pompey (the sonne of Pompey the
> Great) only for her beawtie; she began to have good hope
> that she might more easily win Antonius. For Caesar and
> Pompey knew her when she was but a young thing, and knew
> not then what the world ment : but now she went to Antonius,
> at the age when a womans beawtie is at the prime, and she
> also of best judgement.

"At the prime" are Plutarch's words ; for in point
of fact she was then twenty-eight years of age.
In this Shakespeare follows and goes beyond his
authority ; he gives us the impression of her being
somewhat older. Pompey talks of her contemptuously as " Egypt's widow," and prays :

All the charms of love,
Salt Cleopatra, soften thy waned lip. (II. i. 20.)

She herself in ironical self-disparagement avows
that she is " wrinkled deep in time " (I. v. 29) and
exclaims :

Though age from folly could not give me freedom,
It does from childishness. (I. iii. 57.)

But what then ? Like Helen and Gudrun and
the ladies of romance, or like Ninon de Lenclos in
actual life, she never grows old. As even the cynical
Enobarbus proclaims, "age cannot wither her." She
has only gained skill and experience in the use and
embellishment of her physical charms, and with these
the added charms of grace, culture, expressiveness.
She knows how to set off her attractions with all the

aids of art, wealth and effect, as we see from the *mise-en-scène* at the Cydnus : and her mobility and address, her wit, her surprises, her range of interest do the rest. Again Shakespeare has got the clue from Plutarch :

> Now her beawtie (as it is reported) was not so passing, as unmatchable of other women,[1] nor yet suche, as upon present viewe did enamor men with her; but so sweete was her companie and conversacion, that a man could not possiblie but be taken. And besides her beawtie, the good grace she had to talke and discourse, her curteous nature that tempered her words and dedes, was a spurre that pricked to the quick. Furthermore, besides all these, her voyce and words were marvelous pleasant; for her tongue was an instrument of musicke to divers sports and pastimes, the which she easely turned to any language that pleased her.

In one respect Shakespeare differs from Plutarch ; he bestows on her surpassing and unmatchable beauty, so that she transcends the artist's ideal as much as that transcends mortal womanhood ; she o'er-pictures

that Venus where we see

The fancy outwork nature.[2]   (II. ii. 205.)

But he agrees with Plutarch in making her beauty the least part of her spell. Generally speaking it is taken for granted rather than pointed out ; and of its great triumph on the Cydnus we hear only in the enraptured reminiscences of Enobarbus. Thus it is removed from the sphere of sense to the sphere of imagination, and is idealised in the fervour of his delight ; but, though this we never forget, it is of her other charms that we think most when she is present on the scene.

---

[1] The sense is : " Her beauty was not so surpassing as to be beyond comparison with other women's," etc. Compare the Greek : " καὶ γὰρ ἦν, ὡς λέγουσιν, αὐτὸ μὲν καθ' αὐτό, τὸ κάλλος αὐτῆς οὐ πάνυ δυσπαράβλητον, οὐδ' οἷον ἐκπλῆξαι τοὺς ἰδόντας."

[2] Plutarch in the corresponding passage merely says that she was "apparelled and attired like the goddesse Venus commonly drawen in picture."

She is all life and movement, and never the same, so that we are dazzled and bewildered, and too dizzy to measure her by any fixed standard. Her versatility of intellect, her variety of mood, are inexhaustible ; and she can pass from gravity to gaiety, from fondness to banter, with a suddenness that baffles conjecture. We can forecast nothing of her except that any forecast will be vain. At her very first entrance the languishing gives place in a moment to the exasperating vein :

> If it be love indeed, tell me how much.   (I. i. 14.)

> Fulvia perchance is angry ; or, who knows
> If the scarce-bearded Caesar have not sent
> His powerful mandate to you.   (I. i. 20.)

For she turns to account even the gibe and the jeer, stings her lover with her venomous punctures, and pursues a policy of pin-pricks not to repel but to allure. The hint comes from Plutarch.

> When Cleopatra found Antonius jeasts and slents to be but grosse and souldier-like, in plaine manner ; she gave it him finely and without feare taunted him throughly.

And on the other hand she can faint at will, weep and sob beyond measure.

> We cannot call her winds and waters sighs and tears : they are greater storms and tempests than almanacs can report.   (I. ii. 152.)

Here, too, the hint is given by Plutarch, but in a later passage, when she fears Antony may return to Octavia :

> When he went from her, she fell a weeping and blubbering, looked rufully of the matter, and still found the meanes that Antonius should often tymes finde her weeping.

In the play, when he announces his departure, she is ready to fall ; her lace must be cut ; she plays the seduced innocent ; but she mingles wormwood with her pathos and overwhelms him with all sorts of

opposite reproaches. Since he does not bewail
Fulvia, that is proof of infidelity :

> O most false love !
> Where be the sacred vials thou shouldst fill
> With sorrowful water ? Now I see, I see,
> In Fulvia's death, how mine received shall be. (I. iii. 62.)

When his distress is not to be confined, she taxes
him with mourning for his wife :

> I prithee, turn aside and weep for her ;
> Then bid adieu to me, and say the tears
> Belong to Egypt. (I. iii. 76.)

When he loses patience, she mocks at him :

> *Ant.* You'll heat my blood : no more.
> *Cle.* You can do better yet ; but this is meetly.
> *Ant.* Now, by my sword,—
> *Cle.*   And target   Still he mends ;
> But this is not the best. Look, prithee, Charmian,
> How this Herculean Roman does become
> The carriage of his chafe. (I. iii. 80.)

But at the word of his leaving she is at once all
wistful tenderness :

> Courteous lord, one word.
> Sir, you and I must part, but that's not it :
> Sir, you and I have loved, but there's not it ;
> That you know well : something it is I would,—
> O, my oblivion is a very Antony,
> And I am all forgotten.[1] (I. iii. 86.)

But thence again she passes on the instant to grave
and quiet dignity :

> All the gods go with you ! upon your sword
> Sit laurel victory ! and smooth success
> Be strew'd before your feet ! (I. iii. 99.)

It is the unexpectedness of her transitions, the im-
possibility of foreseeing what she will say or do, the
certainty that whatever she says or does will be a

---

[1] See Appendix E.

surprise, that keeps Antony and everyone else in perpetual agitation.[1] Tranquillity and dullness fly at the sound of her name. Her love relies on provocation in both senses of the word, and to a far greater extent in Shakespeare than in Plutarch. Thus Plutarch tells how Octavius' expedition in occupying Toryne caused dismay amōng Antony's troops : "But Cleopatra making light of it : 'And what daunger, I pray you,' said she, 'if Caesar keepe at Toryne?'" On which North has the long marginal note :

> The grace of this tawnt can not properly be expressed in any other tongue, bicause of the equivocation of this word Toryne, which signifieth a citie of Albania, and also, a ladell to scoome the pot with : as if she ment, Caesar sat by the fire side, scomming of the pot.

Shakespeare makes no attempt to find an equivalent for the untranslatable jest, but substitutes one of those bitter mocks before which Antony has so often to wince. When he expresses wonder at his rival's dispatch, she strikes in :

> Celerity is never more admired
> Than by the negligent. (III. vii. 25.)

[1] The love she inspires and feels is of the kind described by La Rochefoucauld : "L'amour, aussi bien que le feu, ne peut subsister, sans un mouvement continuel ; et il cesse de vivre dès qu'il cesse d'espérer ou de craindre." He has another passage that suggests an explanation of the secret of Cleopatra's permanent attraction for the volatile Antony : "La constance en amour est une inconstance perpétuelle, qui fait que notre cœur s'attache successivement à toutes les qualités de la personne que nous aimons, donnant tantôt la préférence à l'une, tantôt à l'autre ; de sorte que cette constance n'est qu'une inconstance arrêtée et renfermée dans un même sujet." It is curious how often an English reader of La Rochefoucauld feels impelled to illustrate the Reflections on Love and Women by reference to Shakespeare's Cleopatra, but it is very natural. His friend the Duchess of Longueville and the other great ladies of the Fronde resembled her in their charm, their wit, their impulsiveness ; and when they engaged in the game of politics, subordinated it like her to their passions and caprices. So his own experience would familiarise La Rochefoucauld with the type, which he has merely generalised, and labelled as the only authentic one.

And she does this sort of thing on principle.   She
tells Alexas :

> See where he is, who's with him, what he does :
> I did not send you : if you find him sad,
> Say I am dancing ; if in mirth, report
> That I am sudden sick.   (I. iii. 2.)

Is it then all artifice ?   Are all her eddying whims
and contradictions mere stratagems to secure her
sway ?   For a moment Antony seems to think so.
" She is cunning past man's thought," he says in
reference to her swooning : and perhaps it is because
of her cunning as well as her sinuous grace that his
endearing name for her is his "Serpent of old Nile "
(I. v. 25).   Enobarbus' reply is in effect that her
displays of emotion are too vehement to be the
results of art ; they are the quintessence of feeling :
" her passions are made of nothing but the finest part
of pure love " (I. ii. 151).

And both these views are correct.   It is her deliberate programme to keep satiety afar by the
swiftness and diversity of the changes she assumes ;
but it is a programme easy to carry out, for it corresponds to her own nature.   She is a creature of
moods.   Excitement, restlessness, curiosity pulse in
her life-blood.   In Antony's absence she is as flighty
with herself as ever she was with him.   She feeds
on memories and thoughts of him, but they plague
rather than soothe her.   In little more than a
breathing-space she turns to music, billiards, and
fishing ; and abandons them all to revel once in her
day-dreams.

When the messenger arrives after Antony's
marriage, she in her ungovernable eagerness interrupts him and will not let him disclose the tidings
for which she longs.   When she hears what they
are, she loses all restraint ; she stuns him with
threats, curses, blows ; she hales him by the hair
and draws a knife upon him.   Then, sinking down

in a faint, she suddenly recovers herself with that irrepressible vitality and inquisitiveness of hers, that are bone of her bone and flesh of her flesh :

> Go to the fellow, good Alexas ; bid him
> Report the feature of Octavia, her years,
> Her inclination, let him not leave out
> The colour of her hair. (II. v. 111.)

And while we are still smiling at the last little touch, comes that moving outburst of a sensitive and sorely stricken soul :

> Pity me, Charmian,
> But do not speak to me. (II. v. 118.)

Not long, however, is she in despair. Her knowledge of Antony's character, her knowledge of her own charms, even her vanity and self-illusion combine to give her assurance of final triumph ; and when we next meet her, she is once more hopeful and alert. "Why, methinks," she sums up at the close of her not very scientific investigation, "this creature's no such thing" (III. iii. 43) ; and she concludes, "All may be well enough" (III. iii. 50).

The charm and piquancy of this nimble changefulness are obvious, and it is not without its value as a weapon in the warfare of life. But it is equally true that such shifting gusts will produce unreliability, and even shiftiness. It is quite natural that Cleopatra, a queen and the daughter of kings, should, in her presumptuous mood, insist on being present in the campaign and on leading to battle her own sixty ships. It is no less natural that amid the actual horrors of the conflict, the luxuriously bred lady should be seized with panic and take to flight. Indeed it is precisely what we might expect. For despite the royalty of soul she often displays, there is in Cleopatra a strain of physical timidity, for which Shakespeare has already prepared us. When the messenger of woe is to give his tidings to Antony, he hesitates and says :

> The nature of bad news infects the teller,

and Antony answers nobly and truly :

> When it concerns the fool or coward.   (I. ii. 99.)

We cannot help remembering Antony's words when Cleopatra visits on the bearer the fault of the bad news to her :

> Hadst thou Narcissus in thy face, to me
> Thou wouldst appear most ugly.   (II. v. 96.)

Such a reception according to Antony stamps the fool or the coward. Cleopatra is no fool, but there is a touch of cowardice in her, that appears over and over again.

Thus it is perhaps fear, fear blended with worldliness, that gains a hearing for Thyreus. There is absolutely no indication that she is playing a part and temporising, out of faithfulness to Antony. She had already sent her own private petition to Caesar, confessing his greatness, submitting to his might, and requesting " the circle of the Ptolemies " for her heirs. This, otherwise than in Plutarch, she had done without Antony's knowledge, who tells her, as though for her information, that he had sent his schoolmaster to bear his terms ; with which Cleopatra's were not associated. Her whole behaviour shows that she dreads Octavius' power, and dreads the loss of her own wealth and dignities. But, in the scene with Thyreus, is she really prepared to desert and betray her lover? Antony suspects that she is, and appearances are indeed against her. Enobarbus believes that she is, and Enobarbus generally hits on the truth. Yet we have always to remember the temptation she would feel to try her spells on Thyreus and his master :

and even after Enobarbus' desertion she remains with Antony, clings to him, encourages him, arms him, is proud of him. In any case it would not be cold-blooded perfidy, but one of those flaws of weakness, of fear, of self-pity, of self-interest, that take her unawares.[1] For the final treason of the fleet at any rate, of which Antony imagines her guilty, she seems in no way responsible. Plutarch mentions Antony's infuriated suspicion but adds no word in confirmation, and Shakespeare, who would surely not have left us without direction on so important a matter, is equally reticent. Such hints as he gives, point the other way. We may indeed discount the disclaimers of Mardian and Diomedes who would probably say anything they were told to say. But when Antony greets Cleopatra, "Ah, thou spell! avaunt!" her exclamation,

> Why is my lord enraged against his love? (IV. xii. 31.)

seems to express genuine amazement rather than assumed innocence. And in her conversation with her attendants her words, to all appearance, imply that she cannot understand his rage: to her it is merely inexplicable frenzy:

> Help me, my women! O, he is more mad
> Than Telamon for his shield; the boar of Thessaly
> Was never so emboss'd. (IV. xiii. I.)

Moreover, if she had packed cards with Caesar, it is difficult to see why she should not claim a price for her treachery, instead of locking herself up in the Monument as she does, and trying to keep the Romans out. All the negociations and interviews after Antony's death seem to imply that she had no previous understanding with Octavius.

But she recoils from her lover's desperation, as she always does when he is deeply moved. She

---

[1] " L'on fait plus souvent des trahisons par foiblesse que par un dessein formé de trahir."—*La Rochefoucauld.*

has ever the tact to feel the point at which her blandishments and vexations are out of place and will no longer serve her turn. Just as after the disaster of Actium she only sobs :

> O my lord, my lord,
> Forgive my fearful sails ! (III. xi. 54.)

and then can urge no plea but "pardon"; just as after her interview with Thyreus, with no hint of levity, she solemnly imprecates curses on herself and her offspring if she were false ; so now she bows before his wrath and flees to the monument. Then follows the fiction of her death, a fiction in which the actress does not forget the *finesses* of her art.

> Say, that the last I spoke was " Antony,"
> And word it, prithee, piteously. (IV. xiii. 8.)

It is not the most candid nor dignified expedient, but probably it is the most effective one ; for violent ills need violent cures ; and perhaps there was nothing that could allay Antony's storm of distrust but as fierce a storm of regret. At any rate it has the result at which Cleopatra aims ; but she knows him well, and presently foresees that the antidote may have a further working than she intends. Diomedes seems to state the mere truth when he says that her prophesying fear dispatched him to proclaim the truth.

But it is too late ; and there only remains the lofty parting-scene, when if she still fears to open the gates lest Caesar should enter, she draws her lover up to the monument, and lightens his last 'moments no less with her queenliness than with her love. She feels the fitness and the pathos in his ending, that none but Antony should conquer Antony : she not obscurely hints that she will take the same path. When he bids her :

> Of Caesar seek your honour, with your safety ; (IV. xv. 47.)

she answers well, "They do not go together."   Her
passionate ejaculation ere she faints above his corpse,
her appeal to her frightened women,

what's brave, what's noble,
Let's do it after the high Roman fashion,   (v. xv. 87.)

have a whole-heartedness and intensity that first
reveal the greatness of her nature.

And yet even now she seems to veer from the
prouder course on which she has set out.   We soon
find her in appearance paltering with her Roman
decision.   She sends submissive messages to Caesar ;
she delays her death so long that Proculeius can
surprise her in her asylum ; she accepts her conqueror's condescension ; she stoops to hold back
and conceal the greater part of her jewels.

It is a strange riddle that Shakespeare has here
offered to the student, and perhaps no certain solution of it is to be found.   In this play, even more
than in most, he resorts to what has been called
his shorthand, to the briefest and most hurried
notation of his meaning, and often it is next to
impossible to explain or extend his symbols.

The usual interpretation, which has much to commend it, accepts all these apparent compliances of
Cleopatra for what on the face they are.   They are
taken as instances of Shakespeare's veracious art
that abstains from sophisticating fact for the sake
of effect, and attains a higher effect through this
very conscientiousness and self-restraint.   Just as
he makes the enthusiastic fidelity of Enobarbus fail
to stand the supreme test, so he detects a flaw in
the resolute yearning of Cleopatra.   The body of
her dead past weighs her down, and she cannot
advance steadily in the higher altitudes.   She wavers
in her determination to die, as is implied by her
retention of her treasure, and " the courtesan's instincts of venality and falsehood "[1] still assert their

[1] Boas, *Shakespeare and his Predecessors.*

sway. She has too easily taken to heart Antony's advice, and is but too ready, despite all her brave words, to grasp at her safety along with her honour, or what she is pleased to consider her honour to be. And, just as in the case of Enobarbus, an external stimulus is needed to urge her to the nobler course. The gods in their unkindness are kind to her. Dolabella's disclosures and her own observations convince her that Caesar spares her only for his own glory and for her shame; that, as she foreboded, her safety and her honour do not go together. Then, at the thought of the indignity, all her royal and aristocratic nature rises in revolt, and she at last chooses as she ought.

On the other hand it is possible to maintain that all these apparent lapses are mere subterfuges forced on Cleopatra to ensure the success of her scheme; and this interpretation receives some support not only from the text of the play, but from the comparison of it with North, and a consideration of what in the original narrative Shakespeare takes for granted, of what he alters, and of what he adds.[1]

After her more or less explicit statements in Antony's death scene, her suppliant message from the monument is an interpolation of the dramatist's; but so is the very different declaration which she subsequently makes to her confidantes and in which her purpose of suicide seems unchanged:

> My desolation does begin to make
> A better life. 'Tis paltry to be Caesar;
> Not being Fortune, he's but Fortune's knave,
> A minister of her will: and it is great
> To do the thing that ends all other deeds;
> Which shackles accidents and bolts up change;
> Which sleeps, and never palates more the dung,[2]
> The beggar's nurse and Caesar's. (v. ii. 1.)

[1] This was first suggested in A. Stahr's *Cleopatra*. I prefer to give the arguments in my own way.

[2] So in folio: some modern editions alter unnecessarily to "dug."

Which of these two utterances gives the true
Cleopatra, the one transmitted at second hand for
Octavius' consumption, or the one breaking from
her in private to her two women who will be true to
her till death? Quite apart from the circumstances
in which, and the persons to whom, they are spoken,
there is a marked difference -in tone between the
ceremonious official character of the first, and the
spontaneous sincerity of the second.

Then just at this moment Proculeius arrives and
engages her in talk. It is not wonderful that she
should look for a moment to the man Antony had
recommended to her; but, though she is deferential
to Octavius, her one request is not for herself but
for her son. And when the surprise is effected,
there is no question of the genuineness of her
attempt at self-destruction. Even when she is
disarmed, she persists, as with Plutarch, in her
resolution to kill herself if need be by starvation.
In Plutarch she is dissuaded from this by threats
against her children; in Shakespeare events proceed
more rapidly, and she has no time to put such a
plan in practice; nor is any serious use made of the
maternal "motif." From first to last it is, along
with grief for Antony, resentment at the Roman
triumph that moves her. And these feelings are in
full activity when immediately afterwards she is left
in charge of Dolabella, This passage also is an
addition, and it is noteworthy that it begins with
her deification of Antony, and ends with Dolabella's
assurance, which in Plutarch only follows later where
the play repeats it, of her future fate.

> Cle. He'll lead me, then, in triumph?
> Dol. Madam, he will; I know't.   (v. ii. 109.)

It is just then that Caesar is announced; and it is
hard to believe that Cleopatra, with her two master
passions excited to the height, should really contem-

plate embezzling treasure as provision for a life which surely, in view of the facts, she could not care to prolong. Moreover, in Plutarch's narrative there is a contradiction or ambiguity which North's marginal note brings into relief, and which would be quite enough to set a duller man than Shakespeare thinking about what it all meant.

> At length, she gave him a breefe and memoriall of all the readie money and treasure she had. But by chaunce there stoode Seleucus by, one of her Treasorers, who to seeme a good servant, came straight to Caesar to disprove Cleopatra, that she had not set in al, but kept many things back of purpose. Cleopatra was in such a rage with him, that she flew upon him and tooke him by the heare of the head, and boxed him wellfavoredly. Caesar fell a laughing, and parted the fray. "Alas," said she, "O Caesar: is not this a great shame and reproche, that thou having vouchsaved to take the peines to come unto me, and hast done me this honor, poore wretche, and caitife creature, brought into this pitiefull and miserable estate: and that mine owne servaunts should come now to accuse me, though it may be I have reserved some juells and trifles meete for women, but not for me (poore soule) to set out my selfe withall, but meaning to geve some pretie presents and gifts unto Octavia and Livia, that they making meanes and intercession for me to thee, thou mightest yet extend thy favor and mercie upon me?" Caesar was glad to heare her say so, *perswading him selfe thereby that she had yet a desire to save her life.* So he made her answere, that he did not only geve her that to dispose of at her pleasure, which she had kept backe, but further promised to use her more honorably and bountifully then she would thinke for: and so he tooke his leave of her, *supposing he had deceived her, but in deede he was deceived him selfe.*

And North underlines the suggestive clauses with his comment:

> Cleopatra finely deceiveth Octavius Caesar, as though she desired to live.

It is not hard therefore to see how the whole episode may be taken as contrived on her part. It would be a device of the serpent of old Nile, one of her

triumphs of play-acting, by means of which she gets
the better of her conqueror and makes him indeed
an ass unpolicied.   And though the suggestion
would come from Plutarch, whom Shakespeare
follows in the main very closely throughout this
passage, it is pointed out that some of Shakespeare's
modifications in detail seem to favour this view.

And to begin with it should be noticed that in
all this episode he passes over what is abject or
hysterical or both in Plutarch's Cleopatra, and gives
her a large measure of royal self-respect and self-
command.   This is how Octavius finds her in the
original story :

> Cleopatra being layed upon a little low bed in poore estate,
> when she sawe Caesar come in to her chamber, she sodainly
> rose up, naked in her smocke, and fell downe at his feete
> marvelously disfigured : both for that she had plucked her
> heare from her head, as also for that she had martired all
> her face with her nailes, and besides, her voyce was small
> and trembling, her eyes sonke into her heade with continuall
> blubbering.

Thus, and with other traits that we omit, Plutarch
describes her "ougly and pitiefull state," when
Caesar comes to see and comfort her.   We cannot
imagine Shakespeare's Cleopatra ever so forgetting
what was due to her beauty, her rank, and herself.
Then the narrative proceeds :

> When Caesar had made her lye downe againe, and sate by
> her beddes side ; Cleopatra began to cleere and excuse her
> selfe for that she had done, laying all to the feare she had of
> Antonius.   Caesar, in contrarie maner, reproved [1] her in
> every poynt.

In the play this suggestion is put back to the interview with Thyreus ; and is made, not refuted, on
the authority of Octavius.

> *Thy.* He knows that you embrace not Antony
> As you did love, but as you fear'd him.
> *Cle.*   O !

[1] *i.e.* confuted.

Thy. The scars upon your honour, therefore, he
Does pity as constrained blemishes,
Not as deserved.
  Cle.   He is a god, and knows
What is most right: mine honour was not yielded,
But conquer'd merely.   (III. xiii. 56.)

But this was before the supreme sorrow had come
to quicken in her her nobler instincts. Now she
has no thought of incriminating Antony and excul-
pating herself. She says with quiet dignity :

    Sole sir o' the world,
I cannot project mine own cause so well
To make it clear : but do confess I have
Been laden with like frailties, which before
Have often shamed our sex.   (V. II. 120.)

Even her wrath at Seleucus is less outrageous than
in Plutarch. She threatens his eyes, but does not
proceed to physical violence. She does not fly
upon him and seize him by the hair of the head and
box him well-favouredly. These vivacities Shakespeare had remarked, but he transfers them to the
much earlier scene when she receives news of
Antony's marriage and strikes the messenger to the
ground, and strikes him again, and drags him up
and down. Now she has somewhat more self-
control, and is no longer carried beyond all limits of
decency by her ungovernable moods. Shakespeare,
therefore, gives her a new dignity and strength even
in this most equivocal scene ; and how could these
be reconciled with a craven hankering for life and a
base desire to retain by swindling a share of its
gewgaws ?

But a further alteration, we are told, gives a
definite though unobtrusive hint that all the while
she is in collusion with Seleucus, and that the whole
affair is a comedy arranged between them to keep
open the door of death. Not only does the treasurer
escape unpunished after his disclosure, but he is

invited to make it.   In Plutarch he merely happens
to stand by, and intervenes "to seeme a good
servant."   Here Cleopatra calls for him ; bids Caesar
let him speak on his peril ; and herself orders him,
"Speak the truth, Seleucus."

Moreover his statement and her excuse point to
a much more serious embezzlement than Plutarch
suggests, and just in so far would give Octavius a
stronger impression of her desire to live.   In the
biography Seleucus confines himself to saying that
"she had not set in al, but kept many things back
of purpose ": and she confesses only to "some juells
and trifles meete for women . . . meaning to geve
some pretie presents and gifts unto Octavia and
Livia."   In the play to her question : " What have
I kept back ? " Seleucus answers :

Enough to purchase what you have made known :   (v. ii. 148.)

and she, after the express proviso she makes in
advance, that she has not admitted petty things in
the schedule, now acknowledges that she has reserved not only "lady trifles, immoment toys"—
these were already accounted for—but some "nobler
token " for Octavius' sister and wife.

If these clues are unduly faint, we are reminded
that such elliptical treatment is not without parallel
in other incidents of the drama.   Octavius' policy in
regard to Octavia's marriage, for example, has, in
just the same way, to be gathered from the general
drift of events and the general probabilities of the
case, from an unimportant suggestion in Plutarch,
from the opportunity furnished to Agrippa, and his
agency in that transaction, which are not more
explicit than the opportunity furnished to Seleucus,
and his agency in this.

These arguments are ingenious and not without
their cogency, but they leave one unconvinced.   The
difficulties in accepting them are far greater than in

the analogous question of Antony's marriage. For in the latter the theory of Octavius' duplicity does not contradict the impression of the scene. Nor does it contradict but only supplements the statement of the historian : the utmost we can say is that it is not made sufficiently prominent. And, lastly, the doubt that is thus left possible does not concern a protagonist of the drama, but at most the chief or one of the chief of the minor characters. But in the present case the impression produced on the un-sophisticated reader is certainly that Cleopatra is convicted of fraud : and however that impression may be weakened by a review of the circumstances as a whole, there is no single phrase or detail that brings the opposite theory home to the imagination. Besides, the complicity of Seleucus would be a much bolder fabrication than the complicity of Agrippa : the latter is not recorded, but the opposite of the former is recorded, and was accepted by all who dealt with this episode from Jodelle to Daniel, and probably by all who read Plutarch : the treasurer was present by accident and used the opportunity to ingratiate himself. So Shakespeare, without giving adequate guidance himself, would leave people to the presuppositions they had formed under the guidance of his author. Surely this is a very severe criticism on his art. But this is not all. The miscon-struction which he did nothing to prevent and everything to produce, would concern the heroine of the piece, an even more important personage than the hero, as is shown by her receiving the fifth act to herself, while Antony is dismissed in the fourth.

These objections, however, only apply to the view that the suppression and discovery of the treasure were parts of a deliberate stratagem. They do not affect the arguments that Cleopatra has virtually accepted death as the only practical solution, and that the rest of her behaviour at this stage accords ill with mercenary imposture.

In a word both these antagonistic theories approve themselves in so far as they take into account the facts alleged and the impressions produced by the drama. If we credit our feelings, it is quite true that Cleopatra is taken by surprise and put out of countenance, that she seeks to excuse herself and passionately resents the disloyalty of Seleucus. And again, if we credit our feelings, it is quite true that from the time the mortally wounded Antony is brought before her, she has made up her mind to kill herself, and that she is nobler and more queenly for her decision than she was before or than Plutarch makes her.

Of course, buoyant and versatile, feeling her life in every limb, and quick to catch each passing chance, she may even now without really knowing it, without really believing it, have hoped against hope that she might still obtain terms she could accept undisgraced. And the hope of life would bring with it the frailties of life, for clearly it is only the resolve to die that lifts her above herself. So here we should only have another instance of the complexity of her strange nature that can consciously elect the higher path, and yet all the while in its secret councils provide, if it may be, for following the lower.

But is there not another interpretation possible? What are these " lady trifles " and " nobler tokens " that together would purchase all the wealth of money, plate and jewels she has declared. Plutarch, talking of her magnificence when she obeyed Antony's first summons, evidently does not expect to be believed, and adds that it was such "as is credible enough she might bring from so great a house, and from so wealthie a realme as Ægypt was." And now she is "again for Cydnus," and

needs her "crown and all." Already to all intents
and purposes she has resolved on her death, as is
shown by her frequent assurances. She has also
resolved on the means of it ; for scarcely has Caesar
left, than she tells Charmian :

I have spoke already, and it is provided. (v. ii. 195.)

Will she not also have resolved on the manner of it ;
and both in the self-consciousness of her beauty and
in memory of her first meeting with Antony, does
she not desire to depart life for the next meeting
with due pomp and state? If we imagine she
was keeping back her regalia for this last display,
we can understand why Shakespeare inserted the
"nobler token" in addition to the unconsidered
trifles which she was quite ready to own she had
reserved, and of which indeed in Shakespeare
though not in Plutarch she had already made express mention as uninventoried.[1] We can understand her consternation and resentment at the disclosure ; for just as in regard to the "nobler token"
she could not explain her real motives without
ruining her plan. And we can admire her "cunning
past man's thought" in turning the whole incident
to account as proof that she was willing to live on
sufferance as *protégée* of Caesar.

No doubt this suggestion is open to the criticism
that it is nowhere established by a direct statement ;
but that also applies to the most probable explanation
of some other matters in the play. And meanwhile
I think that it, better than the two previous theories

---

[1] It is a rather striking coincidence that Jodelle, too, heightens Plutarch's account of the treasures she has retained, and includes among
them the crown jewels and royal robes. Seleucus finishes a panegyric
on her wealth :

> Croy, Cesar, croy qu'elle a de tout son or
> Et autres biens tout le meilleur caché.

And she says in her defence :

> Hé ! si j'avois retenu les joyaux
> Et quelque part de mes habits royaux,
> L'aurois-je fait pour moy, las ! malheureuse !

we have discussed, satisfies the conditions, by con-
forming with the *data* of the play, the treatment of
the sources, and the feelings of the reader.   On the
one hand it fully admits the reality of Cleopatra's
fraud and of her indignation at Seleucus.   On the
other it removes the discrepancy between her dissimulation, and the loftiness of temper and readiness
for death, which she now generally and but for the
usual interpretation of this incident invariably displays.   It tallies with what we may surmise from
Shakespeare's other omissions and interpolations ;
and if it goes beyond Plutarch's account of Caesar's
deception by Cleopatra, it does not contradict it,
and therefore would not demand so full and definite
a statement as a new story entirely different from
the original.

Be that as it may, there is at least no trace of
hesitation or compliance in the Queen from the
moment when she perceives that Octavius is merely
" wording " her.   Her self-respect is a stronger or,
at any rate, a more conspicuous motive than her
love.   Antony, when he believed her false had said
to her :

> Vanish, or I shall give thee thy deserving,
> And blemish Caesar's triumph.   Let him take thee,
> And hoist thee up to the shouting plebeians :
> Follow his chariot, like the greatest spot
> Of all thy sex ; most monster-like be shown
> For poor'st diminutives, for doits : and let
> Patient Octavia plough thy visage up
> With her prepared nails.   (IV. xii. 32.)

These words of wrath have lingered in her memory
and she echoes them in his dying ears:

> Not the imperious show
> Of the full-fortuned Caesar ever shall
> Be brooch'd with me ; if knife, drugs, serpents have
> Edge, sting, or operation, I am safe :
> Your wife Octavia, with her modest eyes
> And still conclusion, shall acquire no honour
> Demuring upon me.   (IV. xv. 23.)

The loathsomeness of the prospect grows in her imagination, and compared with it the most loathsome fate is desirable.   She tells Proculeius :

> Know, sir, that I
> Will not wait pinion'd at your master's court ;
> Nor once be chastised with the sober eye
> Of dull Octavia.   Shall they hoist me up
> And show me to the shouting varletry
> Of censuring Rome ?   Rather a ditch in Egypt
> Be gentle grave unto me ! rather on Nilus' mud
> Lay me stark naked, and let the water-flies
> Blow me into abhorring ! rather make
> My country's high pyramides my gibbet,
> And hang me up in chains.   (v. ii. 52.)

And now in the full realisation of the scene, she brings it home to her women :

> *Cle.*   Now, Iras, what think'st thou ?
> Thou, an Egyptian puppet, shalt be shown
> In Rome, as well as I : mechanic slaves
> With greasy aprons, rules and hammers, shall
> Uplift us to the view ; in their thick breaths,
> Rank of gross diet, shall we be enclouded,
> And forced to drink their vapour.
> *Iras.*   The gods forbid !
> *Cle.* Nay, 'tis most certain, Iras : saucy lictors
> Will catch at us, like strumpets ; and scald rhymers
> Ballad us out of tune.   (v. ii. 207.)

Such thoughts expel once for all her mutability and flightiness :

> My resolution's placed and I have nothing
> Of woman in me : now from head to foot
> I am marble constant ; now the fleeting moon
> No planet is of mine.   (v. ii. 238.)

And the scene that follows with the banalities and trivialities of the clown who supplies the aspics among the figs, brings into relief the loneliness of a queenly nature and a great sorrow.   Yet not merely the loneliness, but the potency as well. Who would have given the frivolous waiting-women

of the earlier scenes credit for devotion and heroism?
Yet inspired by her example they learn their lesson
and are ready to die as nobly as she.   Iras has
spoken for them all :

> Finish, good lady ; the bright day is done,
> And we are for the dark.   (v. ii. 193.)

Now she brings the robe and crown Cleopatra wore
at Cydnus, and then, like Eros, ushers the way.
Charmian stays but to close the eyes and arrange
the diadem of her dead mistress :

> Downy windows, close ;
> And golden Phoebus never be beheld
> Of eyes again so royal.   Your crown's awry ;
> I'll mend it, and then play.   (v. ii. 319.)

Thereupon she too applies the asp and provokes
its fang.

> O, come apace, dispatch.   (v. ii. 325.)

Even in the last solemn moment there is vanity,
artifice, and voluptuousness in Cleopatra.   She is
careful of her looks, of her state, of her splendour,
even in death ; and doubtless would have smiled if
she could have heard Caesar's tardy praise :

> She looks like sleep,
> As she would catch another Antony
> In her strong toil of grace.   (v. ii. 349.)

And she does not depart quite in the high Roman
fashion.   She has studied to make her passage easy,
and has taken all measures that may enable her to
liken the stroke of death to a lover's pinch and the
biting of the asp to the suckling of a babe, and to
say :

> As sweet as balm, as soft as air, as gentle.   (v. ii. 314.)

None the less her exit in its serene grace and
dignity is imperial, and deserves the praise of the
dying Charmian and the reluctant Octavius.

CHAPTER VII

ANTONY AND CLEOPATRA

HITHERTO this discussion of *Antony and Cleopatra* has so far as possible passed over the most distinctive thing in the history of the hero and heroine, the fatal passion that binds them together, gives significance to their lives, and makes their memories famous. Knowing their environment and their nature we are in a better position to see in some measure what it meant.

We have noted how in that generation all ties of customary morality are loosed, how the individual is a law to himself, and how selfishness runs riot in its quest of gratification, acquisition, material ambition. Among the children of that day those make the most sympathetic impression who import into the somewhat casual and indefinite personal relations that remain—the relation of the legionary to his commander, of the freedman to his patron, of the waiting-woman to her mistress—something of universal validity and worth. But obviously no connection in a period like this at once arises so naturally from the conditions, and has the possibilities of such abiding authority, as the love of the sexes. On the one hand it is the most personal bond of all. Love is free and not to be compelled. It results from the spontaneous motion of the individual. Were we to conceive the whole social fabric dissolved, men and women would still be drawn together by mutual inclination in more or less permanent unions of pairs.   And yet this attraction that seems to be and that is so completely dictated by choice, that is certainly quite beyond the domain of external compulsion, is in another aspect quite independent of the will of the persons concerned, and sways them like a resistless natural force.   It has been said that the highest compliment the lover can pay the beloved is to say, " I cannot help loving you."   Necessity is laid upon him, and he is but its instrument.   If then the inclination is so pervasive and imperious that it becomes a master passion, clearly it will supply the grand effective bond when other social bonds fail.   When nothing else can, it will enable a man and woman to overleap a few at least of the barriers of their selfishness, and in some measure to merge their egoism in sympathy.   This is what justifies Antony's idolatry of Cleopatra to our feelings.   The passion is enthusiastic, and in a way is self-forgetful ; and passion, enthusiasm, self-forgetfulness, whatever their aberrations, always command respect.   They especially do so in this world of greeds and cravings and calculating self-interest. This infinite devotion that shrinks from no sacrifice, is at once the greatest thing within Antony's reach, and witness to his own greatness in recognising its worth.   The greatest thing within his reach : when we remember what the ambitions of his fellows and his rivals were, there is truth in the words with which he postpones all such ambitions to the bliss of the mutual caress :

> Let Rome in Tiber melt, and the wide arch
> Of the ranged empire fall !   Here is my space.
> Kingdoms are clay ; our dungy earth alike
> Feeds beast as man : the nobleness of life

Is to do thus : when such a mutual pair   (*embracing*)
And such a twain can do't, in which I bind,
On pain of punishment, the world to weet
We stand up peerless.   (I. i. 33.)

And only one of grand general outlook could feel
like this, when he had tasted the sweets of conquest
and power, and when all the kingdoms of the world
were reached to his hand as the alternative for the
kingdom of his love. It takes a hero, with such
experiences behind him and such opportunities before,
to make the disastrous choice. Heine tells us how
he read Plutarch at school and how the master
"impressed on us that Antony for this woman
spoiled his public career, involved himself in domestic unpleasantnesses, and at last plunged himself in ruin. In truth my old master was right,
and it is extremely dangerous to establish intimate
relations with a person like Cleopatra. It may be
the destruction of a hero ; but only of a hero.
Here as everywhere there is no danger for worthy
mediocrity."

But despite the sympathy with which Shakespeare
regards Antony's passion both as an object of pursuit
and as an indication of nobility, he is quite aware
that it is pernicious and criminal. Relatively it may
be extolled : absolutely it must be condemned. It
is rooted in breach of troth and duty, and it bears
within itself the seeds of infidelity and wrong. It
has none of the inviolability and security of a lawful
love. After all, Cleopatra's gibes about Antony's
relations with "the married woman" and herself,
despite their affectation of petulance, are only too
much to the point, so far as he is concerned ; and
when she has yielded to Julius, Pompey, and Antony
in turn, what guarantee has the last favourite that
she will not do so again to some later supplanter?
In point of fact each is untrue to the other, Antony
by his marriage with Octavia, Cleopatra by her

traffickings with Octavius and Thyreus.[1] She forfeits in the sequel her right to be angry at his
truancy; he has forfeited in advance the right to
be angry at hers. But it is their penalty that these
resentments should come between them ; and at the
very time when they most need each other's support,
their relation, being far from the perfect kind that
casts out mistrust, is vitiated by jealousy on the one
side and fear on the other. She flees to the Monument, shuts herself up from his blind rage in craven
panic, and seeks to save her life by lies. At the
sight of the liberties she has allowed Thryeus to
take, he loses himself in mad outbursts which have
but a partial foundation in the facts. Then he
jumps to the conclusion that she has arranged for
the desertion of the sailors, and dooms her to
death, when in reality she seems to know nothing
about it.

> Betray'd I am :
> O this false soul of Egypt ! this grave charm,—
> Whose eye beck'd forth my wars. and call'd them home ;
> Whose bosom was my crownet, my chief end,—
> Like a right gipsy, hath, at fast and loose,
> Beguiled me to the very heart of loss. (IV. xii. 24.)

These terrors and suspicions are inevitable in such
love as theirs.

Or is their feeling for each other to be called love
at all ? The question has been asked even in regard
to Antony. From first to last he is aware not only
of her harmfulness but of her pravity. He is under
no illusions about her cunning, her boggling, her
falsity. And can this insight co-exist with devotion ?

Much more frequently it has been asked in regard
to Cleopatra. She frankly avows even in retrospect

---

[1] I take it as certain that with Thyreus she is for the moment at least
"a boggler," and then she has already sent her private message to
Caesar.

her policy of making him her prey. Thus does she
mimic fact in her pastime :

> Give me mine angle : we'll to the river ; there,
> My music playing far off, I will betray
> Tawny-finn'd fishes ; my bended hook shall pierce
> Their slimy jaws ; and, as I draw them up,
> I'll think them every one an Antony,
> And say, "Ah, ha ! you're caught." (II. v. 10.)

Moreover, her first capture of him at that banquet
where he paid his heart as ordinary, was a mere
business speculation. He has been useful to her
since, for he is the man to piece her opulent throne
with kingdoms. When he seems lost to her, she
realises that she can no longer gratify her caprices
as once she did.

> *Alex.* Herod of Jewry dare not look upon you
> But when you are well pleased.
> *Cle.* That Herod's head
> I'll have : but how, when Antony is gone
> Through whom I might command it ? (III. iii. 4.)

Or, if other motives supervene, they belong to wanton
whim and splendid coquetry. Her deliberate allure-
ments, her conscious wiles, her calculated tenderness,
are all employed merely to retain her command of
the serviceable instrument, and at the same time
minister to her vanity, since Antony would accept
such a rôle only from her.

If both or either of these theories were adopted,
the whole interest and dignity of the theme would
be gone. If Antony were not genuinely in love,
his follies and delinquencies would cast him beyond
the pale of our tolerance. If Cleopatra were not
genuinely in love, she would at best deserve the
description of Ten Brink, "a courtesan of genius."
If the love were not mutual, Antony would be
merely the toy of the courtesan, Cleopatra merely
the toy of the sensualist.

But in point of fact, it is mutual and sincere. Antony's feeling has to do with much more than the senses. It goes deeper and higher; and even when he doubts Cleopatra's affection, he never doubts his own :

> (Her) heart I thought I had, for she had mine. (IV. xiv. 16.)

Cleopatra's feeling may have originated in self-interest and may make use of craft. But in catching Antony she has been caught herself; and though interest and vanity are not expelled, they are swallowed up in vehement admiration for the man she has ensnared. Her artifices are successful, because they are the means made use of by a heart that is deeply engaged; and it is no paradox to say that they are evidence of her sincerity. So often as she refers to her lover seriously, it is with something like adoration. After the first separation, he is her "man of men." In her first bitterness at his marriage, she cannot let him go, for

> Though he be painted one way like a Gorgon,
> The other way's a Mars. (II. v. 116.)

Even when he is fallen and worsted, she has no doubt how things would go were it a merely personal contest between him and his rival. When he returns from his last victory, she greets him : " Lord of lords ! O infinite virtue ! " (IV. viii. 16). When he dies, the world seems to her " no better than a sty " (IV. xv. 62). When she recalls his splendour, his bounty, his joyousness, it seems not a reality, but a dream, which yet must be more than a dream.

> If there be, nor ever were, one such,
> It's past the size of dreaming : nature wants stuff
> To vie strange forms with fancy; yet, to imagine
> An Antony, were nature's piece 'gainst fancy,
> Condemning shadows quite. (V. ii. 96.)

Various interpretations have been given of these lines, but on any possible interpretation they exalt

Antony alike above fact and fancy.[1]   And when we run through the whole gamut of the words and deeds of the pair, from their squabbles to their death, it seems to me possible to doubt their love only by isolating some details and considering them to the exclusion of the rest.

But the truth is that the love of Antony and Cleopatra is genuine and intense ; and if it leads to shame as well as to glory, this is to be explained, apart from the circumstances of the time, apart from the characters of the lovers, in the nature of the variety to which it belongs.

Plutarch, whose thoughts when he is discussing such subjects are never far from Plato's, has a passage in which he characterises Antony's passion by reference to the famous metaphor in the *Phaedrus.*

> In the ende, the horse of the minde, as Plato termeth it, that is so hard of rayne (I meane the unreyned lust of concupiscence), did put out of Antonius' heade all honest and commendable thoughts.

Certainly it is not the milder and more docile steed that takes the lead in Antony's affection.   But it is perhaps a little surprising that Plutarch did not rather go for his Platonic illustration to the *Symposium*, where the disquisitions of Aristophanes and Diotima explain respectively what Antony's love is and is not.   Aristophanes, with his myth that men, once four-legged and four-armed, were split in two because they were too happy, and now are pining to find their counterparts, gives the exact description of what the love of Antony and Cleopatra is.

[1] To me the sense seems to be : Supposing the Antony I have depicted never existed, still the conception is too great to be merely my own.   It must be an imagination of Nature herself, which she may be unable to embody, but which shames our puny ideals.   In other words, Antony is the "form" or "type" which Nature aims at even if she does not attain.   I see no reason for changing the "nor" of the first line as it is in the folio to "or."

Q

> Each of us when separated is but the indenture of a man,
> having one side only like a flat-fish, and he is always looking
> for his other half. . . . When one of them finds his other
> half, . . . the pair are lost in an amazement of love and
> friendship and intimacy, and one will not be out of the
> other's sight, as I may say, even for a moment.[1]

And, on the other hand, Diotima's opposite theory
does not apply to this particular case, at least, to
begin with or superficially :

> You hear people say that lovers are seeking for their other
> half; but I say that they are seeking neither for the half of
> themselves, nor for the whole, unless the half or the whole
> be also a good.   And they will cut off their own hands and
> feet and cast them away, if they are evil. . . . For there is
> nothing which men love but the good.[2]

We may put the case in a somewhat more popular
and modern fashion.   All love that really deserves
the name must base more or less completely on
sympathy, on what Goethe called *Wahlverwand-
schaft*, or elective affinity.   But such affinity may
be of different kinds and degrees, and according to
its range will tend to approximate to one of two
types.   It may mean sympathy with what is deepest
and highest in us, our aspiration after the ideal, our
bent towards perfection ; or it may mean sympathy
with our whole nature and with all our feelings and
tendencies, alike with those that are high and with
those that are low.   The former is the more exacting though the more beneficent.   It implies the
suppression and abnegation in us of much that is
base, of much that is harmless, of much, even, that
may be good, for the sake of the best.   In it we
must inure ourselves to effort and sacrifice for the
sake of advance in that supersensible realm where
the union took place.

The second is less austere, and, for the time being,
more comprehensive.   It is founded on a correspondence in all sorts of matters, great and small,

[1] Jowett's *Plato*, Vol. II., pages 42-43.   [2] *Ibid*, pages 56-57.

noble and base, of good or of bad report. If it lacks
the exclusive loftiness of the other, it affords many
more points of contact and a far greater wealth of
daily fellowship. / And of this latter variety, the love
of Antony and Cleopatra is perhaps the typical
example. At first sight it is evident that they are,
as we say, made for each other. They are both
past the first bloom of youth. Cleopatra, whom at
the outset Plutarch makes twenty-eight years of age,
and of whose wrinkles and waned lip Shakespeare,
though in irony and exaggeration, finds it possible
to speak, has relatively reached the same period of
life as Antony, whom Plutarch makes at the outset
forty-three or forty-six years of age, and whom
Shakespeare represents as touched with the fall of
eld. And they correspond in their experiences.
Neither is a novice in love and pleasure : Cleopatra,
the woman with a history, Antony, the masquer and
reveller of Clodius' set, have both seen life. They
are alike in their emotionalism, their impressibility,
their quick wits, their love of splendour, their genial
power, their intellectual scope, their zest for everything. Plutarch narrates—and it is strange that
à propos of this he did not quote Aristophanes'
saying in the *Symposium*—

> She, were it in sport, or in matter of earnest, still devised
> sundrie new delights to have Antonius at commaundement,
> never leaving him night nor day, nor once letting him go out
> of her sight. For she would play at dyce with him, drinke
> with him, and hunt commonly with him, and also be with
> him when he went to any exercise or activity of body. And
> sometime, also, when he would goe up and downe the citie
> disguised like a slave in the night, and would peere into
> poore men's windowes and their shops, and scold and brawle
> with them within the house : Cleopatra would be also in a
> chamber-maides array, and amble up and downe the streets
> with him, so that oftentimes Antonius bare away both mockes
> and blowes.

Here we have a picture of the completest *camara-
derie* in things serious and frivolous, athletic and

intellectual, decorous and venturesome, with memories of which the play is saturated. We are
witnesses of Cleopatra's impatience when he is away
for a moment : we hear of her drinking him to bed
before the ninth hour, and of their outdoor sports.
Antony proposes to roam the streets with her and
note the qualities of the people. Perhaps it was
some such expedition that gave Enobarbus material
for his description :

> I saw her once
> Hop forty paces through the public street ;
> And having lost her breath, she spoke, and panted,
> That she did make defect perfection,
> And, breathless, power breathe forth.   (II. ii. 233.)

It is such doings that raise the gorge of the
genteel Octavius, who has no sense for popular
pleasures, whether we call them simple or vulgar.
But the daughter of the Ptolemies is less fastidious,
and is as ready as Antony to escape from the
etiquette of the court and take her share in these
unceremonious frolics. Yet it is not only these
lighter moods and moments that draw them together.
In the depth of his mistrust, Antony recalls the
"grave charm" of his enchantress ; and she, when
he is no more, remembers that

> his voice was propertied
> As all the tuned spheres.   (v. ii. 83.)

But what of serious and elevated they have in common gains warmth and colour by their mutual
delight in much that is neither one nor other. He
tells her,

> But that your royalty
> Holds idleness your subject, I should take you
> For idleness itself.   (I. iii. 91.)

And he pays homage to her in every mood :

> Fie, wrangling queen !
> Whom everything becomes, to chide, to laugh,
> To weep ; whose every passion fully strives
> To make itself, in thee, fair and admired !   (I. i. 48.)

It is as genuine and catholic admiration as Florizel's for Perdita :

> What you do
> Still betters what is done. . . .
> Each your doing,
> So singular in each particular,
> Crowns what you are doing in the present deed,
> That all your acts are queens.   (*W.T.* iv. iv. 135.)

But apart from their sincerity and range, how different are the two tributes : Florizel's all innocence and simplicity, Antony's *raffiné* and sophisticated. We feel from his words that he would endorse Shakespeare's ambiguous praise of his own dark lady :

> Whence hast thou this becoming of things ill,
> That in the very refuse of thy deeds
> There is such strength and warrantise of skill,
> That, in my mind, thy worst all best exceeds ?
> (*Sonnet* CL. 5.)

Does not Enobarbus speak in almost exactly the same way of the Cleopatra that Antony adores ?

> Vilest things
> Become themselves in her ; that the holy priests
> Bless her when she is riggish.   (II. ii. 243.)

Thus the two are alike not only in great and indifferent things, but in their want of steadfastness, their want of principle, their compliance with baseness. Hence they encourage each other in what debilitates and degrades, as well as in what fortifies and exalts. At its worst their love has something divine about it, but often it seems a divine orgy rather than a divine inspiration. Not seldom does it lead to madness and ignominy. That Antony loses the world for it is a small matter and even proves his grandeur of soul. But for it, besides " offending reputation," he profanes his inward honour as well ; and that unmasks it as the Siren and Fury of their lives.   Indeed, such love is self-destructive, and for it the lovers sacrifice the means of securing it against the hostile power of things. Yet, just because it is so plenary and permeating, it becomes an inspiration too.   When its prodigal largesse fails, at the hour when it is stripped of its inessential charms, the lovers are thrown back on itself ; and at once it elevates them both.   Antony, believing Cleopatra dead, and not yet undeceived as to the part that he fancies she played at the last, thinks only of following her to entreat and obtain a reconciliation.

> I will o'ertake thee, Cleopatra, and
> Weep for my pardon.   (IV. xiv. 44.)

When he learns that she still lives, no reproach crosses his lips for the deceit ; his only wish as the blood flows from his breast is to be borne " where Cleopatra bides " to take a last farewell.   He wrestles with death till he receives the final embrace :

> I am dying, Egypt, dying : only
> I here importune death awhile, until
> Of many thousand kisses the poor last
> I lay upon thy lips.   (IV. xv. 18.)

Thereafter he has no thought of himself but only of her, counselling her in complete self-abnegation to seek of Cæsar her honour with her safety, and recommending her to trust only Proculeius—one who, as we soon learn, would be eager to preserve her life.

And her love, too, though perhaps more fitfully, yet all the more strikingly, is deepened and solemnised by trial.   After Actium it quite loses its element of mockery and petulance.   Her flout at Antony's negligence before the battle is the last we hear her utter.   Henceforth, whether she protests her faith, or speeds him to the fight, or welcomes him on his return, her words have a new seriousness

and weight.[1] Her feeling seems to become simpler
and sincerer as her fortunes cloud, and at her lover's
death it is nature alone that triumphs. In the first
shock of bereavement Iras, attempting consolation,
addresses her as "Royal Egypt, Empress"; and
she replies :

> No more, but e'en a woman, and commanded
> By such poor passion as the maid that milks
> And does the meanest chares.   (IV. XV. 72.)

Her grief for her great loss, a grief, perhaps, hardly
anticipated by herself, is in her own eyes her teacher,
and "begins to make a better life." Even now she
may falter, if the usual interpretation of her fraud
with the treasure is correct. Even now, at all
events, she has to be urged by the natural and royal
but not quite unimpeachable motive, the dread of
external disgrace. Cleopatra is very human to the
last. Her weaknesses do not disappear, but they
are but as fuel to the flames of her love by which
they are bred and which they help to feed. It is
still as the "curled Antony" she pictures her dead
lover, and it is in "crown and robe" that she will
receive that kiss which it is her heaven to have.
But even in this there is a striking similarity to
Antony's expectation of the land where "souls do
couch on flowers," and where they will be the cyno-
sure of the gazing ghosts. Their oneness of heart
and feeling is indeed now complete, and their love
is transfigured. It is at his call she comes, and his
name is the last word she utters, before she lays the
second asp on her arm. The most wonderful touch
of all is that now she feels her right to be considered
his wife. This, of course, is due to Shakespeare,
but it is not altogether new. It occurs in Daniel's

[1] Le plus grand miracle de l'amour, c'est de guérir de la coquet-
terie.—*La Rochefoucauld.*

tragedy, when she calls on Antony's spirit to pray the gods on her behalf :

> O if in life we could not severd be,
> Shall death divide our bodies now asunder?
> Must thine in Egypt, mine in Italy,
> Be kept the Monuments of Fortune's wonder?
> If any powres be there whereas thou art
> (Sith our country gods betray our case),
> O worke they may their gracious helpe impart
> To save thy wofull *wife* from such disgrace.

It also occurs twice in Plutarch, from whom Daniel probably obtained it. In the *Comparison of Demetrius and Marcus Antonius*, he writes : [1]

> Antonius first of all married two wives together, the which never Romane durst doe before, but him self.

In the biography, when Cleopatra has lifted him to the Monument, we are told :

> Then she dryed up his blood that had berayed his face, and called him her Lord, *her husband*, and Emperour, forgetting her owne miserie and calamity for the pitie and compassion she tooke of him.

It is not, therefore, the invention of the idea, but the new position in which he introduces it, that shows Shakespeare's genius. It has no great significance, either in Plutarch or Daniel. In the one, Cleopatra is speaking in compassion of Antony ; in the other, she is bespeaking Antony's compassion for herself. But in Shakespeare, when she scorns life for her love, and prefers honour with the aspic's bite to safety with shame, she feels that now at last their union has the highest sanction, and that all the dross of her nature is purged away from the pure spirit :

> Husband, I come :
> Now to that name my courage prove my title !
> I am fire and air : my other elements
> I give to baser life. (v. ii. 290.)

---

[1] Cleopatra was actually married to Antony, as has been proved by Professor Ferrero. But Plutarch nowhere else mentions the circumstance, and it contradicts the whole tenor of his narrative.

Truly their love, which at first seemed to justify Aristophanes against Diotima, just because it is true love, turns out to answer Diotima's description after all.   Or perhaps it rather suggests the conclusion in the *Phaedrus* : " I have shown this of all inspirations to be the noblest and the highest, and the offspring of the highest ; and that he who loves the beautiful, is called a lover, because he partakes of it." Antony and Cleopatra, with all their errors, are lovers and partake of beauty, which we cannot say of the arid respectability of Octavius.   It is well and right that they should perish as they do : but so perishing they have made their full atonement ; and we can rejoice that they have at once triumphed over their victor, and left our admiration for them free.

CORIOLANUS

CHAPTER I

POSITION OF THE PLAY BEFORE THE ROMANCES. ITS POLITICAL AND ARTISTIC ASPECTS

Coriolanus seems to have been first published in the folio of 1623, and is one of the sixteen plays described as not formerly "entered to other men." In this dearth of information there has naturally been some debate on the date of its composition, yet the opinions of critics with few exceptions agree as to its general position and tend more and more to limit the period of uncertainty to a very few months.

This comparative unanimity is due to the evidence of style, versification, and treatment rather than of reminiscences and allusions. Though a fair number of the latter have been discovered or invented, some of them are vague and doubtful, some inapposite or untenable, hardly any are of value from their inherent likelihood.

Of these, one which has been considered to give the *terminus a quo* in dating the play was pointed out by Malone in the fable of Menenius. Plutarch's account is somewhat bald :

> On a time all the members of mans bodie, dyd rebell against the bellie, complaining of it, that it only remained in the middest of the bodie, without doing any thing, neither

dyd beare any labour to the maintenaunce of the rest:
whereas all other partes and members dyd labour payne-
fully, and was very carefull to satisfie the appetites and
desiers of the bodie. And so the bellie, all this notwithstanding, laughed at their follie, and sayed: "It is true,
I first receyve all meates that norishe mans bodie: but
afterwardes I send it againe to the norishement of other
partes of the same. Even so (quoth he) O you, my masters,
and cittizens of Rome: the reason is a like betwene the
Senate, and you. For matters being well digested, and their
counsells throughly examined, touching the benefit of the
common wealth; the Senatours are cause of the common
commoditie that commeth unto every one of you."

This is meagre compared with Shakespeare's full-
blooded and dramatic narrative, and though in any
case the chief credit for the transformation would be
due to the poet, who certainly contributes most of
the picturesque and humorous details and all of the
interruptions and rejoinders, it has been thought
that he owes something to the expanded version
in Camden's *Remaines concerning Britaine*, which
appeared in 1605.

All the members of the body conspired against the
stomacke, as against the swallowing gulfe of all their
labors; for whereas the eies beheld, the eares heard, the
handes labored, the feete traveled, the tongue spake, and
all partes performed their functions, onely the stomacke lav
idle and consumed all. Here uppon they ioyntly agreed
al to forbeare their labors, and to pine away their lasie
and publike enemy. One day passed over, the second
followed very tedious, but the third day was so grievous
to them all, that they called a common Counsel; the eyes
waxed dimme, the feete could not support the bodie, the
armes waxed lasie, the tongue faltered, and could not lay
open the matter; therefore they all with one accord desired
the advise of the Heart. Then Reason layd open before
them that hee against whome they had proclaimed warres,
was the cause of all this their misery: For he as their
common steward, when his allowances were withdrawne of
necessitie withdrew theirs fro them, as not receiving that
he might allow. Therefore it were a farre better course
to supply him, than that the limbs should faint with hunger.
So by the perswasion of Reason, the stomacke was served,
the limbes comforted, and peace re-established. Even so

it fareth with the bodies of Common-weale; for albeit the Princes gather much, yet not so much for themselves, as for others: So that if they want, they cannot supply the want of others; therefore do not repine at Princes heerein, but respect the common good of the whole publike estate.

It has been pointed out,[1] in criticism of Malone's suggestion, that in some respects Shakespeare's version agrees with Plutarch's and disagrees with Camden's. Thus in Camden it is the stomach and not the belly that is denounced, the members do not confine themselves to words but proceed to deeds, it is not the belly but Reason from its seat in the heart that sets forth the moral. This is quite true, but no one doubted that Shakespeare got from Plutarch his general scheme; the only question is whether he fitted into it details from another source. It has also been objected that Shakespeare was quite capable of making the additions for himself; and this also is quite true as the other and more vivid additions prove, if it needed to be proved. Nevertheless, when we find Shakespeare's expansions in the play following some of the lines laid down by Camden in the *Remaines*, occasionally with verbal coincidence, it seems not unlikely that the *Remaines* were known to him. Thus he does not treat the members like Plutarch in the mass, but like Camden enumerates them and their functions; the stomach in Camden like the belly in Shakespeare is called a gulf, a term that is very appropriate but that would not occur to everyone; the heart where Reason dwells and to which Camden's mutineers appeal for advice, is the counsellor heart in Shakespeare's list.[2] Moreover, it has been shown by

---

[1] *E.g.*, by Delius. *Shakespeare's Coriolanus in seinem Verhältniss zum Coriolanus des Plutarch (Jahrbuch der D.-Sh. Gesellschaft*, xi. 1876).

[2] In some respects Shakespeare's details remind me more of Livy than either of Plutarch or Camden; *e.g.*, Inde apparuisse ventris quoque haud segne ministerium esse, nec magis ali quam alere eum,

Mr. Sidney Lee that there were friendly relations between the two men. So it is a conjecture no less probable than pleasing that Shakespeare owed a few hints to the great and patriotic scholar whom Ben Jonson hailed as "most reverend head."

It is clear, however, that if the debt to Camden was more certain than it is, this would only give us the year before which *Coriolanus* could not have been written, and it would not of itself establish a date shortly after the publication of the *Remaines*.

reddentem in omnis corporis partes hunc, quo vivimus vigemusque, divisum pariter in venas maturum confecto cibo sanguinem." (II. 32.)

Cf.
> I receive the general food at first,
> Which you do live upon ; . . .
> . . . but, if you do remember,
> I send it through the rivers of your blood, . . .
> And through the cranks and offices of man,
> The strongest nerves and small inferior veins
> From me receive that natural competency
> Whereby they live. (I. i. 135 seq.)

This certainly is liker Livy than Plutarch ; and besides the chances of Shakespeare having read Livy in the original, we have to bear in mind that in 1600 Philemon Holland published the *Romane Historie written by Titus Livius of Padua*. His version, as it is difficult to procure, may be quoted in full :

> Whilome (quoth he) when as in mans bodie, all the parts thereof agreed not, as now they do in one, but each member had a several interest and meaning, yea, and a speech by it selfe ; so it befel, that all other parts besides the belly, thought much and repined that by their carefulness, labor, and ministerie, all was gotten, and yet all little enough to serve it : and the bellie it selfe lying still in the mids of them, did nothing else but enjoy the delightsome pleasures brought unto her. Wherupon they mutinied and conspired altogether in this wise, That neither the hands should reach and convey food to the mouth, nor the mouth receive it as it came, ne yet the teeth grind and chew the same. In this mood and fit, whiles they were minded to famish the poore bellie, behold the other lims, yea and the whole bodie besides, pined, wasted, and fel into an extreme consumption. Then was it wel seen, that even the very belly also did no smal service, but fed the other parts, as it received food it selfe : seeing that by working and concocting the meat throughlie, it digesteth and distributeth by the veines into all parts, that fresh and perfect blood whereby we live, we like, and have our full strength. Comparing herewith, and making his application, to wit, how like this intestine, and inward sedition of the bodie, was to the full stomacke of the Commons, which they had taken and borne against the Senatours, he turned quite the peoples hearts.

Such a date has been suggested, but the reference to Camden has been made merely auxiliary to the argument of a connection between the play and the general circumstances of the time. This surmise, for it can hardly be called more, will presently be noticed, and meanwhile it may be said that the internal evidence is all against it.

On the other hand, an excessively late date has been proposed for *Coriolanus* on the ground of its alleged indebtedness to the fourth edition of North, of which it is sometimes maintained that Shakespeare possessed a copy. Till 1612, Volumnia says in her great appeal :

> Think now with thy selfe, how much more *unfortunatly*, then all the women livinge we are come hether ;

but in the fourth edition this becomes *unfortunate*, and so Shakespeare has it :

> Think with thyself
> How more unfortunate than all living women
> Are we come hither. (v. iii. 96.)

But the employment of the adjectival for the adverbial form is a very insignificant change, and is, besides, suggested by the rhythm. Moreover, such importance as it might have, is neutralised by a counter argument on similar lines, which would go to prove that one of the first two editions was used. In them Coriolanus tells Aufidius :

> If I had feared death, I would not have come hither to have put my life in hazard : but prickt forward with *spite* and desire I have to be revenged of them that thus have banished me, etc.

In 1603, this suffers the curtailment, "pricked forward with desire to be revenged, etc." But Shakespeare says :

> If
> I had fear'd death, of all men i' the world
> I would have 'voided thee, but in mere *spite*,
> To be full quit of those my banishers,
> Stand I before thee here. (IV. v. 86.)

This argument is no doubt of the same precarious kind as the other ; still in degree it is stronger, for the persistence of *spite* is much more distinctive than the disappearance of a suffix.

In any case this verbal detail is a very narrow foundation to build a theory upon, which there is nothing else to support, except one of those alluring and hazardous guesses that would account for the play in the conditions of the time. This, too, as in the previous case, may be reserved for future discussion. Meanwhile the dating of *Coriolanus*, subsequently to 1612, is not only opposed to internal evidences of versification and style, but would separate it from Shakespeare's tragedies and introduce it among the romantic plays of his final period.

If, however, we turn to the supposed allusions that make for the intermediate date of 1608 or 1609, we do not find them much more satisfactory.

Thus it has been argued that the severe cold in January, 1608, when even the Thames was frozen over, furnished the simile :

> You are no surer, no,
> Than is the coal of fire upon the ice.   (i. i. 176.)

But surely there must have been many opportunities for such things to present themselves to Shakespeare's observation or imagination, by the time that he was forty-four years old.

Again Malone found a reference to James's proclamation in favour of breeding silk-worms and the importation of young mulberry trees during 1609, in the expression :

> Now humble as the ripest mulberry
> That will not hold the handling.   (iii. ii. 79.)

But even in *Venus and Adonis* Shakespeare had told how, in admiration of the youth's beauty, the birds

> Would bring him mulberries and ripe-red cherries ;   (1103.)

and in *Midsummer-Night's Dream*, Titania orders the fairies to feed Bottom

With purple grapes, green figs, and mulberries.   (III. i. 170.)

A third of these surmises is even more gratuitous. Chalmers calls attention to the repeated references in the play to famine and dearth, and supposes they were suggested by the scarcity which prevailed in England during the years 1608 and 1609. But the lack of corn among the people is one of the pre-suppositions of the story, to which Plutarch also recurs.

There is only one allusion that has strength to stand by itself, though even it is doubtful; and it belongs to a different class, for, if authentic, it is suggested not to Shakespeare by contemporary events, but to a contemporary writer by Shake-speare. Malone noticed the coincidence between the line, " He lurch'd all swords of the garlànd" (II. ii. 105), and a remark in *Epicoene :* " You have lurched your friends of the better half of the garland (v. i.) ; and considered that here, as not infrequently, Ben Jonson was girding at Shakespeare. After-wards he withdrew his conjecture because he found a similar expression in one of Nashe's pamphlets, and concluded that it was proverbial; but it has been pointed out in answer to this [1] that Nashe has only the *lurch* and not the supplementary words, *of the garland*, while it is to the phrase as a whole, not to the component parts, that the individual character belongs. This, if not absolutely beyond challenge, is at least very cogent, and probably few will deny that *Coriolanus* must have been in existence before *Epicoene* was acted in January 1609, old style.

How long before? And did it succeed or precede *Antony and Cleopatra*?

[1] Introduction to the Clarendon Press Edition.

Attempts have been made to find in that play immediate anticipations of the mental attitude and of particular thoughts that appear in *Coriolanus*. Thus Octavia's dilemma in her petition has been quoted :

> A more unhappy lady,
> If this division chance, ne'er stood between,
> Praying for both parts :
> The good gods will mock me presently,
> When I shall pray, " O, bless my lord and husband ! "
> Undo that prayer, by crying out as loud,
> " O, bless my brother ! "   Husband win, win brother,
> Prays, and destroys the prayer ; no midway
> 'Twixt these extremes at all.   (III. iv. 12.)

And this has been taken as a link with Volumnia's perplexity :

> And to poor we
> Thine enmity's most capital : thou barr'st us
> Our prayers to the gods, which is a comfort
> That all but we enjoy : for how can we,
> Alas, how can we for our country pray,
> Whereto we are bound, together with thy victory,
> Whereto we are bound ?   Alack, or we must lose
> The country, our dear nurse, or else thy person,
> Our comfort in the country.   We must find
> An evident calamity, though we had
> Our wish, which side should win.   (v. iii. 103.)

But then the same sort of conflict puzzles the Lady Blanch in *King John* :

> Which is the side that I must go withal?
> I am with both : each army hath a hand ;
> And in their rage, I having hold of both,
> They whirl asunder and dismember me.
> Husband, I cannot pray that thou mayst win ;
> Uncle, I needs must pray that thou mayst lose ;
> Father, I may not wish the fortune thine ;
> Grandam, I will not wish thy wishes thrive :
> Whoever wins, on that side shall I lose
> Assured loss before the match be play'd.   (III. i. 327.)

Could not this style of argument be used to prove that *Coriolanus* and *Antony and Cleopatra* immediately followed *King John*?

Or again the contemptuous descriptions of the people by Octavius, Cleopatra and Antony himself have been treated as preludes to the more savage vituperations in *Coriolanus*. But *Julius Caesar* gives an equally unflattering account of mob law, and some of Casca's gibes would quite fit the mouth of Coriolanus or Menenius. On these lines we should be as much entitled to make this play the direct successor of the first as of the second of its companions, a theory that would meet with scant acceptance. The truth is that whenever Shakespeare deals with the populace, he finds some one to disparage it in the mass.

Still there is little doubt that *Coriolanus* does occupy the position these arguments would assign to it, but the real evidence is of another kind. To begin with there is what Coleridge describes in *Antony and Cleopatra* as the "happy valiancy of style," which first becomes marked in that play, which is continued in this, and which henceforth in a greater or less degree characterises all Shakespeare's work. Then even more conclusive are the peculiarities of metre, and especially the increase in the total of weak and light endings together with the decrease of the light by themselves. Finally, there is the conduct of the story to a conclusion that proposes no enigma and inflicts no pang, but even more than in the case of *Macbeth* satisfies, and even more than in the case of *Antony and Cleopatra* uplifts the heart, without troublesome questionings on the part of the reader. "As we close the book," says Mr. Bradley, "we feel more as we do at the close of *Cymbeline* than as we do at the close of *Othello*." We cannot be far wrong in placing it in the last months of 1608 or the first months of 1609.

Attempts have been made to find suggestions of a personal kind for Shakespeare's choice of the subject. The extreme ease with which they have been discovered for the various dates proposed may well teach us caution. Thus Professor Brandl who assigns it an earlier position than most critics and discusses it before *Lear* sees in it the outcome of events that occurred in the first years of the century.

The material for *Coriolanus* was perhaps put in Shakespeare's way by a contemporary tragedy which keenly excited the Londoners, and especially the courtly and literary circles, about 1603 and 1604. Sir Walter Raleigh had been one of the most splendid gentlemen at the court of Elizabeth, was a friend of Spenser and Ben Jonson, had himself tried his hand at lyric poetry, and in addition as adventurous officer had discovered Virginia and annexed Guiana. He was the most highly considered but also the best hated man in England: for his behaviour was domineering, in the consciousness of his innate efficiency he showed without disguise his contempt for the multitude, the farm of wine-licenses granted him by the Queen had made him objectionable to the pothouse politicians, and his opposition in parliament to a bill for cheapening corn had recently drawn on him new unpopularity. He, therefore, shortly after the accession of James succumbed to the charge, that he, the scarred veteran of the Spanish wars, the zealous advocate of new expeditions against Spain, had involved himself in treasonous transactions with this, the hereditary foe of England. In November 1603 the man who had won treasure-fleets and vast regions for his country, almost fell a victim to popular rage as he was being transferred from one prison to another.[1] A month later he was condemned to death on wretched evidence : he was not yet executed however but locked up in the Tower, so that men were in suspense as to his fate for many years. To depict his character his biographer Edwards involuntarily hit on some lines of Shakespeare's *Coriolanus*. The figure of the Roman, who had deserved well but incurred hatred, of the patriot whom his aristocratic convictions drive to the enemy, was already familiar to the dramatist from North's translation of Plutarch ; and Camden's *Remaines concerning Britaine*, which had newly appeared in 1605 contributed a more detailed version of the fable of the belly and the members, first set forth by Livy. From this mood and about this time *Coriolanus*, for the dating of which only the very relative evidence of metre and style is available, may most probably have proceeded.[2]

[1] Strictly speaking, from the Tower to Winchester for trial.
[2] *Shakespeare*, in the *Führende Geister* Series.

In this passage, Professor Brandl has brought out some of the considerations that would lend the case of Raleigh a peculiar interest in the eyes of men like Shakespeare, and has made the most of the parallels between his story and the story of Coriolanus.[1] It is necessary of course to look away from almost all the points except those enumerated, for when we remember Sir Walter's robust adulation of Elizabeth, and tortuous policy at court, it is difficult to pair him with tne Roman who "would not flatter Neptune for his trident," and of whom it was said, " his heart's his mouth." Still the analogies in career and character are there, so far as they go ; but they are insufficient to prove that the actual suggested the poetical tragedy, still less to override the internal evidence, relative though that be ; for they could linger and germinate in the poet's mind to bring forth fruit long afterwards : as for example the treason and execution of Biron in 1602 inspired Chapman to write *The Conspiracie* and *The Tragedie* which were acted in 1608.

Again, in connection with what seems to be the actual date, an attempt has been made to explain one prominent characteristic of the play from a domestic experience through which Shakespeare had just passed. His mother died in September 1608, and her memory is supposed to be enshrined in the picture of Volumnia. As Dr. Brandes puts it :[2]

> The death of a mother is always a mournfully irreparable loss, often the saddest a man can sustain. We can realise how deeply· it would go to Shakespeare's heart when we

---

[1] Rather more than the most. It is special pleading to interpret Raleigh's arguments against the *Act for sewing Hemp* and the *Statute of Tillage* in 1601, as directed against cheap corn. His point was rather that coercive legislation in regard to agriculture hindered production and was oppressive to poor men. Nor am I aware that his speeches on these occasions increased his unpopularity,—which, no doubt, was already great.

[2] *William Shakespeare, a critical study.*

remember the capacity for profound and passionate feeling with which nature had blessed and cursed him. We know little of his mother; but judging from that affinity which generally exists between famous sons and their mothers, we may suppose she was no ordinary woman. Mary Arden, who belonged to an old and honourable family, which traced its descent (perhaps justly) back to the days of Edward the Confessor, represented the haughty patrician element in the Shakespeare family. Her ancestors had borne their coat of arms for centuries, and the son would be proud of his mother for this among other reasons, just as the mother would be proud of her son. In the midst of the prevailing gloom and bitterness of his spirits,[1] this fresh blow fell upon him, and out of his weariness of life as his surroundings and experiences showed it to him, recalled this one mainstay to him—his mother. He remembered all she had been to him for forty-four years, and the thoughts of the man and the dreams of the poet were thus led to dwell upon the significance in a man's life of this unique form, comparable to no other—his mother. Thus it was that, although his genius must follow the path it had entered upon and pursue it to the end, we find, in the midst of all that was low and base in his next work, this one sublime mother-form, the proudest and most highly-wrought that he has drawn, Volumnia.

Thus Shakespeare, in a mood of pessimism, and in the desolation of bereavement, turned to a subject that he treated on its seamy side, but redeemed from its meanness by exalting the idea of the mother in obedience to his own pious regrets. Even, however, if we grant the assumptions in regard to Mary Arden's pedigree and her aristocratic family pride, and the unique support she gave to her son, does this statement give a true account of the impression the play produces? Is it the fact that, apart from the figure of Volumnia, the story is " low and base," and is it not rather the record of grand though perverted heroism? Is it the fact that Volumnia stands

[1] In point of fact "gloom and bitterness" can be less justly attributed to *Antony and Cleopatra* and *Coriolanus* than to any of the later tragedies, and less justly to *Coriolanus* than to *Antony and Cleopatra* ; but Dr. Brandes treats *Troilus and Cressida* as coming between them, and if that position could be vindicated for it, the phrase would be defensible.

out as a study of motherhood, such as the first heart-
ache at a mother's death would inspire ? The most
sympathetic traits in her portrait are drawn by
Plutarch. Shakespeare's many touches supply the
harshness, the ambition, the prejudice. If these
additions are due to Shakespeare's wistful broodings
on his own mother, a woman with a son of genius
may well hope that he will never brood on her.

Then, especially by those who advocate a later
date for the play, a political motive for it has been
discovered. Mr. Whitelaw, who would assign it to
1610, when James's first parliament was dissolved,
conjectures that " in *Coriolanus* Shakespeare intended a two-fold warning, to the pride of James,
and to the gathering resistance of the Commons." [1]
Mr. Garnett, [2] on the other hand, maintains that
" Coriolanus, to our apprehension, manifestly reflects
the feelings of a conservative observer of the contests
between James and his refractory parliaments," and
placing it after the *Tempest*, would connect it with
the dissolution of the Addled Parliament in 1614.
But since the friction between King and Commons,
though it intensified with the years, was seldom
entirely absent, this theory adapts itself pretty well
to any date, and Dr. Brandes, while refusing to
trace the spirit of the play to any "momentary
political situation," adopts the general principle as
quite compatible with the state of affairs in 1608.
He puts the case as follows :

> Was it Shakespeare's intention to allude to the strained
> relations existing between James and his parliament ? Does
> *Coriolanus* represent an aristocratically-minded poet's side-
> glance at the political situation in England ? I fancy it does.
> Heaven knows there was little resemblance between the
> amazingly craven and vacillating James and the haughty,

[1] *Coriolanus.* Rugby Edition.

[2] In the conclusion of his essay on the *Date and Occasion of the
Tempest. Universal Review, 1889.*

resolute hero of Roman tradition, who fought a whole garrison single-handed. Nor was it personal resemblance which suggested the comparison, but a general conception of the situation as between a beneficent power on the one hand, and the people on the other. He regarded the latter wholly as mob, and looked upon their struggle for freedom as mutiny, pure and simple.

This theory, however, in all its varieties seems to attribute too definite an influence to the controversies of the hour, and to turn Shakespeare too much into the politician prepense. Certainly *Coriolanus* is not meant to be a constitutional manifesto ; probably it does not, even at unawares, idealise a contemporary dispute ; it is hardly likely that Shakespeare so much as intrudes conscious allusions to the questions then at issue. And this on account not only of the particular opinions attributed to him, but, much more, of his usual practice in poetic creation. Do any of these alleged incentives in the circumstances, public or private, of his life go far to explain his attraction to a story and selection of it, its power over him and his power over it ? Doubtless in realising the subject that took his fancy, he would draw on the stores of his experience as well as his imagination. In dealing with the tragedy of a proud and unpopular hero of antiquity, very possibly he would be helped by what he knew of the tragedy of a proud and unpopular worthy of his own time. In dealing with the influence of a mother and the reverence of a son, very probably the memories of his own home would hover before his mind. In dealing with the plebeians and patricians of Rome, he would inevitably fill in the details from his knowledge of the burgesses and nobles of England, and he might get hints for his picture of the by-gone struggle, from the struggle that he himself could watch. But it is the story of Coriolanus that comes first and that absorbs all such material into itself, just as the seed in its growth assimilates nourishment from the earth and sunshine and rain. These things are not the seed. The experiences are utilised in the interest of the play ; the play is not utilised in the interest of the experiences.

It is particularly important to emphasise this in view of the circumstance that *Coriolanus* has often been regarded as a drama of principles rather than of character, even by those who refrain from reading into it any particular reference. But Shakespeare's supreme preoccupation is always with his fable, which explains, and is explained by, human nature in action. He does not set out to commend or censure or examine a precept or a theory or a doctrine. Of course the life of men is concerned with such matters, and he could not exclude them without being untrue to his aim. Thus, to take the most obvious example, it is impossible to treat of character with a total omission of ethical considerations, since character is connected with conduct, and conduct has its ethical aspect ; and, indeed, success in getting to the truth of character depends very much on the keenness of the moral insight. It is very largely Shakespeare's moral insight that gives him his unrivalled position among the interpreters of men ; and we may, if we like, derive any number of improving lessons from his works. But he is an artist, not a moralist ; and he wrote for the story, not for the moral. Just in the same way an architect seeks to design a beautiful or convenient building, not to illustrate mechanical laws. Nevertheless, in proportion as these are neglected, the building will not rise or will not last ; and if they are obeyed, however unconsciously, the illustration of them will be provided. In Charlotte Brontë's *Shirley*, when Caroline gives Robert Moore this very play to read, he asks, " Is it to operate like a sermon ? " And she answers : " It is to stir you ; to give you new sensations. *It is to make you feel life strongly*"—(that is the main thing, and then comes the indirect consequence)—"not only your virtues but your vicious perverse points."

Now just as in all Shakespeare's dramas, though or rather because they are personal, the ethical considerations cannot be excluded ; so in a drama that moves through a constitutional crisis, though or rather because it, too, is personal, political considerations cannot be excluded. They are there, though it is on the second plane. And just as his general delineation of character would be unsatisfactory if his moral insight were at fault, so his delineation of the characters that play their part in this history would be unsatisfactory if his political insight were at fault. He is not necessarily bound to appreciate correctly the conditions that prevailed in reality or by report : that is required only for historical accuracy or fidelity to tradition. But he is bound to appreciate the conditions as he imagines them, and not to violate in his treatment of them the principles that underlie all political society.

Yet this he has been accused of doing. He has been charged with a hatred of the people that is incompatible even with a benevolent tyranny, and with a glorification of the protagonist's ruthless disregard of popular claims. Thus Dr. Brandes, in the greater part of a chapter, dwells upon Shakespeare's "physical aversion for the atmosphere of the people," and "the absence of any humane consideration for the oppressed condition of the poor"; and, on the other hand, upon his "hero-worship" for Marcius, whom he glorifies as a demigod. Though admitting the dramatist's detestation of the crime of treason, this critic sees no implicit censure of what preceded it. To him Shakespeare's impression of life as conveyed in the play is that "there must of necessity be formed round the solitary great ones of the earth, a conspiracy of envy and hatred raised by the small and mean."

It is no doubt true that this and many other
Shakespearian plays abound in hostile or scornful
vituperation of the people ; and not only of their
moral and mental demerits ; their sweaty clothes,
their rank breaths, their grossness and uncleanness
are held up to derision and execration. But are we
to attribute these sentiments to Shakespeare ? Such
utterances are *ex hypothesi* dramatic, and show us
merely the attitude of the speakers, who are without
exception men of the opposite camp or unfriendly
critics. Only once does Shakespeare give his personal, or rather, impersonal estimate. It is in the
Induction to the second part of *Henry IV.*, when
Rumour, whose words, in this respect at least, cannot
be influenced by individual bias, speaks of

> the blunt monster of uncounted heads,
> The still-discordant, wavering multitude.   (line 18.)

That is, the populace as a whole is stupid, disunited,
fickle. And this is how, apart from the exaggerations
of their opponents, Shakespeare invariably treats
crowds of citizens, whether in the ancient or modern
world. He therefore with perfect consistency regards
them as quite unfit for rule, and when they have it
or aspire to it, they cover themselves with ridicule
or involve themselves in crime. But this is by no
means to hate them. On the contrary he is kindly
enough to individual representatives, and he certainly
believes in the sacred obligation of governing them
for their good. Where then are the governors to
be found ? Shakespeare answers : in the royal and
aristocratic classes. It is the privilege and duty of
those born in high position to conduct the whole
community aright. Shakespeare can do justice to
the Venetian oligarchy and the English monarchy.
But while to him the rule of the populace is impossible, he also recognises that nobles and kings
may be unequal to their task. The majority of his

kings indeed are more or less failures ; his nobles—
and in this play, the patricians—often cut a rather
sorry figure. In short, popular government must be
wrong, but royal or aristocratic government need not
be right.

And this was exactly what historical experience
at the time seemed to prove. The Jacqueries, the
Peasants' Wars, the Wat Tyler or Jack Cade
Insurrections, were not calculated to commend demo-
cratic experiments ; and, on the other hand, the
authority of king and nobles had often, though not
always, secured the welfare of the state.

Now, holding these opinions, would Shakespeare
be likely to glorify Coriolanus ? Of course, in a
sense he does. There is a *Lues Boswelliana* to
which the dramatist like the biographer should and
must succumb. He must have a fellow-feeling for
his hero and understand from within all that can
be urged on his behalf. So Shakespeare glorifies
Coriolanus in the same way that he glorifies Hamlet or Brutus or Antony. That is, he appreciates
their greatness and explains their offences so that
we sympathise with them and do not regard them
as unaccountable aberrations ; but offences they
remain and they are not extenuated. On the
contrary they receive all due prominence and are
shown to bring about the tragic catastrophe. This
is even more the case with Coriolanus than with
some of the others. So much stress is laid on
his violence and asperities that to many he is anti-
pathetic, and the antipathy is reflected on the cause
that he champions. Gervinus says very truly :

> It will be allowed that from the example of Brutus many
> more would be won over to the cause of the people, than
> would be won over to aristocratic principles by Coriolanus.

Quite apart from the final apostasy he strikes the
unprejudiced reader as an example to eschew rather

than to imitate.   Charlotte Brontë, not a Shakespearian scholar but a woman of no less common
sense than genius, gives the natural interpretation
of his career in the passage I have already referred
to.   After Caroline and Moore have finished the
play, she makes the former ask concerning the hero :

> "Was he not faulty as well as great ? "
> Moore nodded.
>   "And what was his fault ?   What made him hated by the
> citizens ?   What caused him to be banished by his country-
> men ? "

She answers her own question by quoting Aufidius'
estimate, and proceeds :

> "And you must not be proud to your work people ; you
> must not neglect the chance of soothing them ; and you must
> not be of an inflexible nature, uttering a request as austerely
> as if it were a command."

That, so far as it goes, is a quite legitimate "moral "
to draw from the story ; and it is the obvious one.
   How then does Shakespeare conceive the political
situation ?   On the one side there is a despised and
famished populace, driven by its misery to demand
powers in the state that it cannot wisely use, and
trusting to leaders that are worse than itself.   On
the other side there is a prejudiced aristocracy, num-
bering competent men in its ranks, but disorganised
and, to some extent, demoralised by plebeian encroachments, so that it can no longer act with
its old efficiency and consistency.   And there is
one great aristocrat, pre-eminently consistent and
efficient, but whose greatness becomes mischievous
to himself and others, partly because it is out of
harmony with the times, partly because it is corrupted by his inordinate pride.   And to all these
persons, or groups of persons, Shakespeare's attitude,
as we shall see, is at once critical and sympathetic.
Admitting the conditions, we can only agree with
Coleridge's verdict : "This play illustrates the won-

derfully philosophic impartiality of Shakespeare's
politics.[1] And there is no reason why the conditions
should not be admitted. It is easy to imagine a
society in which the masses are not yet ripe for
self-government, and in which the classes are no
longer able to steer the state, while a gifted and
bigoted champion of tradition only makes matters
worse. Indeed, something similar has been exemplified in history oftener than once or twice.
Whether in point of fact Shakespeare's conception
is correct for the particular set of circumstances he
describes is quite another question, that concerns
neither the excellence of *Coriolanus* as a drama
nor the fairness of its political views, but solely its
fidelity to antiquarian truth and the accuracy of its
antiquarian *data.*

Clearly it was impossible for Shakespeare to
revive the spirit of the times in *Coriolanus*, even
to the extent that he had done so in *Julius Caesar*
or *Antony and Cleopatra*, for the simple reason that
in them, with whatever trespasses into fiction on the
part of himself or his authority, he was following the
record of what had actually taken place, while now
he was dealing with a legend that seems to have the
less foundation in fact the more it is examined. The
tribunate, with the establishment of which the whole
action begins, the opposition to which by Marcius is
his main offence, and the occupants of which play so
important a part in the proceedings, is now generally
held to be of much later origin than the supposed
date of the story. There is no agreement as to the
names of the chief persons ; Coriolanus is Cneius or
Caius, his mother is Veturia or Volumnia, his wife
is Volumnia or Vergilia, the Volscian leader Tullus
Aufidius or Amfidius or Attius Tullius. Even the
appellation Coriolanus rouses suspicion, for the be-
stowal of such titles seems to have been unknown

[1] *Notes on Plays of Shakespere*, 1818.

till long afterwards, and, in the view of some, points not to conquest but to origin ; and there are contradictory accounts of the hero's end. It has been conjectured [1] that the whole story arose in connection with religious observances and contains a large mythological admixture ; and we may remember how at the end it is associated with the erection of the temple to *Fortuna Muliebris*.

This much at least is beyond doubt, that the account given by Plutarch, from whom Shakespeare took his material, and even by Livy, whom he may have read, has much less matter-of-fact reality than characterises the later Roman lives. There are many discrepancies and contradictions, especially in Plutarch's description. Now he gives what we may consider an idealised picture of the plebs, attributing to it extraordinary self-control and sagacity, and again it is to him merely the rascal vulgar. Now he seems to approve the pliancy which the Senate showed on the advice of the older and wiser men, and again he seems to blame it as undignified. And the mixture of bravado and pusillanimity during the siege is almost unintelligible. Now the city sends the humblest embassages to the rebel, now it haughtily refuses to treat till he has withdrawn from Roman soil, and again it despatches what North calls " a goodly rabble of superstition and priestes " with new supplications.

From a narrative that teemed with incongruities like the above, Shakespeare was entitled to select the alternatives that would combine to a harmonious whole, and he rightly chose those that were nearest to his own comprehension and experience, though perhaps in doing so he failed to make the most of such elements of historic truth as the tradition may contain, and certainly effaced some of the antique colouring.

[1] By Ettore Pais. *Storia di Roma.* Vol. I.

But if Plutarch's *Coriolanus* has less foundation in fact than some of the later Lives, it is not without compensating advantages. The circumstance that it is in so large measure a legend, implies that the popular imagination has been busy working it up, and it already falls into great scenic crises which lend themselves of their own accord to the dramatist's art. It is rather remarkable in view of this that it had received so little attention from the tragedians of the time. Perhaps its two-fold remoteness, from world-wide historical issues on the one hand, and from specifically romantic feeling on the other, may have told against it. The stories of Lucretia and Virginia had as primitive and circumscribed a setting, and were nevertheless popular enough : but they have an emotional interest that appeals to the general taste. The story of Julius Caesar lacks the sentimental lure, but concerns such mighty issues that it was the best beloved of all. And next comes the story of Antony and Cleopatra, which in a high degree unites both attractions. But *Coriolanus*, even as treated by Shakespeare, is unsympathetic to many, and the legend is of so little historic significance that it is often omitted from modern handbooks of Roman history ; so, for these reasons, despite its pre-eminent fitness for the stage, it was generally passed over.

Not universally, however. It seems already to have engaged the attention of one important dramatist in France, the prolific and gifted Alexandre Hardy. Hardy began to publish his works only in 1623, and the volume containing his *Coriolan* appeared only in 1625 ; so there is hardly any possibility of Shakespeare's having utilised this play. And, on the other hand, it was certainly written before 1608, probably in the last years of the sixteenth century, but in any case by 1607, so there is even less possibility of its being influenced by

Shakespeare's treatment. All the more interesting is it to observe the coincidences that exist between them, and that are due to their having selected a great many of the same *motifs* from Plutarch's story. It shows that in that story Plutarch met the playwright half way, and justifies the statement of Hardy in his argument that " few subjects are to be found in Roman history which are worthier of the stage."[1] The number of subsequent French dramas with Coriolanus as hero proves that he was right, though in England, as so frequently, Shakespeare's name put a veto on new experiments.

Hardy's tragedy in style and structure follows the Senecan manner of Jodelle and Garnier, but he compromised with mediaeval fashions in so far as to adopt the peculiar modification of the "simultaneous" or " complex " decoration which is usual in his other plays. In accordance with that, several scenes were presented at the same time on the stage, and actors made their first speeches from the area appropriated to that one of them which the particular phase of the action required. There was thus considerable latitude in regard to the unity of place, and even more in regard to the unity of time ; but the freedom was not so great as in the Elizabethan theatre, for after all there was space only for a limited number of scenes, or " mansions " as they would formerly have been called. Generally there were five, two at each side and one at the back. In the *Coriolan* there were six, and there is as well a seventh place indicated in the play without scenical decoration.[2] Even so they are few, compared with the two and twenty[3] that Shakespeare employs ; and though no

---

[1] See *Théâtre d'Alexandre Hardy*, ed. Stengel.

[2] See M. Rigal's admirable treatise on *Hardy*.

[3] Of course these scenes are not marked in the folio, but on the whole there are good grounds for the division that has been adopted by modern editors.

doubt that number might be considerably reduced without injury to the effect, by running together localities that approximate in character and position, one street with another street, the forum with a public place and the like, still it would in any case exceed what Hardy allows himself. This may account for some of his omissions as compared with Shakespeare.

His scenarium includes the house of Coriolanus and the forum at Rome, the house of Coriolanus and the house of Amfidius at Antium, the Volscian camp near Rome, the council-hall at Antium, and in addition to these an indeterminate spot where Coriolanus soliloquises after his expulsion.[1] There is no room for Corioli, and this may be why Hardy begins somewhat later than Shakespeare with the collision between the hero and the people, and gets as far as the banishment by the end of the first act. In the second, Marcius leaves Rome, presents himself to Amfidius, and obtains the leadership of the Volscians. The third portrays the panic of the Romans and the reception of their embassage by Coriolanus. In the fourth, the Roman ladies make ready to accompany Volumnia on her mission, Amfidius schemes to use all Coriolanus' faults for his destruction, Volumnia arrives in the camp and makes her petition, which her son at length grants though he foresees the result. The fifth is occupied with his murder in the Senate House at Antium, and concludes with his mother's reception of the news.

Thus the sequence and selection of episodes are much the same in the two tragedies, except that Hardy, perhaps, as I have said, owing to the exigencies of his decorative system, does not begin till the exploit at Corioli is over, and adds, as he could do so by using once more Coriolanus' house in Rome, the final scene with Volumnia. Otherwise the

[1] See footnote 2 on previous page.

R

scaffolding of the plays is very similar, and it is because both follow closely the excellent guidance of Plutarch. But it is interesting also to note that some of their additions are similar, for when they were independently made, it shows how readily Plutarch's narrative suggested such supplements. Thus, as in Shakespeare, but not as in Plutarch, Volumnia counsels her son to bow his pride before the people, and he, though in the end consenting, at first refuses.

> *Volomnie.* Voicy le jour fatal qui te donne (mon fils)
> Par une humilité tes hayneurs deconfits ;
> Tu vaincras, endurant, la fiere ingratitude
> Et le rancoeur malin de ceste multitude.
> Tu charmes son courroux d'une submission ;
> Helas ! ne vueille donc croire à ta passion.
> Cede pour un moment, et la voila contente,
> Et tu accoiseras une horrible tourmente,
> Que Rome divisée ébranle à ton sujet :
> La pieté ne peut avoir plus bel objet,
> Et faire mieux paroistre à l'endroit d'une mere,
> A l'endroit du païs, qu'escoutant ma priere.
> *Coriolan.* Madame, on me verroit mille morts endurer,
> Plustôt que suppliant sa grace procurer,
> Plustôt qu'un peuple vil à bon tiltre se vante
> D'avoir en mon courage imprimé l'épouvante,
> Que ceux qui me devroient recognoistre seigneur,
> Se prévallent sur moy du plus petit honneur :
> Moy, fléchir le genoüil devant une commune !
> Non, je ne le veux faire, et ne crains sa rancune.

Thus Coriolanus, again as in Shakespeare but not as in Plutarch, accepts his banishment as a calamity to those that inflict it.

> Je luy obeirai, ouy ouy, je mettrai soin
> De quitter ces ingrats plustost qu'ils n'ont besoin.

Thus the machinations of Amfidius before the final cause of offence are amplified far beyond the limits of Plutarch, and these are in part excused by his previous rivalry with Coriolanus which, as in Shakespeare, is made ever so much more personal and graphic.

Un esperon d'honneur cent fois nous a conduits,
Aveugles de fureur, à ces termes reduits
De sentre-deffier [1] au front de chaque armée,
Vouloir mourir, ou seul vaincre de renommée.

In short, though Hardy's drama, as compared with
Shakespeare's, is a work of talent as compared with
a work of genius, it shows that the *Life* had in it
the material for a tragedy already rough-dressed,
with indications, obvious to a practised playwright,
of some of the processes that still were needed.

Shakespeare, then, was now dealing with a much
more tractable theme than in his previous Roman
plays, and this is evident in the finished product.
Technically and artistically it is a more perfect
achievement than either of them.   In *Julius Caesar*
the early disappearance of the titular hero does not
indeed affect the essential unity of the piece, but it
does, when all is said and done, involve, to the
feelings of most readers, a certain break in the
interest.   In *Antony and Cleopatra* the scattering
of the action through so many short scenes does not
interfere with the main conception, but it does
make the execution a little spasmodic.   In both
instances Shakespeare had to suit his treatment to
the material.   But that material in the case of
Coriolanus offered less difficulty.   It lay ready to
the dramatist's hand and took the shape that he
imposed, almost of itself.   The result is a masterpiece that, as an organic work of art, has been placed
on the level of Shakespeare's most independent
tragedies.[2]

Thus it is easy to see how the personality of the
hero dominates the complex story, as the heart
transmits the life-blood through the body and its

[1] S'entre-défier.

[2] *E.g.* by Viehoff, in his interesting essay, *Shakespeare's Coriolan*
(*Jahrbuch der D.-Sh. Gesellschaft*, Bd. iv. 1869), which has been used
in the following paragraphs.

members, and receives it back again; how his
character contains in itself the seeds of his offence
and its reparation; how the other figures are related
to him in parallel and contrast; how the two grand
interests, the conflict between Coriolanus and
Aufidius, the conflict between Coriolanus and the
people, intertwine, but always so that the latter
remains the principal strand; how the language is
suited to the persons, the circumstances, and the
prevailing tone. In short, whatever the relations in
which we consider the play, they seem, like the
radii of a circle, to depart from and meet in one
centre.

Hardly less admirable are the balance and
composition of the whole, which yet in no wise
impair the interest of the individual scenes. Dr.
Johnson indeed makes the criticism: "There is
perhaps too much bustle in the first act and too
little in the last." This possibly is more noticeable
when the play is acted than when it is read; but it
is fitting that from the noise and hubbub of the
struggle there should be a transition to the outward
quietude of the close that harmonises with the
inward acquiescence in the mind of reader or
spectator. Nor is the element of tumult entirely
lacking at the last. To the uproar in the street of
Rome, where the life of Marcius is threatened,
corresponds the uproar in the public place of Antium
where it is actually taken. But Dr. Johnson was
probably thinking of those battle scenes beloved by
Elizabethan audiences and generally wearisome to
modern taste. There are no fewer than five of
them in the first act, a somewhat plentiful allowance.
But they are written by no means exclusively in the
drum-and-trumpet style. On the contrary they are
rich in psychological interest, and bring home to us
many characteristics of the hero that we have to
realise. Not only are we witnesses of his prowess,

but his pride in Rome, his contempt of baseness, his rivalry with Aufidius, his power of rousing enthusiasm in the field, are all shown in relief. Such things lift these concessions to temporary fashion above the level of outworn crudities.

And the construction is very perfect too. Perhaps the crisis, understood as the acme of Coriolanus' success, when he is voted to the consulship in the middle of the third scene of the second act comes a little early. But crisis may bear another meaning. It may denote the decisive point of the conflict, and this is only reached in the centre of the play. To the supreme tension of the scenes that describe Coriolanus' denunciation of the Tribunes, the consultations in his house, his final condemnation, all that goes before gradually leads up, and from that all that follows after gradually declines. In the first act we are introduced to the circumstances, the opposition between the Romans and the Volsces, the Senate and the Plebs, and to all the leading characters, as well as Coriolanus and his friends and opponents, in an exposition that is not merely declaratory but is full of action and life : and we see that the situation is fraught with danger. In the second act we are shown more definitely how the grand disaster will come from the collision of Coriolanus with the people, and the cloud gathers even in the instant of his success. In the third the storm breaks, and, despite a momentary lull, in the end sweeps away all wonted land-marks. The fourth presents the change that follows in the whole condition of things : the rival of Aufidius has recourse to his generosity, the champion of Rome becomes her foe, and the people, after its heedless triumph, is plunged into dismay. In the fifth we proceed by carefully considered ways to the catastrophe : the deliverance of Rome from material and the hero from moral perdition, the expiation of his passion in death and the fruitless triumph of his rival.

But through this symmetrical rise and fall of the excitement, there is no abatement of the interest. Attention and suspense are always kept on the alert. They are secured partly by the diversity of the details and the swiftness of the fluctuations. Dr. Johnson says :

> The Tragedy of *Coriolanus* is one of the most amusing of our author's performances. The old man's merriment in Menenius, the lofty lady's dignity in Volumnia, the bridal modesty in Virgilia, the patrician and military haughtiness in Coriolanus, the plebeian malignity and tribunition insolence in Brutus and Sicinius, make a very pleasing and interesting variety ; and the various revolutions of the hero's fortune fill the mind with anxious curiosity.

This is so because, while the agitation culminates in the third act, the emotion is neither overtaxed in the two that precede nor allowed to subside in the two that follow. For though this movement, first of intensification, then of relaxation, is discernible in the play as a whole, it is not uniform or uninterrupted. There is throughout a throb and pulse, an ebb and flow. The quieter scenes alternate with the more vehement : Coriolanus' fortune by turns advances and retires. Only when we reflect do we become aware that we have risen so high out of our daily experience, and have returned "with new acquist" of wisdom to a spot whence we can step back to it once more.

But to produce so consummate a masterpiece from the material of history, no matter how dramatic that material was, Shakespeare was bound to reshape it more freely than he was wont to do when dealing with historical themes. We have seen from Hardy's example what stores of half-wrought treasure Plutarch's narrative offered to a dramatist who knew his business. Still it was only half-wrought, and in working it up Shakespeare consciously or unconsciously allowed himself more liberties than in his other Roman plays. His loans indeed are none the fewer or the less on that account; nowhere has he borrowed more numerous or so lengthy passages. But it almost seems as though with the tact of genius he had the feeling that he was at work, not on fact, but on legend. Though he is far from recasting the Roman tradition as he recast the pseudo-historic traditions of his own island in *Lear* and *Macbeth*, yet he gives a new colouring to the picture as he hardly does to genuine histories like *Richard II.* or *Antony and Cleopatra.*

This will appear from a comparison of the play with the *Life*.

CHAPTER II

PARALLELS AND CONTRASTS WITH PLUTARCH

THE first impression produced by a comparison of the biography and the play is that the latter is little more than a scenic replica of the former. Shakespeare has indeed absorbed so many suggestions from the translation that it is difficult to realise how much he has modified them, or to avoid reading these modifications into his authority when we try to distinguish what he has received from what he has supplied. And the illusion is confirmed by the frequency with which we light on familiar words, familiar traits, familiar incidents. For the similarity seems at first to pervade the language, the characterisation, and the action.[1]

In the language it is most marked. Nowhere has Shakespeare borrowed so much through so great a number of lines as in Volumnia's appeal to the piety of her son. This passage, even if it stood alone, would serve to make the play a notable example of Shakespeare's indebtedness to North.[2] But it does not stand alone. Somewhat shorter, but still longer than any loan in the other plays, is Coriolanus' announcement of himself to Aufidius, and in it

---

[1] A good many of the parallels and contrasts noted in this chapter are to be found in the excellent paper by Delius already cited.

[2] See Appendix B.

Shakespeare follows North even more closely than in the former instance.

> If thou knowest me not yet, Tullus, and seeing me, dost not perhappes beleeve me to be the man I am in dede, I must of necessitie bewraye my selfe to be that I am. I am that Caius Martius, who hath done to thy self particularly, and to all the Volsces generally, great hurte and mischief, which I cannot denie for my surname of Coriolanus that I beare. For I never had other benefit nor recompence, of all the true and paynefull service I have done, and the extreme daungers I have bene in, but this only surname: a good memorie and witnes, of the malice and displeasure thou showldest beare me. In deede the name only remaineth with me: for the rest, the envie and crueltie of the people of Rome have taken from me, by the sufferance of the dastardlie nobilitie and magistrates, who have forsaken me, and let me be banished by the people. This extremitie hath now driven me to come as a poore suter, to take thy chimney harthe, not of any hope I have to save my life thereby. For if I had feared death, I would not have come hither to have put my life in hazard: but prickt forward with strife and desire I have to be revenged of them that thus have banished me, whom now I beginne to be avenged on, putting my persone betweene their enemies. Wherefore, if thou hast any harte to be wrecked [1] of the injuries thy enemies have done thee, spede thee now, and let my miserie serve thy turne, and so use it, as my service maye be a benefit to the Volsces: promising thee, that I will fight with better good will for all you, then ever I dyd when I was against you, knowing that they fight more valliantly, who know the force of their enemie, then such as have never proved it. And if it be so that thou dare not, and that thou art wearye to prove fortune any more; then am I also weary to live any lenger. And it were no wisedome in thee, to save the life of him, who hath bene heretofore thy mortall enemie, and whose service now can nothing helpe nor pleasure thee.

Shakespeare gives little else than a transcript, though, of course, a poetical and dramatic transcript, of this splendid piece of forthright prose.

> *Coriolanus.* If, Tullus,
> Not yet thou knowest me, and, seeing me, dost not
> Think me for the man I am, necessity
> Commands me name myself.

[1] wreaked, avenged.

Aufidius.   What is thy name?
Coriolanus. A name unmusical to the Volscians' ears,
And harsh in sound to thine.
    Aufidius.   Say, what's thy name?
Thou hast a grim appearance, and thy face
Bears a command in't: though thy tackle's torn,
Thou show'st a noble vessel: what's thy name?
    Coriolanus. Prepare thy brow to frown; know'st thou me yet?
    Aufidius. I know thee not: thy name?
    Coriolanus. My name is Caius Marcius, who hath done
To thee particularly, and to all the Volsces
Great hurt and mischief: thereto witness may
My surname, Coriolanus: the painful service,
The extreme dangers, and the drops of blood
Shed for my thankless country are requited
But with that surname; a good memory,
And witness of the malice and displeasure
Which thou should'st bear me: only that name remains;
The cruelty and envy of the people,
Permitted by our dastard nobles, who
Have all forsook me, hath devoured the rest:
And suffer'd me by the voice of slaves to be
Whoop'd out of Rome. Now this extremity
Hath brought me to thy hearth; not out of hope—
Mistake me not—to save my life, for if
I had fear'd death, of all men i' the world
I would have 'voided thee, but in mere spite,
To be full quit of those my banishers,
Stand I before thee now. Then if thou hast
A heart of wreak in thee, that wilt revenge
Thine own particular wrongs and stop those maims
Of shame seen through thy country, speed thee straight,
And make my misery serve thy turn: so use it
That my revengeful services may prove
As benefits to thee, for I will fight
Against my canker'd country with the spleen
Of all the under fiends. But if so be
Thou darest not this and that to prove more fortunes
Thou'rt tired, then, in a word, I also am
Longer to live most weary, and present
My throat to thee and to thy ancient malice;
Which not to cut would show thee but a fool,
Since I have ever follow'd thee with hate,
Drawn tuns of blood out of thy country's breast
And cannot live but to thy shame, unless
It be to do thee service.   (IV. v. 60.)

As much material, though it is amplified and re-arranged, has been incorporated, as we shall have to point out, in Coriolanus' invective against the tribunate and the distribution of corn. Within a narrower compass we see the same adherence to North's phraseology in Brutus' instructions to the people, where, very notably, Shakespeare's fidelity to his author has made it possible to supply an omission in the text with absolute certainty as to the sense and great probability as to the wording. The opening sentences of the *Life* run as follows :

> The house of the Martians at Rome was of the number of the patricians, out of the which hath sprong many noble personages : whereof Ancus Martius was one, King Numaes daughters sonne, who was king of Rome after Tullus Hostilius. Of the same house were Publius, and Quintus, who brought Rome their best water they had by conducts. Censorinus also came of that familie, that was so surnamed, bicause the people had chosen him Censor twise.

Shakespeare puts the notifications in the Tribune's mouth :

> Say we read lectures to you,
> How youngly he began to serve his country,
> How long continued, and what stock he springs of,
> The noble house o' the Marcians, from whence came
> That Ancus Martius, Numa's daughter's son,
> Who, after great Hostilius, here was king :
> Of the same house Publius and Quintus were,
> That our best water brought by conduits hither :
> *And Nobly nam'd, so twice being Censor,*
> *Was his great Ancestor.* (II. iii. 242.)

Many editors saw that something had dropped out, but no attempt to fill the gap was satisfactory, till Delius, having recourse to North, supplemented,

> [And Censorinus, that was so surnamed]
> And nobly named so, twice being censor.[1]

[1] This seems preferable to the reading of the Cambridge Editors
> And [Censorinus,] nobly named so,
> Twice being [by the people chosen] censor.

In the first place it is closer to North, and agrees with Shakespeare's usual practice of keeping to North's words so far as possible. In the

These lines also show how Shakespeare reproduces Plutarch's statement even when they are for him not quite in keeping. Plutarch, writing in the second century, could instance Publius, Quintus and Censorinus as ornaments of the Marcian gens ; but Brutus' reference to them is an anachronism as they come after the supposed date of the play. So too Plutarch says of the attack⁻ on the Romans before Corioli :

> But Martius being there at that time, ronning out of the campe with a fewe men with him, he slue the first enemies he met withall, and made the rest of them staye upon a sodaine, crying out to the Romaines that had turned their backes, and calling them againe to fight with a lowde voyce. For he was even such another, as Cato would have a souldier and a captaine to be : not only terrible, and fierce to laye about him, but to make the enemie afeard with the sounde of his voyce, and grimnes of his countenaunce.

Shakespeare makes short work of chronology by putting this allusion into the mouth of Titus Lartius :

> Thou wast a soldier
> Even to Cato's[1] wish, not fierce and terrible
> Only in strokes ; but, with thy grim looks, and
> The thunder-like percussion of thy sounds,
> Thou madest thine enemies shake, as if the world
> Were feverous and did tremble. (I. iv. 56.)

Occasionally even mistakes in North's text or marginal notes, or in Shakespeare's interpretation or recollection of what he had read, have passed into the play. Thus it has been shown[2] that North, owing to a small typographical error in the French, misunderstood the scope of Cominius' offer to Marcius. Amyot says :

second place, it is closer to the Folio text, involving only the displacement of a comma. In the third place, it is simpler to suppose that a whole single line has been missed out than that parts of two have been amputated, and the remainders run together.

[1] Here again Plutarch has furnished an emendation : Folio, *Calues*.

[2] By Büttner, *Zu Coriolan und seiner Quelle* (*Jhrbch. der D.-Sh. Gesellschaft*, Bd. xli. 1905).

> "Et en fin lui dit, que de *tous les cheveaux prisonniers,*
> et autres biens qui avoient esté pris et gaignés en grande
> quantité, il en choisist dix de chaque sorte à sa volonté, avant
> que rien en fust distribué, ni desparti aux autres.

There should be a comma after *cheveaux,* as appears
on reference to the Greek,[1] and Marcius is told to
select ten of the horses, prisoners, and other chattels;
but North took the *prisonniers* as used adjectivally
in agreement with the preceding noun and translated:

> So in the ende he willed Martius, he should choose *out of
> all the horses they had taken* of their enemies, and of all the
> goodes they had wonne (whereof there was great store) tenne
> of every sorte which he liked best, before any distribution
> should be made to other.

Further there is the quite incorrect abridgment in
the margin :

> The tenth parte of the enemies goods offered Martius for
> rewarde of his service by Cominius the Consul.

Shakespeare combines these misstatements :

> Of all the horses,
> Whereof we have ta'en good and good store, of all
> The treasure in this field achieved and city,
> We render you the tenth, to be ta'en forth,
> Before the common distribution, at
> Your only choice. (I. ix. 31.)

Of great frequency are the short sentences from
North that are embedded in Shakespeare's dialogue.
Thus, the preliminary announcement of Marcius'
hardihood is introduced with the remark :

> Now in those dayes, valliantnes was honoured in Rome
> above all the other vertues.

Cominius begins his panegyric :

> It is held
> That valour is the chiefest virtue, and
> Most dignifies the haver. (II. ii. 87.)

---

[1] πολλῶν χρημάτων καὶ ἵππων γεγονότων αἰχμαλώτων καὶ ἀνθρώπων, ἐκέλευσεν
αὐτὸν ἐξελέσθαι δέκα πάντα πρὸ τοῦ νέμειν τοῖς πολλοῖς. Ἄνευ δὲ ἐκείνων ἀρισ-
τεῖον αὐτῷ κεκοσμημένον ἵππον ἐδωρήσατο.

When Marcius drives the Volscians back to Corioli
and the Romans hesitate to pursue, we are told :

> He dyd encorage his fellowes with wordes and deedes,
> crying out to them, that fortune had opened the gates of the
> cittie more for the followers, then for the flyers.

Compare his exhortation :

> So, now the gates are ope : now prove good seconds :
> 'Tis for the followers fortune widens them,
> Not for the fliers.   (I. iv. 43.)

When the proposal to distribute the corn is being
discussed, many senators are in favour of it :

> But Martius standing up on his feete, dyd somewhat
> sharpely take up those, who went about to gratifie the people
> therein, and called them people pleasers and traitours to the
> nobilitie.

Brutus charges him with this in the play :

> When corn was given them gratis, you repined ;
> Scandal'd the suppliants for the people, call'd them
> Time-pleasers, flatterers, foes to nobleness.   (III. i. 43.)

Sometimes the debt is confined to a single phrase or
word and yet is unmistakable. When Coriolanus
has reached Antium, Plutarch quotes Homer on
Ulysses :

> So dyd he enter into the enemies towne.

In the play Coriolanus before the house of Aufidius
soliloquises :

>   My love's upon
> This enemy town. I'll enter.   (IV. iv. 23.)

Now and then some apparently haphazard detail can
be explained if we trace it to its source. Thus,
Cominius talks of the "seventeen battles" which
the hero had fought since his first exploit. Why
seventeen ? Doubtless Shakespeare had in his mind
the account of the candidature, when Marcius showed
the wounds "which he had receyved in seventeene

yeres service at the warres, and in many sundrie battells." In Plutarch the number of years is prescribed by his mythical chronology, for he dates the beginning of Marcius' career from the wars with the Tarquins, which were supposed to have broken out in 245 A.U.C., while Corioli was taken in 262 : but when transferred to the battles it becomes a mere survival which serves at most to give apparent definiteness.

But occasionally such survivals have a higher value. It is instructive, for example, to notice how Shakespeare utilises the tradition dear to Plutarch's antiquarian tastes but not very interesting to an Elizabethan audience of the acknowledgment made to the goddess, *Fortuna Muliebris*, after the withdrawal of Coriolanus from Rome.

> The Senate ordeined, that the magistrates to gratifie and honour these ladyes, should graunte them all that they would require. And they only requested that they would build a temple of Fortune of the women, for the building whereof they offered them selves to defraye the whole charge of the sacrifices, and other ceremonies belonging to the service of the goddes. Nevertheles, the Senate commending their good will and forwardnes, ordeined, that the temple and image should be made at the common charge of the cittie.

And the marginal note sums up : "The temple of Fortune built for the women." This seems to be the archaeological ore from which is forged Coriolanus' gallant hyperbole :

> Ladies, you deserve
> To have a temple built you. (v. ii. 206.)

From the worshippers they become the worshipped.

Sometimes in the survival the fact is transformed to figure, the prose to poetry. After Marcius' miracles of valour at Corioli, Cominius gives him, "in testimonie that he had wonne that day the price of prowes above all other, a goodly horse with a

capparison, and all furniture to him." This Shakespeare does not omit. Cominius declares :

> Caius Marcius
> Wears this war's garland : in token of the which
> My noble steed,[1] known to the camp, I give him
> With all his trim belonging.   (I. ix. 59.)

But the same episode furnishes Titus Lartius with
his imagery as he points to the wounded and
victorious hero :

> O general,
> Here is the steed, we the caparison !   (I. ix. 11.)

This illustrates the sort of sea-change that always
takes place in the language of North under the
hands of the magician, though it may not always be
equally perceptible.   But it is never entirely lacking,
even where we are at first more struck by the
amount that Shakespeare has retained without
alteration.   The *Life*, for instance, describes what
takes place after Marcius has joined Cominius,
before they hurry off to the second fight.

> Martius asked him howe the order of their enemies battell
> was, and on which side they had placed their best fighting
> men.   The Consul made him aunswer, that he thought the
> bandes which were in the voward of their battell, were those
> of the Antiates, whom they esteemed to be the war-likest
> men, and which for valliant corage would give no place, to
> any of the hoste of their enemies.   Then prayed Martius
> to be set directly against them.

Here is what Shakespeare makes of this :

> *Mar.* How lies their battle?   Know you on which side
> They have placed their men of trust?
> *Com.*   As I guess, Marcius,
> Their bands in the vaward are the Antiates,
> Of their best trust ; o'er them Aufidius,
> Their very heart of hope.

---

[1] Shakespeare, following North ("Martius accepted the gift of *his*
horse") makes it, instead of *a* horse, Cominius' own horse, which
would be a violation of antique usage.   See Büttner as above.

Mar.   I do beseech you,
By all the battles wherein we have fought,
By the blood we have shed together, by the vows
We have made to endure friends, that you directly
Set me against Aufidius and his Antiates;
And that you not delay the present, but,
Filling the air with swords advanced and darts,
We prove this very hour.   (I. vi. 51.)

Here to begin with Shakespeare hardly does more
than change the indirect to the direct narrative and
condense a little, but presently he adds picturesqueness, passion, and, by the introduction of Aufidius,
dramatic significance. And this is invariably his
method. It is unfair to quote the parallel passages
without the context, for, apart from the subtle
transmutation they have undergone, they are
preludes to original utterance and almost every one
of them is a starting point rather than the goal.
Shakespeare's normal practice is illustrated in the
fable of Menenius, in which, with every allowance
made for possible assistance from Camden, the words
of his authority or authorities are only so many spur-
pricks that set his own imagination at a gallop. And
what goes before and comes after is pure Shakespeare.

And it should be noticed that his textual ap-
propriations from North, long or short, obvious or
covert, never clash with his more personal contributions, which in bulk are far more important. They
are all subdued to the tone that the purpose of the
dramatist imposes. Delius says with absolute
truth : "This harmonious colouring would make it
impossible for us, in respect of style, to discover real
or supposititious loans from Plutarch in Shakespeare's drama, and definitely identify them as such,
if by chance North's translation were inaccessible."
Yet this harmonious colouring, that has its source in
the author's mind and that is required by the
theme, does not prevent an individualisation in
the utterance, whether wholly original or partly

borrowed, that fits it for the lips of the particular speaker. The language, even when it is suggested by North, is not only spontaneous and consistent, it is dramatic as well, and apposite to the strongly marked characters of whom the story is told.

To these characters, and their development by Shakespeare, we now turn. It may be remarked that all of them, except the quite episodical Adrian and Nicanor, are nominally to be found in Plutarch, by whom the hero himself is drawn at full length and in great detail. For his delineation then there was a great deal to borrow and Shakespeare has borrowed a great deal. In his general bearing and in many of his features the Coriolanus of the play is the Coriolanus of the *Life*, though of course imagined with far more firmness and comprehension. Only on very close scrutiny do we see that each has a physiognomy of his own, and that the difference in the impressions they produce is due not merely to the execution but to the conception. This will become clear as the general discussion proceeds and will incidentally occupy our attention from time to time. Meanwhile it should be noticed that, Coriolanus excepted, Plutarch's persons are very shadowy and vague. If we compare this biography with those that Shakespeare had used for his earlier Roman plays, it is obvious that it is much more of a monograph. In the others room is found for sketches of many subordinate figures in connection with the titular subject, but Marcius stands out alone and the remaining personages are scarcely more than names. In the tragedy, too, he is in possession of the scene, but his relatives, his friends, and his enemies are also full of interest and life; and for their portraiture Shakespeare had to depend almost entirely on himself.

Next to the hero, for example, it is his mother who is most conspicuous in the play; and how much did Plutarch contribute to the conception of her concrete personality? He supplies only one or two hints, some of which Shakespeare disregards or contradicts. They both attribute to her the sole training of the boy, but Plutarch implies that her discipline was slack and her instruction insufficient, while in Shakespeare she incurs no such blame except in so far as we infer a certain lack of judiciousness from her peculiar attitude to her grandson and from her son's exaggeration of some of her own traits. But injudiciousness is not quite the same as the laxity that Plutarch's apologetic paragraph would insinuate :

> Caius Martius, whose life we intend now to write, being left an orphan by his father, was brought up under his mother a widowe, who taught us by experience, that orphanage bringeth many discommodities to a childe, but doth not hinder him to become an honest man, and to excell in vertue above the common sorte ; as they, are meanely borne, wrongfully doe complayne, that it is the occasion of their casting awaye, for that no man in their youth taketh any care of them to see them well brought up, and taught that were meete. This man is also a good proofe to confirme some mens opinions, that a rare and excellent witte untaught, doth bring forth many good and evill things together ; like as a fat soile bringeth forth herbes and weedes, that lieth unmanured.[1] For this Martius naturell wit and great harte dyd marvelously sturre up his corage, to doe and attempt notable actes. But on the other side for lacke of education, he was so chollericke and impacient, that he would yeld to no living creature ; which made him churlishe, uncivill, and altogether unfit for any mans conversation.

Again, in reference to Marcius' strenuous career, Plutarch writes :

> The only thing that made him to love honour, was the joye he sawe his mother dyd take of him. For he thought nothing made him so happie and honorable, as that his mother might heare every bodie praise and commend him, that she might allwayes see him returne with a crowne upon his head, and that she might still embrace him with teares ronning downe her cheekes for joye.

[1] *Unworked, untilled*, from *manoeuvrer*.

In the play, it is not with tears of joy that Volumnia welcomes her warrior home.

Here is another instance of piety that Plutarch cites :

> Martius thinking all due to his mother, that had bene also due to his father if he had lived ; dyd not only content him selfe to rejoyce and honour her, but at her desire tooke a wife also, by whom he had two children, and yet never left his mothers house therefore.

In Shakespeare there is no word of Marcius' marrying at his mother's desire, and though she apparently lives with him, it is in his, not in her house.

All these notices occur in the first pages of the *Life*. Thenceforward till her intervention at the close there is only a passing mention of her affliction at her son's banishment.

> When he was come home to his house againe, and had taken his leave of his mother and wife, finding them weeping, and shreeking out for sorrowe, and had also comforted and persuaded them to be content with his chaunce ; he immediately went to the gate of the cittie.

Even in regard to the intercession, where Shakespeare follows Plutarch most closely, he makes one significant omission. In the original, it is the suggestion of Valeria "through the inspiration of some god above," that the women should sue for peace, and she visits Marcius' kinswoman to secure their help : by the suppression of this circumstance, the prominent place is left to Volumnia. And in the appeal itself Shakespeare, besides the various vivifying and personal touches, makes one important addition. In Plutarch her words are throughout forcible and impassioned, but they do not burst into the wrathful indignation of the close, which alone is sufficient to break down Coriolanus' resolution.

Now it is clear that the presence of Volumnia does not pervade the *Life* as it does the play, and she has not nearly so much to do. Moreover, besides being less important, she is less masculine and masterful. Indeed, from Plutarch's hints it would be possible to construct for her a character that differed widely from that of Shakespeare's heroine. She is like the latter in her patriotism, her love for and delight in her son, and, at the critical moment, in her influence over him. But even her influence is less constant, and seems to be stronger in the way of unconscious inspiration than of positive direction. It would be quite legitimate to picture her as an essentially womanly woman, high-souled and dutiful, but finding her chosen sphere in the home, overflowing with sympathy and affection, and failing in her obligations as widowed mother only by a lack of sternness.

And if Shakespeare has given features to Volumnia, much more has he done so to Virgilia and young Marcius. Both, of course, are presented in the merest outline, but in Plutarch the wife is only once named and the children are not named at all. Shakespeare's Virgilia, on the other hand, by the few words she speaks and the few words spoken to her, by her very restraint from speech and the atmosphere in which she moves, produces a very definite as well as a very pleasing impression. Ruskin, after enumerating some other of Shakespeare's female characters, concludes that they "and last and perhaps loveliest, Virgilia, are all faultless; conceived in the highest heroic type of humanity." This enthusiasm may be, as Ruskin's enthusiasms sometimes were, exaggerated and misplaced, but it could not be roused by a nonentity; and a nonentity Plutarch's Virgilia is.

Young Marcius, again, is not merely one of the two children mentioned in the *Life*. As Mr. Verity remarks,[1] in this case "the half is certainly better

---

[1] *Coriolanus*. (The Students' Shakespeare, Cambridge University Press.) Volumnia indeed refers to "children" in her petition (v. iii. 118), but this seems merely a reminiscence of Plutarch's language, for everywhere else young Marcius is treated as an only child.

than the whole "; and the named half has a whole-
ness of his own that the anonymous brace can
lay no claim to. He is a thorough boy, and an
attractive though boisterous one. If he is cruel to
winged things, he is brave .and circumspect withal.
He has a natural objection to be trodden on even
for a patriotic cause ; if the risk is too great, " he'll
run away till he's bigger, but then he'll fight."

Passing from Coriolanus' kinsfolk to his friends,
we meet with very similar results. Titus Lartius is
sketched very slightly in Shakespeare, but a good
deal more visually than in Plutarch, who says of him
in two sentences that he was " one of the valliantest
men the Romaines had at that time," and that, having
entered Corioli with Marcius, he, " when he was
gotten out, had some leysure to bring the Romaines
with more safetie into the cittie." Cominius is hardly
more distinct. As Consul he conducts the campaign
against Corioli ; welcomes Marcius from his first
exploit, and gives him the opportunity for his second,
in the double engagement that then took place ;
thereafter officially rewards and eulogises his gallan-
try, which " he commended beyond the moone " ;
and that is practically all that is said about him. In
the play, though in it too his part was a small one,
he has characteristics of his own which Shakespeare
has created for him without much help from these
vague suggestions. Nor has Marcius, in the original
story, any intimate association with either of his
fellow soldiers. It is stated that at first he is in
Lartius' division of the army, and afterwards joins
Cominius and wins his praises, but it is only in the affair
of Corioli that their names are mentioned together.

In the drama, however, Menenius is undoubtedly
the chief of the young man's friends as well as one
of the most prominent persons ; and what has Plutarch to say about him ? He is introduced only in
connection with the fable which he tells the seceders

to the Holy Hill, and, apart from the fable, all that we
hear of him is confined to the following few sentences:

> The Senate being afeard of their departure, dyd send unto
> them certaine of the pleasauntest olde men, and the most
> acceptable to the people among them. Of those, Menenius
> Agrippa was he, who was sent for chief man of the message
> from the Senate. He, after many good persuasions and
> gentle requestes made to the people, on the behalfe of the
> Senate, knit up his oration in the ende, with a notable tale.
> . . . These persuasions pacified the people, conditionally,
> that the Senate would graunte there should be yerely chosen
> five magistrates, which they now call *Tribuni Plebis*.

Even the few particulars given in this passage
Shakespeare alters or neglects. It is not to the
secessionists on the Mons Sacer, but to a street mob
in Rome, that the fable is told. It not merely serves
to lubricate in advance the negotiations that result
in the tribunate, but effectually discomfits the mur-
murers, and Menenius learns only subsequently and
to his surprise that the Senate has meanwhile conceded the political innovation. There is no hint in
Plutarch of his being himself one of the patricians,
and if Shakespeare glanced at Holland's Livy he
would see that in point of fact tradition assigned to
him a plebeian origin.[1] Above all he has no dealings
whatever with Marcius, and, according to Livy, died
a year before his banishment. Plutarch thus furnishes hardly anything for the portrait of the man,
and nothing at all for his relations with the hero.

And it is the same, or nearly the same, if we turn
from Marcius' friends to his enemies.

The tribunes, for example, are comparatively
colourless. On the institution of the new magis-
tracy,

> Junius Brutus, and Sicinius Vellutus were the first tribunes
> of the people that were chosen, who had only bene the causes
> and procurers of this sedition.

[1] Placuit igitur oratorem ad plebem mitti Menenium Agrippam,
facundum virum et, quod inde oriundus erat, plebi carum. (11. 32
Weissenborn & Müller's edition.)

Then we hear of their opposition to the colonisation of Velitrae because it was infected with the plague, and to a new war with the Volscians, because it was in the interest only of the rich ; but they have nothing to do with the rejection of Marcius when he is candidate for the consulship.   Only at a later time, when he inveighs against the relief of the people and the tribunitian power, do they stir up a popular tumult and insist that he shall answer their charges, adopting tactics not unlike those that are attributed to them in the play.

> All this was spoken to one of these two endes, either that Martius against his nature should be constrained to humble him selfe, and to abase his hawty and fierce minde : or els if he continued still in his stowtnes, he should incurre the peoples displeasure and ill will so farre, that he should never possibly winne them againe.   Which they hoped would rather fall out so, then otherwise ; as in deede they gest unhappely, considering Martius nature and disposition.

He answers not only with his wonted boldness, but " gave him selfe in his wordes to thunder and looke therewithall so grimly as though he made no reckoning of the matter."   This affords his opponents their chance :

> Whereupon Sicinius, the cruellest and stowtest of the Tribunes, after he had whispered a little with his companions, dyd openly pronounce in the face of all the people, Martius as condemned by the Tribunes to dye.

Matters do not end here.   A formal trial is agreed to, at which the resourceful magistrates procure the sentence of banishment, partly by arranging that the votes shall be taken not by centuries but by tribes, so that " the poore needy people " and the rabble may be in the majority, partly by eking out the indictments to which they are pledged to confine themselves, with other accusations.   Then they drop out.

It may be observed that Brutus is only once

named, and nothing is said of his disposition or ways. Even of Sicinius, who is more conspicuous, we only read that he was "the cruellest and stowtest" of the two. But it is less their character than their policy that occupies Plutarch, and even their policy is presented in an ambiguous light. They are described as the only authors of the rising which culminated in the exodus from the city; but with that exodus Plutarch on the whole seems to sympathise. They are described as "seditious tribunes" when they oppose the colonisation of Velitrae and the renewal of the war; but Plutarch shows they had good grounds for doing so. Even their action against Coriolanus for opposing the grant of corn and advocating the abolition of their office, was from their own point of view, and perhaps from any point of view, perfectly legitimate. We can only say that in the measures they took they were violent and unscrupulous. Yet when we consider the bitterness of party feeling and the exigencies of public life, they seem no worse than many statesmen who have been accounted great. Even their overt policy then is more respectable than that of Shakespeare's pair of demagogues, and of course it is Shakespeare who has created, or all but created, for them their vulgar but life-like characters.

Nor are things greatly different in the case of the third of Marcius' enemies, Tullus Aufidius, though Plutarch tells us somewhat more about him, and Shakespeare in the main fills in rather than alters Plutarch's sketch. The first mention of him occurs when the exile determines on his revenge.

> Now in the cittie of Antium, there was one called Tullus Aufidius, who for his riches, as also for his nobilitie and valliantnes, was honoured emong the Volsces as a king. Martius knewe very well that Tullus dyd more malice and envie him, then he dyd all the Romaines besides: bicause that many times in battells where they met, they were ever at the encounter one against another, like lustie coragious

youthes, striving in all emulation of honour, and had encoun-
tered many times together. In so muche, as besides the
common quarrell betweene them, there was bred a marvelous
private hate one against another. Yet notwithstanding, considering that Tullus Aufidius was a man of a greate minde.
and that he above all other of the Volsces, most desired
revenge of the Romaines, for the injuries they had done unto
them; he dyd an act that confirmed the true wordes of an
auncient Poet, who sayed:

It is a thing full·harde, mans anger to withstand.

After the welcome at Antium, Tullus and Coriolanus
combine to bring on the war and are entrusted with
the joint command; but Tullus chooses to remain at
home to defend his country, while Coriolanus conducts the operations abroad, in which he is wonderfully successful. A truce he grants the Romans is
however the occasion for a rift in their alliance.

This was the first matter wherewith the Volsces (that most
envied Martius glorie and authoritie) dyd charge Martius
with. Among those, Tullus was chief: who though he had
receyved no private injurie or displeasure of Martius, yet the
common faulte and imperfection of mans nature wrought
in him, and it grieved him to see his owne reputation
bleamished, through Martius great fame and honour, and so
him selfe to be lesse esteemed of the Volsces, then he was
before.

We do not hear of him after this till Coriolanus has
come back from the siege of Rome.

Now when Martius was returned againe into the cittie of
Antium from his voyage, Tullus that hated him and could no
lenger abide him for the feare he had of his authoritie;
sought divers meanes to make him out of the waye, thinking
that if he let slippe that present time, he should never recover
the like and fit occasion againe.

So he contrives and effects the assassination of his
rival.

Thus the chief features of Aufidius' character
and the story of its development, the emulation
that is dislodged by generosity, the generosity that
is submerged in envy, were already supplied for

Shakespeare's use. But the darker hues are lacking in the earlier picture. There is neither the un-scrupulous rancour in his initial relations with Marcius that Shakespeare attributes to them, nor the hypocritical pretence at the close. Plutarch does not bring the contrast with Coriolanus to a head. And in connection with this it should be observed that Tullus appears late and intervenes only incidentally. Less than a sentence is spared to his earlier antagonism with Coriolanus, nor is he present in the march on Rome or during the siege. And this is typical of Plutarch's treatment of all the subordinate persons. They enter for a moment, and are dismissed. But in Shakespeare they accompany the action throughout, and do this in such a way that they illustrate and influence the character and career of the hero, and have their own characters and careers illustrated and influenced by him. They are all, even young Marcius by description, intro-duced in the first four scenes, with an indication of their general peculiarities and functions, and with the single exception of Titus Lartius, they continue to reappear almost to the end.

The recurrent presence of the agents of itself involves considerable modification in the conduct of the plot, but in this respect too we are at first more struck by the resemblances than the differences between the two versions; and it is possible to exhibit the story in such a manner that its main lines seem the same in both.

The setting is furnished by the primitive Roman state when it has newly assumed its republican form. Less than a score of years before, it passed through its first great crisis in its successful rejection of the kingship, and ever since has been engaged in a life-and-death struggle with representatives of the exiled dynasty and with jealous neighbours some-what similar in power and character to itself. It has made good its position under the direction of a proud and valiant aristocracy, but not without paying the price. The constant wars have resulted in widespread poverty and distress among the lower classes till they can bear it no longer and demand constitutional changes by which, as they think, their misery may be redressed. Rome is thus confronted with the internal peril of revolution as well as the foreign peril of invasion, and the future mistress of the world runs the risk of being cut off at the outset of her career by tribal broils and domestic quarrels. It is this that gives the legend a certain grandeur of import. The Senate, finding itself and its partisans in the minority, concedes to the commons rights which have the effect of weakening its old authority, and for that reason are bitterly resented by upholders of the old order. Meanwhile, however, Rome is able to take the field against the Volscians and gains a decisive victory over them, mainly owing to the soldiership of the young patrician, Marcius, who wins for himself in the campaign the name of Coriolanus. The ability he has shown, the glory he has achieved, the gratitude that is his due, seem to mark him out for a leading role. He almost deserves, and almost attains, the highest dignity the little state has to confer : but he has already given proof of his scorn for popular demands and opposition to the recent innovations, and at the last moment he is set aside. Not only that, but the new magistrates, in dread of his influence, incite the people against him and procure his condemnation to death, which, however, is afterwards mitigated to banishment. His friends of the nobility dare not or cannot interpose, and he departs into exile. Then his civic virtue breaks beneath the strain, and, reconciling himself with the Volscians, he leads them against his country. Nothing can stay his advance, and he is on the point of reducing the city, when, yielding to filial affection what he had refused to patriotic obligation, he relinquishes his revenge when he has it within his grasp. But this gives a pretext to those among his new allies who envy his greatness, and soon afterwards he is treacherously slain.

This general scheme is common to the biography and the play, and many of the details, whether presented or recounted, are derived from the former by the latter. Such, in addition to those already mentioned in another connection, are Marcius' first exploit in the battle with Tarquin, when he bestrides a citizen, avenges his injury, and is crowned with the garland of oak ; the dispersion of the soldiers to take spoil in Corioli, and Marcius' consequent indignation ; the response to his call for volunteers ; his petition on behalf of his former host ; the initial approval of his candidature by the plebs from a feeling of shame ; the custom of candidates wearing the humble gown and showing their old wounds at an election ; the popular joy at his banishment ; the muster of nobles to see him to the gates ; his popularity with the Volscian soldiery and their eagerness to serve under him ; the perturbation and mutual recriminations in Rome at his approach ; his reception of former friends when they petition him for mercy ; the device of interrupting his speech in Antium lest his words should secure his acquittal.

To this extent Shakespeare and Plutarch agree, and the agreement is important and far-reaching. Has the dramatist then, been content to embellish and supplement the diction of the story, and give new life to the characters, while leaving the fable unchanged except in so far as these other modifications may indirectly affect it ? On the contrary we shall see that the design is thoroughly recast, that each of the borrowed details receives a new interpretation or a heightened colouring, that significant insertions and no less significant omissions concur to alter the effect of the whole.

Sometimes Shakespeare's innovations followed almost necessarily and without any remoter result from the greater fullness and concreteness of his picture, and the care with which he grouped the persons round his hero. Such are many of the conversations and subordinate scenes, by means of which the story is conveyed to us in all its reality and movement; the episode of Valeria's call, the description and words of Marcius' little son, Aufidius' self-disclosure to his soldiers and his lieutenant, even the interview between the Volscian scout and the Roman informer.

Still in this class, but more important, are the inventions that have no authority in Plutarch, but that are not opposed to and may even have been suggested by some of his hints. Thus in the *Life*, Volumnia's interposition is not required to make Marcius submit himself to the judgment of the people, and in this connection she is not mentioned at all; but at any rate her action in Shakespeare does not belie the influence that Plutarch ascribes to her.

Occasionally, again, the deviation from and observance of the biographer's statements follow each other so fast, and are both so dominated by truth to his spirit, that it needs some vigilance to note all the points where the routes diverge or coincide. Take, for example, the account of the candidature :

> Shortely after this, Martius stoode for the Consulshippe ; and the common people favored his sute, thinking it would be a shame to denie, and refuse, the chiefest noble man of bloude, and most worthie persone of Rome, and specially him that had done so great service and good to the common wealth. For the custome of Rome was at that time, that such as dyd sue for any office, should for certen dayes before be in the market place, only with a poore gowne on their backes, and without any coate underneath, to praye the

cittizens to remember them at the daye of election: which was thus devised, either to move the people the more, by requesting them in suche meane apparell, or els bicause they might shewe them their woundes they had gotten in the warres in the service of the common wealth, as manifest markes and testimonie of their valliantnes. . . . Now Martius following this custome, shewed many woundes and cuttes upon his bodie, which he had receyved in seventeene yeres service at the warres, and in many sundrie battells, being ever the formest man that dyd set out feete to fight. So that there was not a man emong the people, but was ashamed of him selfe, to refuse so valliant a man: and one of them sayed to another, " We must needes chuse him Consul, there is no remedie." But when the daye of election was come, and that Martius came to the market place with great pompe, accompanied with all the Senate, and the whole Nobilitie of the cittie about him, who sought to make him Consul, with the greatest instance and intreatie they could, or ever attempted for any man or matter: then the love and good will of the common people, turned straight to an hate and envie toward him, fearing to put this office of soveraine authoritie into his handes, being a man somewhat partiall toward the nobilitie, and of great credit and authoritie amongest the Patricians, and as one they might doubt would take away alltogether the libertie from the people.

Now Shakespeare borrows from Plutarch the explanation of the rather remarkable circumstance that the people at first gave Martius their support, and, like Plutarch, he emphasises it by giving it twice over, though he avoids the dullness of repetition by making one of the statements serious and one humorous. The first is put in the mouth of the official of the Capitol:

> He hath so planted his honours in their eyes, and his actions in their hearts, that for their tongues to be silent, and not confess so much, were a kind of ingrateful injury: to report otherwise, were a malice, that giving itself the lie, would pluck reproof and rebuke from every ear that heard it.
>
> (II. ii. 32.)

The second is given in the language of the plebeians themselves:

> *First Citizen.* Once, if he do require our voices, we ought not to deny him.

Second Citizen. We may, sir, if we will.

Third Citizen. We have power in ourselves to do it, but it is a power that we have no power to do : for if he show us his wounds and tell us his deeds, we are to put our tongues into those wounds and speak for them ; so, if he tell us his noble deeds, we must also tell him our noble acceptance of them. Ingratitude is monstrous, and for the multitude to be ingrateful, were to make a monster of the multitude : of the which we being members, should bring ourselves to be monstrous members. (II. iii. I.)

But this is only before he wears the candidate's gown, for, otherwise than in Plutarch, he does not show his wounds—"No man saw them," say the citizens (III. iii. 173)—and gives such offence by his contumacy that it is on this the tribunes are able to take further action. In the biography he is rejected only because the indiscreet advocacy of the nobles makes the plebeians fear that he will be too much of a partizan. He shows no reluctance either to stand or to comply with the conditions. All these things are the inventions of Shakespeare, and are made to bring about the catastrophe which in his authority was due to very different causes. Nevertheless, they are suggested by Plutarch in so far as they are merely additional illustrations of that excess of aristocratic pride, on which Plutarch, too, insists as the source of Marcius' offences and misfortunes.

But this example merges into another kind of alteration which may primarily have been due to the need of greater economy and dramatic condensation, but which in its results involves a great deal more. In Plutarch, Coriolanus' unsuccessful candidature has, except as it adds to his private irritation, no immediate result ; and only some time later does his banishment follow on quite another occasion. Corn had come from Sicily, and in the dearth it was proposed to distribute it gratis : but Marcius inveighed against such a course and urged that the time was opportune for the abolition of the Tribunate, in a speech which, in the play, he "speaks again" when his election is challenged. But the *Life* reports it only as delivered in the Senate ; and the tribunes, who are present, at once leave and raise a tumult, attempt to arrest him and are resisted. The senators, to allay the commotion, resolve to sell the corn cheap, and thus end the discontent against themselves, but the tribunes persist in their attack on the ringleader, hoping, as we have seen, that he will prove refractory and give a handle against himself. When he does this and the death-sentence is pronounced, there is still so much feeling of fairness that a legal trial is demanded, which the tribunes consent to grant him, and to which he consents to submit on the stipulation that he shall be charged only on the one count of aspiring to make himself king. But when the assembly is held the tribunes break their promise and accuse him of seeking to withhold the corn and abolish the Tribunate, and of distributing the spoils of the Antiates only among his own followers. For shortly after the fall of Corioli, the people had refused to march against the Volsces, and Coriolanus, organising a private expedition, had won a victory, taken great booty, and given it to all those who had been of the party. So the unexpectedness and injustice of this last indictment throws him out.

> This matter was most straunge of all to Martius, looking least to have been burdened with that, as with any matter of offence. Whereupon being burdened on the sodaine, and having no ready excuse to make even at that instant : he beganne to fall a praising of the souldiers that had served with him in that jorney. But those that were not with him, being the greater number, cried out so lowde, and made such a noyse, that he could not be heard. To conclude, when they came to tell the voyces of the Tribes, there were three voyces odde, which condemned him to be banished for life.

Now there are several things to notice in Shakespeare's very different version. The first is the tact

s

with which he compresses a great many remotely connected incidents into one. He antedates the affair about the corn with Marcius' speech against the distribution and the Tribunate, and only brings it in as a supplementary circumstance in the prosecution. The real centre of the situation is Coriolanus' behaviour when a candidate, and round this all else is grouped : and this behaviour, it will be remembered, is altogether a fabrication on Shakespeare's part. Two other things follow from this.

In the first place, the unreasonableness of the Romans as a whole is considerably mitigated. More prominence, indeed, is given to the machinations of the tribunes, but on the other hand the body of electors is not only acting less on its own initiative than on the prompting of its guides, but it proceeds quite properly to avenge grievances that do exist and avert dangers that do threaten. And this excuse is to some extent valid for the leaders too. In Plutarch, the Senate has come to terms on the question of the corn, yet Coriolanus is hounded down for an opposition which has turned out to be futile. In the play, though he has met with a check, both he and his friends hope that even now he may win the election, and the evils that would result to the people from his consulship are still to be feared.

Again, Plutarch dwells on the unfairness of the arrangements for taking the votes, which has the effect of packing the jury :

> And first of all the Tribunes would in any case (whatso-ever became of it) that the people would proceede to geve their voyces by Tribes, and not by hundreds : for by this meanes the multitude of the poore needy people (and all such rabble as had nothing to lose, and had lesse regard of honestie before their eyes) came to be of greater force (bicause their voyces were numbered by the polle) then the noble honest cittizens : whose persones and purse dyd duetifully serve the common wealth in their warres.

This is not exactly omitted in the drama, but it is slurred over, and Plutarch's clear explanation is entirely suppressed, so that few of Shakespeare's readers and still fewer of his hearers could possibly suspect the significance.

> *Sicinius.* Have you a catalogue
> Of all the voices that we have procured
> Set down by the poll ?
> *Ædile.* I have ; 'tis ready.
> *Sicinius.* Have you collected them by tribes ?
> *Ædile.* I have. (III. iii. 8.)

Above all, the accusations brought against Coriolanus, in Shakespeare, are substantially just. He may not seek to wind himself into a power tyrannical, if we take *tyrant*, as Plutarch certainly did but as Shakespeare probably did not, in the strict classical sense of *tyrannus*, but with his disregard of aged custom and his avowed opinions of the people, there can be no doubt that he would have wielded the consular powers tyrannically, in the ordinary acceptation of the word. For there can be as little doubt about his ill-will to the masses and his abhorrence of the tribunitian system. And it is on these grounds that he is condemned. It is very noticeable that the division of the Antiate spoil, which in Plutarch is the most decisive and unwarrantable allegation against him, is mentioned by Shakespeare only in advance as a subordinate point that may be brought forward, but, as a matter of fact, it is never urged.

> *Brutus.* In this point charge him home, that he affects
> Tyrannical power : if he evade us there,
> Enforce him with his envy to the people,
> And that the spoil got on the Antiates
> Was ne'er distributed. (III. iii. 1.)

Shakespeare makes no further use of a circumstance to which Plutarch attaches so great importance that he dwells on it twice over and gives it the prominent place in the narrative of the trial. This piece of sharp practice becomes quite negligible in the play, and the only chicanery of which the tribunes are guilty in the whole transaction is that, as in the *Life*, but more explicitly, they goad Coriolanus to a fit of rage in which he avows his real sentiments—a tactical expedient that many politicians would consider perfectly permissible. Shakespeare, as has often been pointed out, in some ways shows even less appreciation than Plutarch of the merits of the people ; so it is all the more significant that, at the crisis of the play, he softens down and obliterates the worst traits in their proceedings against their enemy.

And the second thing we observe is that by all this Shakespeare emphasises the insolence and truculence of the hero. It is Coriolanus' pride that turns his candidature, which begins under the happiest auspices, to a snare. It is still his pride that plays into the tribunes' hands and makes him repeat in mere defiance his offensive speech. It is again his pride, not any calumny about his misapplying the profits of his raid, that gives the signal for the adverse sentence. Just as in this respect the plebs is represented as on the whole less ignoble than Plutarch makes it, so Coriolanus' conduct is portrayed as more insensate.

And this two-fold tendency, to palliate the guilt of Rome and to stress the violence that provoked it, appears in the more conspicuous of Shakespeare's subsequent deviations from his authority.

In Plutarch, Tullus and Aufidius have great difficulty in persuading the magnates of Antium to renew the war, and only succeed when the Romans expel the Volscian residents from their midst.

> On a holy daye common playes being kept in Rome, apon some suspition, or false reporte, they made proclamation by sound of trumpet, that all the Volsces should avoyde out of Rome before sunne set. Some thincke this was a crafte and deceipt of Martius, who sent one to Rome to the Consuls,

to accuse the Volsces falsely, advertising them howe they had made a conspiracie to set upon them, whilest they were busie in seeing these games, and also to sette their cittie a fyre.

At any rate, the proclamation brings about a declaration of hostilities, and war speedily follows.

Now in Shakespeare, Lartius, for fear of attack, has to surrender Corioli even before Coriolanus meets with his rebuff.

> *Coriolanus.* Tullus Aufidius then had made new head?
> *Lartius.* He had, my lord, and that it was which caused
> Our swifter composition.   (III. i. 1.)

Moreover, all the preparations of the Volsces are complete for a new incursion. Cominius, indeed, cannot believe that they will again tempt fortune so soon.

> They are worn, lord consul, so
> That we shall hardly in our ages see
> Their banners wave again.   (III. i. 6.)

But Cominius is wrong. In the little intercalated scene between the Roman and the Volsce, we learn that they have mustered an army which the latter thus describes :

> A most royal one; the centurions and their charges, distinctly billeted, already in the entertainment, and to be on foot at an hour's warning.   (IV. iii. 47.)

And Aufidius welcomes Coriolanus to the feast with the words :

> O, come, go in,
> And take our friendly senators by the hands :
> Who now are here, taking their leaves of me,
> Who am prepared against your territories,
> Though not for Rome itself.   (IV. v. 137.)

The arrival of such an auxiliary, however, at once alters that plan, and we presently learn that they are now going to make direct for the city :

> To-morrow; to-day; presently; you shall have the drum struck up this afternoon: 'tis, as it were, a parcel of their feast, and to be executed ere they wipe their lips.
>   (IV. v. 229.)

Now in Plutarch we cannot but be struck by the pusillanimous part the Romans play when menaced by their great peril. They answer the declaration of war with a bravado which events quite fail to justify, but, despite the warning they have received, they make no resistance and do not even prepare for it. In Shakespeare there is more excuse for them. They are taken completely by surprise. Their foe has almost been their match before, when they were equipped to meet him, and had their champion on their side. Now that champion is not only gone, but is at the head of the invading army.

Nor is this all. In Plutarch, Coriolanus begins operations by making a raid on the Roman territories with light-armed troops, retiring again with his plunder. Still the Romans do not take any precautions. In a second campaign he gets within five miles of the city, and still they do nothing but send an embassage. Even when, at the peril of his popularity, he grants them a truce of thirty days, they make no use of it for defence, but only continue to transmit arrogant or abject messages. This further opportunity, too, which they so strangely neglect, is wisely omitted by Shakespeare. With him the irruption is swift and sudden beyond the grasp of human thought. Coriolanus breaks across the border and strikes straight for Rome. There is no time for defensive measures, no possibility of aid. Even so, the part the Romans play is not so heroic as might be expected, but it is at least intelligible and much less dastardly than in the history.

Or take another instance. In describing the first inroad of Coriolanus, Plutarch writes :

> His chiefest purpose was, to increase still the malice and dissention betweene the nobilitie, and the communaltie : and to drawe that on, he was very carefull to keepe the noble mens landes and goods safe from harme and burning, but spoyled all the whole countrie besides, and would suffer no

man to take or hurte any thing of the noble mens. This
made greater sturre and broyle betweene the nobilitie and
people, then was before. For the noble men fell out with
the people, bicause they had so unjustly banished a man of
so great valure and power. The people on thother side,
accused the nobilitie, how they had procured Martius to
make these warres, to be revenged of them : bicause it pleased
them to see their goodes burnt and spoyled before their eyes,
whilest them selves were well at ease, and dyd behold the
peoples losses and misfortunes, and knowing their owne goods
safe and out of daunger : and howe the warre was not made
against the noble men, that had the enemie abroad, to keepe
that they had in safety.

In Shakespeare there is no word of Coriolanus
making any such distinction either from policy or
partisanship : he is incensed against all the inhabi-
tants of Rome, "the dastard nobles" quite as much
as the offending plebeians. And, on the other hand,
though the patricians revile the populace and its
leaders, there is no division between the orders, and
they show no inclination to disregard the solidarity
of their interests. This contrast becomes more
marked in the sequel. According to Plutarch, the
people in panic desire to recall the exile ; but the

Senate assembled upon it, would in no case yeld to that.
Who either dyd it of a selfe will to be contrarie to the
peoples desire : or bicause Martius should not returne through
the grace and favour of the people.

Afterwards, however, when he encamps so near
Rome, the majority has its way :

For there was no Consul, Senatour, nor Magistrate, that
durst once contrarie the opinion of the people, for the calling
home againe of Martius.

Accordingly, the first envoys are instructed to
announce to him his re-instatement in all his rights.
In Shakespeare's account the action of Rome
becomes much more dignified. In none of the
negociations, in no chance word of citizen, tribune
or senator, is there any hint of the sentence on

Coriolanus being revoked. Only when peace is concluded does his recall follow quite naturally, as an act of gratitude, in the burst of jubilant relief :

> Unshout the shout that banish'd Marcius,
> Repeal him with the welcome of his mother.   (v. v. 4.)

This, too, is one of the indications of Shakespeare's feeling for Roman greatness, that we should bear in mind when elsewhere he seems to show less sense even than Plutarch of her civic virtue.

The last notable deviation of the play from the biography occurs in the passage which deals with the murder of Coriolanus, and the difference is such as to make the victim far more responsible for the crime.

In Plutarch, after his return to Antium, Tullus, wishing to make away with him, demands that he should be deposed from his authority and taken to task. Marcius replies that he is willing to resign, if this be required by all the lords, and also to give account to the people if they will hear him. Thereupon a common council is called, at which proceedings begin by certain orators inciting popular feeling against him.

> When they had tolde their tales, Martius rose up to make them aunswer. Now, notwithstanding the mutinous people made a marvelous great noyse, yet when they sawe him, for the reverence they bare unto his valliantnes, they quieted them selves, and gave still audience to alledge with leysure what he could for his purgation. Moreover, the honestest men of the Antiates, and who most rejoyced in peace, shewed by their countenaunce that they would heare him willingly, and judge also according to their conscience. Whereupon Tullus fearing that if he dyd let him speake, he would prove his innocencie to the people, bicause emongest other things he had an eloquent tongue, besides that the first good service he had done to the people of the Volsces, dyd winne him more favour, then these last accusations could purchase him displeasure : and furthermore, the offence they layed to his charge, was a testimonie of the good will they ought him, for they would never have thought he had done

them wrong for that they tooke not the cittie of Rome, if they had not bene very neare taking of it, by meanes of his approche and conduction. For these causes Tullus thought he might no lenger delaye his pretence and enterprise, neither to tarie for the mutining and rising of the common people against him : wherefore those that were of the conspiracie, beganne to crie out that he was not to be heard, nor that they would not suffer a traytour to usurpe tyrannicall power over the tribe of the Volsces, who would not yeld up his estate and authoritie. And in saying these wordes, they all fell upon him, and killed him in the market place, none of the people once offering to rescue him. Howbeit it is a clear case, that this murder was not generally consented unto, of the most parte of the Volsces : for men came out of all partes to honour his bodie, and dyd honorablie burie him, setting out his tombe with great store of armour and spoyles, as the tombe of a worthie persone and great captaine.

Here the conspirators do not give him a chance, but kill him before a word passes his lips. In the tragedy, on the contrary, all might have been well, if in his rage of offended pride at Tullus' insults and taunts, he had not been carried away with his vaunts and reminders to excite and excuse the passions of his hearers. And thus with Shakespeare his ungovernable insolence is now made the cause of his death, just as before it has been accentuated as the cause of his banishment.

Still, though the exasperation against Coriolanus in Rome as in Corioli is thus in a measure justified, his own violence also receives its apology. In the latter case it is the provocation of Aufidius that rouses him to frenzy. In the former, it is the ineptitude of the citizens that fills him with scorn for their claims. And it is with reference to this and his whole conception of the Roman plebs that Shakespeare has made the most momentous and remarkable change in his story, the consideration of which we have purposely left to the last. The discussion of the difference in Plutarch's and in Shakespeare's attitude to the people will show us some of the most important aspects of the play.

CHAPTER III

THE GRAND CONTRAST. SHAKESPEARE'S CONCEPTION OF THE SITUATION IN ROME

IT is difficult to describe with any certainty the reasons for Shakespeare's variations from Plutarch in his treatment of the people. They may, like some of those already discussed, be due to the dramatic requirement of compression. They may be due to the deliberate purpose of exonerating the hero. They may, and this is more likely, have arisen quite naturally and unconsciously from Shakespeare's indifference to questions of constitutional theory and his inability to understand the ideals of an antique self-governing commonwealth controlled by all its free members as a body. In any case the result is a picture of the primitive society, from which some of Plutarch's inconsistencies, but with them some of the most typical traits, have been removed. The grand characteristic which the Tudor Englishman rejects, or all but rejects, is the intuitive political capacity which Plutarch, perhaps in idealising retrospect, attributes to all classes of citizens in the young republic, and which at any rate in after development formed the distinctive genius of the Roman state. He has indeed an inarticulate sense of it that enables him to suggest the general impression. He could not but have a sense of it ; for few men have been so penetrated with the greatness of later Rome as he, and he seems to have felt, as the shapers of the tradition and as Plutarch felt, that such a tree must have sprung from a healthy seed. So when we examine what his story involves, we have evidence enough of a general spirit of moderation, accommodation, compromise, that flow from and minister to an efficient practical patriotism; an ingrafted love of the city; and a conviction of the community of interests among high and low alike. Mr. Watkiss Lloyd puts this with great emphasis, and on the whole with great truth.

> Rome is preserved from cleaving in the midst by the virtues of the state, the reverence for the political majority which pervades both contending parties. The senate averts the last evil by the timely concession of the tribunitian power first, and then by sacrifice of a favourite champion of their own order, rather than civil war shall break out and all go to ruin in quarrel for the privilege and supremacy of a part. Rather than this they will concede, and trust to temporising, to negociating, to management, to the material influence of their position and the effect of their own merits and achievements, to secure their power or recover it hereafter. Among the people, on the other hand, there is also a restraining sentiment, a religion that holds back from the worst abuses of successful insurrection and excited faction. The proposition to kill Marcius is easily given up. Even the tribunes are capable of being persuaded to forego the extremity of rancour against the enemy of the people and of their authority, when he is fairly in their power, and commute death for banishment; and, the victory achieved, they counsel tranquility, as Menenius, on the other hand, softens down; and all goes smoothly again like a reconciled household, after experience of the miseries of adjusting wrongs by debate and anger.

Similarly the interests of the country are supreme when Coriolanus, with his new allies, advances to the attack:

> Some impatience of the people against the tribunes is natural, but the tribunes with all their faults, take their humiliation not ignobly, and the nobles never for a moment dream of getting a party triumph by foreign aid. The danger

of the country engrosses all, and at last Volumnia presses
upon her son the right and the noble, and employs all the
influences of domestic and natural affection—but all entirely
to the great political and national end,—and is as disregardful
of the fortunes or interests of the aristocratical party, which
might have hoped to seize the opportunity for recovering lost
ground, as she is apparently unaware, unconscious, regardless
of what may be the consequences personally to her much
loved son.

And Mr. Lloyd clinches his plea by his estimate of
the catastrophe.

In the concluding scene we appear to see the supremacy
of Rome assured . . .   In the senate-house of the Volscians
is perpetrated the assassination, from the disgrace of which
the better spirit of the Romans preserved their city : Aufidius
and his fellows with equal envy and ingratitude take the place
of the plotting tribunes, and the senators are powerless to
control the conspirators and mob of citizens who abet them.

They are, in short, in comparison with Rome self-
condemned ; and this becomes more manifest if we
contrast the finale of the play with the concluding
sentences in Plutarch, which Shakespeare leaves
unused.

Now Martius being dead, the whole state of the Volsces
hartely wished him alive again.   For first of all they fell out
with the Æques (who were their friendes and confederates)
touching preheminence and place : and this quarrell grew on
so farre betwene them, and frayes and murders fell out apon
it one with another.   After that, the Romaines overcame
them in battell, in which Tullus was slaine in the field, and
the flower of all their force was put to the sworde : so that
they were compelled to accept most shameful conditions of
peace, in yelding them selves subject unto the conquerors,
and promising to be obedient at their commandement.

It is at first sight rather strange that Shakespeare
should give no indication that the Volscians, first
by condoning Tullus' crime, the breach of friendship
from desire for pre-eminence, then by repeating it
as a community, prepare the way for their own
downfall.   Perhaps he felt that no finger-post was
necessary, and that all must see how in the long

run such a state must inevitably succumb to the greater moral force of Rome.

A few slight qualifications would have to be made in Mr. Lloyd's statement of his thesis to render it absolutely correct, but it is true in the main. Nevertheless, true though it be, it makes no account of two very important considerations. One of these is that despite the general appreciation which Shakespeare shows for the attitude of the Roman *Civitas*, he has no perception of the real issues between the plebeians and the patricians, or of the course which the controversy took, though these matters constitute the chief claim of the citizens of early Rome to the credit they receive in Plutarch's narrative. And the other consideration is, that Shakespeare's general appreciation of the community he describes is perceptible only when we view the play at a distance and in its mass : the impression in detail as we follow it from scene to scene is by no means so favourable to either party.

The first point is well brought out by the total omission in the drama of the initial episode in the discussion between the populace and the senate, and between the populace and Marcius. And the omission is all the more noticeable since Plutarch gives it particular prominence as directly leading to the establishment of the tribunate, which the drama, as we shall see, ascribes merely to an insignificant bread riot. Here is what Shakespeare must have read, and what slips from him without leaving more than a trace, though to modern feeling it is one of the most impressive passages in the whole *Life*.

> Now (Martius) being growen to great credit and authoritie in Rome for his valliantnes, it fortuned there grewe sedition in the cittie, bicause the Senate dyd favour the riche against the people, who dyd complaine of the sore oppression of userers, of whom they borowed money. For those that had litle, were yet spoyled of that litle they had by their creditours, for lack of abilitie to paye the userie : who offered their

goodes to be solde, to them that would geve most. And
suche as had nothing left, their bodies were layed holde of,
and they were made their bonde men, notwithstanding all the
woundes and cuttes they shewed, which they had receyved
in many battells, fighting for defence of their countrie and
common wealth : of the which, the last warre they made,
was against the Sabynes, wherein they fought apon the
promise the riche men had made them, that from thence-
forth they would intreate them more gently, and also upon
the worde of Marcus Valerius chief of the Senate, who by
authoritie of the counsell, and in the behalfe of the riche,
sayed they should performe that they had promised. But
after that they had faithfully served in this last battell of all,
where they overcame their enemies, seeing they were never a
whit the better, nor more gently intreated, and that the
Senate would geve no eare to them, but make as though they
had forgotten their former promise, and suffered them to be
made slaves and bonde men to their creditours, and besides,
to be turned out of all that ever they had ; they fell then
even to flat rebellion and mutinie, and to sturre up daunger-
ous tumultes within the cittie. The Romaines enemies,
hearing of this rebellion, dyd straight enter the territories of
Rome with a marvelous great power, spoyling and burning
all as they came. Whereupon the Senate immediatly made
open proclamation by sounde of trumpet, that all those which
were of lawfull age to carie weapon, should come and enter
their names into the muster masters booke, to goe to the
warres : but no man obeyed their commaundement. Whereupon their chief magistrates, and many of the Senate,
beganne to be of divers opinions emong them selves. For
some thought it was reason, they should somewhat yeld to
the poore peoples request, and that they should a little
qualifie the severitie of the lawe. Other held hard against
that opinion, and that was Martius for one. For he alleaged,
that the creditours losing their money they had lent, was not
the worst thing that was thereby : but that the lenitie that
was favored, was a beginning of disobedience, and that the
prowde attempt of the communaltie, was to abolish lawe,
and to bring all to confusion. Therefore he sayed ; if the
Senate were wise, they should betimes prevent, and quenche
this ill favored and worse ment beginning. The Senate met
many dayes in consultation about it : but in the end they
concluded nothing. The poore common people seeing no
redresse, gathered them selves one daye together, and one
encoraging another, they all forsooke the cittie, and encamped
them selves upon a hill, called at this daye the holy hill,
alongest the river of Tyber, offering no creature any hurte

or violence, or making any shewe of actuall rebellion ; saving
that they cried as they went up and down, that the riche men
had driven them out of the cittie, and that all Italie through
they should finde ayer, water and ground to burie them in.
Moreover, they sayed, to dwell at Rome was nothing els but
to be slaine, or hurte with continuell warres and fighting for
defence of the riche mens goodes.

Plutarch goes on to tell how in this crisis the Senate
adopts a conciliatory attitude, and how after the
fable of Menenius, the mutineers are pacified by
the concession of five *Tribuni plebis*, "whose office
should be to defend the poore people from violence
and oppression." Then he concludes this part of
his recital :

Hereupon the cittie being growen againe to good quiet
and unitie, the people immediatly went to the warres, shewing
that they had a good will to doe better than ever they dyd, and
to be very willing to obey the magistrates in that they would
commaund concerning the warres.

Now, in this account there is no question which side
is on the right and has a claim on our sympathies.
The plebs is reduced to distress by fighting for the
state and for the aristocratic *régime* that was set up
some twenty years before : its misery is aggravated
by harsh and inadequate laws, the redress of which
it seeks by a policy of passive resistance ; its
demands are so equitable that they are approved by
a portion of the Senate, and so urgent that they are
conceded by the Senate as a whole : but such is the
strength of class selfishness, that when the hour of
need is past, the patricians violate their explicit promise, and the grievances become more intolerable than
before. Even now the plebeians break out in no
violent rebellion, and hardly show their discontent in
a casual riot. In their worst desperation they merely
secede, and in their very secession they are far from
stubborn. They admit Menenius' moral that the
Senate has an essential function in the state : and
as a preliminary to their return, only stipulate for a

machinery that will protect them against further oppression.

But hardly a line in the description of this move-ment which the plebeians conducted so moderately and sagaciously to a successful end, has passed into the picture of Shakespeare. He ignores the reason-ableness of their cause, the reasonableness of their means, and fails to perceive the essential efficiency and steadiness of their character, though all these things are expressed or implied in Plutarch's narrative. This episode, in which the younger contemporary of Nero favours the people, the elder contemporary of Pym summarily dismisses, and substitutes for it another far less important, in which they appear in no very creditable light, but which had nothing to do with the institution of the Tribunate, and occurred in consequence of the dearth only after the capture of Corioli.

> Now when this warre was ended, the flatterers of the people beganne to sturre up sedition againe, without any newe occasion, or just matter offered of complainte. For they dyd grounde this seconde insurrection against the Nobilitie and Patricians, apon the people's miserie and mis-fortune, that could not but fall out, by reason of the former discorde and sedition, betweene them and the Nobilitie. Bicause the most parte of the errable land within the territorie of Rome, was become heathie and barren for lacke of plowing, for that they had no time nor meane to cause corne, to be brought them out of other countries to sowe, by reason of their warres which made the extreme dearth they had emong them. Now those busie pratlers that sought the peoples good will, by suche flattering wordes, perceyving great scarsitie of corne to be within the cittie, and though there had bene plenty enough, yet the common people had no money to buye it : they spread abroad false tales and rumours against the Nobilitie, that they in revenge of the people, had practised and procured the extreme dearthe emong them.

This circumstance, combined with the still later demand for a distribution of corn, Shakespeare transposes, and makes the surely rather inappro-

priate cause of the appointment of the tribunes.
Inappropriate, that is, to what the logic of the
situation requires, and to what the sagacity of the
traditional plebs would solicit. They ask for bread
and they get a magistrate. But not inappropriate
to the unreasoning demands of a frenzied proletariat.
Many parallels might be cited from the French
revolutions. But this is just an instance of Shakespeare's inability to conceive a popular rising in
other terms than the outbreak of a mob.

And this leads us to the second point. The
general moderation and dignity implied in the attitude of Rome, viewed broadly and comprehensively,
almost disappears when we are confronted with
the full concrete life of the participants in all its
picturesque and incisive details.

For consider first a little more closely the treatment of the people. We have seen that in many
ways the proceedings which it and its representatives take against Coriolanus are more defensible
in Shakespeare than in Plutarch : but, on the other
hand, they have less rational grounds for the original
insurrection, and are much less clear-sighted and
consequent in choosing the means of redress. They
are comparatively well-meaning and fair, neither
bitter nor narrow-minded, but they are quite
inefficient, far from self-reliant, very childish and
helpless. They are conspicuously lacking in political
aptitude, but they make up for it by a certain sound-
ness of feeling. Plutarch's plebeians go the right
way about protecting themselves from unjust laws,
but they pursue Coriolanus with rancorous chicane
even when his policy has been overturned. Shakespeare's plebeians seek to legislate against a natural
calamity, but at the crisis they turn quite justifiably,
if a little tardily, on a would-be governor who makes
no secret of his ill-will. Taken as separate units,
they may be unwashed and puzzle-headed, but they

are worthy fellows whom misery has driven desperate, yet whose misery claims compassion, though their desperation makes them meddle in things too high for them. In the opening scene, the First Citizen, even when calling for the death of Marcius, does so merely because he imagines that it is the preliminary to getting cheap food :

> The gods know I speak this in hunger for bread, not in
> thirst for revenge. (I. i. 15.)

But even among the maddened and famishing crowd, Marcius is not without his advocate. The Second Citizen admonishes them :

> Consider you what services he has done for his country?
> (I. i. 30.)

And though these the ringleader discounts on the ground that they were due not to patriotism, but to personal pride and filial affection, his apologist, persisting in his defence, points out that he is not responsible for his inborn tendencies.

> What he cannot help in his nature, you account a vice in
> him. (I. i. 42.)

All this is candid enough : a benevolent neutral could not say more. These rioters have no thought of libelling their adversary. They deny neither his claims nor his merits ; they only assert that these are outweighed by his offences. The Second Citizen proceeds in his plea :

> You must in no way say he is covetous ;

and the First rejoins :

> If I must not, I need not be barren of accusations ; he
> hath faults, with surplus, to tire in repetition. (I. i. 43.)

We have seen how Shakespeare adopts from Plutarch the motive for the plebeians' initial support of Coriolanus at the election, but he makes it a more striking instance of their fairness, for he represents them as quite aware and mindful of the reasons on the other side.

> *Fourth Citizen.* You have deserved nobly of your country, and you have not deserved nobly.
> *Coriolanus.* Your enigma?
> *Fourth Citizen.* You have been a scourge to her enemies, you have been a rod to her friends; you have not indeed loved the common people. (II. iii. 94.)

It is all very well for the candidate to turn this off with a flout, but it is the sober truth. That the despised plebeian should see both sides of the case shows in him more sanity of judgment than Coriolanus ever possessed : that he should nevertheless cast his vote for such an applicant shows more generosity as well. And the generosity, if also the simplicity, of the electors is likewise made more pronounced than in Plutarch by their persevering in their course despite the scorn with which Coriolanus treats them ; of which Plutarch of course knows nothing. Even that they forgive till the tribunes irritate the wounds and predict more fatal ones from the new weapon that has been put into such ruthless hands.

> Did you perceive
> He did solicit you in free contempt
> When he did need your loves, and do you think
> That his contempt shall not be bruising to you,
> When he hath power to crush? (II. iii. 207.)

All these instances of right feeling and instinctive appreciation of greatness are in Shakespeare's picture, while they are either not at all or in a much less degree in Plutarch's. And these citizens are capable of following good leadership as well as bad. They listen to Menenius, and are "almost persuaded" by his argument, without, as in Plutarch, making their acceptance of it merely provisional. Under Cominius they quit themselves, as he says, "like Romans," and he gives them the praise :

> Breathe you, my friends : well fought. (I. vi. 1.)

Afterwards too he recognises that they are earning their share of the spoil, even as before they had borne themselves stoutly :

> March on, my fellows :
> Make good this ostentation, and you shall
> Divide in all with us. (I. vi. 85.)

This is said to the volunteers who come forward at Marcius' summons, an episode for which there is hardly a hint in Plutarch. There, indeed, we read that he cannot call off the looters from the treasures of Corioli :

> Whereupon taking those that willingly offered them selves he went out of the cittie :

which supplies the sentence,

> I, with those that have the spirit, will haste
> To help Cominius. (I. v. 14.)

But this hint, if hint it were, Shakespeare uses anew with far stronger and brighter colouring in the incident of Marcius' stirring appeal to Cominius' men and their enthusiastic response : which is to be found only in the drama :

> If any such be here—
> As it were sin to doubt—that love this painting
> Wherein you see me smear'd : if any fear
> Lesser his person than an ill report ;
> If any think brave death outweighs bad life
> And that his country's dearer than himself ;
> Let him alone, or so many so minded,
> Wave thus, to express his disposition,
> And follow Marcius.
> [*They. all shout and wave their swords, take him up in their arms, and cast up their caps.*] (I. vi. 67.)

If they are handled in the right way, these citizen soldiers can play their part well. But they need to be rightly handled, they need to have their feelings stirred. They have no rational initiative of their own, and cannot do without inspiration and guidance.

For, consider the grounds for their rising. Shakespeare not only completely suppresses the remarkable
secession to the Mons Sacer, but barely mentions
the social grievances that led to it. The First
Citizen says indeed of the patricians :

> [They] make edicts for usury, to support usurers ; repeal
> daily any wholesome act established against the rich, and
> provide more piercing statutes daily, to chain up and restrain
> the poor. If the wars eat us not up, they will.   (I. i. 83.)

But this is a mere passing remark, and no stress is
laid on these, the real causes of the discontent, in
comparison with the dearth, which for the rest seems
to end with the Coriolan campaign, when there is,
as Cominius promises, a "common distribution" of
the spoils. Now the dearth is represented as a
mere disastrous accident, for which no one is
responsible, and for which there is no remedy save
prayer—or such a foray as presently took place.
Menenius expressly says so :

> For the dearth,
> The gods, not the patricians, made it, and
> Your knees to them, not arms, must help.   (I. i. 74.)

It is alleged, no doubt, by the mutineers that the
"storehouses are crammed with grain," but there is
no confirmation of this in the play, and the way in
which "honest" Menenius reports the rumour, and
Marcius, who is never less than honest receives it,
implies that it is mere tittle tattle and gossip of the
chimney corner.

> *Marcius.*   What's their seeking?
> *Menenius.* For corn at their own rates : whereof, they say,
> The city is well stored.
> *Marcius.*   Hang 'em ! They say !
> They'll sit by the fire, and presume to know
> What's done i' the Capitol ; who's like to rise,
> Who thrives and who declines ; side factions and give out
> Conjectural marriages ; making parties strong
> And feebling such as stand not in their liking
> Below their cobbled shoes. They say there's grain enough !
>   (I. i. 192.)

In short their temper is hardly parodied in the modern skit,

> Who fills the butchers' shops with large blue flies?

And if they resemble the ignorant fanatics of later days in the unreasonableness of their complaints, they resemble them too, as we have seen, in the unreasonableness of their remedies. If things were as the play implies what help would lie in constitutional reform? They are no better than the starving *Sansculottes* who sought to allay their hunger by snatching new morsels of the royal prerogative. It really reads like a scene in Carlyle's Paris of 1790 A.D., and not like any scene in Plutarch's Rome of 494 B.C., when Coriolanus describes the delight of the famine-stricken crowds at getting their representatives:

> They threw their caps
> As they would hang them on the horns o' the moon,
> Shouting their emulation.   (I. i. 216.)

Moreover, when left to themselves, or when their sleeping manhood is not awakened, these plebeians, otherwise than those of Plutarch, have not even the average of physical courage. They can fight creditably under the competent management of Cominius, or heroically under the stimulus of Marcius' rousing appeal: but if such influences are lacking, they fail. Menenius says of them:

> Though abundantly they lack discretion,
> Yet are they passing cowardly.   (I. i. 206.)

Marcius ironically invites them to the wars by indicating what would be, and turns out to be, provision for their needs:

> The Volsces have much corn: take these rats thither
> To gnaw their garners. Worshipful mutineers,
> Your valour puts well forth: pray, follow.   (I. i. 253.)

And the citizens steal away.   In truth the low
opinion of their mettle seems justified by events.   At
Corioli the troops under Cominius do well, but those
in Marcius' division, perhaps because his treatment
does not call out what is best in them, seem to deserve
a part at least of his imprecations :

> All the contagion of the south light on you,
> You shames of Rome !   You herd of——.   Boils and plagues
> Plaster you o'er, that you may be abhorr'd
> Further than seen, and one infect another
> Against the wind a mile !   You souls of geese,
> That bear the shapes of men, how have you run
> From slaves that apes would beat !   Pluto and hell !
> All hurt behind ! backs red, and faces pale
> With flight and agued fear !   (i. iv. 30.)

Nor do they appear in a better light in the moment
of partial victory, for they at once fall to plunder
instead of following it up and helping their fellows.
This touch, of course, Shakespeare derived from
Plutarch.

> The most parte of the souldiers beganne incontinently to
> spoyle, to carie awaye, and to looke up the bootie they had
> wonne.   But Martius was marvelous angry with them, and
> cried out on them, that it was no time now to looke after
> spoyle, and to ronne straggling here and there to enriche
> them selves, whilest the other Consul and their fellowe
> cittizens peradventure were fighting with their enemies ; and
> howe that leaving the spoyle they should seeke to winde
> them selves out of daunger and perill.   Howbeit, crie, and
> saye to them what he could, very fewe of them would hearken
> to him.

But Shakespeare is not content with this.   He quite
without warrant describes the articles as worthless,
to emphasise the baseness of the pillagers.

> See here these movers that do prize their hours
> At a crack'd drachma !   Cushions, leaden spoons,
> Irons of a doit, doublets that hangmen would
> Bury with those that wore them, these base slaves,
> Ere yet the fight be done, pack up.   (i. v. 5.)

This strain of baseness appears in another way
afterwards, when they yell and hoot at their banished

enemy, like a pack of curs at a retreating mastiff, or when at his threatened return they eat their words and their deeds.

> *First Citizen.*   For mine own part,
> When I said, banish him, I said 'twas pity.
> *Second Citizen.* And so did I.
> *Third Citizen.* And so did I : and, to say the truth, so did very many of us. . . .
> *First Citizen.* I ever said we were i' the wrong when we banished him.
> *Second Citizen.* So did we all.   (IV. vi. 139 and 155.)

What then is Shakespeare's opinion of the people as a whole ? Despite his sympathy with those of whom it is composed, it is to him a giant not yet in his teens, with formidable physical strength, with crude natural impulses to the good and the bad, kindly-natured and simple-minded, not incapable of fair-dealing and generosity ; but rude, blundering, untaught, and therefore subject to spasms of fury, panic, and greed, fit for useful service only when it finds the right leader, but sure to go wrong if abandoned to its own or evil guidance.

To the danger of evil guidance, however, it is specially exposed, for it loves flattery and is imposed on by professions of goodwill : so Shakespeare reserves his severest treatment for those who cajole it, the demagogues of the Tribunate. No doubt in his tolerant objective way he concedes even to them a measure of justification. He was bound to do so, else they would have been outside the pale of dramatic sympathy ; and also the culpability of Coriolanus would have been obscured. So there is something to be said even for their policy and management. They are quite right in fearing the results of Coriolanus' elevation to the chief place in Rome :

> *Sicinius.*   On the sudden,
> I warrant him consul.
> *Brutus.*   Then our office may
> During his power, go sleep.   (II. i. 237.)

Their admonitions to the electors are such as the organisers of a party are not only entitled but bound to give to a constituency :

> Could you not have told him
> As you were lesson'd, when he had no power,
> But was a petty servant to the state,
> He was your enemy, ever spake against
> Your liberties and the charters that you bear
> I' the body of the weal : and now, arriving
> A place of potency and sway o' the state,
> If he should still malignantly remain
> Fast foe to the plebeii, your voices might
> Be curses to yourselves.   (II. iii. 180.)

These forebodings of what is likely to occur are not only thoroughly justifiable but obvious.

Then, though their abandonment of the methods of violence and acceptance of a trial are discounted partly by the perils of open force, partly by their confidence in and manipulation of a verdict to their minds, their willingness to substitute the penalty of banishment for the extreme sentence of death, must stand, as we have seen, to the credit, if not of their placability, at least of their moderation and prudence. Moreover, if we could disregard the dangers of war, their "platform," as we should now call it, seems approved by its success.   One cannot but sympathise with the satisfaction of Sicinius at the results of Marcius' expulsion :

> We hear not of him, neither need we fear him :
> His remedies are tame i' the present peace
> And quietness of the people, which before
> Were in wild hurry.   Here do we make his friends
> Blush that the world goes well, who rather had,
> Though they themselves did suffer by 't, behold
> Dissentious numbers pestering streets, than see
> Our tradesmen singing in their shops and going
> About their functions friendly.   (IV. vi. 1.)

And when the citizens pass with their greetings, the tribune has a right to say to Menenius :

This is a happier and more comely time
Than when these fellows ran about the streets,
Crying confusion.   (IV. vi. 27.)

Even Menenius has to give a modified and grudging
approval of the new position of things:

All's well: and might have been much better, if
He could have temporised.   (IV. vi. 16.)

And when the disastrous news comes in, after the
first outburst of incredulous wrath and terrified
impatience, the two colleagues bear themselves well
enough. There is shrewdness and good sense in
Sicinius' words to the citizens:

Go, masters, get you home: be not dismay'd;
These are a side that would be glad to have
This true which they so seem to fear. Go home,
And show no sign of fear.   (IV. vi. 149.)

When this very natural and probable conjecture
proves false, they both rise to the occasion, or seek
to do so, the cross-grained Sicinius somewhat more
effectually than the glib-tongued Brutus, and show a
certain dignity and justness of feeling. Their remonstrance with and petition to Menenius, if we grant
the patriotism on the one side as well as the other,
are not without their cogency:

Nay, pray, be patient: if you refuse your aid
In this so never-needed help, yet do not
Upbraid's with our distress.   (V. i. 33.)

When Menenius objects that his mission will be
futile, Sicinius' reply comes near being noble:

Yet your good will
Must have that thanks from Rome, after the measure
As you intended well.   (V. i. 45).

When Menenius, returning from his fruitless mission,
describes Coriolanus in his unapproachable, inexorable power, the tribune's rejoinder is again the true
one:

Menenius. He wants nothing of a god but eternity and a heaven to throne in.

Sicinius. Yes, mercy, if you report him truly. (v. iv. 24.)

Yet these various traits so little interfere with the general impression, that perhaps many tolerably careful readers who are familiar with the play, hardly take them into account. In the total effect they both seem to us pitiful busybodies, whose ill-earned influence only leads to disaster ; or, as Menenius describes them :

> A pair of tribunes that have rack'd for Rome,
> To make coals cheap. (v. i. 16.)

The first feature we notice in them is their pride, a vice which they blame in Coriolanus, and with which their own is expressly contrasted. For his is the haughty, unbending self-consciousness that is based on the sense of indwelling force, and has a shrinking disgust for praise. Theirs, on the other hand, revels in popularity, and their power depends entirely on the support which that popularity secures them. As Menenius tells them :

> You are ambitious for poor knaves' caps and legs. (ii. i. 76.)

> Your helps are many, or else your actions would grow wondrous single : your abilities are too infant-like for doing much alone. (ii. i. 39.)

They are really consequential and overweening rather than proud. And magnifying their importance and their office, they are apt to take too seriously any trifle in which they are concerned, and to become irritated at any mishap to their own convenience. Having no standard but themselves by which to measure the proportion of things, they are fussy over minor points and lose their tempers over petty troubles. This is the point of Menenius' banter.

> You wear out a good wholesome forenoon in hearing a cause between an orange-wife and a fosset-seller ; and then

rejourn the controversy of three pence to a second day of audience. When you are hearing a matter between party and party, if you chanced to be pinched with the colic, you make faces like mummers; set up the bloody flag against all patience; and, in roaring for a chamber-pot, dismiss the controversy bleeding, the more entangled by your hearing: all the peace you make in their cause is, calling both the parties knaves. (II. i. 77.)

This is, they are disposed to treat a mole-hill as a mountain, but if they are galled, to break out in indiscriminate and unjustified abuse. Menenius gives it them home in respect of these foibles:

You talk of pride: O that you could turn your eyes toward the napes of your necks, and make but an interior survey of your good selves! O that you could!
Brutus. What then, sir?
Menenius. Why, then you should discover a brace of un-meriting, proud, violent, testy magistrates, alias fools, as any in Rome. (II. i. 41.)

This is the utterance of an enemy; nevertheless it is confirmed by their behaviour, and is moreover a prophecy of their action in regard to Marcius. In the first place their pride has been insulted by his:

Sicinius. Was ever man so proud as is this Marcius?
Brutus. He has no equal.
Sicinius. When we were chosen tribunes of the people,—
Brutus. Mark'd you his lip and eyes?
Sicinius. Nay, but his taunts.
Brutus. Being moved, he will not spare to gird the gods—
Sicinius. Bemock the modest moon. (I. i. 256.)

A man who gibes at the gods, the moon, and above all the tribunes, is evidently a profane and irreverent fellow who should be got rid of. And perhaps it is anxiety not only for the public good but for their own authority that makes them dread their office may "go sleep," during his consulship. At any rate the disrespect with which they have been treated is one main motive of their indignation: " *Our* Aediles

smote, *ourselves* resisted!" they exclaim in pardonable horror (III. i. 319).

Then the means they take to ruin Coriolanus,
though not without its astuteness, and similar enough
to what is practised every day in parliamentary
tactics, is altogether base : it is the device of mean,
paltry, inferior natures.   They speculate on the
defect of their enemy's greatness, they reckon on
his heroic vehemence and forcefulness to destroy
him, and lay plans to betray his nobility to a passion
that will embroil him with the people.   It is as easy,
says Sicinius, to drive him to provocation "as to set
dogs on sheep" (II. i. 273).   But easy though it is,
they are careful to give minute directions to their
gang.   Sicinius tells them that any condition proposed to him,

> Would have gall'd his surly nature,
> Which easily endures not article
> Tying him to aught; so putting him to rage,
> You should have ta'en the advantage of his choler
> And pass'd him unelected.   (II. iii. 203.)

Then, after engineering the disavowal of the elected
candidate, Brutus calculates

> If, as his nature is, he fall in rage
> With their refusal, both observe and answer
> The vantage of his anger.   (II. iii. 266.)

And here are his final instructions for the behaviour
of the people at the trial :

> Put him to choler straight : he hath been used
> Ever to conquer, and to have his worth
> Of contradiction : being once chafed, he cannot
> Be rein'd again to temperance ; then he speaks
> What's in his heart; and that is there which looks
> To break his neck.   (III iii. 25.)

The suggestion for these proceedings comes, as
we saw, from Plutarch ; but in this one respect his
tribunes are by no means so wily.   They contrive
a dilemma in which Coriolanus will have either to

humble or to compromise himself; but though they would prefer the latter alternative, they do nothing to bring it about.

Yet with all their activity in the matter, they are meanly desirous of evading responsibility and saving their own skins.

> *Brutus.*   Lay
> A fault on us, your tribunes; that we labour'd,
> No impediment between, but that you must
> Cast your election on him.
> *Sicinius.*   Say you chose him
> More after our commandment than as guided
> By your own true affections, and that your minds,
> Pre-occupied with what you rather must do
> Than what you should, made you against the grain
> To voice him consul: lay the fault on us.   (II. iii. 234.)

And parallel with this is the crowning vulgarity of their triumph :

> Go, see him out at gates, and follow him,
> As he hath follow'd you, with all despite;
> Give him deserved vexation.   (III. iii. 138.)

This is perhaps the supreme instance of their headstrong, testy and inconsiderate violence, for, as we shall see, it embitters the wavering Marcius and drives him to alliance with the foe. But the same violence has abundantly appeared before. The rest do all in their power to appease the tumult and procure a hearing for Sicinius, he uses the opportunity to add fuel to the fire and deserves Menenius' rebuke :

> This is the way to kindle, not to quench.   (III. i. 197.)

When Brutus proceeds in the same way, Cominius interrupts :

> That is the way to lay the city flat;
> To bring the roof to the foundation,
> And bury all, which yet distinctly ranges,
> In heaps and piles of ruin.   (III. i. 204.)

Menenius has to admonish them :

> Do not cry havoc, where you should but hunt
> With modest warrant.   (III. i. 274.)

And again :

> One word more, one word.
> This tiger-footed rage, when it shall find
> The harm of unscann'd swiftness, will too late
> Tie leaden pounds to 's heels.   (III. i. 311.)

They do yield at last, but clearly the game they were playing in unreflecting impatience was most hazardous for the populace itself.   Indeed, even when they have accepted more moderate counsels, the expulsion of Coriolanus seems an act not only of ingratitude but of recklessness.   Their low cunning has attained an end, good perhaps in itself for the party they represent, but even for that party of insignificant advantage in view of the wider issues.   Volumnia's taunt is very much to the point :

> Hadst thou foxship
> To banish him that struck more blows for Rome
> Than thou hast spoken words?   (IV. ii. 18.)

For after all, the pressing need in that period of constant war, as Plutarch and Shakespeare imagine it, was defence of the whole state, the plebs as well as the senate, against the foreign enemy, and the danger of an invasion was one of the ordinary probabilities of the case.   Most men who had any sense of proportion would, in the circumstances, pause before they banished the sword and soldiership of Rome.   No doubt the tribunes were to be excused for not foreseeing the renegacy of Coriolanus; when it is announced as a fact Menenius can hardly credit it.

> This is unlikely :
> He and Aufidius can no more atone
> Than violentest contrariety.   (IV. vi. 71.)

It is less excusable that they should neglect the danger of a new attack from the Volsces, for though Cominius, as we saw, makes a similar error, he does so when Marcius is still on the side of the Romans. Menenius' exclamation, when the invasion actually takes place and when the news of it is first brought to Rome, describes a situation, the possibility or probability of which every public man should have anticipated.

> 'Tis Aufidius,
> Who, hearing of our Marcius' banishment,
> Thrusts forth his horns again into the world :
> Which were inshell'd when Marcius stood for Rome,
> And durst not once peep out. (IV. vi. 42.)

This, though of course an understatement, for in point of fact Aufidius did not wait for Marcius' banishment, is at any rate the least that was to be expected. But the tribunes, with a sanguine and criminal shortsightedness that suggests a distinguished pair of British politicians in our own day, refuse to admit as conceivable a fact the likelihood of which the circumstances of the case and recent experience avouch.

> *Brutus.* It cannot be
> The Volsces dare break with us.
> *Menenius.* Cannot be !
> We have record that very well it can,
> And three examples of the like have been
> Within my age. (IV. vi. 47.)

Besides, the Volscians were not the only jealous neighbours the young republic had to guard herself against.

But their reception of the unwelcome tidings is a new instance of the ignoble strain in the tribunes' nature. The first effect they have on Brutus is to enrage him against the informant : "Go see this rumourer whipp'd"; and Sicinius seconds the humane direction, but improves on it that the public may be duly cautioned against telling unpalatable truths : "Go whip him 'fore the people's eyes." Menenius may well remonstrate :

> Reason with the fellow,
> Before you punish him, where he heard this,
> Lest you shall chance to whip your information,
> And beat the messenger who bids beware
> Of what is to be dreaded.   (IV. vi. 51.)

This is not merely an illustration of their habitual touchiness and irritability at whatever thwarts them. Once more we think of the words of the messenger in *Antony and Cleopatra* when he fears to report the worst : " The nature of bad news infects the teller"; and of Antony's reply : "When it concerns the fool and coward." There is beyond doubt more than a spice of folly and cowardice in the self-important quidnuncs, with their purblind temerity and shifty meanness. We are very glad to hear in the end of Brutus being mishandled by the mob and very sorry that Sicinius goes free : but at least he has had his dose of alarm and mortification, and in the future his influence will be gone ; which is well. Yet they are not bad men. They are very like the majority of the citizens of Great and Greater Britain, and no inconsiderable portion of those who govern the Empire and its members. They have a certain amount of principle, shrewdness, and, if the test of misfortune comes, even of proper feeling. They would have made very worthy aldermen of a small municipality. But measured against the greatness of Rome, or even of Coriolanus, they are as gnats to the lion.

The picture, then, of the people and its elect is not flattering if we follow it in detail, but a similar examination is hardly more favourable to the nobles. Of course their behaviour is to a certain extent accounted for by the peculiarity of their position. Hitherto, since the expulsion of the kings, the

T

" honoured number " have had it all their own way in
the state, and Shakespeare imputes no blame to their
management, unless it be their excessive arrogance
towards the populace they rule and employ.   But
now bad times have made that populace seditious,
and they have discovered that, rightly or wrongly,
they must give it a share of the power.   Their pride,
their traditions, the consciousness of their faculty
for government, pull them one way, the necessities
of the case pull them another.   A dominant caste is
placed in a false position when it is forced to capitu-
late to assailants for whom it feels an unreasonable
contempt and a reasonable mistrust.   When we
consider the difficulties of the situation and the
broad results, the patricians, as we saw, come off
respectably enough, and we must give them credit
for circumspection, adaptability, and civic cohesion.
But in detail their attitude betrays the uncertainty
and weakness that cannot but ensue in a man or a
body of men when there is a conflict between conviction and expediency, and an attempt to obey
them both.   Their scorn of the plebeians, followed
by the very brief effort for their champion and very
prompt acquiescence in his expatriation, makes an
unpleasant impression ; and this is more noticeable
in the drama than in the biography.   Plutarch
repeatedly states that they disagree among themselves, many of them sympathising with the popular
demands and only the younger men favouring the
harsh and reactionary views of Coriolanus.[1]   This
distinction has left no trace in the play except in the

[1] See especially the passage that describes his behaviour after he
has been rejected for the consulship : " Coriolanus went home to his
house, full fraighted with spite and malice against the people, being
accompanied with all the lustiest young gentlemen, whose mindes
were nobly bent, as those that came of noble race, and commonly
used for to followe and honour him.   But then specially they floct
about him, and kept him companie, to his muche harme ; for they dyd
but kyndle and inflame his choller more and more, being sorie with
him for the injurie the people offred him."

stage-direction which represents him as departing into exile escorted to the gates by his friends, his relatives, and " the young nobility of Rome": but otherwise Shakespeare makes no use of it. Coriolanus is mouthpiece for the ideals not of heedless youth but of all the aristocracy, though most of them may be more politic than he and not so frank. Nevertheless his presuppositions are theirs, and therefore they seem temporisers and poltroons beside their outspoken advocate. Indeed, through Menenius, they admit they have been to blame :

> We loved him ; but, like beasts
> And cowardly nobles, gave way unto your clusters,
> Who did hoot him out o' the city.   (IV. vi. 121.)

Nor do they act very vigorously when destruction threatens Rome. They do not indeed seek to separate their cause from that of the whole community and make terms with their former friend for their own class. Beyond some naturally bitter gibes at the "clusters" and their leaders, not unaccompanied for the rest by bitter outbursts against themselves, there is no trace of the dissensions with the people which Plutarch describes. But they have no thought of organising any attempt at resistance. True, there are circumstances in Shakespeare that account for this supineness as it is not explained in his authority. It is partly due to the feeling that they are in the wrong, which Shakespeare in a much greater degree than Plutarch attributes to them. As their own words show :

> *Cominius.*   For his best friends, if they
> Should say, " Be good to Rome," they charged him even
> As those should do that had deserved his hate,
> And therein show'd like enemies.
> *Menenius.*   'Tis true :
> If he were putting to my house the brand
> That should consume it, I have not the face
> To say, " Beseech you, cease."   (IV. vi. 111.)

And again :

> If he could burn us all into one coal,
> We have deserved it.   (IV. vi. 137.)

Partly, too, there has been no time for preparation, for, as we have seen, the invasion is a bolt from the blue, and after it has first struck there is no convenient truce of thirty days_ before its recurrence. Entreaty, says Sicinius, might help

> More than the instant army we can make ;   (V. i. 37.)

and it is the opinion of all.

Partly, too, the inertness of Rome is a tribute to the greatness of the adversary, which is enhanced beyond the hyperboles of Plutarch, and with which to inspire them the Volscians are irresistible.

> He is their god : he leads them like a thing
> Made by some other deity than nature
> That shapes men better : and they follow him,
> Against us brats, with no less confidence
> Than boys pursuing summer butterflies,
> Or butchers killing flies.   (IV. vi. 90.)

But contrition, unpreparedness, despair of success hardly excuse the palsy of incompetence into which this proud aristocracy has now fallen. It does not of course sink so low as in Plutarch. Of the first of the repeated deputations he narrates :

> The ambassadours that were sent, were Martius familliar friendes and acquaintaunce, who looked at the least for a curteous welcome of him, as of their familliar friende and kynesman. Howbeit they founde nothing lesse. For at their comming, they were brought through the campe, to the place where he was set in his chayer of state, with a marvelous and unspeakable majestie, having the chiefest men of the Volsces about him : so he commaunded them to declare openly the cause of their comming. Which they delivered in the most humble and lowly wordes they possiblie could devise, and with all modest countenaunce and behaviour agreeable for the same. When they had done their message ; for the injurie they had done him, he aunswered them very hottely and in great choller.

This is evidently the foundation of the interviews with Cominius and Menenius respectively, and it is worth while noting the points of difference.

In the first place single individuals are substituted for an unspecified number. Just in the same way the final deputation consists of "Virgilia, Volumnia, leading young Marcius, Valeria, and Attendants," without any of "all the other Romaine Ladies" that accompany them in Plutarch. In the last case it is the members and the friend of Coriolanus' family, in the previous cases it is his sworn comrade Cominius and his idolatrous admirer Menenius who make the appeal : and this at once gives their intercessions more of a personal and less of a public character. One result of this with which we are not now concerned, is that the rigour of Coriolanus' first two answers is considerably heightened ; but at present it is more important to observe that the impression of a formal embassy is avoided. Cominius and Menenius strike us less as delegates from the Roman state, than as private Romans who may suppose that their persuasions will have special influence with their friend. There is nothing to indicate that Cominius was official envoy of the republic, and we know that Menenius went without any authorisation, in compliance with the request made by Sicinius and Brutus in the street. Shakespeare's senate is spared the ignominy of the recurring supplications to which Plutarch's senate condescends. If these are not altogether suppressed, the references to them are very faint and vague.

And also the suppliants bear themselves more worthily. Menenius is far from employing "the most humble and lowly wordes" that could possibly be devised or "the modest countenaunce and behaviour agreeable for the same." Cominius indeed tells how at the close of the interview, we may suppose as a last resort, he "kneeled before" Coriolanus, but there was no more loss of dignity in his doing so, consul and general though he had been, than there was afterwards in Volumnia's doing the same ; and his words as he repeats them do not show any lack of self-respect.

Still the inactivity, the helplessness, the want of nerve in the Roman nobles in the hour of need are somewhat pitiful. It was the time to justify their higher position by higher patriotism, resourceful-ness and courage. They do not make the slightest effort to do so. Remorse for their desertion of Coriolanus need not have lamed their energies, since now they would be confronting him not for themselves but for the state. Even their "instant armies" might do something if commanded and inspired by devoted captains. At the worst they could lead their fellow-citizens to an heroic death. One cannot help feeling that if a Coriolanus, or anyone with a tithe of his spirit, had been among them, things would have been very different. But while they retain much of the old caste pride, they have lost much of the old caste efficiency.

Thus Shakespeare, when he comes to the concrete, views with some severity both the popular and the senatorial party. They show themselves virulent and acrimonious in their relations with each other, yet inconsequent even in their virulence and acrimony : then, after having respectively enforced and permitted the banishment of their chief defender, they are ready to succumb to him without a blow when, it has well been said, he returns not even as an *émigré* using foreign aid to restore the privileges of his own order and the old *régime*, but as a barbarian bringing the national foe to exterminate the state and all its members. And we cannot help asking : Is this an adequate representation of the young republic that was ere long to become the mistress of the world? We must look steadily at those general aspects of the story which we have noticed above, as well as at the doings of the persons and parties amidst which Coriolanus is set, if we would get the total effect of the play. Then it produces something of the feeling which prompted Heine's description of the ancient Romans :

> They were not great men, but through their position they were greater than the other children of earth, for they stood on Rome. Immediately they came down from the Seven Hills, they were small. . . . As the Greek is great through the idea of Art, the Hebrew through the idea of one most holy God ; so the Romans are great through the idea of their eternal Rome ; great, wheresoever they have fought, written or builded in the inspiration of this idea. The greater Rome grew, the more this idea dilated : the individual lost himself in it : the great men who remain eminent are borne up by this idea, and it makes the littleness of the little men more pronounced.[1]

The Idea of Rome! It is the triumph of that which yields the promise and evidence of better things that the final situation contains. The titanic intolerance of Coriolanus after being expelled by fear and hatred from within, has threatened destruction from without, and the threat has been averted. The presumptuous intolerance of the demagogues, after imperilling the state, has been discredited by its results, and their authority is destroyed. The Idea of Rome in the patriotism of Volumnia has led to her self-conquest and the conquest of her son, and is acclaimed by all alike. Thus we have borne in upon us a feeling of the majesty and omnipotence of the Eternal City, and we understand how it not only inspires and informs the units that compose it, but stands out aloft and apart from its faulty representatives as a kind of mortal deity that overrules their doings to its own ends, and against which their cavilling and

---

[1] *Reisebilder*, 2ter Theil ; "Italien, Reise nach Genua," Cap. xxiv.

opposition are vain.   What Menenius says to the
rioters applies to all dissentients :

> You may as well
> Strike at the heaven with your staves as lift them
> Against the Roman state, whose course will on
> The way it takes, cracking ten thousand curbs
> Of more strong link asunder than can ever
> Appear in your impediment.   (I. i. 69.)

This, then, is the background against which are
grouped with more or less prominence, as their importance requires, Coriolanus' family, his associates,
his rival, round the central figure of the hero
himself.

CHAPTER IV

THE KINSFOLK AND FRIENDS OF CORIOLANUS

Of the subordinate persons, by far the most imposing and influential is Volumnia, the great-hearted mother, the patrician lady, the Roman matron. The passion of maternity, whether interpreted as maternal love or as maternal pride, penetrates her nature to the core, not, however, to melt but to harden it. In her son's existence she at first seems literally wrapped up, and she implies that devotion to him rather than to her dead husband has kept her from forming new ties:

> Thou hast never in thy life
> Show'd thy dear mother any courtesy,
> When she, poor hen, fond of no second brood,
> Has cluck'd thee to the wars and safely home,
> Loaden with honour.   (v. iii. 160.)

Marcius is thus the only son of his mother and she a widow; but these reminiscences show how strictly the tenderness, and still more the indulgence, usual in such circumstances, have been banished from that home. In Plutarch the boy seeks a military career from his irresistible natural bent:

> Martius being more inclined to the warres, then any young gentleman of his time: beganne from his Childehood to geve him self to handle weapons, and daylie dyd exercise him selfe therein.

In Shakespeare the direction and stimulus are much

more directly attributed to his mother, and it is she who first despatches him to the field. This she herself expressly states in her admonition to Virgilia:

Volumnia. I pray you, daughter, sing; or express yourself in a more comfortable sort: if my son were my husband, I should freelier rejoice in that absence wherein he won honour, than in the embracements of his bed where he would show most love. When yet he was but tender-bodied and the only son of my womb, when youth with comeliness plucked all gaze his way, when for a day of kings' entreaties a mother should not sell him an hour from her beholding, I, considering how honour would become such a person, that it was no better than picture-like to hang by the wall, if renown made it not stir, was pleased to let him seek danger where he was like to find fame. To a cruel war I sent him; from whence he returned, his brows bound with oak. I tell thee, daughter, I sprang not more in joy at first hearing he was a man-child than now in first seeing he had proved himself a man.

Virgilia. But had he died in the business, madam; how then?

Volumnia. Then his good report should have been my son; I therein would have found issue. Hear me profess sincerely: had I a dozen sons, each in my love alike, and none less dear than thine and my good Marcius, I had rather had eleven die nobly for their country than one voluptuously surfeit out of action. (I. iii. I.)

He is the object of her love because he is to be the ideal which she adores. She trains him to all the excellence she understands, and would have him a captain of Rome's armies and a force in the state. She has to the full the sentiment of *noblesse oblige*, and is inspired by the same feeling which in Plutarch moves Marcius to bid the patricians show that

they dyd not so muche passe the people in power and riches as they dyd exceede them in true nobilitie and valliantnes.

She is full of the virtues and prejudices of her class, and, with the self-consciousness of an aristocrat, looks from the plebs only for the obedience and approval due to their betters. They are quite unqualified for self-government or for the criticism of those above

them. In comparison with the noble Coriolanus,
the people, whom she calls the rabble, are " cats "
(IV. ii. 34). Naturally she is tenacious of the
supremacy of her order, and would fain see it make
good its threatened privileges. She remonstrates
with her son for his contumacy :

> I am in this,
> Your wife, your son, these senators, the nobles ;
> And you will rather show our general louts
> How you can frown than spend a fawn upon 'em,
> For the inheritance of their loves and safeguard
> Of what that want might ruin. (III. ii. 64.)

Her dream has been that Marcius shall be consul
to establish once more the power of the patricians.
When he enters in his great triumph from Corioli,
she exclaims in expectation of that result :

> I have lived
> To see inherited my very wishes,
> And the buildings of my fancy : only
> There's one thing wanting, which I doubt not but
> Our Rome will cast upon thee. (II. i. 214.)

Yet she has one feeling that outweighs both her
maternal and her aristocratic instincts, and that is
devotion to her country. This is the first and last
and noblest thing in her. It is the basis and mainspring of the training of her son ; she wishes him to
serve the fatherland. It is the basis and mainspring
of her patrician partisanship ; she honestly believes
that the nobles alone are fit to steer Rome to safety
and honour. And to it she is willing to sacrifice the
two other grand interests of her life. When the call
comes she is ready for Rome, with its mechanics and
tribunes as well as its senators and patricians, to persuade her son to the step that will certainly imperil
and probably destroy him. It is public spirit of no
ordinary kind that makes such a nature disregard
the dearest ties of family and caste, and all personal

motives of love and vengeance, to intercede for the
city as a whole. But she puts her country first, and
her words show that she never even questions the
sacredness of its claim :

> Thou know'st, great son,
> The end of war's uncertain, but this certain,
> That, if thou conquer Rome, the benefit
> Which thou shalt thereby reap is such a name,
> Whose repetition will be dogg'd with curses ;
> Whose chronicle thus writ : " The man was noble,
> But with his last attempt he wiped it out :
> Destroy'd his country, and his name remains
> To the ensuing age abhorr'd." (v. iii. 140.)

She feels, as well she may, that she is basing her
plea on eternal right, and is willing to stake her
success on the irresistible truth of her argument.

> Say my request's unjust,
> And spurn me back : but if it be not so,
> Thou art not honest. (v. iii. 164.)

Such a woman is made to be the mother of heroes.
It is no wonder that she has bred that colossal *Über-
mensch*, her son. But she has the defects of her
qualities. Her devotion is narrow in its intensity,
and in normal circumstances spares little recognition
or tolerance for those beyond its pale. Her contempt for the plebeians is open and unrestrained.
She was wont, says Coriolanus,

> To call them woollen vassals, things created
> To buy and sell with groats, to show bare heads
> In congregations, to yawn, be still and wonder,
> When one but of my ordinance stood up
> To speak of peace or war. (iii. ii. 9.)

Even when trying to pacify her son, she cannot
bridle her own resentment. When he recklessly
cries of his opponents : " Let them hang !" she

instinctively approves: "Ay, and burn too."[1] The
energy of her love of glory has nothing sentimental
about it, but often becomes savage and sanguinary.
She gloats over her robust imaginings of the fight:

> Methinks I hear hither your husband's drum,
> See him pluck Aufidius down by the hair,
> As children from a bear, the Volsces shunning him:
> Methinks I see him stamp thus, and call thus:
> "Come on, you cowards! you were got in fear,
> Though you were born in Rome": his bloody brow
> With his mail'd hand then wiping, forth he goes,
> Like to a harvest-man that's tasked to mow
> Or all or lose his hire.
>   *Virgilia.* His bloody brow! O Jupiter, no blood!
>   *Volumnia.* Away, you fool! it more becomes a man
> Than gilt his trophy: the breasts of Hecuba,
> When she did suckle Hector, look'd not lovelier
> Than Hector's forehead when it spit forth blood
> At Grecian sword, contemning.   (I. iii. 32.)

And when she has heard the actual news, she trium-
phantly exclaims:

> O, he is wounded; I thank the gods for't.   (II. i. 133.)

As Kreyssig points out, even great-hearted mothers,
proud of their warrior sons, do not often like to dwell
so realistically on havoc and slaughter and blood.
But tenderness and humanity are alien to her nature.
When Valeria narrates how young Marcius tore in
pieces the butterfly, she interrupts with obvious satisfaction: "One on's father's moods" (I. iii. 72). At
her hearth Coriolanus would not be taught much
kindliness for Volscians or plebeians or any other
of the lower animals. Indeed, her own relations with
her son depend on his reverence rather than on his
fondness. In the two collisions of their wills he
resists all her entreaties and endearments, but yields
in a moment to her anger and indignation. She

---

[1] There is no authority for taking this most characteristic utterance
from Volumnia and assigning it to "a patrician" as some editions do.

beseeches him to submit to the judgment of the
people—all in vain till she loses patience :

> At thy choice, then :
> To beg of thee, it is my more dishonour
> Than thou of them.   Come all to ruin : let
> Thy mother rather feel thy pride than fear
> Thy dangerous stoutness, for I mock at death
> With as big heart as thou.   Do as thou list.   (III. ii. 123.)

At this his efforts to propitiate her are almost
amusing :

> Pray, be content :
> Mother, I am going to the market-place :
> Chide me no more.   I'll mountebank their loves,
> Cog their hearts from them, and come home beloved
> Of all the trades in Rome.   Look, I am going.
> (III. ii. 130.)

Similarly, at the end, all argument and complaint, all
pressure on the affections of Coriolanus are without avail, till she turns upon him with a violence for
which, as in the previous case, Shakespeare found
no authority in Plutarch :

> Come, let us go :
> This fellow had a Volscian to his mother ;
> His wife is in Corioli, and his child
> Like him by chance.   Yet give us our dispatch :
> I am hush'd until our city be afire,
> And then I'll speak a little.   (v. iii. 177.)

And the great warrior and rebel cannot bear her
rebuke.

These are instances both of the degree and the
manner in which Volumnia's forceful character influences her son.   Indeed it is easy to see that for
good and evil he is what she has made him.   She
is entitled to say :

> Thou art my warrior :
> I holp to frame thee.   (v. iii. 62.)

And though elsewhere she puts it,

> Thy valiantness was mine, thou suck'dst from me,
> But owe thy pride thyself ;   (III. ii. 129.)

the impartial onlooker cannot make the distinction.
He is bone of her bone and blood of her blood ; and
all her master impulses reappear in him, though not
so happily commingled or in such beneficent proportion. The joint operation is different and in some
respects opposite, but there is hardly a feature in
him that cannot be traced to its origin in Volumnia,
whether by heredity or education. This is just what
we might expect. Modern conjecture points to the
mother rather than the father as the source of will-
power and character in the offspring ; and in the
up-bringing of the boy Volumnia has had it all her
own way. Plutarch, as we saw, in his simple fashion,
notices this as a disadvantage : and though we may
be sure that Plutarch's insinuation of laxity could
never be breathed against Shakespeare's Volumnia,
still she could not give her son more width and
flexibility than her own narrow and rigid ideals
enjoined. Moreover, her limitations when transferred to the larger sphere of his public efforts,
would cramp and congest his powers, and displace
his interests.

Nor was there any other agency to divide the
young man's allegiance to his mother or to counteract or temper her authority. Generally the most
powerful rivals of home influence are the companionship of friends, and the love that founds
a new home in marriage. But both of these
are either wanting in Coriolanus' life, or serve
only to deepen the impressions made on him by
Volumnia.

If, for example, we consider the relation of friendship, we cannot but notice that Shakespeare gives
him no intimate of his own years. A French
tragedian would infallibly have placed by his side
the figure of a confidant. Shakespeare was dis-
pensed from the necessity by the freer usage of the
Elizabethan stage and was at liberty to follow out

the hints which he found in Plutarch. Marcius was

> churlishe, uncivill, and altogether unfit for any mans conver-
> sation. . . . They could not be acquainted with him, as one
> cittizen useth to be with another in the cittie. His behaviour
> was so unpleasaunt to them, by reason of a certaine insolent
> and sterne manner he had, which bicause it was to lordly,
> was disliked.

So in Shakespeare he has no personal relations with
any of the younger generation, even their resort
to him as their congenial leader surviving, as has
already been pointed out, only in the desiccated
phrase of a stage direction ; and his only associates
are old or elderly men like Titus Lartius, the
Consul Cominius, and Menenius Agrippa. What
sort of antidote could they supply against his
mother's intolerant virtue ? As Shakespeare conceives them, they respectively follow in Marcius' wake,
or are powerless to change and check his course, or
even urge him forward.

Take Lartius, whom Shakespeare has drawn in
a few rapid and vigorous strokes. He is old and
stiff, but ready if need be to lean on one crutch and
fight with the other, prompt to take a sporting
wager, and, when he wins, eager to remit the stake
in his admiration for the noble youngster, to whom
with all his years he grants priority, whom on his
supposed death he laments as an irreplaceable jewel,
whom he hails as the living force that dwells within
the trappings of their armament. Clearly from this
cheery old fighting man, with his reverential enthusiasm for Marcius' fighting powers in voice, looks
and blows, we need not expect much correction of
Marcius' restiveness at the civic curb.

Cominius would seem more likely to prove a
fitting Mentor, for to his love and esteem he adds
discretion. In Shakespeare, though he "has years
upon him," he is the avowed friend and comrade-
in-arms of the younger man ; the brave and prudent

general, "neither foolish in his stands, nor cowardly
in retire"; who, perhaps from seniority, holds the
position to which the other might aspire, but who
confidently appeals to his promise of service. For
their mutual affection is untouched by jealousy,
and Cominius not only extols his heroism in the
camp, but is his warmest advocate in the Senate.
He resents the citizens' fickleness and the tribunes'
trickery at the election as unworthy of Rome as well
as insulting to her hero, and is indignant at the
attempt to arrest Coriolanus; but he abhors civil
brawls, and, just as in the field so in the city, he
bows to "odds beyond arithmetic," and considers
that

> Manhood is call'd foolery, when it stands
> Against a falling fabric.   (III. i. 246.)

So he counsels Marcius' withdrawal from the hostile
mob, and afterwards dispassionately states the three
courses open to him, with some hesitation sanction-
ing the method of compromise if the hothead can
bring himself to give it fair play. When his doubts
prove true, he interposes first with a remonstrance
to his friend, and then with a solemn appeal to
the people; and though in neither case is he allowed
to finish, his efforts do not flag. He wishes to
accompany the exile for a month, and maintain a
correspondence with him and have everything in
readiness for his recall. And if, when the invasion
takes place, he rails at those who have brought
about the calamity, that does not hinder him from
his vain but zealous attempt at intercession. Altogether a sagacious, loyal, generous, but somewhat
ineffective character, who wins our respect rather
for what he essays than for what he achieves; for
he brings nothing to a successful issue. With the
best will in the world, which he has, and with more
freedom from class prejudice than can in point of

fact be attributed to him, such an one could do little
to tame or bridle his friend.

There remains Menenius, with his much more
strongly marked character, and with the fuller opportunities that a close · intimacy could procure.
Were Marcius and he of the same flesh and blood,
their affection could hardly be greater. When
debating with himself whether to try his mediation,
this thought encourages the old man : " He call'd
me father" (v. i. 3). He tells the Volscian sentinel:

> You shall perceive that a Jack guardant cannot office me
> from my son Coriolanus. (v. ii. 67.)

And when they meet, he hails him :

> The glorious gods sit in hourly synod about thy particular
> prosperity, and love thee no worse than thy old father Men-·
> enius does! O, my son, my son! (v. ii. 72.)

Nor are these statements idle brags ; they are borne
out by Coriolanus' own words when he dismisses
him :

> For I loved thee,
> Take this along ; I writ it for thy sake, [*Gives a letter*
> And would have sent it. (v. ii. 95.)

And again he tells Aufidius :

> This last old man,
> Whom with a crack'd heart I have sent to Rome,
> Loved me above the measure of a father ;
> Nay, godded me, indeed. (v. iii. 8.)

But the last expression may give an explanation
both of the young man's condescension to fondness
and of the unprofitableness of Menenius' influence.
He is too much dazzled by the glories of his splendid
adoptive son. His enthusiasm knows no bounds.
No lover is more enraptured at receiving a *billet
doux* from his mistress, than is the old man when the
youth on whom he dotes, deigns to write to him.

> A letter for me! it gives me an estate of seven years' health; in which time I will make a lip at the physician; the most sovereign prescription in Galen is but empiricutic, and, to this preservative, of no better report than a horse-drench.
>
> (II. i. 125.)

He may occasionally interpose a mild hint of re-monstrance against Marcius' vehemence, but it is solely on the ground of expediency, not at all on the ground of principle; and on the whole he belongs to that not very edifying class of devotees who can say of a friend,

> Whate'er he does seems well done to me.

Of which he himself is not altogether unaware. He tells the Volscian sentinel:

> I tell thee, fellow,
> Thy general is my lover: I have been
> The book of his good acts, whence men have read
> His fame unparallel'd, haply amplified:
> For I have ever verified my friends,
> Of whom he's chief, with all the size that verity
> Would without lapsing suffer: nay, sometimes,
> Like to a bowl upon a subtle ground,
> I have tumbled past the throw; and in his praise
> Have almost stamp'd the leasing.
>
> (v. ii. 13.)

This attitude, then, accounts for Coriolanus' pre-dilection for the old senator, and also reduces the value of the relation as an educative agency. Youthful recklessness will meet with no inconvenient thwarting, i.e. with no salutary rebuke, from such an adorer. But of course in the blindest friendship there is always the unconscious influence and criticism of the admirer's own walk and conversation. And at first sight it might seem that this influence and criticism Menenius was well fitted to supply. He, too, like Volumnia, puts Rome before all other con-siderations, as is shown not only by his undertaking the mission to the Volscian camp, but by his action all through the drama. He is ever willing to play the part of mediator. Now we find him soothing

the people, now we find him soothing Coriolanus.
When the banishment is an accomplished fact, he
endeavours to mitigate the outbursts of Volumnia ;
and Sicinius bears witness :

> O, he is grown most kind of late. (IV. vi. 11.)

During all the tumult of the election and the *émeute*
he keeps his head and his heart ; for he is inspired
by the right civic feeling that there must be no civil
war.

> Proceed by process ;
> Lest parties, as he is beloved, break out,
> And sack great Rome with Romans. (III. i. 314.)

And with this patriotism, partly as its result, he
combines singular moderation, at least in principle
and thought, if not in language. He is always
ready to commend and accept compromises. He
says to the tribune,

> Be that you seem, truly your country's friend,
> And temperately proceed to what you would
> Thus violently redress. (III. i. 218.)

On the other hand, when Marcius draws he sees the
mistake and interposes : " Down with that sword "
(III. i. 226) ; and only when the tribunes persist in
their attack does he himself resort to force, which,
however, he is glad to abandon at the first opportunity.
And this moderation comes the more easily to him
that he has a real kindliness even for the plebeians.
It is assuredly no small compliment that at the very
height of the popular violence this patrician and
senator, the known and avowed friend of Coriolanus,
should be chosen by the tribunes themselves as their
own delegate :

> Noble Menenius,
> Be you then as the people's officer. (III. i. 329.)

This confirms the testimony given him by the First
Citizen in the opening scene : " He's one honest

enough " (i. i. 54) ; and the Second Citizen describes him as

> Worthy Menenius Agrippa ; one that hath always loved
> the people.   (i. i. 52.)

He has indeed a sympathy with them, that shows itself in the russet and kersey of his speech.   The haughty Coriolanus despises the household words of the common folk, and cites them only to ridicule them, but Menenius' phrases of their own accord run to the homespun and proverbial.   He addresses the obtrusive citizen : "You, the great toe of this assembly " (i. i. 159).   The dissension at Rome is a rent that "must be patch'd with cloth of any colour " (iii. i. 252).   Coriolanus' rough words he excuses on the ground that he is

> ill school'd
> In bolted language : meal and bran together
> He throws without distinction.   (iii. i. 321.)

He figures the relentlessness of the returned exile as "yon coign o' the Capitol, yon corner-stone " (v. iv. 1), and is at no loss for illustrations of the change that has come over the outcast :

> There is a differency between a grub and a butterfly, yet
> your butterfly was a grub.   (v. iv. 11.)

And with similes for Coriolanus' present temper he positively overflows :

> He no more remembers his mother now than an eight-
> year-old horse.   The tartness of his face sours ripe grapes.
>   (v. iv. 16.)
> There is no more mercy in him than there is milk in a
> male tiger.   (v. iv. 29.)

All his thoughts clothe themselves in the pat, familiar image, and this is no doubt a great help to him in persuading his auditors, for which he has an undeniable talent.   His famous apologue, besides being a masterpiece in its kind, worthy of La Fontaine at his best, completely answers its immediate purpose ;

and in the later scene he is able to lull the storm that Coriolanus and the tribunes have raised, and obtain from the infuriated demagogues what are in some sort favourable terms. But he is assisted in this by his genuine joviality and *bonhomie*. He is one of those people who permit themselves a little indulgence that we hardly blame, for it is only one side of their pervasive good nature. Menenius is in truth something of a belly-god and wine-bibber. When he hears news of Marcius he promptly decides how to celebrate the occasion:

> I will make my very house reel to-night;   (II. i. 121.)

and he has already confessed that he is known to be

> one that loves a cup of hot wine with not a drop of allaying Tiber in't; . . . one that converses more with the buttock of the night than with the forehead of the morning.
>
> (II. i. 52 and 56.)

It is almost comic to hear him consoling Volumnia on her son's banishment when she moves off to lament "in anger, Juno-like," with an invitation: "You'll sup with me?" (IV. ii. 49). And wholly comic is his explanation of Cominius' rebuff by Coriolanus, an explanation suggested no doubt by subjective considerations:

> He was not taken well; he had not dined:
> The veins unfill'd, our blood is cold, and then
> We pout upon the morning, are unapt
> To give or to forgive; but when we have stuff'd
> These pipes and these conveyances of the blood
> With wine and feeding, we have suppler souls
> Than in our priest-like fasts; therefore I'll watch him
> Till he be dieted to my request,
> And then I'll set upon him.   (v. i. 50.)

But the worthy *bon-vivant* is thoroughly in earnest, and in the crisis of his altercation with the sentinel harks back to this key of the position, as he supposes it to be:

> Has he dined, canst thou tell? for I would not speak with him till after dinner.   (v. ii. 36.)

All these, however, are very human weaknesses, that
sort well with the geniality of the man, and, just
because they are very human weaknesses, might
have a wholesome rather than a prejudicial effect
on the overstrained tensity of Marcius.   So far then,
despite the excessive and uncritical in Menenius'
love, his patriotism, his moderation, his popular
bent, commended by his persuasive tongue and
companionable ways, might tend to supplement the
defects and transcend the limitations of Volumnia's
training.   But Menenius has other qualities akin to,
or associated with, those that we have discussed,
which would have a more questionable and not less
decisive influence.   He admits that he is

said to be something imperfect in favouring the first complaint.
(II. i. 53.)

That is, he neglects the wise counsel, "Hear the
other side," and jumps to his conclusion at once.
This is quite in keeping with the partiality that
makes him magnify the virtues of his friends,
and with his assumption that, since his own intercession has failed, that of Volumnia can have no
effect.   He prejudges, in other words he is prejudiced.   We do not have any instance of this in
his acts, but we have many in his unconsidered
sayings, that, as he imagines, are to have no consequence beyond the moment.

Then he goes on to confess that he has the
reputation of being "hasty and tinder-like upon too
trivial motion" (II. i. 55), which means that he loses
patience and fires up without adequate ground ; and
of this too we have ample evidence.   He is wonderfully forbearing and longsuffering if matters of any
moment are at stake, but if he has gained his point,
or if there is nothing to gain and nothing to lose, he
rails and mocks in Coriolanus' own peculiar vein.
Thus, when he has convinced the mob, he feels free

to make the ringleader his butt. When the tribunes profess to "know him," that is, to understand his character, he overwhelms them with peppery banter. When the news of Coriolanus' invasion arrives, in unrestrained indignation he upbraids the people and their blind guides with their imbecility. But it will be observed that no harm ever comes by any of these ebullitions. They have no after-effects. If something has to be done, no one could be more sagacious and conciliatory than Menenius. Dr. Johnson said of him, perhaps more in exercise of his right as a sturdy old Tory to twit those in high places, than in deliberate appreciation of the facts : "Shakespeare wanted a buffoon and he went to the Senate House for that with which the Senate House would certainly have supplied him." Similarly, in the play Brutus is rash enough to answer him back :

> Come, come, you are well understood to be a perfecter giber for the table than a necessary bencher in the Capitol.
>
> (II. i. 90.)

But Menenius deserves neither taunt. It was no parliamentary wag or social lampooner whom the Senate entrusted with the task of addressing the rioters, or who persuaded the triumphant tribunes to a compromise. The charges nevertheless have a foundation in so far that Menenius, partly in jest, partly in irritation, gives his tongue rein unless he sees reason to curb it, and allows his choleric impulses full expression. These random ejaculations are taken at their proper value by himself and others. As he says :

> What I think I utter, and spend my malice in my breath.
>
> (II. i. 58.)

He is obviously one of those estimable and deservedly popular people whose deliberate views are just and penetrating, and who are gifted with the power of commending them, but who are none the less liked because they do not always think it necessary to have themselves in hand, but let themselves go on the full career of their own half-jocular, half-serious likes and dislikes, when for the moment they are free from graver responsibilities.

Now this of itself was no very good example for Coriolanus. He adopts Menenius' headlong frankness, but without Menenius' tacit presupposition of good-humoured hyperbole. He utters what he thinks but he does not spend his malice in his breath. His friend would do nothing to teach him restraint and reserve, but would rather, if he influenced him at all, influence him to surcharge his invectives and double-barb his flouts.

But not only so. These instinctive likes and dislikes, which the old patrician could not but feel but which he never allowed to interfere with his practical policy, were the guiding principles of his less cautious friend. It must be admitted that there is no abuse of the citizens or their officers to which Coriolanus gives vent, but can be paralleled with something as strong from the mouth of Menenius. This worthy senior who hath always loved the people, turns from the tribunes with the insult:

> God-den to your worships: more of your conversation would infect my brain, being the herdsmen of the beastly plebeians. (II. i. 103.)

In this mood he asks them in regard to Coriolanus:

> Your multiplying spawn how can he flatter—
> That's thousand to one good one? (II. ii. 82.)

He has to the full the aristocratic loathing for the uncleanly populace:

> You are they
> That made the air unwholesome, when you cast
> Your stinking greasy caps in hooting at
> Coriolanus' exile. (IV. vi. 129.)

> You are the musty chaff: and you are smelt
> Above the moon. (V. i. 31.)

These are his authentic innate prejudices that he controls and represses by the help of his reason and his patriotism, when the emergency requires : but they are there ; and he would be no more careful to restrain them in his familiar circle than a squatter at his club feels called upon to restrain his opinions about the Labour Party, though he may be very proud of Australia, and a very kindly master, and though he would neither publish them in an election address nor perhaps justify them in his serious moments to himself. And this, we may suppose, was the sort of conversation Marcius would hear as a lad from his old friend. There would be little in it to modify the pride and prejudice he derived from his mother.

And lastly, coming to the other possible corrective, would his wife be likely to soften the asperities of temper and opinion that were his by nature and by second nature ? At first we might say Yes. She takes comparatively little pleasure in the brilliance of his career and is more concerned for his life than for his glory. When Volumnia recalls how she sent him forth as a lad to win honour, Virgilia's heart pictures his possible death, and how would that have been compensated ? For she loves in the first place not the hero but the husband, and her love makes her timorous. She has none of her mother-in-law's assurance that his prowess is without match and beyond comparison. When " wondrous things " are told of him how characteristic are their respective comments :

> *Virgilia.* The gods grant them true !
> *Volumnia.* True ! pow, wow. (II. i. 154.)

How differently they feel about his contest with his rival :

> *Virgilia.* Heavens bless my lord from fell Aufidius !
> *Volumnia.* He'll beat Aufidius' head below his knee
> And tread upon his neck. (I. iii. 48.)

So she shrinks from the thoughts of blood and wounds over which Volumnia gloats, and trembles at the dangers of the campaign. Devoured by suspense, she is in no mood to meet the ordinary social claims on her rank and sex, but shuts herself up within her four walls, and wears out the time over household tasks. Her seclusion, and the attempts to withdraw her from it, must not be misunderstood. They have sometimes been taken as pictures of domestic narrow-mindedness on the one hand, and callous frivolity on the other. But frivolity is unthinkable in Volumnia ; we may be sure she would never advise or do anything unbefitting the Roman matron. And it is quite opposed to the impression Valeria produces ; we may be sure she would never suggest it. In Plutarch's story it is she who proposes and urges the deputation of women to Coriolanus, and though Shakespeare, to suit his own purpose, transfers by implication the credit of this to Volumnia, Plutarch's statement was enough to prevent him from transforming the true authoress of the idea into the fashionable gadabout that some critics have alleged her to be. On the contrary, with him she calls forth the most purely poetical passage in the whole play, and she does so by the vestal dignity and severity of her character. Coriolanus greets her in the camp :

> The noble sister of Publicola,
> The moon of Rome, chaste as the icicle
> That's curdied by the frost of purest snow
> And hangs on Dian's temple : dear Valeria !
>
> (v. iii. 65.)

The woman to whom this splendid compliment is paid by one who never speaks otherwise than he thinks, is assuredly no more obnoxious than Volumnia herself to the charge of levity. They are both great high-hearted Roman ladies who do not let their private or public solicitudes interfere with their customary social routine, and Valeria visits her friend to cheer her in her anxiety, as she would have her, in turn, visit and comfort their common acquaintance. But Virgilia is cast in a gentler mould ; though neither is she lacking in character, spirit and magnanimity. Of course she is not an aggressive woman, and she feels that the home is the place for her. She speaks seldom, and when she does her words are few. It is typical that she greets her husband when he returns a victor with no articulate welcome, but with her more eloquent tears. He addresses her in half humorous, half tender reproach :

> My gracious silence, hail !
> Wouldst thou have laugh'd had I come coffin'd home,
> That weep'st to see me triumph ? (II. i. 192.)

A wonderful touch that comes from a wonderful insight. It may well be asked, as it has been asked, how Shakespeare *knew* that Virgilia's heart was too full for words.

But with all this, she shows abundant resolution, readiness and patriotism. She is adamant to the commands of her imperious mother-in-law and the entreaties of her insistent friend when they urge her to break her self-imposed retirement. She, too, has her rebuke for the insolent tribunes. Above all, she, too, plays her part in turning Coriolanus from his revenge. In that scene, after her wont, she does not say much, less than two lines in all, that serve to contain the simple greeting and the quick answer to her husband's warning that he no longer sees things as he did :

> The sorrow that delivers us thus changed
> Makes you think so. (v. iii. 39.)

But who shall say that

> those dove's eyes
> Which can make gods forsworn, (v. iii. 27.)

did not shed their influence on his mother's demand,
and help him to break his vindictive vow. Remember, too, that the sacrifice this implied would
mean more to her than to Volumnia, for though she
likewise can dedicate what she holds dearest on the
altar of her country, her affections, her home, Marcius as an individual, bulk more largely in her life.

And if she loves him, we see how fondly he loves
her. More than once or twice he alludes to his
happiness as bridegroom, husband, and father.
When she appears before him, his ejaculations and
the tenderness of his appeal,

> Best of my flesh,
> Forgive my tyranny,   (v. iii. 42.)

speak volumes in a mouth like his for the keenness
of his affection. To express the bliss that he feels
in the salute of re-union, this hero-lover can find
analogues only in his banishment and his vengeance :

> O, a kiss
> Long as my exile, sweet as my revenge !
> Now, by the jealous queen of heaven, that kiss
> I carried from thee, dear : and my true lip
> Hath virgin'd it e'er since.   (v. iii. 44.)

This woman, then, with her love and sweetness,
that strike such responsive chords in the rude breast
of her lord, is apparently well fitted to smooth the
harshness of his dealings with his fellow-men : and
this would seem all the more likely since her gentle-
ness is not of that flabby kind that cannot hold or
bind, but is strengthened by firmness of will and
largeness of feeling.

All the same, she exerts no influence whatever
before the very end on her husband's public life or
even on his general character, because she has no
interest in or aptitude for concerns of his busy, practical career. She has chosen her own orbit in her
home, and her love has no desire to step beyond.

We have seen that, according to Plutarch, Volumnia was entrusted with the selection of her son's wife. This Shakespeare omits, perhaps as incongruous with the spontaneousness of the relation between his wedded lovers, but it may have left a trace in the position he assigns to Virgilia. The mother-in-law has and claims the leading place ; and, as Kreyssig remarks, with a woman of the daughter-in-law's steady inflexibility, collisions more proper for comedy than for tragedy must inevitably ensue, unless there were a strict delimitation of spheres. Volumnia continues to be prompter and guide in all matters political. She has all the outward precedence. On his return from Corioli, her son gives her the prior reverence and salutation, and, only as it were by her permission, turns to his wife. When the deputation of ladies appears in his presence before Rome, he seems for a moment to be surprised out of his de-corum, and his first words of passionate greeting are for Virgilia ; but he presently recovers, and, with a certain accent of reproof, turns on himself :

> You gods ! I prate,
> And the most noble mother of the world
> Leave unsaluted : sink, my knee, i' the earth :
> Of thy deep duty more impression show
> Than that of common sons.   (v. iii. 48.)

Evidently, his love for his wife, intense though it be, is a thing apart, a sanctuary of his most inmost feeling, and is quite out of relation with the affairs of the jostling world. In them his mother has supreme sway, and Virgilia's unobtrusive gracious-ness does not exercise even an indirect influence on his ingrained principles and prejudices. She is no makeweight against the potent authority of Volumnia.

CHAPTER V

THE GREATNESS OF CORIOLANUS. AUFIDIUS

IN the atmosphere then of Volumnia's predominance
we are to imagine young Marcius growing up from
infancy to boyhood, from boyhood to youth, en-
vironed by all the most inspiring and most exclusive
traditions of an old Roman family of the bluest
blood. After the expulsion of the Tarquins, we
must suppose that there was no more distinguished
gens than his. The tribune Brutus gives the long
bead-roll of his ancestry, the glories of which, as has
already been shown, are even exaggerated in his
statement through Shakespeare's having made a
little mistake in regard to Plutarch's account, and
having included representatives of later among those
of former generations. But Volumnia is not the
mother to let him rest on the achievements of his
predecessors; he must make them his own by
equalling or excelling them. He begins as a boy,
and already in his maiden fight his exploits rouse
admiration. Plutarch describes the circumstance:

> The first time he went to the warres, being but a strippling,
> was when Tarquine surnamed the prowde . . . dyd come to
> Rome with all the ayde of the Latines, and many other
> people of Italie. . . . In this battell, wherein were many
> hotte and sharpe encounters of either partie, Martius valliantly
> fought in the sight of the Dictator; and a Romaine souldier
> being throwen to the ground even hard by him, Martius
> straight bestrid him, and slue the enemie with his owne

handes that had overthrowen the Romaine. Hereupon, after the battell was wonne, the Dictator dyd not forget so noble an acte, and therefore first of all he crowned Martius with a garland of oken boughs.

This furnishes Cominius with the prologue to his eulogy :

>   At sixteen years,
> When Tarquin made a head for Rome, he fought
> Beyond the mark of others : our then dictator,
> Whom with all praise I point at, saw him fight,
> When with his Amazonian chin he drove
> The bristled lips before him : he bestrid
> An o'erpress'd Roman and i' the consul's view
> Slew three opposers : Tarquin's self he met
> And struck him on his knee : in that day's feats,
> When he might act the woman in the scene,
> He proved the best man i' the field, and for his meed
> Was brow-bound with the oak.   (II. ii. 91.)

But it will be noticed that in Shakespeare's version Marcius' prowess is enhanced : not one opponent but three fall before him ; he confronts the arch-enemy himself, and has the best of it. Similarly his derring-do at Corioli is raised to the super-human. Plutarch's statement, as he feels, makes demands, but it is moderate compared with Shakespeare's.

> Martius being in the throng emong the enemies, thrust him selfe into the gates of the cittie, and entred the same emong them that fled, without that any one of them durst at the first turne their face upon him, or els offer to slaye him. But he looking about him and seeing he was entred the cittie with very fewe men to helpe him, and perceyving he was envirouned by his enemies that gathered round about to set apon him : dyd things then as it is written, wonderfull and incredible : . . . By this meanes, Lartius that was gotten out, had some leysure to bring the Romaines with more safetie into the cittie.

Here he is accompanied at least by a few, among whom, it is implied, the valiant Lartius is one, and Lartius having extricated himself, comes back with reinforcements to help him. But in Shakespeare he

is from beginning to end without assistance, and his
boast, "Alone I did it," is the literal truth. The
first soldier says, discreetly passing over the disobedience of the men :

> Following the fliers at the very heels,
> With them he enters ; who, upon the sudden,
> Clapp'd to their gates : he is himself alone
> To answer all the city. (I. iv. 49.)

And Cominius reports :

> Alone he enter'd
> The mortal gate of the city, which he painted
> With shunless destiny ; aidless came off. (II. ii. 114.)

But he is not merely, though he is conspicuously, a
soldier. He is also a general who once and again
gives proof of his strategic skill. Nor do his qualifications stop here. He has the forethought and
insight of a statesman, at any rate in matters of
foreign and military policy. He has anticipated the
attack of the Volsces with which the play begins, as
we learn from the remark of the First Senator :

> Marcius, 'tis true that you have lately told us ;
> The Volsces are in arms. (I. i. 231.)

So after their disaster at Corioli, he estimates the
situation aright, when even Cominius is mistaken,
and conjectures that the enemy is only waiting an
opportunity for renewing the war :

> So then the Volsces stand but as at first,
> Ready, when time shall prompt them, to make road
> Upon 's again. (III. i. 4.)

And this, as we presently learn, is quite correct.

Even in political statesmanship, the department
in which he is supposed to be specially to seek, he
has a sagacity and penetration that show him the
centre of the problem. This does not necessarily
mean that his solution is the true one ; and still less
does it mean that he is wise in proclaiming his views
when and where he does so : but the views themselves are certainly deep-reaching and acute, and

U

such as would win approval from some of the greatest builders of states, the Richelieus, the Fredericks, the Bismarcks. He is quite right in denying that his invectives against the policy of concession are due to "choler":

> Choler!
> Were I as patient as the midnight sleep,
> By Jove, 'twould be my mind! (III. i. 84.)

His objections are in truth no outbreaks of momentary exasperation, though that may have added pungency to their expression, but mature and sober convictions, that have a worth and weight of their own. As we might expect; for Shakespeare derives almost all of them from Plutarch; and Plutarch, who had thought about these things, puts several of his favourite ideas in Coriolanus' mouth, even while condemning Coriolanus' bigotry and harshness; and while, for dramatic fitness, suppressing the qualifications and provisos that he himself thought essential.

To Marcius the root of the matter is to be found in the fact that the Roman Republic is not a democracy but an aristocracy, and in this respect he contrasts it with some of the Greek communities.

> Therefore sayed he, they that gave counsell, and persuaded that the corne should be geven out to the common people *gratis*, as they used to doe in citties of Graece, where the people had more absolute power; dyd but only nourishe their disobedience, which would breake out in the ende, to the utter ruine and overthrowe of the whole state.

Shakespeare's transcription is, but for the interpolated interruption, fairly close:

> *Coriolanus.* Whoever gave that counsel, to give forth
> The corn o' the storehouse gratis, as 'twas used
> Sometime in Greece,—
> *Menenius.* Well, well, no more of that.
> *Coriolanus.* Though there the people had more absolute power,
> I say, they nourished disobedience, fed
> The ruin of the state. (III. i. 113.)

That being so, he regards it as a kind of treason to the constitution to pay court to the plebs, or let it have a share of the government.

> He sayed they nourished against them selves, the naughty seede and cockle of insolencie and sedition, which had bene sowed and scattered abroad emongest the people, whom they should have cut of, if they had bene wise, and have prevented their greatnes.

This is only a little more explicit in Shakespeare :

> I say again,
> In soothing them, we nourish 'gainst our senate
> The cockle of rebellion, insolence, sedition,
> Which we ourselves have plough'd for, sow'd, and scatter'd,
> By mingling them with us, the honour'd number,
> Who lack not virtue, no, nor power, but that
> Which they have given to beggars.   (III. i. 68.)

For, and this is one of Shakespeare's additions, if they have any share at all, being the majority they will swamp the votes of the superior order.

> You are plebeians,
> If they be senators ; and they are no less,
> When, both your voices blended, the great'st taste
> Most palates theirs.   (III. i. 101.)

And their magistrate, strong in the support he receives, dictates his ignorant will to the experience and wisdom of the senate.

> [They should] not to their owne destruction to have suffered the people, to stablishe a magistrate for them selves, of so great power and authoritie, as that man had, to whom they had graunted it. Who was also to be feared, bicause he obtained what he would, and dyd nothing but what he listed, neither passed for any obedience to the Consuls, but lived in all libertie acknowledging no superiour to commaund him, saving the only heades and authors of their faction, whom he called his magistrates : . . . [The Tribuneshippe] most manifestly is the embasing of the Consulshippe.

This arraignment of the populace and its elect as mischief-makers whenever they try to rule and interfere with competent authority, goes to Shakespeare's heart, and he makes the passage much more nervous and vivid ; but the idea is the same.

> O good but most unwise patricians ! why,
> You grave but reckless senators, have you thus
> Given Hydra here to choose an officer,
> That with his peremptory "shall," being but
> The horn and noise of the monster's, wants not spirit
> To say he'll turn your current in a ditch,
> And make your channel his. (III. i. 91.)

> By Jove himself !
> It makes the consuls base. (III. i. 107.)

The result must be division and altercation with all the resulting anarchy.

> The state [of the cittie] as it standeth, is not now as it was wont to be, but becommeth dismembred in two factions, which mainteines allwayes civill dissention and discorde betwene us, and will never suffer us againe to be united into one bodie.

Here, too, with some variation in the wording Shakespeare keeps close to the sense.

> My soul aches
> To know, when two authorities are up,
> Neither supreme, how soon confusion
> May enter 'twixt the gap of both, and take
> The one by the other. (III. i. 108.)

The grand mistake was the distribution of corn, for, as Plutarch puts it very clearly :

> They will not thincke it is done in recompense of their service past, sithence they know well enough they have so ofte refused to goe to the warres, when they were commaunded : neither for their mutinies when they went with us, whereby they have rebelled and forsaken their countrie : neither for their accusations which their flatterers have preferred unto them, and they have receyved, and made good against the Senate : but they will rather judge we geve and graunt them this, as abasing our selves, and standing in feare of them, and glad to flatter them every waye.

These weighty arguments, which Coriolanus is quite

entitled to call his "reasons," for reasons they are,
are substantially reproduced in Shakespeare :

> They know the corn
> Was not our recompense, resting well assured
> They ne'er did service for't : being press'd to the war,
> Even when the navel of the state was touched,
> They would not thread the gates.   This kind of service
> Did not deserve corn gratis.   Being i' the war,
> Their mutinies and revolts, wherein they show'd
> Most valour, spoke not for them : the accusation
> Which they have often made against the senate,
> All cause unborn could never be the motive
> Of our so frank donation.   Well, what then ?
> How shall this bisson multitude digest
> The senate's courtesy ?   Let deeds express
> What's like to be their words : "We did request it ;
> We are the greater poll, and in true fear
> They gave us our demands."   Thus we debase
> The nature of our seats and make the rabble
> Call our cares fears : which will in time
> Break ope the locks o' the senate, and bring in
> The crows to peck the eagles.   (III. i. 120.)

That seems convincing enough.   Their refusal of
military service shows that the citizens merited no
leniency from the state, the charge that the patricians
were hoarding stores was universally known to be
baseless, so the malcontents can only infer that
the senate gave the largesse in fright, and find in
this encouragement for their usurpations.   And in
the meantime, while doubt exists as to the real
centre of authority, the effect must be vacillation in
the policy of the republic and neglect of the most
urgent measures.   This was a consideration that
came home to Shakespeare, who never forgot the
weakness and misery of his own country when it
was torn by civil strife, so he calls urgent attention
to it at the close.   This is the only portion of the
speech that is quite original so far as the thought
is concerned.

> This double worship,
> Where one part does disdain with cause, the other

Insult without all reason, where gentry, title, wisdom,
Cannot conclude but by the yea and no
Of general ignorance,—it must omit
Real necessities, and give way the while
To unstable slightness : purpose so barr'd, it follows,
Nothing is done to purpose.   (III. i. 142.)

                    Your dishonour
Mangles true judgment and bereaves the state
Of that integrity which should become 't,
Not having the power to do the good it would,
For the ill which doth control 't.   (III. i. 157.)

All this contains a measure of truth that is valid
in all times ; from the point of view of the aristocratic republican it is absolutely true. Coriolanus'
diagnosis of the case is minutely correct and every
one of his prognostics is fulfilled. The plebs does
proceed with its encroachments ; the power of Rome
is strangely weakened as the immediate result of
the struggle ; the foreign policy is short-sighted
and unwise ; the pressing need of defence is overlooked. Of course the answer is that his uncompromising suggestions might have led to a worse
revolution, and that in the long run a great deal
more was gained than lost : but the important point
to note is that his views are certainly arguable, that
much could be said for them, that at the very
least they assert one aspect of the real facts, and are
as far as possible from being the mere tirades of
a brainless aristocratic swashbuckler. As already
pointed out they give just the sort of estimate that
some of the wisest statesmen who have ever lived
would have formed of the situation. It is quite
conceivable that his proposals if carried through with
vigour and ruthlessness would have settled things
satisfactorily at least for the moment. So besides
his pre-eminence in war and generalship and his
foresight in foreign affairs, we may claim for Coriolanus not indeed political tact but political grip.
   And to these qualifications of physical prowess

and intellectual force he adds others of a more distinctively moral description.

Among these the most obvious is his extreme truthfulness. He has no idea of equivocation or even of reticence. Menenius says of him :

> His heart's his mouth :
> What his breast forges, that his tongue must vent.
>
> (III. i. 257.)

Nor is his veracity confined to words ; he is honest and genuine to the core of his nature and will not stoop to a gesture that belies his feeling :

> I will not do 't
> Lest I surcease to honour mine own truth
> And by my body's action teach my mind
> A most inherent baseness.   (III. ii. 120.)

And following on this is his innate loyalty. Nothing revolts him like a breach of that obligation, and in the crises of his career it is the accusation of treason that rouses him to a frenzy. Thus, after his imprudent speech, Sicinius cries :

> Has spoken like a traitor, and shall answer
> As traitors do.   (III. i. 162.)

And Coriolanus bursts out :

> Thou wretch, despite o'erwhelm thee.

It is the same word that scatters his prudent resolutions in the trial scene :

> *Sicinius.*   You are a traitor to the people.
> *Coriolanus.* How ! traitor !
> *Menenius.*   Nay, temperately ; your promise.
> *Coriolanus.* The fires i' the lowest hell fold-in the people !
> Call me their traitor ! Thou injurious tribune !
> Within thine eyes sat twenty thousand deaths,
> In thy hands clutch'd as many millions, in
> Thy lying tongue both numbers, I would say
> " Thou liest " unto thee with a voice as free
> As I do pray the gods.   (III. iii. 66.)

And similarly when Aufidius calls him traitor, he repeats the word "Traitor! how now!" in a wrath that is for the moment almost speechless, till it overflows in a torrent of reckless abuse. It is part of the tragic irony of the play that with his ingrained horror of such an offence, he should yet in very truth let himself be hurried into treason against his country. For all his instincts are on the side of faith and troth and obligation. When he wishes to express his hostility to Aufidius he can think of no better comparison than this :

> I'll fight with none but thee ; for I do hate thee
> Worse than a promise-breaker.　　　　(I. viii. I.)

One result of this is that he has a simple reverence for all prescriptive ties, which suffuses his stern nature with a certain tinge of kindly humanity. His piety to his mother comes of course from Plutarch ; but his tenderness for his wife and delight in his son, lightly but strongly marked, are Shakespearean traits. So is the intimacy with Menenius, which greatly removes the impression of " churlishness " and " solitariness " that Plutarch's portrait conveys ; and his self-effacement in obedience to the powers that be and to the word that he has pledged, appears in his willing acceptance of a subordinate rank. The tribunes wonder that

> His insolence can brook to be commanded
> Under Cominius ;　　　　(I. i. 266.)

and attribute it to base calculation in keeping with their own natures ; but to this view Shakespeare's story gives no support. The real explanation is simpler : it is his former promise and he is constant (I. i. 241).

Even more pleasant is the famous instance of his respect for the claims of hospitality. This episode is obtained from Plutarch, but in several respects it

is completely altered. After describing how Coriolanus declined all special reward, the original narrative
proceeds :

> "Only this grace (sayed he) I crave, and beseeche you to
> graunt me. Among the Volsces there is an olde friende and
> hoste of mine, an honest wealthie man and now a prisoner,
> who living before in great wealthe in his owne countrie, liveth
> now a poore prisoner in the handes of his enemies : and yet
> notwithstanding all this his miserie and misfortune, it would
> do me great pleasure if I could save him from this one
> daunger : to keepe him from being solde as a slave." The
> souldiers hearing Martius wordes, made a marvelous great
> showte among them.

Compare this with the scene in Shakespeare :

> *Coriolanus.* The gods begin to mock me. I, that now
> Refused most princely gifts, am bound to beg
> Of my lord general.
> *Cominius.* Take 't ; 'tis yours. What is 't ?
> *Coriolanus.* I sometime lay here in Corioli
> At a poor man's house : he used me kindly :
> He cried to me ; I saw him prisoner ;
> But then Aufidius was within my view,
> And wrath o'erwhelmed my pity : I request you
> To give my poor host freedom.
> *Cominius.*   O well begg'd !
> Were he the butcher of my son, he should
> Be free as is the wind. Deliver him, Titus.
> *Lartius.* Marcius, his name ?
> *Coriolanus.*   By Jupiter ! forgot.
> I am weary ; yea, my memory is tired.
> Have we no wine here ?
>   (I. ix. 79.)

The postponement of pity to wrath is a new characteristic detail which shows how these gentler impulses
in Coriolanus must yield to his ruling passions. On
the other hand his host is transformed from a rich to
a poor man, and thus his humanity acquires a wider
range, and we see how it can extend beyond his own
class if only there is a personal claim on it. Above
all there is the new illuminating touch of the lapse of
memory. Sometimes this has been taken as betray-
ing the indifference of the aristocrat for an inferior

whose name he does not think it worth while to remember. Surely not. Coriolanus is experiencing the collapse that follows his superhuman exertions, the exhaustion of body and mind when one cannot think of the most familiar words : but he rallies his strength for a last effort, and is just able to intercede for his humble guest-friend ere he succumbs.

And this last passage brings before us another of his magnanimous qualities. He has refused most princely gifts. No one can accuse him of covetousness. His patrician bigotry aims at power and leadership, not at material perquisites. After the double battle, won almost entirely by his instrumentality, when Cominius offers him the tenth, he makes the generous answer :

> I thank you, general ;
> But cannot make my heart consent to take
> A bribe to pay my sword : I do refuse it.   (i. ix. 36.)

He deserves the encomium of the consul :

> Our spoils he kick'd at,
> And look'd upon things precious as they were
> The common muck of the world : he covets less
> Than misery itself would give ; rewards
> His deeds with doing them, and is content
> To spend the time to end it.   (ii. ii. 128.)

He "rewards his deeds with doing them," without thought of ulterior profit or of anything beyond the worthy occupation of the moment. This leads to the next point, his cult of honour ; and it must be confessed that he conceives it in a very lofty and noble way. His view of it reminds one of Arthur's saying in Tennyson's *Idylls* :

> For the deed's sake my knighthood do the deed,
> Not to be noised of.

Honour, of course, is not the highest possible principle. It implies a certain quest for recognition, and in so far has a personal and even selfish aspect. But in the right kind of honour the recognition is sought, in the first place, for real excellences that, in the second place, are determined only by competent judges, in some cases only by the individual's own conscience. In both respects Coriolanus bears examination.

Of course, when there is any pursuit of honour at all, it is almost impossible to exclude some admixture of rivalry and emulation : for the desire of recognition, if only by oneself, carries with it the desire of being recognised as having achieved the very best : and rivalry and emulation must to that extent have an egoistic direction. Coriolanus has these feelings to the full, and often gives them extreme expression in regard to his one possible competitor Aufidius. He calls him " the man of my soul's hate " (I. v. 11) ; and tells him : "I have ever followed thee with hate" (IV. v. 104). Aufidius has equal animosity against Coriolanus. His correspondent, to give an idea of his rival's unpopularity with his townsmen, writes of

> Marcius your old enemy,
> Who is of Rome worse hated than of you.   (I. ii. 12.)

Lartius reports how the Volscian has said,

> That of all things upon the earth, he hated
> Your person most.   (III. i. 14.)

Marcius, hearing he is at Antium, sums up for both :

> I wish I had a cause to seek him there,
> To oppose his hatred fully.   (III. i. 19.)

As Tullus sums up on his side :

>   We hate alike ;
> Not Afric owns a serpent I abhor
> More than thy fame and envy.   (I. viii. 2.)

Still, it is precisely in his relations with Aufidius, and in comparison with Aufidius' passions and purposes, that Coriolanus' finer conception of honour becomes apparent. The true warrior values these encounters for themselves, and has a rapture in them second to none that he knows. He exclaims :

> Were half to half the world by the ears, and he
> Upon my party, I'ld revolt, to make
> Only my wars with him : he is a lion
> That I am proud to hunt. (I. i. 237.)

This has sometimes been regarded as a hint in advance of Marcius' readiness to desert the national cause. But that seems to be taking *au pied de la lettre* one of those conversational audacities that much discreeter men than he often permit themselves. It is rather an exaggerated expression of his delight in the contest, and an ironical comment on his later abandonment of it for the sake of revenge. At anyrate, even if the worst interpretation be put on it, it suggests a more respectable motive for desertion than the parallel outburst of Aufidius :

> I would I were a Roman ; for I cannot,
> Being a Volsce, be that I am. (I. x. 4.)

For Coriolanus would change sides in order to confront the severest test, Aufidius would do so in order not to be of the defeated party. There is a meanness and bitterness in Tullus from which his rival is wholly free. All through, Marcius shows the generosity of conscious heroism. He is very handsome in his acknowledgment of Aufidius' merits :

> They have a leader,
> Tullus Aufidius, that will put you to 't.
> I sin in envying his nobility,
> And were I anything but what I am,
> I would wish me only he. (I. i. 232.)

In their trials of valour he takes no advantage, but rather makes a point, first of facing his foe though he himself is wearied and wounded, and, second, of rousing him to put forth all his strength.

> The blood I drop is rather physical
> Than dangerous to me : to Aufidius thus
> I will appear, and fight. (I. v. 19.)

Then, when they meet, he dissembles his hurts, and cries :

> Within these three hours, Tullus,
> Alone I fought in your Corioli walls,
> And made what work I pleased : *'tis not my blood*
> Wherein thou seest me mask'd : for thy revenge
> Wrench up thy power to the highest. (I. viii. 7.)

They are pledged to slay each other or be slain. Tullus has told the senators :

> If we and Caius Marcius chance to meet,
> 'Tis sworn between us we shall ever strike
> Till one can do no more. (I. ii. 34.)

And to this he adds boasts of his own, which Coriolanus omits. Nevertheless, though his professions are the loudest, Aufidius makes good neither pledge nor boasts, but lets himself be driven back despite the assistance of his friends. And then, just as he would rather be a successful Roman than a defeated Volsce, his thoughts turn to getting the better of his victor by whatever means ; he cannot take his beating in a sportsmanlike way, and thus shows finally how hollow is the honour after which he strives. Whether intentionally or not, Lartius' report gives a true description of his feeling :

> He would pawn his fortunes
> To hopeless restitution, so he might
> Be call'd your vanquisher. (III. i. 15.)

" Be call'd " ; as though the vain ascription of superiority were all that he desired. But in truth he has already made the same confession in so many words, with the more damaging admission that he now feels as though he no longer cared by what foul play such ascription is won.

> By the elements,
> If e'er again I meet him beard to beard,
> He's mine, or I am his : mine emulation
> Hath not that honour in't it had : for where
> I thought to crush him in an equal force,

True sword to sword, I'll potch at him some way
Or wrath or craft may get him.   (I. x. 10.)

                              My valour's poison'd
With only suffering stain by him : for him
Shall fly out of itself: nor sleep, nor sanctuary,
Being naked, sick, nor fane nor Capitol,
The prayers of priests, nor times of sacrifice,
Embarquements all of fury, shall lift up
Their rotten privilege and custom 'gainst
My hate to Marcius: where I find him, were it
At home, upon my brother's guard, even there,
Against the hospitable canon, would I
Wash my fierce hand in's blood.   (I. x. 17.)

On this passage Coleridge comments :

> I have such deep faith in Shakespeare's heart-lore, that I
> take for granted that this is in nature, and not as a mere
> anomaly ; although I cannot in myself discover any germ of
> possible feeling, which could wax and unfold itself into such
> a sentiment as this.

It seems strange that Coleridge should say this, for it is proved by not a few examples that baffled emulation may issue in an envy which knows few restraints. Perhaps it was the avowal rather than the temper which struck him as verging on the unnatural or abnormal. Those who deliberately adopt such an attitude do not usually admit it to themselves, still less to their victims, and least of all to a third party. Which may admonish us that Aufidius' threats were not deliberate, but mere frantic outcries wrung from him in rage and mortification. Yet they spring from authentic impulses in his heart, and though they may for a time be hidden by his superficial chivalry, they will spread and thrive if the conditions favour their growth. When they have overrun his nature and choked the wholesome grain, he will not point to them so openly and will name them by other names. But they are the same and differ from what they were only as the thorny thicket differs from its parent seeds. They

have always been there and it is well that we should
be aware of their presence from the first.   Coleridge
concludes his criticism : " However I perceive that
in this speech is meant to be contained a prevention
of the shock at the after-change in Aufidius'
character."   In short. it is not to be taken as his
definite programme from which he inconsistently
deviates when the opportunity is offered at Antium
for carrying it out, but as the involuntary presentiment, which the revealing power of anguish awakens
in his soul, of the crimes he is capable of committing
for his master passion, a presentiment that in the
end is realised almost to the letter.

And in the fulfilment, as in the anticipation, he
has an eye merely to the results, and seeks only to
obtain the first place for himself whether he deserve
it or no.   When Coriolanus consents to the peace
with Rome, Aufidius soliloquises :

> I am glad thou hast set thy mercy and thy honour
> At difference in thee : out of that I'll work
> Myself a former fortune.   (v. iii. 200.)

It is the adventitious superiority and the judgment
by appearances that always appeal to him.   Listen
to the interchange of confidences between his accom-
plice and himself :

> *Third Conspirator.* The people will remain uncertain whilst
> 'Twixt you there's difference ; but the fall of either
> Makes the survivor heir of all.
> *Aufidius.*   I know it :
> And my pretext to strike at him admits
> A good construction.   (v. vi. 17.)

He will be heir of all, and his action will admit a
good construction ; that is enough for him.   It only
remains to keep another construction from being
suggested ; and he approves the conspirator's advice :

> When he lies along,
> After your way his tale pronounced shall bury
> His reasons with his body.   (v. vi. 57.)

It has sometimes been questioned whether such a man would give his fugitive rival a welcome which at the first and for some time seems so magnanimous, and if he did, whether the magnanimity was sincere. But Aufidius, though he is above all a lover of pre-eminence at whatever cost and therefore cannot for long stand the ordeal of being surpassed, is not without a soldier's generosity ; and moreover, the course which he was moved to adopt (and this is a more important consideration) would be one congenial to his meretricious love of ostentation and display. There is no rôle more soothing to worsted vanity and at the same time more likely to gain it the admiration it prizes, than that of patron to a formerly successful and now unfortunate rival. In the reflected glory, the benefactor seems to acquire the merits of the other in addition to a magnificence all his own. This, we may assume, was in part the motive of Aufidius ; as appears from his own words, in which he shows himself well aware of his own generous behaviour :

> He came unto my hearth ;
> Presented to my knife his throat : I took him ;
> Made him joint-servant with me ; gave him way
> In all his own desires ; nay, let him choose
> Out of my files, his projects to accomplish,
> My best and freshest men ; served his designments
> In mine own person ; holp to reap the fame
> Which he did end all his ; and *took some pride*
> *To do myself this wrong ;* till, at the last,
> I seem'd his follower, not partner, and
> He waged me with his countenance, as if
> I had been mercenary. (v. vi. 30.)

The hasty flash of generosity, the hope of winning new credit, would soon be extinguished or transmuted by such persistent success, superiority and pride. And Coriolanus' popularity with the troops at the expense of his Volscian colleague, would be bitter to the most high-minded benefactor. It is

brought out to us by his question to his lieutenant
in the camp near Rome : " Do they still fly to the
Roman ? " (IV. vii. 1). Evidently the soldiers of
Antium flock to the banners of this foreigner rather
than to those of their own countrymen. The
suggestion for this is furnished by Plutarch, but
with Shakespeare a sting is added. In the *Life*
Tullus stays behind as reserve with half the army
to guard against any inroad, while Coriolanus acts
on the offensive and captures a number of towns.
Thereupon,

> the other Volsces that were appointed to remaine in garrison
> for defence of theur countrie, hearing this good newes, would
> tary no lenger at home, but armed them selves, and ranne
> to Martius campe, saying they dyd acknowledge no other
> captaine but him.

It is much less wounding to Aufidius that his men
should wish to exchange inaction for the excitement
of war, than that he should witness their resort to
his rival who is, in name, only his equal in command.
Indeed his lieutenant in the play regrets that he
did not do precisely what he did do according to
Plutarch.

> I wish, sir,—
> I mean for your particular,—you had not
> Join'd in commission with him ; but either
> Had borne the action of yourself, or else
> To him had left it solely.   (IV. vii. 12.)

Thus Shakespeare gives Tullus a stronger motive,
and in so far a better policy for his treason. On
the other hand he bases it more exclusively on personal envy. For in Plutarch the truce of thirty
days which Coriolanus grants Rome is the original
occasion of the movement against him, in which
other Volscians besides Aufidius share ; and this
movement culminates only after he has conceded
peace on conditions which even Plutarch considers
unfair to his employers. But in the play, as we have

seen, the truce is omitted, and Tullus has determined on the destruction of his supplanter even at a time when he confidently expects that Rome cannot save herself :

> When, Caius, Rome is thine,
> Thou art poor'st of all : then shortly art thou mine.
>
> (IV. vii. 56.)

Thus the last shred of public spirit is torn away from his selfish ambition and spite.

In contrast with all this lust for precedence and vainglorious egotism, we cannot but feel that Marcius is striving for the reality of honour and is eager to fulfil the conditions on which honour is due.

And connected with this is another point which we might regard as the natural and inevitable consequence, but which Shakespeare only inferred and did not obtain from Plutarch, who gives no indication of it. This is Marcius' indifference to or rather detestation of all professed praise. His distaste for eulogy does not of course lead him to reject a distinction and acknowledgment like the surname of *Coriolanus* that he is conscious of having deserved. On the contrary he prizes it and clings to it, and among the circumstances that overthrow his self-control in the final scene, the fact that Aufidius withholds from him this appellation has a chief place.

> *Aufidius.*　　　　　　　Marcius !
> *Coriolanus.*　　　　　　　Marcius !
> *Aufidius.* Ay, Marcius, Caius Marcius ; dost thou think
> I'll grace thee with that robbery, thy stol'n name
> Coriolanus in Corioli ?

Just in the same way, his aversion from mercantile profit does not lead him to refuse a gift from a friend when he feels that he has earned that friend's approval. So when Cominius bestows on him the charger, and bids the host hail him with his new title, he answers graciously enough if a little awkwardly :

> I will go wash ;
> And when my face is fair, you shall perceive
> Whether I blush or no : howbeit I thank you.
> I mean to stride your steed, and at all times
> To undercrest your good addition
> To the fairness of my power. (I. ix. 68.)

But except on such semi-official occasions, which he is obliged to recognise, any sort of commendation abashes him and puts him out. Even Lartius' burst of admiration he immediately checks :

> Pray now, no more : my mother,
> Who has a charter to extol her blood,
> When she does praise me, grieves me. (I. ix. 13.)

When Cominius persists, he would fain cut him short :

> I have some wounds upon me, and they smart
> To hear themselves remember'd. (I. ix. 28.)

When the host spontaneously breaks out in acclamation, he feels it is over much, and is more irritated than pleased :

> May these same instruments, which you profane,
> Never sound more ! When drums and trumpets shall
> I' the field prove flatterers, let courts and cities be
> Made all of false-faced soothing !
> When steel grows soft as the parasite's silk,
> Let him be made a coverture for the wars !
> No more, I say ! For that I have not wash'd
> My nose that bled, or foil'd some debile wretch,—
> Which, without note, here's many else have done,—
> You shout me forth
> In acclamations hyperbolical ;
> As if I loved my little should be dieted
> In praises sauced with lies. (I. ix. 42.)

So, too, with the welcome of the crowd at his home-coming :

> No more of this ; it does offend my heart ;
> Pray now, no more. (II. i. 185.)

Where the formal, and therefore up to a certain point, conventional panegyrics have to be pronounced in the senate, he is honestly ill at ease and would rather go away. To the senator who seeks to stay him, he answers :

> Your honour's pardon :
> I had rather have my wounds to heal again
> Than hear say how I got them. (II. ii. 72.)

And he adds, as he actually leaves his seat :

> I had rather have one scratch my head i' the sun
> When the alarum were struck, than idly sit
> To hear my nothings monster'd. (II. ii. 79.)

He can dispense with the admiration of others, because he seeks "the perfect witness" of his own approval, and abhors any extravagant applause because he measures his actions by the standard of absolute desert. In other words, both his self-respect and his ideal of attainment are abnormally, one might say morbidly, developed. And this explains both his humility and his self-assertion. Volumnia tells him :

> Thou hast affected the fine strains of honour,
> To imitate the graces of the gods. (V. iii. 149.)

If that is the goal, how far must even the mightiest fall short of it, and how much must he resent the adulation of his prowess as the highest to be attained. On the contrary he "waxes like the sea," sets himself to advance

> From well to better, daily self surpassed ;

and every glory he achieves is, as Shakespeare read in Plutarch, less a wage that he has earned than a pledge that he must redeem.

> It is daylie seene, that honour and reputation lighting on young men before their time, and before they have no great corage by nature, the desire to winne more, dieth straight in

them, which easely happeneth, the same having no deepe roote in them before. Where contrariwise, the first honour that valliant mindes doe come unto, doth quicken up their appetite, hasting them forward as with force of winde, to enterprise things of highe deserving praise. For they esteeme, not to receave reward for service done, but rather take it for a remembraunce and encoragement, to make them doe better in time to come : and be ashamed also to cast their honour at their heeles, not seeking to increase it still by like deserte of worthie valliant dedes. This desire being bred in Martius, he strained still to passe him selfe in manlines : and being desirous to shewe a daylie increase of his valliantnes, his noble service dyd still advaunce his fame.

But, on the other hand, though he, as not having attained, presses forward to the mark of his high calling, he has but to spend a glance on his fellows, and being an honest man he must perceive that his performance quite eclipses theirs. When the citizen asks him what has brought him to stand for the consulship, his reply is from the heart : " Mine own desert " (II. iii. 71). He feels poignantly the indignity of having to ask for what seems to him his due, and this partly explains the reluctance, which Shakespeare invents for him, to face a popular election.

> Better it is to die, better to starve,
> Than crave the hire which first we do deserve.
>
> (II. iii. 120.)

In bitter self-irony he belies the disinterestedness of his exploits, and libels them as mere contrivances to win favour :

> Your voices : for your voices I have fought ;
> Watch'd for your voices ; for your voices bear
> Of wounds two dozen odd ; battles thrice six
> I have seen and heard of ; for your voices have
> Done many things, some less, some more. (II. iii. 133.)

His fault lies in an opposite direction. His sense of dignity and self-esteem makes him inflexible to any concession that would seem to disparage himself and the truth.

> His nature is too noble for the world :
> He would not flatter Neptune for his trident,
> Or Jove for's power to thunder. (III. i. 255.)

And he is entitled to this consciousness of his worth, for it is not merely individual. It collects in a focus the most valued traits of various social fellowships that are greater and wider than himself. He is—he has been taught to consider himself and to become—the peculiar representative of the great family of the great aristocracy of the great city of Rome. If he transcends the dimensions of ordinary human power and human error, this consideration enables us to see how he has come to do so, and brings him back to our ordinary human sympathies. These are the three concentric orbits in which his universe revolves, the three well-heads that feed the current of his life. They give impetus to his love of honour and volume to his pride.

His civic patriotism he lives to abjure, but at first it is eager and intense. It is this feeling that is affronted by the retreat of his townsmen before Corioli and that boils over in curses and abuse : he is wroth with them because they are "shames of Rome." The climax to his appeal for volunteers is to ask if any thinks "that his country's dearer than himself" (I. vi. 72) : and in the moment of triumph he classes himself unreservedly among all his comrades who have been actuated by his own and the only right motive, love for the *patria*.

> I have done
> What you have done ; that's what I can : induced
> As you have been ; that's for my country :
> He that hath but effected his good will
> Hath overta'en my act. (I. ix. 15.)

He cherishes a transcendent idea of the state, and

is wounded to the heart that its members fall short
of it.

> I would they were barbarians—as they are,
> Though in Rome litter'd—not Romans—as they are not,
> Though calved i' the porch o' the Capitol.   (III. i. 238.)

And he is similarly, but more closely bound up in
his own order. The nobles, the patricians, the
senate, are to him the core of the commonwealth,
the very Rome of Rome. They are, as he says,
"the fundamental part of state" (III. i. 151). His
first thought on his return from the campaign is to
pay his due respects to their dignity :

> Ere in my own house I do shade my head,
> The good patricians must be visited.   (II. i. 211.)

He is scandalised by the insolence of the plebs in
revolting against such authority :

> What's the matter,
> That in these several places of the city
> You cry against the noble senate, who,
> Under the gods, keep you in awe?   (I. i. 188.)

His gorge rises at the thought of a representative
of the people imposing his mandate on so august a
body.

> They choose their magistrate,
> And such a one as he, who puts his "shall,"
> His popular "shall" against a graver bench
> Than ever frown'd in Greece.   (III. i. 104.)

He hates any innovation that is likely

> To break the heart of generosity
> And make bold power look pale.   (I. i. 215.)

For to him the power that is vested in the generous,
that is, the high-born classes, is a sacred thing.

But the domestic tie is the closest of all. The
whole story brings out its compulsive pressure and
no particular passages are needed to illustrate it.
Yet in some passages we are made to realise with

special vividness how it binds and entwines him, as in that exclamation when he sees the deputation of women approaching :

> My wife comes foremost; then the honour'd mould
> Wherein this trunk was framed, and in her hand
> The grandchild to her blood.   (v. iii. 22.)

It is as son, husband and father that the depths of Coriolanus' nature can be reached. In his greetings to his wife, in his prayers for his boy, we have glimpses of his inward heart; but of course this family feeling is concentrated on his mother who, as it were, sums up his ancestry to him, and who, by her personal qualities and her parental authority, fills his soul with a kind of religious reverence. We have seen how she has fashioned him, how she commands and awes him. When she inclines her head as she appears before him, he already feels that it is incongruous and absurd :

> My mother bows :
> As if Olympus to a molehill should
> In supplication nod.   (v. iii. 29.)

When she kneels, it is prodigious, incredible; he cannot believe his eyes :

> What is this?
> Your knees to me? to your corrected son?
> Then let the pebbles on the hungry beach
> Fillip the stars; then let the mutinous winds
> Strike the proud cedars 'gainst the fiery sun :
> Murdering impossibility, to make
> What cannot be, slight work.   (v. iii. 56.)

Not only then is Coriolanus in other respects a singularly noble personality, but even his pride is certainly not devoid of ethical content when it embodies the consciousness of the city republic, the governing estate, the organised family, with all their claims and obligations. These are the constituent elements that have supplied matter for his self-esteem, and all of them are formative, and capable, as we saw, of producing such a lofty, though limited moral character as that of Volumnia. Yet it is precisely to them, or at least to the way in which they are mingled in his pride, that Coriolanus' faults and misfortunes may be traced.

CHAPTER VI

THE DISASTERS OF CORIOLANUS AND THEIR CAUSES

FEELING for his country, feeling for his caste, feeling for his family thus form the triple groundwork of Coriolanus' nobleness, but they fail to uphold it in the storm of temptation. As furnishing the foundations of conduct they have dangers and defects, inherent in themselves, or incident to their combination, and these it is to which the guilt and ruin of Coriolanus are due.

These drawbacks may be illustrated under three heads. They are unfit completely to transfigure egoism, for they have all an egoistic aspect, and are indeed merely extended forms of selfishness. They are primarily the products of nature, instinct, passion ; and may exist without being raised to the rank of rational principles and without having their just scope delimited and defined. And, lastly, for that reason their relative importance may be mistaken, and one that is the stronger natural impulse may usurp the place of one that is of more binding moral authority.

It has often been pointed out, and sometimes as a matter of complaint, that family affection is very restricted in its range and may conflict with the larger interests of mankind. It produces an intense unity within the one household, but it is apt to be jealous, repellent, aggressive as regards other households and their members. Further, in so far as it is *my* parents, *my* brothers, *my* children, whose welfare I promote, the ground of preference has nothing to do with impartial equity : it is determined by the nearness of the persons to *me*, by *my* fondness for them, by my looking on them as appurtenances of *mine*; in short it is selfish. And those who maintain the sacredness of the family give this no absolute denial, but reply, first, that in the long run the true interests of one family, rightly understood, do not conflict with the true interests of other families, of the state, or the rest of mankind ; and, second, that even before the true interests are rightly grasped, the family relation forms at least a stage in the process by which the individual learns to enlarge his self-interest, a preliminary stage but an inevitable stage, and still for the vast majority of men the stage of most practical importance. Many a one is ready to give up his personal pleasure or advantage for those of his own house, who would be deaf to all more general appeals. Thus the family so widens self-love as to include in it some other people, but in one of its aspects it nevertheless depends on self-love.

And the same thing holds good of the enlarged kindred that we call an aristocracy. The nobility of blood forms a sort of family on a large scale, a family of caste, an amplified household united by common pursuits, privileges, education and ideals, and often further blended by frequent intermarriage. The aristocrat finds himself born into this artificial, which is in some respects almost like a natural fraternity ; and his ethos to his order, ethos though it be, is largely the ethos of the individual who recognises his own reflection in his fellow nobles.

Nor is it otherwise with the state, especially, we may say, the antique city state, where often the

aristocracy really was the native nucleus, and which
in the greatest expansion of which it was capable,
did not exceed the dimensions of a modern municipality. The patriotism of the citizens had the fervour
of domestic piety, their disputes had the bitterness
of family quarrels. In the community its sons
exulted and lived and moved and had their being :
it was theirs and they were its, in opposition to the
alien states, the states of other people, to which they
were apt to be indifferent or hostile.

Now it is evident that all these principles in the
case of a man with a strong consciousness of his
own worth and superlative self-respect, might give
substance and validity to his egoism, but would
rather encourage than counteract it. And so with
Coriolanus. His independent, individual, isolated
sufficiency passes all bounds. He derives sustenance
for it from the three layers of atmosphere that
envelope him, but he thinks he can if necessary
dispense with these external aids. In so far as he
can separate the people in his mind from the whole
body politic of Rome, he excludes them from his
sympathy, or even his tolerance, and glories in his
ostentation of antagonism. Take his speech about
the popular demonstration :

They said they were an-hungry, sigh'd forth proverbs,
That hunger broke stone walls, that dogs must eat,
That meat was made for mouths, that the gods sent not
Corn for the rich men only : with these shreds
They vented their complainings. (I. i. 209.)

In reference to this Archbishop Trench has a very
true remark. He points out that where there is a
marked and conscious division of ranks,

[proverbs] may go nearly or quite out of use among the so-
called upper classes. No gentleman, says Lord Chesterfield,
" ever uses a proverb." And with how true a touch of nature,
Shakespeare makes Coriolanus, the man who with all his
greatness, is entirely devoid of all sympathy with the people,

to utter his scorn of them in scorn of their proverbs and of
their frequent employment of them.

He has indeed no sense of their homely wisdom or
their homely virtues. He has no common charity
for them, and his attitude to them if they venture
to assert themselves, is that of a less human slave-
holder to refractory slaves.

> Would the nobility lay aside their ruth,
> And let me use my sword, I'ld make a quarry
> With thousands of these quarter'd slaves, as high
> As I could pick my lance. (I. i. 201.)

After such counsel, we feel that the exclamation of
Sicinius is not without its warrant :

> Where is this viper
> That would depopulate the city, and
> Be every man himself? (III. i. 263.)

His self-centred confidence and egotism culminates
in his retort to his sentence :

> You common cry of curs? whose breath I hate
> As reek o' the rotten fens, whose loves I prize
> As the dead carcasses of unburied men
> That do corrupt my air, I banish you. (III. iii. 120.)

But it is characteristic of this spirit which really
makes a man a law to himself and the measure of
things, that though by all his training and prejudices
inclined to the traditional and conservative in politics,
yet, if use-and-wont presses hard against his own
pride, he shows himself an innovator of the most
uncompromising kind. He objects once and again
to the prescriptive forms of election, and at last
breaks out :

> Custom calls me to 't !
> What custom wills, in all things should we do 't,
> The dust on antique time would lie unswept
> And mountainous error be too highly heapt
> For truth to o'er-peer. (II. iii. 124.)

Here he blossoms out as the reddest of radicals,
though a radical of the Napoleonic type.

But, further, his feeling for family, class and country is pre-eminently feeling. It belongs to those natural tendencies that almost seem to come to us by heredity and environment, and have analogies with the instincts of animals. It is, at least in the form it assumes with him, not to be ranked among the moral convictions which can stand the examination of conscience and reason, and in the production of which conscience and reason have co-operated. It is rather an innate impulse, a headlong passion, and resembles a blind physical force of which he can give no account. His understanding is without right of entry into this part of his life. We have seen, no doubt, that his presuppositions once granted he can form a very acute estimate of the situation. But he never uses his judgment either in examining his presuppositions or in discovering the treatment that the situation requires. He has not the width of outlook or the self-criticism that enable Menenius and Cominius, and even the ordinary senators, to see the relative importance of the principles for which they contend, and prefer any compromise to laying the city flat and sacking great Rome with Romans. He has not the astuteness of Volumnia, who perceives that strategy is to be used in government as in war and bids him stoop to conquer :

> I have a heart as little apt as yours,
> But yet a brain that leads my use of anger
> To better vantage. (III. ii. 29.)

> If it be honour in your wars to seem
> The same you are not, which, for your best ends,
> You adopt your policy, how is it less or worse,
> That it shall hold companionship in peace
> With honour, as in war, since that to both
> It stands in like request? (III. ii. 46.)

Both in regard to end and means, he listens to the counsels not of his reason but of his passion and hot blood. As how could he do otherwise? It is

passion not reason that oversways his nature, determining everything in him from these first fundamental principles to the most transitory mood.
More particularly, that tyrannous self-respect of his,
the personal flame in which all his interests, domestic,
aristocratic, national, are fused, is his central passion,
and one that gives more heat than light. Sometimes, indeed, it kindles him to great things. When
the Volscian army abandons the shelter of Corioli
he feels it an insult to his country, therefore to
himself; and the outrage to his *amour propre* incites
him to do wonders.

> They fear us not, but issue forth their city.
> Now put your shields before your hearts, and fight
> With hearts more proof than shields. Advance, brave Titus:
> *They do disdain us much beyond our thoughts,*
> *Which makes me sweat with wrath.* (I. iv. 23.)

But again, it may make it impossible for him to take
the right path. When asked to show some outward
submission to the people, he answers :

> To the market-place!
> You have put me now to such a part which never
> I shall discharge to the life. (III. ii. 104.)

He was justified in objecting to methods of dissimulation and flattery, but, if only he had been
reasonable, a middle course would not have been
hard to find, which should safeguard his self-respect
while pacifying the populace. It is because his
self-respect is of passion not of reason, that he is so
unconciliatory, and therefore almost as culpable as
if he were guilty of the opposite fault. Plutarch,
indeed, thinks he is more so. In his comparison
between him and Alcibiades, he is in this matter
more lenient to the latter :

> He is lesse to be blamed, that seeketh to please and
> gratifie his common people; then he that despiseth and
> disdaineth them, and therefore offereth them wrong and
> injurie, bicause he would not seeme to flatter them, to winne

the more authoritie. For as it is an evill thing to flatter the
common people to winne credit; even so it is besides dishonesty, and injustice also, to atteine to credit and authoritie,
for one to make him selfe terrible to the people, by offering
them wrong and violence.

This passage has inspired the criticism of the officer
of the Capitol; who, however, impartially holds the
scales.

If he did not care whether he had their love or no, he
waved indifferently 'twixt doing them neither good nor harm:
but he seeks their hate with greater devotion than they can
render it him; and leaves nothing undone that may fully
discover him their opposite. Now, to seem to affect the
malice and displeasure of the people is as bad as that which
he dislikes, to flatter them for their love. (II. ii. 18.)

With this temper it is natural that the arrogance
of success, lack of nous, and want of adaptability
—which is often merely another form of self-will—
should bring about his ruin; and it is these three
characteristics, or a modicum of them, to which
Aufidius in point of fact attributes his banishment.

> First he was
> A noble servant to them; but he could not
> Carry his honours even: whether 'twas pride,
> Which out of daily fortune ever taints
> The happy man; whether defect of judgement,
> To fail in the disposing of those chances
> Which he was lord of; or whether nature,
> Not to be other than one thing, not moving
> From the casque to the cushion, but commanding peace
> Even with the same austerity and garb
> As he controll'd the war; but one of these —
> As he hath spices of them all, not all,
> For I dare so far free him—made him fear'd,
> So hated, and so banish'd. (IV. vii. 35.)

But, lastly, not only are the three objective ethical
principles that give Coriolanus his moral equipment,
inadequate in so far as their range is largely selfish
and their origin largely natural; he misplaces the
order in which they should come. In the case of
Volumnia, despite all her maternal preference and

patrician prejudice, Rome is the grand consideration, as her deeds unequivocally prove. Nor is she singular; she is only the most conspicuous example among others of her caste. Cominius, too, post-pones the family to the state:

> I do love
> My country's good with a respect more tender,
> More holy and profound, than mine own life,
> My dear wife's estimate, her womb's increase,
> And treasure of my loins. (III. iii. 111.)

And this is more or less the attitude of the rest. But Coriolanus reverses the sequence, and gives his chief homage precisely to the most restricted and elementary, the most primitive and instinctive principle of the three. He loves Rome indeed, fights for her, grieves for her shames, and glories in her triumphs; but he loves the nobility more, and would by wholesale massacre secure their supremacy. He loves the nobility indeed, but when they, no doubt for the common good, suffer him to be expelled from Rome, they become to him the "dastard nobles"; and he makes hardly any account of his old henchman and intimate Menenius, and none at all of his old comrade and general Cominius. But he loves his family as himself, and though he strives to root out its claims from his heart, the attempt is vain. He may exclaim:

> Out, affection!
> All bond and privilege of nature, break! (v. iii. 24.)

> I'll never
> Be such a gosling to obey instinct, but stand,
> As if a man were author of himself
> And knew no other kin. (v. iii. 34.)

But it is mere histrionic make-believe and pretence: at the first words of Virgilia he cries:

> Like a dull actor now,
> I have forgot my part, and I am out,
> Even to a full disgrace. (v. iii. 40.)

x

How could this man, whose personal pride and family pride are so interwoven, whose self-love and whose virtues are so much an inheritance of his line, ever hope to sever himself from what makes up his very being ? The home instincts must triumph.

It is well that they should, and this is the redeeming touch that cancels much of the guilt of apostasy which brands the close of his career. But all the same we feel that his self-surrender to the obligations of the family is a less noble thing than his mother's self-surrender to the obligations of the state. Of course, in a way, family and class must with all come before the whole community. Men, that is, are bound to be more interested in those of their own circle and their own set than in their fellow-citizens with whom they have less relation. That gives a very good ground for a man's constant unremitting occupation with his nearest and dearest. But, nevertheless, when the call comes, it is the wider community that has the more imperative claim.

And it is easy to see that Volumnia, though at the supreme moment she shows that she herself has the right feeling for the relation, is responsible for the inverted order in the conception of her son. Her contempt for the masses, her exaltation of the patricians, her high-handed insistence on the family authority were almost bound to be exaggerated in a child growing up under her influence and subjected to no corrective views. And she must have added to the dangers of her tuition by dangling before his eyes the ideal personal honour as the grand prize of life. He wins it and lets it slip again and again, and when he grasps it at last, it is rent and mangled in his hands. There is something typical in the episode of his son and the butterfly, as Valeria narrates it :

> I saw him run after a gilded butterfly ; and when he caught it, he let it go again ; and after it again ; and over and over

> he comes, and up again; catched it again; or whether his
> fall enraged him, or how 'twas, he did so set his teeth and
> tear it : O, I warrant, how he mammocked it !   (I. iii. 65.)

Young Marcius is described as the facsimile and
"epitome" of his father, and Volumnia is well
pleased with this example of the family bent. She
must not disclaim her share in the preparation, when
the father enacts the apologue in the larger theatre
of life.

And she is even responsible for some of the mistaken courses that directly lead to the disaster.

For Coriolanus, with all his blind sides and rough
corners, might still be the faithful and honoured
champion of Rome if he were left to follow his own
predestined and congenial path as military leader.
In the field he can rouse the courage of the citizens
and fire their enthusiasm, while on his part, when he
wins their recognition and devotion, he lays aside
some of his asperity to them, and is even gracious
in his awkward, convincing way. They forget their
hatred, he forgets his scorn. And to him as warrior
the whole population, not only the portion of it
that has the franchise, is ready to do honour. The
description which the chagrined tribune gives of
his triumphal progress through the streets shows
with what cordial pride all ranks were eager to
pay him homage. There is no reason why he should
not continue to discharge in this his proper sphere
the functions that none could discharge so well.
His political weight is from the first small. Despite
his urgent dissuasion he has been powerless to
prevent the distribution of corn or the concession of
the tribunate. And when he does not intrude into
this outlying domain, where he effects nothing, he
seems to go his own way peaceably enough, occupied
mainly in watching for the common good the
movements of Aufidius and the Volscians ; so that,
so far as his antipathy to the people is concerned,

his bark is worse than his bite. That is the point of the similes that Brutus and Menenius exchange about him when Menenius has compared the plebs to a wolf and Coriolanus to a lamb. Says the tribune :

He's a lamb indeed, that baes like a bear.

And the senator answers :

He's a bear indeed, that lives like a lamb. (II. i. 12.)

But thrust him into a position that involves political authority, and all will be changed. It will be impossible for him to confine himself to harmless growls ; the bear will have the people in his hug, and they are not to blame if they take to their weapons. In short the antagonism, which before was, so to speak, academic and led to nothing, must become a matter of life and death. Now it must not be overlooked that it is in obedience to his mother's ambitions and in opposition to his own better judgment that Coriolanus stands for the consulship. Of course, in a way, it is the natural goal of his career. Even Menenius is so blinded by the glamour of the situation that he interposes no prudent warning. Nevertheless, if he had only exercised his accustomed shrewdness he would have seen the mischievousness of such a course ; for in a remark to the tribune he sums up admirably the perils it involves :

He loves your people ;
But tie him not to be their bedfellow ; (II. ii. 68.)

yet for all that, Menenius is the candidate's most active electioneering agent. When his sagacity so neglects its own suggestions, it is perhaps not wonderful that Volumnia's narrower intellect should ignore everything but her visions of glory for herself and her son. And yet she might have laid to heart his sincere remonstrance :

> Know, good mother,
> I had rather been their servant in my way,
> Than sway with them in theirs.   (II. i. 218.)

She cannot be acquitted of driving him into the false position.

And she is equally responsible for the fiasco and disaster in which his attempted submission ends. Observe that this is not the only course he might have adopted. Cominius, entering in the middle of the discussion, suggests two others :

> I have been i' the market-place ; and, sir, 'tis fit
> You make strong party, or defend yourself
> By calmness or by absence.   (III. ii. 93.)

The first expedient of making strong party and resorting to force is out of the question, both because, as Cominius has already pointed out, it is practically hopeless in face of the odds, and because, as he and others have also pointed out, even if successful it would ruin the state. The second expedient of calmness and conciliation is the one that Volumnia and Menenius in their pertinacious craving to see Coriolanus consul, strongly advocate ; and in the abstract it is the right one. But it suffers from a drawback which makes it worse than hopeless, and which Cominius has the foresight to recognise. "Only fair speech," says Menenius, and Cominius rejoins very doubtfully :

> I *think* 't will serve, *if* he
> Can thereto frame his spirit.   (III. ii. 95.)

That is just the point ; and one wonders how anyone who knew Coriolanus could expect of him so impossible a feat. There remains the expedient of absence, which Cominius, from the third place he assigns to it, himself seems to prefer. And in the circumstances it is obviously the best. If only the accused had withdrawn for a time, he would soon have been recalled. It is inconceivable that when the new expedition of the Volscians, which he alone foresaw, broke into Roman territory, the state would not at once have had recourse to the great commander. Nor would there have been much difficulty in doing so, since he would merely have betaken himself to voluntary retirement ; and even had he been exiled in default, the mutual exasperation on both sides, which the last collision was to produce, would have been avoided. But again it is Volumnia's overbearing self-will that imposes on him the pernicious choice. And though, as I have said, this proposal is ideally the best, for in such cases management and compromise are legitimate enough and may be laudable, it is not only the worst in the present instance, but she gives it a turn that must have made it peculiarly revolting to her son. In her covetousness for the consular dignity she recommends such hypocrisy, trickery and base cringing as the self-respect of no honest man, much less of a Coriolanus, could tolerate :

> I prithee now, my son,
> Go to them, with this bonnet in thy hand ;
> And thus far having stretch'd it—here be with them—
> Thy knee bussing the stones—for in such business
> Action is eloquence, and the eyes of the ignorant
> More learned than the ears—waving thy head,
> Which often, thus, correcting thy stout heart.
> Now humble as the ripest mulberry
> That will not hold the handling : or say to them,
> Thou art their soldier, and being bred in broils
> Hast not the soft way which, thou dost confess,
> Were fit for thee to use as they to claim,
> In asking their good loves, but thou wilt frame
> Thyself, forsooth, hereafter theirs, so far
> As thou hast power and person.   (III. ii. 72.

The amicable policy need not have been painted in such colours as these. It is inevitable that Coriolanus, already inclined to regard it as a degradation, should after these words construe it in the most humiliating sense :

>   Well, I must do 't :
> Away, my disposition, and possess me
> Some harlot's spirit ! My throat of war be turn'd,
> Which quired with my drum, into a pipe
> Small as an eunuch, or the virgin voice
> That babies lulls asleep ! The smile of knaves
> Tent in my cheeks, and schoolboys' tears take up
> The glasses of my sight ! a beggar's tongue
> Make motion through my lips, and my arm'd knees,
> Who bow'd but in the stirrup, bend like his
> That hath received an alms.   (III. ii. 110.)

What wonder that his conclusion is to reject such tactics lest they should dishonour his integrity and degrade his soul ? His mother's anger indeed makes him abandon this decision, but his instincts are right. It is a part that of course he could not play under any circumstances, but she has done nothing to show it in its more honourable aspect, and everything to confirm and increase his feeling of its vileness. His sourness and recalcitrance at being false to himself makes him boil over the more fiercely at the first provocation, and all is lost.

It is sometimes said that defeat and the desire for vengeance teach him the lessons which his mother had inculcated in vain, and that henceforth he shows himself a master of dissimulation, flattery, and deception. In proof of this it is usual to cite, in the first place, the farewell scene, when he breathes no word to Cominius, Menenius, Virgilia, or Volumnia of his intention to join the Volscians and return to overthrow Rome. But was any such intention as yet in his mind ? In Plutarch he has adopted no definite plan before he sets out. After telling how he comforts his family, the biography proceeds :

> He went immediatly to the gate of the cittie, accompanied with a great number of Patricians that brought him thither, from whence he went on his waye with three or foure of his friendes only, taking nothing with him, nor requesting any thing of any man. So he remained a fewe dayes in the countrie at his houses, turmoyled with sundry sortes and kynde of thoughtes, suche as the fyer of his choller dyd sturre

up. In the ende, seeing he could resolve no waye, to take a
profitable or honorable course, but only was pricked forward
still to be revenged of the Romaines, he thought to raise up
some great warres against them, by their neerest neighbours.

Of course it is quite true, and it has been one
purpose of this essay to show, that Shakespeare
often completely recasts Plutarch. But it is also
true that, when he does not expressly do so, he
often keeps Plutarch's statements in his mind, even
when, as in the case of the voting by tribes, he does
not cite them. It counts for something, then, that
in the *Life*, Coriolanus on leaving Rome has no
fixed purpose of seeking foreign help. And if we
turn to the parting scene in the tragedy, and let it
make its own impression, without reading into it
suggestions from subsequent occurrences, I think we
feel not so much that he is still undecided as that
the idea has not yet entered into his head. We
seem to hear the very accent of sincerity in his
repetition of the maxims that erewhile he learned
from his mother's own lips, and that he clinches with
the reminder :

You were used to load me

With precepts that would make invincible
The heart that conn'd them. (IV. i. 9.)

Surely it is a real attempt at consolation, when he
interrupts her maledictions on the plebeians who
have banished him :

What, what, what !

I shall be loved, when I am lack'd. (IV. i. 14.)

He seems to hint at seeking out new adventures and
a new career in new regions beyond the reach of
Rome, when he says :

My mother, you wot well

My hazards still have been your solace : and
Believe 't not lightly—though I go alone,
Like to a lonely dragon, that his fen
Makes fear'd and talk'd of more than seen—your son
Will or exceed the common or be caught
With cautelous baits and practice. (IV. i. 27.)

It was not cautelous baits and practice that he would have to fear, but the open violence of Aufidius if he already thought of going to Antium, and the simile of the lonely dragon more talked of than seen would be abundantly inappropriate if it referred to his re-appearance at the head of the Volscian forces : but the expressions would be quite apt if he meant to make his name redoubtable by his single prowess in strange places amidst the risks of an errant life. It is in professed anticipation of this that he rejects the companionship which Cominius offers :

> Thou hast years upon thee ; and thou art too full
> Of the wars' surfeits, to go rove with one
> That's yet unbruised. (IV. i. 45.)

Are these utterances mere pretence ? And have not his last farewells the genuine note of cordiality and good will ? If we could imagine that he would bring himself to address those whom he afterwards called the "dastard nobles" as "my friends of noble touch," it would still be impossible to believe him guilty of cold-hearted deceit to Virgilia and Volumnia.

> Come, my sweet wife, my dearest mother, and
> My friends of noble touch, when I am forth
> Bid me farewell, and smile. I pray you, come.
> While I remain above the ground, you shall
> Hear from me still, and never of me aught
> But what is like me formerly. (IV. i. 48.)

It would not be like the former champion of Rome to return as its assailant ; but we may take it that at this moment he is expecting to carve his way to glory in a different world and perhaps eventually be recalled to his country, but in any case to proceed merely on the old lines in so far as that is possible, and meanwhile to be reported of, as Menenius con-tinues, "worthily as any ear can hear."

If, then, he is speaking honestly in this scene, how are we to account for his change of purpose when we next meet him a renegade in Antium? No explanation was needed in Plutarch, for the circumstances were not quite the same. There he had only not resolved to join the enemy; here he apparently has resolved to do something else. In the *Life* after leaving the city he merely comes to a decision, in the play he reverses the decision he has formed. So some statement is needed of the cause for the alteration of his plans, and at first sight there seems to be none. Yet there is a hint and a fairly emphatic one, though it has not been worked out; a hint, moreover, which is the more significant that it is one of Shakespeare's interpolations.

When the sentence of banishment is pronounced and Coriolanus has retired to his house, there follows a passage which has no parallel or foundation in Plutarch. It is the one already referred to in another connection in which Sicinius gives his mean and malicious order to the people:

> Go, see him out at gates, and follow him,
> As he hath follow'd you, with all despite:
> Give him deserved vexation. (III. iii. 138.)

And the citizens promptly agree:

> Come, come; let's see him out at gates; come. (III. iii. 141.)

This is at the very close of the Third Act, and the Fourth Act begins in " Rome, before a gate of the city" with the scene of leave-taking discussed above. We naturally expect that it will be interrupted by the popular demonstrations which the tribunes have contrived, especially as these exist only in Shakespeare's imagination; but it passes off without any hint of them. Only patrician persons appear by whom Coriolanus is beloved and who are beloved by him: and no hostile murmur jars on the solemnity of their grief. But that does not mean that it may not do so even now. He is not yet beyond the walls, and

towards the close bids his friends : " Bring me out
at gate "; which, we assume, they do forthwith.
There is still time for the plebeians to execute their
masters' orders, and though we witness nothing of
the kind, there is no reason to believe that they
failed to do so. It is easy to conjecture why Shakespeare thought it unnecessary to present this incident
to eye and ear. It would have disturbed the quiet
dignity of the parting interview ; it would have
repeated at a lower pitch, without the accompani-
ment of suspense, and therefore with the risk of
monotony and flatness, the tumultuary *motif* of preceding scenes. But Shakespeare's variations from
his authority are not idle, and we cannot suppose
that the tribune's direction, though we do not
actually see it carried out, was a meaningless tag.
There is room enough in the economy of the play
for its fulfilment beyond the stage. We may imagine
that just as Coriolanus' friends proceed to " bring
him out at gate " the insulting irruption takes place ;
and in the next scene, "a street near the gate,"
we find the tribunes, the work done, dismissing their
agents :

> Bid them all home; he's gone, and we'll no further. (IV. ii. I.)

It seems probable that this last indignity, a hurt to
his pride more galling than any refusal of office or
sentence of banishment, drives Coriolanus to his
fury of vindictiveness ; and that the failure of the
nobles to protect him from the outrage has in his
eyes confounded them with his more ignoble enemies.
Indeed, he almost says as much in his speech to
Aufidius. In that speech, as we have seen, Shakespeare adheres more closely to North than in any
other continuous passage in the play, and the greatest
variation occurs in a line that would apply with
peculiar aptness to the purely Shakespearian episode
of the last affront, and that sets forth the main cause

of the exile's resentment. In Plutarch, after saying
that only the surname of Coriolanus remains to him,
he continues :

> The rest the envie and crueltie of the people of Rome have
> taken from me, by the sufferance of the dastardly nobilitie
> and magistrates, who have forsaken me, and let me be
> banished by the people.

This becomes :

> The cruelty and envy of the people,
> Permitted by our dastard nobles, who
> Have all forsook me, hath devour'd the rest :
> *And suffer'd me by the voice of slaves to be*
> *Whoop'd out of Rome.* (IV. v. 80.)

Considering all these things there seems to be no
evidence in Marcius' parting professions of acquired
duplicity.

But, again, it is said that for his revenge he condescends to fawn upon Aufidius and the Volscians.
This is not very plausible. His speech of greeting
certainly shows no servile propitiation, and according
to Tullus it is conspicuously absent in his subsequent
behaviour :

> He bears himself more proudlier,
> Even to my person, than I thought he would
> When first I did embrace him : yet his nature
> In that's no changeling ; and I must excuse
> What cannot be amended. (IV. vii. 8.)

And elsewhere Tullus complains that his guest has
"waged him with his countenance." The only
ground for saying that he paid court to the Volsces
is alleged in Tullus' speech that just precedes this
accusation of haughtiness to himself :

> He water'd his new plants with dews of flattery,
> Seducing so my friends ; and, to this end,
> He bow'd his nature, never known before
> But to be rough, unswayable and free. (V. vi. 23.)

But the speaker is an enemy, and an enemy who
has to account for the disagreeable circumstance

that his own adherents have gone over to his rival, and who, moreover, at the time is looking for a plea that "admits of good construction." There is nothing that we see or hear of Coriolanus elsewhere that supports the charge. We are told, indeed, that the Volscians throng to him and do him homage. The very magnates of Antium, Aufidius included, treat him like a demi-god:

> Why, he is so made on here within, as if he were son and heir to Mars; set at upper end o' the table: no question asked by any of the senators, but they stand bald before him: our general himself makes a mistress of him; sanctifies himself with 's hand and turns up the white o' the eye to his discourse. (IV. v. 203.)

Recruits throng to his standard and the army worships him. The Lieutenant tells Aufidius:

> I do not know what witchcraft's in him, but
> Your soldiers use him as the grace 'fore meat,
> Their talk at table, and their thanks at end. (IV. vii. 2.)

Doubtless this enthusiasm would have its effect on Marcius. Eagerness of service, coupled with confidence in himself, has before now warmed him to graciousness, and in his own despite wrung from him inspiring compliments. When at Cominius' camp before Corioli the volunteers crowded round him, waved their swords, and took him up in their arms, he was almost hyperbolical in his praises:

> O, me alone! make you a sword of me?
> If these shows be not outward, which of you
> But is four Volsces? none of you but is
> Able to bear against the great Aufidius
> A shield as hard as his. (I. vi. 76.)

So we may well believe that his soldierly spirit would respond promptly and lavishly when the Volscians rallied round him. But such appreciation, however his outstripped competitor might interpret it, would have nothing in common with the arts of the

sycophant and the time-server; nor is there anything else in Coriolanus' conduct that explains or
confirms ever so slightly the charge of the interested
and envious Aufidius.

On the contrary he remains true, and even too
true, to his original nature. It is the outrage on his
self-respect that drives him to the Volscians, and his
self-respect still gives the law to his life, and would
forbid all petty vices, though it enjoins heroic crime.
A man like this could not be expected to palliate or
overlook the profanation of his cherished dignity.
The passion of pride at his ear, he sets himself to
rupture all weaker ties of passion or instinct. And
yet he himself is half aware of his mistake, and he
has to fortify himself in his obstinate perversity.
This is shown in two ways: first, he has a smothered
sense of the inadequacy of his justification; and,
second, he cannot with all his efforts be quite consistent in his revenge.

Of his repressed feeling that the offence does not
excuse the retaliation, we have repeated confessions
on his part, all the more striking that they are
involuntary and perhaps unconscious. Thus, just
after he has sought out the enemy of his country,
he soliloquises:

> O world, thy slippery turns! Friends now fast sworn,
> Whose double bosoms seem to wear one heart,
> Whose hours, whose bed, whose meal, and exercise,
> Are still together, who twin, as 'twere, in love
> Unseparable, shall within this hour,
> On a dissension of a doit, break out
> To bitterest enmity: so, fellest foes,
> Whose passions and whose plots have broke their sleep
> To take the one the other, by some chance,
> Some trick not worth an egg, shall grow dear friends
> And interjoin their issues. So with me:
> My birth-place hate I, and my love's upon
> This enemy town. (IV. iv. 12.)

Here he acknowledges that his change of sides has

the most trivial occasion. Friends fall out on a dissension of a doit while foes are reconciled for some trick not worth an egg ; and he applies this principle to his own case : " So with me." After all he has infinitely more in common with the Romans than he can ever have in common with the Volscians, infinitely more reason for hating this enemy town than he can ever have for hating his own birthplace.

Or again, when on the point of dismissing Menenius, he says :

> That we have been familiar
> Ingrate forgetfulness shall poison, rather
> Than pity note how much.   (v. ii. 91.)

He admits, then, that his wilful oblivion is "ingrate," and realises that pity would consider the old relations.

Or, once more, almost at the close, when he feels himself in danger of yielding to the voice of nature, he utters the truculent prayer :

> Let it be virtuous to be obstinate ;   (v. iii. 26.)

which implies that he knew it was not.

On the other hand, with all his doggedness, he cannot be quite consequent in his rancour. He may lead her foes against his " thankless country " as he calls it, but he has a lurking kindliness even for the Rome he thinks he detests. As we learn from Aufidius' speech :

> Although it seems,
> And so he thinks, and is no less apparent
> To the vulgar eye, that he bears all things fairly,
> And shows good husbandry for the Volscian state,
> Fights dragon-like, and does achieve as soon
> As draw his sword ; yet he hath left undone
> That which shall break his neck or hazard mine,
> Whene'er we come to our account.   (iv. vii. 19.)

This is no doubt suggested by the incident of the thirty days' truce, of which Plutarch makes so much and which Shakespeare totally suppresses. But the vague reference becomes all the more pregnant, when we are to understand that Coriolanus has at unawares and against his purpose granted some little concessions to the victims of his wrath. That Aufidius' statement has some foundation, is made probable by the words of the First Antium Lord, who is no enemy to Marcius, but reproaches Tullus with his murder and reverently bewails his death :

> What faults he made before the last, I think,
> Might have found easy fines. (v. vi. 64.)

Faults, then, from the Volscian point of view he has committed in the opinion of a sympathetic and impartial onlooker : which means that as a Roman he has shown forbearance.

So much for the toll that he pays to his patriotism; but neither can he quite uproot the old associations with his class. He may denounce the "dastard nobles," but he does concede something to Menenius, the patrician whose aristocratic prejudices are most akin to his own :

> Their latest refuge
> Was to send him ; for whose old love I have,
> Though I show'd sourly to him, once more offer'd
> The first conditions, which they did refuse
> And cannot now accept : to grace him only
> That thought he could do more, *a very little
> I have yielded to.* (v. iii. 11.)

And, coming to the chief in his trinity of interests, he may seek to break all bond and privilege of nature and refuse to be such a gosling to obey instinct, but the natural instinct of the family is too strong for him ; before it his resolution crumbles to pieces, though he foresees the result.

> O mother, mother !
> What have you done? Behold, the heavens do ope,
> The gods look down, and this unnatural scene
> They laugh at. O my mother, mother ! O !

> You have won a happy victory to Rome ;
> But for your son,—believe it, O, believe it,
> Most dangerously you have with him prevail'd,
> If not most mortal to him.   (v. iii. 182.)

Still this collapse of Coriolanus' purpose means
nothing more than the victory of his strongest
impulse. There is no acknowledgment of offence,
there is no renovation of character, there is not
even submission to the highest force within his
experience. Our admiration of his surrender is not
unmixed. It is a moving spectacle to see a man,
despite all the solicitations of wrath and revenge,
of interest and fear, obedient to what is on the
whole so salutary an influence as domestic affection.
But loyalty to this will not of itself avail to safeguard
anyone from criminal entanglements, or to equip
him for beneficent public action, or to change the
current of his life. It may mean the triumph of a
natural tendency that happens to be good over other
natural tendencies that happen to be bad, but it
does not mean acceptance of duty as duty, or
anxiety to satisfy the claims that different duties
impose. Hence Coriolanus, to the very end, leaves
unredeemed his inherited obligations to Rome, while
he leaves unfulfilled his voluntary pledges to his
allies. Even in Plutarch's narrative Shakespeare's
insight is not required to detect this underlying
thought, but in the *Comparison*, which there is proof
that Shakespeare had studied, it is set forth so
clearly that he who runs may read.

> He made the Volsces (of whome he was generall) to lose
> the oportunity of noble victory. Where in deede he should
> (if he had done as he ought) have withdrawen his armie with
> their counsaill and consent, that had reposed so great affiance
> in him, in making him their generall : if he had made that
> accompt of them, as their good will towards him did in duety
> binde him. Or else, if he did not care for the Volsces in the
> enterprise of this warre, but had only procured it of intent to
> be revenged, and afterwards to leave if of, when his anger
> was blowen over ; yet he had no reason for the love of his

mother to pardone his contrie; but rather he should in pardoning his contrie have spared his mother, bicause his mother and wife were members of the bodie of his contrie and cittie, which he did besiege. For in that he uncurteously rejected all publike petitions . . . to gratifie only the request of his mother in his departure; that was no acte so much to honour his mother with, as to dishonour his contrie by, the which was preserved for the pitie and intercession of a woman, and not for the love of it selfe, as if it had not bene worthie of it. And so was this departure a grace, to say truly, very odious and cruell, and deserved no thanks of either partie, to him that did it. For he withdrew his army, not at the request of the Romaines, against whom he made warre: nor with their consent, at whose charge the warre was made.

That Shakespeare, with his patriotism and equity, perceived the double flaw in Coriolanus' act of grace can hardly be doubted. He was the last man to put the household above the national gods, or to glorify breach of contract if only it were sanctioned by domestic tenderness. In point of fact, he does not acquit his hero on either count.

On the one hand, if Coriolanus remits the extreme penalty, he neither forgets nor forgives, and has no thought of return to the offending city or resumption of the old ties. Scarcely has he granted the ladies their boon, when he addresses Aufidius:

> For my part
> I'll not to Rome, I'll back with you.   (v. iii. 197.)

And his speech to the senators of Antium shows no revival of former loyalties:

> Hail, lords! I am return'd your soldier,
> No more infected with my country's love
> Than when I parted hence, but still subsisting
> Under your great command. You are to know
> That prosperously I have attempted and
> With bloody passage led your wars even to
> The gates of Rome. Our spoils we have brought home
> Do more than counterpoise a full third part
> The charges of the action. We have made peace
> With no less honour to the Antiates
> Than shame to the Romans.   (v. vi. 71.)

The insolent announcement of the invasion carried
to the gates of the capital, of the plunder that
substantially exceeds the cost, of the humiliating
terms imposed on his countrymen, is ample proof
that in Coriolanus there is no recrudescence of
patriotism.

Yet, despite his words, he has been false to
the Volscians. However base were his motives,
Aufidius speaks the truth when he says :

> Perfidiously
> He has betray'd your business, and given up,
> For certain drops of salt, your city Rome,
> I say "your city," to his wife and mother ;
> Breaking his oath and resolution like
> A twist of rotten silk, never admitting
> Counsel o' the war.   (v. vi. 91.)

It is the opinion of the First Lord, despite his
impartiality and his sympathy with Marcius :

> There to end
> Where he was to begin, and give away
> The benefit of our levies, answering us
> With our own charge ; making a treaty where
> There was a yielding,—this admits no excuse.   (v. vi. 65.)

Thus both his native and his adopted country have
reason to complain. He remains a traitor to the
one, while yet he breaks faith with the other.

Of course, in theory there was a middle course
possible, which would have served the best interests
of the two states equally.   He might have used his
influence to establish a lasting and intimate alliance ;
and this was the policy that Volumnia outlined in
her plea :

> If it were so that our request did tend
> To save the Romans, thereby to destroy
> The Volsces whom you serve, you might condemn us
> As poisonous to your honour : no ; our suit
> Is, that you reconcile them : while the Volsces
> May say, "This mercy we have show'd " ; the Romans,
> "This we received " ; and each in either side
> Give the all-hail to thee, and cry " Be blest
> For making up this peace ! "   (v. iii. 132.)

But such an all-hail was not for Coriolanus to win. It is one of the charges which Plutarch brings against him in the *Comparison*, that he neglected the opportunity.

> By this dede of his he tooke not away the enmity that was betwene both people.

But how could he, when he had no special desire for the well-being of either, and when his heart was unchanged? His family affection has got the better of his narrower egoism, but even after sacrificing a portion of his revenge, he remains essentially the man he was, and is no more capable of pursuing a judicious and conciliatory policy now for the good of the whole and his own good, than of old in the market-place of Rome.

For to the end he is imprudent, headstrong, and violent as ever. He sees quite clearly that his compliance with his mother's prayer must be dangerous, if not mortal, to him. Dangerous it is, mortal it need not be. With a little more self-restraint and circumspection, a little less aggressiveness and truculence, he might still preserve both his life and his authority. It is his unchastened spirit, not the questionable treaty, that is the direct cause of his death. Indeed, in a sense, the treaty had nothing to do with it. In Shakespeare, though not in Plutarch, Tullus, as we have seen, when he still anticipated the capture of Rome, determined to make away with his rival so soon as that should take place; and from what we know of Coriolanus' character, and Tullus' comprehension of it[1] and general astuteness in management, we feel sure that the scheme was bound to succeed, if Coriolanus persisted in his old ways. Even as things have turned out, Marcius has all the odds in his favour. His triumphal entry into Antium is a repetition of

[1] See Appendix F.

his triumphal entry into Rome. When, according
to the stage direction, "Drums and trumpets sound,
with great shouts of the People," the malcontents
turn to Aufidius :

> *First Conspirator.* Your native town you enter'd like a post,
> And had no welcomes home ; but he returns,
> Splitting the air with noise.
>   *Second Conspirator.*   And patient fools,
> Whose children he hath slain, their base throats tear
> With giving him the glory.   (v. vi. 50.)

That is, the admiration of the populace, constrained
by his prowess, is the same sort of obstacle to these
factionaries as it formerly was to the tribunes ; and
with that, and his great services as well, he commands the situation. He needs only a minimum of
skill and moderation to carry all before him. So
the problem of his antagonists is the same in both
cases : namely, to neutralise these advantages by
rousing his passion, and provoking him to show his
pride, his recklessness, his uncompromising rigour.
In both cases he falls into the trap, and converts the
popular goodwill to hatred by defiantly harping on
the injuries he has inflicted on his admirers. He is
the unregenerate "superman" to the last. The
suppression of his victorious surname, the taunts of
"traitor" and "boy," drive him mad. He lets
himself be transported to a bravado that must
shake from sleep all the latent hostility of the
Volscians.

> Measureless liar, thou hast made my heart
> Too great for what contains it. Boy ! O slave !
> Pardon me, lords, 'tis the first time that ever
> I was forc'd to scold. Your judgements, my grave lords,
> Must give this cur the lie : and his own notion—
> Who wears my stripes impress'd upon him ; that
> Must bear my beating to his grave—shall join
> To thrust the lie unto him.
>   *First Lord.* Peace, both, and hear me speak.

Coriolanus. Cut me to pieces, Volsces; men and lads,
Stain all your edges on me.   Boy! false hound!
If you have writ your annals true, 'tis there,
That like an eagle in a dove-cote, I
Flutter'd your Volscians in Corioli;
Alone I did it.   Boy!

The patient fools, whose children he had slain, are not patient now, and no longer tear their throats in acclaiming his glory. Their cries, "Tear him to pieces," "He killed my son," and the like, give the conspirators the cue, and Aufidius is presently standing on his body.

It is not, then, as a martyr to retrieved patriotism that Coriolanus perishes, but as the victim of his own passion. In truth, the victory he won over himself under the influence of his mother, though real, is very incomplete. His piety to the hearth saves him from the superlative infamy of destroying his country, which is something, and even a good deal; but it is not everything; and beyond that it has no result, public or personal. On the contrary, Coriolanus' isolated and but partly justified act of clemency receives its comment from the motives that induced it, the troth-breach that accompanied it, and the rage in which he passed away. If, like his son with the butterfly, he did grasp honour at the close, it was disfigured by his rude handling. But at least he never belies his own great though mixed nature, and it is fitting that his death, needless but heroic, should have its cause in his nature and be such as his nature would select. Indeed, it is both his nemesis and his guerdon. For he would not be a Roman, he could not be a Volsce; what part could he have played in the years to come? Perhaps Shakespeare read in Philemon Holland's rendering the alternative account that Livy gives of the final scene.

I find in Fabius, a most ancient writer, that he lived untill he was an old man: who repeateth this of him: that oftentimes in his latter daies he used to utter this speech : *A heavie case and most wretched, for an aged man to live banisht.*

At all events some such feeling as his regrets in this variant tradition suggest, makes us prefer the version that Plutarch followed and that Shakespeare adapted. Coriolanus deserves to be spared the woes that the future has in store.   As it is, he falls in the fulness of his power, inspired by great memories to greater audacity, and, no doubt, elated at the thought of challenging and outbraving death, when death is sure to win.

APPENDIX A

NEAREST PARALLELS BETWEEN GARNIER'S *CORNELIE*, IN THE FRENCH AND ENGLISH VERSIONS, AND *JULIUS CAESAR*

IT should be remembered that it is not on these particular equivalents, mostly very loose, that those who uphold the theory of connection between the two plays rely, but on the general drift of the corresponding scenes which in this respect strikingly resemble each other and in no way produce the same impression as the narrative of Plutarch.

French.	English.
Cassie. Miserable Cité, tu armes contre toy	*Cassius.* Accursed Rome, that arm'st against thy selfe
La fureur d'un Tyran pour le faire ton Roy :	A Tyrants rage, and mak'st a wretch thy King :
Tu armes tes enfans, injurieuse Romme,	For one mans pleasure (O injurious Rome !)
Encontre tes enfans, pour le plaisir d'un homme :	Thy chyldren gainst thy chyldren thou hast arm'd :
Et ne te souvient plus *d'avoir faict autrefois*	*And thinkst not of the riuers of theyr bloode,*
Tant ruisseler de sang pour n'avoir point de Rois,	*That earst were shed to saue thy libertie,*
Pour n'estre point esclave, et ne porter flechie	*Because thou euer hatedst Monarchie.*[1] . . .
Au service d'un seul, le joug de Monarchie.[1] (line 1065.)	

| . . . Quoy Brute ? et nous faut-il trop craignant le danger, | But, Brutus, shall wee dissolutelie sitte |
| Laisser si laschement sous un Prince ranger ? | And see the tyrant liue to tyranize ? |

[1] Shall Rome stand under one man's awe ? What, Rome? My ancestors did from the streets of Rome The Tarquin drive when he was call'd a King. (II. i. 51.)

Faut-il que tant de gens morts pour nostre franchise
Se plaignent aux tombeaux de nostre couardise ?
Et que les peres vieux voisent disant de nous,
"Ceux-là ont mieux aimé, tant ils ont le coeur mous,
Honteusement servir en dementant leur race,
Qu'armez pour le païs mourir dessus la place." [1] (line 1101.)

Or shall *theyr ghosts, that dide to doe us good,*
Plaine in their Tombes of our base cowardise . . .

"See where they goe that haue theyr race forgot!
And rather chuse, (unarm'd) to serue with shame,
Then, (arm'd), to saue their freedom and their fame!" [1]

Brute. Je jure par le Ciel, thrône des Immortels,
Par leurs images saincts, leurs temples, leurs autels,
De ne souffrir, vray Brute, aucun maistre entreprendre
Sur nostre liberte, si je la puis defendre.
J'ai Cesar en la guerre ardentement suyvi,
Pour maintenir son droit, non pour vivre asservi . . .
. . . Il verra que Decime a jusques aujourdhuy
Porté pour luy l'estoc qu'il trouvera sur luy.
. . . *Je l'aime cherement, je l'aime, mais le droit*
Qu'on doit à son païs, qu'à sa naissance on doit,
Tout autre amour surmonte. [2] . . .
(line 1109.)

Brutus. I swear by heauen, th' Immortals highest throne.
Their temples, Altars, and theyr Images,
To see (for one) that Brutus suffer not
His ancient liberty to be represt.
I freely marcht with Caesar in hys warrs,
Not to be subject, but to ayde his right, . . .
But he shall see, that Brutus thys day beares
The self-same Armes to be aueng'd on hym. . . .
I loue, I loue him deerely. But the loue
That men theyr Country and theyr birth-right beare,
Exceeds all loues. [2] . . .

Cassie. Tandisque Cassie aura goutte de sang
En son corps animeux, il voudra vivre franc,
Il fuira le servage ostant la tyrannie,

Cassius. . . . Know, while Cassius hath one drop of blood
To feede this worthles body that you see,
What reck I death, to doe so many good?

---

[1]
Age, thou art shamed !
Rome, thou hast lost the breed of noble bloods !   (I. ii. 150.)
Our fathers' minds are dead
And we are govern'd by our mothers' spirits,
Our yoke and sufferance show us womanish.   (I. iii. 82.)

[2] If there be any in this assembly, any dear friend of Caesar's, to him I say, that Brutus' love to Caesar was no less than his. If then that friend demand why Brutus rose against Caesar, this is my answer :—Not that I loved Caesar less but that I loved Rome more.   (III. ii. 19.)

Ou l'ame de son corps il chassera bannie.[1]

Brute. Toute ame genereuse indocile a servir Deteste les Tyrans.

Cassie. Je ne puis m'asservir, Ny voir que Rome serve, et plustost la mort dure M'enferre mille fois, que vivant je l'endure. . . . O chose trop indigne! *Un homme effeminé* . . . *Commande a l'Univers, la terre tient en bride,*[3] Et maistre donne loy au peuple Romulide, Aux enfants du dieu Mars. . . .

O Brute, O Servilie, Qu'ores vous nous laissez une race avilie!

Brute est vivant, il sçait, il voit, il est present, Que sa chere patrie on va tyrannisant : Et comme s'il n'estoit qu'une vaine semblance De Brut son ayeul, non sa vraye semence, S'il n'avoit bras ny mains, sens ny coeur, pour oser, Simulacre inutile, aux Tyrans s'opposer : Il ne fait rien de Brute, et d'heure en heure augmente Par trop de lascheté la force violente. (line 1201.)

In spite of Caesar, Cassius will be free.[1]

Brutus. A generous or true enobled spirit Detests to learne what tasts of seruitude. *Cassius.* Brutus, I cannot serue nor see Rome yok'd : No, let me rather die a thousand deaths. . . .

O base indignitie! *A beardles youth*[2] . . . *Commaunds the world, and brideleth all the earth,*[3] And like a prince controls the Romulists ; Braue Roman Souldiers, sterneborne sons of Mars. . . . O Brutus, speake! O say, Servilius! Why cry you aime,[4] and see us used thus ? But Brutus liues, and sees, and knowes, and feeles, That there is one that curbs their Countries weale. Yet (as he were the semblance, not the sonne, Of noble Brutus, his great Grandfather) ; As if he wanted hands, sence, sight or hart, He doth, deuiseth, sees, nor dareth ought, That may extirpe or raze these tyrannies : Nor ought doth Brutus that to Brute belongs, But still increaseth by his negligence His owne disgrace and Caesars violence.

[1] Cassius from bondage will deliver Cassius . . .
  Life being weary of these worldly bars
Never lacks power to dismiss itself. (I. iii. 90.)

[2] Notice the inept rendering.

[3]   It doth amaze me,
A man of such a feeble temper should
So get the start of the majestic world,
And bear the palm alone. (I. ii. 128.)

[4] Approve or agree.

APPENDIX B

THE VERBAL RELATIONS OF THE VARIOUS VERSIONS OF PLUTARCH ILLUSTRATED BY MEANS OF VOLUMNIA'S SPEECH

THIS passage, though it does not show the successive modifications of the text quite so fully and strikingly as some others, is the most interesting in so far as it is the longest in which Shakespeare closely follows the lead of the original.

The Latin version of the Renaissance is placed first, both because in definite form it is chronologically the earliest, and because for the reasons already given it cannot be held to have had much influence on Amyot, North and Shakespeare.

It is of course impossible to reconstruct the Greek text that Amyot put together for himself. I have taken that of the edition of 1599, published half a dozen years after his death, as a fair approximation. The chief variations from the Latin are given in spaced type.

In the extract from Amyot the chief variations from the Greek are printed in Italics; the few phrases or words in which the influence of the Latin may be suspected are underlined.

In the extract from North the chief variations from the French are printed in Italics.

In the extract from Shakespeare, it is, as we might expect, more convenient to reverse the process and italicise what he has taken over.

[The Version

The Version[1] of the elder Guarini, styled Guarinus Veronensis, in the Edition of the *Vitae Parallelae* issued by Udalricus Gallus in 1470 (?)

Tum pueros ac Vergiliam unacum reliquis secum mulieribus ducens castra Volscorum adiit. Earum miseranda facies hosti reverentiam injecit atque silentium. Hic Martius in suggesto inter Volscorum proceres sedens, ubi eas adventare mulieres vidit, admiratione confectus est, imprimis venientem uxorem noscitans immoto et obstinato persistere animo[2] voluit : verum consternatus affectu et ad ipsarum confusus intuitum haud tulit ut se sedentem adirent,[3] ac pernici devotas gradu obviam prodiit. Et matre primo diutissimeque salutata, inde uxore ac filiis, nullo jam pacto frenare lacrimas poterat. Ut vero dulces incepti sunt amplexus, virum parentis amore perinde ac secundo fluminis cursu deferri cerneres.[4] Caeterum cum inchoantem jam verba matrem intelligeret, acceptis Volscorum primoribus Volumniam talia orantem audivit. " Etsi fili taceamus, ipse, tum veste, tum miseri corporis apparatu, cernis qualem domesticae rei conditionem tuum nobis confecerit exilium. Existima vero quam caeteris longe mulieribus infeliciores accessimus, quibus dulcissimum aspectum fecit fortuna terribilem : te mihi filium, huic vero maritum, patriae muros obsidentem aspicimus. Et quod caeteris calamitatis et malorum solet esse solacium, deos orare, quam procul nobis ablatum est : non enim et patriae victoriam et tibi salutem implorare fas est : quaeque atrociora quispiam nobis impraecaretur hostis, ea nostris insunt[5] praecibus. Uxorem enim ac liberos aut patria aut te orbari necesse est. Ego vero, dum haec viventi mihi bellum dijudicet, haud morabor, teque nisi positis inimicitiis ad pacem atque concordiam conciliavero ; ita ut utrique[6] potius beneficum quam alteri perniciosum te reddas. Hoc tibi persuade sicque conformatus et paratus accede, ut non ante hostiles patriae manus conferas quam caesam calcaveris parentem. Nec enim ea mihi expectanda dies est qua filium aut in triumpho tractum a civibus aut de patria triumphantem aspiciam. Quod si pro conservanda patria

---

[1] I have modernised the punctuation, and extended the contractions throughout, but wherever there is any possibility of misinterpretation I have noted it.

[2] aĩo.   [3] adiret.   [4] cernēs.   [5] Insinit.   [6] uterque.

profligari a te Volscos exorarem, grave fili iniquumque tibi fateor imminere consilium ; namque necque cives perdere bonum est, necque tuos commissos fidei perdere justum. Nunc malorum finem imploramus simulque populis utrisque salutem. Quae res maximam Volscis gloriam comparabit : quod cum ingentia nobis bona et victores quidem tribuerint, non minus jocundam ipsi pacem et amicitiam sint consecuturi : quae si effecta fuerint, tu tantorum profecto dux eris et causa bonorum : sin ea infecta permanserint, utrique noxam in te solum crimenque rejicient. Cumque incertus belli sit eventus, hoc certi secum affert : ut siquidem vincas immanissimus patriae vastator appellandus sis, sin victus succumbas, ob tuam videberis iracundiam benefactoribus et amicis ingentium origo malorum extitisse." Haec dum oraret Volumnia, nullum respondens verbum Martius intentis excipiebat auribus. Ut vero desierat, cum is diuturnum teneret silentium, rursus Volumnia ; "Quid siles," inquit. "Nate, num irae receptarumque injuriarum memoriae omnia concedere satius arbitraris an depraecanti talia matri largiri pulcherrimum munificentiae genus non est ? Magnine interesse viri putas acceptorum meminisse malorum ? Suscepta autem a parentibus beneficia eorum cultui ac venerationi reddere num excelso potius ac bono dignissimum viro munus censes? Caeterum gratiam habere tuerique magisquam tu debuit nemo, cum tamen per acerbissimam adeo ingratitudinem eas. Et cum permagnas jam patriae paenas exegeris acceperisque, nullas adhuc matri grates retulisti. Erat vero aequissimum atque sanctissimum ut abs te vel nulla ingruenti necessitate tam honesta tamque justa postulans impetrarem. Quid cum in meam te verbis sententiam deflectere nequeam, extremae jam parco spei ?" Haec affata cum uxore simul ac liberis pedibus advoluta procumbit. Tum conclamans Martius, "Qualia mihi" ait "factitasti mater" ; et jacentem sustulit : et pressa dextera inquit ; "Vicisti patriae quidem prosperam, nimis atque nimis perniciosam autem[1] mihi victoriam. Abs te tantum superatus abscedam."

PLUTARCH'S GREEK IN THE EDITION OF 1599

Ἐκ τούτου, τά τε παιδία καὶ τὴν Οὐεργιλίαν ἀναστήσασα μετὰ τῶν ἄλλων γυναικῶν, ἐβάδιζεν εἰς τὸ στρατόπεδον τῶν Οὐολούσκων. ἡ δ' ὄψις αὐτῶν τότε οἰκτρὰν καὶ τοῖς πολεμίοις

[1] aut.

ἐνεποίησεν αἰδὼ καὶ σιωπήν. ἔτυχε δ' ὁ Μάρκιος ἐπὶ βήματος
καθεζόμενος μετὰ τῶν ἡγεμονικῶν. ὡς οὖν εἶδε προσιούσας
τὰς γυναῖκας, ἐθαύμασεν· ἐπιγνοὺς δὲ τὴν γυναῖκα πρώτην
βαδίζουσαν, ἐβούλετο μὲν ἐμμένειν τοῖς ἀτρέπτοις ἐκείνοις
καὶ ἀπαραιτήτοις λογισμοῖς· γενόμενος δὲ τοῦ πάθους
ἐλάττων καὶ συνταραχθεὶς πρὸς τὴν ὄψιν, οὐκ ἔτλη καθεζομένῳ
προσελθεῖν, ἀλλὰ κ α τ α β ὰ ς θᾶττον ἢ βάδην, καὶ ἀπαν-
τήσας, πρώτην μὲν ἠσπάσατο τὴν μητέρα, καὶ πλεῖστον
χρόνον, ἔτι δὲ τὴν γυναῖκα καὶ τὰ τέκνα, μήτε δακρύων
ἔτι, μ ή τ ε τ ο ῦ φ ι λ ο φ ρ ο ν ε ῖ σ θ α ι φειδόμενος, ἀλλ'
ὥσπερ ὑπὸ ῥεύματος φέρεσθαι τοῦ πάθους ἑαυτὸν ἐνδεδωκώς.
ἐ π ε ὶ δ ὲ τ ο ύ τ ω ν ἅ δ η ν ε ἶ χ ε, καὶ τὴν μητέρα βουλομένην
ἤδη λόγων ἄρχειν ᾔσθετο, τοὺς τῶν Οὐολούσκων προβούλους
παραστησάμενος, ἤκουσε τῆς Οὐολουμνίας τοιαῦτα λεγούσης,
"Ὁρᾷς μὲν, ὦ παῖ, κἂν αὐταὶ μὴ λέγωμεν, ἐσθῆτι καὶ μορφῇ
τῶν ἀθλίων σωμάτων τεκμαιρόμενος, οἵαν οἰκουρίαν ἡμῖν ἡ
σὴ φυγὴ περιποίησε. λόγισαι δὲ νῦν ὡς ἀτυχέσταται πασῶν
ἀφίγμεθα γυναικῶν, αἷς τὸ ἥδιστον θέαμα, φοβερώτατον ἡ
τύχη πεποίηκεν, ἐμοὶ μὲν υἱόν, ταύτῃ δ' ἄνδρα τοῖς τῆς
πατρίδος τείχεσιν ἰδεῖν ἀντικαθήμενον. ὃ δ' ἔστι τοῖς ἄλλοις
ἀτυχίας πάσης καὶ κακοπραγίας παραμύθιον, εὔχεσθαι θεοῖς,
ἡμῖν ἀπορώτατον γέγονεν. οὐ γὰρ οἷόν τε καὶ τῇ πατρίδι
νίκην ἅμα καὶ σοὶ σωτηρίαν αἰτεῖσθαι παρὰ τῶν θεῶν, ἀλλ'
ἅ τις ἂν ἡμῖν καταράσαιτο τῶν ἐχθρῶν, ταῦτα ταῖς ἡμετέραις
ἔνεστιν εὐχαῖς. ἀνάγκη γὰρ ἢ τῆς πατρίδος ἢ σου στέρεσθαι
γυναικὶ σῇ καὶ τέκνοις. ἐγὼ δ' οὐ περιμένω ταύτην μοι
διαιτῆσαι τὴν τύχην ζώσῃ τὸν πόλεμον· ἀλλ' εἰ μή σε
πείσαιμι φιλίαν καὶ ὁμόνοιαν διαφορὰς καὶ κακῶν θέμενον,
ἀμφοτέρων γενέσθαι εὐεργέτην μᾶλλον, ἢ λυμεῶνα τῶν
ἑτέρων, οὕτω διανοοῦ καὶ παρασκεύαζε σεαυτόν, ὡς τῇ πατρίδι
μὴ προσμίξαι δυνάμενος πρὶν ἢ νεκρὰν ὑπερβῆναι τὴν τεκοῦσαν.
οὐ γὰρ ἐκείνην με δεῖ τὴν ἡμέραν ἀναμένειν ἐν ᾗ τὸν υἱὸν
ἐπόψομαι θριαμβευόμενον ὑπὸ τῶν πολιτῶν, ἢ θριαμβεύοντα
κατὰ τῆς πατρίδος. εἰ μὲν οὖν ἀξιῶ σε τὴν πατρίδα σῶσαι
Οὐολούσκους ἀπολέσαντα, χαλεπή σοι καὶ δυσδιαίτητος, ὦ
παῖ, πρόκειται σκέψις, οὔτε γὰρ διαφθεῖραι τοὺς πολίτας
καλόν, οὔτε τοὺς πεπιστευκότας προδοῦναι δίκαιον. νῦν δ'
ἀπαλλαγὴν κακῶν αἰτιούμεθα, σωτήριον μὲν ἀμφοτέροις
ὁμοίως, ἔνδοξον δὲ καὶ καλὴν μᾶλλον Οὐολούσκοις, ὅτι τῷ
κρατεῖν δόξουσι διδόναι τὰ μέγιστα τῶν ἀγαθῶν, ο ὐ χ
ἧ τ τ ο ν λ α μ β ά ν ο ν τ ε ς, εἰρήνην καὶ φιλίαν, ὧν μάλιστα
μὲν αἴτιος ἔσῃ γινομένων, μὴ γινομένων δὲ, μόνος αἰτίαν
ἕξεις παρ' ἀμφοτέροις. ἄδηλος δ' ὢν ὁ πόλεμος τοῦτ'
ἔχει πρόδηλον, ὅτι σοὶ νικῶντι μὲν, ἀλάστορι τῆς πατρίδος

εἶναι περίεστιν· ἡττώμενος δὲ, δόξεις ὑπ' ὀργῆς εὐεργέταις
ἀνδράσι καὶ φίλοις τῶν μεγίστων συμφορῶν αἴτιος γεγονέναι."
ταῦτα τῆς Οὐολουμνίας λεγούσης ὁ Μάρκιος ἠκροάτο μηδὲν
ἀποκρινόμενος.· ἐπεὶ δὲ καὶ παυσαμένης, εἱστήκει σιωπῶν
πολὺν χρόνον, αὖθις ἡ Οὐολουμνία, "Τί σιγᾷς (εἶπεν) ὦ παῖ,
πότερον ὀργῇ καὶ μνησικακίᾳ πάντα συγχωρεῖν καλόν; οὐ
καλὸν δὲ μητρὶ χαρίσασθαι δεομένῃ περὶ τηλικούτων; ἢ τὸ
μεμνῆσθαι πεπονθότα κακῶς ἀνδρὶ μεγάλῳ προσήκει, τὸ δ'
εὐεργεσίας αἷς εὐεργετοῦνται παῖδες ὑπὸ τῶν τεκόντων
σέβεσθαι καὶ τιμᾶν, οὐκ ἀνδρὸς ἔργον ἐστὶ μεγάλου καὶ
ἀγαθοῦ; καὶ μὴν οὐδενὶ μᾶλλον ἔπρεπε τηρεῖν χάριν ὡς σοι,
πικρῶς οὕτως ἀχαριστίαν ἐπεξιόντι. καίτοι
παρὰ τῆς πατρίδος ἤδη μεγάλας δίκας ἀπείληφας, τῇ μητρὶ
δ' οὐδεμίαν χάριν ἀποδέδωκας. ἦν μὲν οὖν ὁσιώτατον ἄνευ
τινὸς ἀνάγκης τυχεῖν με παρὰ σοῦ δεομένην οὕτω καλῶν καὶ
δικαίων· μὴ πείθουσα δὲ τί φείδομαι τῆς ἐσχάτης ἐλπίδος;"
καὶ ταῦτ' εἰποῦσα προσπίπτει τοῖς ποσὶν αὐτοῦ μετὰ τῆς
γυναικὸς ἅμα καὶ τῶν τέκνων. ὁ δὲ Μάρκιος ἀναβοήσας,
"Οἷα εἴργασαί με, ὦ μᾶτερ;" ἐξανίστησιν αὐτὴν, καὶ τὴν
δεξιὰν πιέσας σφόδρα, "Νενίκηκας (εἶπεν) εὐτυχῆ μὲν τῇ
πατρίδι νίκην, ἐμοὶ δ' ὀλέθριον· ἄπειμι γὰρ ὑπὸ σοῦ μόνης
ἡττώμενος."

AMYOT'S VERSION.

Elle prit sa belle fille et ses enfans quand et[1] elle, et avec
toutes les autres Dames Romaines s'en alla droit au camp
des Volsques, lesquelz eurent eulx-mesmes une compassion
meslee de reverence quand ils la veirent *de maniere qu'il n'y
eut personne d'eulx qui luy ozast rien dire.* Or estoit lors
Martius assis en son tribunal, *avec les marques de souverain
Capitaine*,[2] et *de tout loing* qu'il apperceut venir des femmes,
s'esmerveilla que ce pouvoit estre ; mais peu apres recog-
noissant sa femme, qui marchoit la premiere, il voulut *du
commencement* perseverer en son obstinee et inflexible
rigueur ; mais à la fin, vaincu de l'affection naturelle, estant
tout esmeu de les voir, il *ne peut* avoir le *coeur si dur* que de
les attendre en son siege, ains[3] en descendant plus viste que
le pas, leur alla au devant, et baisa sa mere la premiere, et
la teint assez longuement embrassee, puis sa femme et ses

---

[1] *together with.*

[2] A mistranslation of the Greek phrase, μετὰ τῶν ἡγεμονικῶν, from which it
must come.   The Latin is correct and unmistakable.

[3] But.

petits enfants, ne se pouvant plus tenir que les *chauldes*
larmes ne luy vinssent *aux yeux*, ny se garder de leur faire
caresses, ains se laissant aller à l'affection *du sang* ne plus
ne moins qu'à la force d'un impetueux torrent. Mais
apres qu'il leur eut assez faict *d'aimable recueil*, et qu'il
apperceut que sa mere Volumnia vouloit commencer a luy
parler, il appella les principaux du conseil des Volsques
pour *ouyr ce qu'elle proposeroit*, puis elle parla en ceste
maniere : "Tu peux assez cognoistre de toy mesme, mon
filz, encore que nous ne t'en dissions rien, à voir noz accous-
tremens, et l'estat auquel sont noz pauvres corps, quelle a
esté nostre vie en la maison depuis tu en es dehors ; mais
considere encore maintenant combien plus *mal heureuses* et
plus infortunees nous sommes icy venues que toutes les
femmes du monde, attendu que ce qui est à toutes les autres
le plus doulx a voir, la fortune nous l'a rendu le plus
effroyable, faisant voir à moy mon filz, et à celle-ci, son
mary, assiegeant les murailles de son propre païs ; telle-
ment que ce qui est à toutes autres le *souverain* renconfort
en leurs adversitez, de *prier* et invoquer les Dieux à leur
secours, c'est ce qui nous met en plus grande perplexité,
pource que nous ne leur sçaurions demander en noz prieres
victoire a nostre païs et preservation de ta vie tout ensemble,
ains toutes les plus griefves maledictions que sçauroit
imaginer contre nous un ennemy sont *necessairement*
encloses en noz oraisons, pource qu'il est force à ta femme
et à tes enfans qu'ilz soyent privez de l'un de deux, ou de
toy, ou de leurs païs : car quant a moy, je ne suis pas deli-
beree d'attendre que la fortune, moy vivante, decide *l'issue
de ceste guerre* : car si je ne te puis persuader que tu vueilles
plus tost bien faire à toutes les deux parties, que d'en *ruiner*
et destruire l'une, en preferant amitie et concorde aux
miseres et calamitez de la guerre, je veux bien que tu saches
et le tienes pour asseuré que tu n'iras jamais assaillir ny
combattre ton païs que premierement tu ne passes par
dessus le corps de celle qui t'a mis en ce monde, et ne doy
point differer jusques à voir le jour, ou que mon filz *prison-
nier* soit mené en triumphe par ses citoyens, ou que luy
mesme triumphe de son païs. Or si ainsi estoit que je te
requisse de sauver ton païs en destruisant les Volsques, ce
te serait certainement une deliberation trop mal-aisee à
resoudre ; car comme il n'est point licite de ruiner son païs,
aussi n'est-il point juste de trahir ceulx qui se sont fiez en
toy. Mais ce que je te demande est une delivrance de

maulx, laquelle est egalement *profitable* et salutaire à l'un
et à l'autre peuple, mais plus honorable aux Volsques,
pource qu'il semblera qu'ayans la victoire en main, ils nous
auront de grace donné deux souverains biens, la paix et
l'amitié, encore qu'ilz n'en prennent pas moins pour eulx,
duquel tu seras principal autheur, s'il se fait ; et, s'il ne se
fait, tu en auras seul le reproche et le blasme[1] total envers
l'une et l'autre des parties : ainsi estant l'issue de la guerre
incertaine,[2] cela neantmoins est bien tout certain que, si tu
en demoures vaincueur, il t'en restera *ce profit*, que tu en
seras estimé la *peste* et la ruine de ton païs : et si tu es
vaincu, on dira que pour un *appetit de venger tes propres
injures* tu auras esté cause de tres griefves calamitez à
ceulx qui t'avoient humainement et amiablement recueilly."
Martius escouta ces paroles de Volumnia sa mere sans
l'interrompre, et apres qu'elle eut acheve de dire demoura
longtemps tout *picqué* sans luy respondre. Parquoy elle
reprit la parole et recommencea à luy dire : "Que ne me
respons-tu, mon filz ? Estimes-tu qu'il soit licite de con-
ceder tout à son ire et à son appetit de vengeance, et non
honeste de condescendre et *incliner* aux prieres de sa mere
en si grandes choses ? Et *cuides-tu* qu'il soit convenable a
un grand personnage, se souvenir des torts qu'on luy a faits
et *des injures passees*, et que ce ne soit point acte d'homme
de bien et de grand cueur, *recognoistre* les bienfaicts que
reçoyvent les enfans de leurs peres et meres, en leur portant
honneur et reverence ? Si[3] n'y a il homme en ce monde
qui deust mieux observer tous les poincts de gratitude que
toy, veu que tu poursuis si asprement une ingratitude : et
si[3] y a davantage, que tu as ja fait payer a ton païs de
grandes amendes pour les torts que l'on t'y a faits, et n'as
encore fait aucune recognoissance a ta mere; pourtant
seroit-il plus honeste que sans autre contrainte j'impetrasse[4]
de toy une requeste si juste et si raisonnable. Mais puis
que *par raison* je ne le te puis persuader, à quel besoing
espargne-je plus, et *differe-je* la derniere esperance." En
disant ces paroles elle se jetta elle mesme, avec sa femme
et ses enfans, a ses pieds. Ce que Martius *ne pouvant sup-
porter*, la releva tout aussi tost en s'escriant : "O mere, que
m'as tu faict ?" et un luy serrant estroittement la main

---

[1] Greek αἰτίαν, Latin noxam crimenque.

[2] Latin : cumque incertus belli sit eventus.   [3] Yet.

[4] An unusual word in French. Compare the *impetrare* of the Latin.

Y

droite: " Ha," dit il, " Mere, tu as vaincu une victoire heureuse pour ton païs mais bien *malheureuse* et mortelle pour ton filz, car je m'en revois [1] vaincu par toy seule.

NORTH'S VERSION.

She tooke her daughter in lawe, and Martius children with her, and being accompanied with all the other Romaine ladies, they went *in troupe* together unto the Volsces camp : whome when they sawe, they of them selves did both pitie and reverence her, and there was not a man amonge them that once durst say a worde unto her. Nowe was Martius set then in his chayer of state, with all the honours of a generall, and when he had spied the women coming a farre of, he marveled what the matter ment : but afterwardes knowing his wife which came formest, he determined at the first to persist in his obstinate and inflexible rancker. But overcomen in the ende with naturall affection, and being altogether altered to see them; his harte *would not serve him* to tarie their comming to his chayer, but comming down in hast, he went to meete them, and first he kissed his mother, and imbraced her a pretie while, then his wife and litle children. And *Nature so wrought with him*, that the [2] teares fell from his eyes, and he coulde not keepe him selfe from making much of them, but yeelded to the affection of his bloode as if he had bene *violently* caried with the furie of a most swift running streame. After he had thus lovingly received them, and perceiving that his mother Volumnia would beginne to speake to him, he called the chiefest of the counsell of the Volsces to heare what she would say. Then she spake in this sorte : " If we held our peace, (my sonne) and *determined not to speake,* the state of our poor bodies, and *present* sight of our rayment, would easely bewray to thee what life we have led at home, since thy exile and abode abroad. But thinke nowe with thy selfe, how much more unfortunatly,[3] then all the women livinge we are come hether, considering that the sight which should be most pleasaunt to all other to beholde, *spitefull* fortune hath made most fearefull to us: making my selfe to see my sonne, and my daughter here, her husband, besieging the

---

[1] ἄπειμι, *revais* = retourne.   [2] No *chauldes.*

[3] Adverb for adjective, omission of one duplicate.

walles of his native countrie. So as that which is thonly comforte to all other in their adversitie and *miserie*, to pray unto the goddes and to call to them for aide ; is the *onely* thinge which *plongeth* us into most deepe perplexitie. For we can not (alas) together pray, both for victorie, for our countrie, and for safetie of thy life also : but a *worlde* of grievous curses, *yea more then* any *mortall* enemie can heape uppon us, are forcibly wrapt up in our prayers. For the *bitter soppe of most hard choyce* is offered thy wife and children, to forgoe the one of the two : either to lose the *persone* of thy selfe, or the *nurse* of[1] their native contrie. For my selfe (my sonne) I am determined not to tarie, till fortune in my life time do make an ende of this warre. For if I cannot persuade thee, rather to doe good unto both parties than to overthrowe and destroye the one, preferring love and *nature* before the *malice* and calamitie of warres : *thou shalt* see, my sonne, and trust unto it,[2] thou shalt no soner marche forward to assault thy countrie, but thy foote shall treade upon thy mothers *wombe*, that brought thee first into this world. And I maye not deferre to see the daye, either that my sonne be led prisoner in triumphe by his *naturall* country men, or that he him selfe doe triumphe *of them*, and of his *naturall* countrie. For if it were so, that my request tended to save thy countrie, in destroying the Volsces : *I must confesse*, thou wouldest hardly and *doubtfully* resolve on that. For as to destroye thy naturall countrie it is altogether *unmete* and unlawfull ; so were it not just, and *lesse honorable*, to betraye those that put their trust in thee. But my only demaunde consisteth to make a *gayle*[3] deliverie of all evills, which delivereth equall benefit and safety both to the one and the other, but most honorable for the Volsces. For it shall appeare, that having victorie in their hands, they have of speciall favour graunted us singular graces ; peace, and amitie, albeit them selves have no lesse parte of both, then we. Of which *good*, if so it came to passe, thy selfe is thonly authour, *and so hast thou thonly honour*. But if it faile, *and fall out contrarie* : thy selfe alone *deservedly* shall carie the *shameful* reproche and burden of either partie. So, though the ende of warre be uncertaine, yet this notwithstanding is most certaine : that if it be thy chaunce to conquer, this benefit shalt thou *reape* of *thy goodly conquest*, to be chronicled the plague and destroyer of thy

---

[1] *of*, appositional.   [2] Not so clear as the French.   [3] gaol.

countrie. And if fortune also overthrowe thee, then the
worlde will saye, that through desire to revenge thy private
injuries, thou hast *for ever* undone thy good friendes, who
dyd most lovingly and curteously receyve thee." Martius
gave good eare unto his mothers wordes, without interrupting
her speache at all: and after she had sayed *what she would*,
he held his peace a prety while,[1] and annswered not a worde.
Hereupon she beganne again to speake unto him, and sayed :
" My sonne, why doest thou not aunswer me ? Doest thou
think it good altogether to geve place unto thy choller and
desire of revenge, and thinkest thou it not honestie for thee
to graunt[2] thy mothers request in so weighty a cause ?
doest thou take it honorable for a noble man, to remember
the wrongs and injuries done him : and doest not in like
case thinke it an honest noble man's parte, to be thankefull
for the goodnes that parents doe shewe to their children,
acknowledging the duety and reverence *they ought to beare
unto them* ?[3] No man living is more bounde to shewe him
selfe thankefull in all partes and respects then thy selfe :
who so unnaturally sheweth all ingratitude.[4] Moreover
(my sonne) thou hast sorely taken of thy countrie, exacting
grievous payments apon them, in revenge of the injuries
offered thee : besides, thou hast not hitherto shewed thy
poore mother any curtesie.[5] And therefore it is *not only*
honest, *but due unto me*, that without compulsion I should
obtaine my so just and reasonable request of thee. But
since by reason I cannot persuade thee to it, to what
purpose do I deferre[6] my last hope ? " And with these
wordes her selfe, his wife and children fell downe upon their
knees before him. Martius seeing that could refraine no
longer but *went straight* and lifte her up, crying out : " Oh
mother, what have you done to me ? " And holding her
hard by the right hand, " Oh mother," sayed he, " You have
wonne a happy victorie for your countrie, but mortall and

[1] picqué not translated.

[2] One of Amyot's duplicates wanting.

[3] Important connective particle omitted.

[4] Quite wrong. The French means : " Since you so bitterly pursue in-gratitude."

[5] In this sentence North again misses the point of the argument. The
meaning is " And there is this further point as well, that you have already in a
measure requited your wrongs, but never yet shown your gratitude."

[6] One of Amyot's duplicate expressions omitted.

unhappy for your sonne : for I see [1] myself vanquished by you alone."

SHAKESPEARE'S VERSION

The narrative which ushers in the speech is of course left to the actors. It is interesting, however, to observe that Shakespeare varies from his authorities in making Coriolanus embrace not his mother but his wife in the first instance. He inserts too the conversation, that, at first merely personal, leads up to the grand question. Then Volumnia proceeds with her speech. It is impossible to note all the minute changes that Shakespeare makes. The Italics in the following reprint represent most generously what he has borrowed, for even in the clauses and phrases indicated as loans there is abundant evidence of his own irrepressible dramatic and poetic originality.

> *Vol. Should we be silent and not speak, our raiment*
> *And state of bodies would bewray what life*
> *We have led since thy exile. Think with thyself*
> *How more unfortunate than all living women*
> *Are we come hither : since that thy sight,* which should
> Make our eyes flow with joy, hearts dance with comforts,
> Constrains them weep and shake with fear and sorrow ;
> *Making the mother, wife,* and child to see
> *The son, the husband,* and the father tearing
> His country's bowels out. *And to poor we*
> *Thine enmity's most capital : thou barr'st us*
> *Our prayers to the gods, which is a comfort*
> *That all but we enjoy; for how can we,*
> *Alas, how can we for our country pray,*
> Whereto we are bound, *together with thy victory,*
> Whereto we are bound? *alack, or we must lose*
> *The country, our dear nurse, or else thy person,*
> Our comfort in the country. We must find
> An evident calamity, though we had
> Our wish, which side should win : for *either thou*
> *Must,* as a foreign recreant, *be led*
> With manacles thorough our streets, or *else*
> *Triumphantly tread on thy country's ruin*
> And bear the palm for having bravely shed
> Thy wife and children's blood. *For myself, son,*
> *I purpose not to wait on fortune till*
> *These wars determine : if I cannot persuade thee*
> *Rather to show a noble grace to both parts*
> *Than seek the end of one, thou shalt no sooner*
> *March to assault thy country than to tread—*

[1] A pardonable mistranslation of the French ; which, however, proves that in this passage at least North consulted neither the Greek nor the Latin.

Trust to't thou shalt not—on thy mother's womb,
That brought thee to this world.
   Vir.   Ay, and mine,
That brought you forth this boy, to keep your name
Living to time.
   Young Mar. A' shall not tread on me ;
I'll run away till I am bigger, but then I'll fight.
   Cor. Not of a woman's tenderness to be,
Requires nor child nor woman's face to see.
I have sat too long.   [*Rising.*
   Vol.   Nay, go not from us thus,
If it were so that our request did tend
To save the Romans, thereby to destroy
The Volsces whom you serve, you might condemn us,
As poisonous of your honour : no ; *our suit*
Is, that you reconcile them : while the Volsces
May say " This mercy we have show'd" ; the Romans,
" This we received" ; and each in either side
Give the all-hail to thee ; and cry " Be blest
For making up this peace ! " Thou know'st, great son,
The end of war's uncertain, but this certain
That, if thou conquer Rome, the benefit
Which thou shalt thereby reap is such a name,
Whose repetition will be dogg'd with curses ;
Whose chronicle thus writ : " The man was noble,
But with his last attempt he wiped it out :
Destroy'd his country, and his name remains
To the ensuing age abhorr'd." Speak to me, son :
Thou hast affected the fine strains of honour,
To imitate the graces of the gods ;
To tear with thunder the wide cheeks o' the air,
And yet to charge thy sulphur with a bolt
That should but rive an oak. Why dost not speak ?
Think'st thou it honourable for a noble man
Still to remember wrongs ? Daughter, speak you :
He cares not for your weeping. Speak thou, boy :
Perhaps thy childishness will move him more
Than can our reasons. *There's no man in the world*
More bound to's mother ; yet here he lets me prate
Like one i' the stocks. *Thou hast never in thy life*
Show'd thy dear mother any courtesy,
When she, poor hen, fond of no second brood,
Has cluck'd thee to the wars and safely home,
Loaden with honour. *Say my request's unjust,*
And spurn me back : but if it be not so,
Thou art not honest ; and the gods will plague thee,
That thou restrain'st from me the duty which
To a mother's part belongs. He turns away :
Down, ladies ; let us shame him with our knees.
To his surname Coriolanus 'longs more pride
Than pity to our prayers. Down : an end ;
This is the last : so we will home to Rome,
And die among our neighbours. Nay, behold's :
This boy, that cannot tell what he would have,

But kneels and holds up hands for fellowship,
Does reason our petition with more strength
Than thou hast to deny 't.   Come, let us go :
This fellow had a Volscian to his mother ;
His wife is in Corioli and his child
Like him by chance.   Yet give us our dispatch :
I am hush'd until our city be afire,
And then I 'll speak a little.   [*He holds her by the hand, silent.*
  Cor.   *O mother, mother !*
What have you done ?   Behold, the heavens do ope,
The gods look down, and this unnatural scene
They laugh at.   O my mother, mother !   O !
You have won a happy victory to Rome ;
But, for your son,—believe it, O, believe it,
Most dangerously you have with him prevail'd,
If not most mortal to him.   But, let it come.

APPENDIX C

SHAKESPEARE'S ALLEGED INDEBTEDNESS TO APPIAN IN *JULIUS CAESAR*

PLUTARCH gives little more than the situation and the *motif* for Antony's oration. He has two accounts of the incident.

> (*a*) When Caesars body was brought into the Market Place, Antonius making his funeral oration in praise of the dead according to the ancient custom of Rome, and perceiving that his wordes moved the common people to compassion ; he framed his eloquence to make their harts yerne the more, and taking Caesars gowne all bloudy in his hand, he layed it open to the sight of them all, shewing what a number of cuts and holes it had upon it. Therewithall the people fell presently into such a rage and mutinie, that there was no more order kept amongs the common people.
>
> (*Marcus Brutus.*)
>
> (*b*) When Caesars body was brought to the place where it should be buried, he made a funeral oration in commendacion of Caesar, according to the auncient custom of praising noble men at their funerals. When he saw that the people were very glad and desirous to heare Caesar spoken of, and his praises uttered : he mingled his oration with lamentable wordes, and by amplifying of matters did greatly move their harts and affections unto pitie and compassion. In fine to conclude his oration, he unfolded before the whole assembly the bloudy garments of the dead, thrust through in many places with their swords, and called the malefactors, cruell and cursed murtherers. With these words he put the people into . . . a fury. (*Marcus Antonius.*)

Shakespeare certainly did not get much of the stuff for Antony's speech from these notices.

Appian, on the other hand, gives a much fuller report, which was quite accessible to ordinary readers, for Appian had been published in 1578 by Henrie Bynniman.[1]

---

[1] Under the title : "An auncient Historie and exquisite Chronicle of the Romanes warres, both Ciuile and Foren. Written in Greeke by the noble Orator and Historiographer Appian of Alexandria."

The English version of the most important passages runs thus:

> Antony marking how they were affected, did not let it slippe, but toke upon him to make Caesars funeral sermon, as Consul, of a Consul, friend of a friend, and kinsman, of a kinsman (for Antony was partly his kinsman) and to use craft againe. And thus he said: "I do not thinke it meete (O citizens) that the buriall praise of suche a man, should rather be done by me, than by the whole country. For what you have altogither for the loue of hys vertue giuen him by decree, aswell the Senate as the people, I thinke your voice, and not Antonies, oughte to expresse it."
>
> This he uttered with sad and heauy cheare, and wyth a framed voice, declared euerything, chiefly upon the decree, whereby he was made a God, holy and inuiolate, father of the country, bene-factor and gouernor, and suche a one, as neuer in al things they entituled other man to the like. At euery of these words Antonie directed his countenance and hands to Caesars body, and with vehemencie of words opened the fact. At euery title he gaue an addition, with briefe speach, mixte with pitie and indignation. And when the decree named him father of the country, then he saide: "This is the testimony of our duety."
>
> And at these wordes, *holy, inuiolate* and *untouched*, and *the refuge of all other*, he said: "None other made refuge of hym. But he, this holy and untouched, is kylled, not takyng honoure by violences whiche he neuer desired, and then be we verye thrall that bestowe them on the unworthy, neuer suing for them. But you doe purge your selves (O Citizens) of this unkindnesse, in that you nowe do use suche honoure towarde hym being dead."
>
> Then rehearsing the othe, that all shoulde keepe Caesar and Caesars body, and if any one wente about to betraye hym, that they were accursed that would not defende him: at this he extolled hys voice, and helde up his handes to the Capitoll, saying:
>
> "O Jupiter, Countries defendour, and you other Gods, I am ready to reuenge, as I sware and made execration, and when it seemes good to my companions to allowe the decrees, I desire them to aide me."
>
> At these plaine speeches spoken agaynst the Senate, an uproare being made, Antony waxed colde, and recanted hys wordes. "It seemeth, (O Citizens)," saide hee, "that the things done haue not bin the worke of men but of Gods, and that we ought to haue more consideration of the present, than of the past, bycause the thyngs to come, maye bring us to greater danger than these we haue, if we shall returne to oure olde [dissentions], and waste the reste of the noble men that be in the Cittie. Therefore let us send thys holy one to the number of the blessed, and sing to him his due hymne and mourning verse."
>
> When he had saide thus, he pulled up his gowne lyke a man beside hymselfe, and gyrded it, that he might the better stirre his handes: he stoode ouer the Litter, as from a Tabernacle, looking into it and opening it, and firste sang his Himne, as to a God in heauen. And to confirme he was a God, he held up his hands, and with a swift voice he rehearsed the warres, the fights, the

victories, the nations that he had subdued to his countrey, and the great booties that he had sent, making euery one to be a maruell. Then with a continuall crie, " This is the only unconquered of all that euer came to hands with hym. Thou (quoth he) alone diddest reuenge thy countrey being iniured, 300 years, and those fierce nations that only inuaded Rome, and only burned it, thou broughtest them on their knees."

And when he had made these and many other inuocations, he tourned hys voice from triumphe to mourning matter, and began to lament and mone him as a friend that had bin uniustly used, and did desire that he might giue hys soule for Caesars. Then falling into moste vehement affections, uncouered Caesars body, holding up his vesture with a speare, cut with the woundes, and redde with the bloude of the chiefe Ruler, by the which the people lyke a Quire, did sing lamentation unto him, and with this passion were againe repleate with ire. And after these speeches, other lamentations wyth voice after the Country custome, were sung of the Quires, and they rehearsed again his acts and his hap.

Then made he Caesar hymselfe to speake as it were in a lamentable sort, to howe many of his enimies he hadde done good by name, and of the killers themselues to say as in an admiration, " Did I saue them that haue killed me ? " This the people could not abide, calling to remembraunce, that all the kyllers (only Decimus except) were of Pompey's faction, and subdued by hym, to whom, in stead of punishment, he had giuen promotion of offices, gouernments of prouinces and armies, and thought Decimus worthy to be made his heyre and son by adoption, and yet conspired his death.[1]

Now, this is not very like the oration in the play. It may be analysed and summarised as follows :

Antony begins by praising the deceased as a consul a consul, a friend a friend, a kinsman a kinsman. He recites the public honours awarded to Caesar as a better testimony than his private opinion, and accompanies the enumeration with provocative comment. He touches on Caesar's sacrosanct character and the unmerited honours bestowed on those who slew him, but acquits the citizens of unkindness on the ground of their presence at the funeral. He avows his own readiness for revenge, and thus censures the policy of the Senate, but admits that that policy may be for the public interest. He intones a hymn in honour of the deified Caesar ; reviews his wars, battles, victories, the provinces annexed and the spoils transmitted to Rome, and glances at the subjugation of the Gauls as the payment of an ancient score. He uncovers the body of Caesar and displays the pierced and blood-stained garment to the

---

[1] In Schweighäuser's Edition II. cxliii. to cxlvi.

wrath of the populace. He puts words in the mouth of the dead, and makes him cite the names of those whom he had benefited and preserved that they should destroy him. And the people brook no more.

Thus Appian's Antony differs from Shakespeare's Antony in his attitude to his audience, in the arrangement of his material, and to a considerable extent in the material itself. Nevertheless, in some of the details the speeches correspond. It is quite possible that Shakespeare, while retaining Plutarch's general scheme, may have filled it in with suggestions from Appian. The evidence is not very convincing, but the conjecture is greatly strengthened by the apparent loans from the same quarter in *Antony and Cleopatra,* which would show that he was acquainted with the English translation. See Appendix D.

APPENDIX D

SHAKESPEARE'S LOANS FROM APPIAN IN
ANTONY AND CLEOPATRA

I DO not think there can be any serious doubt about Shakespeare's having consulted the 1578 translation of the *Bella Civilia* for this play, at any rate for the parts dealing with Sextus Pompeius. The most important passage is the one (*A. and C.* III. v. 19) which records Antony's indignation at Pompey's death. Now of that death there is no mention at all in the *Marcus Antonius* of Plutarch ; and even in the *Octavius Caesar Augustus* by Simon Goulard, which was included in the 1583 edition of Amyot and in the 1603 edition of North, it is expressly attributed to Antony. Here is Goulard's statement : [1]

> Whilst Antonius made war with the Parthians, or rather infortunately they made war with him to his great confusion, his lieutenant Titius found the means to lay hands upon Sextus Pompeius ; that was fled into the ile of Samos, and then forty years old : whom he put to death by Antonius' commandment.

Appian at least leaves it an open question whether Antony was responsible or not, and thus gives his apologist an opportunity :

> Titius commaunded hys (*i.e.* Pompey's) army to sweare to Antony, and put hym to death at Mileto, when he hadde lyved to the age of fortye yeares, eyther for that he remembered late displeasure and forgot olde good turnes, or for that he had such commaundemente of Antony.
> *There bee that saye that Plancus, and not Antony did commaunde hym to dye, whyche beeyng president of Syria had Antonyes signet, and in greate causes wrote letters in hys name.* Some thynke it

---

[1] I quote from *Shakespeare's Plutarch* (Prof. Skeat), the 1603 edition of North being at present inaccessible to me.

was done wyth Antonyes knowledge, he fearyng the name of Pompey, or for Cleopatra, who fauoured Pompey the Great.

Some thynke that Plancus dyd it of hymselfe for these causes, and also that Pompey shoulde gyve no cause of dissention between Caesar and Antony, or for that Cleopatra would turn hyr favour to Pompey.   (V. cxiv.)

I do not think indeed that there is any indication that Shakespeare had read, or at all events been in any way impressed by, Goulard's *Augustus*: no wonder, for compared with the genuine *Lives*, it is a dull performance. The only other passages with which a connection might be traced, do no more than give hints that are better given in Appian. Thus Sextus Pompeius' vein of chivalry, of which there is hardly a suggestion in Plutarch's brief notices, is illustrated in Goulard by his behaviour to the fugitives from the proscription.

> Pompeius had sent certain ships to keep upon the coast of Italy, and pinnaces everywhere, to the end to receive all them that fled on that side ; giving them double recompence that saved a proscript, and honourable offices to men that had been consuls and escaped, comforting and entertaining the others with a most singular courtesy.

But Appian says all this too in greater detail, and adds the significant touch :

> So was he moste profitable to hys afflicted Countrey, and wanne greate glory to hymselfe, *not inferioure to that he hadde of hys father*.   (IV. xxxvi.)

Note particularly this reference to his father's reputation, for which there is no parallel in Plutarch or Goulard ; and compare

Our slippery people
. . . . begin to throw
Pompey the Great, and all his dignities
Upon his son.   (*A. and C.* I. ii. 192.)

and

Rich in his father's honour.   (*Ib.* I. iii. 50.)

Again, Goulard, talking of the last struggle, says :

> After certain encounters, where Pompey ever had the better, insomuch as Lepidus was suspected to lean on that side, Caesar resolved to commit all to the hazard of a latter battle.

The insinuation in regard to Lepidus might be taken as

the foundation for Shakespeare's statement, which has no sanction in Plutarch, that Caesar

> accuses him of letters he had formerly wrote to Pompey.
> (*A. and C.* III. v. 10.)

But it seems a closer echo of a remark of Appian's about some transactions shortly after Philippi:

> Lepidus was accused to favour Pompey's part. (v. iii.)

There are, moreover, several touches in Shakespeare's sketch, that he could no more get from Goulard than from Plutarch, but that are to be found in Appian. Thus there is Pompey's association with the party of the " good Brutus" and the enthusiasm he expresses for "beauteous freedom" (*A. and C.* II. vi. 13 and 17). Compare passages like the following in Appian:

> Sextus Pompey, the seconde son of Pompey the Great being lefte of that faction, was sette up of Brutus friends. (v. i.)

> Pompey's friends hearing of this, did marvellously rejoyce, crying now to be time to restore their Countrey's libertie. (III. lxxxii.)

Thus, too, Shakespeare refers to Pompey's command of "the empire of the sea" (*A. and C.* I. ii. 191), which, if Plutarch were his authority, would be an unjustifiable exaggeration. Yet it exactly corresponds to the facts of the case as Appian repeatedly states them, and perhaps one of Binniman's expressions suggested the very phrase.

> Pompey *being Lorde of the Sea* . . . caused famine in the cittie all victuall beyng kepte away. (v. xv.)

> The Citie in the meane time was in great penurie, their provision of corne beyng stopped by Pompey. (v. xviii.)

> In the meane time the cytie was oppressed with famine, for neyther durst the Merchauntes bring any corn from the East bicause of Pompeis beeing in Sicelie, nor from the Weast of Corsica and Sardinia, where Pompeis ships also lay: nor from Africa, where the navies of the other conspiratours kepte their stations. Being in this distresse, they (*i.e.* the people) alleaged that the discorde of the rulers was the cause, and therefore required that peace might be made with Pompey, unto the whiche when Caesar woulde not agree, Antonie thought warre was needefull for necessitie. (v. lxvii.)

Then there are the frequent references of Antony (*A. and C.* I. ii. 192, I. iii. 148), of the messenger (I. iv. 38, I. iv. 52), of Pompey himself (II. i. 9), to Pompey's popularity and the

rush of recruits to his standard. Neither Goulard nor
Plutarch makes mention of these points, but Appian does
often, and most emphatically in the following passage:

> Out of Italy all things were not quiet, for Pompey by resorte of
> condemned Citizens, and auntient possessioners was greatly in-
> creased, both in mighte, and estimation: for they that feared
> their life, or were spoyled of their goodes, or lyked not the present
> state, fledde all to hym. And this disagreemente of Lucius aug-
> mented his credite: beside a repayre of yong men, desirous of
> gayne and seruice, not caring under whome they went, because
> they were all Romanes, sought unto him. And among other,
> hys cause seemed most just. He was waxed rich by booties of
> the Sea, and he hadde good store of Shyppes, with their furniture.
> . . . Wherefore me thynke, that if he had then inuaded Italy, he
> might easily have gotte it, which being afflicted with famine and
> discord loked for him. But Pompey of ignorance had rather
> defend his owne, than inuade others, till so he was ouercome also.
> (v. xxv.)

It should be noted too that Menas, to whom Appian
always gives his full formal name of Menodorus, not only
as in Plutarch proposes to make away with the Triumvirs
after the compact, but as in the play (II. vi. 84 and 109) and
not as in Plutarch, disapproves the cessation of hostilities.

> All other persuaded Pompey earnestly to peace, only Menodorus
> wrote from Sardinia that he should make *open warre, or dryve
> off*,[1] whyles the dearth continued, *that he might make peace with*
> the better conditions. (v. lxxi.)

I have not noticed any other points of importance in
which there is an apparent connection between the drama
and the *Roman History*: unless indeed Antony's passing
compunction for Fulvia's death may be so regarded.

> Newes came that Antonies wyfe was dead, who coulde not bear
> his unkyndenesse, leavyng her sicke, & not bidding hyr farewell.
> Hir death was thought very commodius for them both. For
> Fulvia was an unquiet woman, & for ielousie of Cleopatra, raysed
> suche a mortall warre. Yet the matter vexed Antony bicause he
> was compted the occasion of her death. (v. lix.)

Here, however, the motive of Antony's regret differs from
that which Shakespeare attributes to him; and on the
whole the references to Fulvia in the play deviate even
more from Appian's account than from Plutarch's. So far
as I am in a position to judge, Shakespeare derived all
his other historical data, as well as the general scheme into
which he fitted these trifling loans, from Plutarch's *Life*,

---

[1] *i.e.* put off. Greek, βραδύνειν.

and can be considered a debtor to Appian only in the points that are illustrated in my previous extracts.

But there are two qualifications I should like to make to this statement.

In the first place, I have not seen the 1578 version of Appian, the passages I have quoted being merely transcripts made by my direction. I have had only the original text to work upon, and it is possible that the Tudor Translation might offer verbal coincidences that of course would not suggest themselves to me.

In the second place, the book is not merely a translation of Appian. The descriptive title runs: " An auncient historie and exquisite chronicle of the Romanes warres, both civile and foren . . . with a continuation . . . from the death of Sextus Pompeius to the overthrow of Antonie and Cleopatra."

Appian's History of the Civil Wars, as now extant, concludes at the death of Sextus Pompeius. The Tudor translator's continuation till the deaths of Antony and Cleopatra may be responsible for some of the later deviations from Plutarch, which I have described as independent modifications of Shakespeare's. The matter is worth looking into.

Meanwhile, from my collation I draw two conclusions, the first definitive, the second provisional :

(1) That Shakespeare laid Appian under contribution to fill in the details of his picture.

(2) That he borrowed from him, that is, from his English translator, only for the episode of Sextus Pompeius.

APPENDIX E

CLEOPATRA'S *ONE WORD*

PROFESSOR TH. ZIELINSKI of St. Petersburg suggests a peculiar interpretation of this passage in his *Marginalien* (*Philologus*, N.F., Band xviii. 1905). He starts from the assertion that Shakespeare had in his mind Ovid's *Epistle from Dido* (*Heroid.* vii.) when he composed the parting scene between Antony and Cleopatra. This statement is neither self-evident nor initially probable. Shakespeare was no doubt acquainted with portions of Ovid both in the original and in translation, but there is not much indication that his knowledge extended to the *Heroides*. Mr. Churton Collins, indeed, in his plea for Shakespeare's familiarity with Latin, calls attention to the well-known pair of quotations from these poems, the one in *3 Henry VI.*, the other in the *Taming of the Shrew.* But though Mr. Collins makes good his general contention, he hardly strengthens it with these examples : for Shakespeare's share in both plays is so uncertain that no definite inference can be drawn from them. Apart from these more than doubtful instances, there seems to be no reference in Shakespeare to the *Heroides*, either in the Latin of Ovid or in the English of Turberville ; and it would be strange to find one cropping up here.

But Professor Zielinski gives his arguments, and one of them is certainly plausible. He quotes :

> What says the married woman? You may go :
> Would she had never given you leave to come ;
>
> (*A. and C.* I. iii. 20.)

and compares

> " Sed iubet ire deus." Vellem vetuisset adire.
>
> (*Her.* VII. 37.)

There is a coincidence, but it is not very close, and scarcely implies imitation. Moreover, it becomes even less striking in the English version; which, after all, Shakespeare is more likely to have known, if he knew the poem at all:

> But God doth force thee flee ; would God had kept away
> Such guilefull guests, and Troians had in Carthage made no stay.[1]

Professor Zielinski's next argument is singularly unconvincing. He says: " The situation (*i.e.* in the Epistle and in the Play) is parallel even in details, as everyone will tell himself: moreover the poet himself confesses it :

> Where souls do couch on flowers, we'll hand in hand,
> And with our sprightly port make the ghosts gaze :
> Dido and her Æneas shall want troops
> And all the haunt be ours." (IV. xiv. 51.)

But in the first place this has reference not to the separation but to the reunion: and in the second place, of the reunion there is no word in the Epistle. I cannot therefore see how Shakespeare's lines can be taken as a confession of indebtedness to Ovid. But these analogies, real or imaginary, lead up to Professor Zielinski's main point. He quotes as what he calls the " Motiv des Kindes" and considers the distinctive feature of Ovid's treatment, Dido's reproach :

> Forsitan et gravidam Didon, scelerate, relinquas,
> Parsque tui lateat corpore clausa meo. (line 131.)

He admits that it is not easy to find this " Motiv" in the play, but argues that Shakespeare was always very reticent in such regards. Then he proceeds: " Hier nun war Kleopatra tatsächlich schwanger, als Antonius sie verliess : Plutarch setzt es c. 36 voraus, und Shakespeare wird es gewusst haben, da er Act III. die Kinder erwähnt. Sollte er in der grossen Abschieds-scene das dankbare Motiv haben entgehen lassen? Sehn wir zu. Kleopatra spielt die nervöse, ihr ist bald gut, bald schlecht : ' schnür mich auf . . . nein, lass es sein.' Ihre ungerechten Vorwürfe bringen den Antonius endlich auf ; er will gehn. Sie hält

---

[1] *The Heroycall Epistles of the learned poet Publius Ouidius Naso in English verse : set out and translated by George Turberville, gent*, etc. Transcribed from a copy in the Bodleian, which Malone, who owned it, conjecturally dated 1569.

ihn zurück : *courteous lord, one word.* Wir erwarten eine wichtige Erklärung ; was wird das ' eine Wort ' sein ?

> Sir, you and I must part—but that's not it :
> Sir, you and I have loved—but there's not it ;
> That you know well : something it is I would—
> O, *my oblivion is a very Antony,*
> And I am all forgotten.

Es ist für den klassischen Philologen erheiternd und tröst-lich, die Commentare zum hervorgehoben verse zu lesen : dieselben Torheiten, wie bei uns, wenn einer das erklären muss, was er selber nicht versteht.   Man wollte sogar *oblivion* hinausconjiciren : andere befehlen es = *memory* zu nehmen.   Was wird dadurch gewonnen ?   Ich verlange das versprochene ' eine wort.'—' Ja, das hat sie eben ver-gessen '—Ich danke.   Nein, sie hat es ausgesprochen : ihr ' Vergessen ' war in der Tat ' ein echter Antonius,' wenn auch ein ganz kleiner.   Und als der Freund die Anspielung nicht versteht—*I should take you for idleness itself*—fährt sie bitter fort :

> 'Tis sweating labour
> *To bear such idleness so near the heart,*
> As Cleopatra *this.*

(das *this* mit discret hinweisender Geberde) . . . Es wäre Mangel an Zartgefühl, mehr zu verlangen.—Und wirklich, besser als die Erklärer hat ein Dichter den Dichter ver-standen ; ich meine Puschkin, der in einer Stelle seiner lieblichen ' Nixe' (Rusalka) die oben ausgeschriebenen Worte der Kleopatra offenbar nachahmen wollte :

> *Fürst.*   Leb' wohl.
> *Mädchen.*   Nein, wart . . . ich muss dir etwas sagen . . .
> Weiss nimmer was.
> *Fürst.*   So denke nach !
> *Mädchen.*   Für dich
> Wär ich bereit . . . Nein das ist's nicht . . . So wart doch.
> Ich kann's nicht glauben, dass du mich auf ewig
> Verlassen willst . . . Nein, das ist's immer nicht . . .
> Jetzt hab' ich's : heut war's, dass zum ersten Mal
> Dein kind sich unter'm Herzen mir bewegte."

This is very ingenious, and the parallel from Puschkin is very interesting.   What makes one doubtful is that from first to last Shakespeare slurs over the motherhood of Cleopatra, to which the other tragedians of the time give great prominence.   On the whole he obliterates even those references that Plutarch makes to this aspect of his heroine, and it would therefore be odd if he went out of his way to invent an allusion which does not fit in with the rest of the picture, and which is without consequence and very obscure. If one were forced to conjecture the "missing word," it would be more plausible to suppose that she both wishes and hesitates to suggest marriage with Antony. At the close, her exclamation :

Husband, I come :
Now to that name my courage prove my title ! (v. ii. 290.)

shows that she recognises the dignity of the sanction. At the outset, she feels the falsity of her position, as we see from her reference to "the married woman"; and in Plutarch Shakespeare had read the complaint of her partisans, that "Cleopatra, being borne a Queene of so many thousands of men, is onely named Antonius Leman." In Rome the marriage is assumed to be quite probable ; and in this very scene Antony, after announcing the removal of the grand impediment by Fulvia's death, has just professed his unalterable devotion to his Queen. Why should there not be a marriage, unless he regards her merely as a mistress ; and why should she not propose it, except that she fears to meet with this rebuff ? The "sweating labour" she bears would thus be her unsanctioned love and its disgrace.

This, however, is not put forward as a serious interpretation, but only as a theory quite as possible as Professor Zielinski's. The most obvious and the most satisfactory way is to suppose, as probably almost every reader does and has done, that she is merely making pretexts to postpone the separation. And there is surely no great difficulty about the phrase : "My oblivion is a very Antony." Here too the obvious explanation is the most convincing : "My forgetfulness is as great as Antony's own."

APPENDIX F

THE "INEXPLICABLE" PASSAGE IN *CORIOLANUS*

COLERIDGE, in his *Notes on Shakespeare* (1818, Section IV.), calls attention to the difficulty of Aufidius' speech to his lieutenant :

> All places yield to him ere he sits down ;
> And the nobility of Rome are his :
> The senators and patricians love him too :
> The tribunes are no soldiers ; and their people
> Will be as rash in the repeal, as hasty
> To expel him thence.   I think he'll be to Rome
> As is the osprey to the fish, who takes it
> By sovereignty of nature.   First he was
> A noble servant to them ; but he could not
> Carry his honours even : whether 'twas pride,
> Which out of daily fortune ever taints
> The happy man ; whether defect of judgement,
> To fail in the disposing of those chances
> Which he was lord of ; or whether nature,
> Not to be other than one thing, not moving
> From the casque to the cushion, but commanding peace
> Even with the same austerity and garb
> As he controll'd the war ; but one of these—
> As he hath spices of them all, not all,
> For I dare so far free him—made him fear'd,
> So hated, and so banish'd, but he has a merit,
> To choke it in the utterance.   So our virtues
> Lie in the interpretation of the time ;
> And power, unto itself most commendable,
> Hath not a tomb so evident as a chair
> To extol what it hath done.
> One fire drives out one fire ; one nail, one nail ;
> Rights by rights falter, strengths by strengths do fail.
> Come, let's away.   When, Caius, Rome is thine,
> Thou art poor'st of all : then shortly art thou mine.
>
> (IV. vii. 28.)

Here there are puzzling expressions in detail, but they have on the whole been satisfactorily explained, and it is not to them that Coleridge refers.[1] He says: "I have always thought this in itself so beautiful speech the least explicable from the mood and full intention of the speaker of any in the whole works of Shakespeare." It strikes one indeed as a series of disconnected jottings that have as little to do with each other as with the situation and attitude of Aufidius. First he gives reason for expecting the capture of Rome; then he enumerates defects in Coriolanus that have led to his banishment with a supplementary acknowledgment of his merits; next he makes general reflections on the relation of virtue to the construction put upon it, and on the danger that lies in conspicuous power: thereafter he points out that things are brought to nought by themselves or their likes; and finally he predicts that when Rome is taken, he will get the better of his rival.

Is there here a mere congeries of thoughts as one chance suggestion leads to another with which it happens to be casually associated; or does one thread of continuous meaning run through the whole? I would venture to maintain the latter opinion with more confidence than I do, if Coleridge had not been so emphatic.

In the first place we have to remember what goes before. The report of the Lieutenant confirms the jealousy of Aufidius, who is further embittered by the hint that he is losing credit, but reflects that he can bring weighty charges against Coriolanus, and concludes:

> He hath left undone
> That which shall break his neck or hazard mine,
> Whene'er we come to our account.

Thereupon the Lieutenant meaningly rejoins:

> Sir, I beseech you, think you he'll carry Rome?

It is a contingency to be reckoned with, for clearly if Rome falls, any previous mistakes or complaisances alleged against the conqueror will find ready pardon. So Aufidius discusses the matter in the light of these two main considerations: (1) that he must get rid of his rival, and (2) that his rival may do the state a crowning service. He

---

[1] Of these the most perplexing to me is the distinction Shakespeare makes between "the nobility" on the one hand, and "the senators and patricians" on the other. What was in his mind? I fail to find an explanation even on trying to render his thought in terms of contemporary arrangements in England. "Peers," "parliament men," and "gentry" would not do.

admits that Coriolanus, what with his own efficiency, what with the friendliness of one class in Rome and the helplessness of the remainder, is likely to achieve the grand exploit. How then will Aufidius' chances stand? Formerly Marcius deserved as well of his own country when he had overthrown Corioli, yet that did not secure him. What qualities in himself discounted his services to Rome and may again discount his services to Antium? Pride of prosperity, disregard of his opportunities, his unaccommodating peremptory behaviour—all of these faults which in point of fact afterwards contributed to his death—brought about his banishment, though truly he had merit enough to make men overlook such trifles. This shows how worth depends on the way it is taken, and how ability, even when of the sterling kind that wins its own approval, may find the throne of its public recognition to be, more properly, its certain grave. Thus likes counteract likes; the greater the popularity, the greater the reaction; the greater the superiority, the more certainly it will balk itself. So, and this is the conclusion of the whole matter, even when Marcius has won Rome by a greater conquest than when he won Corioli, the result will be the same. His proud, imprudent and overbearing conduct will obscure his high deserts. These will be construed only by public opinion, and the very prowess in which he delights will rouse an adulation, which, when he is no longer required, will swing round to its opposite. So his success will correct itself. His very triumph over Rome will be guarantee for Aufidius' triumph over him.

If this amplified paraphrase give the meaning, that meaning is coherent enough and is quite suitable to the mood and attitude of the speaker.

INDEX

DATE DUE

JUL 3 0 '70			
AUG 5 '70			
AUG 1 8 '70			
JY 6'71			
OCT 9 '73			
MAR 1 '7?			
MAR 1 8 1992			
GAYLORD			PRINTED IN U.S.A.